The Book of Canadian Prose: Volume 2

To Jeannie, with love

THE CANADIAN CENTURY

ENGLISH-CANADIAN WRITING SINCE CONFEDERATION

Edited by A. J. M. Smith

GAGE EDUCATIONAL PUBLISHING LIMITED

PREFACE

I suppose I shall be expected to make some sort of excuse for the long delay in the publication of this volume, but beyond saying that I have followed the advice of Horace, as transmitted by my favorite poet Alexander Pope, and kept my piece nine years — even that is something of an understatement—I do not propose to explain or apologise, particularly since the delay has been actually an advantage. It has made it possible to include some outstanding recent work by Alice Munro, Dave Godfrey, and Ramsay Cook, and to take a fresh look at some of the outstanding prose authors who made their reputation mainly in the sixties, Hugh Hood, for example, and Jack Ludwig. A special effort has been made to include original and outstanding material by well-known men of letters that is as worthy of attention as some of their more frequently anthologized pieces. I am thinking particularly of Morley Callaghan's little comic gem *A Predicament,* Northrop Frye's brilliant distinctions between "ordinary speech, verse, and prose," Thomas Raddall's pregnant satire on Grey Owl, Margaret Laurence's striking up-dating of the Oedipus myth, and the scholar-poet George Whalley's tragic narrative of the deaths of John Hornby and Edgar Christian.

Perhaps I might take the risk of including here a remarkable short story for which no place could be found in the text. It was written by a certain "John Goodwin of West Vancouver, B.C., . . . when he was aged twelve and in Grade 7," according to the note by the late John Sutherland who printed it in the October-November 1951 issue of his influential *Northern Review*. It was rediscovered many years later by

Ethel Wilson, who published it again in an article entitled "Where Is John Goodwin?" in *The Tamarack Review*, No. 33. I am sure that Mrs. Wilson and Mrs. Sutherland will not mind another attempt to bring this story to the attention of the public, and if the author should see it and would communicate with me I shall be happy to pay him what so excellent a piece of writing richly deserves. Here it is:

The Mysterious Question, by John Goodwin

How many beautiful young ladies in this world wear black velvet ribbons around their necks? Marcel did, and John wondered why the first time he met her. They had been going together for three weeks before John got enough courage to ask her. Marcel looked worried and changed the subject quickly. Their love blossomed and one day he asked her, "Marcel, why do you wear that black ribbon around your neck?" She burst into tears and said, "I thought I told you not to ask that question!" The incident was not forgotten and quickly the years passed by, John was in his fifties when again he asked. "Marcel, darling, will you please tell me the reason you wear that black ribbon around your beautiful neck?" She burst into tears again as she had done long ago and said nothing. As the time passed and John lay in his deathbed, he said "Marcel, since I am to die in a few hours, I wish, as my last request, that you would tell me why you wear that black ribbon around your neck?" There were no tears from Marcel as she said, "All right, I'll show you." Her fingers trembled as she lifted them towards her neck. She felt for the ribbon. Her hands groped for the clasp. Carefully she undid it and her head fell off.

In the Preface to the first volume of this work I thanked the many friends, scholars, and critics who in one way or another gave me their generous assistance. To all of them an expression of gratitude is once more due, and to their names must be added that of George Woodcock, founder and editor of the indispensable quarterly *Canadian Literature*. I owe much too to discussions with my students in courses in Canadian literature at Dalhousie, McGill, and Sir George Williams universities.

February, 1973   A.J.M.S.

CONTENTS

2. Local Color, Sentiment, and Satire

3. Essays and Belles-Lettres

INTRODUCTION

When we look back over the historical development of Canadian literature written in English, we find that, like our political and social history, it falls into three clearly marked divisions, the products of each being sharply distinguished in tone, attitude, and purpose from those of others. The first is the pre-Confederation period illustrated in the first volume of this work, the second is the period of roughly half a century from 1867 to the end of the first world war, and the last is the nearly sixty years of rapidly accelerating change and development that bring us to the present.

During the decades following the establishment of a federated Dominion, national enthusiasm in politics and business gradually carried all before it. During these years, literature became self-conscious and professional or, more often, commercial, and the novel tended to become a pale reflection of popular fiction in England or the United States. Consequently, much that was produced in the eighteen-seventies and eighties is quite dead today. The once much-praised historical romance *The Golden Dog* by William Kirby and the historical fiction of Charles G. D. Roberts or Gilbert Parker, written in the style of Sir Walter Scott and Fenimore Cooper, are no longer read, unlike the still vital narratives of the explorers and fur traders.

There was, however, some prose of an original if minor excellence produced in the late nineteenth century. It is found in the animal stories of Charles G. D. Roberts and in a few of the regional novels of the local color school.

Roberts, who had already made a reputation as a poet, published most of his animal stories in the eighteen-nineties and in the first decade of the new century. In these, acute and accurate observation was illuminated by poetic imagination and a graceful style. What strikes the reader at once about Roberts' animal stories is that they are *animal* stories: wild beasts, birds, insects, fish—often the most unromantic and inconsiderable of living things—are treated dramatically and with respect. The human figures that intrude occasionally into the action are comparatively colorless, drawn in rough outline, and crudely or sentimentally motivated: the best stories are those in which no desecrating human touch is felt at all. In such tales as "The Watchers in the Swamp" our sympathies are engaged in the deadly struggles that go on in a world that is normally below our knowledge or sympathy. We can take pleasure in the uncompromising way Roberts presents a clear-eyed picture of nature red in tooth and claw, without any of the pessimistic overtones of Arnold or Hardy. While these stories are less scientifically knowledgeable than the animal biographies of the Canadian naturalist Ernest Thompson Seton, written at about the same time, they are much less didactic and subjective. They belong to poetic literature, but they are a part of life.

The other literary development of interest in this period was the rise of a school of local color in the short story and the novel. Some of the tales of the Ottawa poet Duncan Campbell Scott, collected in *In the Village of Viger,* deal with grace and charm, but not very much vitality, with life in rural Quebec, as do the novels of S. Frances Harrison. A great popular success was achieved by L. M. Montgomery's idyllic picture of a Prince Edward Island girlhood in *Anne of Green Gables,* but its rather sugary sentimentalism makes it representative of the weaknesses rather than the virtues of the local color school. For these, modest though they are, we may turn to Ralph Connor's interpretations of rural Scottish life in Glengarry County, Ontario. Such books as *Glengarry Schooldays* and *The Man from Glengarry* and the short stories of Edward W. Thomson and Norman Duncan helped to develop around the turn of the century a national awareness based on regional knowledge and warm local sympathies.

Humor, usually of a gentle and sympathetic sort, is often a feature of the local color novel, but it has been handled with complete and triumphant success by only two writers of superior talent—Thomas

Haliburton at the beginning of the nineteenth century and Stephen Leacock a hundred years later. Leacock's most assured successes are certainly the two volumes of 1912 and 1914, *Sunshine Sketches of a Little Town* and *Arcadian Adventures with the Idle Rich.* Each is aptly and accurately titled. The sketches of the "characters" who dwell in the little town of Mariposa (Orillia, Ontario) are indeed filled with sunshine and a gentle laughter, but there is also a note of regret for a pastoral innocence that even as Leacock wrote was disappearing. Of course *Sunshine Sketches* is not, and does not pretend to be, realism. It is impressionism, and impressionism of a high order. What we get from "The Great Election in Missinaba County," along with the humanity and gently ironic humor, is a strong impression of the muddled but powerful emotions in a Protestant Anglo-Saxon small Ontario town during the crucial Reciprocity election of 1911 that ended the dominance of Sir Wilfrid Laurier and the Liberal party. The point of view is sympathetic and indeed loving, because, while Leacock has the wit to see the absurdity of his characters' emotional involvements, he himself shares them. He implies an irresistible argument in their favor as being human and natural—much more important than being reasonable. Stephen Leacock might have made a humane, kindly, and effective political boss.

When we turn to the *Arcadian Adventures*, we find that the satire, mild in the small town milieu of the *Sketches,* has become sharper and more brittle as we move to the city. Indeed at times it is almost edgy. The writer here is much more of an outsider. He was separated from the good townsfolk of Mariposa only by his education, but he is separated from the businessmen and administrators by a wider gulf. The rich have more money—and hence more power—and to envy them, as I think Leacock did, is something a good and honest man must try to put aside, or at least to fight against. The author of *Arcadian Adventures* fights it by showing once again the weakness of human nature in the unbridged gap between the announced intention and the real performance, between the declared motive and the actual one. But to make the satirical exposure acceptable, the author has had to pose as a member of the Club, one who knows and understands and has the confidence of the businessmen, university administrators, and clergymen he shows up—though, it must be admitted, without ever calling them hypocrites, perhaps without even thinking of them as hypocrites. The *Adventures* has never been as popular as the *Sketches.*

A little earlier than Leacock we find in the more serious novels of Sara Jeannette Duncan an amalgam of satire and social realism. *The Imperialist,* published in 1904, is still one of the more penetrating studies of politics and culture in Canadian fiction. It is the only one of this writer's many novels that has a Canadian setting. Witty and intelligent as it is, *The Imperialist* has had as little effect on the later social realists—Grove, Callaghan, and MacLennan—as the novels of Edith Wharton had on Theodore Dreiser or Sherwood Anderson.

When we consider the essays and belles-lettres of the period from Confederation to the first world war we find something of the same gentle humanism that characterizes the local color novels. The three essays included here are illustrative of the variety and modest goodness to be found in the miscellaneous prose of the period. They are taken from a regional history—*In the Days of the Canada Company,* written in 1896 by two remarkable sisters, Robina and Kathleen Lizars; from the poet Duncan Campbell Scott's occasional essays of the early years of the century; and from a curious little volume of highly individual papers entitled *Chinook Days* by the west coast poet Tom MacInnes, which though written earlier was published in 1926.

All three of these selections are of somewhat special interest. The chapter from the Lizars sisters' history of the Canada Company is a rather rambling anecdotal study of one of the most interesting figures in Upper Canada in the early decades of the nineteenth century, "Tiger" Dunlop (a selection from his own account of his experiences as an army surgeon in the War of 1812 is found in the first volume of this anthology). The personal animation of the Lizars' book is in pleasing contrast to the usual solemnity of the ordinary amateur local historian. Wit and vigor also, along with a good deal of unusual learning, distinguish MacInnes' study of the pidgin English of the Indians and traders of the northwest Pacific coast. D. C. Scott's "The Last of the Indian Treaties" illustrates in prose the interest in and sympathetic knowledge of Indian affairs shown in such poems as "The Forsaken," "The Half-Breed Girl," "At Gull Lake: August 1810," and many others that grew out of his life-long work in the Department of Indian Affairs.

The political essays and addresses, which have been placed at the beginning of this anthology because they reflect the controversies and conflicts of the first three decades of Canadian nationhood, are examples of a different and perhaps more firmly "engaged" kind of writing. The speech delivered in 1874 at Aurora, Ontario, by Edward Blake, the brilliant and unorthodox leader of the Liberals, pledged an allegiance to the Canada First movement and looked forward to an eventually independent Canada as an equal partner of Great Britain, Goldwin Smith, in his *Canada and the Canadian Question* of 1891, offered an entirely different solution to the economic and political difficulties of the young nation: political union with the United States. This, he felt, was bound to happen because of the geographic divisions of the country and the division between the French and English inhabitants.

In the interval between the writing of Blake's speech and Goldwin Smith's book Canada was agitated and divided by the two rebellions in the West led by Louis Riel. Riel's defence of his actions and his speech before sentence has an eloquence and humanity which, like the final speech of Vanzetti, gains rather than loses by the speaker's imperfect command of English. It is followed here by the bitter but dignified denunciation of the courts that was subsequently made by Sir Wilfrid Laurier, one of the great Canadian statesman's finest speeches.

The second and major part of our book is concerned with the increasingly rapid changes in the moral, social, and economic life of the nation and with the emotional and spiritual experience of individuals. All these, particularly as they are reflected in Canadian fiction, seemed to crest in two great waves, the first between the two world wars, and the second in the last two decades.

The most notable development in prose literature was the rise of critical realism, especially in the work of three ambitious and successful professional novelists: Frederick Philip Grove, Morley Callaghan, and Hugh MacLennan. This was accomplished mainly in the thirties and forties.

Grove is the most original of the three writers, though this is not, alas, to praise him. He is, indeed, a very special case. Dogged, persistent, dour, touched with megalomania, a bad writer often, sometimes an excellent one, Grove, as seen through his grim and uncompromising novels and his "autobiographical" books, nevertheless impresses one as a heroic figure. He did much to liberate the Cana-

dian literary scene from the sexual inhibitions and cheerful sentimen-
talities of the earlier years of the century. He is a kind of native—or
rather, naturalized—Strindberg or Knut Hamsun, though reduced, it
cannot be denied, to a lower denominator. Yet the man was an artist,
slowly and obstinately working his way into and through a subject.
The astonishing chapter "I Come in Contact with Humanity Again,"
from the supposedly autobiographical *A Search for America*, shows
his seemingly naive but actually very sophisticated artistry at its rare
best.

Morley Callaghan too is a dedicated and self-conscious artist who
carefully and painfully learned his trade. His apprenticeship included
newspaper work in Toronto, where he became friendly with Ernest
Hemingway, and a kind of "coming of age" in the Paris of Hemingway, Fitzgerald, Gertrude Stein, and Joyce. His first short stories
were praised by Sinclair Lewis and Hemingway, and the names of
Flaubert and Tolstoy were invoked in much the same way as Edmund Wilson was later to call up that of Turgenev. The stories dealt
simply, objectively, and sympathetically with the lives of the poor
and humble in a Canadian city, unmistakably Toronto, and they
were first published in the *avant-garde* literary journals run by expatriate Americans—*transition*, *This Quarter*, and Ezra Pound's
Exile, as well as in *The Canadian Forum*. Returning to Toronto at
the onset of the depression, Callaghan devoted himself with single-
minded energy to the writing of stories, novellas, and novels, the best
of which are among the most distinguished contributions to our
literature by a living writer.

The earliest novels were published between 1928 and 1932, along
with the collection of short stories, *A Native Argosy*, in 1929. Then
in the years between 1934 and 1937 came Callaghan's three most
impressive successes: *Such is my Beloved*, the story of a young priest's
ill-starred efforts to help two unfortunate prostitutes; *They Shall Inherit the Earth*, a dramatic study of the relations between a father
and son; and *More Joy in Heaven*, a tragic account of the sacrificial
figure of a reformed convict who becomes the victim of society when
he champions the cause of the oppressed.

In the three novels mentioned and in his short stories Callaghan's
philosophy of style finds its most perfect expression. Writing, he has
affirmed, must be uncomplicated and direct. Avoiding metaphor and
symbol, it should present the object, not seek to change it into something else. Such a style was placed at the service of a moral seriousness

that differentiates his work from naturalistic fiction and from the social propaganda that invalidates so many American novels of the thirties. In each of the novels an implied moral dilemma is worked out in terms of character and action. The problem is how to become a *person* and attain or preserve human integrity in the face of a mechanized and amoral social condition. Father Dowling in *Such is my Beloved*, Kip Caley in *More Joy in Heaven*, and Andrew Aikenhead in *They Shall Inherit the Earth*, while they fail or suffer in the eyes of the world, find an ultimate salvation in some aspect of Christian love. The underlying religious implication of these novels is not found in their biblical titles alone.

This kind of "engagement" is also found in the later novels, *The Loved and the Lost* (1951), *The Many Coloured Coat* (1960), and *A Passion in Rome* (1961), which appeared after a long silence. In these the austerity of style which gave the three earlier successes their peculiar effectiveness has been replaced by something more ambitious, complex, and conventional. In spite of the seriousness and scope of the intention the later books are comparatively diffuse and sometimes sentimental. As the critic George Woodcock has pointed out, Callaghan's best work since the three middle novels and the early short stories is the fascinating autobiographical volume, *That Summer in Paris* (1963).

Much of the success of the third novelist mentioned, Hugh MacLennan, can be attributed to his dealing in every one of his books with themes of immense importance to Canadians—the problem of individual and national identity in *Barometer Rising;* the relations between the French and English in *Two Solitudes* and *Return of the Sphinx;* and the fate of the practical liberal in *The Watch that Ends the Night*. It is the insistence of these problems themselves rather than the originality or cogency of their analysis or solution that has made these books a part of the national consciousness.

Actually, however, MacLennan's real superiority lies in what might be called "pure," or, better perhaps, "heroic" narrative. The masterly account of the Halifax explosion in *Barometer Rising* or the powerful episode from *The Watch that Ends the Night* included here are cases in point. In these the speed of the writing, its convincing reality, and its faithfulness to human instinct and emotion place MacLennan firmly in the tradition of Hearne or David Thompson and show him to be a forerunner of the movement towards symbolic fiction we have mentioned above and shall return to in a moment.

The work of realists younger than Callaghan and MacLennan reveals an increasing subtlety and experimentation in theme and style, though the range is narrower and the scope less ambitious. Examples of these trends are found here in the stories by Sinclair Ross, Hugh Garner, and Hugh Hood, and indeed in the stories of Jack Ludwig, Mordecai Richler, and Alice Munro, which because of their peculiar amalgam of irony and sentiment have been grouped in the section entitled "Character and Comedy."

These stories are perhaps more conventional than some in our final section, but they should not be thought of as any the less accomplished or less cogent. Such writings are a development from the local color novels of the earlier period and from the soberer realism of the thirties, but the tone is sharp, the characterization vivid, and a spirit of irony, gentle and sympathetic or bitter and sometimes savage, informs them all. As novelists, Ethel Wilson and Robertson Davies, because of the bulk of their output and its consistently high standard of technique, are quite as important as Callaghan, MacLennan, or Mordecai Richler. They are *humourists* in the Jonsonian sense, inheritors—one might almost say "guardians"—of an older English culture. Their work is given relevance by a lively intelligence and an informed delight. So too is the sensitive and quietly malicious account by John Glassco of his sojourn in a Laurentian mountain sanitarium, a fitting epilogue to his *Memoirs of Montparnasse,* an incomparable evocation of the literary and bohemian Paris of the twenties.

The ironic tone, gentle and humorous in the pieces by Ethel Wilson, Robertson Davies, and W. O. Mitchell, is seen as acidly critical in Thomas Raddall's "Bald Eagle" and hilariously raucous in Mordecai Richler's "Mortimer Griffin, Shalinsky, and How They Settled the Jewish Question." The stories by Raddall and Richler are pointedly satiric, and they deal with a theme of vital significance—the relations between different ethnic groups. "Bald Eagle" is the more oblique and the subtler of the two. It is not primarily concerned with the Red Man, noble or otherwise, but with the Britisher who tries —and indeed succeeds—to become more native than the native: an impostor who takes in everybody but Mr. Raddall. He may stand also for the fake literary man who deceives the public and wins acclaim (although Grey Owl, Raddall's model for the story, was in fact a writer of considerable talent).

In the late fifties and all through the sixties into the seventies there has been a marked change in the dominant trend of Canadian fiction, a movement away from but growing out of realism, naturalistic or critical—a movement in the direction of symbolism, influenced if only obliquely by such modern writers as Lawrence, Kafka, Graves, and Joyce. This "new fiction" is illustrated chiefly in the concluding section, which in some ways is the most rewarding of all. Especially notable are the glittering *tour de force* from A. M. Klein's unique evocation of modern Jewish history, *The Second Scroll,* and the auto-biographical novella "Through the Panama" by Malcolm Lowry. Equally distinguished is the Conradian account of the Homeric fight with the bear from Howard O'Hagan's too long neglected novel *Tay John.* In the stories by Sheila Watson and Margaret Laurence some of the themes of classical tragedy are presented with a contemporary and northern relevance. In George Whalley's factual narrative of the death of John Hornby in the Arctic and in Dave Godfrey's strange story, we see history and fact changing into myth before our eyes. In all these tales we have a creative application of the theories of myth in the literary criticism of Northrop Frye and Robert Graves, so that they form a kind of prose parallel to the poetry of such Canadian writers as Jay Macpherson, James Reaney, and Eli Mandel.

The criticism of Frye, which has had an effect on modern theories of literature that extends far beyond the borders of Canada, is represented here by one of the most useful and stimulating analyses of prose style—or rather, styles—that has been formulated in modern times, and as such has a special interest for the reader or student of this book. So, too, should the fine discussion of the difficulties the Canadian writer has always had to face in overcoming the limitations of Colonialism, by the distinguished scholar-critic E. K. Brown, who died in 1951 at the age of forty-six. Criticism itself is lucidly examined in the essay by George Woodcock, who, as writer and as editor of *Canadian Literature,* has contributed prolifically and wisely to our understanding of many of the writers and developments represented in this book. Quite as boldly original as Frye, and even more famous, is the critic and philosopher Marshall McLuhan. McLuhan is as experimental as any writer who has come upon the scene in Canada during the fifties and sixties—and these include the symbolist novelists and the "new wave" poets. He is experimental both in thought and style, and, indeed, in his later books the style *is* the thought—"The medium *is* the message." Style has become for McLuhan what it is for the advertising layout man, the typographer, or the billboard display artist—a means of enlisting the eye and ear in order to affect a reader accustomed to radio and TV rather than to books. It is

important therefore to have some reassurance from an enthusiast of
the new electronic age that the humanities, which since Gutenberg
have been fostered by books, are not inevitably doomed by the new
science of instant communication.

Historical writing also became original and bold, and such works
as Creighton's *Commercial Empire of the St. Lawrence,* Underhill's
In Search of Canadian Liberalism, and Lower's *From Colony to
Nation* are classics of our literature as well as of our scholarship.
Among Canadian historians of the present day the most distinguished are these three—Donald Creighton, the late Frank Underhill, and Arthur Lower. The first is a conservative nationalist; the
second stood a little to the left of liberalism; and the third is an
eclectic individualist who somehow manages to keep to the middle
road of practical nationalism. The contribution of all three is discussed with insight and scholarship in the essay by Ramsay Cook
from his post-centennial study, *The Maple Leaf Forever.*

The suspicion of irony in Professor Cook's title, the need to admit
the possibility, however remote, that the Maple Leaf may not flourish
forever, leads us to examine before we leave these considerations
whether the survey of English-Canadian prose literature since Confederation can tell us anything about the much discussed and sometimes tedious question of Canadian identity. Do we find here, for
instance, a unity, a harmony, a set of common characteristics, rising
perhaps out of a common confrontation of common experience, or,
if it is too much to expect *identity,* are there perhaps analogies and
agreements, a sharing and an equitable distribution of common
possessions and responsibilities, so that Canada is really a nation as
certainly as the ethnically and geographically even more diverse
United States?

These questions will have to be left to the consensus of opinion
formed by readers and critics. The editor's opinion perhaps finds
expression in the pieces of literature he has chosen to include, though
his criterion has been in every case literary, not social, political, or
historical. He believes, however, that the genuine, deep, and therefore
significant emotions and ideas are the ones that produce works of art
of permanent value, whether in poetry or prose, painting, music, or
architecture, and conversely therefore it is from art in all its forms
that the true essence, *soul,* if you will, of a country can best be discerned. Here then is a book of testimony—something for the record.

PART I

THE EXPANDING DOMINION, 1867-1914

1. Affirmation and Conflict

EDWARD BLAKE

1833-1912

Born in Adelaide, Upper Canada, and educated at Upper
Canada College and the University of Toronto, Edward Blake
had a long and distinguished career as a liberal politician,
though it is an ironic fact that the loftiness of his ideals and
his intellectual distinction kept him from the highest office.
He was a member of Alexander Mackenzie's liberal cabinet
for a few months in 1873 and 4, but he resigned to announce
his adherence to the new Canada First party and to deliver
the remarkable speech from which a selection is printed below.
He returned to the Liberal Party in 1875 and became Minister
of Justice. He was leader of the opposition from 1877 to 1887.
He attacked the proposal for the construction of the cpr, supported efforts to commute the death sentence on Riel, and
opposed Laurier's advocacy of reciprocity with the United
States. This brought about his refusal to stand for re-election
in 1891. He went to Ireland and was elected to the British
House of Commons as an Irish supporter of Home Rule.
Ill-health forced his retirement in 1907, and he returned to
Canada, dying in Toronto five years later.

The speech which he delivered in Aurora, Ontario, on
October 3, 1874, was an early statement of an enthusiastic and
enlightened Canadian imperialism. It advocated federation of
the Empire and some radical constitutional reforms. The
Canadian people were described as four million of Britons
who are not free. The speech aroused enthusiasm among

the younger members of the Liberal Party but alarmed the older and more conventional reformers. It was printed as a pamphlet entitled *"A National Sentiment," Speech of Hon. Edward Blake at Aurora*, Ottawa, 1874, and reprinted as *Edward Blake's Aurora Speech*, Toronto, 1921. Sir Wilfrid Laurier, in spite of his disagreement with Blake over reciprocity, called him "the most powerful intellectual force in Canadian political history."

belong. We have been invited by Mr Gladstone and other English statesmen—notably by Mr. Gladstone, in the House of Commons, very shortly before his Government fell, to come forward. Mr. Gladstone, speaking as Prime Minister of England, expressed the hope he cherished, that the Colonies would some day come forward, and express their readiness and desire to accept their full share in the privileges and responsibilities of Britons. It is for us to determine— not now, not this year, not perhaps during this Parliamentary term, but yet, at no distant day—what our line shall be. For my part I believe that while it was not unnatural, not unreasonable, pending that process of development which has been going on in our new and sparsely settled country, that we should have been quite willing—we so few in numbers, so busied in our local concerns, so engaged in subduing the earth and settling up the country—to leave the cares and privileges to which I have referred in the hands of the parent State; the time will come when that national spirit which has been spoken of will be truly felt among us, when we shall realize that we are four millions of Britons who are not free, when we shall be ready to take up that freedom, and to ask what the late Prime Minister of England assured us we should not be denied—our share of national rights. To-morrow, by the policy of England, in which you have no voice or control, this country might be plunged into the horrors of a war. It is but the other day, that without your knowledge or consent, the navigation of the St. Lawrence was ceded forever to the United States. That is a state of things of which you may have no right to complain, as long as you can choose to say, "We prefer to avoid the cares, the expenses and charges, and we are unequal in point of ability to discharge the duties which appertain to us as free-born Britons"; but while you say this, you may not yet assume the lofty air, or speak in the high-pitched tones, which belong to a people wholly free. The future of Canada, I believe, depends very largely upon the cultivation of a national spirit. We are engaged in a very difficult task—the task of welding together seven Provinces which have been accustomed to regard themselves as isolated from each other, which are full of petty jealousies, their Provincial questions, their local interests. How are we to accomplish our work? How are we to effect a real union between these Provinces? Can we do it by giving a sop now to one, now to another, after the manner of the late Government? By giving British Columbia the extravagant terms which have been referred to; by giving New Brunswick $150,000 a year for an export duty which cannot be made out as worth more than $65,000 a year? Do you hope to create or to preserve harmony and good feeling upon such a false and sordid and mercenary basis as that? Not so! That day I hope is done for ever, and we must find some other and truer ground for Union than that by which the late Government sought to buy love and purchase peace. We must find some common ground on which to unite, some common aspiration to be shared, and I think it can be found alone in the cultivation of that national spirit to which I have referred. I observe that those who say a word on this subject are generally struck at by the cry that they are practically advocating annexation. I believe that the feeling in the neighbouring Republic has materially changed on this subject, and that the notions which were widely spread there some years ago, and the desire to possess, as one Republic, under one Government, the whole of this continent, from north to south, have died away. A better and a wiser spirit, I believe, now prevails—largely due, per- haps, to the struggles which are unhappily occurring in that country. The attempt to reorganize the South has been going on for some years, and owing, I think, to a very great error in judgment as to the way in which it should be effected, it has been largely a failure. There is great difficulty, and there are frequent disorders in the South. Then there are the conflicts of interest between the Eastern and Western States, very great conflicts and heartburnings. Then there are the alarming difficulties and complications arising from the inordinate political power which has been grasped by great corpora- tions. And I think that the best and wisest minds in the United States have settled down to the conviction that the management of the United States with its present territory is just as difficult a task as their best men can accomplish, and that it would not be wise to add to their existing complications and difficulties by any such unwieldy accession or unmanageable increase as this great domain, the larger half of the whole continent, would be. I think that among those circles in the United States which are to be looked to as influencing the future, there is a great modification of view on this point, and there would be, even were we disposed, as I hope we shall never be disposed, to offer to join them, a great reluctance to take us. But I believe we have a future of our own here. My opinion coincides with those to which I have been referring in the United States. I believe that that country is even larger than it ought to be in order to be well governed, and that an extension of its territory would be very unfortunate in the interests of civilisation. "Cribbed, cabined, and confined" as we ourselves are to the South by the unfortunate acts of English diplomatists in the past, giving up to the United States territory which, if we had it today, would make our future absolutely assured, but still retaining as we do the great North-west, I believe we can show that there is room and verge enough in North America for the maintenance of two distinct governments, and that there is nothing to be said in favour, but on the contrary everything to be said against, the notion of annexation. These are the material reasons, independent altogether of the very strong and justly adverse feeling arising from our affection for and our association with England, and the well settled conviction which I believe exists among the people of this country, that a Constitutional Monarchy is preferable to a Republican Government. The Monarchical Government of England is a truer application of real Republican principles than that of the United States, and I have no hesitation in saying that the Government of Canada is far in advance, in the application of real Republican principles, of the Government of either England or the United States. But, with the very great advantages which we enjoy over that portion of our fellow-subjects living in England, by reason of our having come into a new country, having settled it for ourselves, and adapted our institutions to modern notions, by reason of our not being cumbered by the constitution of a legislative chamber on the hereditary principle, by reason of our not being cumbered with an aristocracy or with the unfortunate principle of primogeniture and the aggregation of the land in very few hands, by reason of our not being cumbered with the difficulties which must always exist where a community is composed of classes differing from one another in worldly circumstances so widely as the classes in England differ, where you can go into one street of the City of London and find the extreme of wealth, and a mile or two away the very extreme of poverty; living, as we do, in a country where these difficulties do not exist, where we early freed ourselves from the incubus of a State Church, where we early provided for the educational needs of our people, under these happy circumstances, with these great privileges, there are corresponding responsibilities. Much remains to be done even here before we can say that the ideal of true popular Government has been reached; and some mistakes have been made, in my poor judgment, in the course already taken.

LOUIS RIEL
1844-1885

Born in St. Boniface in what is now the province of Manitoba, Louis Riel was educated at the Jesuit College in Montreal. Of French and Indian ancestry, he championed the cause of the Métis landholders and buffalo hunters in the Red River district in resisting the encroachment of English-Canadian immigrants from the East. In 1869-1870 he organized a provincial government at Fort Garry but fled to the United States when his ill-judged and irresponsible execution of one of his prisoners, Thomas Scott, led the Canadian government to despatch a punitive force under Colonel Wolseley. Though under indictment, he was elected to the House of Commons in 1873 and again in February, 1874. Risking arrest, he signed the register as a Member of Parliament, but once more fled the country and was expelled from the House. He was re-elected in September, 1874, but did not take his seat. In 1875 he was banished for five years. He returned to Canada in 1884 and took command of rebel forces in Saskatchewan. After some successes, he was taken prisoner at Batoche when a powerful force quickly sent from the East made further resistance impossible. Riel was tried in Regina on a charge of treason and in spite of appeals and protests, particularly from French Canada, was hanged on November 16, 1885.

Mason Wade speaks of the "remarkable, if confused, eloquence" of the two speeches which Riel made at his trial and asserts that Riel's "deep religiosity was very manifest in a

moving plea which is quite as effective . . . as Bartolomeo
Vanzetti's."

Riel's religious verse was published in a small pamphlet in
Montreal in the year after his execution under the title *Poésies
réligieuses et politiques par Louis "David" Riel.* The speeches
below were printed in *Epitome of Parliamentary Documents
in connection with the North-West Rebellion* 1885, Ottawa,
Printed by Order of Parliament, 1886.

Prisoner—Your Honours, gentlemen of the jury: It would be easy for me to-day to play insanity, because the circumstances are such as to excite any man, and under the natural excitement of what is taking place to-day (I cannot speak English very well, but am trying to do so, because most of those here speak English), under the excitement which my trial causes me would justify me not to appear as usual, but with my mind out of its ordinary condition. I hope with the help of God I will maintain calmness and decorum as suits this honourable court, this honourable jury.

You have seen by the papers in the hands of the Crown that I am naturally inclined to think of God at the beginning of my actions. I wish, if you—I do it, you won't take it as a mark of insanity, that you won't take it as part of a play of insanity. Oh my God, help me through Thy grace and the divine influence of Jesus Christ. Oh, my God, bless me, bless this honourable court, bless this honourable jury, bless my good lawyers who have come 700 leagues to try to save my life, bless also the lawyers for the Crown, because they have done, I am sure, what they thought their duty. They have shown me fairness which at first I did not expect from them. Oh, my God, bless all those who are around me through the grace and influence of Jesus Christ Our Saviour, change the curiosity of those who are paying attention to me, change that curiosity into sympathy with me. The day of my birth I was helpless and my mother took care of me although she was not able to do it alone, there was some one to help her to take care of me and I lived. To-day, although a man, I am as helpless before this court, in the Dominion of Canada and in this world, as I was helpless on the knees of my mother the day of my birth.

The North-West is also my mother, it is my mother country, and although my mother country is sick and confined in a certain way, there are some from Lower Canada who came to help her to take care of me during her sickness and I am sure that my mother country will not kill me more than my mother did forty years ago, when I came into the world, because a mother is always a mother, and even if I have my faults, if she can see I am true, she will be full of love for me.

When I came into the North-West in July, the first of July, 1884, I found the Indians suffering. I found the half-breeds eating the rotten pork of the Hudson Bay Company and getting sick and weak every day. Although a half-breed, and having no pretension to help the whites, I also paid attention to them. I saw they were deprived of responsible government, I saw that they were deprived of their public liberties, I remembered that half-breed meant white and Indian, and while I paid attention to the suffering Indians and the half-breeds, I remembered that the greatest part of my heart and blood was white, and I have directed my attention to help the Indians, to help the half-breeds and to help the whites to the best of my ability. We have made petitions, I have made petitions with others to the Canadian Government asking to relieve the condition of this country. We have taken time; we have tried to unite all classes even if I may so speak, all parties. Those who have been in close communication with me know I have suffered, that I have waited for months to bring some of the people of the Saskatchewan to an understanding of certain important points in our petition to the Canadian Government and I have done my duty. I believe I have done my duty. It has been said in this box that I have been egotistic. Perhaps I am egotistic. A man cannot be an individuality without paying attention to himself. He cannot generalize himself, though he may be general. I have done all I could to make good petitions with others, and we have sent them to the Canadian Government, and when the Canadian Government did answer, through the Under-Secretary of State to the secretary of the joint committee of the Saskatchewan, then I began to speak of myself, not before; so my particular interests passed after the public interests. . . .

No one can say that the North-West was not suffering last year, particularly the Saskatchewan, for the other parts of the North-West I cannot say so much; but what I have done, and risked, and to which I have exposed myself, rested certainly on the conviction, I had to do, was called upon to do something for my country.

It is true, gentlemen, I believed for years I had a mission, and when

I speak of a mission, you will understand me not as trying to play the role of insane before the grand jury so as to have a verdict of acquittal upon that ground. I believe that I have a mission, I believe that I had a mission at this very moment. What encourages me to speak to you with more confidence in all the imperfections of my English way of speaking, it is that I have yet and still that mission, and with the help of God, who is in this box with me, and He is on the side of my lawyers, even with the honourable court, the Crown and the jury, to help me and to prove by the extraordinary help that there is a Providence to-day in my trial, as there was a Providence in the battles of the Saskatchewan.

I have not assumed to myself that I had a mission. I was working in Manitoba first, and I did all I could to get free institutions for Manitoba; they have those institutions to-day in Manitoba, and they try to improve them, while myself, who obtained them, I am forgotten as if I was dead. But after I had obtained, with the help of others, a constitution for Manitoba, when the Government at Ottawa was not willing to inaugurate it at the proper time, I have worked till the inauguration should take place, and that is why I have been banished for five years. I had to rest five years, I was willing to do it. I protested. I said: "Oh, my God, I offer You all my existence for that cause, and please to make of my weakness an instrument to help men in my country." And seeing my intentions, the late Archbishop Bourget said: "Riel has no narrow views, he is a man to accomplish great things," and he wrote that letter of which I hope that the Crown has at least a copy. And in another letter, when I became what doctors believed to be insane, Bishop Bourget wrote again and said: "Be blessed by God and man and take patience in your evils." Am I not taking patience? Will I be blessed by man as I have been by God?

I say that I have been blessed by God, and I hope that you will not take that as a presumptuous assertion. It has been a great success for me to come through all the dangers I have in that fifteen years. If I have not succeeded in wearing a fine coat myself I have at the same time the great consolation of seeing that God has maintained my views; that He has maintained my health sufficiently to go through the world, and that He has kept me from bullets, when bullets marked my hat. I am blessed by God. It is this trial that is going to show that I am going to be blessed by man during my existence, the benedictions are a guarantee that I was not wrong when by circumstances I was taken away from my adopted land to my native land. When I see British people sitting in the court to try me, remembering that the English people are proud of that word "fair-play," I am confident that I will be blessed by God and by man also.

Not only Bishop Bourget spoke to me in that way, but Father Jean-Baptiste Bruno, the priest of Worcester, who was my director of conscience, said to me : "Riel, God has put an object into your hands, the cause of the triumph of religion in the world, take care, you will succeed when most believe you have lost." I have got those words in my heart, those words of J.-B. Bruno and the late Archbishop Bourget. But last year, while I was yet in Montana, and while I was passing before the Catholic church, the priest, the Reverend Father Frederick Ebeville, curate of the church of the Immaculate Conception, at Benton, said to me : "I am glad to see you; is your family here?" I said : "Yes." He said : "Go and bring them to the altar, I want to bless you before you go away." And with Gabriel Dumont and my family we all went on our knees at the altar, the priest put on his surplice and he took holy water and was going to bless us, I said : "Will you allow me to pronounce a prayer while you bless me?" He said : "Yes, I want to know what it is." I told him the prayer. It is speaking to God : "My Father, bless me according to the views of Thy Providence which are bountiful and without measure." He said to me : "You can say that prayer while I bless you." Well, he blessed me and I pronounced that prayer for myself, for my wife, for my children, and for Gabriel Dumont.

When the glorious General Middleton fired on us during three days, and on our families, and when shells went and bullets went as thick as mosquitoes in the hot days of summer, when I saw my children, my wife, myself and Gabriel Dumont were escaping, I said that nothing but the blessing without measure of Father Frederick Ebeville could save me, and that can save me to-day from these charges. . . .

The agitation in the North-West Territories would have been constitutional, and would certainly be constitutional to-day if, in my opinion, we had not been attacked. Perhaps the Crown has not been able to find out the particulars, that we were attacked, but as we were on the scene it was easy to understand. When we sent petitions to the Government, they used to answer us by sending police, and when the rumours were increasing every day that Riel has been shot here or there, or that Riel was going to be shot by such and such a man, the police would not pay any attention to it. I am glad that I have mentioned the police, because of the testimony that has been given in the box during the examination of many of the witnesses. If I had been allowed to put questions to the witnesses, I would have asked them when it was I said a single word against a single police-man or a single officer. I have respected the policemen, and I do to-day, and I have respected the officers of the police; the paper that I sent to Major Crozier is a proof of it: "We respect you, Major." There are papers which the Crown has in its hands, and which show that demoralization exists among the police, if you will allow me to say it in the court, as I have said it in writing.

Your Honours, gentlemen of the jury: If I was a man of to-day perhaps it would be presumptuous to speak in that way, but the truth is good to say, and it is said in a proper manner, and it is without any presumption, it is not because I have been libelled for fifteen years that I do not believe myself something. I know that through the grace of God I am the founder of Manitoba. I know that though I have no open road for my influence, I have big influence, concen-trated as a big amount of vapour in an engine. I believe by what I suffered for fifteen years, by what I have done for Manitoba and the people of the North-West, that my words are worth something. If I give offence, I do not speak to insult. Yes, you are the pioneers of civilization, the whites are the pioneers of civilization, but they bring among the Indians demoralization. Do not be offended, ladies, do not be offended, here are the men who can cure that evil; and if at times I have been strong against my true friends and fathers, the reverend priests of the Saskatchewan, it is because my convictions are strong. There have been witnesses to show that immediately after great passion I could come back to the great respect I have for them. . . .

As to religion, what is my belief? What is my insanity about that? My insanity, your Honours, gentlemen of the jury, is that I wish to leave Rome aside, inasmuch as it is the cause of division between Catholics and Protestants. I did not wish to force my views, because in Batoche to the half-breeds that followed me I used the word, *carte blanche*. If I have any influence in the new world it is to help in that way and even if it takes 200 years to become practical, then after my death that will bring out practical results, and then my children's children will shake hands with the Protestants of the new world in a friendly manner. I do not wish these evils which exist in Europe to be continued, as much as I can influence it, among the half-breeds. I do not wish that to be repeated in America. That work is not the work of some days or some years, it is the work of hundreds of years.

My condition is helpless, so helpless that my good lawyers, and they have done it by conviction (Mr. Fitzpatrick in his beautiful speech has proved he believed I was insane) my condition seems to be so helpless that they have recourse to try and prove insanity to try and save me in that way. If I am insane, of course I don't know it, it is a property of insanity to be unable to know it. But what is the kind of mission that I have? Practical results. It is said that I had myself acknowledged as a prophet by the half-breeds. The half-breeds have some intelligence. Captain Young who has been so polite and gentle during the time I was under his care, said that what was done at Batoche, from a military point of view was nice, that the line of defence was nice, that showed some intelligence.

It is not to be supposed that the half-breeds acknowledged me as a prophet if they had not seen that I could see something into the future. If I am blessed without measure I can see something into the future, we all see into the future more or less. As what kind of a prophet would I come, would it be a prophet who would all the time have a stick in his hand, and threatening, a prophet of evil? If the half-breeds had acknowledged me as a prophet, if on the other side priests come and say that I am polite, if there are general officers, good men, come into this box and prove that I am polite, prove that I am decent in my manner, in combining all together you have a decent prophet. An insane man cannot withhold his insanity, if I am insane my heart will tell what is in me.

Last night while I was taking exercise the spirit who guides and assists me and consoles me told me that to-morrow somebody will come *t'aider,* five English and one French word *t'aider,* that is to help you. I am consoled by that. While I was recurring to my God, to our God, I said, but woe to me if you do not help me, and these words came to me in the morning, in the morning some one will come *t'aider,* that is to-day. I said that to my two guards and, you can go for the two guards. I told them that if the spirit that directs me is the spirit of truth it is to-day that I expect help. This morning the good doctor who has care of me came to me and said, you will speak to-day before the court. I thought I would not be allowed to speak; those words were given to me to tell me that I would have liberty to speak. There was one French word in it, it meant I believe that there was to be some French influence in it, but the most part English. It is true that my good lawyers from the Province of Quebec have given me good advice. . . .

You have given me your attention, your Honours; you have given me your attention, gentlemen of the jury, and this great audience, I see that if I go any further on that point I will lose the favour you have granted me up to this time, and as I am aiming all the time at practical results, I will stop here, master of myself, through the help of God. I have only a few more words to say, your Honours. Gentlemen of the jury, my reputation, my liberty, my life, are at your discretion. So confident am I, that I have not the slightest anxiety, not even the slightest doubt, as to your verdict. The calmness of my mind concerning the favourable decision which I expect, does not come from any unjustifiable presumption upon my part. I simply trust, that through God's help, you will balance everything in a conscientious manner, and that, having heard what I had to say, that you will acquit me. I do respect you, although you are only half a jury, but your number of six does not prevent you from being just and conscientious; your number of six does not prevent me giving you my confidence, which I would grant to another six men. Your Honour, because you appointed these men, do not believe that I disrespect you. It is not by your own choice, you were authorised by those above you, by the authorities in the North-West; you have acted according to your duty, and while it is, in our view, against the guarantees of liberty, I trust the Providence of God will bring out good of what you have done conscientiously.

Although this court has been in existence for the last fifteen years, I thought I had a right to be tried in another court. I do not disrespect this court. I do respect it, and what is called by my learned and good lawyers, the incompetency of the court must not be called in disrespect, because I have all respect.

The only things I would like to call your attention to before you retire to deliberate are:—1st. That the House of Commons, Senate and Ministers of the Dominion, and who make laws for this land and govern it, are no representation whatever of the people of the North-West.

2nd. That the North-West Council generated by the Federal Government has the great defect of its parent.

3rd. The number of members elected for the Council by the people make it only a sham representative legislature and no representative government at all.

British civilization which rules to-day the world, and the British constitution has defined such government as this is which rules the North-West Territories as irresponsible government, which plainly means that there is no responsibility, and by all the science which has been shown here yesterday you are compelled to admit if there is no responsibility, it is insane.

Good sense combined with scientific theories lead to the same conclusion. By the testimony laid before you during my trial witnesses on both sides made it certain that petition after petition had been sent to the Federal Government, and so irresponsible is that Government to the North-West that in the course of several years, besides doing nothing to satisfy the people of this great land, it has even hardly been able to answer once or to give a single response. That fact would indicate an absolute lack of responsibility, and therefore insanity complicated with paralysis.

The Ministers of an insane and irresponsible Government and its little one—the North-West Council—made up their minds to answer my petitions by surrounding me slyly and by attempting to jump upon me suddenly and upon my people in the Saskatchewan. Happily when they appeared and showed their teeth to devour, I was ready: that is what is called my crime of high treason, and to which they hold me to-day. Oh, my good jurors, in the name of Jesus Christ, the only one who can save and help me, they have tried to tear me to pieces.

If you take the plea of the defence that I am not responsible for my acts, acquit me completely since I have been quarrelling with an insane and irresponsible Government. If you pronounce in favour of the Crown, which contends that I am responsible, acquit me all the same. You are perfectly justified in declaring that having my reason and sound mind, I have acted reasonably and in self defence, while the Government, my accuser, being irresponsible, and consequently insane, cannot but have acted wrong, and if high treason there is it must be on its side and not on my part.

His Honour.—Are you done?

Prisoner.—Not yet, if you have the kindness to permit me your attention for a while.

His Honour.—Well, proceed.

Prisoner.—For fifteen years I have been neglecting myself. Even one of the most hard witnesses on me said that with all my vanity, I never was particular to my clothing; yes, because I never had much to buy any clothing. The Rev. Father André has often had the kindness to feed my family with a sack of flour, and Father Fourmand. My wife and children are without means, while I am working more than any representative in the North-West. Although I am simply a guest of this country—a guest of the half-breeds of the Saskatchewan —although as a simple guest, I worked to better the condition of the people of the Saskatchewan at the risk of my life, to better the condition of the people of the North-West, I have never had any pay. It has always been my hope to have a fair living one day. It will be for you to pronounce—if you say I was right, you can conscientiously acquit me, as I hope through the help of God you will. You will console those who have been fifteen years around me only partaking in my sufferings. What you will do in justice to me, in justice to my family, in justice to my friends, in justice to the North-West, will be rendered a hundred times to you in this world, and to use a sacred expression, life everlasting in the other.

I thank your Honour for the favour you have granted me in speaking; I thank you for the attention you have given me, gentlemen of the jury, and I thank those who have had the kindness to encourage my imperfect way of speaking the English language by their good attention. I put my speech under the protection of my God, my Saviour, He is the only one who can make it effective. It is possible it should become effective, as it is proposed to good men, to good people, and to good ladies also. . . .

On the jury returning, after having retired to consider their verdict, the clerk of the court says, gentlemen are you agreed upon your verdict? How say you, is the prisoner guilty or not guilty?

The jury find the prisoner guilty.

Clerk.—Gentlemen of the jury, hearken to your verdict as the court records it, "You find the prisoner, Louis Riel, guilty, so say you all." The jury answer "guilty."

A Juror.—Your Honours, I have been asked by my brother jurors to recommend the prisoner to the mercy of the Crown.

Mr. Justice Richardson.—I may say in answer to you that the recommendation which you have given will be forwarded in proper manner to the proper authorities.

Mr. Robinson.—Do your Honours propose to pass sentence now? I believe the proper course is to ask the sentence of the court upon the prisoner.

Mr. Justice Richardson.—Louis Riel, have you anything to say why the sentence of the court should not be pronounced upon you, for the offence of which you have been found guilty?

Prisoner.—Yes, your Honour—

Mr. Fitzpatrick.—Before the accused answers or makes any re-marks, as suggested by your Honours, I would beg leave to ask your Honours to kindly note the objections which I have already taken to the jurisdiction of the court.

Mr. Justice Richardson.—It is noted, Mr. Fitzpatrick. You under-stand of course why I cannot rule upon it.

Mr. Fitzpatrick.—It is simply so as to reserve any recourse the law may allow us hereafter.

Prisoner.—Can I speak now?

Mr. Justice Richardson.—Oh, yes.

Prisoner.—Your Honours, gentlemen of the jury—

Mr. Justice Richardson.—There is no jury now, they are discharged.

Prisoner.—Well, they have passed away before me.

Mr. Justice Richardson.—Yes, they have passed away.

Prisoner.—But at the same time I consider them yet still there, still in their seats. The court has done the work for me, and although at first appearance it seems to be against me, I am so confident in the ideas which I have had the honour to express yesterday, that I think it is for good, and not for my loss. Up to this moment I have been considered by a certain party as insane, by another party as a criminal, by another party as a man with whom it was doubtful whether to have any intercourse. So there was hostility, and there was contempt, and there was avoidance. To-day, by the verdict of the court, one of those three situations has disappeared.

I suppose that after having been condemned, I will cease to be

called a fool, and for me, it is a great advantage. I consider it as a
great advantage. If I have a mission—I say "if," for the sake of
those who doubt, but for my part it means "since," since I have a
mission, I cannot fulfil my mission as long as I am looked upon as an
insane being—human being, as the moment I begin to ascend that
scale I begin to succeed.

You have asked me, your Honours, if I have anything to say why
my sentence should not be passed. Yes, it is on that point particularly
my attention is directed.

Before saying anything about it, I wish to take notice that if there
has ever been any contradiction in my life, it is at this moment, and
do I appear excited? Am I very irritable? Can I control myself? And
it is just on religion and on politics, and I am contradicted at this
moment on politics, and the smile that comes to my face is not an
act of my will so much as it comes naturally from the satisfaction
that I proved that I experienced seeing one of my difficulties disappearing. Should I be executed—at least if I were going to be
executed—I would not be executed as an insane man. It would be a
great consolation for my mother, for my wife, for my children, for
my brothers, for my relatives, even for my protectors, for my countrymen. I thank the gentlemen who were composing the jury for having
recommended me to the clemency of the court. When I expressed
the great hopes that I have just expressed to you, I don't express it
without grounds. My hopes are reasonable, and since they are recommended, since the recommendation of the jury to the Crown is
for clemency, it would be easy for me, your Honours, to make an in-
cendiary protest and take the three reasons which have been reasonably put forward by my good lawyers and learned lawyers about the
jury, about their selection, about the one who selected them, and
about the competency of the court; but why should I do it since the
court has undertaken to prove that I am a reasonable man? Must not
I take advantage of the situation to show that they are right, and
that I am reasonable? And yesterday, when I said, by repeating the
evidence which had been given against me, when I said in conclusion
that you had a decent prophet, I have just to-day the great opportunity of proving it is so. Besides clearing me of the stain of insanity,
clearing my career of the stain of insanity, I think the verdict that
has been given against me is a proof that I am more than ordinary
myself, but that the circumstances and the help which is given to me
is more than ordinary, are more than ordinary, and although I con-

sider myself only as others, yet by the will of God, by His Providence, by the circumstances which have surrounded me for fifteen years, I think that I have been called on to do something which, at least in the North-West, nobody has done yet. And in some way I think, that, to a certain number of people, the verdict against me to-day is a proof that maybe I am a prophet, maybe Riel is a prophet, he suffered enough for it. Now, I have been hunted as an elk for fifteen years. David has been seventeen, I think I will have to be about two years still. If the misfortunes that I have had to go through were to be as long as those of old David, I would have two years still, but I hope it will come sooner. I have two reasons why I would ask that sentence should not be passed upon me, against me. You will excuse me, you know my difficulty in speaking English, and have had no time to prepare, your Honours, and even had I prepared anything, it would have been imperfect enough, and I have not prepared, and I wish you would excuse what I have to say, the way which I will be able to perhaps express it.

The troubles of the Saskatchewan are not to be taken as an isolated fact. They are the result of fifteen years' war. The head of that difficulty lies in the difficulty of Red River. The troubles of Red River were called the troubles of the North-West, and I would like to know if the troubles of the Saskatchewan have not the name to-day of being the troubles of the North-West. So the troubles of 1869 being the troubles of the North-West, and the troubles of 1885 being still the troubles of the North-West, the suggestion comes naturally to the mind of the observer if it is a continuation. The troubles of the North-West in 1885 are the continuation of the troubles in 1869, or if they are two troubles entirely different — I say they are not. Canada — no, I ought not to say Canada, because it was a certain number of individuals, perhaps 700 or 800, that can have passed for Canada, but they came to the Red River, and they wanted to take possession of the country without consulting the people. True, it was the half-breed people. There were a certain number of white pioneers among the population, but the great majority were half-breeds. We took up arms against the invaders of the east without knowing them. They were so far apart of us, on the other side of the lakes, that it cannot be said that we had any hatred against them. We did not know them. They came without notification, they came boldly. We said, who are they, they said, we are the possessors of the country. Well, knowing that it was not true, we done against those parties coming from the east, what we used to do against the Indians from the south and the west, when they would invade us. Public opinion in the States helped us a great deal. . . . I don't mean to say that it is need to obtain justice on this side of the line that the States should interfere, but, at that time, as there was no telegraph communication between the eastern Provinces and the North-West, no railroad, and as the natural way of going to Canada was through the United States, naturally all the rumours, all the news, had to pass by the States, and on their passage they had to meet the remarks and observations of the American people. The American people were favourable to us. Besides, the opposition in Canada done the same thing, and said to the Government: Well, why did you go into the North-West without consulting the people? We took up arms, as I stated, and we made hundreds of prisoners, and we negotiated. A treaty was made. That treaty was made by a delegation of both parties. Whether you consider that organization of the Red River people at that time a provisional government, or not, the fact is that they were recognized as a body tribal, if you like to call it, as a social body with whom the Canadian Government treated. . . .

Our delegates had been invited three times, how were they received in Canada? They were arrested—to show exactly what is the right of nations. They were arrested, they had not a formal trial, but the fact remains that they were arrested, and the protest of the Rev. Father Richot is still in the document. However, there was a treaty. Sir John A. Macdonald was delegated, the late Sir George Cartier was delegated to treat with the people, with those three delegates. Now, how were they acknowledged? Were they acknowledged as the delegates of Riel? Oh, no, they were acknowledged as the delegates of the North-West. The late Mr. Howe, in his acknowledgment of the delegates, and in notifying them who had been delegated by the Canadian Government to treat with them, told them that they were acknowledged as the delegates of the North-West. Then it was the cause of the North-West that they represented. It is acknowledged by the Canadian Government by that very same fact that fifteen years ago the treaty of which I am speaking was a treaty of the North-West, of the delegates of the North-West, and if, by trying to say that it was the delegates of the North-West, they wanted to avoid the fact that I was no being at all, the whole world knows that it is not so; they cannot avoid me. And Sir John A. Macdonald himself, in the report of the committee of enquiry about those very same troubles—the committee sat in 1874—Sir John A. Macdonald said, I think we acknowledge Riel in his status of a governor. What was the treaty? Was it an Indian affair? If it had been an Indian affair Manitoba would not have been as it is, would not be as it is. We have the Manitoba Act. There was an agreement between the two delegates how the whole North-West interest would be considered and how the Canadian Government would treat with the North-West. And then, having settled on the matters of principle, those very principles, the agreement was made that those very principles would be inaugurated in Manitoba first. There was a province erected with responsible government; the lands, they were kept by the Dominion. As the half-breed people were the majority of Manitoba, as at their stage of civilization they were not supposed to be able to administer their lands, we thought that at that time it was a reasonable concession to let them go, not because we were willing to let them go, but because it seemed impracticable to have the administration of the lands. Still, one of the conditions was that the lands were—that the people of the North-West wanted the administration of their lands. The half-breeds had a million, and the land grant of 1,400,000 acres owned about 9,500,000, if I mistake not, which is about one-seventh of the lands of Manitoba. You will see the origin of my insanity and of my foreign policy. One-seventh of the land was granted to the people, to the half-breeds of Manitoba—English and French, Protestant and Catholic; there was no distinction whatever. But in the sub-division, in the allotment of those lands between the half-breeds of Manitoba, it came that they had 240 acres of land. Now, the Canadian Government say that we will give to the half-breeds of the North-West 240 acres. If I was insane I would say yes, but as I have had, thank God, all the time the consciousness that I had a certain degree of reason, I have made up my mind to make use of it, and to say that one-seventh of the lands in Manitoba, as to the inauguration of a principle in the North-West, had to bring to the half-breeds of the North-West at least as soon as possible the guarantee for the future that a seventh of the lands will also be given to them; and seeing and yourself understanding how it is difficult for a small population, as the half-breed population, to have their voices heard, I said what belongs to us ought to be ours. . . .

But somebody will say, on what grounds do you ask one-seventh of the lands? Do you own the lands? In England, in France, the French and the English have lands, the first who were in England, they were the owners of the soil and they transmitted to generations. Now, by the soil they have had their start as a nation. Who starts the nations? The very one who creates them, God. God is the master of the universe, our planet is his land, and the nations and the tribes are members of His family, and as a good father, He gives a portion of his lands to that nation, to that tribe, to everyone, that is his heritage, that is his share of the inheritance, of the people, or nation or tribe. Now, here is a nation strong as it may be, it has its inheritance from God. When they have crowded their country because they had no room to stay any more at home, it does not give them the right to come and take the share of all tribes besides them. When they come they ought to say, well, my little sister, the Cree tribe, you have a great territory, but that territory has been given to you as our own land, it has been given to our fathers in England or in France and of course you cannot exist without having that spot of land. This is the principle: God cannot create a tribe without locating it. We are not birds. We have to walk on the ground, and that ground is enriched with many things, which besides its own value, increases its value in another manner, and when we cultivate it we still increase that value. Well, on what principle can it be that the Canadian Government have given one-seventh to the half-breeds of Manitoba? I say it must be on this ground, civilization has the means of improving life that Indians or half-breeds have not. So when they come in our savage country, in our uncultivated land, they come and help us with their civilization, but we helped them with our lands, so the question comes: Your land, you Cree or you half-breed, your land is worth to-day one-seventh of what it will be when civilization will have opened it? Your country unopened is worth to you only one-seventh of what it will be when opened. I think it is a fair share to acknowledge the genius of civilization to such an extent as to give, when I have seven pair of socks, six, to keep one. . . .

This court was not in existence when the difficulties of which we speak now in the Saskatchewan, began; it is the difficulties of 1869, and what I say is, I wish that I have a trial. My wish is this, your

Honour, that a commission be appointed by the proper authorities, but amongst the proper authorities of course I count on English authorities, that is the first proper authorities; that a commission be appointed; that that commission examines into this quesion, or if they are appointed to try me, if a special tribunal is appointed to try me, that I am tried first on this question: Has Riel rebelled in 1869? Second question. Was Riel a murderer of Thomas Scott, when Thomas Scott was executed? Third question. When Riel received the money from Archbishop Taché, reported to be the money of Sir John, was it corruption money? Fourth. When Riel seized, with the council of Red River, on the property of the Hudson Bay Company, did he commit pillage? Fifth. When Riel was expelled from the House as a fugitive of justice in 1874, was he a fugitive of justice? . . .

Am I insulting? No, I do not insult. You don't mean to insult me when you declare me guilty; you act according to your convictions, I do also according to mine. I speak true. I say they should try me on this question, whether I rebelled on the Saskatchewan in 1885. There is another question. I want to have one trial; I wish to have a trial that will cover the space of fifteen years, on which public opinion is not satisfied. I have, without meaning any offence, I have heard, without meaning any offence, when I spoke of one of the articles I mentioned, some gentlemen behind me saying, "yes, he was a murderer." You see what remarks. It shows there is something not told. If told by law it would not be said. I wish to have my trial, as I am tried for nothing; and as I am tried for my career, I wish my career should be tried; not the last part of it. On the other side I am declared to be guilty of high treason, and I give myself as a prophet to the new world. If I am guilty of high treason I say that I am a prophet of the new world. I wish that while a commission sits on one side a commission of doctors should also sit and examine fully whether I am sane, whether I am a prophet or not; not insanity, because it is disposed of, but whether I am a deceiver and impostor. I have said to my good lawyers, I have written things which were said to me last night and which have taken place to-day; I said that before the court opened. Last night the spirit that guides and assists me told me the court will make an effort—your Honour, allow me to speak of your charge, which appeared to me to go on one side—the court made an effort, and I think that word is justified. At the same time there was another thing said to me; a commission will sit; there will be a commission. I did not hear yet that a commission is to take place. I ask for it. You will see if I am an impostor thereby. The doctors will say when I speak of these things whether I am deceiving. If they say I am deceiving, I am not an impostor by will. I may be declared insane because I seek an idea which drives me to something right. I tell you in all what I say in most things I do, I do according to what is told to me. In Batoche any things which I said have already happened. It was said to me not far from here and that is why I never wanted to send the half-breeds far, I wanted to keep them, and it was said to me I will not begin to work before 12 o'clock, and when the first battle opened I was taking my dinner at Duck Lake. When the battle began it was a little after 12 o'clock. I will not begin to work before 12 o'clock, and what has happened? And it was said to me if you do not meet the troops on such a road, you will have to meet them at the foot of a hill, and the half-breeds facing it. It is said my papers have been published. If they have been published, examine what took place, and you will see we had to meet General Middleton at the foot of the hill. It was also told me that men would stay in the "belle prairie," and the spirit spoke of those who would remain on the "belle prairie," and there were men who remained on the "belle prairie." And he admits it was looked upon as something very correct in the line of military art, it was not come from me or Dumont, it was the spirit that guides me.

I have two reasons why I wish the sentence of the court should not be passed upon me. The first, I wish my trial should take place as I said, whether that wish is practical or not, I bow respectfully to the court. I ask that a commission of doctors examine me. As I am declared guilty I would like to leave my name, as far as conscience is concerned, all right. If a commission of doctors sits and if they examine me, they can see if I was sincere or not. I will give them the whole history, and I think while I am declared guilty of high treason it is only right I should be granted the advantages of giving my proofs whether I am sincere, that I am sincere. Now, I am judged a sane man, the cause of my guilt is that I am an impostor, that would be the consequence. I wish a commission to sit and examine me. There have been witnesses around me for ten years, about the time they have declared me insane, and they will show if there is in me the character of an impostor. If they declare me insane, if I have been astray, I have been astray not as an impostor, but according to my conscience. Your Honour that is all what I have to say.

SENTENCE

Mr. Justice Richardson.—Louis Riel, after a long consideration of your case, in which you have been defended with as great ability as I think counsel could have defended you with, you have been found by a jury who have shown, I might almost say, unexampled patience, guilty of a crime the most pernicious and greatest that man can commit. You have been found guilty of high treason. You have been proved to have let loose the flood-gates of rapine and bloodshed, you have, with such assistance as you had in the Saskatchewan country, managed to arouse the Indians and have brought ruin and misery to many families whom if you had simply left alone were in comfort, and many of them were on the road to affluence.

For what you did, the remarks you have made form no excuse whatever. For what you have done the law requires you to answer. It is true that the jury in merciful consideration have asked Her Majesty to give your case such merciful consideration as she can bestow upon it. I had almost forgotten that those who are defending you have placed in my hands a notice that the objection which they raised at the opening of the court must not be forgotten from the record, in order that if they see fit they may raise the question in the proper place. That has been done. But in spite of that, I cannot hold out any hope to you that you will succeed in getting entirely free, or that Her Majesty will, after what you have been the cause of doing, open her hand of clemency to you.

For me, I have only one more duty to perform, that is, to tell you what the sentence of the law is upon you. I have, as I must, given time to enable your case to be heard. All I can suggest or advise you is to prepare to meet your end, that is all the advice or suggestion I can offer. It is now my painful duty to pass the sentence of the court upon you, and that is, that you be taken now from here to the police guard-room at Regina, which is the gaol and the place from whence you came, and that you be kept there till the 18th of September next, that on the 18th of September next you be taken to the place appointed for your execution, and there be hanged by the neck till you are dead, and may God have mercy on your soul.

SIR WILFRID LAURIER

1841-1919

Sir Wilfrid Laurier, who was born at Saint Lin, Canada East, ranks with Sir John A. Macdonald as the greatest of Canada's statesmen and perhaps her greatest political orator. From his early days as a member of the *Institut canadien* at McGill University he actively supported a policy of political liberalism that was opposed by the forces of conservative clericalism in Quebec. Nevertheless, after serving for three years in the provincial legislature he was elected a member of Parliament in 1874 and in 1877 delivered a major political affirmation, his *Discours sur le libéralisme politique*, in which he drew a sharp distinction between the doctrinaire anti-clericalism of France and the British tradition of political liberty. He asserted his faith in a progressive liberalism that could appeal to all advocates of political liberty irrespective of religion or language. In spite of serious opposition, he was able to maintain his position in Parliament after only a temporary setback. After the Liberal government's defeat in 1878, Laurier served as Edward Blake's chief lieutenant and in 1887 became leader of the party. His speech on the execution of Louis Riel delivered in the House of Commons on 10 March, 1886, was a powerful and generous appeal whose influence extends far beyond the immediate tragic occasion and can be read here as an example of the power of Laurier as an orator and of his cultivated humanism as a statesman.

In 1896, five years after the death of Sir John A. Macdonald,

Laurier became Prime Minister upon the defeat of the Conservative government. During the sixteen years he was in office he dealt successfully with many problems, including the right of separate schools for French-speaking Catholics in Manitoba and Canada's relations with England and the Empire during the South African war. In 1911 he was defeated over the question of commercial reciprocity with the United States. When he died in 1919, still a member of parliament, members of all parties acknowledged his greatness, echoing the words of a journalist (L. O. David, *Courrier de Montréal,* October 14, 1874) early in Laurier's career: "Mr. Laurier speaks English as fluently as French, a precious advantage destined to give him considerable influence in a House almost wholly English . . . the most remarkable Parliamentary orator of the day possessed by Lower Canada. Others may have more brilliant eloquence, more captivating imagery; he has neither the voice, the gesture, nor the fire of the tribune; his temperament like his nature does not lend itself to those impetuous movements, those energetic inspirations for which certain men are noted, . . . but more than our distinguished orators he has the tone, the method, the loftiness of ideas, the correct reasoning, the purity of diction and the elegance of language which constitute the Parliamentary orator. . . ."

FROM *Speech on the Execution of Riel*, 1886

Mr. Speaker, . . . in all that has been said so far, and that has fallen from the lips of honorable gentlemen opposite, there is one thing in which we can all agree, and one thing only—we can all agree in the tribute which was paid to the volunteers by the Minister of Public Works when he entered into a defence of the Government. The volunteers had a most painful duty to perform, and they performed it in a most creditable manner to themselves and the country. Under the uniform of a soldier there is generally to be found a warm and merciful heart. Moreover, our soldiers are citizens who have an interest in this country; but when they are on duty they know nothing but duty. At the same time it can fairly be presumed that when on duty the heart feels and the mind thinks; and it may be fairly presumed that those who were on duty in the North-West last spring thought and felt as a great soldier, a great king, King Henry IV of France, thought and felt when engaged in battle for many years of his life, in fighting his rebellious subjects. Whenever his sword inflicted a wound he used these words: "The king strikes thee, God heal thee."

It may be presumed that perhaps our soldiers, when fighting the rebellion, were also animated by a similar spirit, and prayed to God that he would heal the wounds which it was their duty to inflict, and that no more blood should be shed than the blood shed by themselves. The Government, however, thought otherwise. The Government thought that the blood shed by the soldiers was not sufficient, but that another life must also be sacrificed. We heard the Minister of Public Works attempting to defend the conduct of the Government, and stating that its action in this matter was a stern necessity which duty to our Queen and duty to our country made inevitable. Mr. Speaker, I have yet to learn—and I have not learned it from anything that has fallen from the lips of gentlemen opposite—that duty to Queen and country may ever prevent the exercise of that prerogative of mercy which is the noblest prerogative of the Crown. The language of the honourable gentleman was not the first language of the same nature. This was not the first occasion when responsible or irresponsible advisors of the Crown attempted to delude the public, and perhaps themselves as well, into the belief that duty to Queen and country required blood, when mercy was a possible alternative.

When Admiral Byng was sentenced to be shot for no other crime than that of being unfortunate in battle, there were men at the time, who said to the King that the interests of the country required that the sentence should be carried out, though the court, which had convicted him, strongly recommended him to mercy. Those evil counsels prevailed, and the sentence was carried out; but the verdict of history, the verdict of posterity—posterity to which honourable gentlemen now appeal—has declared long ago that the carrying out of the sentence against Admiral Byng was a judicial murder. And I venture to predict, Mr. Speaker, that the verdict of history will be the same in this instance. In every instance in which a Government has carried out the extreme penalty of the law, when mercy was suggested instead, the verdict of history has been the same. Sir, in the province to which I belong, and especially amongst the race to which I belong, the execution of Louis Riel has been universally condemned as being the sacrifice of a life, not to inexorable justice, but to bitter passion and revenge. . . .

It has been said by sober-minded people that the execution, even if unjust, of the man who was executed and who is believed to have been insane by those who sympathize with him, does not make this a case for the outburst of feeling which has taken place in Quebec on the occasion of Riel's execution. I differ from that view. In our age, in our civilization, every single human life is valuable, and is entitled to protection in the councils of the nation. Not many years ago England sent an expedition and spent millions of her treasure and some of her best blood simply to rescue prisoners whose lives were in the hands of the King of Abyssinia. In the same manner I say that the life of a single subject of Her Majesty here is valuable, and is not to be treated with levity. If there are members in the House who believe that the execution of Riel was not warranted, that under the circumstances of the case it was not judicious, that it was unjust, I say they have a right to arraign the Government for it before this country, and if they arraign the Government for it and the Government have to take their trial upon it, it must be admitted as a consequence that certain parties will feel upon the question more warmly than others. It is not to be supposed that the same causes which influenced public opinion in Lower Canada acted in the same manner with all classes of the community; that the causes which actuated the community at large were identical in all classes of the community. Some there were who believed that the Government had not meted out the same measure of justice to all those that were accused and who took part in the rebellion. Others believed that the state of mind of Riel was such that it was a judicial murder to execute him; but the great mass of the people believed that mercy should have been extended to all the prisoners, Riel included, because the rebellion was the result of the policy followed by the Government against the half-breeds. That was the chief reason which actuated them, and it seems to me that it is too late in the day now to seriously attempt to deny that the rebellion was directly the result of the conduct of the Government towards the half-breeds. It is too late in the day to dispute that fact. Yet we have heard it disputed in this House. By whom? By the last man who, I should have expected, would have disputed it—by the hon. member for Provencher (Mr. Royal). He gave us the other day his version of the origin of the trouble.

Everybody is responsible for the rebellion except one body. The *Globe* is responsible for it; the Farmers' Union is responsible for it; the white settlers are responsible for it. Everybody you can conceive of is responsible for it, except the Government. The Government is perfectly innocent of it, as innocent as a new-born child! Such was the statement made by the hon. member the other day. But if the hon. member is now in earnest as to that matter, how is it that the half-breeds alone have been prosecuted? If the *Globe* is the cause of that rebellion, the *Globe* should have been the first to be indicted. If the white settlers were the instigators of the rebellion, the white settlers should have been indicted also. There is more than that. The counsel for the Crown received authority and even instructions specially to proceed against the instigators of the rebellion, the white settlers, who certainly would have been more guilty than the half-breeds whom they had instigated to rebellion. . . .

When the seeds of discontent have long been germinating, when hearts have long been swelling with long accumulating bitternesses, and when humiliations and disappointments have made men discontented and sullen, a small incident will create a conflagration, just as a spark dropped on the prairie, under certain circumstances, will kindle a widespread and unquenchable fire. Then the Government moved, but it was too late. The incident occurred—what was it? The honourable member for Provencher told us what it was. After the Government had announced a commission, a man had the imprudence to say that a commission would not come, but that bullets would come instead; and this statement of the honourable gentleman is corroborated by a statement of Archbishop Taché in a letter published in December last, in which, speaking of the commencement of the rebellion, he said:

> The assurance that a commission would be sent was not accepted. People preferred to believe a rumor which went to show that, instead of granting them their rights, the authorities were to send irons for their leader and bullets for those who would protect him. That conviction produced the result which was to be expected. The half-breeds thought they would resist and defend themselves. Badly armed, without ammunition or provisions, they took possession of the stores in the vicinity. The unfortunate attack made against them at Duck Lake was a declaration of war.

It will strike many minds now that there is a great analogy between the origin of this rebellion and the origin of the rebellion in Lower Canada in 1837. An agitation had been going on in Lower Canada for many years, as it had been going on in the North-West for many years, and it was when the Government attempted to arrest the leaders of the movement that the rebellion broke out; and, without going any further, I am glad to recall the fact that, deplorable as was this rebellion in Lower Canada, it secured at once to the Lower Canadians the rights which they had been vainly seeking for so many years, and it secured this further result: That although the population had been hitherto in favour of rebellion they at once became the most faithful subjects England ever had. In the same manner, though the last result has not yet been obtained, it may be and will be obtained, I have no doubt, in the North-West, because the immediate result of the rebellion there has been to secure to the half-breeds the rights which had been denied to them up to that time. I have charged the Government with not only having been negligent in the duty they owed to the half-breeds, but with denying to the half-breeds the rights to which they were entitled. I charge them again with, not ignoring only, but actually refusing, of design aforethought, the rights to which the half-breeds were entitled. . . .

In ten days, from the 26th of March to the 6th of April, the Government had altered their policy and had given what they had refused for years. What was the cause? The bullets of Duck Lake; the rebellion in the North-West. The Government had been refusing for years, and at last these men took their lives and liberties in their hands, and at last the Government came down and gave them what they were entitled to. I appeal now to any friend of liberty in this House; I appeal not only to the Liberals who sit beside me, but to any man who has a British heart in his breast, and I ask, when subjects of Her Majesty have been petitioning for years for their rights, and those rights have not only been ignored, but have been denied, and when these men take their lives in their hands and rebel, will anyone in this House say that these men, when they got their rights, should not have saved their heads as well, and that the criminals, if criminals there were, in this rebellion, are not those who fought, and bled and died, but the men who sit on those Treasury benches? Sir, rebellion is always an evil, it is always an offence against the positive law of a nation, it is not always a moral crime. . . .

Mr. Speaker, such were my sentiments, and I spoke them elsewhere. I appeal, upon this occasion, as I did elsewhere, to every friend of liberty, to all those who, during these twenty-five years past, have felt their hearts thrill whenever a struggle for freedom was going on in any corner of the world; with the Italians, when they delivered their country from the yoke of Austria; with the Americans, in their stupendous struggle for national unity and for the suppression of African slavery; with the Mexicans, in their successful attempt to resist the foreign domination which the French Emperor sought to impose on them; with the French themselves in their generous though often misguided efforts to establish amongst themselves the bulwark of freedom, parliamentary and responsible government; with the Danubian populations, when they attempted to rid themselves of the degrading domination of the Turks; and when at last —at last—a section of our own countrymen rose in arms to claim

rights long denied them, rights which were immediately acknowledged to be just, as soon as they were asked with bullets, are we to
have no sympathy with them? Though, Mr. Speaker, these men
were in the wrong; though the rebellion had to be put down; though
it was the duty of the Canadian Government to assert its authority
and vindicate the law; still, I ask any friend of liberty, if there is not
a feeling rising in his heart, stronger than all reasoning to the contrary, that these men were excusable? Such were, Mr. Speaker, my
sentiments. I spoke them elsewhere. I have had, since that time,
occasion to realize that I have greatly shocked Tory editors and Tory
members. Sir, I know what Tory loyalty is. Tories have always been
famous for preaching loyalty to others. Tories have always been
famous for being loyal, as long as it was profitable to be so. Under
the reign of James, the Tories were gushing in their loyalty as long
as the tyranny of the king fell upon Whigs and Dissenters; but when
at last the tyranny of James fell upon the Tories themselves and the
Church of their heart, their slavish notions received a most salutary
shock. They took side with the Whigs, and horror of horrors, they
shouldered the musket, joined the Prince of Orange and put him on
the throne; and I believe that to this day the Tories will say that it
was a happy day for England when that rebellion took place. If we
pass from England to this country, we have the same tale to tell. In
1849 the Tories were gushing in their loyalty as long as they expected
the Governor General to be disloyal to the people, but when they
found the Governor General was loyal to the people, their own loyalty
oozed out of their bodies and vanished into thin air. They did not
shoulder the musket—that would have been too noble a weapon—
but with eggs and stones they pelted the representative of Her
Majesty. They did not shoulder the musket, but with pen and ink
they wrote and signed annexation manifestoes. And, Mr. Speaker, if
we continue the story, even down to the days since this Government
has been in power, we find that when they introduced the National
Policy, and when it was objected that the policy was unfair and
ungenerous to England, and that it might possibly endanger British
connection, the cool Tory answer was: "So much the worse for
British connection." Sir, this is Tory loyalty. Ready they are to-day
to sacrifice British connection, if British connection stands between
them and their selfishness; ready they are to-day to sacrifice British
connection if it stands between them and their enjoyment of power;
ready they are to sacrifice British connection for mere sordid greed,

SIR WILFRID LAURIER 37

but they affect, forsooth, to be shocked when we profess sympathy for men who, in the west, have been vindicating their rights long denied. Sir, I will not receive any lectures on loyalty from men with such a record. I am a British subject, and I value the proud title as much as anyone in this House. But if it be expected of me that I shall allow fellow-countrymen unfriended, undefended, unprotected and unrepresented in this House, to be trampled under foot by this Government, I say that is not what I understand by loyalty, and I would call that slavery. I am a British subject, but my loyalty is not of the lips. If honourable gentlemen opposite will read history, they will find that my ancestors, in all their struggles against the British Crown in the past, never sought anything else than to be treated as British subjects, and as soon as they were treated as British subjects, though they had not forgotten the land of their ancestors, they became amongst the most loyal subjects that England ever had. . . .

Now, is it not manifest, as was stated by the honourable member for West Huron the other night, that if Riel had supposed that in surrendering he would meet with the same fate as if he was taken prisoner, he would never have surrendered, but would have done as Gabriel Dumont and several others did? Recurring to the American case, who can doubt that of those two men, Andrew Johnson and General Grant, the true statesman, the true patriot, was the one who advocated clemency? You see the result to-day. Scarcely twenty years have passed away since that rebellion, the most terrible that ever shook a civilized nation, was put down, and because of the merciful course adopted by the victors, the two sections of that country are now more closely united than ever before, more closely even than they were when fighting for their independence. The Canadian Government should have followed this example, and I repeat again that we cannot make a nation of this new country by shedding blood, but only by extending mercy and charity for all political offences. The Government say they were desirous of giving a lesson. In the last paragraph of their written defence, they say:

> In deciding for the application for the commutation of sentence passed upon the prisoner the Government were obliged to keep in view the need of exemplary and deterrent punishment committed in a country situated in regard to settlement and

population as are the North-West Territories; the isolation and
defenceless position of the settlers already there; the horrors to
which they have been exposed in the event of an Indian outbreak; the effect upon intending settlers of any weakness in the
administration of law, and the consequences which must follow
such a course in a country if it came to be believed that such
crimes as Riel's could be committed without incurring the
extreme penalty of the law, by any one who was either subject
to delusions, or could lead people to believe he was so subject.

Indeed the Government have convinced all the people here mentioned, the half-breeds, the Indians, the white settlers, that their arm
is long and strong, and that they are powerful to punish. Would to
heaven that they had taken as much pains to convince them all, the
half-breeds, Indians and white settlers, of their desire and their
willingness to do them justice, to treat them fairly. Had they taken
as much pains to do right, as they have taken to punish wrong, they
never would have had any occasion to convince those people, that the
law cannot be violated with impunity, because the law would never
have been violated at all. But to-day, not to speak of those who have
lost their lives, our prisons are full of men who, despairing ever to
get justice by peace, sought to obtain it by war, who, despairing of
ever being treated like freemen, took their lives in their hands, rather
than be treated as slaves. They have suffered a great deal, they are
suffering still; yet, their sacrifices will not be without reward. Their
leader is in the grave; they are in durance, but from their prisons
they can see that that justice, that liberty which they sought in vain,
and for which they fought not in vain, has at last dawned upon their
country. Their fate well illustrates the truth of Byron's invocation to
liberty, in the introduction to the Prisoner of Chillon : —

Eternal Spirit of the chainless mind!
Brightest in dungeons, Liberty thou art!
For there thy habitation is the heart—
The heart which love of thee alone can bind;
And when thy sons to fetters are consigned—
To fetters and the damp vault's dayless gloom,
Their country conquers with their martyrdom.

Yes, their country has conquered with their martyrdom. They are
in durance to-day; but the rights for which they were fighting have

been acknowledged. We have not the report of the commission yet, but we know that more than two thousand claims so long denied have been at last granted. And more—still more. We have it in the Speech from the Throne that at last representation is to be granted to those Territories. This side of the House long sought, but sought in vain, to obtain that measure of justice. It could not come then, but it came after the war; it came as the last conquest of that insurrection. And again I say that their country has conquered with their martyrdom, and if we look at that one fact alone there was cause sufficient, independent of all others, to extend mercy to the one who is dead and to those who live.

GOLDWIN SMITH

1823-1910

Born in England and educated at Eton and Magdalen College, Oxford, Goldwin Smith left his chair as Regius Professor of Modern History at Oxford to become an unsalaried teacher of English constitutional history at the newly established Cornell University, Ithaca, New York, in 1868. Three years later he moved to Toronto, where he lived until his death. He took an active part in politics, journalism, education, and the social sciences, and was associated as editor or contributor to a number of influential Canadian periodicals, among them *The Canadian Monthly, The Bystander,* and *The Week,* originally edited by the poet Charles G. D. Roberts. He was a prolific essayist both on literary topics and on questions of the day. Among his works were *Lectures and Essays* (1881), *The Moral Crusader, William Lloyd Garrison* (1892), *Bay Leaves,* translations from the Latin poets (1893), *My Memory of Gladstone* (1904), and, most controversial and significant of all, *Canada and the Canadian Question* (1891), from which the following selection is taken. The seeds of the ideas expressed in the chapter "Political Union" appeared as early as March, 1862, in a letter to the *Daily News* of London. Goldwin Smith's advocacy of the political union of Canada and the United States stirred up a controversy that is not without significance for the present as well as for the past.

POLITICAL UNION

Annexation is an ugly word; it seems to convey the idea of force or pressure applied to the smaller State, not of free, equal, and honourable union, like that between England and Scotland. Yet there is no reason why the union of the two sections of the English-speaking people on this Continent should not be as free, as equal, and as honourable as the union of England and Scotland. We should rather say their reunion than their union, for before their unhappy schism they were one people. Nothing but the historical accident of a civil war ending in secession, instead of amnesty, has made them two. When the Anglo-Saxons of England and those of Scotland were reunited they had been many centuries apart; those of the United States and Canada have been separated for one century only. The Anglo-Saxons of England and Scotland had the memory of many wars to estrange them: the Anglo-Saxons of Canada and the United States have the memory, since their separation, only of one war.

That a union of Canada with the American Commonwealth, like that into which Scotland entered with England, would in itself be attended with great advantages cannot be questioned, whatever may be the considerations on the other side or the reasons for delay. It would give to the inhabitants of the whole Continent as complete a security for peace and immunity from war taxation as is likely to be attained by any community or group of communities on this side of the Millenium. Canadians almost with one voice say that it would greatly raise the value of property in Canada; in other words, that it would bring with it a great increase of prosperity. The writer has seldom heard this seriously disputed, while he has heard it admitted in the plainest terms by men who were strongly opposed to Union on political or sentimental grounds, and who had spent their lives in the service of Separation. The case is the same as that of Scotland or Wales in relation to the rest of the island of which they are parts, and upon their union with which their commercial prosperity depends. The Americans, on the other hand, would gain in full proportion as England gains by her commercial union with Wales and Scotland. These inducements are always present to the minds of the Canadian people, and they are specially present when the trade of Canada, with the rest of her Continent, is barred by such legislation as the M'Kinley Act, when her security is threatened by the imminence of war in Europe, or when from internal causes she happens to be acutely feeling the commercial atrophy to which her isolation condemns her. Canadians who live on the border, and who from the shape of the country form a large proportion of the population, have always before their eyes the fields and cities of a kindred people, whose immense prosperity they are prevented from sharing only by a political line, while socially, and in every other respect, the identity and even the fusion is complete.

On the other hand, there is the affection of the Colonists for the mother country, which has always been kind to them in intention, even if she has not had the power to defend their rights and her interference has ceased to be useful. This might prevail if union with the rest of the race on this Continent, under the sanction of the mother country, would really be a breach of affection for her. But it would be none. It would be no more a breach of affection than the naturalization, now fully recognized by British law, of multitudes both of Englishmen and of Canadians in the United States. Let us suppose that the calamitous rupture of the last century had never taken place, that the whole race on this Continent had remained united, and had parted, when the time came, from the mother country in peace; where would the outrage on love or loyalty have been? Admitted into the councils of their own Continent, and exercising their fair share of influence there, Canadians would render the mother country the best of all services, and the only service in their power, by neutralizing the votes of her enemies. Unprovoked hostility on the part of the American Republic to Great Britain would then become impossible. It is now unlikely, but not impossible, since there is no wickedness which may not possibly be committed by demagogism pandering to Irish hatred.

Nor need Canada give up any of the distinctive character or historical associations which she has preserved through the continuance of her connection with the mother country. Scotland is still Scotch, and her idol Sir Walter Scott was the type at once of patriotic Britons and of Scotchmen. The Federal system admits wide local diversities, and if Ontario or Nova Scotia clings to the British statute-book, to the British statute-book it may cling. There is no reason even why Canadians, who like to show their spirit by military cele-brations, should not celebrate Canadian victories as the Scotch cele-brate Bannockburn. Americans would smile. Of the antipathy to Americans sedulously kept up within select circles and in certain interests, there is absolutely none among the Canadian people at large. It would be strange if there were any, considering that half of them have brothers, sons, or cousins on the American side of the Line. "Bombard New York!" said a Canadian to the writer when somebody was declaiming in that vein; "why, my four sons live there!" On the Pacific Coast of the United States a British shell could scarcely burst without striking a Canadian home. The masses do not read much history or cherish antiquarian feuds. If the President of the United States were to visit Canada, he would be received as cordially as he is in any part of his own Republic; more cordially, perhaps, since in Canada the people of both parties would unite in the ovation.

If the language held by Canadian Jingoes or "Paper Tigers," as they are called, about American character were the truth or anything like the truth, union with such people ought indeed to be declined at any sacrifice of military security or commercial profit. But even those who hold it hardly believe it. An Imperialist journal in London the other day ended an article on the influence of Americans in England by saying that they are too like the English in all essential respects to produce any possible change in English character. That, as regards the normal American, is the fact. The present writer has known the Americans not, like most of their critics, only in the cities, but in the country and the country town. As a lecturer and resident in an American University he has been brought into contact with American youth; he has friends among Americans of all voca-tions and professions; he has seen the people under the ordeal of civil war, seen their conduct in the field, their care of the wounded, and their treatment of their captured enemies; and to him the idea that Canadians would undergo moral disparagement by the Union seems of all reveries the most absurd. Sheer snobbishness, to tell the truth, has not a little to do with the affectation of contempt for Yankees. This is one of the ways in which vulgarity tries to make itself genteel. The good feeling of Canadians towards their mother country is strong, genuine, disinterested, and cannot be too highly prized. But there is a blatant loyalty which it is very easy to prize too highly. If a man makes a violent and offensive demonstration of it against those whom he accuses of American sympathies, you are apt presently to find him in the employment of some American company, peddling for an American house, or accepting a call to the other side of the Line. We have already, in our historical retrospect, had occasion to observe that when by untoward circumstances interest is divorced from sentiment, the loyalism which before had been the most fiery in its manifestations can suddenly grow cold. If England ever has occasion to call on her children in Canada for a real sacrifice, she may chance to repeat the experience of King Lear.

There are varieties too little noticed by critics of American character in different parts of the Union. These are black spots. In certain districts lawlessness and want of respect for human life remain as the traces of slavery, whose cause Canadian Jingoism ardently espoused. New York has its shoddy wealth which the better Americans despise, and which British aristocracy, though scornful of American democracy, sometimes takes to its arms. Rapid commercial development has bred gambling speculation, and with it unscrupulousness, of which Canada also has her proportionate share, though in both cases the amount of knavery is small compared with that of sound and honest trade. Party politics are the same on both sides of the Line, and on neither side, happily, are they the whole of life. The Canadian politician exactly resembles the American, and none the less when he has been knighted. Both countries would be in a bad way if the demagogue ruled society and trade. Political corruption is on a far larger scale in the wealthier country, but it is more shameless in the poorer country. About the American Press there is a good deal to be said, but not more than there is about the successive personal organs of a Prime Minister of Canada. Canada has the advantage of not having broken with her history, or bearing on her political character, like the American, the trace of a revolution; but America is gradually renewing her historical associations, and since she has had herself to contend with rebellion and been threatened within by the Anarchists, the revolutionary sentiment has been losing force. In the wealthier country and that which had the start in civilization is found a higher standard of living, with more of science and culture; in the other, more frugality and simplicity of life. Both communities are threatened by the same social dangers and disturbances, nor is there any conservative force in one which there is not in the other, the phantom of monarchy in Canada being, as has been shown, no conservative force at all, but rather serving to disguise the action of forces the reverse of conservative. There is continual harping on the laxity of the American divorce law, and Canada was told that if she traded more with the Americans Canadian wedlock would be in danger of the contagion. Illinois and Indiana, where the laxity prevails, are not the United States. However, scarcely had the warning been penned, when we had proof that, even as it is, no impassable gulf of sentiment divides us from Indiana and Illinois.

The fear that with the addition of Canada the Union would be too large and that its cohesion might give way, which is felt both by Canadians and Americans, though natural, seems not to be well-founded. Slavery being extinct there is no longer any visible line of cleavage. So long as the freedom of the system is preserved, there seems to be no limit to its possible extension, provided the territory, though vast, is within a ring fence. Nobody is likely to rebel against an arrangement which, within fettering local self-development, gives safety against attack from without, peace and freedom of inter-course within. People must be revolutionary indeed if they can take arms against mere immunity from evils. The tariff question does not form a line of cleavage, and is in a fair way to be settled by the ballot. If 300,000,000 Chinese can get on well together under a centralized Government, surely 100,000,000 of the higher race can get on to-gether under a government much more elastic. The problem of races at the South no doubt is still serious, but there is no tendency to re-newal of secession, and the South is becoming daily smaller and less important in proportion to the Union. The growth there of manu-facturing industries will both modify political character and bind the States to their Northern market. Socialistic revolution, such as would take a State out of the Republic, and the occupation of the Pacific Coast by the Chinese, are contingencies which might threaten the Union, but at present they are very remote, while to Chinese irruption Canada on the Pacific is more open than the United States.

Again, Canadians who heartily accept democracy wish that there should be two experiments in it on this Continent rather than one, and the wish is shared by thoughtful Americans not a few. But we have seen that in reality the two experiments are not being made. Universal suffrage and party government are the same, and their effects are the same in both Republics. Differences there are, such as that between the Presidential and the Cabinet system, of a subordinate kind, yet not unimportant, and such as might make it worth while to forego for a time at least the advantages of union, supposing that the dangers and economical evils of separation were not too great, and if the territorial division were not extravagantly at variance with the fiat of Nature. The experiments of political science must be tried with some reference to terrestrial convenience. Besides, those who scan the future without prejudice must see that the political fortunes of the Continent are embarked in the great Republic, and that Canada will best promote her own ultimate interests by contributing without unnecessary delay all that she has in the way of political character and force towards the saving of the main chance and the fulfilment of the common hope. The native American element in which the tradition of self-government resides is hard pressed by the foreign element untrained to self-government, and stands in need of the reinforcement which the entrance of Canada into the Union would bring it. Canadians feel all this without being distinctly conscious of it: they are taking less interest in British and more in American politics: in British politics they would take but little interest if their attention were not turned that way by the efforts of the Irish to drag everybody into their clan feud. A Presidential election now makes almost as much stir in Canada as it does in the United States. There is something to be said in favour of recognizing destiny without delay. The reasoning of Lord Durham with regard to French Canada holds good in some measure with regard to Canada altogether in its relation to the Anglo-Saxon Continent. He thought it best to make the country at once that which after the lapse of no long time it must be. And this reminds us of another reason for not putting off the unification of the English-speaking race, since it is perfectly clear that the forces of Canada alone are not sufficient to assimilate the French element or even to prevent the indefinite consolidation and growth of a French nation. Either the conquest of Quebec was utterly fatuous or it is to be desired that the American Continent should belong to the English tongue and to Anglo-Saxon civilization.

The Americans in general are not insensible, perhaps they are more sensible than they sometimes affect to be, of the advantages and the accession of greatness which would accrue to the Republic by the entrance of Canada into the Union. They expect that some day she will come to them, and are ready to welcome her when she does. But few of them much desire to hasten the event, and hardly any of them think of hastening it by coercion. The M'Kinley Act was not intended to coerce Canada into the Union. Its objects were to rivet Protection and catch the farmer's vote, though it was welcomed by the Tory Prime Minister of Canada and his following as a plausible ground for insulting demonstrations against the Americans, and this at the moment when Great Britain was carrying on difficult negotiations at Washington on Canada's behalf. Of conquest there is absolutely no thought. The Southern violence and the Western lawlessness which forced the Union into the War of 1812 are things of the past. The American people could not now be brought to invade the homes of an unoffending neighbour. They have no craving for more territory. They know that while a despot who annexes may govern through a viceroy with the strong hand, a republic which annexes must incorporate, and would only weaken itself by incorporating disaffection. The special reason for wishing to bring Canada at once into the Union, that she might help to counterbalance the Slave Power, has with the Slave Power departed. So far as the Americans are concerned, Canada is absolute mistress of her own destiny, while she is welcome to cast in her lot with the Republic. Such is the impression made upon the writer by his intercourse with Americans of all classes during twenty years.

Of Canadian opinion the one thing that can be said with certainty is that the great mass of the people, and especially those who dwell along the border of Ontario, in the Maritime Provinces, in Manitoba or other districts of the North-West, and those who are engaged or wish to be engaged in the mining, lumbering, or shipping trade, strongly desire freedom and commercial intercourse with their own Continent. Such appears to be the wish of the people and of the politicians in Quebec also, as well indeed it may be, since the American market is the only market which Quebec has. The tendency of the priesthood is isolation, as the safeguard of their dominion and of their tithe; but their position is in all respects somewhat altered by the exodus, and it is doubtful whether they would dare to oppose themselves directly to the material welfare of the masses. Nothing apparently can save the restrictive policy of the present Government and its confederate, the protected manufacturer, except the use of the same engines which have so long sustained a similar policy in the United States. On the question of political union apart from commercial union there are no means of gauging popular sentiment, the question never having been brought definitely before the people and expression not being free. But the English inquirer had better be cautious in receiving the confident reports of official persons, or listening to public professions of any kind. The very anxiety shown to gag opinion by incessant cries of disloyalty and treason shows that there is an opinion which needs to be gagged. People were taken by surprise when in 1849, under the pressure of commercial distress, a manifesto in favour of annexation appeared with the signatures of a number of the leading men of the country. In these democracies, where everybody from his cradle is thinking of votes, and to be in a minority is perdition, political courage, whether in action or speech, is not a common virtue. Politicians especially tremble at the very thought of a premature declaration of any kind. But the notion that a man who at a meeting of ordinary Canadians should avow his belief in an ultimate reunion of the two sections of his race would be "stoned" or even hissed, may be proved from experience to be a mistake. A bold man had avowed annexationist opinions in official company at Ottawa. One of the company, horrified at his profanities, told him that he should feel it his duty to denounce them if he were not restrained by social confidence. "Come down," was the reply, "into the street, collect the biggest crowd you can, and I will soon relieve you of the restraint of social confidence." The other day an ex-Governor-General undertook to assure the world that the slightest suspicion of annexationism would be absolutely fatal to a candidate in an election. Almost on the very day on which his ex-Excellency's paper reached Canada an avowed annexationist was elected by a large majority for a county in Ontario. Annexation is not the platform of either party, and as a rule, nobody can get himself elected without a party nomination. But supposing a candidate had the party nomination and were locally strong the suspicion of annexationism would do him very little harm. Of this, indeed, we have already had practical proofs, besides the example just cited. Since the passing of the Jesuits' Estates Act and the revelation in connection with it of priestly influence and designs, the saying of Lord Durham's Report that the day might come when English Canadians to remain English would have to cease to be British, or something like it, has been heard on many sides.

There is a conflict of forces, and we must judge each for himself which are the primary forces and likely to prevail. Prevail the primary forces will in the end, however long their action may be suspended by a number of secondary forces arrayed against them. In the case of

German and in that of Italian unity the number and strength of the secondary forces arrayed against the event were such, and the action of the great forces was so long suspended by them, that it seemed even to sagacious observers as if the event would never come. It came, irresistible and irreversible, and we see now that Bismarck and Cavour were the ministers of destiny.

In the present case there are, on one side, geography, commerce, identity of race, language, and institutions, which with the mingling of population and constant intercourse of every kind, acting in ever-increasing intensity, have brought about a general fusion, leaving no barriers standing but the political and fiscal lines. On the other side, there is British and Imperial sentiment, which, however, is confined to the British, excluding the French and Irish and other nationalities, and even among the British is livelier as a rule among the cultivated and those whose minds are steeped in history than among those who are working for their bread; while to set against it there is the idea, which can hardly fail to make way, of a great continent with an almost unlimited range of production forming the home of a united people, shutting out war and presenting the field as it would seem for a new and happier development of humanity. Again, there are bodies of men, official, political, and commercial, whose interests are bound up with the present state of things, whose feelings naturally go with those interests, who in many cases suffer little from the economical consequences of isolation, and who, gathered in the capital or in the great cities, exercise an influence out of proportion to their numbers on public opinion and its organs. Great public undertakings involving a large expenditure, produce fortunes to which titles are sometimes added, and which form strong supports of the existing system, though they are no indications of general prosperity, and the interest of their possessors is as far as possible from being identical with that of the farmer, who meantime is paying ruinous duties on his farm implements and on some of the necessaries of life. Repulsion is also created by the scandals of American politics, by the corruption which has reigned of late, by the turmoil of Presidential elections, and by such enormities as the Pension List, while political scandals and evils at home, being familiar, are less noted. Men of British blood, more-over, even when they are friendly to closer relations with the United States, are disgusted by the anti-British language of the American Press and of some of the American politicians. Above all there is the difficulty of getting any community, but especially a democracy in which there is no strong initiative, to quit the groove in which it has long been running. On the American side there is, to countervail the promptings of high policy and natural ambition, the partisan's fear of disturbing the adjustment of parties. There is the comparative indifference of the Southern States of the Union to an acquisition in the North. There is, moreover, a want of diplomatic power to negotiate a Union. The southern politicians were statesmen after their kind, secure in their seats and devoted to public life. They governed the country as a nation, though with ends of their own. Their successors, besides being by no means safe in their seats, are to a great extent delegates of local interests, each of which, like the members of a Polish diet, has and exercises a veto in the councils of the nation. Upon successive attempts to pursue a definite policy towards Canada the veto has been put by one local interest or another. If negotiations for a Union were set on foot, the party out of power would of course do its best to make them miscarry, and a patriotic Press would not fail to lend its aid. Every sort of susceptibility and jealousy on such occasions is wide awake. The great English statesmen, trained in the highest school of diplomacy, who negotiated the Union with Scotland, found their task hard though they operated under far easier conditions. However, if the primary forces are working towards an event, sooner or later the crisis arrives; the man appears, and the bidding of Destiny is done.

2. Local Color, Sentiment, and Satire

CHARLES G. D. ROBERTS
1860-1943

Charles George Douglas Roberts, son of an Anglican clergyman, was born near Fredericton, New Brunswick, of United
Empire Loyalist stock. He studied Greek and Latin in secondary school and at the University of New Brunswick. For a
time he taught school, and in 1883 he became editor of Goldwin Smith's periodical, *The Week*. He resigned after a few
months owing to his disapproval of Smith's annexationist
ideas. In 1885 Roberts was appointed Professor of English and
French at King's College in Windsor, Nova Scotia. In 1897,
he moved to New York, where he lived with his cousin, Bliss
Carman, devoting himself to the production of tales, historical
romances, poems, and a series of animal stories that became
world famous. In 1907 he went to England where he lived
until after the first world war. He served with the British
army and Canadian Forces Overseas, and later travelled in
Africa and Europe. When he returned to Canada in 1925, he
toured the country giving lectures and readings. For a time
Roberts, the first recipient of the Lorne Pierce Medal for
literature, was president of the Canadian Authors' Association.
He was knighted in 1935.

Roberts became recognized as a poet in the 1880's. His first
book, *Orion and Other Poems* (1880), reflects his classical
studies. His best work in verse is to be found in his sober
studies of nature and country life in his native New Brunswick, published in *In Divers Tones* (1886), *Songs of the
Common Day* (1893), and *The Book of the Native* (1896).

FROM *Wisdom of the Wilderness*, 1922

THE WATCHERS IN THE SWAMP

Under the first pale lilac wash of evening, just where the slow
stream of the Lost Water slipped placidly from the open meadows
into the osier and bulrush tangles of the swamp, a hermit thrush,
perched in the topmost spray of a young elm tree, was fluting out
his lonely and tranquil ecstasy to the last of the sunset. *Spheral—
spheral—oh—holy—holy—clear*—he sang; and stopped abruptly, as
if to let the brief, unfinished, but matchlessly pure and poignant
cadence sink unjarred into the heart of the evening stillness. One
minute—two minutes—went by; and the spaces of windless air were
like a crystal tinged with faint violet. And then this most reticent of
singers loosed again his few links of flawless sound—a strain which,
more than any other bird song on this earth, leaves the listener's
heart aching exquisitely for its completion. *Spheral—spheral—oh—
holy—holy*—but this time, as if seeking by further condensation to
make his attar of song still more rare and precious, he cut off the
final note, that haunting, ethereal—*clear*.

Again the tranced stillness. But now, as if too far above reality to
be permitted to endure, after a few seconds it was rudely broken.
From somewhere in the mysterious and misty depths of the swamp
came a great booming and yet strangulated voice, so dominant that
the ineffable colors of the evening seemed to fade and the twilight to
deepen suddenly under its somber vibrations. Three times it sounded
—*Klunk-er-glungk . . . Klunk-er-glungk . . . Klunk-er-glungk*—
an uncouth, mysterious sound, sonorous, and at the same time half-
muffled, as if pumped with effort through obstructing waters. It was
the late cry of the bittern, proclaiming that the day was done.

The hermit thrush, on his tree top against the pale sky, sang
no more, but dropped noiselessly to his mate on her nest in the
thickets. Two bats flickered and zigzagged hither and thither above
the glimmering stream. And the leaf-scented dusk gathered down

broodingly, with the dew, over the wide solitudes of Lost Water Swamp.

It was high morning in the heart of the swamp. From a sky of purest cobalt flecked sparsely with silver-white wisps of cloud, the sun glowed down with tempered, fruitful warmth upon the tender green of the half-grown rushes and already rank water grasses—the young leafage of the alder and willow thickets—the wide pools and narrow, linking lanes of unruffled water already mantling in spots with lily pad and arrow weed. A few big red-and-black butterflies wavered aimlessly above the reed tops. Here and there, with a faint, elfin clashing of transparent wings, a dragon fly, a gleam of emerald and amethyst fire, flashed low over the water. From every thicket came a soft chatter of the nesting red-shouldered blackbirds.

And just inside the watery fringe of the reeds, as brown and erect and motionless as a mooring stake, stood the bittern.

Not far short of three feet in length, from the tip of his long and powerful, dagger-pointed bill to the end of his short, rounded tail, with his fierce, unblinking eyes, round, bright, and hard, with his snaky head and long, muscular neck, he looked, as he was, the formidable master of the swamp. In coloring he was a streaked and freckled mixture of slaty grays and browns and ochres above, with a freckled whitish throat and dull buff breast and belly—a mixture which would have made him conspicuous amid the cool, light green of the sedges but that it harmonized so perfectly with the earth and the roots. Indeed, moveless as he stood, to the indiscriminating eye he might have passed for a decaying stump by the waterside. His long legs were of a dull olive which blended with the shadowy tones of the water.

For perhaps ten minutes the great bird stood there without the movement of so much as a feather, apparently unconcerned while the small inhabitants of the swamp made merry in the streaming sunshine. But his full, round eyes took in, without stirring in their sockets, all that went on about him, in air or sedge or water. Suddenly, and so swiftly that it seemed one motion, his neck uncoiled and his snaky head darted downward into the water near his feet, to rise again with an eight-inch chub partly transfixed and partly gripped between the twin daggers of his half-opened bill. Squirming, and shining silverly, it was held aloft, while its captor stalked solemnly in through the sedges to a bit of higher and drier turf. Here he proceeded to hammer his prize into stillness upon an old, half-buried log. Then, tossing it into the air, he caught it adroitly by the head, and swallowed it, his fierce eyes blinking with the effort as he slowly forced it down his capacious gullet. It was a satisfying meal, even for such a healthy appetite as his, and he felt no immediate impulse to continue his fishing. Remaining where he was beside the old log, thigh deep in the young grasses and luxuriously soaking in the sunshine, he fell once more into a position of rigid movelessness. But his attitude was now quite different from that which he had affected when his mind was set on fish. His neck was coiled backward till the back of his head rested on his shoulders, and his bill pointed skyward, as if the only peril he had to consider seriously during his time of repose might come, if at all, from that direction. And though he rested, and every nerve and muscle seemed to sleep, his gemlike eyes were sleeplessly vigilant. Only at long intervals a thin, whitish membrane flickered down across them for a fraction of an instant, to cleanse and lubricate them and keep their piercing brightness undimmed.

Once a brown marsh hawk, questing for water rats, winnowed past, only ten or a dozen feet above his head. But he never stirred a muscle. He knew it would be a much more formidable and daring marauder than the marsh hawk that would risk conclusions with the uplifted dagger of his bill.

In about half an hour—so swift is the digestion of these masters of the swamp—the bittern began to think about a return to his easy and pleasant hunting. But, always deliberate, except when there was need for instant action, at first he did no more than uncoil his long neck, lower his bill to a level, and stand motionlessly staring over the sedge tops. One of the big red-and-black butterflies came wavering near, perhaps under the fatal delusion that that rigid yellow bill would be a good perch for him to alight on. A lightning swift dart of the snaky head, and those gay wings, after curiously adorning for a moment the tip of the yellow bill, were deftly gathered in and swallowed—an unsubstantial morsel, but not to be ignored when one is blest with a bittern's appetite.

After a few minutes more of statuesque deliberation, having detected nothing in the landscape particularly demanding his attention, the bittern lazily lifted his broad wings and flapped in slow flight, his long legs almost brushing the sedge tops, back to the post of vantage where he had captured the chub. As soon as he alighted he stiffened himself erect, and stared about as if to see whether his flight had been noticed. Then, presently, he seemed to remember something of importance. This was the season of mating joys and cares. It was time he signalled his brown mate. First he began snapping his bill sharply, and then he went through a number of contortions with his throat and neck, as if he were trying to gulp down vast quantities of air, and finding the effort most difficult. At length, however, the painful-looking struggle was crowned with achievement. Once more, as on the preceding evening, that great call boomed forth across the swamp, sonorous yet strangulated, uncouth yet thrilling and haunting, the very voice of solitude and mystery—*Klunk-er-glungk—Klunk-er-glungk—Klunk-er-glungk*.

Almost immediately came an acknowledgment of this untuneful love song—a single hoarse *guaw-awk*; and another snaky, brown head and yellow dagger bill were raised above the tops of the sedges. The hen bittern, in response to her mate's cry, had just come off her nest.

For some tranquil moments the two eyed each other without stirring, and it almost seemed as if their very immobility was a mode of expression, a secret code for communication between them. The result, if so, appeared to be satisfactory. The hen came stalking solemnly through the grass and sedges toward the water's edge, only pausing on the way to transfix and gulp down a luckless frog. And the stately male, once more spreading his spacious vanes, flapped slowly over and dropped again into the grass some ten or a dozen feet from the nest.

The nest was a rather casual structure of dry grass and weeds, in a hollow of the turf, and more or less concealed by leaning tufts of swamp grass. It contained three large eggs of a dull greenish buff, clouded with darker tones, and blending elusively with the soft colorings of the nest. These precious eggs the male bittern was to stand guard over with jealous vigilance, while his mate was away foraging. The sun was softly warm upon them through the thin shadows of the grass blades, and he knew they would not chill during her brief absence. He took his post just near enough to keep his eye upon the nest, without unduly drawing attention to its hiding place.

This patch of water meadow, perhaps a half acre in extent, on which the bitterns had their nest, was one of many such tiny islands scattered amid the interlacing channels of Lost Water Swamp. It formed a congenial refuge for all that small life of the wilderness which loves to be near water without being in it. It was particularly beloved of the meadow mice, because the surrounding watercourses and morasses were an effectual barrier to some of their worst enemies, such as foxes, skunks, and weasels; and they throve here amazingly. To be sure the bittern would take toll of them when they came his way, but he did not deliberately hunt them, rather preferring a diet of frogs and fish; and moreover his depredations upon the mice were more than counterbalanced by his eager hostility to their dreaded foes, the snakes. So, on the whole, he might have been regarded by the mouse community as a benefactor, though a rather costly one.

Even now, as he stood there apparently thinking of nothing but his guardianship of the nest, he gave a telling example of his beneficence in this regard. There was a tiny, frightened squeak, a desperate small rustling in the grass stems, and a terrified mouse scurried by, with a two-foot black snake at its tail. The bittern's head flashed down, unerringly, and rose again, more slowly, with the snake gripped by the middle, held high in air, as if on exhibition, between the knife-edge tips of that deadly, yellow bill. The victim writhed and twisted, coiling itself convulsively around its captor's head and neck. But with two or three sharp jerks it was drawn further back, toward the base of the mandibles; and then, with an inexorable pressure, bitten clean in two; the halves uncoiled and fell to the ground still wriggling spasmodically. With grave deliberation the bittern planted one foot upon the head half, and demolished the vicious head with a tap of his bill. This done, he swallowed it with determined and strenuous gulpings. Then he eyed the other half doubtfully, and decided that he was not yet ready for it. So, placing one foot upon it with a precise air, he lifted his head again and resumed his motionless guarding of the nest.

A little later in the morning—perhaps fifteen or twenty minutes after the incident of the snake—the mice found yet another potent reason for congratulating themselves on the presence of their expensive champion. The hen bittern, apparently, had not been very successful in her foraging. She had shown as yet no sign of returning to the nest. The male was just beginning to get impatient. He even went so far as to move his head, though ever so slightly. Indeed, he was on the very point of beginning those grotesque snappings of the bill and gulpings of air which would be followed by his booming triple call when he caught sight of a dark form moving through the grass, beyond the nest. Instantly he stiffened again into rigidity.

Only, very slowly, the long, slender feathers which crowned his head and lay along his neck began to rise.

The dark form gliding stealthily among the grasses was that of an animal about two feet in length, low on the legs, slender, sinuous, quick-darting. The bittern had never chanced to observe a mink before, but he needed no one to tell him that this creature was dangerous. Ferocity and efficiency were written all over the savage, triangular head and lithe, swift body. But the intruder had evidently not yet discovered the precious nest. He was half a dozen paces away from it, and not moving directly toward it. In the very next moment he pounced upon a mouse, which he tore and devoured with an eagerness which showed him to be hungry. The bittern waited, and hoped anxiously that the nest might escape discovery.

The mink was not at the moment thinking of any such luxury as eggs. He had entered the swamp in the hope of finding just such a happy hunting ground as this bit of mouse-thronged meadow. He had just arrived, and he was now full of bloodthirsty excitement over the success of his venture. His nose sniffed greedily the subtle, warm, mousy smells. His ears detected the innumerable, elusive, mousy squeaks and rustlings. His eyes, lit now with the red spark of the blood lust, were less fortunate than his ears and nose, because word of a new and dreadful foe had gone abroad among the mouse folk, and concealment was the order of the day. But already, he had made one kill—and that so easily that he knew the quarry here was not much hunted.

He was preparing to follow a very distinct mouse trail, when a chance puff of air bore him a scent which instantly caught his attention. The scent of the bittern was new to him, as it chanced. He knew it for the scent of a bird, a water bird of some kind—probably, from its abundance, a large bird, and certainly, therefore, a bird worth his hunting.

Curious and inquiring, he rose straight up on his hind quarters in order to get a good view, and peered searchingly over the grass tops. He saw nothing but the green and sun-steeped meadow with the red-and-black butterflies wavering over it, the gleam of the unruffled water, and the osier thickets beyond. He looked directly at, and *past*, the guardian bittern, probably mistaking that rigid, vigilant shape for an old brown stump. For the mink's eyes, like those of many other animals, were less unerring than his ears and nostrils, and much quicker to discern motion than fixed form. Had the bittern stirred by so much as a hair's breadth, the mink would have detected him at once. But the mink looked at him and saw him not; nor saw another similar form, unstirring, intensely watchful, over by the waterside.

Having failed to detect the source of that strange, intriguing smell, the mink concluded that it must come from a brooding mother, hiding on a nest in the grass. Nothing could be more satisfactory. His eyes blazed blood-red at the prospect of slaughter. Dropping down again upon all fours, he darted forward up the trail of the scent, and came full upon the nest with its three unsheltered eggs. Instantly seizing the nearest one between his agile forepaws, he crunched the shell and began greedily sucking up the contents.

But the savor of the feast had hardly thrilled his palate when it seemed as if the skies had fallen upon him. A scalding anguish stabbed his shoulders, a smother of buffeting wings enveloped him, and he was borne backward from the nest, the broken eggshell still clinging to his nose.

At the moment when he had darted forward toward the nest, all the immobility of the watching bittern had vanished. His long crest standing straight up in his fury, he had launched himself to the attack, covering the intervening distance with two tremendous thrusts of his powerful wings, and fallen like a cyclone upon the violator of his home. The dagger of his bill had struck deeply, and the impetus of his charge had carried him clear of his foe and a couple of paces past, but he turned adroitly in the air and landed facing about, ready for the inevitable counterattack.

Amazed and startled though he was, and handled with a roughness quite new to his experience, the mink was in no way daunted. Rather he was so boiling with rage that his wonted wariness forsook him completely. With a snarl he sprang straight at the long, exposed, inviting throat of his adversary. His leap was swift, true, deadly. But equally true, and more swift, was the counterstroke. He was met, and stopped in mid-air by a thrust of the bittern's bill, which, had he not twisted his head just in time, would have split his skull. As it was, it laid open one side of his snarling face, and brought him heavily to the ground. Even under this punishment, however, he would not acknowledge defeat. Springing aside, with a lightning, zigzag movement to confuse the aim of that terrific bill, he darted low and made a leap at his antagonist's long, vulnerable legs. He missed only by a hair's breadth, as the bittern leapt nimbly aside and balked him with a stiff wing stroke. He seized the baffling wing and strove to pull his tall adversary down. But two great pinion feathers came away in his jaws, and the next moment he got another terrible, driving stab from the dagger beak, well forward on the flank. It was a slanting thrust, or it would have pierced his lungs; but it nearly knocked the wind out of him, and ploughed a deep, red gash in his glossy coat.

Screeching furiously, he doubled on himself like a snake to meet this attack. But at the same moment he cringed under another excruciating stab in the haunch; and looking up, he saw himself enveloped in a cloud of blinding wings. The hen bittern had arrived to join in the defense of her nest.

Now, bloodthirsty and merciless marauder though he was, the mink's courage was a thing beyond dispute; and terribly though the fight had so far gone against him, with a single foe to confront he would probably have held on to the death. But for all his fury he was not quite mad; and this reinforcement of the enemy was too much for him. Suddenly straightening himself out long and narrow like an eel, he slipped from under the terrifying storm of wings and stabs, and made off through the grass at the best speed he had ever attained. He made for the water, which he felt would be his safest refuge. The angry bitterns were after him on the instant, flying as low as possible and stabbing down at him. But his cunning and slippery zigzags enabled him to dodge most of their thrusts; and in their eagerness they got in each other's way—which probably saved him his bare life. At length streaming with blood, and leaving behind him a red trail he reached the water and dived in. Without daring to come to the surface he swam across the channel and cautiously raised his head behind a screen of overhanging weeds. He saw his two pursuers standing, motionless and erect, on the opposite bank, watching with fierce eyes for him to reappear. Submerging himself again, he swam on downstream till he had rounded a sharp bend of the channel. When he thought it prudent to show himself once more, he was sheltered by a dense screen of alder and willows. He hurried through the thicket, and on down the bank till he found an ancient muskrat hole. Into this he crept eagerly, and lay down in the grateful dark to nurse his wounds and his humiliation.

After the disappearance of the mink the hen bittern soon returned to her nest. But the male stayed where he was. From time to time he would spear a passing frog or chub or sucker. But always his indignant heart was hoping that the mink would return. After an hour or two, however, his wrath died down and he began to forget.

Later in the day, when the osiers were beginning to throw long shadows across the water, and the red-and-black butterflies had grown too indolent to dance, the great bittern, full-fed and at ease with life, flapped languidly up from the waterside and dropped close beside the nest. His brooding mate lifted her head, as if in greeting, and laid it back at once between her shoulders, with her yellow bill pointed skyward as was her vigilant custom.

Soon the first warm tints of sunset began to stain the edges of the clouds above the far fringes of the swamp. Motionless and erect beside his mate, the bittern watched the oncoming of the enchantment as his day drew to its quiet close. Suddenly the colored quiet of the air was disturbed by the throbbing of hurried wings. He glanced upward, without moving. A mallard drake, in frantic flight, whirred past, making for the water. Close after the fugitive, and swiftly overhauling him with long tremendous thrusts of his mighty wings, came that most dreaded cutthroat of the air, a great, blue goshawk. Had the water been two feet farther away the fate of the glossy drake would have been sealed. He would have been overtaken, his throat torn out in mid-air, his body carried off to the nearest tree top to be plucked and devoured. But this time the inscrutable Fates of the wilderness, too seldom so lenient to the weak, decided to favor him. With a heavy sounding splash he shot down into the blessed water, and disappeared into safety.

The destroying talons of the great hawk clutched convulsively at the dandy curled tips of his tail as he vanished.

With his arrowy speed, his precision of stroke, his audacity and fiery spirit, the blue goshawk was little accustomed to the experience of being balked of his prey. With a sharp yelp of wrath he swept up from the water on a long, graceful curve, and sailed back low above the bittern's island seeking other prey. And his piercing gaze fell upon the bittern standing rigid beside the nest.

His swoop was instantaneous, straight and swift as a bolt from a crossbow. But that coiled steel spring of the bittern's neck was even swifter; and as his talons struck downward, the bittern's dagger thrust caught him in the very center of the impending claw, splitting the foot fairly and disabling it. Nevertheless, by the shock of the attack, the bittern was borne downward, and would have been caught in the breast or throat by the other talon, but at the same instant his watchful mate, who had half risen on the nest that her eggs might not be crushed in the *mêlée*, delivered her thrust. It went true. It caught the goshawk full in the base of the neck, pierced clean through, and severed the spine. And in a wild confusion of sprawled legs and pounding wings, the three great birds fell in a heap in the grass, just beyond the nest.

The two bitterns nimbly extricated themselves, stabbing savagely at the unresisting body of the hawk. Presently, as if by one impulse, they both stood up, erect and still as images, their yellow bills dripping with blood. The male had a bleeding gash along the side of his head. But this concerned him little. His heart swelled with triumph. He was forced to give it utterance. He snapped his bill sharply, gulped a few mouthfuls of air, and then sent forth his booming challenge across the swamp—*Klunk-er-glungk—Klunk-er-glungk—Klunk-er-glungk*.

His mate spread her broad wings, shook her self till her ruffled plumage fell into place, wiped her conquering bill on the grass, stepped delicately back into the nest, and softly settled herself down upon her two eggs, so miraculously preserved.

Silence fell on Lost Water Swamp. The air became gradually transfused with amethyst and pale rose. And then, far and faint, tranquil and poignant, came the entrancing cadence—*Oh—spheral, spheral, Oh holy, holy—spheral*—the silver vesper ecstasy of the hermit thrush, in his tree top against the pellucid sky.

RALPH CONNOR
1860-1937

Ralph Connor was the pseudonym of Charles William Gordon, a Presbyterian minister who began writing serialized missionary adventure stories for a church paper in 1898. His father was a Presbyterian minister who came from Scotland to Glengarry County, Ontario, where Connor was born. In 1871, the family moved to western Ontario. Connor graduated from the University of Toronto in 1883, and from Knox College in 1887. After serving as a student minister in southern Manitoba and an ordained missionary in Banff, Alberta, he became minister of St. Stephen's Church, Winnipeg, in 1894. During the first world war he was first chaplain of the Cameron Highlanders, and then senior chaplain of the Canadian forces in England. When he returned to Canada, he went back to St. Stephen's in Winnipeg to continue as minister and writer.

Connor wrote some twenty-eight novels. Among the most successful were those drawn from his early boyhood: *The Man From Glengarry* (1901) and *Glengarry School Days* (1902). Other popular and well-written novels in which a didactic moral purpose does not entirely destroy the interest of local verisimilitude and exciting action are *Black Rock* (1898) and *The Sky Pilot* (1899). A posthumous autobiography, *Postscript to Adventure*, was edited by Ralph Connor's son, J. King Gordon, in 1938, and reveals a man of great energy, charm, and integrity.

The first days of that week were days of strife. Murdie Cameron and Bob Fraser and the other big boys succeeded in keeping in line with the master's rules and regulations. They were careful never to be late, and so saved themselves the degradation of bringing an excuse. But the smaller boys set themselves to make the master's life a burden, and succeeded beyond their highest expectations, for the master was quick of temper, and was determined at all costs to exact full and prompt obedience. There was more flogging done those first six days than during any six months of Archie Munro's rule. Sometimes the floggings amounted to little, but sometimes they were serious, and when those fell upon the smaller boys, the girls would weep and the bigger boys would grind their teeth and swear.

The situation became so acute that Murdie Cameron and the big boys decided that they would quit the school. They were afraid the temptation to throw the master out would some day be more than they could bear, and for men who had played their part, not without credit, in the Scotch River fights, to carry out the master would have been an exploit hardly worthy of them. So, in dignified contempt of the master and his rules, they left the school after the third day.

Their absence did not help matters much; indeed, the master appeared to be relieved, and proceeded to tame the school into submission. It was little Jimmie Cameron who precipitated the crisis. Jimmie's nose, upon which he relied when struggling with his snickers, had an unpleasant trick of failing him at critical moments, and of letting out explosive snorts of the most disturbing kind. He had finally been warned that upon his next outburst punishment would fall.

It was Friday afternoon, the drowsy hour just before recess, while the master was explaining to the listless Euclid class the mysteries of the forty-seventh proposition, that suddenly a snort of unusual violence burst upon the school. Immediately every eye was upon the master, for all had heard and had noted his threat to Jimmie.

"James, was that you, sir?"

There was no answer, except such as could be gathered from

Jimmie's very red and very shamed face.

"James, stand up!"

Jimmie wriggled to his feet, and stood a heap of various angles.

"Now, James, you remember what I promised you? Come here, sir!"

Jimmie came slowly to the front, growing paler at each step, and stood with a dazed look on his face, before the master. He had never been thrashed in all his life. At home the big brothers might cuff him good-naturedly, or his mother thump him on the head with her thimble, but a serious whipping was to him an unknown horror.

The master drew forth his heavy black strap with impressive deliberation and ominous silence. The preparations for punishment were so elaborate and imposing that the big boys guessed that the punishment itself would not amount to much. Not so Jimmie. He stood numb with fear and horrible expectation. The master lifted up the strap.

"James, hold out your hand!"

Jimmie promptly clutched his hand behind his back.

"Hold out your hand, sir, at once!" No answer.

"James, you must do as you are told. Your punishment for disobedience will be much severer than for laughing." But Jimmie stood pale, silent, with his hands tight clasped behind his back.

The master stepped forward, and grasping the little boy's arm, tried to pull his hand to the front; but Jimmie, with a roar like that of a young bull, threw himself flat on his face on the floor and put his hands under him. The school burst into a laugh of triumph, which increased the master's embarrassment and rage.

"Silence!" he said, "or it will be a worse matter for some of you than for James."

Then turning his attention to Jimmie, he lifted him from the floor and tried to pull out his hand. But Jimmie kept his arms folded tight across his breast, roaring vigorously the while, and saying over and over, "Go away from me! Go away from me, I tell you! I'm not taking anything to do with you."

The big boys were enjoying the thing immensely. The master's rage was deepening in proportion. He felt it would never do to be beaten. His whole authority was at stake.

"Now, James," he reasoned, "you see you are only making it worse for yourself. I cannot allow any disobedience in the school. You must hold out your hand."

But Jimmie, realizing that he had come off best in the first round, stood doggedly sniffing, his arms still folded tight.

"Now, James, I shall give you one more chance. Hold out your hand."

Jimmie remained like a statue.

Whack! came the heavy strap over his shoulders. At once Jimmie set up his refrain, "Go away from me, I tell you! I'm not taking anything to do with you!"

Whack! whack! whack! fell the strap with successive blows, each heavier than the last. There was no longer any laughing in the school. The affair was growing serious. The girls were beginning to sob, and the bigger boys to grow pale.

"Now, James, will you hold out your hand? You see how much worse you are making it for yourself," said the master, who was heartily sick of the struggle, which he felt to be undignified, and the result of which he feared was dubious.

But Jimmie only kept up his cry, now punctuated with sobs, "I'm —not—taking—anything—to do—with—you."

"Jimmie, listen to me," said the master. "You must hold out your hand. I cannot have boys refusing to obey me in this school." But Jimmie caught the entreaty in the tone, and knowing that the battle was nearly over, kept obstinately silent.

"Well, then," said the master, suddenly, "you must take it," and lifting the strap, he laid it with such sharp emphasis over Jimmie's shoulders that Jimmie's voice rose in a wilder roar than usual, and the girls burst into audible weeping.

Suddenly, above all the hubbub, rose a voice, clear and sharp.

"Stop!" It was Thomas Finch, of all people, standing with face white and tense, and regarding the master with steady eyes.

The school gazed thunderstruck at the usually slow and stolid Thomas.

"What do you mean, sir?" said the master, gladly turning from Jimmie. But Thomas stood silent, as much surprised as the master at his sudden exclamation.

He stood hesitating for a moment, and then said, "You can thrash me in his place. He's a little chap, and has never been thrashed."

The master misunderstood his hesitation for fear, pushed Jimmie aside, threw down his strap, and seized a birch rod.

"Come forward, sir! I'll put an end to your insubordination, at any rate. Hold out your hand!"

Thomas held out his hand till the master finished one birch rod. "The other hand, sir!"

Another birch rod was used up, but Thomas neither uttered a sound nor made a move till the master had done, then he asked, in a strained voice, "Were you going to give Jimmie all that, sir?"

The master caught the biting sneer in the tone, and lost himself completely.

"Do you dare to answer me back?" he cried. He opened his desk, took out a rawhide, and without waiting to ask for his hand, began to lay the rawhide about Thomas's shoulders and legs, till he was out of breath.

"Now, perhaps you will learn your place, sir," he said.

"Thank you," said Thomas, looking him steadily in the eye.

"You are welcome. And I'll give you as much more whenever you show that you need it." The slight laugh with which he closed this brutal speech made Thomas wince as he had not during his whole terrible thrashing, but still he had not a word to say.

"Now, James, come here!" said the master, turning to Jimmie. "You see what happens when a boy is insubordinate." Jimmie came trembling. "Hold out your hand!" Out came Jimmie's hand at once. Whack! fell the strap.

"The other!"

"Stop it!" roared Thomas. "I took his thrashing."

"The other!" said the master, ignoring Thomas.

With a curious savage snarl Thomas sprung at him. The master, however, was on the alert, and swinging round, met him with a straight facer between the eyes, and Thomas went to the floor.

"Aha! my boy! I'll teach you something you have yet to learn."

For answer came another cry. "Come on, boys!" It was Ranald Macdonald, coming over the seats, followed by Don Cameron, Billy Ross, and some smaller boys. The master turned to meet them.

"Come along!" he said, backing up to his desk. "But I warn you it's not a strap or a rawhide I shall use."

Ranald paid no attention to his words, but came straight toward him, and when at arm's length, sprung at him with the cry, "Horo, boys!"

But before he could lay his hands upon the master, he received a blow straight on the bridge of the nose that staggered him back, stunned and bleeding. By this time Thomas was up again, and rushing in was received in like manner, and fell back over a bench.

"How do you like it, boys?" smiled the master. "Come right along."

The boys obeyed his invitation, approaching him, but more warily, and awaiting their chance to rush. Suddenly Thomas, with a savage snarl, put his head down and rushed in beneath the master's guard, paid no attention to the heavy blow he received on the head, and locking his arms round the master's middle, buried his head close into his chest.

At once Ranald and Billy Ross threw themselves upon the struggling pair and carried them to the floor, the master underneath. There was a few moments of fierce struggling, and then the master lay still, with the four boys holding him down for dear life.

It was Thomas who assumed command.

"Don't choke him so, Ranald," he said. "And clear out of the way, all you girls and little chaps."

"What are you going to do, Thomas?" asked Don, acknowledging Thomas's new-born leadership.

"Tie him up," said Thomas. "Get me a sash."

At once two or three little boys rushed to the hooks and brought one or two of the knitted sashes that hung there, and Thomas proceeded to tie the master's legs.

While he was thus busily engaged, a shadow darkened the door, and a voice exclaimed, "What is all this about?" It was the minister, who had been driving past and had come upon the terrified, weeping children rushing home.

"Is that you, Thomas? And you, Don?"

The boys let go their hold and stood up, shamed but defiant.

Immediately the master was on his feet, and with a swift, fierce blow, caught Thomas on the chin. Thomas, taken off his guard, fell with a thud on the floor.

"Stop that, young man!" said the minister, catching his arm. "That's a coward's blow."

"Hands off!" said the master, shaking himself free and squaring up to him.

"Ye would, would ye?" said the minister, gripping him by the neck and shaking him as he might a child. "Lift ye'r hand to me, would ye? I'll break ye'r back to ye, and that I will." So saying, the minister seized him by the arms and held him absolutely helpless. The master ceased to struggle, and put down his hands.

"Ay, ye'd better, my man," said the minister, giving him a fling backward.

Meantime Don had been holding snow to Thomas's head, and had brought him round.

"Now, then," said the minister to the boys, "what does all this mean?"

The boys were all silent, but the master spoke.

"It is a case of rank and impudent insubordination, sir, and I demand the expulsion of those impudent rascals."

"Well, sir," said the minister, "be sure there will be a thorough investigation, and I greatly misjudge the case if there are not faults on both sides. And for one thing, the man who can strike such a cowardly blow as you did a moment ago would not be unlikely to be guilty of injustice and cruelty."

"It is none of your business," said the master, insolently.

"You will find that I shall make it my business," said the minister. "And now, boys, be off to your homes, and be here Monday morning at nine o'clock, when this matter shall be gone into."

The news of the school trouble ran through the section like fire through a brûlé. The younger generation, when they heard how Thomas Finch had dared the master, raised him at once to the rank of hero, but the heads of families received the news doubtfully, and wondered what the rising generation was coming to.

The next day Billy Jack heard the story in the Twentieth store, and with some anxiety waited for the news to reach his father's ears, for to tell the truth, Billy Jack, man though he was, held his father in dread.

"How did you come to do it?" he asked Thomas. "Why didn't you let Don begin? It was surely Don's business."

"I don't know. It slipped out," replied Thomas. "I couldn't stand Jimmie's yelling any longer. I didn't know I said anything till I found myself standing up, and after that I didn't seem to care for anything."

"Man! it was fine, though," said Billy Jack. "I didn't think it was in you." And Thomas felt more than repaid for all his cruel beating. It was something to win the approval of Billy Jack in an affair of this kind.

It was at church on the Sabbath day that Donald Finch heard about his son's doings in the school the week before. The minister, in his sermon, thought fit to dwell upon the tendency of the rising generation to revolt against authority in all things, and solemnly laid upon parents the duty and responsibility of seeing to it that they ruled their households well.

It was not just the advice that Donald Finch stood specially in need of, but he was highly pleased with the sermon, and was enlarging upon it in the churchyard where the people gathered between the services, when Peter McRae, thinking that old Donald was hardly taking the minister's advice to himself as he ought, and not knowing that the old man was ignorant of all that had happened in the school, answered him somewhat severely.

"It is good to be approving the sermon, but I would rather be seeing you make a practical application of it."

"Indeed, that is true," replied Donald, "and it would not be amiss for more than me to make application of it."

"Indeed, then, if all reports be true," replied Peter, "it would be well for you to begin at home."

"Mr. McRae," said Donald, earnestly, "it is myself that knows well enough my shortcomings, but if there is any special reason for your remark, I am not aware of it."

This light treatment of what to Peter had seemed a grievous offense against all authority incensed the old dominie beyond all endurance.

"And do you not think that the conduct of your son last week calls for any reproof? And is it you that will stand up and defend it in the face of the minister and his sermon upon it this day?"

Donald gazed at him a few moments as if he had gone mad. At length he replied, slowly, "I do not wish to forget that you are an elder of the church, Mr. McRae, and I will not be charging you with telling lies on me and my family——"

"Tut, tut, man," broke in Long John Cameron, seeing how the matter stood; "he's just referring to yon little difference Thomas had with the master last week. But it's just nothing. Come away in."

"Thomas?" gasped Donald. "My Thomas?"

"You have not heard, then," said Peter, in surprise, and old Donald only shook his head.

"Then it's time you did," replied Peter, severely, "for such things are a disgrace to the community."

"Nonsense!" said Long John. "Not a bit of it! I think none the less of Thomas for it." But in matters of this kind Long John could hardly be counted an authority, for it was not so very long ago since he had been beguiled into an affair at the Scotch River which, while it brought him laurels at the hands of the younger generation, did not add to his reputation with the elders of the church.

It did not help matters much that Murdie Cameron and others of his set proceeded to congratulate old Donald, in their own way, upon his son's achievement, and with all the more fervor that they perceived that it moved the solemn Peter to righteous wrath. From one and another the tale came forth with embellishments, till Donald Finch was reduced to such a state of voiceless rage and humiliation that when, at the sound of the opening psalm the congregation moved into the church for the Gaelic service, the old man departed for his home, trembling, silent, amazed.

How Thomas could have brought this disgrace upon him, he could not imagine. If it had been William John, who, with all his good nature, had a temper brittle enough, he would not have been surprised. And then the minister's sermon, of which he had spoken in such open and enthusiastic approval, how it condemned him for his neglect of duty toward his family, and held up his authority over his household to scorn. It was a terrible blow to his pride.

"It is the Lord's judgment upon me," he said to himself, as he tramped his way through the woods. "It is the curse of Eli that is hanging over me and mine." And with many vows he resolved that, at all costs, he would do his duty in this crisis and bring Thomas to a sense of his sins.

It was in this spirit that he met his family at the supper-table, after their return from the Gaelic service.

"What is this I hear about you, Thomas?" he began, as Thomas came in and took his place at the table. "What is this I hear about you, sir?" he repeated, making a great effort to maintain a calm and judicial tone.

Thomas remained silent, partly because he usually found speech difficult, but chiefly because he dreaded his father's wrath.

"What is this that has become the talk of the countryside and the disgrace of my name?" continued the father, in deepening tones.

"No very great disgrace, surely," said Billy Jack, lightly, hoping to turn his father's anger.

"Be you silent, sir!" commanded the old man, sternly. "I will ask for your opinion when I require it. You and others beside you in this house need to learn your places."

Billy Jack made no reply, fearing to make matters worse, though he found it hard not to resent this taunt, which he knew well was flung at his mother.

"I wonder at you, Thomas, after such a sermon as yon. I wonder you are able to sit there unconcerned at this table. I wonder you are not hiding your head in shame and confusion." The old man was lashing himself into a white rage, while Thomas sat looking stolidly before him, his slow tongue finding no words of defense. And indeed, he had little thought of defending himself. He was conscious of an acute self-condemnation, and yet, struggling through his slow-moving mind there was a feeling that in some sense he could not define, there was justification for what he had done.

"It is not often that Thomas has grieved you," ventured the mother, timidly, for, with all her courage, she feared her husband when he was in this mood.

"Woman, be silent!" blazed forth the old man, as if he had been waiting for her words. "It is not for you to excuse his wickedness. You are too fond of that work, and your children are reaping the fruits of it."

Billy Jack looked up quickly as if to answer, but his mother turned her face full upon him and commanded him with steady eyes, giving, herself, no sign of emotion except for a slight tightening of the lips and a touch of color in her face.

"Your children have well learned their lesson of rebellion and deceit," continued her husband, allowing his passion a free rein. "But I vow unto the Lord I will put an end to it now, whatever. And I will give you to remember, sir," turning to Thomas, "to the end of your days, this occasion. And now, hence from this table. Let me not see your face till the Sabbath is past, and then, if the Lord spares me, I shall deal with you."

Thomas hesitated a moment as if he had not quite taken in his father's words, then, leaving his supper untouched, he rose slowly, and without a word climbed the ladder to the loft. The mother followed him a moment with her eyes, and then once more turning to Billy Jack, held him with calm, steady gaze. Her immediate fear was for her eldest son. Thomas, she knew, would in the meantime simply suffer what might be his lot, but for many a day she had lived in terror of an outbreak between her eldest son and her husband. Again Billy Jack caught her look, and commanded himself to silence.

"The fire is low, William John," she said, in a quiet voice. Billy Jack rose, and from the woodbox behind the stove, replenished the fire, reading perfectly his mother's mind, and resolving at all costs to do her will.

At the taking of the books that night the prayer, which was

spoken in a tone of awful and almost inaudible solemnity, was for the most part an exaltation of the majesty and righteousness of the government of God, and a lamentation over the wickedness and rebellion of mankind. And Billy Jack thought it was no good augury that it closed with a petition for grace to maintain the honor of that government, and to uphold that righteous majesty in all the relations of life. It was a woeful evening to them all, and as soon as possible the household went miserably to bed.

Before going to her room the mother slipped up quietly to the loft and found Thomas lying in his bunk, dressed and awake. He was still puzzling out his ethical problem. His conscience clearly condemned him for his fight with the master, and yet, somehow he could not regret having stood up for Jimmie and taken his punishment. He expected no mercy at his father's hands next morning. The punishment he knew would be cruel enough, but it was not the pain that Thomas was dreading; he was dimly struggling with the sense of outrage, for ever since the moment he had stood up and uttered his challenge to the master, he had felt himself to be different. That moment now seemed to belong to the distant years when he was a boy, and now he could not imagine himself submitting to a flogging from any man, and it seemed to him strange and almost impossible that even his father should lift his hand to him.

"You are not sleeping, Thomas," said his mother, going up to his bunk.

"No, mother."

"And you have had no supper at all."

"I don't want any, mother."

The mother sat silent beside him for a time, and then said, quietly, "You did not tell me, Thomas."

"No, mother, I didn't like."

"It would have been better that your father should have heard this from—I mean, should have heard it at home. And—you might have told me, Thomas."

"Yes, mother, I wish now I had. But, indeed, I can't understand how it happened. I don't feel as if it was me at all." And then Thomas told his mother all the tale, finishing his story with the words, "And I couldn't help it, mother, at all."

The mother remained silent for a little, and then, with a little tremor in her voice, she replied: "No, Thomas, I know you couldn't help it, and I"—here her voice quite broke—"I am not ashamed of you."

"Are you not, mother?" said Thomas, sitting up suddenly in great surprise. "Then I don't care. I couldn't make it out well."

"Never you mind, Thomas, it will be well," and she leaned over him and kissed him. Thomas felt her face wet with tears, and his stolid reserve broke down.

"Oh, mother, mother, I don't care now," he cried, his breath coming in great sobs. "I don't care at all." And he put his arms round his mother, clinging to her as if he had been a child.

"I know, laddie, I know," whispered his mother. "Never you fear, never fear." And then, as if to herself, she added, "Thank the Lord you are not a coward, whatever."

Thomas found himself again without words, but he held his mother fast, his big body shaking with his sobs.

"And, Thomas," she continued, after a pause, "your father—we must just be patient." All her life long this had been her struggle. "And—and—he is a good man." Her tears were now flowing fast, and her voice had quite lost its calm.

Thomas was alarmed and distressed. He had never in all his life seen his mother weep, and rarely had heard her voice break.

"Don't, mother," he said, growing suddenly quiet himself. "Don't you mind, mother. It'll be all right, and I'm not afraid."

"Yes," she said, rising and regaining her self-control, "it will be all right, Thomas. You go to sleep." And there were such evident reserves of strength behind her voice that Thomas lay down, certain that all would be well. His mother had never failed him.

The mother went downstairs with the purpose in her heart of having a talk with her husband, but Donald Finch knew her ways well, and had resolved that he would have no speech with her upon the matter, for he knew that it would be impossible for him to persevere in his intention to "deal with" Thomas, if he allowed his wife to have any talk with him.

The morning brought the mother no opportunity of speech with her husband. He, contrary to his custom, remained until breakfast in his room. Outside in the kitchen, he could hear Billy Jack's cheerful tones and hearty laugh, and it angered him to think that his displeasure should have so little effect upon his household. If the house had remained shrouded in gloom, and the family had gone about on tiptoes and with bated breath, it would have shown no more than a proper appreciation of the father's displeasure; but as Billy Jack's cheerful words and laughter fell upon his ear, he renewed his vows to do his duty that day in upholding his authority, and bringing to his son a due sense of his sin.

In grim silence he ate his breakfast, except for a sharp rebuke to Billy Jack, who had been laboring throughout the meal to make cheerful conversation with Jessac and his mother. At his father's rebuke Billy Jack dropped his cheerful tone, and avoiding his mother's eyes he assumed at once an attitude of open defiance, his tones and words plainly offering to his father war, if war he would have.

"You will come to me in the room after breakfast," said his father, as Thomas rose to go to the stable.

"There's a meeting of the trustees at nine o'clock at the school-house at which Thomas must be present," interposed Billy Jack, in firm, steady tones.

"He may go when I have done with him," said his father, angrily, "and meantime you will attend to your own business."

"Yes, sir, I will that!" Billy Jack's response came back with fierce promptness.

The old man glanced at him, caught the light in his eyes, hesitated a moment, and then, throwing all restraint to the winds, thundered out, "What do you mean, sir?"

"What I say. I am going to attend to my own business, and that soon." Billy Jack's tone was quick, eager, defiant.

Again the old man hesitated, and then replied, "Go to it, then."

"I am going, and I am going to take Thomas to that meeting at nine o'clock."

"I did not know that you had business there," said the old man, sarcastically.

"Then you may know it now," blazed forth Billy Jack, "for I am going. And as sure as I stand here, I will see that Thomas gets fair play there if he doesn't at home, if I have to lick every trustee in the section."

"Hold your peace, sir!" said his father, coming nearer him. "Do not give me any impertinence, and do not accuse me of unfairness."

"Have you heard Thomas's side of the story?" returned Billy Jack.

"I have heard enough, and more than enough."

"You haven't heard both sides."

"I know the truth of it, whatever, the shameful and disgraceful truth of it. I know that the country-side is ringing with it. I know that in the house of God the minister held up my family to the scorn of the people. And I vowed to do my duty to my house."

The old man's passion had risen to such a height that for a moment Billy Jack quailed before it. In the pause that followed the old man's outburst the mother came to her son.

"Hush, William John! You are not to forget yourself, nor your duty to your father and to me. Thomas will receive full justice in this matter." There was a quiet strength and dignity in her manner that commanded immediate attention from both men.

The mother went on in a low, even voice, "Your father has his duty to perform, and you must not take upon yourself to interfere."

Billy Jack could hardly believe his ears. That his mother should desert him, and should support what he knew she felt to be injustice and tyranny, was more than he could understand. No less perplexed was her husband.

As they stood there looking at each other, uncertain as to the next step, there came a knock at the back door. The mother went to open it, pausing on her way to push back some chairs and put the room to rights, thus allowing the family to regain its composure.

"Good morning, Mrs. Finch. You will be thinking I have slept in your barn all night." It was Long John Cameron.

"Come away in, Mr. Cameron. It is never too early for friends to come to this house," said Mrs. Finch, her voice showing her great relief.

Long John came in, glanced shrewdly about, and greeted Mr. Finch with great heartiness.

"It's a fine winter day, Mr. Finch, but it looks as if we might have a storm. You are busy with the logs, I hear."

Old Donald was slowly recovering himself.

"And a fine lot you are having," continued Long John. "I was just saying the other day that it was wonderful the work you could get through."

"Indeed, it is hard enough to do anything here," said Donald Finch, with some bitterness.

"You may say so," responded Long John, cheerfully. "The snow is that deep in the bush, and——"

"You were wanting to see me, Mr. Cameron," interrupted Donald. "I have a business on hand which requires attention."

"Indeed, and so have I. For it is——"

"And indeed, it is just as well you and all should know it, for my disgrace is well known."

"Disgrace!" exclaimed Long John.

"Ay, disgrace. For is it not a disgrace to have the conduct of your family become the occasion of a sermon on the Lord's Day?"

"Indeed, I did not think much of yon sermon, whatever," replied Long John.

"I cannot agree with you, Mr. Cameron. It was a powerful sermon, and it was only too sorely needed. But I hope it will not be without profit to myself."

"Indeed, it is not the sermon you have much need of," said Long John, "for every one knows what a——"

"Ay, it is myself that needs it, but with the help of the Lord I will be doing my duty this morning."

"And I am very glad to hear that," replied Long John, "for that is why I am come."

"And what may you have to do with it?" asked the old man.

"As to that, indeed," replied Long John, coolly, "I am not yet quite sure. But if I might ask without being too bold, what is the particular duty to which you are referring?"

"You may ask, and you and all have a right to know, for I am about to visit upon my son his sins and shame."

"And is it meaning to wheep him you are?"

"Ay," said the old man, and his lips came fiercely together.

"Indeed, then, you will just do no such thing this morning."

"And by what right do you interfere in my domestic affairs?" demanded old Donald, with dignity. "Answer me that, Mr. Cameron."

"Right or no right," replied Long John, "before any man lays a finger on Thomas there, he will need to begin with myself. And," he added, grimly, "there are not many in the county who would care for that job."

Old Donald Finch looked at his visitor in speechless amazement. At length Long John grew excited.

"Man alive!" he exclaimed, "it's a quare father you are. You may be thinking it disgrace, but the section will be proud that there is a boy in it brave enough to stand up for the weak against a brute bully." And then he proceeded to tell the tale as he had heard it from Don, with such strong passion and such rude vigor, that in spite of himself old Donald found his rage vanish, and his heart began to move within him toward his son.

"And it is for that," cried Long John, dashing his fist into his open palm, "it is for that that you would punish your son. May God forgive me! but the man that lays a finger on Thomas yonder, will come into sore grief this day. Ay, lad," continued Long John, striding toward Thomas and gripping him by the shoulders with both hands, "you are a man, and you stood up for the weak yon day, and if you ever will be wanting a friend, remember John Cameron."

"Well, well, Mr. Cameron," said old Donald, who was more deeply moved than he cared to show, "it may be as you say. It may be the lad was not so much in the wrong."

"In the wrong?" roared Long John, blowing his nose hard. "In the wrong? May my boys ever be in the wrong in such a way!"

"Well," said old Donald, "we shall see about this. And if Thomas has suffered injustice it is not his father will refuse to see him righted." And soon they were all off to the meeting at the school-house.

Thomas was the last to leave the room. As usual, he had not been able to find a word, but stood white and trembling, but as he found himself alone with his mother, once more his stolid reserve broke down, and he burst into a strange and broken cry, "Oh, mother, mother," but he could get no further.

"Never mind, laddie," said his mother, "you have borne yourself well, and your mother is proud of you."

At the investigation held in the school-house, it became clear that, though the insubordination of both Jimmie and Thomas was undeniable, the provocation by the master had been very great. And though the minister, who was superintendent of instruction for the district, insisted that the master's authority must, at all costs, be upheld, such was the rage of old Donald Finch and Long John Cameron that the upshot was that the master took his departure from the section, glad enough to escape with bones unbroken.

SARA JEANNETTE DUNCAN
1862-1922

Sara Jeannette Duncan was born in Brantford, Canada West, in 1862, and educated in the public schools there. After a short period of school teaching she became a journalist and in 1885 travelled to the New Orleans Exposition as correspondent for a number of Canadian newspapers. She wrote for the *Washington Post* and worked for the *Toronto Globe*, Goldwin Smith's *The Week*, and the *Montreal Star*, becoming Ottawa correspondent for the last paper in 1888. The following year she and another newspaperwoman, Mrs. Lilian Rood, travelled west on the newly completed Canadian Pacific Railway and continued on around the world. Their syndicated letters and articles formed the substance of her first book, *A Social Departure: How Orthodocia and I went Round the World by Ourselves* (1890). In India she met Everard Charles Cotes, curator of the Indian Museum in Calcutta, whom she married in 1891. Most of her later life was spent in Calcutta and Simla, though with a number of lengthy visits to England and Canada. Mrs. Cotes died in England in 1922.

   She wrote many novels of Anglo-Indian life, of which *The Simple Adventures of a Mem-sahib* (1893) has a characteristic excellence. *An American Girl in London* (1891) and *Cousin Cinderella: A Canadian Girl in London* (1908) are neat, albeit minor, examples of the Jamesian school of transatlantic analysis. Her one exclusively Canadian novel is *The Imperialist* (1904). In this she displays an intelligence and wit that had been notably absent from Canadian fiction since Mrs. Brooke and Judge Haliburton and was not to be equalled until Leacock's *Sunshine Sketches* and its more mordant successor, *Arcadian Adventures,* and later the novels of Robertson Davies.

THE ORATOR FROM ENGLAND

Social precedents are easily established in the country. The accident that sent the first Liberal canvasser for Jordanville votes to the Crow place for his supper would be hard to discover now; the fact remains that he has been going there ever since. It made a greater occasion than Mrs. Crow would ever have dreamed of acknowledging. She saw to it that they had a good meal of victuals, and affected indifference to the rest; they must say their say, she supposed. If the occasion had one satisfaction which she came nearer to confessing than another, it was that the two or three substantial neighbours who usually came to meet the politicians left their wives at home, and that she herself, to avoid giving any offence on this score, never sat down with the men. Quite enough to do it was, she would explain later, for her and the hired girl to wait on them and to clear up after them. She and Bella had their bite afterward when the men had hitched up, and when they could exchange comments of proud congratulation upon the inroads on the johnny-cake or the pies. So there was no ill feeling, and Mrs. Crow, having vindicated her dignity by shaking hands with the guests of the evening in the parlour, solaced it further by maintaining the masculine state of the occasion, in spite of protests or entreaties. To sit down opposite Mr. Crow would have made it ordinary "company"; she passed the plates and turned it into a function.

She was waiting for them on the parlour sofa when Crow brought them in out of the nipping early dark of December, Elmore staying behind in the yard with the horses. She sat on the sofa in her best black dress with the bead trimming on the neck and sleeves, a good deal pushed up and wrinkled across the bosom, which had done all that would ever be required of it when it gave Elmore and Abe their start in life. Her wiry hands were crossed in her lap in the moment of waiting: you could tell by the look of them that they were not often crossed there. They were strenuous hands; the whole worn figure was strenuous, and the narrow set mouth, and the eyes which had looked after so many matters for so long, and even the way the hair was drawn back into a knot in a fashion that would have given a phrenologist his opportunity. It was a different Mrs. Crow from the one that sat in the midst of her poultry and garden-stuff in the Elgin market square; but it was even more the same Mrs. Crow, the sum of a certain measure of opportunity and service, an imperial figure in her bead trimming, if the truth were known.

The room was heated to express the geniality that was harder to put in words. The window was shut; there was a smell of varnish and whatever was inside the "suite" of which Mrs. Crow occupied the sofa. Enlarged photographs—very much enlarged—of Mr. and Mrs. Crow hung upon the walls, and one other of a young girl done in that process which tells you at once that she was an only daughter and that she is dead. There had been other bereavements; they were written upon the silver coffin-plates which, framed and glazed, also contributed to the decoration of the room; but you would have had to look close, and you might feel a delicacy.

Mrs. Crow made her greetings with precision, and sat down again upon the sofa for a few minutes' conversation.

"I'm telling them," said the husband, "that the sleighin's just held out for them. If it 'ud been tomorrow they'd have had to come on wheels. Pretty soft travellin' as it was, some places, I guess."

"Snow's come early this year," said Mrs. Crow. "It was an open fall, too."

"It has certainly," Mr. Farquharson backed her up. "About as early as I remember it. I don't know how much you got out here; we had a good foot in Elgin."

" 'Bout the same, 'bout the same," Mr. Crow deliberated, "but it's been layin' light all along over Clayfield way—ain't had a pair of runners out, them folks."

"Makes a more cheerful winter, Mrs. Crow, don't you think, when it comes early?" remarked Lorne. "Or would you rather not get it till after Christmas?"

"I don't know as it matters much, out here in the country. We don't get a great many folks passin', best of times. An' it's more of a job to take care of the stock."

"That's so," Mr. Crow told them. "Chores come heavier when there's snow on the ground, a great sight, especially if there's drifts."

And for an instant, with his knotted hands hanging between his knees, he pondered this unvarying aspect of his yearly experience. They all pondered it, sympathetic.

"Well, now, Mr. Farquharson," Mrs. Crow turned to him. "An' how reely *be* ye? We've heard better, an' worse, an' middlin'— there's ben such contradictory reports."

"Oh, very well, Mrs. Crow. Never better. I'm going to give a lot more trouble yet. I can't do it in politics, that's the worst of it. But here's the man that's going to do it for me. Here's the man!"

The Crows looked at the pretendant, as in duty bound, but not any longer than they could help.

"Why, I guess you were at school with Elmore?" said Crow, as if the idea had just struck him.

"He may be right peart, for all that," said Elmore's mother, and Elmore, himself, entering with two leading Liberals of Jordanville, effected a diversion, under cover of which Mrs. Crow escaped, to superintend, with Bella, the last touches to the supper in the kitchen.

Politics in and about Jordanville were accepted as a purely masculine interest. If you had asked Mrs. Crow to take a hand in them she would have thanked you with sarcasm, and said she thought she had about enough to do as it was. The schoolhouse, on the night of such a meeting as this, was recognized to be no place for ladies. It was a man's affair, left to the men, and the appearance there of the other sex would have been greeted with remark and levity. Elgin, as we know, was more sophisticated in every way, plenty of ladies attended political meetings in the Drill Shed, where seats as likely as not would be reserved for them; plenty of handkerchiefs waved there for the encouragement of the hero of the evening. They did not kiss him; British phlegm, so far, had stayed that demonstration at the southern border.

The ladies of Elgin, however, drew the line somewhere, drew it at country meetings. Mrs. Farquharson went with her husband because, since his state of health had handed him over to her more than ever, she saw it a part of her wifely duty. His retirement had been decided upon for the spring, but she would be on hand to retire him at any earlier moment should the necessity arise. "We'll be the only female creatures there, my dear," she had said to Dora on the way out, and Hesketh had praised them both for public spirit. He didn't know, he said, how anybody would get elected in England without the ladies, especially in the villages, where the people were obliged to listen respectfully.

"I wonder you can afford to throw away all the influence you get in the rural districts with soup and blankets," he said; "but this is an extravagant country in many ways." Dora kept silence, not being sure of the social prestige bound up with the distribution of soup and blankets, but Mrs. Farquharson set him sharply right.

"I guess we'd rather do without our influence if it came to that," she said.

Hesketh listened with deference to her account of the rural district which had as yet produced no Ladies Bountiful, made mental notes of several points, and placed her privately as a woman of more than ordinary intelligence. I have always claimed for Hesketh an open mind; he was filling it now, to its capacity, with care and satisfaction.

The schoolroom was full and waiting when they arrived. Jordan-ville had been well billed, and the posters held, in addition to the conspicuous names of Farquharson and Murchison, that of Mr. Alfred Hesketh (of London, England). There was a "send-off" to give to the retiring member, there was a critical inspection to make of the new candidate, and there was Mr. Alfred Hesketh, of London, England, and whatever he might signify. They were big, quiet, expectant fellows, with less sophistication and polemic than their American counterparts, less stolid aggressiveness than their parallels in England, if they have parallels there. They stood, indeed, for the development between the two; they came of the new country but not of the new light; they were democrats who had never thrown off the monarch—what harm did he do there overseas? They had the air of being prosperous, but not prosperous enough for theories and doctrines. The Liberal vote of South Fox had yet to be split by Socialism or Labor. Life was a decent rough business that required all their attention; there was time enough for sleep but not much for speculation. They sat leaning forward with their hats dropped be-tween their knees, more with the air of big schoolboys expecting an entertainment than responsible electors come together to approve their party's choice. They had the uncomplaining bucolic look, but they wore it with a difference; the difference, by this time, was enough to mark them of another nation. Most of them had driven to the meeting; it was not an adjournment from the public house. Nor did the air hold any hint of beer. Where it had an alcoholic drift the flavor was of whisky; but the stimulant of the occasion had been tea or cider, and the room was full of patient good will.

The preliminaries were gone through with promptness; the Chair had supped with the speakers, and Mr. Crow had given him a friendly hint that the boys wouldn't be expecting much in the way of trimmings from *him*. Stamping and clapping from the back benches greeted Mr. Farquharson. It diminished, grew more sub-dued, as it reached the front. The young fellows were mostly at the back, and the power of demonstration had somehow ebbed in the old ones. The retiring member addressed his constituents for half an hour. He was standing before them as their representative for the last time, and it was natural to look back and note the milestones behind, the changes for the better with which he could fairly claim association. They were matters of Federal business chiefly, beyond the immediate horizon of Jordanville, but Farquharson made them a personal interest for that hour at all events, and there were one or two points of education policy which he could illustrate by their own schoolhouse. He approached them, as he had always done, on the level of mutual friendly interest, and in the hope of doing mutual friendly business. "You know and I know," he said more than once; they and he knew a number of things together.

He was afraid, he said, that if the doctors hadn't chased him out of politics, he never would have gone. Now, however, that they gave him no choice, he was glad to think that though times had been pretty good for the farmers of South Fox all through the eleven years of his appearance in the political arena, he was leaving it at a mo-ment when they promised to be better still. Already, he was sure, they were familiar with the main heads of that attractive prospect and, agreeable as the subject, great as the policy was to him, he would leave it to be further unfolded by the gentleman whom they all hoped to enlist in the cause, as his successor for this constituency, Mr. Lorne Murchison, and by his friend from the old country, Mr. Alfred Hesketh. He, Farquharson, would not take the words out of the mouths of these gentlemen, much as he envied them the oppor-tunity of uttering them. The French Academy, he told them, that illustrious body of literary and scientific men, had a custom, on the death of a member and the selection of his successor, of appointing one of their number to eulogize the newcomer. The person upon whom the task would most appropriately fall, did circumstances permit, would be the departing academician. In this case, he was happy to say, circumstances did permit—his political funeral was still far enough off to enable him to express his profound confidence in and his hearty admiration of the young and vigorous political heir whom the Liberals of South Fox had selected to stand in his shoes. Mr. Farquharson proceeded to give his grounds for this confidence and admiration, reminding the Jordanville electors that they had met Mr. Murchison as a Liberal standard-bearer in the last general election, when he, Farquharson, had to acknowledge very valuable services on Mr. Murchison's part. The retiring member then thanked his audience for the kind attention and support they had given him for so many years, made a final cheerful joke about a Pagan divinity known as Anno Domini, and took his seat.

They applauded him, and it was plain that they regretted him, the tried friend, the man there was never any doubt about, whose convictions they had repeated, and whose speeches in Parliament they had read with a kind of proprietorship for so long. The Chair had to wait, before introducing Mr. Alfred Hesketh, until the back-benchers had got through with a double rendering of "For He's a Jolly Good Fellow," which bolder spirits sent lustily forth from the anteroom where the little girls kept their hats and comforters, interspersed with whoops. Hesketh, it had been arranged, should speak next, and Lorne last.

Mr. Hesketh left his wooden chair with smiling ease, the ease which is intended to level distinctions and put everybody concerned on the best of terms. He said that though he was no stranger to the work of political campaigns, this was the first time that he had had the privilege of addressing a colonial audience. "I consider," said he handsomely, "that it is a privilege." He clasped his hands behind his back and threw out his chest.

"Opinions have differed in England as to the value of the colonies, and the consequence of colonials. I say here with pride that I have ever been among those who insist that the value is very high and the consequence very great. The fault is common to humanity, but we are, I fear, in England, too prone to be led away by appearances, and to forget that under a rough unpolished exterior may beat virtues which are the brightest ornaments of civilization, that in the virgin fields of the possessions which the good swords of our ancestors wrung for us from the Algonquins and the—and the other savages—may be hidden the most glorious period of the British race."

Mr. Hesketh paused and coughed. His audience neglected the opportunity for applause, but he had their undivided attention. They were looking at him and listening to him, these Canadian farmers, with curious interest in his attitude, his appearance, his inflection, his whole personality as it offered itself to them—it was a thing new and strange. Far out in the Northwest, where the emigrant trains had been unloading all the summer, Hesketh's would have been a voice from home; but here, in long-settled Ontario, men had forgotten the sound of it, with many other things. They listened in silence, weighing with folded arms, appraising with chin in hand; they were slow, equitable men.

"If we in England," Hesketh proceeded, "required a lesson—as perhaps we did—in the importance of the colonies, we had it, need I remind you? in the course of the late protracted campaign in South Africa. Then did the mother country indeed prove the loyalty and devotion of her colonial sons. Then were envious nations compelled to see the spectacle of Canadians and Australians rallying about the common flag, eager to attest their affection for it with their life-blood, and to demonstrate that they, too, were worthy to add deeds to British traditions and victories to the British cause."

Still no mark of appreciation. Hesketh began to think them an unhandsome lot. He stood bravely, however, by the note he had sounded. He dilated on the pleasure and satisfaction it had been to the people of England to receive this mark of attachment from far away dominions and dependencies, on the cementing of the bonds of brotherhood by the blood of the fallen, on the impossibility that the mother country should ever forget such voluntary sacrifices for her sake, when, unexpectedly and irrelevantly, from the direction of the cloakroom, came the expressive comment—"Yah!"

Though brief, nothing could have been more to the purpose, and Hesketh sacrificed several effective points to hurry to the quotation—

What should they know of England
Who only England know?

which he could not, perhaps, have been expected to forbear. His audience, however, were plainly not in the vein for compliment. The same voice from the anteroom inquired ironically, "That so?" and the speaker felt advised to turn to more immediate considerations.

He said he had had the great pleasure on his arrival in this country to find a political party, the party in power, their Canadian Liberal party, taking initiative in a cause which he was sure they all had at heart—the strengthening of the bonds between the colonies and the mother country. He congratulated the Liberal party warmly upon having shown themselves capable of this great function—a point at which he was again interrupted; and he recapitulated some of the familiar arguments about the desirability of closer union from the point of view of the army, of the Admiralty, and from one which would come home, he knew, to all of them, the necessity of a dependable food supply for the mother country in time of war. Here he quoted a noble lord. He said that he believed no definite proposals had been made, and he did not understand how any definite proposals could be made; for his part, if the new arrangement was to be in the nature of a bargain, he would prefer to have nothing to do with it.

"England," he said, loftily, "has no wish to buy the loyalty of her colonies, nor, I hope, has any colony the desire to offer her allegiance at the price of preference in British markets. Even proposals for mutual commercial benefit may be underpinned, I am glad to say, by loftier principles than those of the market-place and the counting-house."

At this one of his hearers, unacquainted with the higher commercial plane, exclaimed, "How be ye goin' to get 'em kept to, then?"

Hesketh took up the question. He said a friend in the audience asked how they were to ensure that such arrangements would be adhered to. His answer was in the words of the Duke of Dartmoor, "By the mutual esteem, the inherent integrity, and the willing compromise of the British race."

Here someone on the back benches, impatient, doubtless, at his own incapacity to follow this high doctrine, exclaimed intemperately, "Oh, shut up!" and the gathering, remembering that this, after all, was not what it had come for, began to hint that it had had enough in intermittent stamps and uncompromising shouts for "Murchison!"

Hesketh kept on his legs, however, a few minutes longer. He had a trenchant sentence to repeat to them which he thought they would take as a direct message from the distinguished nobleman who had uttered it. The Marquis of Aldeburgh was the father of the pithy thing, which he had presented, as it happened, to Hesketh himself. The audience received it with respect—Hesketh's own respect was so marked—but with misapprehension; there had been too many allusions to the nobility for a community so far removed from its soothing influence. "Had ye no friends among the commoners?"

suddenly spoke up a dry old fellow, stroking a long white beard; and the roar that greeted this showed the sense of the meeting. Hesketh closed with assurances of the admiration and confidence he felt toward the candidate proposed to their suffrages by the Liberal party that were quite inaudible, and sought his yellow pinewood schoolroom chair with rather a forced smile. It had been used once before that day to isolate conspicuous stupidity.

They were at bottom a good-natured and a loyal crowd, and they had not, after all, come there to make trouble, or Mr. Alfred Hesketh might have carried away a worse opinion of them. As it was, young Murchison, whose address occupied the rest of the evening, succeeded in making an impression upon them distinct enough, happily for his personal influence, to efface that of his friend. He did it by the simple expedient of talking business, and as high prices for produce and low ones for agricultural implements would be more interesting there than here, I will not report him. He and Mr. Farquharson waited, after the meeting, for a personal word with a good many of those present, but it was suggested to Hesketh that the ladies might be tired, and that he had better get them home without unnecessary delay. Mrs. Farquharson had less comment to offer during the drive home than Hesketh thought might be expected from a woman of her intelligence, but Miss Milburn was very enthusiastic. She said he had made a lovely speech, and she wished her father could have heard it.

A personal impression, during a time of political excitement, travels unexpectedly far. A week later Mr. Hesketh was concernedly accosted in Main Street by a boy on a bicycle.

"Say, mister, how's the dook?"

"What duke?" asked Hesketh, puzzled.

"Oh, any dook," responded the boy, and bicycled cheerfully away.

STEPHEN LEACOCK
1869-1944

Stephen Butler Leacock was born in Hampshire, England. His family emigrated in 1876 to a farm near Lake Simcoe, Ontario. He was educated at Upper Canada College, the University of Toronto, and the University of Chicago, where he received a Ph.D. in 1903. He was a Master at Upper Canada College from 1888 to 1899, and on his return from Chicago he began lecturing in economics and political science at McGill. In 1908 he became head of the department, a position he held until his retirement in 1936. Although best known for his humorous works, Leacock wrote a number of books on economics and political science and a volume on the establishment of responsible government in The Makers of Canada series. He was elected a Fellow of the Royal Society of Canada in 1910.

When Leacock published *Literary Lapses* in 1910 he began a series of humorous books which he produced at the rate of one a year for the next twenty-odd years. Best known, of course, are *Sunshine Sketches of a Little Town* (1912) and *Arcadian Adventures with the Idle Rich* (1914). After his successful lecture tour of Great Britain in 1921 he produced an inversion of the usual traveller's account, *My Discovery of England* (1922). Leacock wrote a number of works of literary criticism, mostly on the theory of humor. Among these are *Mark Twain* (1932) and *Charles Dickens* (1933). He also wrote studies of the art and theory of humor and a fine local history, *Montreal: Seaport and City* (1942). His last work, an autobiography, was published posthumously: *The Boy I Left Behind Me* (1946).

FROM *Sunshine Sketches of a Little Town*, 1912

THE GREAT ELECTION IN MISSINABA COUNTY*

Don't ask me what election it was, whether Dominion or Provincial or Imperial or Universal, for I scarcely know.

It must, of course, have been going on in other parts of the country as well, but I saw it all from Missinaba County which, with the town of Mariposa, was, of course, the storm centre and focus point of the whole turmoil.

I only know that it was a huge election and that on it turned issues of the most tremendous importance, such as whether or not Mariposa should become part of the United States, and whether the flag that had waved over the school house at Tecumseh Township for ten centuries should be trampled under the hoof of an alien invader, and whether Britons should be slaves, and whether Canadians should be Britons, and whether the farming class would prove themselves Canadians, and tremendous questions of that kind.

And there was such a roar and a tumult to it, and such a waving of flags and beating of drums and flaring of torchlights that such parts of the election as may have been going on elsewhere than in Missinaba County must have been quite unimportant and didn't really matter.

Now that it is all over, we can look back at it without heat or passion. We can see—it's plain enough now—that in the great election Canada saved the British Empire, and that Missinaba saved Canada and that the vote of the Third Concession of Tecumseh Township saved Missinaba County, and that those of us who carried the Third Concession—well, there's no need to push it further. We prefer to be modest about it. If we still speak of it, it is only quietly and simply and not more than three or four times a day.

But you can't understand the election at all, and the conventions and the campaigns and the nominations and the balloting, unless you first appreciate the peculiar complexion of politics in Mariposa.

* The election of 1911 that brought about the defeat of Sir Wilfrid Laurier's Liberal government over the question of reciprocity with the United States.

Let me begin at the beginning. Everybody in Mariposa is either a Liberal or a Conservative or else is both. Some of the people are or have been Liberals or Conservatives all their lives and are called dyed-in-the-wool Grits or old-time Tories and things of that sort. These people get from long training such a swift penetrating insight into national issues that they can decide the most complicated question in four seconds: in fact, just as soon as they grab the city papers out of the morning mail, they know the whole solution of any problem you can put to them. There are other people whose aim is to be broad-minded and judicious and who vote Liberal or Conservative according to their judgment of the questions of the day. If their judgment of these questions tells them that there is something in it for them in voting Liberal, then they do so. But if not, they refuse to be the slaves of a party or the henchmen of any political leader. So that anybody looking for henches has got to keep away from them.

But the one thing that nobody is allowed to do in Mariposa is to have no politics. Of course, there are always some people whose circumstances compel them to say that they have no politics. But that is easily understood. Take the case of Trelawney, the postmaster. Long ago he was a letter carrier under the old Mackenzie Government, and later he was a letter sorter under the old Macdonald Government, and after that a letter stamper under the old Tupper Government, and so on. Trelawney always says that he has no politics, but the truth is that he has too many.

So, too, with the clergy in Mariposa. They have no politics—absolutely none. Yet Dean Drone round election time always announces as his text such a verse as: "Lo! is there not one righteous man in Israel?" or "What ho! is it not time for a change?" And that is a signal for all the Liberal business men to get up and leave their pews.

Similarly over at the Presbyterian Church, the minister says that his sacred calling will not allow him to take part in politics and that his sacred calling prevents him from breathing even a word of harshness against his fellow-man, but that when it comes to the elevation of the ungodly into high places in the commonwealth (this means, of course, the nomination of the Conservative candidate) then he's not going to allow his sacred calling to prevent him from saying just what he thinks of it. And by that time, having pretty well cleared the church of Conservatives, he proceeds to show from the scriptures that the ancient Hebrews were Liberals to a man, except those who were drowned in the flood or who perished, more or less deservedly, in the desert.

There are, I say, some people who are allowed to claim to have no politics—the office holders, and the clergy and the school teachers and the hotel keepers. But beyond them, anybody in Mariposa who says that he has no politics is looked upon as crooked, and people wonder what it is that he is "out after."

In fact, the whole town and county is a hive of politics, and people who have only witnessed gatherings such as the House of Commons at Westminster and the Senate at Washington and never seen a Conservative Convention at Tecumseh Corners or a Liberal Rally at the Concession schoolhouse, don't know what politics means.

So you may imagine the excitement in Mariposa when it became known that King George had dissolved the parliament of Canada and had sent out a writ or command for Missinaba County to elect for him some other person than John Henry Bagshaw because he no longer had confidence in him.

The king, of course, is very well known, and favourably known, in Mariposa. Everybody remembers how he visited the town on his great tour in Canada, and stopped off at the Mariposa station. Although he was only a prince at the time, there was quite a big crowd at the depot and everybody felt what a shame it was that the prince had no time to see more of Mariposa, because he would get such a false idea of it, seeing only the station and the lumber yards. Still, they all came to the station and all the Liberals and Conservatives mixed together perfectly freely and stood side by side without any distinction, so that the prince should not observe any party differences among them. And he didn't—you could see that he didn't. They read him an address all about the tranquillity and loyalty of the Empire, and they purposely left out any reference to the trouble over the town wharf or the big row there had been about the location of the new post office. There was a general decent feeling that it wouldn't be fair to disturb the prince with these things: later on, as king, he would, of course, *have* to know all about them, but meanwhile it was better to leave him with the idea that his empire was tranquil.

So they deliberately couched the address in terms that were just as reassuring as possible and the prince was simply delighted with it. I am certain that he slept pretty soundly after hearing that address. Why, you could see it taking effect even on his aides-de-camp and the people round him, so imagine how the prince must have felt!

I think in Mariposa they understand kings perfectly. Every time that a king or a prince comes, they try to make him see the bright side of everything and let him think that they're all united. Judge Pepperleigh walked up and down arm in arm with Dr. Gallagher, the worst Grit in the town, just to make the prince feel fine.

So when they got the news that the king had lost confidence in John Henry Bagshaw, the sitting member, they never questioned it a bit. Lost confidence? All right, they'd elect him another right away. They'd elect him half a dozen if he needed them. They don't mind; they'd elect the whole town man after man rather than have the king worried about it.

In any case, all the Conservatives had been wondering for years how the king and the governor-general and men like that had tolerated such a man as Bagshaw so long.

Missinaba County, I say, is a regular hive of politics, and not the miserable, crooked, money-ridden politics of the cities, but the straight, real old-fashioned thing that is an honour to the country-side. Any man who would offer to take a bribe or sell his convictions for money, would be an object of scorn. I don't say they wouldn't take money—they would, of course, why not?—but if they did they would take it in a straight fearless way and say nothing about it. They might—it's only human—accept a job or a contract from the government, but if they did, rest assured it would be in a broad national spirit and not for the sake of the work itself. No, sir. Not for a minute.

Any man who wants to get the votes of the Missinaba farmers and the Mariposa business men has got to persuade them that he's the right man. If he can do that—if he can persuade any one of them that he is the right man and that all the rest know it, then they'll vote for him.

The division, I repeat, between the Liberals and the Conservatives, is intense. Yet you might live for a long while in the town, between elections, and never know it. It is only when you get to understand the people that you begin to see that there is a cross division running through them that nothing can ever remove. You gradually become aware of fine subtle distinctions that miss your observation at first. Outwardly, they are all friendly enough. For instance, Joe Milligan the dentist is a Conservative, and has been for six years, and yet he shares the same boathouse with young Dr. Gallagher, who is a Liberal, and they even bought a motor boat between them. Pete Glover and Alf McNichol were in partnership in the hardware and paint store, though they belonged on different sides.

But just as soon as elections drew near, the differences in politics became perfectly apparent. Liberals and Conservatives drew away from one another. Joe Milligan used the motor boat one Saturday and Dr. Gallagher the next, and Pete Glover sold hardware on one side of the store and Alf McNichol sold paint on the other. You soon realized, too, that one of the newspapers was Conservative and the other was Liberal, that there was a Liberal drug store and a Conservative drug store, and so on. Similarly round election time, the Mariposa House was the Liberal Hotel, and the Continental, Conservative, though Mr. Smith's place, where they always put on a couple of extra bartenders, was what you might call Independent-Liberal-Conservative, with a dash of Imperialism thrown in. Mr. Gingham the undertaker, was, as a natural effect of his calling, an advanced Liberal, but at election time he always engaged a special assistant for embalming Conservative customers.

So now, I think, you understand something of the general political surroundings of the great election in Missinaba County.

John Henry Bagshaw was the sitting member, the Liberal member, for Missinaba County.

The Liberals called him the old war horse, and the old battle-axe, and the old charger and the old champion and all sorts of things of that kind. The Conservatives called him the old jackass and the old army mule and the old booze fighter and the old grafter and the old scoundrel.

John Henry Bagshaw was, I suppose, one of the greatest political forces in the world. He had flowing white hair crowned with a fedora hat, and a smooth statesmanlike face which it cost the country twenty-five cents a day to shave.

Altogether, the Dominion of Canada had spent over two thousand dollars in shaving that face during the twenty years that Bagshaw had represented Missinaba County. But the result had been well worth it.

Bagshaw wore a long political overcoat that it cost the country twenty cents a day to brush, and boots that cost the Dominion fifteen cents every morning to shine.

But it was money well spent.

Bagshaw of Mariposa was one of the most representative men of the age, and it's no wonder that he had been returned for the county for five elections running, leaving the Conservatives nowhere. Just think how representative he was. He owned two hundred acres out on the Third Concession and kept two men working on it all the time to prove that he was a practical farmer. They sent in fat hogs to the Missinaba County Agricultural Exposition and World's Fair every autumn, and Bagshaw himself stood beside the pig pens with the judges, and wore a pair of corduroy breeches and chewed a straw all afternoon. After that if any farmer thought that he was not properly represented in Parliament, it showed that he was an ass.

Bagshaw owned a half share in the harness business and a quarter share in the tannery and that made him a business man. He paid for a pew in the Presbyterian Church and that represented religion in Parliament. He attended college for two sessions thirty years ago, and that represented education and kept him abreast with modern science, if not ahead of it. He kept a little account in one bank and a big account in the other, so that he was a rich man or a poor man at the same time.

Add to that that John Henry Bagshaw was, perhaps, the finest orator in Mariposa. That, of course, is saying a great deal. There are speakers there, lots of them, that can talk two or three hours at a stretch, but the old war horse could beat them all. They say that when John Henry Bagshaw got well started, say after a couple of hours of talk, he could speak as Pericles or Demosthenes or Cicero never could have spoken.

You could tell Bagshaw a hundred yards off as a member of the House of Commons. He wore a pepper-and-salt suit to show that he came from a rural constituency, and he wore a broad gold watch-chain with dangling seals to show that he also represents a town. You could see from his quiet low collar and white tie that his electorate were a God-fearing, religious people, while the horseshoe pin that he wore showed that his electorate were not without sporting instincts and knew a horse from a jackass.

Most of the time, John Henry Bagshaw had to be at Ottawa (though he preferred the quiet of his farm and always left it, as he said, with a sigh). If he was not in Ottawa, he was in Washington, and of course at any time they might need him in London, so that it was no wonder that he could only be in Mariposa about two months in the year.

That is why everybody knew, when Bagshaw got off the afternoon train one day early in the spring, that there must be something very important coming and that the rumours about a new election must be perfectly true.

Everything that he did showed this. He gave the baggage man

twenty-five cents to take the check off his trunk, the 'bus driver fifty
cents to drive him up to the Main Street, and he went into Callahan's
tobacco store and bought two ten-cent cigars and took them across
the street and gave them to Mallory Tompkins of the Times-Herald
as a present from the Prime Minister.

All that afternoon, Bagshaw went up and down the Main Street
of Mariposa, and you could see, if you knew the signs of it, that there
was politics in the air. He bought nails and putty and glass in the
hardware store, and harness in the harness shop, and drugs in the
drug store and toys in the toy shop, and all the things like that that
are needed for a big campaign.

Then when he had done all this he went over with McGinnis the
Liberal organizer and Mallory Tompkins, the Times-Herald man,
and Gingham (the great Independent-Liberal undertaker) to the back
parlour in the Mariposa House.

You could tell from the way John Henry Bagshaw closed the door
before he sat down that he was in a pretty serious frame of mind.

"Gentlemen," he said, "the election is a certainty. We're going to
have a big fight on our hands and we've got to get ready for it."

"Is it going to be on the tariff?" asked Tompkins.

"Yes, gentlemen, I'm afraid it is. The whole thing is going to
turn on the tariff question. I wish it were otherwise. I think it madness, but they're bent on it, and we got to fight it on that line. Why
they can't fight it merely on the question of graft," continued the old
war horse, rising from his chair and walking up and down, "heaven
only knows. I warned them. I appealed to them. I said, fight the
thing on graft and we can win easy. Take this constituency—why not
have fought the thing out on whether I spent too much money on
the town wharf or the post office? What better issues could a man
want? Let them claim that I am crooked, and let me claim that I'm
not. Surely that was good enough without dragging in the tariff.
But now, gentlemen, tell me about things in the constituency. Is there
any talk yet of who is to run?"

Mallory Tompkins lighted up the second of the Prime Minister's
cigars and then answered for the group:

"Everybody says that Edward Drone is going to run."

"Ah!" said the old war horse, and there was joy upon his face, "is
he? At last! That's good, that's good—now what platform will he
run on?"

"Independent."

"Excellent," said Mr. Bagshaw. "Independent, that's fine. On a program of what?"

"Just simple honesty and public morality."

"Come now," said the member, "that's splendid: that will help enormously. Honesty and public morality! The very thing! If Drone runs and makes a good showing, we win for a certainty. Tompkins, you must lose no time over this. Can't you manage to get some articles in the other papers hinting that at the last election we bribed all the voters in the county, and that we gave out enough contracts to simply pervert the whole constituency. Imply that we poured the public money into this county in bucketfuls and that we are bound to do it again. Let Drone have plenty of material of this sort and he'll draw off every honest unbiassed vote in the Conservative party.

"My only fear is," continued the old war horse, losing some of his animation, "that Drone won't run after all. He's said it so often before and never has. He hasn't got the money. But we must see to that. Gingham, you know his brother well; you must work it so that we pay Drone's deposit and his campaign expenses. But how like Drone it is to come out at this time!"

It was, indeed, very like Edward Drone to attempt so misguided a thing as to come out an Independent candidate in Missinaba County on a platform of public honesty. It was just the sort of thing that anyone in Mariposa would expect from him.

Edward Drone was the Rural Dean's younger brother—young Mr. Drone, they used to call him, years ago, to distinguish him from the rector. He was a somewhat weaker copy of his elder brother, with a simple, inefficient face and kind blue eyes. Edward Drone was, and always had been, a failure. In training he had been, once upon a time, an engineer and built dams that broke and bridges that fell down and wharves that floated away in the spring floods. He had been a manufacturer and failed, had been a contractor and failed, and now lived a meagre life as a sort of surveyor or land expert on goodness knows what.

In his political ideas Edward Drone was and, as everybody in Mariposa knew, always had been crazy. He used to come up to the autumn exercises at the high school and make speeches about the ancient Romans and Titus Manlius and Quintus Curtius at the same time when John Henry Bagshaw used to make a speech about the Maple Leaf and ask for an extra half holiday. Drone used to tell the boys about the lessons to be learned from the lives of the truly great, and

Bagshaw used to talk to them about the lessons learned from the lives of the extremely rich. Drone used to say that his heart filled whenever he thought of the splendid patriotism of the ancient Romans, and Bagshaw said that whenever he looked out over this wide Dominion his heart overflowed.

Even the youngest boy in the school could tell that Drone was foolish. Not even the school teachers would have voted for him.

"What about the Conservatives?" asked Bagshaw presently; "is there any talk yet as to who they'll bring out?"

Gingham and Mallory Tompkins looked at one another. They were almost afraid to speak.

"Hadn't you heard?" said Gingham; "they've got their man already."

"Who is it?" said Bagshaw quickly.

"They're going to put Josh Smith."

"Great Heaven!" said Bagshaw, jumping to his feet; "Smith! the hotel keeper."

"Yes, sir," said Mr. Gingham, "that's the man."

Do you remember, in history, how Napoleon turned pale when he heard that the Duke of Wellington was to lead the allies in Belgium? Do you remember how, when Themistocles heard that Aristogiton was to lead the Spartans, he jumped into the sea? Possibly you don't but it may help you to form some idea of what John Henry Bagshaw felt when he heard that the Conservatives had selected Josh Smith, proprietor of Smith's Hotel.

You remember Smith. You've seen him there on the steps of his hotel—two hundred and eighty pounds in his stockinged feet. You've seen him selling liquor after hours through sheer public spirit, and you recall how he saved the lives of hundreds of people on the day when the steamer sank, and how he saved the town from being destroyed the night when the Church of England church burnt down. You know that hotel of his, too, halfway down the street, Smith's Northern Health Resort, though already they were beginning to call it Smith's British Arms.

So you can imagine that Bagshaw came as near to turning pale as a man in federal politics can.

"I never knew Smith was a Conservative," he said faintly; "he always subscribed to our fund.

"He is now," said Mr. Gingham ominously. "He says the idea of this reciprocity business cut him to the heart."

"The infernal liar!" said Mr. Bagshaw.

There was silence for a few moments. Then Bagshaw spoke again.

"Will Smith have anything else in his platform besides the trade question?"

"Yes," said Mr. Gingham gloomily, "he will."

"What is it?"

"Temperance and total prohibition!"

John Henry Bagshaw sank back in his chair as if struck with a club.

THE CANDIDACY OF MR. SMITH

"Boys," said Mr. Smith to the two hostlers, stepping out onto the sidewalk in front of the hotel—"hoist that there British Jack over the place and hoist her up good."

Then he stood and watched the flag fluttering in the wind.

"Billy," he said to the desk clerk, "get a couple more and put them up on the roof of the caff behind the hotel. Wire down to the city and get a quotation on a hundred of them. Take them signs 'American Drinks' out of the bar. Put up noo ones with 'British Beer at all Hours,' clear out the rye whiskey and order in Scotch and Irish, and then go up to the printing office and get me them placards."

Then another thought struck Mr. Smith.

"Say, Billy," he said, "wire to the city for fifty pictures of King George. Get 'em good, and get 'em coloured. It don't matter what they cost."

"All right, sir," said Billy.

"And Billy," called Mr. Smith, as still another thought struck him (indeed, the moment Mr. Smith went into politics you could see these thoughts strike him like waves), "get fifty pictures of his father, old King Albert."

"All right, sir."

"And say, I tell you, while you're at it, get some of the old queen,

Victorina, if you can. Get 'em in mourning, with a harp and one of them lions and a three-pointed prong."

*   *   *

It was on the morning after the Conservative Convention. Josh Smith had been chosen the candidate. And now the whole town was covered with flags and placards and there were bands in the streets every evening, and noise and music and excitement that went on from morning till night.

Election times are exciting enough even in the city. But there the excitement dies down in business hours. In Mariposa there aren't any business hours and the excitement goes on *all* the time.

Mr. Smith had carried the Convention before him. There had been a feeble attempt to put up Nivens. But everybody knew that he was a lawyer and a college man and wouldn't have a chance by a man with a broader outlook like Josh Smith.

So the result was that Smith was the candidate and there were placard out all over the town with SMITH AND BRITISH ALLEGIANCE in big letters, and people were wearing badges with Mr. Smith's face on one side and King George's on the other, and the fruit store next to the hotel had been cleaned out and turned into committee rooms with a gang of workers smoking cigars in it all day and half the night.

There were other placards, too, with BAGSHAW AND LIBERTY, BAGSHAW AND PROSPERITY, VOTE FOR THE OLD MISSINABA STANDARD BEARER, and up town beside the Mariposa House there were the Bagshaw committee rooms with a huge white streamer across the street, and with a gang of Bagshaw workers smoking their heads off.

But Mr. Smith had an estimate made which showed that nearly two cigars to one were smoked in his committee rooms as compared with the Liberals. It was the first time in five elections that the Conservative had been able to make such a showing as that.

One might mention, too, that there were Drone placards out—five or six of them—little things about the size of a pocket handkerchief, with a statement that "Mr. Edward Drone solicits the votes of the electors of Missinaba County." But you would never notice them. And when Drone tried to put up a streamer across the Main Street with DRONE AND HONESTY the wind carried it away into the lake.

The fight was really between Smith and Bagshaw, and everybody knew it from the start.

I wish that I were able to narrate all the phases and the turns of the great contest from the opening of the campaign till the final polling day. But it would take volumes.

First of all, of course, the trade question was hotly discussed in the two newspapers of Mariposa, and the Newspacket and the Times-Herald literally bristled with statistics. Then came interviews with the candidates and the expression of their convictions in regard to tariff questions.

"Mr. Smith," said the reporter of the Mariposa Newspacket, "we'd like to get your views of the effect of the proposed reduction of the differential duties."

"By gosh, Pete," said Mr. Smith, "you can search me. Have a cigar."

"What do you think, Mr. Smith, would be the result of lowering the *ad valorem* British preference and admitting American goods at a reciprocal rate?"

"It's a corker, ain't it?" answered Mr. Smith. "What'll you take, lager or domestic?"

And in that short dialogue Mr. Smith showed that he had instantaneously grasped the whole method of dealing with the press. The interview in the paper next day said that Mr. Smith, while unwilling to state positively that the principle of tariff discrimination was at variance with sound fiscal science, was firmly of opinion that any reciprocal interchange of tariff preferences with the United States must inevitably lead to a serious per capita reduction of the national industry.

*   *   *

"Mr. Smith," said the chairman of a delegation of the manufacturers of Mariposa, "what do you propose to do in regard to the tariff if you're elected?"

"Boys," answered Mr. Smith, "I'll put her up so darned high they won't never get her down again."

*   *   *

"Mr. Smith," said the chairman of another delegation, "I'm an old free trader——"

"Put it there," said Mr. Smith, "so'm I. There ain't nothing like it."

*   *   *

"What do you think about imperial defence?" asked another questioner.

"Which?" said Mr. Smith.

"Imperial defence."

"Of what?"

"Of everything."

"Who says it?" asked Mr. Smith.

"Everybody is talking of it."

"What do the Conservative boys at Ottaway think about it?" answered Mr. Smith.

"They're all for it."

"Well, I'm fer it, too," said Mr. Smith.

*   *   *

These little conversations represented only the first stage, the argumentative stage of the great contest. It was during this period, for example, that the Mariposa Newspacket absolutely proved that the price of hogs in Mariposa was decimal six higher than the price of oranges in Southern California and that the average decennial import of eggs into Missinaba County had increased four decimal six eight two in the last fifteen years more than the import of lemons in New Orleans.

Figures of this kind made the people think. Most certainly.

After all this came the organizing stage and after that the big public meetings and the rallies. Perhaps you have never seen a county being "organized." It is a wonderful sight. First of all the Bagshaw men drove through crosswise in top buggies and then drove through it again lengthwise. Whenever they met a farmer they went in and ate a meal with him, and after the meal they took him out to the buggy and gave him a drink. After that the man's vote was absolutely solid until it was tampered with by feeding a Conservative.

In fact, the only way to show a farmer that you are in earnest is to go in and eat a meal with him. If you can't eat it, he won't vote for you. That is the recognized political test.

But, of course, just as soon as the Bagshaw men had begun to get the farming vote solidified, the Smith buggies came driving through in the other direction, eating meals and distributing cigars and turning all the farmers back into Conservatives.

Here and there you might see Edward Drone, the Independent candidate, wandering round from farm to farm in the dust of the political buggies. To each of the farmers he explained that he pledged himself to give no bribes, to spend no money and to offer no jobs, and each one of them gripped him warmly by the hand and showed him the way to the next farm.

After the organization of the county there came the period of the public meetings and the rallies and the joint debates between the candidates and their supporters.

I suppose there was no place in the whole Dominion where the trade question—the Reciprocity question—was threshed out quite so thoroughly and in quite such a national patriotic spirit as in Mariposa. For a month, at least, people talked of nothing else. A man would stop another in the street and tell him that he had read last night that the average price of an egg in New York was decimal ought one more than the price of an egg in Mariposa, and the other man would stop the first one later in the day and tell him that the average price of a hog in Idaho was point six of a cent per pound less (or more—he couldn't remember which for the moment) than the average price of beef in Mariposa. People lived on figures of this sort, and the man who could remember most of them stood out as a born leader.

But, of course, it was at the public meetings that these things were most fully discussed. It would take volumes to do full justice to all the meetings that they held in Missinaba County. But here and there single speeches stood out as masterpieces of convincing oratory. Take, for example, the speech of John Henry Bagshaw at the Tecumseh Corners School House. The Mariposa Times-Herald said next day that that speech would go down in history, and so it will—ever so far down.

Anyone who has heard Bagshaw knows what an impressive speaker he is, and on this night when he spoke with the quiet dignity of a man old in years and anxious only to serve his country, he almost surpassed himself. Near the end of his speech somebody dropped a pin, and the noise it made in falling fairly rattled the windows.

"I am an old man now, gentlemen," Bagshaw said, "and the time must soon come when I must not only leave politics, but must take my way towards that goal from which no traveller returns." There was a deep hush when Bagshaw said this. It was understood to imply that he thought of going to the United States.

"Yes, gentlemen, I am an old man, and I wish, when my time comes to go, to depart leaving as little animosity behind me as possible. But before I *do* go, I want it pretty clearly understood that there are more darn scoundrels in the Conservative party than ought to be tolerated in any decent community. I bear," he continued, "malice towards none and I wish to speak with gentleness to all, but what I will say is that how any set of rational responsible men could nominate such a skunk as the Conservative candidate, passes the bounds of my comprehension. Gentlemen, in the present campaign there is no room for vindictive abuse. Let us rise to a higher level than that. They tell me that my opponent, Smith, is a common saloon keeper. Let it pass. They tell me that he has stood convicted of horse stealing, that he is a notable perjurer, that he is known as the blackest hearted liar in Missinaba County. Let us not speak of it. Let no whisper of it pass our lips."

"No, gentlemen," continued Bagshaw, pausing to take a drink of water, "let us rather consider this question on the high plane of national welfare. Let us not think of our own particular interests but let us consider the good of the country at large. And to do this, let me present to you some facts in regard to the price of barley in Tecumseh Township."

Then, amid a deep stillness, Bagshaw read off the list of prices of sixteen kinds of grain in sixteen different places during sixteen years.

"But let me turn," Bagshaw went on to another phase of the national subject, "and view for a moment the price of marsh hay in Missinaba County——"

When Bagshaw sat down that night it was felt that a Liberal vote in Tecumseh Township was a foregone conclusion.

But here they hadn't reckoned on the political genius of Mr. Smith. When he heard next day of the meeting, he summoned some of his leading speakers to him and he said:

"Boys, they're beating us on them statissicks. Ourn ain't good enough."

Then he turned to Nivens and he said:

"What was them figures you had here the other night?"

Nivens took out a paper and began reading.

"Stop," said Mr. Smith, "what was that figure for bacon?"

"Fourteen million dollars," said Nivens.

"Not enough," said Mr. Smith, "make it twenty. They'll stand for it, them farmers."

Nivens changed it.

"And what was that for hay?"

"Two dollars a ton."

"Shove it up to four," said Mr. Smith. "And I tell you," he added, "if any of them farmers says the figures ain't correct, tell them to go to Washington and see for themselves; say that if any man wants the proof of your figures let him go over to England and ask—tell him to go straight to London and see it all for himself in the books."

*   *   *

After this, there was no more trouble over statistics. I must say, though, that it is a wonderfully convincing thing to hear trade figures of this kind properly handled. Perhaps the best man on this sort of thing in the campaign was Mullins, the banker. A man of his profession simply has to have figures of trade and population and money at his fingers' ends and the effect of it in public speaking is wonderful.

No doubt you have listened to speakers of this kind, but I question whether you have ever heard anything more typical of the sort of effect that I allude to than Mullins's speech at the big rally at the Fourth Concession.

Mullins himself, of course, knows the figures so well that he never bothers to write them into notes and the effect is very striking.

"Now, gentlemen," he said very earnestly, "how many of you know just to what extent the exports of this country have increased in the last ten years? How many could tell what per cent of increase there has been in one decade of our national importation?" Then Mullins paused and looked round. Not a man knew it.

"I don't recall," he said, "exactly the precise amount myself—not at this moment—but it must be simply tremendous. Or take the question of population," Mullins went on, warming up again as a born statistician always does at the proximity of figures, "how many of you know, how many of you can state, what has been the decennial percentage increase in our leading cities——?"

There he paused, and would you believe it, not a man could state it.

"I don't recall the exact figures," said Mullins, "but I have them at home and they are positively colossal."

But just in one phase of the public speaking, the candidacy of Mr. Smith received a serious set-back.

It had been arranged that Mr. Smith should run on a platform of total prohibition. But they soon found that it was a mistake. They had imported a special speaker from the city, a grave man with a white tie, who put his whole heart into the work and would take nothing for it except his expenses and a sum of money for each speech. But beyond the money, I say, he would take nothing.

He spoke one night at the Tecumseh Corners social hall at the same time when the Liberal meeting was going on at the Tecumseh Corners school house.

"Gentlemen," he said, as he paused halfway in his speech, "while we are gathered here in earnest discussion, do you know what is happening over at the meeting place of our opponents? Do you know that seventeen bottles of rye whiskey were sent out from the town this afternoon to that innocent and unsuspecting school house? Seventeen bottles of whiskey hidden in between the blackboard and the wall, and every single man that attends that meeting—mark my words, every single man—will drink his fill of the abominable stuff at the expense of the Liberal candidate!"

Just as soon as the speaker said this, you could see the Smith men at the meeting look at one another in injured surprise, and before the speech was half over the hall was practically emptied.

After that the total prohibition plank was changed and the committee substituted a declaration in favour of such a form of restrictive license as should promote temperance while encouraging the manufacture of spirituous liquors, and by a severe regulation of the liquor traffic should place intoxicants only in the hands of those fitted to use them.

*   *   *

Finally there came the great day itself, the Election Day that brought, as everybody knows, the crowning triumph of Mr. Smith's career. There is no need to speak of it at any length, because it has become a matter of history.

In any case, everybody who has even seen Mariposa knows just what election day is like. The shops, of course, are, as a matter of custom, all closed, and the bar rooms are all closed by law so that you have to go in by the back way. All the people are in their best clothes, and at first they walk up and down the street in a solemn way just as they do on the twelfth of July and on St. Patrick's Day, before the fun begins. Everybody keeps looking in at the different polling places to see if anybody else has voted yet, because, of course, nobody cares to vote first for fear of being fooled after all and voting on the wrong side.

Most of all did the supporters of Mr. Smith, acting under his instructions, hang back from the poll in the early hours. To Mr. Smith's mind voting was to be conducted on the same plan as bear-shooting.

"Hold back your votes, boys," he said, "and don't be too eager. Wait till she begins to warm up and then let 'em have it good and hard."

In each of the polling places in Mariposa there is a returning officer and with him are two scrutineers, and the electors, I say, peep in and out like mice looking into a trap. But, if once the scrutineers get a man well into the polling booth, they push him in behind a little curtain and make him vote. The voting, of course, is by secret ballot, so that no one except the scrutineers and the returning officer and the two or three people who may be round the poll can possibly tell how a man has voted.

That's how it comes about that the first results are often so contradictory and conflicting. Sometimes the poll is badly arranged and the scrutineers are unable to see properly just how the ballots are being marked and they count up the Liberals and Conservatives in different ways. Often, too, a voter makes his mark so hurriedly and carelessly that they have to pick it out of the ballot box and look at it to see what it is.

I suppose that may have been why it was that in Mariposa the results came out at first in such a conflicting way.

Perhaps that was how it was that the first reports showed that Edward Drone, the Independent candidate, was certain to win. You should have seen how the excitement grew upon the streets when the news was circulated. In the big rallies and meetings of the Liberals and Conservatives, everybody had pretty well forgotten all about Drone, and when the news got round at about four o'clock that the Drone vote was carrying the poll, the people were simply astounded. Not that they were not pleased. On the contrary. They were delighted. Everybody came up to Drone and shook hands and congratulated him and told him that they had known all along that what the country wanted was a straight, honest, non-partisan representation. The Conservatives said openly that they were sick of party, utterly done with it, and the Liberals said that they hated it. Already three or four of them had taken Drone aside and explained that what was needed in the town was a straight, clean, non-partisan post office, built on a piece of ground of a strictly non-partisan character, and constructed under contracts that were not tainted and smirched with party affiliation. Two or three men were willing to show to Drone just where a piece of ground of this character could be bought. They told him, too, that in the matter of the postmastership itself they had nothing against Trelawney, the present postmaster, in any personal sense, and would say nothing against him except merely that he was utterly and hopelessly unfit for his job and that if Drone believed, as he had said he did, in a purified civil service, he ought to begin by purifying Trelawney.

Already Edward Drone was beginning to feel something of what it meant to hold office, and there was creeping into his manner the quiet self-importance which is the first sign of conscious power.

In fact, in that brief half-hour of office, Drone had a chance to see something of what it meant. Henry McGinnis came to him and asked straight out for a job as federal census-taker on the ground that he was hard up and had been crippled with rheumatism all winter. Nelson Williamson asked for the post of wharf master on the plea that he had been laid up with sciatica all winter and was absolutely fit for nothing. Erasmus Archer asked him if he could get his boy Pete into one of the departments at Ottawa, and made a strong case of it by explaining that he had tried his cussedest to get Pete a job anywhere else and it was simply impossible. Not that Pete wasn't a willing boy, but he was slow—even his father admitted it—slow as the devil, blast him, and with no head for figures, and unfortunately he'd never had the schooling to bring him on. But if Drone could get him in at Ottawa, his father truly believed it would be the very place for him. Surely, in the Indian Department or in the Astronomical Branch or in the New Canadian Navy there must be any amount of opening for a boy like this? And to all of these requests Drone found himself explaining that he would take the matter under his very earnest consideration and that they must remember that he had to consult his colleagues and not merely follow the dictates of his own wishes. In fact, if he had ever in his life had any envy of Cabinet Ministers, he lost it in this hour.

But Drone's hour was short. Even before the poll had closed in Mariposa, the news came sweeping in, true or false, that Bagshaw was carrying the county. The Second Concession had gone for Bagshaw in a regular landslide—six votes to only two for Smith—and all down the township line road (where the hay farms are) Bagshaw was said to be carrying all before him.

Just as soon as that news went round the town, they launched the

Mariposa band of the Knights of Pythias (every man in it is a Liberal) down the Main Street with big red banners in front of it with the motto BAGSHAW FOREVER in letters a foot high. Such rejoicing and enthusiasm began to set in as you never saw. Everybody crowded round Bagshaw on the steps of the Mariposa House and shook his hand and said they were proud to see the day and that the Liberal Party was the glory of the Dominion and that, as for this idea of non-partisan politics, the very thought of it made them sick. Right away in the committee rooms they began to organize the demonstration for the evening with lantern slides and speeches, and they arranged for a huge bouquet to be presented to Bagshaw on the platform by four little girls (all Liberals) all dressed in white.

And it was just at this juncture, with one hour of voting left, that Mr. Smith emerged from his committee-rooms and turned his voters on the town, much as the Duke of Wellington sent the whole line to the charge at Waterloo. From every committee room and sub-committee room they poured out in flocks with blue badges fluttering on their coats.

"Get at it, boys," said Mr. Smith, "vote and keep on voting till they make you quit."

Then he turned to his campaign assistant. "Billy," he said, "wire down to the city that I'm elected by an overwhelming majority and tell them to wire it right back. Send word by telephone to all the polling places in the county that the hull town has gone solid Conservative and tell them to send the same news back here. Get carpenters and tell them to run up a platform in front of the hotel; tell them to take the bar door clean off its hinges and be all ready the minute the poll quits."

It was that last hour that did it. Just as soon as the big posters went up in the windows of the Mariposa Newspacket with the telegraphic despatch that Josh Smith was reported in the city to be elected, and was followed by the messages from all over the county, the voters hesitated no longer. They had waited, most of them, all through the day, not wanting to make any error in their vote, but when they saw the Smith men crowding into the polls and heard the news from the outside, they went solid in one great stampede, and by the time the poll was declared closed at five o'clock there was no shadow of doubt that the county was saved and that Josh Smith was elected for Missinaba.

*   *   *

I wish you could have witnessed the scene in Mariposa that evening. It would have done your heart good—such joy, such public rejoicing as you never saw. It turned out that there wasn't really a Liberal in the whole town and that there never had been. They were all Conservatives and had been for years and years. Men who had voted, with pain and sorrow in their hearts, for the Liberal party for twenty years, came out that evening and owned up straight that they were Conservatives. They said they could stand the strain no longer and simply had to confess. Whatever the sacrifice might mean, they were prepared to make it.

Even Mr. Golgotha Gingham, the undertaker, came out and admitted that in working for John Henry Bagshaw he'd been going straight against his conscience. He said that right from the first he had had his misgivings. He said it had haunted him. Often at night when he would be working away quietly, one of these sudden misgivings would overcome him so that he could hardly go on with his embalming. Why, it appeared that on the very first day when reciprocity was proposed, he had come home and said to Mrs. Gingham that he thought it simply meant selling out the country. And the strange thing was that ever so many others had just the same misgivings. Trelawney admitted that he had said to Mrs. Trelawney that it was madness, and Jeff Thorpe, the barber, had, he admitted, gone home to his dinner, the first day reciprocity was talked of, and said to Mrs. Thorpe that it would simply kill business in the country and introduce a cheap, shoddy American form of hair-cut that would render true loyalty impossible. To think that Mrs. Gingham and Mrs. Trelawney and Mrs. Thorpe had known all this for six months and kept quiet about it! Yet I think there were a good many Mrs. Ginghams in the country. It is merely another proof that no woman is fit for politics.

*   *   *

The demonstration that night in Mariposa will never be forgotten. The excitement in the streets, the torchlights, the music of the band of the Knights of Pythias (an organization which is conservative in all but name), and above all the speeches and the patriotism.

They had put up a big platform in front of the hotel, and on it were Mr. Smith and his chief workers, and behind them was a perfect forest of flags. They presented a huge bouquet of flowers to Mr.

Smith, handed to him by four little girls in white—the same four that I spoke of above, for it turned out that they were all Conservatives.

Then there were the speeches. Judge Pepperleigh spoke and said that there was no need to dwell on the victory that they had achieved, because it was history; there was no occasion to speak of what part he himself had played, within the limits of his official position, because what he had done was henceforth a matter of history; and Nivens, the lawyer, said that he would only say just a few words, because anything that he might have done was now history; later generations, he said, might read it but it was not for him to speak of it, because it belonged now to the history of the country. And, after them, others spoke in the same strain and all refused absolutely to dwell on the subject (for more than half an hour) on the ground that anything that they might have done was better left for future generations to investigate. And, no doubt, this was very true, as to some things, anyway.

Mr. Smith, of course, said nothing. He didn't have to—not for four years—and he knew it.

FROM *Arcadian Adventures with the Idle Rich*, 1914

THE RIVAL CHURCHES OF ST. ASAPH AND ST. OSOPH

The church of St. Asaph, more properly called St. Asaph's in the Fields, stands among the elm trees of Plutoria Avenue opposite the university, its tall spire pointing to the blue sky. Its rector is fond of saying that it seems to him to point, as it were, a warning against the sins of a commercial age. More particularly does he say this in his Lenten services at noonday, when the business men sit in front of him in rows, their bald heads uncovered and their faces stamped with contrition as they think of mergers that they should have made, and real estate that they failed to buy for lack of faith.

The ground on which St. Asaph's stands is worth seven dollars and a half a foot. The mortgagees, as they kneel in prayer in their long frock-coats, feel that they have built upon a rock. It is a beautifully appointed church. There are windows with priceless stained glass that were imported from Normandy, the rector himself swearing out the invoices to save the congregation the grievous burden of the customs duty. There is a pipe organ in the transept that cost ten thousand dollars to instal. The debenture-holders, as they join in the morning anthem, love to hear the dulcet notes of the great organ and to reflect that it is as good as new. Just behind the church is St. Asaph's Sunday School, with a ten-thousand dollar mortgage of its own. And below that again, on the side street, is the building of the Young Men's Guild, with a bowling-alley and a swimming-bath deep enough to drown two young men at a time, and a billiard-room with seven tables. It is the rector's boast that with a Guild House such as that there is no need for any young man of the congregation to frequent a saloon. Nor is there.

And on Sunday mornings, when the great organ plays, and the mortgagees and the bond-holders and the debenture-holders and the Sunday school teachers and the billiard-markers all lift up their voices together, there is emitted from St. Asaph's a volume of praise that is practically as fine and effective as paid professional work.

St. Asaph's is episcopal. As a consequence it has in it and about it all those things which go to make up the episcopal church—brass tablets let into its walls, blackbirds singing in its elm trees, parishioners who dine at eight o'clock, and a rector who wears a little crucifix and dances the tango.

On the other hand, there stands upon the same street, not a hundred yards away, the rival church of St. Osoph—presbyterian down to its very foundations in bed-rock, thirty feet below the level of the avenue. It has a short, squat tower—and a low roof, and its narrow windows are glazed with frosted glass. It has dark spruce trees instead of elms, crows instead of blackbirds, and a gloomy minister with a shovel hat who lectures on philosophy on week-days at the university. He loves to think that his congregation are made of the lowly and the meek in spirit, and to reflect that, lowly and meek as they are, there are men among them that could buy out half the congregation of St. Asaph's.

St. Osoph's is only presbyterian in a special sense. It is, in fact, too presbyterian to be any longer connected with any other body whatsoever. It seceded some forty years ago from the original body to which it belonged, and later on, with three other churches, it seceded from the group of seceding congregations. Still later it fell into a difference with the three other churches on the question of eternal punishment, the word "eternal" not appearing to the elders of St. Osoph's to designate a sufficiently long period. The dispute ended in a secession which left the church of St. Osoph practically isolated in a world of sin whose approaching fate is neither denied nor deplored.

In one respect the rival churches of Plutoria Avenue had had a similar history. Each of them had moved up by successive stages from the lower and poorer parts of the city. Forty years ago St. Asaph's had been nothing more than a little frame church with a tin spire, away in the west of the slums, and St. Osoph's a square, diminutive building away in the east. But the site of St. Asaph's had been bought by a brewing company, and the trustees, shrewd men of business, themselves rising into wealth, had rebuilt it right in the track of the advancing tide of a real estate boom. The elders of St. Osoph, quiet men, but illumined by an inner light, had followed suit and moved their church right against the side of an expanding distillery. Thus both the churches, as decade followed decade, made their way up the slope of the City till St. Asaph's was presently gloriously expropriated by the street railway company, and planted its spire in triumph on Plutoria Avenue itself. But St. Osoph's followed. With each change of site it moved nearer and nearer to St. Asaph's. Its elders were shrewd men. With each move of their church they took careful thought in the rebuilding. In the manufacturing district it was built with sixteen windows on each side and was converted at a huge profit into a bicycle factory. On the residential street it was made long and deep and was sold to a moving picture company without the alteration of so much as a pew. As a last step a syndicate, formed among the members of the congregation themselves, bought ground on Plutoria Avenue, and sublet it to themselves as a site for the church, at a nominal interest of five per cent. per annum, payable nominally every three months and secured by a nominal mortgage.

As the two churches moved, their congregations, or at least all that was best of them—such members as were sharing in the rising fortunes of the City—moved also, and now for some six or seven years the two churches and the two congregations had confronted one another among the elm trees of the Avenue opposite to the university.

But at this point the fortunes of the churches had diverged. St. Asaph's was a brilliant success; St. Osoph's was a failure. Even its own trustees couldn't deny it. At a time when St. Asaph's was not only paying its interest but showing a handsome surplus on everything it undertook, the church of St. Osoph was moving steadily backwards.

There was no doubt, of course, as to the cause. Everybody knew it. It was simply a question of men, and, as everybody said, one had only to compare the two men conducting the churches to see why one succeeded and the other failed.

The Reverend Edward Fareforth Furlong of St. Asaph's was a man who threw his whole energy into his parish work. The subtleties of theological controversy he left to minds less active than his own. His creed was one of works rather than of words, and whatever he was doing he did it with his whole heart. Whether he was lunching at the Mausoleum Club with one of his church-wardens, or playing the flute—which he played as only the episcopal clergy can play it—accompanied on the harp by one of the fairest of the ladies of his choir, or whether he was dancing the new episcopal tango with the younger daughters of the elder parishioners, he threw himself into it with all his might. He could drink tea more gracefully and play tennis better than any clergyman on this side of the Atlantic. He could stand beside the white stone font of St. Asaph's in his long white surplice holding a white-robed infant, worth half a million dollars, looking as beautifully innocent as the child itself, and drawing from every matron of the congregation with unmarried daughters the despairing cry, "What a pity that he has no children of his own!"

Equally sound was his theology. No man was known to preach shorter sermons or to explain away the book of Genesis more agreeably than the rector of St. Asaph's; and if he found it necessary to refer to the Deity he did so under the name of Jehovah or Jah, or even Yaweh, in a manner calculated not to hurt the sensitiveness of any of the parishioners. People who would shudder at brutal talk of the older fashion about the wrath of God listened with well-bred interest to a sermon on the personal characteristics of Jah. In the same way Mr. Furlong always referred to the devil, not as Satan but as Sû or Swâ, which took all the sting out of him. Beelzebub he spoke of as Behel-Zawbab, which rendered him perfectly harmless. The Garden of Eden he spoke of as the Paradeisos, which explained it entirely; the flood as the Diluvium, which cleared it up completely; and Jonah he named, after the correct fashion, Jon Nah, which put the whole situation (his being swallowed by Baloo, or the Great Lizard) on a perfectly satisfactory footing. Hell itself was spoken of as She-ol, and it appeared that it was not a place of burning, but rather of what one might describe as moral torment. This settled She-ol once and for all: nobody minds moral torment. In short, there was nothing in the theological system of Mr. Furlong that need have occasioned in any of his congregation a moment's discomfort.

There could be no greater contrast with Mr. Fareforth Furlong than the minister of St. Osoph's, the Rev. Dr. McTeague, who was also honorary professor of philosophy at the university. The one was young, the other was old; the one could dance, the other could not; the one moved about at church picnics and lawn teas among a bevy of disciples in pink and blue sashes; the other moped around under the trees of the university campus, with blinking eyes that saw nothing and an abstracted mind that had spent fifty years in trying to reconcile Hegel with St. Paul, and was still busy with it. Mr. Furlong went forward with the times; Dr. McTeague slid quietly backwards with the centuries.

Dr. McTeague was a failure, and all his congregation knew it. "He is not up to date," they said. That was his crowning sin. "He don't go forward any," said the business members of the congregation. "That old man believes just exactly the same sort of stuff now that he did forty years ago. What's more, he *preaches* it. You can't run a church that way, can you?"

His trustees had done their best to meet the difficulty. They had offered Dr. McTeague a two-years' vacation to go and see the Holy Land. He refused; he said he could picture it. They reduced his salary by fifty per cent.; he never noticed it. They offered him an assistant; but he shook his head, saying that he didn't know where he could find a man to do just the work that he was doing. Meantime he moaned about among the trees concocting a mixture of St. Paul with Hegel, three parts to one, for his Sunday sermon, and one part to three for his Monday lecture.

No doubt it was his dual function that was to blame for his failure. And this, perhaps, was the fault of Dr. Boomer, the president of the university. Dr. Boomer, like all university presidents of today, belonged to the presbyterian church; or rather, to state it more correctly, he included presbyterianism within himself. He was, of course, a member of the board of management of St. Osoph's, and it was he who had urged, very strongly, the appointment of Dr. McTeague, then senior professor of philosophy, as minister.

"A saintly man," he said, "the very man for the post. If you should ask me whether he is entirely at home as a professor of philosophy on our staff at the university, I should be compelled to say no. We are forced to admit that as a lecturer he does not meet our views. He appears to find it difficult to keep religion out of his teaching. In fact, his lectures are suffused with a rather dangerous attempt at moral teaching which is apt to contaminate our students. But in the Church I should imagine that would be, if anything, an advantage. Indeed, if you were to come to me and say, 'Boomer, we wish to appoint Dr. McTeague as our minister,' I should say, quite frankly, 'Take him.'"

So Dr. McTeague had been appointed. Then, to the surprise of everybody, he refused to give up his lectures in philosophy. He said he felt a call to give them. The salary, he said, was of no consequence. He wrote to Mr. Furlong senior (the father of the episcopal rector, and honorary treasurer of the Plutoria University), and stated that he proposed to give his lectures for nothing. The trustees of the college protested; they urged that the case might set a dangerous precedent which other professors might follow. While fully admitting that Dr. McTeague's lectures were well worth giving for nothing, they begged him to reconsider his offer. But he refused; and from that day on, in spite of all offers that he should retire on double his salary, that he should visit the Holy Land, or Syria, or Armenia, where the dreadful massacres of Christians were taking place, Dr. McTeague clung to his post with a tenacity worthy of the best traditions of Scotland. His only internal perplexity was that he didn't see how, when the time came for him to die, twenty or thirty years hence, they would ever be able to replace him. . . .

3. Essays and Belles-Lettres

ROBINA AND
KATHLEEN LIZARS

[?]-1918   [?]-1931

Collaborators in two lively and valuable works of local history, *In the Days of the Canada Company*, 1825-1850 and *Humours of '37*, Robina and Kathleen Lizars were born in Stratford and spent most of their lives there, though Kathleen was private secretary for a number of years to the Hon. John Robson, premier of British Columbia from 1889 to 1892.

In the Days of the Canada Company is a gossipy, informal history of the early days of the Huron Tract and is notable for its brilliant characterizations of John Galt, Dr. William (Tiger) Dunlop, and other early worthies. It was published in 1896 with an introduction by Principal G. M. Grant, of Queen's University. *Humours of '37*, which appeared the following year, attempted the more difficult task of recalling the incongruities, follies, and confusions of "Rebellious Times in the Canadas." In 1900 the sisters collaborated on a novel of ecclesiastical life in a small Ontario town, presumably Stratford, entitled *Committed to his Charge*. Robina died in Toronto in 1918 and Kathleen in 1931.

The delightful account of "Tiger" Dunlop is abridged from Chapter VIII, "Gairbraid," of *In the Days of the Canada Company*. With it should be read the selections from Dr. Dunlop's *Recollections of the American War*, 1812-1814 in *The Book of Canadian Prose* I. Gairbraid was the name of the house established by Dr. Dunlop and his brother Robert ("the Captain") near Goderich, Ontario. The house was named after their mother's home in Dumbartonshire, Scotland.

FROM *In the Days of the Canada Company*, 1896

TIGER DUNLOP

Gairbraid was built of solid oak logs, the house in form somewhat like the letter H. It contained eight or nine roomy apartments, and like the Castle, on a larger scale, was a series of house, lean-to, porches and passages. The double door of the hall carried a door-plate in brass, "Mr. Dunlop," and the windows looked out upon a scene which even in Canada was not often equalled, and which was said to resemble English scenery more than any other spot in America— up the valley of the Minnesetung, through lovely glades where the red waters glinted against the green, across to the white-washed cottages of the new-made hamlet; and away to the right were the waters of Huron, bluer than the skies above them, white with breakers, sullen as smoke, or wild as the German Ocean itself.

At Gairbraid the two rooms most characteristic of the times and of the occupants were the dining-room and kitchen. In the former stood a large, round dining-table of solid mahogany, fitted to seat twelve persons; and ranged round the room were twelve most solid chairs to match, upholstered in Brussels carpet. In them the Dunlop brothers and their cronies were to gather by that second Table Round for wassail, merriment, and a new series of *Noctes Ambrosianæ* (*Canadensis*). The huge fireplace in the end of the room was flanked by large walnut presses, wherein a wealth of china, silver and glass, was stored, and beside them a napery chest which testified to Scotch thrift and the spinning wheel. In front of the fire was an apparatus, in appearance something like a fender-stool, where plates and hot meats were placed for warmth; for the Dunlopian sense of comfort was well developed. In the centre hollow of the sideboard stood a huge liquors-stand made of mahogany, brass bound, with large brass handles. It measured seventeen and one-half inches high by thirty-three in length and twenty-three in width. It was simply a monster "traveller" on wheels, built to hold twelve gallons of liquid, containing a dozen large bottles from a converted military chest, each carrying a new label and measuring a good sixteen inches by nine, with a half-pound stopper, in itself a handful. These were termed by the irreverent Doctor the "Twelve Apostles"; the brandy bottle was Paul, and Peter held the whiskey, and they went the rounds of the room in pilgrimages suitable to the disposition of the company. The flowing bowl flowed too freely in the days of private stills and whiskey at a York shilling to a shilling per bottle. When hot punch was too hot to be quaffed it was the fashion to cool it with cold whiskey.

On summer evenings the friends would gather at the low windows and look at the lovely view framed in by vines which grew luxuriantly in the new-turned earth, or in winter before a fiery cone of twenty sound maple logs which bade defiance to Canadian cold; or, drawn up by the round table, read the last arrived numbers of *Maga,* *Fraser's,* or *The Times* (all six or eight weeks on the way), which were like handshakes across the ocean from that Britain of blue coats and brass buttons which these emigrants had left behind them. . . .

Between 1833 and 1834 another figure comes upon the scene. This was Louisa McColl, a dairy-woman sent out from the Dumbarton-shire Gairbraid to manage the Canadian household. This she did, in ways that were not at first looked for. She was a shrewd, "pretty-looking" woman, very Highland in her speech; after events proved her to be clever above her class and kind. Her arrival excited a good deal of wonder in the small community.

"How did you come?" she was asked.

"Oh, indeed, shuist py poaste"; and the Doctor was so charmed with her check on idle curiosity that he repeated the question for the pleasure of each guest. Her cap was never straight, and she herself told how her fellows at home were always adjusting it as they passed her; her dress was that of the Highland byre-woman; she had "a most elegant bow"; and she danced the fling whenever bidden, first asking permission to remove her shoes.

Fate had it in store to make her a Laird's Lady. From the first she was devoted to "the deare gentlemen," and one, at least, kept her busy. The Tiger's use of snuff was so incessant and profuse that it was impossible for him to wear the lace ruffle and elaborate toilet which dress then demanded. He still kept to his grey check home-spun, Scotch bonnet and plaid; but for better wear he had suits of snuff-coloured broadcloth. Even these she failed to keep as she wished, for the traces of rappee were always visible. He was once stopped at the Customs, the officer demanding the reason for such an importation of best Irish. He would not believe it could be for private consumption until Dunlop threw a handful in the air and, catching it as best he could on his face, snuffed it up.

"There, that's what I want it for; *that's* the way I use it."

He was terribly careless in many ways, and the light of later days revealed that he was robbed right and left. When travelling he would order a glass of brandy, tender a crown or a pound-note in payment and forget the change. When he changed his clothes away from home he left the old ones on the floor, and marched away in the fresh ones. In money matters the Captain was not so careless; but he was simple as a child, and in his turn was imposed upon. The Doctor's smile and laugh were ever ready; his temper was fierce when roused, but for ordinary wear and tear was one of imperturbable good humour. His impulse was to defend the weak and defy the strong; but he dearly loved a practical joke. The Captain was, for the latter, often a convenient butt.

Small as the community was, simple as were the ways of that primitive society, Mrs. Grundy had arrived, and it was demanded that the Highland lassie should be let go. The Doctor gravely told his brother that there was but one way out of the difficulty, viz., for one of them to marry her; he was willing to decide which of them it should be, by three tosses of a penny—he to provide the coin. Three tosses were solemnly given with a double-headed penny, and the unsuspecting Captain became a candidate for matrimony. Why the Doctor, who "had been proclaimed a J.P. in every county in the province," did not perform the ceremony, history does not tell. In his stead they employed the services of Thompson, the black butler, white-jacketed instead of surpliced. The brothers were no church-goers, for, as the Doctor said, "he did not believe in one having all the chat, nor yet in singing without grog." But besides Mr. McKenzie's services they often had family prayers, conducted by the Captain; and the "Book of Common Prayer," which both much admired, was used. Once, when the lesson for the day was on the story of the Prodigal Son, the Captain, as he came to "filling with husks," in parenthesis mused aloud, "Why didn't the fool kill one of the swine and eat *him*!"

On the Sunday after the tossing of the penny, when prayers were finished, Black Jimmy was solemnly and formally invited to read the marriage service for the first wedding in Colborne. This he did, and the two became man and wife after a peculiar fashion. The Captain was of a retiring disposition, and his brother of a particularly obliging one. The former had a cough, which served as an excuse for not going into society with his more convivial brother. The bride now wished to go to church, and be seen and recognized as a wife. The first intimation which outside friends had of her change of state was owing to a visitor, who had been in the habit of making too free use of Gairbraid, ordering something from her. She was on her knees, scrubbing, and gave him no attention. The man repeated his order, and after a little further unpleasantness, swore at her. She told him not to do that again. He told her to remember that she was Dunlop's servant. She ordered him out of the house forthwith, saying he would soon know what she really was.

By this time a log school-house served for Sunday purposes. The bridegroom could not be persuaded to appear there; so, not to disappoint "dear Lou," the Doctor took her instead. Off they set, she holding up her dove-grey bridal skirt, her hand resting on the kind, brotherly arm; he, in the unaccustomed rigour of corduroy trousers, brass-buttoned blue coat and ruffled shirt; and, for once, the Scotch bonnet was replaced by a beaver of the fashion. In domestic life she maintained she could milk as well in satin gown as in her Highland byre-woman's dress. She tucked up the tail of the former when, with milking-stool and pail, she went to the spacious stable and barn-yard—the barn which cost £300—to do her humble work. But her maids were not easily managed. The Doctor, when nothing more exciting offered, would read for hours together, or, seated before his wooden, home-made desk, with its tray of blotting-sand and vessel of shot for pens, would put down the results of the day or bring into publishing form those articles which he still contributed to *Blackwood's* and *Fraser's*. His serenity was one day disturbed by voices, the bride's broken tongue waxing ever higher and shriller. He stood in the kitchen doorway and viewed the Laird's Lady, all glorious without but disturbed within, as she bestowed plentiful reproaches, in which Gaelic and English strove for the mastery, upon her maids, the quasi-clerical butler and the jottery-man, Malcolm.

"Lou! Lou! What is all this row about—now what's this sound o' flycht?"

"Hech! They will not pay sufficient respect to my reverence."

But she was a dauntless woman, of much ready resource and native wit. She could "keep house" with any lady, she did the honours of the brothers' table creditably, and she made up for her deficiency in learning by keeping an open Bible on her knee when, on Sabbath afternoons, she took her arm-chair in the crimson-curtained, fire-lit parlour. These crimson curtains were over long, trailing some half yard on the floor; the carpet seats of the twelve dining chairs were shabbied; so she took the superfluous length and covered them anew. What matter if the book were upside down, she looked the Laird's Lady, in silken gown and gauze-trimmed cap; and surrounded by the handsome appointments of her home, in time she obtained due "respect for her reverence." One of her maids had red hair, and the Doctor called her Red-top. Mrs. Dunlop, although an indulgent mistress in some ways, was strict in others, and she always charged breakages.

The desk spoken of was one which the Doctor had had made for himself by one of his workmen while on an exploring expedition in 1831, and he writes to Mr. Longworth, asking for hinges and lock to complete it, and for a "further supply of foolscap and post" with which to stock it.

Mrs. Dunlop's sense made her doubt the binding nature of the knot tied by Black Jimmy. The Captain now became Member of Parliament, and when he was absent from home her uneasy doubts grew apace.

The election of 1835, the first in the District, had been won with much difficulty, albeit there were but some sixty voters in the whole Huron Tract. These made up in fervour what was lacked in numbers. The hustings—on the spot where the pump opposite West Street now stands—were burnt; but Mr. Hyndman, Returning Officer, vowed that up they should go until allowed to remain. Nevertheless, the election took place at Feltie Fisher's inn. Colonel Van Egmond, who was the Captain's opponent, had enthusiastic followers who would not allow him to be drawn by horses, but filled that office proudly themselves. The votes were given—thirty-five for the Captain, twenty-five for the Colonel; axe-handles flourished, and there were more heads left broken than whole. The victor was put into a conveyance fitted in appearance for the road it was to travel; a Highlander with his bagpipes got in beside him, and the procession of the victorious thirty-five began—some with bandaged heads, others with a tooth or two less than they had owned the day before. The points of arrest were all the inns in the countryside; the bagpipes shrilled, the whiskey flowed; the Black Hawks, the Tipperary boys and the Far Downs, with axe-handles not as white as might be, dived into the woods again; and Lou, upon the steps of Gairbraid, welcomed home the first Member for Huron. . . .

The Doctor's two-headed coin has found its way, with his eccentric Will, wherever history has mentioned his name. Drinking stories, too, of all degrees, meet one at every point, but in no case do they show up the man apart from his intellectual side. Companionable he always was. Fergusson, dating from Niagara, says: "This has been a day of infinite enjoyment, and the close of it not a little enlivened by Dr. D——, who arrived to dinner, with a budget full of anecdote and fun. He found the canal rather tedious, and ordered his schooner to rendezvous at Buffalo." Next day, after a long talk and hot walk, "thirst, too, had its triumph, and I scarce recollect of anything more welcome than a beverage with which my companion regaled me at Forsyth's, under some odd name, but which consisted of a bottle of good brown stout turned into a quart of iced water, with a *quant. suff.* of ginger, cinnamon and sugar; truly it was a prescription worthy of being filed."

Mrs. Dunlop had her own version of matters, and it is but fair to give it. The Doctor's story was often told in her presence, for one of the delights of his life was to tease her. She always seemed offended, but seldom contradicted him. She used to tell that she was about to be married to someone else, and the "deare Captain" said: "Lou, if you leave us, we may as well shut up shop." To secure her he had to marry her, and he proposed while she was milking "Bloassom." She was much disturbed, as indeed she might be, if the rights of the other man were well established. She left Blossom and the Captain and retired to her bedroom, opened her Bible, and read: "In the mouth of two or three witnesses shall every word be established." She never explained the formula of her exegesis, but "felt divinely called upon to accept the deare Captain." She was not fond of allusion to the first marriage. At the second ceremony she "found herself so faint, and the service so long, that the deare Captain juiste supported her py pooting his arm round her wayisst."

But ere this took place before Rector Campbell, the Captain had gone to Toronto on his Parliamentary duties. Lou became very anxious. After sleepless nights, and Anglo-Gaelic wars of words with maids who now paid still less respect to her reverence, she bade John Morris harness Mungo and his mate, put hot bricks in the sleigh, and prepare to accompany her on her hundred and fifty mile drive. The winter of 1835 was unusually white. The whole Canadian earth seemed to slumber in a ghostly repose as they left Gairbraid one early morning in January. The irreverent maids saw well to their mistress's comforts; the hot bricks were supplemented with other things necessary, and away they flew, the hissing of the sleigh along the dazzling path and the jingling of Mungo's bells the only sounds. They were plentifully provisioned; and for as long as Mungo and his mate were able, they kept on that woful relic of energetic road-making British power. Mungo was bought in Toronto and brought from there when Charlie Abbott, late coachman to some English gentleman, fell in with the Dunlops and took service with them.

To bait the animals, to eat, to sleep, they stopped when necessary; but the anxious wife kept on, till those mythical "blue hills of old Toronto," sung by Moore when he took geographical as well as poetic license, were reached. At the door of the hotel the heart of the Member's wife failed. She remained in the sleigh, and bade John Morris go find the Captain.

"What the d——l are you doing here?" was a pardonable question from the Captain when found.

"Mrs. Dunlop is here, Captain."

"Then come and have a drink."

Explanations followed, John Morris was sent to his lodgings, and the happy wife remained with her equally (let us hope) happy husband.

During Mr. Morris's stay in Toronto, the Captain saw that he was often present at the Parliamentary debates, and his opinion was that the Captain himself and Allan MacNab were the two most gentlemanly men in the House.

On their return, the real marriage took place. . . .

Mrs. Dunlop's relation towards these two men was extraordinary —the wife of one, but the good friend and close companion of the other, by whom, undoubtedly, she was better understood than by her husband. The Doctor had regard and respect for, and not a little awe of her; while she again was much attached to him, and was officiously attentive. She was so careful of his toilet that he feared to let her know when he wished to cross the river to visit his Goderich friends. When she saw him from a distance she would run after him with his shoes in her hand, imploring him to stop, for in order to deceive her he would saunter off in his slippers. He one day ran into a Goderich house, and laughingly told his friends how he had evaded Lou by walking leisurely down his own hill until far enough on his way, when he "put" across the Flats. Expostulated with for not going to church, he solemnly answered that they didn't "know the difficulties I have to contend with. If I propose to go in the morning, Lou requires me to put on a clean shirt. This I might not object to, but on returning from church she requires me to take it off again; and to this I *do* object." She brewed the whiskey, he the beer, and as soon as both fluids were barely matured, they disappeared in a surprisingly short space of time. Gairbraid was not singular. In Britain every house, gentle or simple, farm or manor, made its own beer as it did its preserves or lavender water, although the last were not so variable in results. The outcome of the brew was a thing of anxiety and the event of the week. Although Lou kept a sharp eye on him and the fruit of her labours, he would evade her, go to town, and bring back a following of friends as thirsty as himself. "Lou, bring out the Twelve Apostles." The heavy mahogany case rumbled to the table, and Lou saw Peter broached, emptied and re-filled, and knew the precious outcome of her still was going, and would go to "fill these greedy hounds from town."

"And am I to have a late dinner for them, too," she would ask, when evening drew near and the last drop was gone.

"No, Lou, no; take the broom to them, take the broom to them."

Nevertheless, the dinners, and good ones too, were ready, with a display of snowy linen, bright glass and silver, that was balm to her spirit.

One afternoon the Table Round groaned under the weight of eatables, for there was to be a dinner party of twelve. There was venison and wild duck, pigeon pasty, and ham and poultry of her own curing and raising; and by the time the last compliment was paid to the only lady present, the "Honourable and Reverend and Very Drunken" Cassels Stuart, "the Old Gent," Daw Don, or the Baron de Tuyle, might do as they would. The house stood near the edge of the bank, and benches were fixed beneath the trees upon the sloping green. Here they gathered, twelve knights in a new world, and with what wits were left them sat and discussed their lands, their "crops," the last bundle of literature which had come over sea and corduroy to cheer them, the probability of a mail bag during the coming week, the politics of the day in both countries, the last impudence of the Family Compact, the advent of a new Governor, the mistakes of the old one, the grievances which heralded the coming rebellion; and when talk became too sombre, the Doctor showed them the tricks of his pet fawn and the accomplishments of his gander. The river babbled and flowed at their feet, through the middle of the Flats; on it were Lou's geese, with their white leader, a bird of the size of a swan, and with a voice of surpassing power. David Don was one of the knights, as true a gentleman as ever made the mistake of trying to be a Canadian farmer.

"*Daw*-Don, *Daw*-Don," cried the Doctor; and the gander gravely waddled towards him as it screamed and flapped its wings in reply. Daw Don laughed with the rest, but never grew quite accustomed to the joke. Sunset, with its glories, recalled them to order; and in silence they watched a sight, the fame of which had brought many travellers to the Huron banks. Mountains and castles of molten colour in a great arc of fading light were banded with royal purple; pink backgrounds faded to silver, which changed again to violet behind a floating moon. The lake had become to these men as the face of a friend; they loved its every change, as if it were a thing alive; its glories could awe, its beauties could silence; and they were content to sit and watch, to think on the past, to dream of the future, till the stars and the fireflies came out together, and lights from the windows twinkled a recall.

And then these sweet influences of nature, memory and hope, waned; the Round Table and the Twelve Apostles saw a night of revelry. All grew too merry; but "the Honourable, Reverend and Very Drunken Cassels Stuart" lapsed into unconsciousness. Then these eleven friends put him on the table, placed a saucer of salt upon his breast, covered his face with a sheet, set lighted candles at his head and feet, and so left him. The dimensions of Gairbraid at bedtime seemed to enlarge; capacious sofas turned into beds, hammocks swung and bunks yawned, till sleeping accommodation for the house party was found. Then came the awakening of the corpse, who thought himself in another world and was nearly frightened into a sudden going there.

Justice makes one remember that a case of total abstinence was a phenomenon in any country then, and that these men had been frequenters of the old British taverns, places not unlike Lou's own kitchen, where the floor was sanded and the kettle never off the boil, a department which replaced the waste of ichor with food and liquor; places where they not only ate and drank, but sang, making emphasis with fist-whacks which made the steel-pronged forks and pint glasses ring again. The chorus was always of the "whack fol-de-rol-de-rol-de-dido" kind.

The Round Table was a piece of beautiful wood and it took a high polish. These gentlemen put their hot glasses on it, with the usual result of white discs overlapping on the bright surface. Lou got a large piece of oilcloth, extending some inches beyond the edge, put in a running string, drew it tight, and so saved much polishing and some disfigurement.

Lou, with her high-strung, excitable temperament, her Highland dances, her "elegant bow" and her tailed gown, was never happier than when entertaining guests. If a dinner party formed part of her day she always met her guests at the door, both hands outstretched, an expansive welcome of word and gesture. The gentlemen were at once "offered something," and the same was taken to the ladies in their dressing-room. At parting there was doch-an'-darrach; and she came out, glass and decanter in hand, after her friends were seated in their waggons, and herself dispensed the drops to speed the parting guest. . . .

Like all of her country, she was superstitious and suspicious, and her brother-in-law never tired of exhibiting the former trait. She had heard of the pranks played by witches in the Highland cow-byres, when they tied up the cows' tails with red tape. He managed to have her animals' tails so decorated, and one morning he escorted her and her maids, with their stools and milking pails, to the byre. The dismay and wonder was all he could have desired.

"Hech! but yon's awesome!"

" 'Tis the fell airts o' Brownies!"

"Haud yer nash-gab, an' let me oot!"

"Ech-wow!"

They were frightened nearly to death, and the Tiger's huge frame leant against the doorway, shaking himself and everything about him with the strength of his laughter.

When the butter would not come, "the deare Doctor would take a sixpence and put it between the leaves of the Bible, then lay it on the churn, and in a minute the butter would come. It never failed." If Blossom refused her milk down, he would make passes between her horns and "say something to mek it richt." "And they were deare, kind-hairted gentlemen both. Once I drowned a cat in the swill-barrel, and the deare Captain was so mad. I never saw him so mad in all my life."

What made him still angrier was her ceaseless activity. He would ask her to go for a walk with him about the farm, or down the Flats to hear Daw Don answer to his name, or in the ravine beside the house where a wealth of wild flowers grew. But she would tuck her silken tail under her arm and set fire to stumps, not listening to his botanical discourse nor impressed by the view before them. Her husband would walk off in dudgeon, leaving her to her practical choice.

The year 1840 saw the lean, lithe little Captain begin to fail—not from old age, for he was only in his fifty-first year. Till now he had been always busy, for, unlike his brother, who would read from morning till night when nothing more exciting came in the way, he was always full of schemes. Interest in these now failed him, and he "fairly shrivelled away." But his spirit was still high and his word sharp. Lou fretted to see the change in him, and tended him faithfully. This in turn fretted him, and it is recorded how once he suddenly sat up in bed and shouted, "Lou I don't pity you one bit, for you are well provided for; but I *do* pity my brother Will." But the history does not say whether this was a reflection upon Lou as a companion, or a foreshadow of his brother's loneliness.

It is certain that she was said to have stinted the brother Will in all ways that she could, with a success not in proportion to her efforts. On one occasion, when a house full of guests necessitated the use of the dining-room sofa for a bed, the occupant of it was disturbed by the Doctor at the sideboard. The friend pretended to be asleep, and made no response to the Doctor's question. But when the latter turned again and saw a pair of amused eyes looking at him, he brought the bottle over to the lounge, saying: "Quick, Ned, quick—take your horn and be quick, or Lou will catch us!" The horn disposed of, the Doctor's burly, night-gowned form stole softly from the room—"and Lou never found us out." The Doctor was very fond of his dog "Tag," but was afraid Lou's thrift made her starve him; at any rate, she would not allow him to be fed as he wished. So the Doctor would walk round the table, quietly casual, before the meats were removed, abstract morsels as chance turned Lou's back, and feed Tag unknown to her. Tag entered into the domestic spirit, and was as demure as his master.

One afternoon John Haldane, sr., and John Haldane, jr., walked over to Gairbraid to make a friendly call. They were kept waiting, an unusual thing, for welcomes in that house were from the doorstep ben. At length the Tiger came in, laughing.

"Mr. Haldane, I have just been writing my will. If you like I'll read it to you."

Out came the Twelve Apostles, the brass kettle, the tumblers and ladles, the cut lemon, and the doyleys, squares of sampler-stitch with fringed edges. The Dunlop recipe for hot whiskey toddy, better than any recorded by Mr. J. M. Barrie, was to put the spoon in the tumbler and fill up with boiling water; then, when the glass was thoroughly heated, pour out the water, fill with whiskey, and drink quickly.

Mrs. Dunlop was in the room as the Doctor wrote the first draft of the will; and as he progressed, he read aloud to her. She often expostulated, but with no effect until he came to allusions to herself, outrageous and not to be borne. She tried to get the paper into her hands, but failed; chased him about the Round Table, and so manifested her displeasure that he promised to expunge everything relating to her in any way objectionable. After the famous tossing for her with the penny, and enjoying as he did her many peculiarities and Highland characteristics, it is easy to imagine what pungent paragraphs he might have made. The will and the codicil show he kept his word.

One of the twelve arm-chairs supported the Tiger's burly frame, as he leaned back to read what has since become a curiosity of Surrogate literature.

"In the name of God. Amen.

"I, William Dunlop, of Gairbraid, in the Township of Colborne, County and District of Huron, Western Canada, Esquire, being in sound health of body, and my mind just as usual (which my friends who flatter me say is no great shakes at the best of times), do make this my last Will and Testament as follows, revoking, of course, all former Wills:

"I leave the property of Gairbraid, and all other landed property I may die possessed of, to my sisters Helen Boyle Story and Elizabeth Boyle Dunlop; the former because she is married to a minister whom (God help him) she henpecks. The latter because she is married to nobody, nor is she like to be, for she is an old maid, and not market-rife. And also, I leave to them and their heirs my share of the stock and implements on the farm; provided always, that the enclosure round my brother's grave be reserved, and if either should die without issue, then the other to inherit the whole.

"I leave to my sister-in-law, Louisa Dunlop, all my share of the household furniture and such traps, with the exceptions hereinafter mentioned.

"I leave my silver tankard to the eldest son of old John, as the representative of the family. I would have left it to old John himself, but he would melt it down to make temperance medals, and that would be sacrilege—however, I leave my big horn snuff-box to him: he can only make temperance horn spoons of that.

"I leave my sister Jenny my Bible, the property formerly of my great-great-grandmother, Bethia Hamilton, of Woodhall; and when she knows as much of the spirit of it as she does of the letter, she will be another guise Christian than she is.

"I also leave my late brother's watch to my brother Sandy, exhorting him at the same time to give up Whiggery, Radicalism, and all other sins that do most easily beset him.

"I leave my brother Alan my big silver snuff-box, as I am informed he is rather a decent Christian with a swag belly and a jolly face.

"I leave Parson Chevasse (Magg's husband), the snuff-box I got from the Sarnia Militia, as a small token of my gratitude for the service he has done the family in taking a sister that no man of taste would have taken.

"I leave John Caddle a silver teapot, to the end that he may drink tea therefrom to comfort him under the affliction of a slatternly wife.

"I leave my books to my brother Andrew, because he has been so long a Jungley Wallah [a bushman], that he may learn to read with them.

"I give my silver cup, with a sovereign in it, to my sister Janet Graham Dunlop, because she is an old maid and pious, and therefore will necessarily take to horning. And also my Granma's snuff mull, as it looks decent to see an old woman taking snuff.

"I do hereby constitute and appoint John Dunlop, Esquire, of Gairbraid; Alexander Dunlop, Esquire, Advocate, Edinburgh; Alan C. Dunlop, Esquire, and William Chalk, of Tuckersmith; William Stewart and William Gooding, Esquires, of Goderich, to be the executors of my last Will and Testament.

"In witness whereof I have hereunto set my hand and seal the thirty-first day of August, in the year of our Lord one thousand eight hundred and forty-two.

"W. Dunlop. [L.S.]"

"The above instrument of one sheet was, at the date thereof, declared to us by the Testator, William Dunlop Esquire, to be his last Will and Testament, and he then acknowledged to each of us that he had subscribed the same, and we at his request signed our names hereunto as attesting witnesses.

"JAMES CLOUTING,
"PATRICK McNAUGHTON, } [L.S.]"
"ELIZABETH STEWARD.

* * *

Gairbraid was the centre of hospitality, loyalty, and benevolence and diversion, the last, unhappily, often regulated by what was the crying evil of the time and country. A large flag pole stood in front of the house, made from two maple trees. Under that flag they loved so well, and for which they had fought so bravely, the brothers with their friends used to sit, drinking their hot brandy and water, with an eye to the Flats below or the road skirting the hill, ready with a welcome for every new comer. "Ho, ho, ho! I have plenty, I have plenty; come, come in," was the burden of the Dunlop song. No wonder that they were beloved and that their memory is still green in Colborne. As Lou's tombstone testifies, she too was a good and faithful friend. She idolized and "mothered" both these men, and but for her clever hands and head they would not have had the plenty they were so ready to part with. Even where it was most difficult to restrain them she managed well.

"Gie us a glass, old lady."

"Ye dinna want a glass this time o' day."

"Hoot, woman!" and aside to their guests—"the woman's daft!"

But she tended them faithfully living and closed their eyes in death, true to the last to her Deare Gentlemen.

DUNCAN CAMPBELL SCOTT
1862-1947

Duncan Campbell Scott, one of the leading poets of the so-called Confederation group associated with Archibald Lampman, Charles G. D. Roberts, and Bliss Carman, was a prose writer of distinction. He wrote two volumes of short stories, *In the Village of Viger* (1896), delicate and sensitive local color sketches of life in rural Quebec, and *The Witching of Elspie* (1923), ranging from a ghost story set in Trois Rivières to harsh tales of the northern fur trade; literary criticism, including his contributions (along with those of Lampman and Wilfred Campbell) to a series of familiar essays "At the Mermaid Inn" written for the Toronto *Globe* in 1892 and 1893; and more formal essays collected in *The Circle of Affection* (1947), the most notable of which are "The Last of the Indian Treaties" (1906) and the Presidential Address to the Royal Society of Canada on "Poetry and Progress" (1922); and biographical and historical writings including a life of John Graves Simcoe (1905) and, perhaps finest of all, a "Memoir" of Archibald Lampman published in 1900 in *The Poems of Archibald Lampman*.

THE LAST OF THE INDIAN TREATIES (1906)

The Indian policy of the Canadian Government was inherited from the British procedure in the American colonies, which still survives with additions and modifications. The reserve system appeared at the earliest, and there was but little difference between the policy of the French and British in Canada with the exception that in the French design evangelization was an important feature. So that in 1867, when the Dominion of Canada took over the administration of Indian Affairs, the Government found a certain well-established condition. The Indians of the old provinces of Nova Scotia and New Brunswick had been given lands; in Quebec the grants of the French king had been respected and confirmed; in Ontario the Indian titles had been surrendered by treaty for a consideration in land and money. The first of the treaties was made by Governor Haldimand in 1784.

In the early days the Indians were a real menace to the colonization of Canada. At that time there was a league between the Indians east and west of the River St. Clair, and a concerted movement upon the new settlements would have obliterated them as easily as a child wipes pictures from his slate. The Indian nature now seems like a fire that is waning, that is smouldering and dying away in ashes; then it was full of force and heat. It was ready to break out at any moment in savage dances, in wild and desperate orgies in which ancient superstitions were involved with European ideas but dimly understood and intensified by cunning imaginations inflamed with rum. So all the Indian diplomacy of that day was exercised to keep the tomahawk on the wall and the scalping knife in the belt. It was a rude diplomacy at best, the gross diplomacy of the rum bottle and the material appeal of gaudy presents, webs of scarlet cloth, silver medals, and armlets.

Yet there was at the heart of these puerile negotiations, this control that seemed to be founded on debauchery and licence, this alliance that was based on a childish system of presents, a principle that has been carried on without cessation and with increased vigilance to the present day—the principle of the sacredness of treaty promises. Whatever has been written down and signed by king and chief both will be bound by so long as "the sun shines and the water runs." The policy, where we can see its outcome, has not been ineffectual, and where in 1790 stood clustered the wigwams and rude shelters of Brant's people now stretch the opulent fields of the township of Tuscarora; and all down the valley of the Grand River there is no visible line of demarcation between the farms tilled by the ancient allies in foray and ambush who have become confederates throughout a peaceful year in seed-time and harvest.

The treaty policy so well established when the confederation of the provinces of British North America took place has since been continued and nearly all civilized Canada is covered with these Indian treaties and surrenders. A map colored to define their boundaries would show the province of Ontario clouted with them like a patchwork blanket; as far north as the confines of the new provinces of Saskatchewan and Alberta the patches lie edge to edge. Until lately, however, the map would have shown a large portion of the province of Ontario uncovered by the treaty blanket. Extending north of the watershed that divides the streams flowing into Lakes Huron and Superior from those flowing into Hudson Bay, it reached James Bay on the north and the long curled ribbon of the Albany River, and comprised an area of 90,000 square miles, nearly twice as large as the State of New York.

This territory contains much arable land, many million feet of pulpwood, untold wealth of minerals, and unharnessed water-powers sufficient to do the work of half the continent. Through the map of this unregarded region Sir Wilfrid Laurier, Premier of Canada, had drawn a long line, sweeping up from Quebec and curving down upon Winnipeg, marking the course of the eastern section of the new Transcontinental Railway. The aboriginal owners of this vast tract, aware of the activity of prospectors for timber and minerals, had asked the Dominion Government to treat for their ancient domain, and the plans for such a huge public work as the new railway made a cession of the territory imperative.

In June, 1905, the writer was appointed one of three commissioners to visit the Indian tribes and negotiate a treaty. Our route

lay inland from Dinorwic, a small station on the Canadian Pacific
Railway two hundred miles east of Winnipeg, to reach the Lac Seul
water system, to cross the height of land, to reach Lake St. Joseph,
the first great reservoir of the Albany River. Our flotilla consisted
of three canoes, two large Peterboroughs and one birch-bark thirty-
two feet long which could easily hold eleven or twelve men and
2,500 pounds of baggage and supplies, as well as the treasure-chest
which was heavy with thirty thousand dollars in small notes. Our
party included three commissioners, a physician, an officer of the
Hudson's Bay Company who managed all the details of transport
and commissariat, and two constables of the Dominion police force.
I am bound to say the latter outshone the members of the commission itself in the observance of the Indians. The glory of their
uniforms and the wholesome fear of the white man's law which
they inspired spread down the river in advance and reached James
Bay before the commission. I presume they were used as a bogey
by the Indian mothers for no children appeared anywhere until the
novelty had somewhat decreased and opinion weakened that the
magnificent proportions and manly vigor of our protectors were
nourished upon a diet of babies.

Our crew of half-breeds and Indians numbered not less than
twelve and sometimes seventeen, so that the strength of the party
never fell below nineteen and was often twenty-four.

New men were engaged at Albany and at Moose Factory and
experience was had of many different types. The Scriptures had
seemingly been searched to furnish names for our men and we
had in service at one time or another the prophets, the apostles, and
a goodly number of the saints, even to such minor worthies as
Caleb who went to spy out the land for the children of Israel! A
word or two of the chronicle must be given up to the chief members
of the crew—to David Sugarhead, who had only one lung and
worked as if he had four; to Oombash, the dandy of the party, a
knowing bowsman who wore a magenta and blue sweater and
always paddled in a pair of black woollen gloves; to Simon Small-
boy, a hard man to traffic with, but a past master of poling; of
Daniel Wascowin, who cooked for the crew, and who was a merry
man; and lastly, of Jimmy Swain, the old Albany River guide,
sixty-seven years old, who ran to and fro over the longest portage
carrying the heaviest pack.

He is a fine type of the old half-breed race of packers and voyageurs which is fast disappearing; loyal and disinterested, cautious but fearless, full of that joy of life which consists in doing and possessed by that other joy of life which dwells in retrospect, in the telling of old tales, the playing of old tunes, and the footing of old dance steps. Jimmy was enjoying a mighty old age after a mighty youth. He had been able to carry 600 pounds over a portage nearly a quarter of a mile long. He had run on snow-shoes with the mail from Moose Factory to Michipicoten, a distance of 500 miles, in six days, carrying only one blanket, a little hardtack, and a handful of tea. Now in his sixty-seventh year he was the equal of the best of the young fellows. He took all the portages at a tremendous speed and barefooted, for there was a thick layer of callous flesh on the soles of his feet. He was conscious of his virtues, for in reply to the question, "Well, Jimmy, is there anything left at the other end of the portage?" he would always say, "I was there last myself, surr." That was conclusive. Moreover, Jimmy was an artist. How he could play the violin at all with his huge callous fingers was a matter for wonder, but play he did, all the jigs popular on the Albany for the last fifty years, curious versions of hymn-tunes, "Abide with Me" and "Lead, Kindly Light," a pathetic variation of "Home, Sweet Home," the name of which tune he did not know, but called it after a day or two "The tune the bosses like; it makes them feel bad!" Every night after supper Jimmy withdrew into his tent, closed the flap, and took out his violin. The instrument was as curious as the art employed to play it. "Oh, it's a fine fiddle!" Jimmy would say. "It's an *expensive* fiddle. Dr. Scovil gave it to me, and it must have cost ten dollars." He had scraped the belly and rubbed it with castor oil, and the G-string had two knots in it. But what matter! When Jimmy closed the flap of his tent and drew it forth out of its blue pine box, I doubt whether any artist in the world had ever enjoyed a sweeter pang of affection and desire.

We touched water first at Big Sandy Lake and in three days had reached Frenchman's Head (Ishquahka portage), one of the reserves set apart by an earlier treaty. James Bunting, the chief of the band, when he learned our business sent twelve of his stalwart Indians to help us over the long and difficult portage; as it was the occasion of a lifetime they brought their wives, children, and dogs and made a social event of it. But they doubled our working force and saved us a half-day on the portage. Once again we were to meet with such kindness, at New Post on the Abitibi River, when Chief Esau and five of his men, adherents of the new treaty, gave us an offering of their help for two days. "We do not expect any money, and no food for this. We will feed ourselves. You have brought us much; we have little to give, but that we freely give."

After Osnaburgh, Fort Hope was to come, then Marten's Falls, then English River, then Fort Albany and the salt water, then Moose Factory and New Post. But Osnaburgh had all the importance of a beginning.

It was about two o'clock one afternoon that we sighted Osnaburgh, a group of Hudson's Bay buildings clustered on the lake shore, and upon higher ground the little wooden church of the Anglican mission. Everyone expected the usual welcome, for the advent of a paymaster is always announced by a fusillade, yells, and the barking of dogs. But even the dogs of Osnaburgh gave no sound. The Indians stood in line outside the palisades, the old blind chief, Missabay, with his son and a few of the chief men in the centre, the young fellows on the outskirts, and women by themselves, separated as they are always. A solemn hand-shaking ensued; never once did the stoicism of the race betray any interest in the preparations as we pitched our tents and displayed a camp equipage, simple enough, but to them the matter of the highest novelty; and all our negotiations were conducted under like conditions—intense alertness and curiosity with no outward manifestation of the slightest interest. Everything that was said and done, our personal appearance, our dress and manners, were being written down as if in a book; matter which would be rehearsed at many a campfire for generations until the making of the treaty had gathered a lore of its own; but no one could have divined it from visible signs.

Nothing else is so characteristic of the Indian, because this mental constitution is rooted in physical conditions. A rude patience has been developed through long ages of his contact with nature which respects him no more than it does the beaver. He enriches the fur-traders and incidentally gains a bare sustenance by his cunning and a few gins and pitfalls for wild animals. When all the arguments against this view are exhausted it is still evident that he is but a slave, used by all traders alike as a tool to provide wealth, and therefore to be kept in good condition as cheaply as possible.

To individuals whose transactions had been heretofore limited to computation with sticks and skins our errand must indeed have been dark.

They were to make certain promises and we were to make certain promises, but our purpose and our reasons were alike unknowable. What could they grasp of the pronouncement on the Indian tenure which had been delivered by the law lords of the Crown, what of the elaborate negotiations between a dominion and a province which had made the treaty possible, what of the sense of traditional policy which brooded over the whole? Nothing. So there was no basis for argument. The simpler facts had to be stated, and the parental idea developed that the King is the great father of the Indians, watchful over their interests, and ever compassionate. After gifts of tobacco, as we were seated in a circle in a big room of the Hudson's Bay Company's House, the interpreter delivered this message to Missabay and the other chiefs, who listened unmoved to the recital of what the Government would give them for their lands.

Eight dollars to be paid at once to every man, woman and child; and forever afterward, each, "so long as the grass grows and the water runs" four dollars each; and reserves of one square mile to every family of five or in like proportion; and schools for their children; and a flag for the chief.

"Well for all this," replied Missabay, "we will have to give up our hunting and live on the land you give us, and how can we live without hunting?" So they were assured that they were not expected to give up their hunting-grounds, that they might hunt and fish throughout all the country, but that they were to be good subjects of the King, their great father, whose messengers we were. That was satisfying, and we always found that the idea of a reserve became pleasant to them when they learned that so far as that piece of land was concerned they were the masters of the white man, could say to him, "You have no right here; take your traps, pull down your shanty and begone."

At Fort Hope, Chief Moonias was perplexed by the fact that he seemed to be getting something for nothing; he had his suspicions maybe that there was something concealed in a bargain where all the benefit seemed to be on one side. "Ever since I was a little boy," he said, "I have had to pay well for everything, even if it was only a few pins or a bit of braid, and now you come with money and I have to give nothing in exchange." He was mightily pleased when he understood that he was giving something that his great father the King would value highly.

Missabay asked for time to consider, and in their tents there was great deliberation all night, but in the morning the chiefs appeared, headed by Missabay, led by Thomas, his son, who attended the blind old man with the greatest care and solicitude. Their decision was favorable. "Yes," said Missabay, "we know now that you are good men sent by our great father the King to bring us help and strength in our weakness. All that we have comes from the white man and we are willing to join with you and make promises which will last as long as the air is above the water, as long as our children remain who come after us."

After the payment, which followed the signing of the treaty, the Hudson's Bay store was filled with an eager crowd of traders. The majority of the Indians had touched paper money for the first time; all their trading had been done heretofore with small sticks of different lengths. They had been paid in Dominion notes of the value of one dollar and two dollars, and several times the paymasters had received deputations of honest Indians who thought they had received more in eight "ones" than some of their fellows had in four "twos." But they showed shrewdness in calculation when they understood the difference, and soon the camp was brightened by new white shawls, new hats and boots, which latter they wore as if doing a great penance.

Meantime, the physician who accompanied the party, had visited the tents. He found the conditions that exist everywhere among Indians—the effects of unsanitary habits and surroundings, which are to some extent neutralized by constant changes of camping-ground, by fresh air and pure water; the prevalance of tuberculosis in all forms; and a percentage of cases which at one time might have been relieved by surgical treatment, but which had long passed that stage.

It had become known that a mysterious operation called vaccination was to be performed upon the women and children, but not upon the men, whose usefulness as workers might be impaired by sore arms. Indians are peculiarly fond of medicine, and at least as open to the pleasure of making experiments with drugs as their white neighbours, but operations they dread; and what was this mysterious vaccination? Jenner and his followers had time to carry on a propaganda, but here at Osnaburgh our physician had to conquer superstitious fears and prejudice in a few short hours. I have known a whole tribe take to the woods upon the mere suggestion of vaccination. But this very superstition, aided by the desire to be in the fashion, gained the day. The statement that something rubbed into a little scratch on the arm would have such powerful results savored of magic and "big medicine," but the question was solved by one of the society leaders, Madame Mooniahwinini! She was one of three sisters, all wives of Mooniahwinini, and she appeared with those of his thirteen children for whom she was partly responsible. That settled the matter and children were pulled from their hiding-places and dragged to the place of sacrifice, some howling with fear, others giggling with nervousness. Never in the history of the region had there been such an attempt at personal cleanliness as at Osnaburgh that day, and at the other posts, upon like occasions. To be sure the cleansing extended to only three or four square inches of arm surface, but it was revolutionary in its tendencies.

As soon as the treaty had been signed a feast had been promised by the commissioners and the supplies had been issued by the Hudson's Bay Company. They consisted of the staples, pork and flour, tea and tobacco; with the luxuries, raisins, sugar, baking-powder, and lard. The best cooks in the camp had been engaged for hours upon the preparation of these materials. Bannocks had been kneaded and baked, one kind plain, another shortened with lard and mixed with raisins; the pork, heavy with fat, had been cut into chunks and boiled; the tea had been drawn (or overdrawn) in great tin kettles.

There is a rigid etiquette at these feasts; the food is piled in the centre of the surrounding Indians, the men in the inner circle, the women and children in the outer. When everyone is assembled the food is divided as fairly as possible and until each person is served no one takes a mouthful, the tea grows cold, the hot pork rigid and half the merit of the warm food vanishes, but no one breaks the rule. They still wait patiently until the chiefs address them. At Osnaburgh while Missabay walked to and fro striking his long staff on the ground and haranguing them in short reiterant sentences—the same idea expressed over and over, the power and goodness of the white man, the weakness of the Indian, the kindness of the King, their great father—there they sat and stoically watched the food turn clammy! With us the cloth is cleared and the speeches follow; with the Albany River Indians every formality precedes the true purpose of the feast, the eating of it.

The proceedings at Osnaburgh were repeated at the river posts, but when we reached Fort Albany we seemed to be in a different world. The salutation on the upper river is "Bow jou" the "Bon jour" of the Early French voyageur; on the coast it is "Wat che," the "What cheer" of the English.

Marten's Falls was the last post at which we heard Ojibway spoken; at Fort Albany we met the Crees. In our journey we had been borne by the waters of the Albany through a country where essential solitude abides. Occasionally the sound of a conjurer's drum far away pervaded the day like an aerial pulse; sometimes we heard the clash of iron-shod poles against the stones where a crew was struggling up-stream with a York boat laden with supplies. For days we would travel without seeing a living thing, then a mile away a huge black bear would swim the river, slip into the underbrush through a glowing patch of fire-weed, then a lemming would spring across the portage path into the thick growth of Labrador tea; no birds were to be seen, but a white-throat sparrow seemed to have been stationed at intervals of a hundred miles or so to give us cheer with his bright voice. But at Marten's Falls the blithe sentinel disappeared.

When one has heard even a few of the stories of Indian cruelty and superstition which haunt the river, of the Crane Indians who tied a man and his wife together, back to back, and sent them over the falls because they were sorcerers, of the terrible wendigo of Marten's Falls, the lonely spirit of the stream becomes an obsession. It is ever present, but at night it grows in power. Something is heard and yet not heard; it rises, and dwells, and passes mysteriously, like a suspiration immense and mournful, like the sound of wings, dim and enormous, folded down with weariness.

Below Marten's Falls the Albany flows in one broad stream for three hundred and fifty miles through banks, in some places eighty feet high, unimpeded by rapids or falls rushing gloriously to the sea. One night the canoes were lashed together and floated on under the stars until daybreak. Above Marten's Falls the river is broken by great rapids and cataracts and interrupted by long lake stretches, such as Makikobatan and Miminiska. The shores are flat and the land seems merely an incident in a world of water. Wherever a tent is pitched it is amid flowers; wild roses are enclosed within your canvas house, all about are myriads of twin-flowers, dwarf cornel, and pyrola blossoms. At James Bay the casual effect of the land is yet more apparent. Can these be called shores that are but a few feet high? The bay is vast and shallow; ten miles away the fringes of red willow look like dusky sprays brushed in against the intense steel-gray of the skyline, and the canoe paddles will reach the sandy bottom! No language can convey the effect of loneliness and desolation which hangs over this far-stretching plain of water, treacherous with shifting sands and sudden passionate storms, unfurrowed by any keels but those of the few small boats of the fur-traders.

At the upper river posts the Indians had been stoical, even taciturn but at Fort Albany and Moose Factory the welcome was literally with prayer and songs of praise and sounds of thanksgiving. The Hudson's Bay Company's property at Fort Albany separates the buildings of the Roman Catholic mission from those of the Anglican mission. Moose Factory was until lately the seat of the Anglican Bishop of Moosonee, but that glory and part of the trading glory had departed; the bishop has gone to "the line," as the Canadian Pacific Railway is called, and the Hudson's Bay Company has removed its distributing warehouse to Charlton Island, fifty miles in the Bay.

The Indians are adherents of either one faith or the other. Casuists they are, too, and very brilliant at a theological argument; so the religious element was largely mingled with the business, and here they thanked God as well as the King. The feasts at Moose Factory and New Post seemed like primitive "tea-meetings."

An address written in Cree, in the syllabic character, was presented at Albany; and at Moose Factory the proceedings opened with prayer and were enlivened by hymn singing. The use of the syllabic character is common on the river. Here and there messages from one group of Indians to another were met with, written upon birch bark and fixed to a stick driven into the ground in some prominent position—announcements that the fishing was poor and that they had gone to Winisk; that if Cheena's boy was met with, tell him his father was building canoes two days' journey up the Chepy River.

This method of writing the Indian languages was invented by Rev. James Evans, a Methodist missionary about the middle of the last century. He was then living at Norway House, north of Lake Winnipeg, where he had come from Upper Canada. As the Crees of Norway House are hunting Indians he found it difficult to make any headway with the work of evangelization. It was almost impossible to teach them to read by the English alphabet, and during the greater part of the year they were on their hunting grounds, virtually inaccessible. So he invented the characters in which each sign represents a syllable modified by terminals and prefixes. He made his first type from the lead in which tea was packed, moulded in clay; his first press was a Hudson's Bay Company's fur press, his first paper fine sheets of birch bark. An intelligent Indian can readily learn to read by the aid of the syllabic character and the system is used by the missionaries of all sects to disseminate their teachings.

The effect of education and of contact with a few of the better elements of our civilization were noticeable at Albany and Moose Factory. There was a certain degree of cleanliness in the preparation of food, the Indians were better dressed, and although the fur trade is a sort of slavery, a greater self-reliance was apparent. The crew that took the Commission from Moose Factory to Abitibi were constant in their vespers and every evening recited a litany, sang a hymn and made a prayer. There was something primitive and touching in their devotion, and it marks an advance, but these Indians are capable of leaving a party of travellers suddenly, returning to Moose Factory in dudgeon if anything displeases them, and the leader of the prayers got very much the better of one of the party in an affair of peltries. But any forecast of Indian civilization which looks for final results in one generation or two is doomed to disappointment. Final results may be attained, say, in four centuries by the merging of the Indian race with the whites, and all these four things—treaties, teachers, missionaries and traders—with whatever benefits or injuries they bring in their train, aid in making an end.

The James Bay Treaty will always be associated in my mind with the figure of an Indian who came in from Attawapiskat to Albany just as we were ready to leave. The pay-lists and the cash had been securely packed for an early start next morning, when this wild fel-

TOM MacINNES
1867-1951

Thomas Robert Edward MacInnes was born in Dresden, Ontario. He was educated at the University of Toronto and Osgoode Hall. He went to the west coast and was called to the British Columbia bar in 1893. He was appointed secretary to the Bering Sea Commission in 1896, was a police and customs official at Skagway during the gold rush of 1897, and served as private secretary to his father, who was Lieutenant-Governor of B.C., 1898-1900. He had a distinguished career as a civil servant, particularly in connection with the problem of oriental immigration. From 1916 to 1927 he spent considerable time in China. The ultimate expropriation of his business interests at the hands of the revolutionary government led him to write bitterly against the Chinese immigrants in Vancouver. He had, however, become interested in the philosophy of Lao Tse and in 1927 he published a characteristically lively translation and commentary, *The Teachings of the Old Boy* (1927). *Chinook Days*, from which the essay printed below is taken, appeared in 1926. It is a very rare little paper-bound volume, pocket size and square, printed on cheap paper by the Sun Publishing Co., of Vancouver. The essays are filled with memories of old times in the Pacific northwest and have a curious personal charm that is found in some of MacInnes' poems also. A selection of these from the volume of *Complete Poems* (1923) can be found in *The Book of Canadian Poetry*.

CHINOOK JARGON

What is known as Pidgin English, that is Business English, derives mainly from ordinary English, with addition of a few Cantonese and Portuguese and Malay and Hindustani words, spoken in fashion easy for the Chinese ear; with a sloppy touch of comicality about its delivery and phrasing as a rule; but sometimes attaining a sharp, laconic content equal to Latin. Pidgin English can do on a caricature of Cantonese construction; and sufficient fluency for trade and travel purposes may be acquired in the use of it within a month; whereas command of any Chinese language proper usually costs a foreigner years of intensive study. Likewise, in almost as short a time, one may become proficient in the use of the Chinook jargon; while most of the Indian languages once spoken along this Coast and west of the Rockies, maybe east also for all I know, took long to master because of intricate inflections, and variations of verbs and pronouns according to the rank or relation of the speaker to those addressed; and other ridiculous complexities like in Latin which I am not learned enough to name. Pidgin English still serves at a pinch in China for any necessary business between Chinese from various Provinces and Districts of the Empire who otherwise would be unable to understand each other's speech as spoken; and it is useful also for the foreigners who trade out there. Even so the Chinook jargon once served along the Pacific Coast from Oregon to as far north as the Queen Charlotte Islands. It served for communication between various nations of Indians; differing in language and customs as widely as Spaniards differ from Swedes. It served the purpose also of the pioneer whites and the French and Scotch employees of the Hudson's Bay Company.

About 1870 an Anglican priest, the Rev. Canon Good, compiled a list of about four hundred words of the Chinook in common use. His little dictionary containing them, together with examples of their use, and a version of the Lord's Prayer in Chinook, although not the first of its kind, was the most popular while yet there was a demand for such a thing.

Canon Good had an old book which contained the first written list of Chinook words. It was called "The Captive of Nootka," and was printed at Middletown, Connecticut, in 1815. The author was an English sailor named John Jewett; and I understand his plain narrative was a favourite with Edgar Allan Poe. John Jewett hailed from Boston, England; and at that port he joined an American ship from Boston, United States, which was outfitting there in 1802 under command of Captain Salter. An old British tar by the name of William Thompson, formerly in the Royal Navy, joined along with Jewett. The *Boston* sailed around the Horn and up to Nootka to get a share of the fur trade. Arriving safely there all went well until March, 1803, when Captain Salter, just as his ship was about to sail, insulted the old Chief Makwinna, then well advanced in years, but prouder than ever in his memories of friendship with Captains Cook and Hanna and Meares and Martinez and Quadra and Vancouver. So as a result of the insult the Indians, under Makwinna's command, attacked and captured the *Boston*; killing all the crew except Jewett, because he was an armourer and likely to be of use to them; and also old Thompson, because Jewett pretended Thompson was his father, and said that if Thompson were killed it would cause him such grief he would be unable to make knives and spearheads properly from the ship's metal. It was after this affair with the *Boston* that all Americans became known in Chinook as Boston men; just as all British were known as King George men. During his three years' captivity Jewett wrote down a list of nearly three hundred Chinook words. He was finally rescued in July, 1806, by the original Sam Hill, Yankee captain of the brig Lydia of Boston; his fellow-captive, Thompson, having died shortly before that. Old Thompson had been made personal attendant on Chief Makwinna; and among other duties was required to wash and keep in order the Chief's blankets. On one occasion an insolent Indian from another village, seeing the blankets spread out on the grass to dry, deliberately walked across them to soil them and show his contempt for the white slave. Thompson, in a fury, warned him not to ever do such a thing again or he would kill him. The Indian laughed, and deliberately walked across one of the blankets again. Thompson had always been permitted by Makwinna to carry his cutlass; and the old tar was still handy with it. He sprang forward, expert boarder that he was, and with one blow of the cutlass he cut the Indian's head off clean. Then he rolled the head up in the blanket and took it to Makwinna, who was much pleased when he heard the circumstances explained; and Thompson was advanced in honour thereafter. When the Canon would be telling that, and he told the same story often, he would refer to a Biblical incident which he claimed to be somewhat similar, and justifiable; the time a handsome Jewess delivered the Lord's people by bringing to the Elders of Zion the head of their chief enemy rolled in a blanket. But that Jewess had first gotten her customer dead drunk with wine before she did the business of decapitation; and she must have made a bloody, slow mess of it. Anyway, to me as a child, the outrightness of the English sailor seemed far more commendable.

I conversed with the Canon at different periods over a stretch of twenty-five years. For long he was a character in Nanaimo, a town once noted for odd characters. In his day and in his way he helped to make things pleasant for all, irrespective of creed. He was never so evangelical as to be an affliction to the community. In the matter of Chinook he once informed me, with more or less precision, that about half of its vocabulary came out of the original Chinook, which was a highly inflected language; that about a quarter was derived from other Indian languages; that about a quarter more was made up of English and French disguised; and that half as much again was straight French and English. Seems to me there must have been in addition a few auxiliary fifths, and possibly even tenths, expressed by emphasis and ululation, spaced by comprehensive silences; with a few gestures thrown in for full measure.

But I have forgotten all but a little of my Chinook; and make no claim to be accurate now. The use of English words in the jargon naturally increased after the régime of the Hudson's Bay Company, with its Gaelic factors and French trappers, had ended; what time the King George men and the Boston men were busy founding their towns, and rounding the lands where the Indians lived; taking over all of the immemorial No Man's Land between the recognized reserves. Canon Good told me that the original Chinook Indians were a remarkable but unfortunate people, who for centuries had been the leading traders at Nootka, before the white men came; but after that, being up against the mouth of Columbia and under the administration of Washington, they were soon decimated. Yet they left a name for many things; including this jargon called Chinook.

It was at Nootka, where the tribes met to trade, that Chinook came to form. The Chinook of the Nootkas kept chiefly to the k consonant; although some have disguised the stark kukluxity of the fact by using hard c instead of k, and x instead of ecks, and qu instead of kw in the spelling of it. There was also a lot of yah and wah about Chinook; and it easily ran to l with the French; incorporating the article le or la with the approximate French sound of the word adopted; and sometimes even with an English word. For instance, lecallat was the Chinook word for carrot; and lapuss for cat; hyas puss-puss being a cougar. Compounds were also made of English and Indian; and indiscriminately either way. Thus chuck was Chinook for water; and salt-chuck for the sea. But again the English word water would be joined with a Chinook word, as in the Chinook tumwata, a cascade or water-fall, or the rapids of a river; tum being Chinook for tone or sound. In Chinook variation was by repetition of the same; by such device indicating increase of size or intensity or quality. Thus tum, which meant a sound, by doubling into tumtum served to indicate the identifying tone or keynote of a thing; hence the mind, the heart, the soul, as we would say. The Salish Indians in general seemed incapable of the clear r; slurring it, as one finds r mistreated in utterance by certain of the English; and also by Americans from the lower Southern States; and negroes, and denizens of the Bowery.

A standard spelling for Chinook could hardly be expected by those who compiled its various dictionaries; for one thing, because the Indian accent and the several accents of the French and English-speaking whites were so pronouncedly different. All of them naturally claimed to be right about words out of their own language; and they were not finicky about the others so long as they made their meaning clear.

I have spoken of the prevailing k tone; but that k was sounded for accommodation of our own tongue, and was not quite the sound given by the Indians. For instance: sokalie, meaning high, had a growling k in it when uttered by the Indians, more like what one hears from a sober Scot saying loch. Perhaps if the word were spelled saughalie to convey a throaty gh, it might be nearer to the Indian way. But why be precise about a dead jargon which served a good purpose once, but which is now almost extinct; and which left no literature! So it is not my purpose here to expatiate on the structure and peculiarities of this once easy, useful and odd jargon. I am not qualified, anyway. But I will say this: For all its paleolithic crudity some could work with it for expression as exquisitely as an artisan of the Stone Age worked with his rude stone tools; and he did more than many of us now could do if left to face life in the wilderness

with the best of steel tools. When I recall the grammatic poverty of
Chinook, its limited vocabulary, bare of ornament, and yet remember
the rich syllabic music which could be made to run through it
with right enunciation; and when I recall also the ease with which
an expert in its use could convey accurate directions, and express
strong opinions concerning his enemies, and cover new situations as
they arose; I am wondering if in structure it were not of a kind with
whatever primitive language slowly crystalled in the subconscious of
men before Adam left Lilith and took to Eve; or before the Lunar
Pitris descended; or before the Pithecanthropus Erectus ascended;
or whatever be the truth of the creatures and our origin, if ever we
had any definite origin, which I very much doubt.

The proportion of English increased as time passed. Now many of
the Salish Indians speak only English; and have no such difficulty
with certain letters as once their fathers had; the time when in
Chinook the English words fire, fish and rum became pia, pish and
lum. The root syllable pot, with its give and take significance, became,
when mixed with rum, potlum; meaning the state of being intoxicated; also, by association, any strong drink by which that state was
attained.

This unexpectedly leads me to things of the spirit. There was more
outlet for spiritual expression in Chinook than one knowing it only
in terms of hunting and trade might think. Even obscure spiritual
concepts could be hinted at through Chinook. Naturally the words
and combinations for such were not in the traders' working list of
words; and some of them were left out of the missionary lists because
not comprehended; or because it was considered expedient to ignore
them. I tell in another article about slolikum. An ekonay was a
beneficent spirit; contained of an order above slolikum. The kahwok
was what we mean by a person's guardian angel; one's own special
totem or guiding spirit; kahwok-oo was the topmost reach of a man's
nature when purified and in possession of the other sight and hearing.
A cheehah was generally an evil influence, vague like a hoodoo; but
again it might be concrete as an Arabian jinn, or even one of the
devouring ogres of our own folklore.

Slolikum, and spirits in general, were not thought of as having
any proper sex in our sense; although they may have all the tantrums
of it. When they desire to exist they strike like lightning where right
ethers are assembled; and presto, there you are! They hook on and
explode the stuff; and then grow it to form, seen or unseen in this

world, to exist for a moment or an age; independent and parentless as the spirit of a snowflake or a quartz crystal. Some are gentle, and some are rough; some go straight at a thing, and some travel more quickly by going roundabout. Some succeed by extreme action; and others do by not doing. For that reason, perhaps, we now and then ascribe a gender to their manifestations.

It is difficult for certain spirits to move through our world; but many move like the wind; or radio themselves all around to come out where they please. The Skookum Tah, or Stone Spirits, are connected with the earth. But they are usually remote; and unconcerned with the affairs of men. They make their point of contact with our world through great rocks and mountain peaks; into some of which they may enter and dream. The good influence from their dreaming is received by the land and the right creatures below.

The word tah in Chinook corresponds very nearly to every meaning we ascribe to spiritual; and it was variously conjoined with other words to express aspects of the supernatural. For instance: tah is the qualifying word in tahlapuss, the spirit cat or kyotee ghoul; the loup garou or were-wolf as we would say. At Nootka from the Spanish it would seem as if something like lamana and manus was taken to signify the hand. Then tah was prefixed to this to indicate the spirit hand or touch of wizardry; making the word tahlamanus, and later tahmanawus, to cover every form of sorcery. Also by Tah or Latah was sometimes meant a supernatural race of people next above the human order; and yet an order attainable by living men. These Tah, comparable to the lesser Gods of the Greeks, dwell apart in the Kloosh Illahie, the Delectable Land; which is by no means the abode of ordinary persons who die and wake in ghostland. Just as siyah, meaning distance, meant great distance with the last syllable long drawn, siya-a-ah, so tah-oo, meaning spiritual distance, or distance in time, was intensified by dwelling on the last syllable.

Long ago, and alone under a pine tree on a hilltop, an Indian came and told things to me between sound and silence that were tah-oo. When leaving he gave an all-round wave of his arm and said: "Kwonsum Sokalie Tyhee mamook kopa sokalie. Pe kwonsum Yo mitlite Yo." That is to say: "Forever the Lord on High works high. But forever Yo stays Yo." How about that? How about that notion of Yo, the eternal, unexistent yet potential matrix; anterior to God as the sky is anterior to the sun? Such a notion was neither acceptable, nor perhaps comprehensible, by such of our people as were engaged in giving the comfort of our religion to those who were being killed off by our culture.

I remember how that unusual talk with that unusual Indian came back to me many years after in Dr. George Morrison's library at Pekin. I was being shown characters at the back of a Chinese book, beginning a rare version of the Scripture of the Heavenly Way. Those characters were turned into words for me: "Dau ko dau fay chwang dau!" That is: The doing that can be done is not the regular doing! I knew then without more ado that it meant: The doing that can be done is not the eternal doing! And that is only another way of saying what the Indian said to me on the hilltop under the pine tree when I was a boy. The Divine that can be divined is not the Eternal Divine!

PART II

THE TWENTIETH CENTURY: 1914 TO THE PRESENT

1. Interpretations of Politics and Culture

A. R. M. LOWER
1889-

Distinguished by an incisive style and a genuinely independent
point of view, the historical writings of Arthur Lower have
had an important influence both on the academic interpretation and the popular understanding of Canada's political,
social, and racial development.

Born in Barrie, Ontario, and educated at the University of
Toronto, he served in the Royal Navy during the first world
war. Later he worked for a time at the Canadian Archives in
Ottawa and then studied at Harvard. He taught history at
Tufts College, Massachusetts, at Harvard, and at United College, Winnipeg. Elected to the Royal Society of Canada in
1941, he received the Society's Tyrell Medal in History in
1947. The same year he was appointed to the Douglas Chair
of Canadian and Commonwealth History at Queen's University, a post he held until his retirement in 1959.

Among Professor Lower's most important contributions
to Canadian historical scholarship are *The North American
Assault on the Canadian Forest* (1938), a history of the lumber
trade between Canada and the United States; *Settlement and
the Forest Frontier in Eastern Canada* (1936); *Canada and
the Far East* (1940); and a contribution to a symposium
Evolving Canadian Federalism, lectures given at Duke University, North Carolina. For the general reader Professor
Lower's main significance stems from his three popular works
of historical synthesis *Colony to Nation: A History of Canada*
(1946, revised 1964), *This most Famous Stream: The Liberal
Democratic Way of Life* (1954), and *Canadians in the
Making: A Social History of Canada* (1958).

TWO WAYS OF LIFE: THE SPIRIT OF OUR INSTITUTIONS

A paper presented at the annual meeting of the Canadian Historical Association, May, 1947.

> *"Achieved liberty is the one ethical result that rests on the converging and combined conditions of advancing civilization."*
> Lord Acton, *Inaugural Lecture on the Study of History* (London, 1930)

Anyone who undertakes to investigate the spirit of our institutions must come to grips at once with what I have elsewhere called "Two Ways of Life," for it is an area in which the two races are widely separated. Yet unless we give up altogether the view that Canada is a community—a step for which I cannot believe many Canadians are ready—we must make the attempt to find common ground. There is far more of that than is usually assumed, particularly if scholars from both groups are willing to explore it together.

Naturally in a short paper it is impossible to do more than make a few generalizations, all susceptible of challenge. Nor is it possible to introduce much novelty. Nevertheless, no pardon need be asked for retreading familiar ground, for nothing needs more frequent restatement than the nature of our institutions. The time is coming for that to be summarized and once more read into our constitution, as it has been before. Whether the wisest type of restatement consists in a Bill of Rights[1] is a matter for discussion. That there should be restatement is not. Freedom is everywhere and at all times challenged and never was it more seriously challenged than in the present age. Restatement, therefore, is imperative.

FRENCH INSTITUTIONS PRECEDING THE CONQUEST

Everyone knows that the accepted law in French Canada was the Custom of Paris, the most highly developed of French regional laws.[2] While it never became the common law of metropolitan France, it was the only code introduced into the colonies.[3] In France it was modified by the great reforming and codifying edicts[4] which reorganized French law and laid the basis for the Code Napoléon. The Ordinance of Civil Procedure was registered in the Sovereign Council of Quebec and formally came into force in 1679. The others were not registered. But on the principle that metropolitan law extended to a colony they nevertheless were in force.[5] The Custom of Paris, as modified, remained the basis of law in the province of Quebec until reorganized and caught up into Cartier's code of 1865.

Two points in connection with it immediately attract the attention of a person accustomed to English institutions: the first is that, despite the completion under Louis xiv of the edifice of absolutism, it apparently takes for granted the rule of law; the second is that in contrast with its careful provisions for the rights of one subject as against another, it has no provision for the rights of the subject against the state.

French monarchy, as it worked out in the seventeenth century, has been called totalitarian. It is true that no will could stand against that of the king and that Louis xiv subdued to himself virtually every other element within the state, including the church, but he made no formal abrogation of law. Law may, in the last resort, have been the king's will, but it remained law. The impression received from the books and documents of the time is not of a régime in a high state of flux, with officials acting on the whispered or fancied wishes of the king, but of one in a considerable state of legal stability, which performed its official acts with due ceremony and order. With too much, in fact: one of the objects against which revolutionary and Napoleonic ire was to be directed was the legal system, with its overdose of formalism.

In Canada, the element of distance created its own variations. The monarchy proceeded on the principle of *divide et impera* in its careful avoidance of precise delimitation of duty between governor and intendant. Governor, bishop, and intendant were representative of the three estates in France for the governor was invariably an aristocrat and the intendant a *bourgeois*; the incessant quarrels between them foreshadowed, in miniature, the French Revolution. While divisions between these functionaries perhaps gave to the ordinary man certain irregular liberties which he would not otherwise have enjoyed, the distance from the throne enabled them on occasion to act in a more direct way than might have been normally permitted in France. They sometimes carried direct action to the point of arbitrarily arresting and detaining the king's subjects, without cause shown, a treatment usually reserved in the mother country for great political offenders, under *lettres de cachet.*

The criminal law of the old régime appears to have been a mixture of customary and Roman elements. In Canada, the crown attorney (*procureur du roi*) was the official who initiated prosecutions. Like a commissioner under our Public Inquiries Act, it would seem, he had the right to bring anyone before him for questioning in private. If in this way he accumulated sufficient evidence, he might proceed to a prosecution. Though the prosecution was conducted in public, the crown attorney would hardly be likely to proceed unless he had a very sure case, and in order to make it one, in his private examination, he could go to lengths which shock a modern mind.

The old customary law was bad enough, but all its rigors were incorporated formally in the great Criminal Ordinances of 1670 and 1685, which made escape from conviction, once prosecution had begun, so difficult as to prompt a judge of the time to remark: "Si j'étais accusé d'avoir volé les tours de Notre-Dame, je commencerais par m'enfuir."[6] The code, though not registered by the Sovereign Council, was in force in Canada. It mingled reasonable usage with extreme severity. It established sound rules on the hearing and competence of witnesses, on appeals, and on the maintenance and inspection of prisons. But in the preliminary examinations, the persons examined had no counsel, procedure was secret, and as a means of discovery it was permissible to use torture.

There are too many cases on record to permit us to believe that the severities of this code did not extend to Canada. In so far as humane conduct goes, there is no point in comparing the seventeenth century with our own. French Canada seems to have been neither more nor less cruel than other countries of the time and I am in no sense attempting to put it in the pillory: I am merely trying to indicate what was the nature of its public institutions. That compels me to observe that in addition to executions with accompaniments of a barbarity that would shock the present generation, there is no doubt that it was legal to employ torture, and at a comparatively late date: "En avril 1734, une noire esclave de madame de Francheville causa un grand incendie, qui dévasta une partie de la ville de Montreal."[7] "Elle fut soumise à la question ordinaire et extraordinaire. On voulait lui faire avouer son crime."[8]

"In 1752, Pierre Beaudoin dit Cumberland, with three others, soldiers in a corps called 'Détachement des Troupes de la Marine,' then in garrison in the town of Three Rivers, were accused of having set fire to the Town, in different places, on the night of the 21st May. The crime of arson was proved by witnesses against Beaudoin, but he was placed on the *rack* in order to discover whether he had any accomplices. He suffered this punishment without making any declaration, and was finally executed."⁹

I do not know what "la question ordinaire et extraordinaire" amounted to: "la question ordinaire" seems to have been merely the rack! Yet the impression one gets from reading the documents of the French régime is not that of a dark and bloody tyranny, but of a rather kindly, though highly inefficient, paternalism, whose justice was arbitrary but also speedy—and cheap. The point here is not the practice so much as the law: French criminal law, like French public law, was weighted heavily against the individual.

THE INSTITUTIONS OF THE PROVINCE OF QUEBEC

AFTER THE CONQUEST

The Conquest involved the acceptance in many fields of English law and English public institutions. The English criminal law came in with the Quebec Act, and though it was severe enough, in all conscience, with its scores of capital crimes, it did give the culprit a fighting chance: I have never heard of objections against the introduction of English criminal law, with its essential attribute of publicity. Habeas corpus and jury trial followed within ten years, and in 1791, parliamentary institutions. Parliamentary institutions were received with considerable enthusiasm, and the educated classes were fully seized of the fact that through them there was being conferred the inestimable gift of freedom.

Although the common law of England with respect to crime was formally introduced in 1774, it seems to have taken a long time before its essential nature became familiar to the French-speaking people of Canada: "Ignorant la langue dans laquelle les précédents qui font le droit commun étaient écrits, éloignés de son étude par son formalisme et la bizarrerie de ses termes techniques, quoique pénétrés de sa grande humanité, ils témoignèrent d'abord une grande indifférence à s'en instruire. La pratique de ce droit était restée presque l'apanage exclusif du barreau anglais. . . . De fait, jusqu'à la décentralisation judiciaire en 1857, le droit criminel était resté à l'état de science mystérieuse pour la race française du Bas-Canada. . . ." [10]

English representative institutions, however, were taken up with alacrity. The classical duels between British governors and the House of Assembly followed as a matter of course. Down to within two or three years of the end of his long struggle with the administration, Papineau fought for constitutional goals and followed methods which no Englishman who had any sympathy for the seventeenth century could reprobate. He fought mainly for complete control of finance by the Assembly, and only in the eighteen-thirties did he move on to Jacksonianism in his advocacy of election for the Legislative Council. How far Papineau was tinged with European liberalism before he went into exile, I do not know. His political tactics suggest that he was little more than a rather extreme Whig. Lafontaine was closer still to the model of English Whiggism. With Cartier, who kept calling himself a Reformer until as late as 1857, the wheel came full circle and the former rebel became a conservative. His ascendancy may be taken as marking the full acceptance by the French of English institutions, but not necessarily the full understanding of them, still less the full appreciation of the spirit which had engendered them.

While the people of New France were yet under French rule they had no guarantees of liberty, but they do not seem to have regarded themselves as other than free. The strife of governor and intendant went on far above their heads: it provoked no popular alignments and no germ of partyism. Individuals could be, and were, oppressed, but a class, challenged in that perpetual French tender spot, the pocket, seems to have had its own way of resisting. When in 1680 a royal order came out that the colonists should pay each curé annually 574 livres, a sum greater than the amount of the tithe, we are told that "the seigneurs and habitants assembled and declared that they could not give more than the twenty-sixth part of their grain" and that the execution of the law was successfully hindered. [11] Three-quarters of a century later, Bougainville, as his oft-quoted passage indicates, found this same sturdy spirit of independence among the Canadiens: "Les simples habitants du Canada seraient scandalisés d'être appelés paysans. En effet, ils sont d'un meilleure étoffe et ont plus d'esprit . . . que ceux de France. Ils ne payent aucun impôt et vivent dans une espèce d'indépendance." [12]

Since the Conquest, this collective attitude has been reinforced, mainly by English pressure. French-speaking Canadians are no more successful today in resisting the tax-gatherer than are the rest of us, but they struggle vigorously for the freedom that is dearest to them, the freedom of their religion and of their language. The individual's rights against the state, something not in their tradition, as yet only imperfectly acquired from the English tradition, and a matter of concern to relatively few individuals, do not, it would seem, excite them.

ENGLISH INSTITUTIONS: THEIR GENERAL NATURE

It is exceedingly difficult to characterize English institutions in a word, and for the simple reason that English institutions are English history. If you understand one, you will understand the other, and the spectacle we sometimes see, of political scientists attempting to scale these vast peaks without the full resources of history in their kit, seems foolish indeed. Our own Canadian position is made trebly difficult in that not only are we the heirs of England, but sharers in the spirit of the continent, which has put its mark on institutions as on individuals, and also, as possessors of a written constitution, the subjects of a fundamental law quite different from anything in all but the last eighty years of our experience.

The French historian Petit-Dutaillis, in his book *The Feudal Monarchy in France and England*, pictures the institutions of the two countries during the century and a half or so after the Norman Conquest, or until about the year 1200, as substantially the same: each was French and feudal. But during the century and a quarter from 1154 to 1272, or from the accession of Henry II to the accession of Edward I, a legal revolution occurred in England, and at the end of another century and a quarter a second great institutional revolution had taken place with the growth of parliament.

I have no space to sketch a comparative history of the two countries here, but I might remark in passing that it was neither defect in the French sense of liberty, nor a racial element, nor the lack of political clear-sightedness on the continent, which made for the divergence. "The Constitution ought to combine a limited and elective monarchy, with an aristocracy of merit, and such an admixture of democracy as shall admit all classes to office, by popular election. No government has a right to levy taxes beyond the limit determined by the people. All political authority is derived from popular suffrage, and all laws must be made by the people or their representatives. . . ." [13]

This is not a statement by some late eighteenth-century theorist but by a man writing about the same time that Simon de Montfort was calling together his experimental parliament (1264). It is true the words are not those of the barbarous northerners, either French or Anglo-French, among whom one may seek in vain for political theory of like clarity, but of a supple Neapolitan cleric, one St. Thomas Aquinas by name; nevertheless such thinking was at the disposal of French monarchs, as of others. Needless to say, it was not accepted. France went off on her road to absolutism, and England on a very different road.

The French sense of liberty was probably just as lively as that across the Channel. In fact, then as now, it was probably too lively, and that may be a part of the explanation for French failure to form lasting public institutions of freedom. The solid *bourgeoisie* were no doubt glad to see a curb put at any cost on baronial conceptions of liberty, with their concomitants of brawls, oppression, and private war, even if it involved giving to the crown of France extremely wide powers. To a person of English background, French ideas of liberty seem to go rather far in the direction of anarchy. Even here in Canada, the province of Quebec will furnish more candidates at an election than several other provinces combined; in the last provincial election not only did no party receive a majority, but there were relatively few elected candidates who received as many as half the votes cast.

As for an institutional explanation based on race, look at the situation. The English legal revolution involved the substitution of the king's justice for the old folk-right. It involved the writ system, the new legislation included in the assizes, the jury system, and greatest of all, the creation, by the king's new judges, of the common law. It involved also a counter-revolution, symbolized, *inter alia*, by Magna Carta, which forced the crown to moderate its pace and, by bringing it to book, introduced into English life that greatest of all its principles, compromise, the basis of constitutionalism. Who were the men that accomplished this first and greatest of the English revolutions? Without exception, in so far as I know, they were each and every one—Henry II, Glanville, Stephen Langton, Simon de Montfort, Edward I—Frenchmen, and Catholics!

I make this point because there has always been so much nonsense talked about race. Even in this day of royal commissions, it is whispered that of course one of the two judge-inquisitors of our last unfortunate example of commissions would naturally be inclined to arbitrary methods because he was a French Catholic. Let me say, as an antidote, that I have also heard rumours to the effect that it was the English judge who led the attack, so I do not know where the truth lies. That the French, whether in Europe or in Canada, have not managed to build up the same majestic edifice of institutions protecting the citizen against the state as have the English, I think must be admitted, but it seems foolish to explain the lack on the basis of race and religion, and anyone must admit that, when it comes to protecting our tradition of liberty, French-speaking Canadians have shown no monopoly of negligence.

Let us just thank our lucky stars that we reap the harvest sown by those mediaeval barons, whoever they were, and let it go at that. That harvest is an institutional system which has stood the storms of centuries and will, if we as citizens are moderately faithful to it, stand those of centuries to come. Parliament is "the baby" of the institutional family, and it is seven hundred years old. Sheer duration is in itself not a bad test of validity, but in this case there are plenty of others. Our institutional heritage is quite unique, so far as I know, and while it does not give perfect liberty—what system ever could?—it enables us, if we wish, to come as close to realizing liberty as any people can. Lord Acton, the greatest champion of liberty that the modern intellectual world has produced, and at one and the same time a great liberal and a great Catholic has said: "Liberty is not a means to a political end. It is itself the highest political end." [14]

THE COMMON LAW

Various aspects of English medievalism have from time to time been picked out as in themselves the single greatest contribution to liberty. This is probably not sound, for the elements in it run together, but if one had to be selected, the choice might well be the common law. "Old father antique, the law," said Shakespeare, in one of those sayings of his which put him on the side of all the bright young fellows of the time who could not see beyond the ends of their noses and were against all forms of old fogyism. Perhaps he had Coke in mind, with his last-ditch defences of legal formalism. One can take his choice between the two attitudes, between those who wanted to take short cuts and clean up the mess, and the legal antiquaries, to whom no praise for the law just as it stood was too high. "The nursing mother of liberty," Coke termed the common law. High praise indeed. "The common law is common sense," it has been said. "The law of England is the law of liberty," Mansfield was later driven to admit, in the famous case which decided that slavery could not exist upon English soil. The Bacons and Wentworths desired a clean executive sword to reorder England. For such men as these, the Star Chamber, that bright, sharp judicial blade, was an ideal instrument. One of its modern equivalents has been the judicial machinery of the Canadian income tax administration. For imposing royal or departmental will on the subject, the common law is too slow; it allows of too many escapes. It is not a law for an executive, and that was, and remains, its merit.

Nor was it a law for cloistered virtue, for "genteel," "refined" people, or arm-chair exponents of liberty. On the contrary, it was forged out of hard tussles for property rights. In its formative period, one's "liberty" was some right, franchise, or piece of property that one could seize and hold. It was the common law's virtue that, by generations of interpretation, usually in the direction of safeguarding the property rights which individuals possessed, it wore down "liberties" into what we call "liberty."

The first virtue of the common law is publicity. "It is one of the essential qualities of a court of justice that its proceedings should be public."[15] "The settled judgment of our ancestors and ourselves is that publicity in the administration of the law is on the whole . . . worth more to society than it costs."[16] From this point of view, our recent espionage investigation at once takes on a sinister light. It flies in the face of centuries of experience in resorting to a type of procedure—secret investigation—that the wisdom of our ancestors has many times condemned. For the second great virtue of the common law is that it has at all times set its face against inquisitorial procedure. When Henry II began to use the jury as part of his new machinery of justice, he had in his hands the most powerful of all royal instruments of absolutism, an inquisition, a fact-gathering body without let or hindrance. His ancestor, William the Conqueror, had used it to his own great advantage in the Domesday inquest, a job of fanatical detective work that could hardly be surpassed, in its prying skill, by our own commissioner of income tax. By lucky accident, Henry did not press the advantages that the jury would have given him, and it settled down into, first, a device of ordinary trial, a substitute for the primitiveness of folk-right, and then, after some centuries, into the "palladium of English liberty," which to some degree, it still remains.

In the Roman law countries, on the other hand, inquisitional procedure became customary; from it flow consequences that take on dark colors in English eyes: secret examination, lack of counsel for the examined, no confrontation of witnesses in open court, devices for securing a man's testimony against himself, and lastly, at the end of the court's resources in compelling testimony, torture. In the espionage commission Roman law criminal procedure has lately had an exemplification in this country of which few of us, it is to be hoped, would welcome a second example. In contradiction to this, the very life of the common law, as Sir Frederick Pollock says, is open discussion and unfettered criticism. Freedom is its sister and in the spirit of freedom its greatest work has ever been done.[17]

The common law never felt obliged to go farther than to set up a referee to a dispute: before him, the king's judge, the parties fought out their cases. He was under no necessity of exploring the case to its limits: his job was to come to a reasonably quick, if approximate, decision on the materials put before him. It was easy, in criminal law, to draw the king in, "not as the supreme head of national justice exhibiting and punishing the crimes which his officers had discovered,"[18] but as a party, along with other parties, bound to make his cause good. The rule that the burden of proof is on the plaintiff was therefore easy to carry over from the civil to the criminal law: hence our rule that a man must be presumed innocent until he is proved guilty.[19]

The common law was essentially the king's law; hence the law of the land. There was no room for a Custom of Paris in England: what elements of local custom survived the legal revolution soon atrophied. Since the king himself, the fountain of justice, was present in all his courts, there could be no question of certain privileged persons claiming immunity. "Who should judge the king's servants if not the king's own judges?"[20] In this way, the special character of officials, which virtually everywhere under Roman law puts them beyond the reach of the ordinary courts for acts in their official capacity, does not exist under the common law. Every official, from the prime minister to the policeman, who exceeds the strict letter of his authority under the law, may be sued by the private citizen.

From this exceedingly important principle there follows the logical deduction that, under English law, there can be no "acts of state." "The French Government does in fact exercise . . . a wide discretionary authority which is not under the control of any Court whatsoever. For an act of State, the Executive or its servants cannot be made amenable to the jurisdiction of any tribunal. . . ."[21] "An act of state" (acte de gouvernement) cannot be precisely defined, but, according to Dicey, the tendency of French legal thinking in his day had been to narrow the term. It is possible that the events of two wars, with their necessity for action, have widened it. Never at any time in our history, until the recent wars, so far as the present writer knows, has the conception of "the act of state" been formally recognized under English law.[22] But during the war just over, it made its entrance, naked and unashamed, into Canadian executive thought, this under the guise of "safety of the state." Who, under our Defence of Canada Regulations, was normally the judge of the "safety of the state"? The minister of justice : which term, no doubt, in practice meant subordinate officials in diminishing importance down to the constable of the R.C.M.P. Is there any darker door than that opened by the present government of Canada in admitting into our life "the safety of the state," with its concomitants, "reasons of state," "acts of state," as carrying their own justification, beyond the reach of the law of the land?

THE STRUGGLE BETWEEN THE COMMON LAW AND "REGIMENTATION"

Not only the common law but all English institutions of government had to fight for their existence during the two centuries of disorder and reaction, running from Henry VI to Charles I. The disorder of the Wars of the Roses—the kind of disorder that was the rule rather than the exception in France—was inevitably followed by the restoral of order with a strong hand, which took the form of stress on the residuary, or prerogative, powers of the crown, that well of jurisdiction which could have swallowed up all liberty, just as the regalian rights of the kings of France swallowed up liberty. Such stress produced Courts of Star Chamber and it produced the insidious suggestion of Francis Bacon to King James I, that by proceeding under the writ *de non procedendo rege inconsulto* it would be possible to prevent the judges from proceeding with any case in which the interests of the crown were concerned.

"The writ," said Bacon, "is a mean provided by the ancient law of England to bring any case that may concern your Majesty in profit or power from the ordinary Benches, to be tried and judged before the Chancellor of England, by the ordinary and legal part of this power. And your Majesty knoweth your Chancellor is ever a principal counsellor and instrument of monarchy, of immediate dependence on the King; and therefore like to be a safe and tender guardian of the regal rights." [23]

Bacon may have found his excuse in the obscurantism of common-law judges like Coke, but there is a fairly strong case against him. He was one of those over-clever persons—Wentworth, Lord Strafford, was another—who get impatient with the slow blunderings of ordinary men, and strive for short cuts to efficiency. Our present civil service is probably full of them—men who know so much about their business (which is also ours) that you or I, as plain citizens, can never cope with them—and who, honestly anxious to do a good job, press for the powers which will enable them to do it, but the net result of whose efforts is to bind us until the area of free movement left to us is small indeed—the eternal type of bureaucrat.

The conflict between liberty and order is never-ending, and humanity oscillates between the two. Left to himself, the average man might show small concern for the common good, and anarchy would ensue. But it is equally true that, left to himself, the governor, be he civil servant, minister, or prince, would show small concern for the freedom of the average man, and despotism would ensue. Has the person in authority ever been known who did not wish to add to his powers? Few of our public men in Canada aspire to a dictatorial position. But some of them obviously welcome the indefinite extension of their powers. They have concrete situations to meet and they want to meet them as effectively and quickly as possible; everyone prefers a smooth eight-cylinder car to the Model-T of sacred memory. So on every hand today, the executive is busily extending its powers, arguing vigorously against any abatement of them, seeking to prove that without them, the emergencies which it is sure are just round the corner never could be met. In Canada, our original War Measures Act of 1914 is still on the books; whenever the government of the day (not the Parliament) decides that the emergency is great enough, it can be put into force again, and away go practically all our cherished institutions of freedom. It is the equivalent of the "state of siege" familiar in the constitutions of many Latin American countries not usually considered as advanced as our own. Those who are interested may turn to the debate of May, 1947, in the Canadian Commons, where, more especially in the speeches of Mr. J. G. Diefenbaker and the Honourable J. L. Ilsley,[24] they will see the two attitudes sharply differentiated. Mr. Diefenbaker spoke in terms of the Pyms or the Hampdens, but the Minister echoed the sentiments of the Wentworths, the practical, realistic administrators who ask for the sharp tools which will enable them to do their job. Efficient administration—"the safety of the state"—driven to an extreme, would mean a smooth-running machine of a state, a slave state. Democracy is not compatible with too much order and safety. For the sake of democracy, democrats must take risks, even in the presence of their enemies. It is those who desire excessive powers for "preserving the safety of the state" who are themselves invariably among the greatest dangers to that safety.

In the seventeenth century the plain citizen broke the bonds that such men would have put about him and regained some of his freedom. The rebellion against Charles Stuart was as much a rebellion against the attempt to establish a strong administrative system of the continental type as it was an affair of religion or of economic classes.[25] It was thus distinctly not a movement towards something, but away from something, not forward but backward, back to the old conceptions of administration and common-law methods, against the new bureaucratic efficiency of Stuart advisers (and the nagging of Stuart French wives who expected English kings to cut as great figures as French royal fathers). It is no accident that the revolt against the Stuarts brought a deluge of appeals to past usage, especially medieval usage, for it was essentially a return to the past. The seventeenth century cried out to the thirteenth and both, with their dislike of coercion, of the neatly-ordered, efficient state, stretch out their hands to the nineteenth. Is there much difference between the armored baron, ever on the fighting point for his "liberties," the seventeenth-century Puritan squire or merchant, determined that the king would not take his property or religion away from him, and the nineteenth-century businessman, with his slogan that every pot should stand on its own bottom?

When they confront us, these exhibitions of rugged individualism are not pleasant, for they are selfish and ruthless, but it is through such determined selfishness that our liberties have been mainly secured. Our problem today is to find some bridge between this hard-fisted insistence on personal rights and the wider rights of men as a whole. Bridging the chasm between individualism and collectivism is like squaring the circle. The last Tudor and the first two Stuarts tackled the problem but it proved too much for them, and they have stood under the accusation ever since of conspiring to take away men's liberties. Today we face the task again.

LATER ENGLISH CONTRIBUTIONS TO A JUST SOCIETY

But we are also children of the nineteenth and twentieth centuries, and many other strains have come into our institutional life since those old seventeenth-century days. We have to canvass the bearing on our theme of the American wilderness, and of the new doctrinal aspects of life that came directly or indirectly out of the Reformation. This cannot be done here. Suffice it to say, as to the new world, that it represented the freedom of medievalism over again; anyone who has read Haskin's account of the way in which the Norman ancestor of the kings of Sicily rose to success will have no difficulty in understanding how the Vanderbilts and the Goulds of the last century built their industrial empires. For the less powerful man, who nevertheless had a strong right arm, the new world represented the freedom of space, space where he could carve a home for himself out of the unbroken wilderness, a spot where other people would not be constantly under his feet. The new world carried freedom far beyond that of medievalism, for its remoteness and space represented freedom—at least relative freedom—from interference of every type, including interference with one's religion or lack of religion.

To the English, the new world represented, above all, freedom, and they brought out with them the institutions by which they were able to maintain that freedom. To the French and the Spanish, it represented some considerable degree of freedom too, but neither people had the institutional framework for their freedom which the English possessed, and the Spaniards, who have never received it, as a result have lost much of the freedom that they once may have had.

Doctrinally, the Reformation also meant freedom, the freedom of religious competition, comparable to the freedom of economic competition. The strands of this freedom are complex; one may be picked out, to point up what goes before.

In the eighteenth century, reaching down to a class which the older Puritanism did not touch, there arose a new variant of Protestantism, that which gave rise to Methodism and the evangelical wing of the Church of England. From the first it had qualities in which the older creeds were weak, altruistic qualities as opposed to their absorption in themselves. Its social gospel was strong, and to it we owe a huge program of domestic reform in England, as well as movements on behalf of the peoples throughout the world unfortunate enough not to have white skins; the humanitarian movement succeeded in getting slavery abolished, and it still, in various forms, exerts a most powerful influence upon British officials in dependent countries. To it, the Protestant people of this country have fully contributed. It opens the way for a new kind of thinking about liberty; it goes back not so much to the hard-boiled bishops of the Middle Ages who always saw to it that every re-issue of the Great Charter should begin with the words: *quod ecclesia anglicana libera sit*, as to gentle medieval saints, like St. Francis of Assisi. The liberty it would have us keep in mind is not so much our own as that of others. In short, with the great Protestant revivals of the eighteenth and early nineteenth centuries, we get, amid much dross and much sheer stupidity, a return to something like the spirit which inspired the Christian gospels.

The great truths by which men live have rolled over humanity for many centuries: they all echo the same spirit, the spirit of justice and fairness. The prophet Micah long ago put the question: "and what doth the Lord require of thee, but to do justly, and to love mercy, and to walk humbly with thy God?" The Stoics put the same ideas in terms almost as penetrating as those of the New Testament itself: "We must treat others as we wish to be treated by them, and must persist until death in doing good to our enemies, regardless of unworthiness and ingratitude."[26] Nowhere, of course, does this fundamental ethic get the same eloquent and satisfactory statement as it does in the New Testament: in fact, it is the New Testament.

Now, it is not suggested that the hard assertions of property rights under which English institutions were hammered out were much affected by the gentle teachings of the Gospel, but merely that behind them—often a long way behind them—there *have* lurked certain conceptions of justice. And, further, that within the last two centuries, the direct relationship of this Christian ethic to public action has become increasingly closer. The "love thy neighbour as thyself" view of society was influential throughout the English world all during the nineteenth century, and although it has now in considerable part passed from its direct association with formal religion, it is the basis of the striving for a better society which is so marked an aspect of our own age. It is, indeed, probably the basis of the collectivism of the English-speaking world, but that is another story.

Are Christian conceptions of justice going to be able to do what Baconian conceptions of efficiency failed to do? Are they going to be able to square the circle of liberty and order? No one can tell. They keep on sapping away at injustice, as economic injustice, but will they bring about the just society? That is too much to expect. Men are not able to create just societies, though they may approximate to them. In attempting to create just societies will they destroy liberty? Is there an antithesis, then, between justice and liberty? No, but there may be a strong antithesis between *my* liberty and *your* justice.

It takes all sorts to make a world. It takes all sorts of people to make a free world. Mere niceness will not do it. We owe a great deal to the nasty people, to the men who were not afraid to be obnoxious and unpopular, and often to the scatterbrained who, having got out on limbs, refused to come in from them, to the Wilkes's, the Mackenzies, and the Stubbs's. We owe a great deal to the giants— to the Miltons and the Burkes. We owe a great deal to the saints, among whom may be included the late J. S. Woodsworth. We owe almost as much to the lawyers. We owe a great deal to the philosophers: to such as Aquinas with his definition of the law of nature as the voice of universal reason—or Grotius, with the saying that is tantamount to it, though perhaps more brutal: "The principles of law must stand even if we suppose that there is no God."[27] We owe a great deal to the dissentient Protestant sects, objectionable though some of them may make themselves.[28] Most of all we owe to the long generations of men who each in their own way have built up our institutional heritage. Let not those who seek to establish the reign of justice begin by destroying the excellent ladder to her abode which has been built for us. And let not those who temporarily are in charge of the destinies of our state forget the many men before them who, either through malevolence, or short-sightedness, or because they wished to take shortcuts to their desires, or to constrain other men to their wills, or because they were ignorant and led the people into the wilderness, or because they interpreted the vociferous demands of the few as the urgent and permanent welfare of the many, or because they deemed force a good answer to argument, let them not forget the many men before them who for these reasons have gone down to obscurity or to shame.

1. It should be noted that the Canadian constitution already has its bill of rights. Not only do the federal sections in themselves lay down fundamental divisions of power which may not be transgressed, but there are also special guarantees to special groups of the King's subjects. Of these the most important are Section 133, containing the guarantee of the French language, and Section 93, on education. Any federal constitution is in itself a bill of rights, or, to use another and related term, it is fundamental law. Canada, unlike Great Britain, is not a country of parliamentary supremacy but of fundamental law. Moreover, the English Bill of Rights of 1688 is still in force in Canada, as are all the other great constitutional statutes (such as Magna Carta) enacted previous to 1867.

2. The Custom of Paris was formally written down in 1510 and was reformed under a commission in 1580 ("l'ancienne coutume, la nouvelle coutume").

3. Edmond Lareau, *Histoire du droit canadien*, 2 vols., Montreal, 1888, I, 140 ff.

4. Those on civil procedure of 1667; the criminal ordinance of 1670; the second criminal ordinance of 1685 (*code noir*); the commercial ordinance of 1673 (*code marchand*).

5. "Les tribunaux, présidés par des juges anglais se fiant aux ordonnances du général Murray, introduisaient dans la jurisprudence du pays cette nécessité de l'enregistrement. . . . Mais après ne étude plus approfondie, lorsqu'on remonte à la source même des autorités, on en vient malgré soi à la conclusion que la nécessité de l'enregistrement est venue dans notre législation par suite de la conquête. . . . Cette nécessité a donc une origine toute anglaise et il n'en a jamais été question pendant la domination française. Toutes les ordonnances générales du royaume enregistrées au parlement de Paris étaient en force en Canada." (Lareau, *Histoire du droit canadien*, I, 136-7).

6. *ibid.*, 283.

7. *ibid.*, 294.

8. J. B. A. Ferland, *Cours d'histoire du Canada*, Quebec, 1882, II, 446n.

9. Robert Christie, *A History of the Late Province of Lower Canada* (6 vols., Quebec, 1848), I, 2n. "The authenticity of the above taken from old manuscript judicial records and papers in possession of G. B. Faribault, Esqr., one of the Vice Presidents of the Literary and Historical Society of Quebec, may be relied upon." (*ibid.*, 12n).

10. Lareau, *Histoire du droit canadien*, I, 310.

11. *ibid.*, 425.

12. *ibid.*, 201.

13. Lord Acton, *The History of Freedom*, London, 1922, 36, quoting Thomas Aquinas.

14. *ibid.*, 22.

15. *Daubney* v. *Cooper*, 1829, quoted in Sir F. Pollock, *The Expansion of the Common Law*, London, 1904, 31.

16. *ibid.*, quoting Justice Holmes, 32.

17. *The Genius of the Common Law*, New York, 1912, 124.

18. F. Pollock, *The Expansion of the Common Law*, London, 1904, 42.

19. *ibid.*

20. *ibid.*, 51.

21. A. V. Dicey, *Introduction to the Study of the Law of the Constitution*, London, 1908, 386.

22. It may of course be argued that the king's prerogative will stretch over unlimited distances and that it can be used by the executive to perform actions for which there is no direct legal authority. This was the Royalist argument in the seventeenth century. Charles I's prerogative was curtailed effectively on the scaffold. It may further be argued that at times since then ministers have had to act actually in contravention of the laws, receiving afterward a vote from Parliament of an act of indemnity. Lord John Russell so acted contrary to the Bank Act in 1846. The point is that the knowledge that they are exceeding their powers necessarily limits ministers in the excess. An act of state, on the other hand, seems to carry its own justification. The difference between this French "act of state" and the old Royalist conception of the prerogative seems small. Under our system, the War Measures Act gives a blank cheque to Council, which it can fill in at its own discretion and in its own terms. It gives Council a wider prerogative than any English king ever dreamed of; under it, the old Royal attempt at autocracy has been replaced by cabinet achievement of autocracy.

23. A. V. Dicey, *Introduction to the Law of the Constitution*, 368, quoting E. A. Abbott, *Francis Bacon*, London, 1885, 234.

24. Hansard, May 16, 1947, 3184; May 19, 1947, 3262.

25. A. V. Dicey, *Introduction to the Law of the Constitution*, 365.

26. Lord Acton, *History of Freedom*, 24, 25. Those who heard the Rector of Laval speak to the Canadian Historical Association and the Canadian Political Science Association in their annual meeting at Quebec, 1947, heard an enunciation in precisely the same spirit.

27. *ibid.*, 46.

28. Lord Acton, *Lectures on Modern History*, London, 1930; *The Study of History*, London, 1895, 10, says "Progress towards organized and secured freedom, based on Protestant sectarianism, is the characteristic fact of modern history."

FRANK UNDERHILL

1889-1971

"I was born a North York Presbyterian Grit," wrote Frank
Underhill in the Introduction to his selected essays and
addresses, published in 1960 under the title *In Search of
Canadian Liberalism*; but he soon moved permanently off to
the left. Born in 1889 in Stouffville, Ontario, he was educated
at Toronto and Oxford. He served as a subaltern officer in an
English Infantry battalion during the war of 1914, an experience which, he tells us, sickened him for good of a society,
national or international, run by the British governing classes.
After the war he became a professor of history and of political
science at the University of Saskatchewan and became interested in farmers' co-operatives. In the West he met and became
friends with J. W. Dafoe, editor of the *Winnipeg Free Press,*
and J. S. Woodsworth, whose thought and action influenced
him profoundly. In 1919 he was made one of the first editors
of *The Canadian Forum*, which soon became and still is
Canada's leading intellectual journal of politics and the arts.
In 1927 he joined the History Department of the University
of Toronto, where he remained until 1955. He was one of four
founders of the League for Social Reconstruction and in 1932
of the c.c.f. party, the aims and ideals of which were set
forth in *Social Planning for Canada* (1935), a book of which
he was part author. In 1963 he gave the third series of Massey
lectures. They were published by the Canadian Broadcasting
Corporation as *The Image of Confederation.*

Professor Underhill has received many honors. He was elected president of the Canadian Historical Association in 1946. From 1955 to 1959 he was curator of Laurier House, Ottawa. In 1959 Queen's University gave him the degree of Doctor of Laws, *honoris causa.*

Frank Underhill was the master of a clear forceful style and in his work as historian and political thinker there is a devotion to principles and an understanding of human needs and human rights that mark his work as one of the finest flowerings of culture in Canadian letters.

FROM *The Image of Confederation*, 1963

CONCLUSIONS

My original intention, when I first made plans for these lectures, was to give them the general title of *The Canadian Rainbow*. I was borrowing from a French-Canadian of 1865, who was a member of the Canadian legislature in which the Confederation Debates took place—Henri Joly de Lotbinière. Joly was a Rouge, at that time a critic and opponent of the Confederation scheme, though he was later to have a distinguished career in the Dominion of Canada. He was a polished, urbane gentleman, a sceptic all his life about many of the passions and fanaticisms that swept over his fellow Canadians. On this occasion he allowed himself to wax ironical about the possibilities of the new Canadian nationality:

> I propose the adoption of the rainbow as our emblem. By the endless variety of its tints the rainbow will give an excellent idea of the diversity of races, religions, sentiments and interests of the different parts of the Confederation. By its slender and elongated form the rainbow would afford a perfect representation of the geographical configuration of Confederation. By its lack of consistence—an image without substance—the rainbow would represent aptly the solidity of our Confederation. An emblem we must have, for every great empire has one; let us adopt the rainbow.

I think that we can all see the point of Joly's suggestion today. But I came to feel, considering the seriousness of the crisis that we are now facing as we prepare to enter the second century of Confederation, that I might justly be accused of frivolity if I proposed today, a century after Joly, that we adopt the rainbow as our Canadian emblem. So I decided on a non-committal title, more fitting for a man of my years, and more fitting for this cautious, non-committal country of which I am a citizen; and I have called my series *The Image of Confederation*.

Joly, I hope you will have noticed, was using this concept of "image" as long ago as 1865, though we are apt to think of it as a very modern one, invented on Madison Avenue. I have been trying to suggest in these lectures that we have not yet arrived at any clear, distinctive image of Canada in our minds, that we have not achieved a sufficient degree of consensus about our national purposes and goals to satisfy either ourselves or outsiders as to what the word Canada means. We shall enter our second century without feeling very confident about the nature of our identity.

I have not tried to cover my subject in any comprehensive or complete manner. I have picked out for comment certain periods, such as that of the Unrestricted Reciprocity election of 1891 or of the Boer War, and certain themes, such as that of the Canada First movement or of English-French relations, in order to illustrate some of the major continuing controversies about our national purposes and goals in which we have been engaged. When I have talked about individuals, I have picked out mainly certain detached intellectuals, or some of the more intellectual of our statesmen, such as Laurier and Bourassa, rather than the practical men of action in politics and business on whom the stage-lights are focussed in most of the standard histories of Canada. It strikes me that, if we are to understand ourselves better, we need to devote a great deal more study to our intellectual history, to the values, to the guiding ideas and ideals, that have influenced the minds of different groups of Canadians at different times. This is what I have been trying to do in a sketchy way in these lectures.

"Our national purposes and goals." Some words of warning are needed here. We Canadians are not a people who have ever shown much aptitude or genius for whole-hearted, deeply felt dedication to purposes and goals beyond those of our particular individual lives. We differ from our American neighbours in this; for, from the moment that the Puritans landed in New England, they have conceived themselves as a people uniquely chosen by destiny to give the world a model of a new, finer civilization than Europe had been capable of producing, and to spread that civilization among more backward peoples. We ordinary Canadians lack the capacity to be caught up in a great crusade for an idea. And this statement is true both of French- and of English-Canadians.

The French were taught by their intellectual and spiritual leaders that their true function was to build up an agrarian peasant society, which would be an oasis of Catholic piety and virtue in the great North American desert of Anglo-Saxon industrialized commercialism. And, all the time, while they dutifully said yes to this proposition, they kept flocking into Montreal and smaller urban centres to work in factories. We English-Canadians dedicated ourselves to maintaining an identity separate from the American one; but, all the time, thousands of our best spirits kept emigrating to the United States, while those of us who remained behind steadily Americanized ourselves in our mass culture so that in our everyday life we became more and more indistinguishable from the Americans. And the most indistinguishable Canadians of all are our politicians who daily save us from the United States. Our capacity for a genuine dedication to national purposes and goals is definitely limited.

For, behind all this talk about loftier national purposes and goals, it is obvious that the individuals who make up our community have individual purposes. In a way, the cumulation of these individual purposes makes up a nation-wide purpose. But these individual purposes are what?—more money, more comfort, more apparatus of all kinds for affluent living, more status, more sex, more leisure, more self- and family-indulgence. The cumulation of such purposes stands in the way of a genuine emergence of any national purpose that might involve the disciplining or sacrificing of individual purposes, the putting of the general good ahead of the individual good and pleasure. This universal reaching out for "more" makes the mean sensual Canadian very much like the mean sensual American or Englishman or Frenchman or German. And we need to remember that in the Western world the men who have talked most loudly about national purpose in our generation were those who went on to impose a national purpose arbitrarily upon their people by means of an authoritarian totalitarian government. Perhaps this whole idea of a national purpose should meet with a certain amount of scepticism and suspicion when we contemplate it today.

* * *

With these qualifications in mind, let me turn to consider a little further some of the controversial issues with which I have been dealing in earlier lectures. Firstly, a little more about the form taken by our economic nationalism; and then about the issues of English-French relations within Canada and about Canada's relations with Britain and with the United States.

Firstly, then, as to our Canadian economic nationalism. I pointed out in my third lecture that, during the generation after Confederation, we adopted a national policy based on economic expansion through railway building and tariff protection, a policy carried out under the leadership of, and for the primary benefit of, a group of great capitalist entrepreneurs working in close alliance with the national government. We have since then made no fundamental modification in this form of society. Other interests have learned how to organize themselves into effective pressure-groups; and the government, in the benefits that it has to distribute, tends to become a sort of arbitrator among competing groups. But in the economic jungle that results from this régime of Darwinian competition, the lion's share continues to be distributed to the lions.

At the end of World War I, there was a great protest movement against the domination of our society by these big-business tycoons in their offices in Montreal and Toronto. But the protest failed. The farm leaders of the prairie had a vision of what they called a New National Policy, a vision of an economy and policy based on freer trade with the outer world, on an international policy centring in the League of Nations, on public ownership and operation of the basic economic activities, on a system of politics emancipated from the control of the old parties, which, in their view, had become the instruments of big-business corporations in Montreal and Toronto. When I was a young man living on the prairies in the 1920s, this seemed to me the vision of a new dynamic democracy in which the common man might become an actively participating citizen instead of a passively manipulated consumer.

But the farmers' revolt, from the Progressive movement of the 1920s into the c.c.f. and Social Credit movements of the 1930s, did not turn out to be the springtime of a new era. It was really the last stand of agrarianism against the urbanization and industrialization of our society, against leadership by the big metropolitan centres. The farmers were unable to enlist the co-operation of the industrial workers in their trade unions. And the prairie fire sweeping eastward was stopped by the fire-break of the Ottawa River. For the French-Canadians remained aloof in the 1920s; and, when the depression of the 1930s at last produced upheavals in their society, these were canalized into narrow, racial, nationalistic channels, producing a variety of Sinn Fein nationalist movements. As for the Maritime provinces, nothing, of course, ever happens down finance, and science, of men without whose advice the representatives of populist democracy are likely to go wildly astray.

Nevertheless, it was out of this populist democracy, in its more promising days after World War I, that there came the one creative idea in our contemporary generation of politics. The man whose name is most closely connected with it was J. S. Woodsworth. As Professor W. L. Morton has put it in his recent one-volume history, *The Kingdom of Canada*:

> A social reformer of a prophetic more than a political bent, Woodsworth entered politics in a heroic endeavour to make society more humane. . . . His principal work was a work of the spirit. More than any other Canadian public man, he helped transform Canadian politics from the politics of special sectional interests to the politics of collective concern for the welfare of the individual in a society collectively organized.[1]

Alas, our national life today is once again dominated by the politics of special sectional interests. The idea of a general national interest transcending these special and provincial interests seems unable to be born. It is time for a Canada First movement more sophisticated and more effective than the Canada First movement of the 1870s. We are in search of the next National Policy, on the basis of which a new national consensus can be built up. This will come when our imaginations are once more moved by a conception of the great things that are waiting for us to do together again in the future.

As things are, however, our national government in recent years has approached the ten lusty provincial governments, and especially that of Quebec, in an attitude of timorous politeness, as if apologizing for the fact of its own existence. And the Canadian people as a whole cannot apparently reach any agreement to entrust their fortunes to any one political party with a majority support. They watch apathetically while our unprotected federal quarterback, looking in vain for a pass receiver, is overrun by the big husky linemen of the provincial defensive team and thrown for another loss.

In an environment that changes every decade with the revolutionary advances of science and technology, our future depends on our flexibility, our adaptability to changing conditions. And this depends upon the quality of the education that we make available there. For Canada as a whole, no new form of co-operation among racial and sectional groups in a programme of social reconstruction led by forces of the left came about. No new National Policy was worked out.

Since then, the western farmers, who once considered themselves the pioneers of a new national outlook, have sunk back into becoming a mere pressure-group, getting what they can out of the old society. They no longer aspire to the responsibility of thinking out the forms of a new society. If this task is to be undertaken today, it will have to be done by some groups in our urban centres —some middle-class groups, since the new trade unions of the 1930s have also sunk back into being just another pressure-group.

If we are to acquire a new image of ourselves and a new sense of purpose, what is needed is a great campaign of education and propaganda to raise us out of our narrow, inward-looking protectionism. What is really wrong with us, both French and English, is our belief that we can defend our identity by turning our backs upon the outer world, by retreating into ourselves. The French are going through an acute attack of this isolationist nationalism just now, which we English-Canadians profess to regard with the superior attitude of a broader-minded people. But the anti-Americanism that afflicts us in a virulent form just now is a disease of exactly the same nature. Canada needs an Adam Smith or a Cobden, backed by a movement something like that of the Anti-Corn-Law League of the 1840s, to tell us that the affluent life at which we aim cannot be attained if we shut ourselves into the limited intercourse, economic and intellectual, of our own local markets.

That radical farm movement, while it lasted, represented something else of significance in our Canadian experience. It was an outburst of local populist democracy, a rising up of the common people at the grass roots, who were refusing to accept the leadership that had hitherto provided both the ideology and the practical politics for our country. In our equalitarian North American society these outbursts of populist democracy, protesting against a central authority in the hands of the Top People of the Establishment, are endemic. They are healthy because they provide a popular balance against too much authority in the hands of an oligarchy at the centre. But in the complicated technology of modern society, populist democracy by itself is not enough. We need the guidance at the top of specialists, trained administrators, experts in economics, to our young people. This is a national interest that we all have in common; in the conditions of the second half of the twentieth century, our rigid division of powers in which we insist that education is a function belonging entirely to the provinces is self-defeating. In a world economy in which all groups are becoming daily more interdependent for their economic health and prosperity, we need a strong, well-equipped national government to direct and supervise the growth of our economy as a whole in its relations with the world as a whole. In a world divided as ours is into two great political blocs competing for power and for the minds of men, we need a strong national government to advance our conceptions of what constitutes the good society and to work in concert with like-minded governments. There is a great constructive role to be played in the Atlantic alliance by a power such as Canada, if we have a government equal to playing that role. And within our own domestic society, as we become a more and more industrialized and urbanized people, we need an active national government to deal with these new problems of urban civilization.

Yet it is at this time, confronted as we are by opportunities and dangers so momentous, that our ambitious provincial governments are doing their best to erode the basis of national authority and to add to their own importance and prestige. The assignment of greater responsibilities and greater financial resources to the provincial governments is, of course, in the interest of the provincial politicians and bureaucrats. I can see no evidence that it is necessarily in the interest of the people of the provinces who are also citizens and taxpayers of the Canadian national state.

* * *

In these circumstances, the case of Quebec presents us with a very difficult situation. That we should agree to the demands of the French-Canadians for equality of the French language in the sphere of the federal administration seems inevitable. That the English-speaking provinces should make concessions in the matter of language rights to the French minorities within their boundaries seems reasonable, though the extent of these concessions is debatable. But the Quebec conception of the future nature of our federal structure is another thing.

Quebec, through its premier, demands complete, exclusive control of all the new social services that have developed since Confederation and that—since they were not dreamt of by the Fathers in 1867

—have been assigned by the Privy Council to the provinces. But, while the B.N.A. Act is to be sacrosanct in the fullest interpretation that can be given to it of provincial rights, it is to be of little account in what it says of federal jurisdiction. For Quebec, so it appears, must also be consulted about federal monetary and fiscal policies, about tariffs, even apparently about some aspects of international policy. One wonders how the Quebec premier will find time both to run his own province and to keep the federal prime minister properly advised on how to run the Dominion. One wonders also what financial resources will be left to the Dominion after the claims of Quebec and the other provinces have been satisfied. To go to such lengths as this in the fragmentation of national unity seems a strange, fantastic way of celebrating the centenary of Confederation.

One can sympathize with the passion of French-Canadian leaders for recovering the control of their province from the English-Canadian and American big-business corporations who have come to dominate its economic life. But it must be pointed out also that no little local communities, whether they call themselves nations or not, can achieve full autonomy in this contemporary world of economic interdependence except at the price of seclusion and poverty. Though she is emancipating herself from clerical control, there still seem to be rather too many lay priests among the Quebec intellectuals who are giving the lead in the quiet revolution of their province—with an occasional lay bishop. And they still exhibit rather too much of the dogmatism, inflexibility, and fervour for isolation, that marked those former clerical prophets, Bishops Bourget and Laflèche.

One senses, also, as one reads them, that these intellectuals are suffering from that last infirmity of noble minds, the dream of a community in which intellectuals will function as Platonic philosopher-kings. Alas, intellectuals are always compelled, sooner or later, to wake up from this dream and to discover that the real kings are hard-boiled, practical administrators. It will not matter much whether these managers are at the head of socialist institutions in Quebec or not. They will be very much like the managers who run our English-Canadian, private-enterprise corporations. "There is more in common between two managers, one of whom is a socialist, than there is between two socialists, one of whom is a manager."

* * *

Let me go on to the question of the relations between Canada, Britain, and the United States.

Have we English-Canadians emancipated ourselves sufficiently from our old worship of Britain? It is obvious that most of the sentimental appeal that the Commonwealth has had for us has now degenerated into the ritual of after-dinner oratory. An Englishman[2] a short time ago referred to the Commonwealth in these terms: "As a stimulant nothing could be flabbier than the Commonwealth, that sop to our self-esteem, that dim intermittent vision of universal niceness." The British have, of course, been under the temptation to exalt the significance of the Commonwealth in world affairs in order to hide from themselves their own loss of the position of a great world power. But when Commonwealth ministers now try in conference to do something more specific than to summon up this vision of universal niceness, they usually find that they disagree and cannot reach a common policy.

To Canadians, the Commonwealth has always meant primarily our connection with Great Britain. This has fulfilled a necessary function for us, because, in the North Atlantic Triangle, Britain acted as a counterweight at one corner against the weight of the United States at another. We still need such a counterweight if we are to escape the necessity of confronting the United States all alone by ourselves here in North America. But Britain has no longer the power nor the economic capacity to provide that counterweight. It can only be provided by a strong united Western Europe of which Britain is an active and influential part. The failure of the rather half-hearted British attempt to enter the West European union was a major defeat for Canadian interests. We should have been much more vigorous in pushing Britain into Europe rather than in holding her back, whatever immediate short-term losses our trade might have suffered.

Of course, for the moment, this Atlantic Community, which I am holding up as an object of Canadian policy, has sunk to be almost as much a theme for pious incantation as is the British Commonwealth. President Kennedy's Grand Design was meeting with frustration before his death, both in the European foreign offices and the Congress of his own country. But this does not alter the fact that the Atlantic Community should be the grand design of Canadian policy also.

In the long run, this is the only way in which we shall be able

to free ourselves from all our present neurotic anxiety as to whether
we are capable of achieving a distinctive Canadian identity here on
the North American continent. We need some constructive activity
to take us out of ourselves and to save us from degenerating into
the gloomy, bad-tempered Ulster of North America, forever brooding hysterically on the dangers of absorption by the more numerous
and more lively people to the south of us. If we were playing a
part in a vigorous and progressive Atlantic community, we would
not be so obsessed by doubts as to our ability to continue to play
an independent, self-respecting part in North America.

For we are inescapably North Americans. In the long run our
Canadian civilization will be a North American one. It is foolish
to hope for anything else. If we are eventually to satisfy ourselves
that we have at last achieved a Canadian identity, it will be only
when we are satisfied that we have arrived at a better American
way of life than the Americans have. A better *American* way of
life, not just a better way of life. Whether we have the capacity
to reach that goal, nobody knows. Of course, we cannot produce
such big business corporations and corporation managers as the
American ones. Probably we cannot produce such big racketeers.
We cannot produce such big universities or research laboratories or
advertising agencies or entertainment industries. But we simply do
not know in what fields we may be able to reach better forms of
North American excellence, because we have not yet really tried.

* * *

This brings me to my last point. In the present circumstances, with
our minds intent upon the commemoration of the first century of
our Confederation, we are liable to become too self-centred. An
inward-looking, self-centred nationalism is a dangerous thing. There
are too many such nationalisms rampant in the world at present.
So far as one can see, the nation-state is going to continue to be the
unit in which peoples naturally group themselves. It will be through
his membership in his national group that the individual will
achieve his own personal identity. But the sovereign, autonomous,
separatist nation-state is now obsolescent, and the nationalist faith
of the nineteenth century needs to be expanded and transformed
into something wider.

In 1867, our Fathers created something new, "a new nationality."
The best way in which we can commemorate their work is not by

breaking up what they did but by going forward ourselves to create something new, some wider, international, transnational community, which will unite us more closely with other peoples. At any rate, let us try to make our Confederation a community that is outward- rather than inward-looking, a community that is ambitious to play a worthy part in the world at large.

Our American neighbours, since the tragedy in Dallas, have been going through a crisis of conscience. They are being led to confess to themselves that the assassination of President Kennedy was, only too clearly, the ultimate manifestation of the violence that has never been far from the surface in their national life, and that has erupted too frequently of late in the displays of hatred and bitterness between segregationists and integrationists, between rightists and leftists, between isolationists and internationalists. The more thoughtful of them have been speculating whether this most recent outburst of violence may produce a catharsis in their national life.

We Canadians are largely free from the violence and extremism in action that have marked the American experience. But we have been indulging of late in far too much extreme language to express the differences of opinion among the various groups who make up our Canadian community. And this extreme language has led us into a defeatist attitude of doubt as to whether the bonds that hold us together have any longer the old strength. As we approach 1967, it is time for us to turn our minds once again to the things that unite us as a people. A nation is a body of people who have done great things together in the past and who hope to do great things together in the future.

1. W. L. Morton, *The Kingdom of Canada*, Toronto, 1963, 443.

2. James Morris, *The Manchester Guardian Weekly*.

DONALD G. CREIGHTON

1902-

D. G. Creighton, historian and biographer was born in
Toronto and educated at the University of Toronto and at
Oxford. He was a member of the Department of History at
Toronto from 1927 until his retirement in the 1960's, and was
appointed chairman in 1945. He was elected to the Royal
Society of Canada in 1946 and given the Tyrrell Medal for
history in 1951.

Creighton's *Commercial Empire of the St. Lawrence*, 1760-
1850 (1937, revised 1956) is an epoch-making work, which has
profoundly influenced the study of Canadian history. It is
written with a distinction of style that makes it a work of
literary art as well as a contribution to scholarship. This judgment applies as well to Creighton's concentrated one-volume
history of Canada, *Dominion of the North* (1944, revised and
brought up to date 1958).

Creighton has written the definitive biography of Canada's
first prime minister, the two-volume work *Sir John A.
Macdonald*: Vol. 1 *The Young Politician* (1952) and Vol. 2
The Old Chieftain (1955) and a brilliant study of his colleague
and in some respects master, *Harold Adams Innis: Portrait of
a Scholar* (1957).

Creighton's work on Sir John A. Macdonald bore fruit
also in a valuable study published in 1964, *The Road to
Confederation*, which was followed in 1970 by a somewhat pessimistic summing up of Canadian history and the future pros-
pects of the Dominion in *Canada's First Century, 1867-1967*.

FROM *The Commercial Empire of the St. Lawrence,*
1760–1850, 1937

THE ECONOMY OF THE NORTH

I

When, in the course of a September day in 1759, the British made
themselves the real masters of the rock of Quebec, an event of apparently unique importance occurred in the history of Canada.
There followed rapidly the collapse of French power in North
America and the transference of the sovereignty of Canada to Great
Britain; and these acts in the history of the northern half of the continent may well appear decisive and definitive above all others. In
fact, for France and England, the crisis of 1759 and 1760 was a climax
of conclusive finality. But colonial America, as well as imperial
Europe, had been deeply concerned in the long struggle in the new
continent; and for colonial America the conquest of New France had
another and a more uncertain meaning. For Europe the conquest
was the conclusion of a drama; for America it was merely the curtain
of an act. On the one hand, it meant the final retirement of France
from the politics of northern North America; on the other, it meant
the regrouping of Americans and the reorganization of American
economies.

The conquest had a double significance, American and European,
because the struggle in North America had not been one war, but
two. It was a part of the history of both the old world and the new.
In its more obvious and more imposing aspect, it was an extension of
that war between France and England which filled the century from
the Revolution of 1688 to the Peace of Paris in 1763. North America
was merely one theatre in a world conflict, a struggle between imperial giants, which invaded the extremes of east and west; and this
conflict appeared, in America, as in every other continent which it
visited, to dominate the lives and to decide the destinies of lesser
men. Its shocks and pauses both stimulated effort and imposed quiet
on the seigniories of the St. Lawrence and the towns of New England. And when the war was won by the capture of Montreal and

concluded by the Peace of Paris, it might well have seemed that the struggle in North America was over for ever.

Yet concealed within this majestic imperial drama was a sub-plot, a conflict between the first Americans in America. And for them this secondary drama was the more prolonged and therefore the more important of the two. Two colonial societies, rooted in two different American landscapes, had come into existence on the continent; and while one was scattered sparingly along the giant system of the St. Lawrence and the lakes, the other, more compact and populous, had grown up on the Atlantic seaboard. These two societies differed from each other, and among the differences which distinguished them were some which had been imported from Europe. Fundamentally, the civilization of each society in North America is the civilization of Europe. An inward necessity, instinctive and compelling, had driven the immigrants to preserve the mysterious accumulations of their cultural heritage; and the price they were forced to pay for its preservation should not entirely obscure the extent of their success. Undoubtedly, these two societies, one almost exclusively French and the other predominantly English, were differentiated by race, language, laws and religion. The distinctions which had been inherited from the old world lived on in the new with an almost inextinguishable vitality; and undoubtedly they helped to foster and to prolong the rivalries between the first Americans.

But the society of the St. Lawrence and the society of the Atlantic seaboard were divided by something else, which was perhaps more fundamental and which was purely American. It was, in fact, the continent of North America itself. Immediately these migrants had to come to terms with the new continent. From it they had to wrest a living; and since they were Europeans and not Indians, a living meant not merely the food to sustain life but the amenities of West-European civilization which alone could make it tolerable. They had to find means to produce their own necessities and to pay for their imports from Europe. They had to live in and by the new world; and they were driven, by this double compulsion, to understand the possibilities of the new continent and to exploit its resources. They could escape neither the brutal dictates nor the irresistible seductions of North American geography; and in an undeveloped world the pressure of these prime phenomena was enormous and insistent. Each society, after long trial and recurrent error, had read the meaning of its own environment, accepted its ineluctable compulsions and prepared to monopolize its promises. And each, in the process of this prolonged and painful adjustment, had acquired an American character, a purpose and a destiny in America.

II

Chance flung the first English colonists on the edges of the Atlantic seaboard and opened the single great eastern waterway of the interior to the French. In the history of the different economies, of the cultural patterns which were to dominate North American life, these were acts of first importance. For each cultural group, the English and the French, fell heir to one of America's geographic provinces, and both these regions had their laws, their promises and their portentous meanings. Of the two, the Atlantic seaboard conformed more nearly to the geographic conditions of western Europe, which had been for centuries a forcing-house of nations. It was, for North America, a fairly small and compact area, sharply defined by obvious natural frontiers. From the coastline the land stretched westward to rise at last in the ridges of the Appalachians, which were unbroken from the St. Lawrence valley to the Floridas, save where the Hudson-Mohawk system gave access to the west. It was a boundary; but during colonial times it was not a barrier in the sense that it confined a restless and ambitious people determined upon its assault. Because they shaped the courses of the rivers, the mountains helped to focus the attention of the English-Americans upon that other boundary of the Atlantic seaboard, the ocean. Their faces were turned east rather than west; and during the greater part of the colonial period, the commercial energies of the population were concentrated in the numerous short rivers, in the bays and sounds and harbours which fretted the coastline, and sought their objectives eastward on the sea. For New England especially, whose economy was based upon its fisheries, the pull of the coastline and the submerged continental shelf beyond it, was enormous. The prohibitions, the invitations and the varieties of this seaboard empire directed, in a kindly fashion, the energies of an adaptive people. While the land configuration concentrated their pursuits, the climate and soil gave them variety. The area meant stolidity, gradual settlement, the inescapable necessity to produce and the possibility of diversified production. Seaward, it meant a commercial empire which would cease to be imperial because it would inevitably become oceanic.

The river up which Cartier ventured gave entrance to the totally different dominion of the north. It was a landscape marked off from the other geographic provinces of the new continent by the almost monotonously massive character of its design. A huge triangle of rocky upland lay bounded by a river and a string of giant lakes. It was a solemn country, with that ungainly splendour evoked by great, crude, sweeping lines and immense and clumsy masses. The marks of age and of terrific experience lay heavy upon it. It was an elemental portion of the earth, harshly shaped by the brutal catastrophes of geological history. The enormous flat bulk of the Precambrian formation was not only the core of the whole Canadian system, but it was also the ancient nucleus of the entire continent. It lay, old and sombre and ravaged, nearly two million square miles in extent. The ice masses, during the glacial period, had passed over and beyond it, and they had scarred and wrenched and altered the entire landscape in their advance and their retreat. Scouring the surface of the Shield itself, pouring boulder clay into the valleys to the south, the ice sheets had hollowed the beds of new lakes and had diverted the courses of ancient rivers. There was left a drainage system, grand in its extent and in the volume of its waters, but youthful, wilful and turbulent. The wrinkled senility of the Precambrian formation was touched by a curious appearance of youth. The countless meaningless lakes and lakelets, the intricately meandering rivers and spillways, the abrupt falls and treacherous rapids, which covered the face of the Shield, seemed to express the renewal of its primitive strength. To the south, below the Shield, the ice masses had throttled the waters into new lakes and had dammed the St. Lawrence into a long southern loop, leaving Niagara, the Long Sault and Lachine as evidence of the novelty of its course.

The Canadian Shield and the river system which seamed and which encircled it, were overwhelmingly the most important physical features of the area. They were the bone and the bloodtide of the northern economy. Rock and water complemented each other, fought each other's battles and forced each other's victories. The Shield itself, a huge lop-sided triangle, whose northern points were Labrador and the Arctic east of the Mackenzie, occupied over one-half of the land area which was to become the Dominion of Canada. For the French and for their successors it was unescapable and domineering. It hugged the north shore of the St. Lawrence as the river issued from the continent. Westward, in the centre of the lowlands of the St. Lawrence, the good lands began to peter out a hundred miles north of Lake Ontario in the scarred, blank rock, thin soil sheet and towering evergreens peculiar to the Shield. Relentlessly it followed the north shore of Lakes Huron and Superior and at last struck north and west for the Arctic Ocean. Its long, flat, undeviating plateau effected the complete severance of the St. Lawrence lowlands from the western plains. In the east it helped, with the northern spurs of the Appalachians, to cut off Acadia from Quebec. Settlement starved and shrivelled on the Shield; it offered a sullen inhospitality to those occupations which were traditional in western Europe and which had been transferred by the first immigrants to the Atlantic seaboard of North America. But from the beginning it exercised an imperious domination over the northerners, for though it was a harsh and an exacting country, it offered lavish prizes to the restless, the ambitious and the daring. It was an area of staples, creating simple trades and undiversified extractive industries; and its furs, its forests and its minerals were to attract three great assaulting waves of northerners. Fur was the first great staple of the north. And with the fur trade, the Precambrian formation began its long career in the Canadian economy as a primary, instead of as a subsidiary, economic region. It was upon these ancient rocks that the central emphasis of the Canadian system was placed at first, and the initial importance of the Shield is of deep significance in the history of the economy of the north.

To the south lay the lowlands of the St. Lawrence. Here the intense winters of the Precambrian formation were softened and the hot, bright summers flamed more slowly out of long springtimes and faded gradually into reluctant autumns. North of the lakes, the lowlands stretched from Quebec city to Georgian Bay—a narrow but slowly broadening band of fertility, crowded a little oppressively by the sombre masses of the Shield. South and west, beyond the river and the lakes, they lapsed easily into the central lowlands of the continent and the basin of the Mississippi. In the centre of this rich region lay that immense organization of waters which issued from the continent by the river of Canada; and this drainage system, driving seaward in a great, proud arc from Lake Superior to the city of Quebec, was the fact of all facts in the history of the northern half of the continent. It commanded an imperial domain. Westward, its acquisitive fingers groped into the territory of the plains. Aggressively it entrenched upon the dominion of the Mississippi. It grasped

the Shield, reached southward into the valley of the Hudson and at
last rolled massively seaward between sombre approaches which
curved away southward into the Maritimes and rose north-eastward
past Quebec and Labrador to Newfoundland.

It was the one great river which led from the eastern shore into
the heart of the continent. It possessed a geographical monopoly; and
it shouted its uniqueness to adventurers. The river meant mobility
and distance; it invited journeyings; it promised immense expanses,
unfolding, flowing away into remote and changing horizons. The
whole west, with all its riches, was the dominion of the river. To the
unfettered and ambitious, it offered a pathway to the central mysteries of the continent. The river meant movement, transport, a ceaseless passage west and east, the long procession of river-craft—canoes,
bateaux, timber rafts and steamboats—which followed each other
into history. It seemed the destined pathway of North American
trade; and from the river there rose, like an exhalation, the dream
of western commercial empire. The river was to be the basis of a
great transportation system by which the manufactures of the old
world could be exchanged for the staple products of the new. This
was the faith of successive generations of northerners. The dream
of the commercial empire of the St. Lawrence runs like an obsession
through the whole of Canadian history; and men followed each other
through life, planning and toiling to achieve it. The river was not
only a great actuality: it was the central truth of a religion. Men
lived by it, at once consoled and inspired by its promises, its whispered suggestions, and its shouted commands; and it was a force in
history, not merely because of its accomplishments, but because of its
shining, ever-receding possibilities.

For something stood between the design and its fulfilment. There
was, in the very geography of the region itself, a root defect, a fundamental weakness, which foreshadowed enormous difficulties, even
though it did not pre-determine defeat. In the centre, by Lake
Ontario and the lower reaches of the river, the drive of the great
waterway was unquestioned and peremptory. But this power was not
indefinitely transmissible, and the pull of a system stretching over
two thousand miles was at long last relaxed and weakened. The
outer defences of the St. Lawrence contradicted its inward solidity;
its boundaries were not bold and definite, but a smudged faint
tracery. Between the valley of the St. Lawrence on the one hand and
the valleys of Hudson Bay, the Mississippi and the Hudson river on

the other, the separating heights of land were low and facile; and over these perfunctory defences invasions might pass as easily as sorties.[1] The river's continuity was broken at Niagara: it stumbled and faltered at the Cascades, the Cedars and Lachine. As it drove east and north past Quebec and into its immense estuary, the river was caught, its influence narrowed and focused by the uplands of the Shield to the north and the rolling highlands of the Appalachians below. There were breaks and obstacles; and over both its seaward approaches and its continental extremities the hold of the river closed and again relaxed, uncertainly and unconvincingly. Yet for all its inward contradictions and its outward weakness, the river was a unit, and its central entrance was dominated by the rock of Quebec and the island of Montreal.

III

Each of these two geographic provinces was a matrix in which a distinct American economy was crudely fashioned. The boundaries of these rival economies were coextensive with the limits of two conflicting political dominions and two antipathetic social groups. It was certain that man, with his political capacities and economic resources, would modify the crude stamp of the geographical matrix; and it was equally certain that the geographical matrix itself would alter slightly under the force of human ingenuity and effort. Yet, in the first simplicity of early settlement, the pressure of geography bore with continuous persistence upon an unprotected people; and a brutal necessity drove the first Americans to come to terms with the landscape they had inherited. To exist as men, to live as West Europeans, they must immediately read the meanings of their respective empires, capitalize their obvious resources, fulfil their manifest destinies. The riddle of all migratory peoples confronted them; they must tie together the cut threads of their material and spiritual history, they must weave a new pattern of existence out of the stuffs of their new homeland and of the old world of Europe. It was a gigantic task; and in their deep need and desperate hurry, they turned naturally to the most immediate and most easily obtainable of their resources. What the continent flaunted, they took; they could not be made to seek what it seemingly withheld. Their economies grew naturally, organically out of the very earth of the new world. It was not the sage wisdom of European statesmen which determined their

development, but the brute facts of North American life. And the
character and development of these two economies were to affect
decisively not only their separate relations with the old world, but
their mutual relations in the new.

In the region of the Atlantic seaboard, which by the end of the
first half-century of settlement the English had acquired for their
own, there developed a richly diversified way of life. The area invited a varied agricultural production; it encouraged, on the sea, a
complex cunningly adjusted and truly oceanic trade. From the stubborn soil and stern north temperate climate of New England, the
coastal plain broadened out into the more fertile amplitudes of the
middle colonies and passed southward into the lush richness of a
region warmed by hot skies and watered by innumerable rivers and
creeks. The sub-tropical products, tobacco, rice and cotton, were
added to the homely, traditional roots and fruits and cereals of
western Europe. But everywhere production called for husbandry,
settlement, the consistent effort of a population established on the
land; and, as the hewn forests receded westward, the life of the
ploughed countryside collected in little villages and became concentrated in towns. There was great vitality in this economy, but its
development was conditioned by certain definite limitations. For
the great majority of these migrants trade was inevitably oceanic and
not continental. They were granted a hundred outlets to the sea; but
they were denied the single great eastern entrance to the continent.
What they wanted from the Indians, the inhabitants of the interior,
was chiefly land, not goods; and beyond the established settlements
there extended, not a vast spectacular commercial empire, but a
narrow, laborious land frontier. The rivers broke and dwindled, the
forests and the hills closed in upon this agricultural community; but
eastward, in generous compensation, were the inviting expanses of
the sea. It was a wide horizon, bounded by the old world of England,
France, Spain and Portugal, and by the new world of Newfoundland, Africa and the Indies; and across these expanses the colonial
merchants drew, not a few direct and simple trade lines, but an increasingly intricate network of commercial communications. Neither
they nor the English could prevent it. The abstractions of the mer-
cantile system could not link the colonies and the motherland com-
mercially when the practical needs of Englishmen and Americans did
not necessitate a close commercial relationship. The trade of the
Atlantic seaboard was not to be carried on over commercial trunk-

lines which crossed the ocean undeviatingly to converge upon England. The paths of American commerce radiated over the Atlantic and no mercantilist wisdom could focus them in London.

This commerce, which in part competed with the interests of Great Britain, expanded continuously during the colonial period. Newfoundland, England, southern Europe, Africa and the West Indies were all drawn into the widening circle of American trade. Back of this expansion was the commercial energy of Philadelphia and New England; and back of New England were the resources of the forest and the cod from the "silver mines of the Atlantic." In the north, that eastern pull to which the whole of the seaboard was subject, the pull of the coast and the submerged continental shelf, was irresistible; and the hoard which the fishermen of Marblehead, Gloucester, Plymouth, Salem and Ipswich drew yearly from the banks and shoals and ledges stretching northward from Cape Cod, paid the way of the Americans around the ports of the Atlantic. The fishing industry enhanced the value and quickened the development of the subsidiary industries of the North Atlantic coast—lumbering, ship-building, distilling and the provision business.[2] Under the rapid and magically repeated transmutations of commerce, cod became molasses, molasses rum, and rum turned into furs and manufactures and gold and slaves. The strangely varied component parts of this system were deftly combined into a great integration. It had toughness, elasticity and expansive powers. American trade burst through the imperial system to become international. The slaves which the New Englanders bought on the Guinea coast and sold to the planter plutocrats of Jamaica and Barbados, fulfilled the beneficent dual function of consuming inferior New England fish and of producing molasses for active New England distilleries. At last this southern trade, geared to increasing speed and capable of greater volume, broke into the French West India islands of Martinique and Guadeloupe.[3]

On the continent, expansion paralleled and complemented expansion by the sea. Settlement, in search of closer bases for the ever-expanding fishery, felt its way instinctively and surely from New England up the coast to Acadia, which thus began to play its complicated role as an outpost of both the St. Lawrence and the north Atlantic seaboard.[4] Trade worked more deeply inland, for though Anglo-American commerce was chiefly eastern and oceanic, there had always been an outlet to the west. This was the Hudson river, a

stream of deep significance in North American history, which alone
of all the rivers of the coastal plain threw off the hold of the Appalachians and alone pierced the inner defences of the St. Lawrence. It
became the pathway of both military and commercial aggression.
The easy route by Lake Champlain and the Richelieu led into the
political centre of the St. Lawrence system; the Hudson, the
Mohawk and Lake Ontario gave entrance to the western commercial
empire of the French. Rum, made by New England distilleries out
of molasses paid for by New England fish, English manufactures,
guns, powder, kettles and cheap cloth, enabled both Dutch and
English merchants to compete effectively in an area which the
French regarded as their own preserve.[5] In Albany, Schenectady,
Oswego and the distant interior, was felt the final pressure of the
first great synthesis of industry and commerce created on the Atlantic
seaboard.

The economy of the north was in utter contrast with the industrial
and commercial organization of the Atlantic seaboard. In the north,
geography directed the activities of men with a blunt sternness; and
it had largely helped to create a distinct and special American system. The lower St. Lawrence was for the French, as it is for the
Canadians of today, the destined focus of any conceivable northern
economy; and in response to an invitation which was at least half a
command, settlement became inevitably concentrated on the strip of
territory between Quebec and Montreal. Here were the lowlands of
the St. Lawrence; but the restricted area drew men for other reasons
than for its fertile land, and northern commerce was not to be built
up upon a solid foundation of agricultural production. The river and
the Shield, which seemed physically to overawe the valley with their
force and mass, reduced the lowlands to a position of secondary
economic importance. It was the final trunk-line of the western commercial system driving past Quebec and Montreal, which gave the
rock and the river city their initial economic importance.

Agriculture struggled with an ineffectual persistence against the
lures of the fur trade; and French officialdom, from Colbert on, tried
to preserve settlement and farming from the too damaging encroachments of expansion and commerce.[6] But the first important
Canadian market and the first source of Canadian staples for export
lay, not in the lowlands, but in the west. Settlement, encouraged
rather by the fitful favour of French policy than by the inner necessities of commercial Canada, huddled close to the lower reaches of

the St. Lawrence or ventured timidly down the Richelieu. There it stuck. The seigniory of Beaupré became the eastern limit of continuous settlement and the manor of New Longueuil was to be its outpost on the west: beyond this, east and west, there were only tiny communities and around them the forest and scarred upland closed with appalling abruptness. Population, in a country where mere numbers were unneeded and unwanted, increased slowly; and at the conquest there were but a scant sixty-five thousand French Canadians while the English in the Thirteen Colonies numbered perhaps a million and a half. Unlike the Anglo-American farmers, the peasants of the St. Lawrence valley produced food-stuffs not for export but for subsistence; and right up to the conquest there were years when they could not subsist upon what they had produced.[7] The efforts of Talon and his successors to build up a diversified industrial system and to develop a trade in wheat and provisions were fated to be fruitless.

The trend of expansion from the St. Lawrence valley was towards the west; and the commercial empire of the north, in sharp contrast with that of the Atlantic seaboard, was inland and not oceanic. The St. Lawrence was incapable of playing an effective role in the task of building a vigorous union out of the maritime and continental colonies which had been established by the French. On the map, the number and the variety of these possessions were impressive. In the West Indies, the French held Guadeloupe, Martinique, St. Christopher and Tortuga—tropical islands which produced sugar and molasses. In the north, in that region bounded by Newfoundland, the Gulf of St. Lawrence and Acadia, where political dominion would be determined largely by mastery in the catch of fish, the French established little settlements in Gaspé and Acadia, at Isle St. Jean, Cape Breton and Placentia. These two groups of colonies— the sugar-producing and fish-producing settlements—together with the fur-producing colony of the St. Lawrence, made up the western dominion of the French. Puny and disconnected, they lay raggedly across the face of the new world; and the problem of uniting them in a robust integration despite the opposition of England and New England—of linking the St. Lawrence, the Maritimes and the West Indies together and with continental France—exhausted the strength and ingenuity of Frenchmen.

The New Englanders shouldered their way into the markets of the French West Indies. To the north, the French fishing settlements were overshadowed by Newfoundland which was growing with painful slowness as an outpost of the English fishery; and to the south, England's temporary ally, New England, flung the accumulating strength of its variously nourished economy into the fight for fishing grounds and markets. For over half the year, the connection between Canada and the French Atlantic colonies was broken by the ice barrier in the St. Lawrence; and the proximity of Acadia enabled New England to usurp the economic control of the maritime region. The French lost Acadia by the Treaty of Utrecht: and although within the restricted area of Gaspé, Isle St. Jean and Cape Breton they prolonged their resistance sufficiently to prove that the final fate of the fisheries region was uncertain, they failed either to make their maritime colonies self-sufficient or to link them effectively with the St. Lawrence and the islands to the south. France itself was incapable of exerting the inward pull which would draw these feeble and scattered American communities together. She could not compete effectively with England in the production of rough staple manufactures for colonial consumption; and, while she could take the furs and fish of America, she could not assist her north temperate colonies in supplying an adequate market for the produce of the French sugar islands. The lower St. Lawrence valley was the best possible centre of an integrated American economy of the French; but the St. Lawrence failed almost completely to emulate the example of New England and to offer independent co-operation to the motherland. The frozen river enforced the periodic isolation of Canada; and the colony was beset by the limitations and weaknesses of population, industry and commerce, which were inevitably inherent in a society based upon the river, the Shield and its furs. All this stunted the seaward expansion of the St. Lawrence;[8] and Cape Breton depended for its existence and the French West Indies for their prosperity upon the commercial strength of New England and not of New France.

The St. Lawrence lacked energy in those very spheres where the vitality of the seaboard was abundant and insistent. The lower valley of the river was not the source of the chief Canadian export; nor was it the base of a complex oceanic trade. Canadian expansion drove impulsively westward, along the rivers and into the interior. The energy and initiative which lay dormant in the lowlands grew exuberantly in the western wilderness of rock and water and forest. Radisson, La Salle, La Vérendrye and the other heroes of exploration stand out from the ruck of men who passed westward along the waterways and unremembered out of life because in them the common compulsion troubling a whole society became the intense, solitary excitement of genius. It was trade which drew them all; for the Shield and its outlying fringes gave up the first and simplest of the Canadian staple products, beaver fur. Furs, a product of the Shield, obtainable by the river system of transportation, weighted the already heavy emphasis of the Precambrian formation and the St. Lawrence. Furs impelled the northerners to win that western commercial empire which the river seemed to offer to the daring. The expansion of the French was the penetration, not the occupation, of the west; it meant travel not home-building, and commerce not agriculture. And the future Upper Canada, the first great granary of the north, which was scarcely touched by French settlement, was passed and distanced by French trade.

Thus the society which grew up in the northern geographic province instinctively created that form of endeavour which was to dominate Canadian life until the conquest and for nearly a century thereafter. This was the northern commercial system, of which furs were the first staple; and the fur-trading organization of the French was the elementary expression of the major architectural style of Canadian business life. It was a distinct North American system, peculiar to Canada, with the immensity and simplicity which were characteristic of the landscape itself. From the ports of France, the northern commercial organization plunged in a single trunk-line across the Atlantic and up the river to Quebec and Montreal; but beyond the river city it spread out in increasing amplitude and with infinite ramifications over the enormous bulk of the Precambrian formation and over the central lowlands of the continent. This western territory, where the goods of Europe were exchanged for the goods of America, was the inland commercial empire of the St. Lawrence. The colony, weak in agriculture, weak in industry and seaward commerce, was tied in utter bondage to France; but it revenged this subordination in the east by its extravagantly ambitious pretensions in the hinterland of North America. The whole landscape annexed to the river of Canada, the lands which spread out north and south and westward of the Great Lakes were claimed and largely exploited by the commercial state which was centralized at Quebec and Montreal.

It seemed, in the first assertive youth of the northern society, as if the St. Lawrence might take possession of inland North America, as if the western edges of the continent would be the only limits of this vast, facile, unsubstantial commercial empire. The young fur-trading colony concentrated with passionate intentness upon the fulfilment of its own peculiar destiny. La Salle and La Vérendrye pressed south and westward to assert the ultimate claims of the northern system; and a long struggle began with those competitors who controlled the Hudson river and Hudson Bay, the two routes which rivalled the St. Lawrence as highways to the interior. It became at once the greatest ambition and the chief task of Canadians to enlarge the extent of their commercial dominion, to centralize it upon the lower reaches of the St. Lawrence and to protect it from the encroachments of rivals from the south and from the north.

The pressure of this system was enormous. The colony grew curiously—ungainly, misshapen, almost distorted—stamped by tasks and ambitions which were, on the whole, too great for it. The western commercial organization, which lasted as the dominant economic form for two centuries of Canadian history, rooted certain tendencies deeply in the society of the St. Lawrence: there were virtues and weaknesses, loyalties and antipathies which became fixed and almost ineradicable. It was western commerce which helped largely to determine the part which Canada would act in the affairs of European empires and the role which it would play in the politics of North America. A colony which scarcely rose above the level of feudal industry and which failed completely to develop a diversified trade, required a mature European metropolis both as a market and as a source of manufactures and supplies.[9] Canada continued acquiescent and loyal within the French empire, for it was tied by every basic interest to the motherland. But while the northern commercial system inclined Canadian statesmen and merchants to passivity within the empire, it drove them to competition and conflict upon the North American continent. Their subserviency in the east was complemented by their aggressiveness in the west. Because they desired it as a commercial monopoly, the Canadians struggled to make the entire empire of the St. Lawrence a political unit. They sought to break the commercial competition of Hudson Bay and the Hudson river and to restrict the expansion of the Atlantic seaboard; for the bay and the river threatened to partition the western monopoly, and the march of settlement from the Atlantic seaboard involved the annihilation of the fur trade through the destruction of the hunting races. North and south of the St. Lawrence, Canada discovered its inevitable enemies; but in the centre of the continent, among the Indians, it found its natural allies. The primitive culture of the hunting Indians was essential to the fur-trading state;[10] and the fur-trading state would alone preserve the Indians from extinction. It was more than an alliance: it was a political union. It was even a strange amalgam of two widely different cultures. The commercial system threaded through the native culture of the continent in tiny, intricate ramifications, changing it, debasing it, but effectively prolonging its existence. The Indians, giving up to the new westerners the fruits of their experience, the cunning adjustments of their heritage, and something of their proud, passionate independence, helped, in their turn, to create that curious western world of halftones, that blent society where Europe and America met and mingled.

It was western trade, moreover, which largely determined the style of Canadian politics. Transcontinentalism, the westward drive of corporations encouraged and followed by the supercorporation of the state, is the major theme in Canadian political life; and it was stated, in its first simplicity, by the fur trade. The trade enforced commitments and determined policies. The state was based upon it: it was anterior to the state. Until 1663 Canada was governed by a series of trading corporations; then it became a commercial and military state. Colonial government derived its strength from taxes paid directly or indirectly by the western trade; and that strength was expended in an effort to extend the dominion of the fur trade and to protect it from competition. From the first, the government was committed to the programme of western exploitation by the river system. The St. Lawrence was an expensive monopoly; and its imperious demands could be met—and even then inadequately—only by the corporate effort of the northern society. The immense capital expenditures of the nineteenth and twentieth centuries were anticipated with startling clarity in the expensive military policy, the fortified posts, the presents to the Indians, by which Frontenac and his successors endeavoured to realize the destiny of the north.[11] Inevitably, the instinct of both politicians and business men was towards unity and centralization, both for the management and the support of this monstrous western machine. Strong, centralized government was, of course, imported from old France; but its continuance in the new world was encouraged, rather than opposed, by the northern commercial system.[12] It is true that the distant western trader, whether he was the employee or the debtor of a Montreal merchant, shouldered his aggressive individuality through an inevitably relaxed restraint. But the laxity which obtained on the frontiers of the system was abandoned as the river in its last concentration drove northeastward towards the sea. Here trade, its management and its final defences, were concentrated; and the twin cities, Quebec and Montreal, were the two symbols, military and commercial, of a single unified system.

IV

Two worlds lay over against each other in North America and their conflict was not only portable but certain. Between those who possessed and those who were denied the single great eastern entrance to the continent, the hostility of war could subside only into the competition of peace. With the whole pressure of its material and spiritual being, each society was impelled to maintain its separateness and to achieve its dominion. They contradicted each other, they crowded each other; and the wars and raids and surprises which fill the seventeenth and eighteenth centuries are but outward manifestations of a great, essential and slowly maturing conflict. When Dongan laboured to defy Montreal from Albany, when the British built Halifax to overawe Louisbourg, when Washington toiled westward against Fort Duquesne, they did not so much initiate clashes as reveal the points at which two ponderously moving systems would be forced into reverberating collision. Here were two geographic provinces occupied by culturally distinct peoples; here were two economies controlled by antagonistic national states. Of their essence, the St. Lawrence and the seaboard denied each other. Riverways against seaways, rock against farmland, trading posts against ports and towns and cities, *habitants* against farmers and fur traders against frontiersmen—they combined, geography and humanity, in one prime contradiction.

With the excuse and with the stimulation of the imperial wars, the conflict in North America developed on its own lines, created its own strategy and tactics and discovered its own battlefields. Along the arc which stretched from the Gulf of St. Lawrence to the Mississippi and wherever these two systems touched or threatened each other, the conflict flared or smouldered. The seaward extension of the St. Lawrence cut like a boulevard through the finest fishing grounds in the West European-American world; and the French, weak as they were in the region, were determined to keep the gulf, the islands and Acadia as the outposts of their inland, and as the citadels of their maritime, empire. From Newfoundland, which lay like "a great English ship moored near the Banks," the English fishery expanded competitively into the area. From the south, New England, with the strength of its fused industrial and commercial organization, developed its fishing interests and pushed its settlements into Acadia. A little westward of this, where the river flowed between the Appalachians and the Canadian Shield the St. Lawrence temporarily threw off the clutch of its competitors; and its inner strength was fittingly expressed in the lofty symbol of the fortress of Quebec. But almost immediately beyond this, the inroads of geography and humanity began again. The Hudson river by its two extensions, Lake Champlain and the Richelieu on the one hand and the Mohawk on the other, pierced through the easy outward defences of the St. Lawrence into the quick of the whole system. New York, backed by the industrial and commercial power of the North Atlantic seaboard, developed this natural highway with a chain of outposts from Albany past Schenectady to Oswego; and as middlemen the Iroquois extended competition throughout the west.

In the central lowlands of the continent, La Salle and those who followed him had established a counterfeit dominion. There was deception in the very grandeur of the Great Lakes. The country which spread out around them in such easy undulations was not a single geographic province: and the lakes crowded a territory which was unexpectedly narrow for them. A short way below the northern system, a low and almost indistinguishable height of land separated the waters of the Mississippi from those of the St. Lawrence. On the north, the rivers of James and Hudson Bay—the Rupert, the Moose, the Albany, and the Nelson—pressed dangerously close. Radisson and La Salle passed with easy confidence into territory which, even from a geographical point of view, was competitive; and time could only reveal more fully the enormous northern and southern pull of Hudson Bay and the Mississippi. The Hudson's Bay Company, backed by the great strength of commercial England, began to invade the north-western, fur-trading country of the French which centred at Lake Winnipeg. By the middle of the eighteenth century, land companies began the scramble for grants by the "western waters" of the Mississippi; and the first discontented pioneers from Virginia and Philadelphia began to mark out the trail that led by Cumberland Gap and the Wilderness Road to the Ohio.

At all these points, where the economy of the St. Lawrence clashed with the rival economies of North America, struggles necessarily arose. They were neither haphazard nor transitory, they were rooted in the continent; and they were to reveal an almost indestructible permanence in the future. The first inhabitants of North America did not create these prime contradictions: they discovered them. The vital quarrel in the new continent was not a mere extension of the political rivalries of Europe; it was not wholly a result of those cultural differences which had been imported from Europe by the first migrants. It was, in part, American, it was a product of North America. It was fought, not only by British and French regulars, but also by Americans—by explorers, seigneurs, fur traders and Indians, by fishermen, Boston apprentices, frontiersmen and Virginia planters. Never was this American conflict completely fused in the imperial war which overshadowed it: its beats and pulses could not be perfectly regulated by the timing of European wars and European diplomacy. To be sure, the naval and military strength of Europe helped to magnify these American disputes and European diplomacy marked the main stages in their evolution. But the tumult in the maritime region did not cease with the Peace of Utrecht and the conflict impending in the Ohio country was not prevented by the solemn affirmations of Aix-la-Chapelle. Irrepressibly, the struggle in North America developed in its own way, in response to its own inner urgencies; and, though Europe might enhance or weaken American forces, it could neither create nor destroy them.

The British conquest, therefore, while it made changes and portended others, did not alter certain fundamentals of Canadian life. The conquest did not end the rivalry between the economies of North America, for it could not. The French could be beaten in America; but the St. Lawrence could not surrender in Europe. The northern commercial system remained what it had been—a distinct and competitive American economy, strong enough, despite its undeniable weakness, to arouse jealousy and fear and to enforce a certain respect. The departure of one set of officials and the arrival of another could not change the main trend of its development. In a certain sense, the French were not really the builders of the northern commercial empire: they were its first owners, its first occupants. They read the meaning of the region, they evoked its spirit, and they first dreamed the dream which the river inspired in the minds of all who came to live upon its banks. What the French saw, what they did and what they failed to do formed an experience which had not merely a limited national significance: it was an astonishingly correct anticipation of the experience of successive generations of northerners. With the surrender of the transportation system of the St. Lawrence, there was passed on also to the victors the commercial philosophy based upon it. It was accepted without pause or question. The new northerners, who succeeded to the direction of the St. Lawrence after the conquest, diverged from the lines laid down by the French only in the attempt to repair their failures. They clung to the conquests of the French and they tried to recapture their concessions.

These facts were at first imperfectly understood. After the conquest of Canada, Great Britain held the whole of North America except the south-west sector—an empire which stretched unbrokenly from Labrador to Florida. The British imagined they could unify this empire and standardize its various parts. They tried, in 1763, to make Quebec a typical American colony in a unified continental dominion. But they were wrong: for Quebec was an unusual colony and it had no part or lot in the affairs of the Atlantic seaboard. It had its own organization and its own internal problems. It nursed a special ambition for the west of North America and it was bound by unusually strong ties to the metropolis in Europe. Thus the Peace of Paris and the subsequent efforts of the British to unify and standardize their American empire violated the logic of facts on the St. Lawrence as well as in other parts of the new continent. It is significant that the peace and the imperial reorganization were followed by twenty years of increasing tumult which culminated in the political division of the continent roughly upon the lines which the French had already established. The French and the British were both humbled in America; but through all the curious chances and reverses of the eighteenth century, the St. Lawrence managed to preserve its individuality and its separateness.

The conquest could not change Canada. In fact, in some ways, it strengthened the dominant impulse of Canadian life. It tied Canada to Great Britain, a commercial and maritime power far stronger than France; and it opened the St. Lawrence to the capital and enterprise of Britain and British America. To the defeated society of the north it brought fresh enthusiasm, a new strength and a different leadership. But this injection of new vigour, while it strengthened commercial Canada, necessarily raised the problem of assimilation. The conquest brought two groups of Americans, different even in terms of their Americanism, within the limits of a single colony; and it remained for the future to determine how long and how effectively they could co-operate in the struggle for the western trade. It was certain that the British Canadians would fight to realize the commercial empire of the St. Lawrence; but it was equally certain that they would be forced to fight in company with the Canadians of French descent.

1. M. I. Newbigin, *Canada, the Great River, the Lands and the Men*, London, 1926, 157–161; H. A. Innis, "Interrelations between the Fur Trade of Canada and the United States," *Mississippi Valley Historical Review*, xx, December, 1933, 321–332.

2. H. A. Innis, "An Introduction to the Economic History of the Maritimes," *Canadian Historical Association Report*, 1931, 89–90.

3. F. W. Pitman, *The Development of the British West Indies, 1700–1763*, New Haven, 1917.

4. J. B. Brebner, *New England's Outpost; Acadia before the Conquest of Canada*, New York, 1927; *The Neutral Yankees of Nova Scotia, a Marginal Colony during the Revolutionary Years*, New York, 1937.

5. H. Broshar, "The First Push Westward of the Albany Traders," *Mississippi Valley Historical Review*, vii, December, 1920, 228–241; A. H. Buffinton, "The Policy of Albany and English Westward Expansion," *ibid.*, viii, March, 1922, 327–366.

6. G. P. de T. Glazebrook, "Roads in New France and the Policy of Expansion," *Canadian Historical Association Report*, 1934, 48–56.

7. H. A. Innis, ed., *Select Documents in Canadian Economic History, 1497–1783*, Toronto, 1929, 367.

8. *ibid.*, 106, 113, 140.

9. H. A. Innis, *The Fur Trade in Canada, an Introduction to Canadian Economic History*, New Haven, 1930, 122–123.

10. *ibid.*, 393.

11. Innis, *Select Documents*, 429.

12. Innis, *The Fur Trade in Canada*, 117.

E. K. BROWN

1905-1951

Edward Killoran Brown published in 1943 the first study of
Canadian poetry from a modern critical standpoint. This book
established with A. J. M. Smith's *Book of Canadian Poetry*,
published in the same year, the now orthodox view of the
historical development of Canadian poetry. The book, however, is not limited to poetry but discusses the problem of
identity and originality in our literature generally. Especially
valuable is the analysis of the debilitating effects of the colonial
attitude of mind found in the chapter from the book that
follows below. Brown was a scholarly critic whose writings
were concerned with British and American literature as well
as Canadian. His other writings include *Matthew Arnold: a
Study in Conflict* (1948), *Rhythm in the Novel* (1950), and
Willa Cather, a Critical Biography (completed after his death
by his friend Leon Edel and published in 1953).

Professor Brown was educated at the Universities of Toronto
and Paris and taught English at the Universities of Toronto,
Manitoba, Cornell, and Chicago. He was editor of the *University of Toronto Quarterly* (1932-1941) and the first editor
of the annual survey of English and French Canadian writing
"Letters in Canada" which is still a valuable feature of *UTQ*.

THE PROBLEM OF A CANADIAN LITERATURE

THERE is a Canadian literature, often rising to effects of great beauty, but it has stirred little interest outside Canada. A few of our authors, a very few, have made for themselves a large and even enthusiastic audience in Britain or in the United States or in both. Among these the first in time was Thomas Chandler Haliburton, a Nova Scotian judge, who would not have relished the claim that he was a Canadian. A curious blend of the provincial and the imperialist, he ended his days in England, where long before he himself arrived his humorous sketches were widely read, so widely that Justin McCarthy has reported that for a time the sayings of his most ingenious creation, Sam Slick, were as well known as those of the more durably amusing Sam Weller. Haliburton's papers were also popular in the United States, and their dialectal humour and local colour have left a perceptible stamp upon New England writing. At the mid-century, when Sam Slick was already a figure in English humour, *Saul*, a huge poetic drama by a Montreal poet, Charles Heavysege, had a passing vogue in Britain and in the United States, impressing Emerson and Hawthorne and inducing Coventry Patmore to describe it as "indubitably one of the most remarkable English poems ever written out of Great Britain." Its vogue was lasting enough for W. D. Lighthall, a Montreal poet of a later generation, to recall that "it became the fashion among tourists to Montreal to buy a copy of *Saul*." Today, along with Heavysege's other works, his *Count Filippo* and his *Jephthah's Daughter*, it is unknown within Canada and without. Even the songs and sonnets of Heavysege are absent from recent Canadian anthologies. At the turn of the century the animal stories of C. G. D. Roberts extended the range of North American writing in a direction it might naturally have been expected to take with equal success somewhat sooner—the imaginative presentation of the forms of wild life characteristic of this continent in their relationship to the frontiers of settlement. These tales, simple and at times powerful, continue to hold a high place in the rather isolated and minor kind of literature to which they belong; but there is no doubt that in our time they are more talked of than opened except by youthful readers. There is little need for comment upon the writings of a handful of Canadians who at about this same time began to make their huge and ephemeral reputations as best-selling writers. Gilbert Parker soon left Canada to establish himself in Britain, and it is to English literature, to that group of British novelists who followed in the wake of Stevenson's romantic fiction, that his work belongs. Pre-eminent among the others, Ralph Connor, L. W. Montgomery, and Robert Service, continued to live in Canada, the first two until they died, Service till middle age. They were all more or less aggressively unliterary; and their only significance for our inquiry is the proof they offered that for the author who was satisfied to truckle to mediocre taste, living in Canada and writing about Canadian subjects, was perfectly compatible with making an abundant living by one's pen. The lesson they taught has not been forgotten: fortunately it has not been widely effective.

More recently Canadian work of value comparable with that of Haliburton's sketches and Roberts' animal tales has become known outside the country. There were the humorous papers of Stephen Leacock, the best of which have delighted not only Americans and Englishmen, and the peoples of other parts of the British Commonwealth, but also some Europeans. I can remember hearing M. André Maurois read to a group of students at the Sorbonne the charming study called "Boarding House Geometry"; and I never heard merrier laughter in Paris. The endless Jalna chronicles of Miss Mazo de la Roche maintain a large audience in Britain, and a sizable one in the United States; and in a more restricted group in the latter country the short stories and, to a less degree, the novels of Morley Callaghan are valued. I think I mentioned all the Canadians who have acquired considerable popularity or reputation as imaginative authors, either in the United States or in Great Britain. To the reader outside Canada such works as have been mentioned have not been important as reflections of phases in a national culture; the interest in the work has not spread to become an interest in the movements and the traditions in the national life from which the work emerged. Canadian books may occasionally have had a mild impact outside Canada; Canadian literature has had none.

Even within the national borders the impact of Canadian books and of Canadian literature has been relatively superficial. The almost feverish concern with its growth on the part of a small minority is no substitute for eager general sympathy or excitement. To one who takes careful account of the difficulties which have steadily beset its growth its survival as something interesting and important seems a miracle.

Some of these difficulties, those of an economic kind, may be easily and briefly stated. Economically the situation of our literature is, and always has been, unsound. No writer can live by the Canadian sales of his books. The president of one of our most active publishing companies, the late Hugh Eayrs, estimated that over a period of many years his profit on the sales of Canadian books was 1 per cent; and I should be surprised to learn that any other Canadian publisher could tell a much more cheerful tale unless, of course, the production of textbooks was the staple of his firm's business. Textbooks make money in any country. In general the Canadian market for books is a thin one, for a variety of important reasons. The Canadian population is in the main a fringe along the American border: nine out of ten Canadians live within two hundred miles of it, more than half within a hundred miles. The one important publishing centre is Toronto; and a bookseller in Vancouver, Winnipeg, or Halifax must feel reasonably sure that a book will be bought before he orders a number of copies which must be transported across thousands of miles. Books like *Gone with the Wind* and *The White Cliffs*—to keep to recent successes—he will order in quantity with confidence; but the distinguished work, the experimental novel, the collection of austere verse, the volume of strenuous criticism, is for him a luxury. The population of Canada is less than that of the State of New York; if our population were confined within an area of the same size the problem of distributing books would be soluble. Even if our fewer than twelve million people were confined within the huge triangle whose points are Montreal, North Bay, and Windsor—enclosing an area comparable with that of the region of New England—the problem might be soluble. But it is hard to see how the cultivated minority is to be served when its centres are separated by hundreds if not thousands of miles in which not a single creditable bookstore exists.

Of the fewer than twelve million Canadians who are strung along the American border in a long thin fringe, almost a third are French-speaking. These read little if at all in any language except French, apart from a small, highly conservative minority which studies the classics and scholastic philosophy, and a rather larger minority which keeps abreast of books in English that treat of political and economic subjects. In French Canada the sense of cultural nationality is much stronger than in English Canada, but the nationality is French Canadian, not Canadian *tout court*. French Canada is almost without curiosity about the literature and culture of English Canada; most cultivated French Canadians do not know even the names of the significant English Canadian creative writers, whether of the past or of the present. Occasionally an important Canadian book is translated from the original into the other official language; but it is much more likely that the work of a French Canadian will be translated into English than that the work of an English Canadian will be translated into French. Louis Hémon was a *Français de France*, but it was because *Maria Chapdelaine* dealt with French Canada that a distinguished Ontario lawyer translated the novel into English, making one of the most beautiful versions of our time. W. H. Blake's translation of Hémon's book is a masterpiece in its own right; no French Canadian has as yet laboured with such loving skill to translate any book that deals with English Canada. A symbol of the fissure in our cultural life is to be found in the definition of sections in The Royal Society of Canada. Three sections are assigned to the sciences, one to mathematics, physics, and chemistry, another to the biological sciences, and the third to geology and allied subjects; in these sections French and English fellows sit side by side. But in the two sections assigned to the humanities the French and English fellows are severely separate: in each the subjects run the impossible gamut from the classics to anthropology. It is not too much to say that the maximum Canadian audience that an English Canadian imaginative author can hope for is fewer than eight million people. . . .

The difficulties that have so far appeared, unlike as they are, all have economic roots. It is time to turn to the psychological factors, implied in much that has been said, against which the growth of a Canadian literature must struggle.

Among these most obvious, the most discussed, although *not* the most potent, is the colonial spirit. Long ago Harvard's President Felton doubted that Canada would come to much since a colony was doomed to be second-rate. In a later generation an American who knew us much better than Felton and who wished us well, William Dean Howells, used almost the same language. In *Their Wedding Journey* he conducts his couple from Niagara Falls by way of Kingston and Montreal to the east coast, giving sharp little pictures of the Canadian towns; he concludes that in comparison with the free nation to which they belong this colony is second-rate in the very quality of its life. Just a year or so ago the Halifax novelist, Mr Hugh MacLennan, gave to one of the colonially minded characters in *Barometer Rising* the same thought: "I've wasted a whole lifetime in this hole of a town. Everything in this country is second-rate. It always is in a colony." These are probably independent judgements. What do they mean? That a colony lacks the spiritual energy to rise above routine, and that it lacks this energy because it does not adequately believe in itself. It applies to what it has in standards which are imported, and therefore artificial and distorting. It sets the great good place not in its present, nor in its past nor in its future, but somewhere outside its own borders, somewhere beyond its own possibilities.

The charge that English Canada is colonial in spirit is the most serious of all the many charges that French Canada brings against us. Speaking in the 1942 session of the Canadian House of Commons, Mr Louis Saint Laurent, the leading French member of the government, illustrated what he meant by our colonialism when he cited an interchange that is supposed to have occurred within the last few years between the two living ex-prime ministers of Canada. One said to the other, on the eve of his departure to live in England: "I am glad to be going *home*," and the other replied: "How I envy you!" For these two men—if the interchange did occur—Canada was not the great good place; and every French Canadian would regard their sentiments as justifying his practice of referring to us not as *Canadiens Anglais*, but merely as *Anglais*, or when his blood is up, as *maudits Anglais!* Colonialism of this kind is natural to emigrants. One can easily forgive Sir Daniel Wilson, although he spent almost his entire active career in Canada, for wishing to lie in Scottish earth: and yet for a Canadian who knows what Scotland is like in November it is an awe-inspiring thought that Sir Daniel on one of our autumn days, full of the crashing scarlet glories of the Canadian forests or the mellow radiance of our Indian summers, wished to be amid the "sleety east winds" of his native land. What is odd, and unsatisfactory, is the perpetuation of this kind of colonialism in the descendants of emigrants even to the third and fourth generation. It is clear that those who are content with this attitude will seek the best in literature, where they seek the best in jam and toffee, from beyond the ocean. That anything Canadian could be supremely good would never enter their heads.

It is important to distinguish this attitude of pure colonialism from another, which is steadily confused with it by all French Canadians, and combined with it by a good number of English Canadians. As the nineteenth century drew on and the concept of empire in Britain herself assumed a new colour, the Kipling colour, some Canadians spoke and wrote of a Canada which would be a partner in the destinies of a great undertaking in which Britain would not be the master, but simply the senior partner. Charles Mair, our first important political poet, expressed the view I have in mind when he wrote, in 1888:

> First feel throughout the throbbing land
> A nation's pulse, a nation's pride—
> The independent life—then stand
> Erect, unbound, at Britain's side.

Another poet, Wilfred Campbell, coined an impressive phrase for Canada's destiny: Canada was to be part of "Vaster Britain." "Stronger even than the so-called Canadian spirit," he wrote, "is the voice of Vaster Britain." It is unjust to speak of this version of the imperialist ideal as showing the "butler's mind": it contemplated not serving Britain, but sharing Britain's glories. The psychological source of this intoxicating imperialism was not perhaps so much loyalty to Britain, but rather discontent with the dimensions of the Canadian scene. Canada was at the close of the last century a poor country, mainly concerned with material problems, and steadily losing many of her people to the large, rich, exultant land to the south. Imperialism was a kind of beneficent magic which would cover our nakedness and feed our starving spirits. The imperialist dream still lingers, but it is only a dream, for the mode in which

the empire has evolved has been centrifugal—away from the concept
of imperial federation—and there is nothing sufficiently rich and
various to which the loyalty the dream evokes can attach itself. In
practice the imperialist has drifted unconsciously into a colonial attitude of mind.

As the idea of imperial federation receded—and it was an idea
that we may well judge impractical since French Canada could
never have shared it, nor the Dutch in South Africa, nor the Southern Irish—Canada entered upon a period in which thinking was
extremely confused. I cannot attempt to provide here any account
of the extraordinary political evolution of the Dominions within the
past generation. But the confusion is obvious if one notes merely a
few significant political facts. Canada has no distinct flag, and no
single distinct anthem although Mr Mackenzie King paused on the
very brink of asserting the latter; the relations between Canadian
Provinces and the federal government are subject to review in London; and the Judicial Committee of the Privy Council, also in
London, is our highest court. But Canada has her own ministers in
foreign countries, makes treaties without reference to Britain, and
declares, or refuses to declare, war by the instrument of her own
Parliament. Is it any wonder that Canadian thinking about Canada
is confused, that one set of clear-thinking men demand that we cease
sending ministers and signing treaties and declaring war for ourselves, and that another set of clear-thinking men demand that we
provide ourselves with a distinct flag and anthem and end the
ingestion of the British Parliament and the British Privy Council in
our affairs? The average English Canadian would still like to have
it both ways and is irritated, or nonplussed, by the demand that he
make a resolute choice; at heart he does not know whether Canada
or the Empire is his supreme political value.

In the contemporary world autonomy is the most luxurious of
privileges, one which this anxious country cannot now afford and
will not be able to afford in any measurable future. It is not an
unmixed good. Autonomy almost always breeds chauvinism, and
usually brings as an immediate consequence an unwholesome delight
in the local second-rate. Its advent opposes strong obstacles to international currents of art and thought. This is to be set firmly against
the notion that out of autonomy all good things soon issue. Still it
must be appreciated just as clearly that dependence breeds a state of

mind no less unwholesome, a state of mind in which great art is most unlikely to emerge or to be widely recognized if it did. A great art is fostered by artists and audience possessing in common a passionate and peculiar interest in the kind of life that exists in the country where they live. If this interest exists in the artist he will try to give it adequate expression; if it exists in the audience they will be alert for any imaginative work which expresses it from a new angle and with a new clearness. From what was said a moment ago it will be obvious that in a colonial or semi-colonial community neither artist nor audience will have the passionate and peculiar interest in their immediate surroundings that is required. Canada is a state in which such an interest exists only among a few. I have pointed out how Mr Callaghan and Miss de la Roche have written as they could not have written if they had possessed such interest. It is the same with Canadian readers. A novel which presents the farms of the prairie, or the industrial towns of south-western Ontario, or the fishing villages in the Maritime Provinces will arouse no more interest in the general reader than a novel which is set in Surrey or in the suburbs of Chicago. Canadian undergraduates are much less likely than Americans to write stories about their immediate environment: their fancies take them to night-clubs in Vienna (rather than Montreal), islands in the South Seas (rather than the St Lawrence), foggy nights in London (rather than Halifax). It is almost impossible to persuade Canadians that an imaginative representation of the group in which they live could clarify for the reader his own nature and those of his associates. To the typical Canadian reader such a notion is arty folly. I give this as a fact; and I offer as a partial interpretation, at least, that most Canadians continue to be culturally colonial, that they set their great good place somewhere beyond their own borders.

Somewhere beyond their borders—not necessarily beyond the seas. Canada is colonial not only in its attitude towards Britain, but often in its attitude towards the United States. It is true that the imprint of a London publisher, or of a British university press is a more impressive guarantee of a book or an author than any Canadian sponsorship, even a Governor-General's. When the late Lord Tweedsmuir remarked that a Canadian's first loyalty should be towards Canada (rather than towards Britain or towards the Empire) it was believed in some circles, and these not the least cultivated, that he had been guilty, as one journalist phrased it in cynical fun, of "disloyalty towards himself." It was inevitable that a Scottish man of letters should think in such terms, Scotland being almost wholly free from the spirit of colonialism. Pleas that we should seek to free ourselves from our colonial feelings towards Britain are met with cries of "ingrate!" or "traitor!" There can, of course, be no question of such open and violent objection against efforts to free us from a colonial attitude towards the United States. Our colonialism in relation to the United States is unavowed, but it is deep. The praise of a couple of New York reviewers will outweigh the unanimous enthusiasm of Canadian journals from coast to coast. There is every reason to suppose that as Canadian feeling becomes more and more friendly towards the United States, as it has done during the past quarter century, our cultural dependence on the Americans will grow. If it does, our literature may be expected to become emphatically regionalist; of the dangers of regionalism something will be said a little later.

A more powerful obstacle at present to the growth of a great literature is the spirit of the frontier, or its afterglow. Most Canadians live at some distance from anything that could even in the loosest terms be known as a material frontier; but the standards which the frontier-life applied are still current, if disguised. Books are a luxury on the frontier; and writers are an anomaly. On the frontier a man is mainly judged by what he can do to bring his immediate environment quickly and visibly under the control of society. No nation is more practical than ours; admiration is readily stirred, even more readily than south of the border, by the man who can run a factory, or invent a gadget or save a life by surgical genius. This kind of admiration is a disguised form of the frontier's set of values. No such admiration goes out to any form of the aesthetic or contemplative life. The uneasiness in the presence of the contemplative or aesthetic is to be ascribed to the frontier feeling that these are luxuries which should not be sought at a time when there is a tacit contract that everyone should be doing his share in the common effort to build the material structure of a nation. That a poem or a statue or a metaphysic could contribute to the fabric of a nation is not believed. In a gathering of ruminative historians and economists, speaking their mind one evening in Winnipeg years before the war was imminent, the unanimous opinion was that a destroyer or two would do more than a whole corpus of literature to establish a Canadian nationality. The dissent of two students of literature was heard in awkward silence. If there were any belief in the national value of art or pure thought, the strong desire of the frontiersman that what is being built should eclipse all that was ever built before would make a mileau for art and thought that would at the root be propitious.

In a disguised form of frontier life what function can the arts hold? They are at best recreative. They may be alternatives to the hockey match, or the whiskey bottle, or the frivolous sexual adventure, as means of clearing the mind from the worries of business and enabling it to go back to business refreshed. The arts' value as interpretation is lost in the exclusive emphasis on their value as diversion, and even their value as diversion is simplified to the lowest possible form—a work of art must divert strongly and completely. It must divert as a thriller or a smashing jest diverts, not as an elaborate and subtle romance or a complicated argument diverts. In a word, Canada is a nation where the best-seller is king, as it is on the frontier.

A third factor telling against the appreciation of art is our strong Puritanism. Every foreign observer notes with amazement, both in our French and in our English books, the avoidance of the themes that irk the Puritan, or the language that now irks him more. Canada has never produced a major man of letters whose work gave a violent shock to the sensibilities of Puritans. There was some worry about Carman, who had certain qualities of the *fin de siècle* poet, but how mildly he expressed his queer longings! Mr Callaghan has fallen foul of the censors of morals in some of our more conservative cities, and even among those of his own Roman Catholic faith a novel as *Such Is My Beloved* has had an uneasy path; but how cautious in the description of sordor and how chastened in language he has always been! Imagination boggles at the vista of a Canadian Whitman, or Canadian Dos Passos. The prevailing literary standards demand a high degree of moral and social orthodoxy; and popular writers accept these standards without even such a rueful complaint as Thackeray made in warning that he could not draw his Pendennis as a full man, since no hero of an English novel intended for the general public had been drawn in full since Fielding went to his grave.

Even our Canadian Puritanism, however, has not been proof against the international currents of moral relaxation which have coursed so strongly during the past quarter century. In the poetry of those who are now approaching their fortieth year, there is a broad range of emotion, which does not stop short of carnality, and an equally broad range of speech for which nothing in the Canadian literary past gave a precedent. This poetry does not yet circulate at all widely, most of it is still locked away in periodicals read by few, and it is not possible to be sure whether it could even yet pass the moral test of the general reading public.

If Puritanism operated simply to restrain the arts within the bonds of moral orthodoxy, its effects, though regrettable, would be much less grave than they now are. Puritanism goes beyond the demand for severe morality: it disbelieves in the importance of art. It allows to the artist no function except watering down moral ideas of an orthodox kind into a solution attractive to minds not keen enough to study the ideas in more abstract presentations. At its most liberal Puritanism will tolerate, a little uneasily, the provision through the arts of an innocent passing amusement which is expected to leave no deep trace on character. To popularize orthodox morality and to provide light, clean fun—that is the very limit of what the arts can be allowed to do without alarming the Puritan mind. For the Puritan a life devoted to one of the arts is a life misused: the aesthetic life is not a form of the good life. That profane art, both for artist and for audience, may provide the contemplation of being, may offer an insight into the life of things, is for the Puritan mist and moonshine.

Puritanism is a dwindling force, and the time is not far off when it will no longer exercise its ruinous restraint upon the themes or language of a Canadian writer who is addressing the general public. Regionalism, another force which tells against the immediate growth of a national literature, cannot be expected to dwindle so fast. Canada is not an integrated whole. The Maritime Provinces recall the days—only seventy-five years in the past—when they were separate colonies; Nova Scotia, for instance, has re-established its colonial flag, dating from the eighteenth century and flying now from the Province House at Halifax; French Canada is a civilization apart; Ontario unconsciously accepts itself as the norm of Canadian life; the Prairie Provinces are steeped in their special vivid western past;

and British Columbia has a strong sense of its pre-Confederation life and of its continuing separate identity. Geography confirms the influence of history. Ontario is separated from the Maritime Provinces by the solid enclave of Quebec; between the populous southern part of Ontario and the prairies the Laurentian shield interposes another huge barrier; and this barrier is no stronger, if broader, than the Rocky Mountains create between the prairies and the coastal province of British Columbia. There is little doubt that the Fathers of Confederation, or the majority of the leaders among them, expected and planned for a much more unified whole than has so far come into being. In time of war the tendency to self-aggrandizement on the part of the Provinces is arrested, and even reversed; but there is ground for fearing that the return to peace will start it into vigorous being once more. Among most Canadians there is little eagerness to explore the varieties of Canadian life, little awareness how much variety exists, or what a peril that variety is, in time of crisis, to national unity. It may be that the next important stage of Canadian literature will be strongly particularist and regionalist: one remembers what a force regionalism was in American literature in the years after the Civil War.

Regionalist art may be expected to possess certain admirable virtues. One of these is accuracy, not merely accuracy of fact, but accuracy of tone; and throughout our literature there has been a disposition to force the note, to make life appear nobler or gayer or more intense than Canadian life really is in its typical expressions. It would help us towards cultural maturity if we had a set of novels, or sketches, or memoires that described the life of Canadian towns and cities as it really is, works in which nothing would be presented that the author had not encountered in his own experience. It should also be acknowledged that a warm emotion for one's *petit pays* can lead to very charming art, as in Stephen Leacock's humorous transposition of an Ontario town in his *Sunshine Sketches*. In the end, however, regionalist art will fail because it stresses the superficial and the peculiar at the expense, at least, if not to the exclusion, of the fundamental and universal. The advent of regionalism may be welcomed with reservations as a stage through which it may be well for us to pass, as a discipline and a purgation. But if we are to pass through it, the coming of great books will be delayed beyond the lifetime of anyone now living.

MARSHALL McLUHAN

1911-

Herbert Marshall McLuhan was born in Edmonton, Alberta, and educated at the University of Manitoba and at Cambridge, England. He taught English at St. Louis University, Missouri, and at Assumption College, Windsor. From 1946 to 1967 he was a member of the English Department, St. Michael's College, University of Toronto, and in 1963 became Director of the university's Centre for Culture and Technology. He was appointed to the Albert Schweitzer chair at Fordham University, New York, in 1967.

A convert to Roman Catholicism and one of the New Critics who have specialized in the rigorous examination of a literary text, McLuhan has succeeded in harmonizing an orthodox, if adventurous, religious and philosophical faith with a thoroughly modern and highly original interpretation of the history of western culture, particularly as it has been affected in recent decades by electronics and the mass media.

In the forties McLuhan contributed articles on Keats, Hopkins, Tennyson, and other literary figures to various English and American quarterlies. With the publication of *The Mechanical Bride: the Folklore of Industrial Man* in New York in 1951 his new and cogent social and cultural criticism began. This book was a brilliantly conceived and imaginatively produced exposé of the psychological stimuli exploited by modern advertising and is still one of the most valuable and accessible of McLuhan's books.

The two works which brought McLuhan international recognition were *The Gutenberg Galaxy: the Making of Typographical Man* (1962) and *Understanding Media* (1964), the former celebrating the death of the printed book and the latter the revolutionary changes brought about in habits of feeling and thought by instantaneous universal communication.

The epigrammatic summing up of McLuhan's ideas in the widely repeated slogan "The Medium is the Message" (or as travestied in a best-selling paper-back *The Medium is the Massage* [1967]) needs to be closely examined to determine whether McLuhan's assumed "scientific" objectivity has or has not placed an emphasis on form and technology rather than on substance.

McLuhan's work as an editor (in collaboration with Edmund S. Carpenter) of *Explorations*, a magazine published at the University of Toronto between 1953 and 1959, prepared him for his influential books of the sixties. The pioneer work of the historian H. A. Innis also was influential in stimulating McLuhan's ideas.

McLuhan's method cannot be separated from his style. He writes a vigorous, aphoristic, witty prose. New or amended definitions, truncated dogmatic assertions, puns, jokes, and epigrams all shot off with the fire and explosive energy of a rocket make McLuhan's pages continuously exciting, so that here too (on the printed page) the medium dominates the message.

G. F. Stearn (ed.) *McLuhan: Hot and Cool* (New York, 1967) is a comprehensive analytical critique by various hands both laudatory and critical that the ordinary reader may find helpful and stimulating. Other such works will be found in the Bibliography.

THE MEDIUM IS THE MESSAGE

1

In a culture like ours, long accustomed to splitting and dividing all things as a means of control, it is sometimes a bit of a shock to be reminded that, in operational and practical fact, the medium is the message. This is merely to say that the personal and social consequences of any medium—that is, of any extension of ourselves —result from the new scale that is introduced into our affairs by each extension of ourselves, or by any new technology. Thus, with automation, for example, the new patterns of human association tend to eliminate jobs, it is true. That is the negative result. Positively, automation creates roles for people, which is to say depth of involvement in their work and human association that our preceding mechanical technology had destroyed. Many people would be disposed to say that it was not the machine, but what one did with the machine, that was its meaning or message. In terms of the ways in which the machine altered our relations to one another and to ourselves, it mattered not in the least whether it turned out cornflakes or Cadillacs. The restructuring of human work and association was shaped by the technique of fragmentation that is the essence of machine technology. The essence of automation technology is the opposite. It is integral and decentralist in depth, just as the machine was fragmentary, centralist, and superficial in its patterning of human relationships.

The instance of the electric light may prove illuminating in this connection. The electric light is pure information. It is a medium without a message, as it were, unless it is used to spell out some verbal ad or name. This fact, characteristic of all media, means that the "content" of any medium is always another medium. The content of writing is speech, just as the written word is the content of print, and print is the content of the telegraph. If it is asked, "What is the content of speech?," it is necessary to say, "It is an actual process of thought, which is in itself nonverbal." An abstract painting represents direct manifestation of creative thought processes as they might appear in computer designs. What we are considering here, however, are the psychic and social consequences of the designs or patterns as they amplify or accelerate existing processes. For the "message" of any medium or technology is the change of scale or pace or pattern that it introduces into human affairs. The railway did not introduce movement or transportation or wheel or road into human society, but it accelerated and enlarged the scale of previous human functions, creating totally new kinds of cities and new kinds of work and leisure. This happened whether the railway functioned in a tropical or a northern environment, and is quite independent of the freight or content of the railway medium. The airplane, on the other hand, by accelerating the rate of transportation, tends to dissolve the railway form of city, politics, and association, quite independently of what the airplane is used for.

Let us return to the electric light. Whether the light is being used for brain surgery or night baseball is a matter of indifference. It could be argued that these activities are in some way the "content" of the electric light, since they could not exist without the electric light. This fact merely underlines the point that "the medium is the message" because it is the medium that shapes and controls the scale and form of human association and action. The content or uses of such media are as diverse as they are ineffectual in shaping the form of human association. Indeed, it is only too typical that the "content" of any medium blinds us to the character of the medium. It is only today that industries have become aware of the various kinds of business in which they are engaged. When IBM discovered that it was not in the business of making office equipment or business machines, but that it was in the business of processing information, then it began to navigate with clear vision. The General Electric Company makes a considerable portion of its profits from electric light bulbs and lighting systems. It has not yet discovered that, quite as much as A.T. & T., it is in the business of moving information.

The electric light escapes attention as a communication medium just because it has no "content." And this makes it an invaluable instance of how people fail to study media at all. For it is not till the electric light is used to spell out some brand name that it is noticed as a medium. Then it is not the light but the "content" (or what is really another medium) that is noticed. The message of the electric light is like the message of electric power in industry, totally radical, pervasive, and decentralized. For electric light and power are separate from their uses, yet they eliminate time and space factors in human association exactly as do radio, telegraph, telephone, and TV, creating involvement in depth.

A fairly complete handbook for studying the extensions of man could be made up from selections from Shakespeare. Some might quibble about whether or not he was referring to TV in these familiar lines from *Romeo and Juliet:*

But soft! what light through yonder window breaks?
It speaks, and yet says nothing.

In *Othello,* which, as much as *King Lear,* is concerned with the torment of people transformed by illusions, there are these lines that bespeak Shakespeare's intuition of the transforming powers of new media:

Is there not charms
By which the property of youth and maidhood
May be abus'd? Have you not read Roderigo,
Of some such thing?

In Shakespeare's *Troilus and Cressida,* which is almost completely devoted to both a psychic and social study of communication, Shakespeare states his awareness that true social and political navigation depend upon anticipating the consequences of innovation:

The providence that's in a watchful state
Knows almost every grain of Plutus' gold,
Finds bottom in the uncomprehensive deeps,
Keeps place with thought, and almost like the gods
Does thoughts unveil in their dumb cradles.

The increasing awareness of the action of media, quite independently of their "content" or programming, was indicated in the annoyed and anonymous stanza:

In modern thought, (if not in fact)
Nothing is that doesn't act,
So that is reckoned wisdom which
Describes the scratch but not the itch.

The same kind of total, configurational awareness that reveals why the medium is socially the message has occurred in the most recent and radical medical theories. In his *Stress of Life*, Hans Selye tells of the dismay of a research colleague on hearing of Selye's theory:

> When he saw me thus launched on yet another enraptured description of what I had observed in animals treated with this or that impure, toxic material, he looked at me with desperately sad eyes and said in obvious despair: "But Selye, try to realize what you are doing before it is too late! You have now decided to spend your entire life studying the pharmacology of dirt!"
>
> (Hans Selye, *The Stress of Life*)

As Selye deals with the total environmental situation in his "stress" theory of disease, so the latest approach to media study considers not only the "content" but the medium and the cultural matrix within which the particular medium operates. The older unawareness of the psychic and social effects of media can be illustrated from almost any of the conventional pronouncements.

In accepting an honorary degree from the University of Notre Dame a few years ago, General David Sarnoff made this statement: "We are too prone to make technological instruments the scapegoats for the sins of those who wield them. The products of modern science are not in themselves good or bad; it is the way they are used that determines their value." That is the voice of the current somnambulism. Suppose we were to say, "Apple pie is in itself neither good nor bad; it is the way it is used that determines its value." Or, "The smallpox virus is in itself neither good nor bad; it is the way it is used that determines its value." Again, "Firearms are in themselves neither good nor bad; it is the way they are used that determines their value." That is, if the slugs reach the right people firearms are good. If the TV tube fires the right ammunition at the right people it is good. I am not being perverse. There is simply nothing in the Sarnoff statement that will bear scrutiny, for it ignores the nature of the medium, of any and all media, in the true Narcissus style of one hypnotized by the amputation and extension of his own being in a new technical form. General Sarnoff went on to explain his attitude to the technology of print, saying that it was true that print caused much trash to circulate, but it had also disseminated the Bible and the thoughts of seers and philosophers. It has never occurred to General Sarnoff that any technology could do anything but *add* itself on to what we already are.

Such economists as Robert Theobald, W. W. Rostow, and John Kenneth Galbraith have been explaining for years how it is that "classical economics" cannot explain change or growth. And the paradox of mechanization is that although it is itself the cause of maximal growth and change, the principle of mechanization excludes the very possibility of growth or the understanding of change. For mechanization is achieved by fragmentation of any process and by putting the fragmented parts in a series. Yet, as David Hume showed in the eighteenth century, there is no principle of causality in a mere sequence. That one thing follows another accounts for nothing. Nothing follows from following, except change. So the greatest of all reversals occurred with electricity, that ended sequence by making things instant. With instant speed the causes of things began to emerge to awareness again, as they had not done with things in sequence and in concatenation accordingly. Instead of asking which came first, the chicken or the egg, it suddenly seemed that a chicken was an egg's idea for getting more eggs.

Just before an airplane breaks the sound barrier, sound waves become visible on the wings of the plane. The sudden visibility of sound just as sound ends is an apt instance of that great pattern of being that reveals new and opposite forms just as the earlier forms reach their peak performance. Mechanization was never so vividly fragmented or sequential as in the birth of the movies, the moment that translated us beyond mechanism into the world of growth and organic interrelation. The movie, by sheer speeding up the mechanical, carried us from the world of sequence and connections into the world of creative configuration and structure. The message of the movie medium is that of transition from lineal connections to configurations. It is the transition that produced the now quite correct observation: "If it works, it's obsolete." When electric speed further takes over from mechanical movie sequences, then the lines of force in structures and in media become loud and clear. We return to the inclusive form of the icon.

To a highly literate and mechanized culture the movie appeared as a world of triumphant illusions and dreams that money could buy. It was at this moment of the movie that cubism occurred, and it has been described by E. H. Gombrich (*Art and Illusion*) as "the most radical attempt to stamp out ambiguity and to enforce one reading of the picture—that of a man-made construction, a colored canvas." For cubism substitutes all facets of an object simultaneously for the "point of view" or facet of perspective illusion.

Instead of the specialized illusion of the third dimension on canvas, cubism sets up an interplay of planes and contradiction or dramatic conflict of patterns, lights, textures that "drives home the message" by involvement. This is held by many to be an exercise in painting, not in illusion.

In other words, cubism, by giving the inside and outside, the top, bottom, back, and front and the rest, in two dimensions, drops the illusion of perspective in favor of instant sensory awareness of the whole. Cubism, by seizing on instant total awareness, suddenly announced that *the medium is the message*. Is it not evident that the moment that sequence yields to the simultaneous, one is in the world of structure and of configuration? Is that not what has happened in physics as in painting, poetry, and in communication? Specialized segments of attention have shifted to total field, and we can now say, "The medium is the message" quite naturally. Before the electric speed and total field, it was not obvious that the medium is the message. The message, it seemed, was the "content," as people used to ask what a painting was *about*. Yet they never thought to ask what a melody was about, nor what a house or a dress was about. In such matters, people retained some sense of the whole pattern, of form and function as a unity. But in the electric age this integral idea of structure and configuration has become so prevalent that educational theory has taken up the matter. Instead of working with specialized "problems" in arithmetic, the structural approach now follows the lines of force in the field of number and has small children meditating about number theory and "sets."

Cardinal Newman said of Napoleon, "He understood the grammar of gunpowder." Napoleon had paid some attention to other media as well, especially the semaphore telegraph that gave him a great advantage over his enemies. He is on record for saying that "Three hostile newspapers are more to be feared than a thousand bayonets."

Alexis de Tocqueville was the first to master the grammar of print and typography. He was thus able to read off the message of coming change in France and America as if he were reading aloud from a text that had been handed to him. In fact, the nineteenth century in France and in America was just such an open book to de Tocqueville because he had learned the grammar of print. So he, also, knew when that grammar did not apply. He was asked why he did not write a book on England, since he knew and admired England. He replied:

One would have to have an unusual degree of philosophical folly to believe oneself able to judge England in six months. A year always seemed to me too short a time in which to appreciate the United States properly, and it is much easier to acquire clear and precise notions about the American Union than about Great Britain. In America all laws derive in a sense from the same line of thought. The whole of society, so to speak, is founded upon a single fact; everything springs from a simple principle. One could compare America to a forest pierced by a multitude of straight roads all converging on the same point. One has only to find the center and everything is revealed at a glance. But in England the paths run criss-cross, and it is only by travelling down each one of them that one can build up a picture of the whole.

De Tocqueville, in earlier work on the French Revolution, had explained how it was the printed word that, achieving cultural saturation in the eighteenth century, had homogenized the French nation. Frenchmen were the same kind of people from north to south. The typographic principles of uniformity, continuity, and lineality had overlaid the complexities of ancient feudal and oral society. The Revolution was carried out by the new literati and lawyers.

In England, however, such was the power of the ancient oral traditions of common law, backed by the medieval institution of Parliament, that no uniformity or continuity of the new visual print culture could take complete hold. The result was that the most important event in English history has never taken place; namely, the English Revolution on the lines of the French Revolution. The American Revolution had no medieval legal institutions to discard or to root out, apart from monarchy. And many have held that the American Presidency has become very much more personal and monarchical than any European monarch ever could be.

De Tocqueville's contrast between England and America is clearly based on the fact of typography and of print culture creating uniformity and continuity. England, he says, has rejected this principle and clung to the dynamic or oral common-law tradition. Hence the discontinuity and unpredictable quality of English culture. The grammar of print cannot help to construe the message of oral and nonwritten culture and institutions. The English aristocracy was properly classified as barbarian by Matthew Arnold because its power and status had nothing to do with literacy or with the cultural forms of typography. Said the Duke of Gloucester to Edward Gibbon upon the publication of his *Decline and Fall*: "Another damned fat book, eh, Mr. Gibbon? Scribble, scribble, scribble, eh, Mr. Gibbon?" De Tocqueville was a highly literate aristocrat who was quite able to be detached from the values and assumptions of typography. That is why he alone understood the grammar of typography. And it is only on those terms, standing aside from any structure or medium, that its principles and lines of force can be discerned. For any medium has the power of imposing its own assumption on the unwary. Prediction and control consist in avoiding this subliminal state of Narcissus trance. But the greatest aid to this end is simply in knowing that the spell can occur immediately upon contact, as in the first bars of a melody.

A Passage to India by E. M. Forster is a dramatic study of the inability of oral and intuitive oriental culture to meet with the rational, visual European patterns of experience. "Rational," of course, has for the West long meant "uniform and continuous and sequential." In other words, we have confused reason with literacy, and rationalism with a single technology. Thus in the electric age man seems to the conventional West to become irrational. In Forster's novel the moment of truth and dislocation from the typographic trance of the West comes in the Marabar Caves. Adela Quested's reasoning powers cannot cope with the total inclusive field of resonance that is India. After the Caves: "Life went on as usual, but had no consequences, that is to say, sounds did not echo nor thought develop. Everything seemed cut off at its root and therefore infected with illusion."

A Passage to India (the phrase is from Whitman, who saw America headed Eastward) is a parable of Western man in the electric age, and is only incidentally related to Europe or the Orient. The ultimate conflict between sight and sound, between written and oral kinds of perception and organization of existence is upon us. Since understanding stops action, as Nietzsche observed, we can moderate the fierceness of this conflict by understanding the media that extend us and raise these wars within and without us.

Detribalization by literacy and its traumatic effects on tribal man is the theme of a book by the psychiatrist J. C. Carothers, *The African Mind in Health and Disease* (World Health Organization, Geneva, 1953). Much of his material appeared in an article in *Psychiatry* magazine, November 1959: "The Culture, Psychiatry, and the Written Word." Again, it is electric speed that has revealed the lines of force operating from Western technology in the remotest areas of bush, savannah, and desert. One example is the Bedouin with his battery radio on board the camel. Submerging natives with floods of concepts for which nothing has prepared them is the normal action of all of our technology. But with electric media Western man himself experiences exactly the same inundation as the remote native. We are no more prepared to encounter radio and TV in our literate milieu than the native of Ghana is able to cope with the literacy that takes him out of his collective tribal world and beaches him in individual isolation. We are as numb in our new electric world as the native involved in our literate and mechanical culture.

Electric speed mingles the cultures of prehistory with the dregs of industrial marketeers, the nonliterate with the semiliterate and the postliterate. Mental breakdown of varying degrees is the very common result of uprooting and inundation with new information and endless new patterns of information. Wyndham Lewis made this a theme of his group of novels called *The Human Age*. The first of these, *The Childermass*, is concerned precisely with accelerated media change as a kind of massacre of the innocents. In our own world as we become more aware of the effects of technology on psychic formation and manifestation, we are losing all confidence in our rights to assign guilt. Ancient pre-historic societies regard violent crime as pathetic. The killer is regarded as we do a cancer victim. "How terrible it must be to feel like that," they say. J. M. Synge took up this idea very effectively in his *Playboy of the Western World*.

If the criminal appears as a nonconformist who is unable to meet the demand of technology that we behave in uniform and continuous patterns, literate man is quite inclined to see others who cannot conform as somewhat pathetic. Especially the child, the cripple, the woman, and the colored person appear in a world of visual and typographic technology as victims of injustice. On the other hand, in a culture that assigns roles instead of jobs to people —the dwarf, the skew, the child create their own spaces. They are not expected to fit into some uniform and repeatable niche that is not their size anyway. Consider the phrase "It's a man's world." As a quantitative observation endlessly repeated from within a homogenized culture, this phrase refers to the men in such a culture who have to be homogenized Dagwoods in order to belong at all. It is in our I.Q. testing that we have produced the greatest flood of misbegotten standards. Unaware of our typographic cultural bias, our testers assume that uniform and continuous habits are a sign of intelligence, thus eliminating the ear man and the tactile man.

C. P. Snow, reviewing a book of A. L. Rowse (*The New York Times Book Review*, December 24, 1961) on *Appeasement* and the road to Munich, describes the top level of British brains and experience in the 1930s. "Their I.Q.'s were much higher than usual among political bosses. Why were they such a disaster?" The view of Rowse, Snow approves: "They would not listen to warnings because they did not wish to hear." Being anti-Red made it impossible for them to read the message of Hitler. But their failure was as nothing compared to our present one. The American stake in literacy as a technology or uniformity applied to every level of education, government, industry, and social life is totally threatened by the electric technology. The threat of Stalin or Hitler was external. The electric technology is within the gates, and we are numb, deaf, blind, and mute about its encounter with the Gutenberg technology, on and through which the American way of life was formed. It is, however, no time to suggest strategies when the threat has not even been acknowledged to exist. I am in the position of Louis Pasteur telling doctors that their greatest enemy was quite invisible, and quite unrecognized by them. Our conventional response to all media, namely that it is how they are used that counts, is the numb stance of the technological idiot. For the "content" of a medium is like the juicy piece of meat carried by the burglar to distract the watchdog of the mind. The effect of the medium is made strong and intense just because it is given another medium as "content." The content of a movie is a novel or a play or an opera. The effect of the movie form is not related to its program content. The "content" of writing or print is speech, but the reader is almost entirely unaware either of print or of speech.

Arnold Toynbee is innocent of any understanding of media as they have shaped history, but he is full of examples that the student of media can use. At one moment he can seriously suggest that adult education, such as the Workers Educational Association in Britain, is a useful counterforce to the popular press. Toynbee considers that although all of the oriental societies have in our time accepted the industrial technology and its political consequences: "On the cultural plane, however, there is no uniform corresponding tendency." (Somervell, 1. 267) This is like the voice of the literate man, floundering in a milieu of ads, who boasts, "Personally, I pay no attention to ads." The spiritual and cultural reservations that the oriental peoples may have toward our technology will avail them not at all. The effects of technology do not occur at the level of opinions or concepts, but alter sense ratios or patterns of perception steadily and without any resistance. The serious artist is the only person able to encounter technology with impunity, just because he is an expert aware of the changes in sense perception.

The operation of the money medium in seventeenth-century Japan had effects not unlike the operation of typography in the West. The penetration of the money economy, wrote G. B. Sansom (in *Japan*, Cresset Press, London, 1931) "caused a slow but irresistible revolution, culminating in the breakdown of feudal government and the resumption of intercourse with foreign countries after more than two hundred years of seclusion." Money has reorganized the sense life of peoples just because it is an *extension* of our sense lives. This change does not depend upon approval or disapproval of those living in the society.

Arnold Toynbee made one approach to the transforming power of media in his concept of "etherialization," which he holds to be the principle of progressive simplification and efficiency in any organization or technology. Typically, he is ignoring the *effect* of the challenge of these forms upon the response of our senses. He imagines that it is the response of our opinions that is relevant to the effect of media and technology in society, a "point of view" that is plainly the result of the typographic spell. For the man in a literate and homogenized society ceases to be sensitive to the diverse and discontinuous life of forms. He acquires the illusion of the third dimension and the "private point of view" as part of his Narcissus fixation, and is quite shut off from Blake's awareness or that of the Psalmist, that we become what we behold.

Today when we want to get our bearings in our own culture, and have need to stand aside from the bias and pressure exerted by any technical form of human expression, we have only to visit a society where that particular form has not been felt, or a historical period in which it was unknown. Professor Wilbur Schramm made

236 THE TWENTIETH CENTURY

such a tactical move in studying *Television in the Lives of Our Children*. He found areas where TV had not penetrated at all and ran some tests. Since he had made no study of the peculiar nature of the TV image, his tests were of "content" preferences, viewing time, and vocabulary counts. In a word, his approach to the problem was a literary one, albeit unconsciously so. Consequently, he had nothing to report. Had his methods been employed in 1500 A.D. to discover the effects of the printed book in the lives of children or adults, he could have found out nothing of the changes in human and social psychology resulting from typography. Print created individualism and nationalism in the sixteenth century. Program and "content" analysis offer no clues to the magic of these media or to their subliminal charge.

Leonard Doob, in his report *Communication in Africa*, tells of one African who took great pains to listen each evening to the BBC news, even though he could understand nothing of it. Just to be in the presence of those sounds at 7 P.M. each day was important for him. His attitude to speech was like ours to melody—the resonant intonation was meaning enough. In the seventeenth century our ancestors still shared this native's attitude to the forms of media, as is plain in the following sentiment of the Frenchman Bernard Lam expressed in *The Art of Speaking* (London, 1696):

> 'Tis an effect of the Wisdom of God, who created Man to be happy, that whatever is useful to his conversation (way of life) is agreeable to him . . . because all victual that conduces to nourishment is relishable, whereas other things that cannot be assimilated and be turned into our substance are insipid. A Discourse cannot be pleasant to the Hearer that is not easie to the Speaker; nor can it be easily pronounced unless it be heard with delight.

Here is an equilibrium theory of human diet and expression such as even now we are only striving to work out again for media after centuries of fragmentation and specialism.

Pope Pius XII was deeply concerned that there be serious study of the media today. On February 17, 1950, he said:

> It is not an exaggeration to say that the future of modern society and the stability of its inner life depend in large part on the maintenance of an equilibrium between the strength of the techniques of communication and the capacity of the individual's own reaction.

Failure in this respect has for centuries been typical and total for mankind. Subliminal and docile acceptance of media impact has made them prisons without walls for their human users. As A. J. Liebling remarked in his book *The Press,* a man is not free if he cannot see where he is going, even if he has a gun to help him get there. For each of the media is also a powerful weapon with which to clobber other media and other groups. The result is that the present age has been one of multiple civil wars that are not limited to the world of art and entertainment. In *War and Human Progress,* Professor J. U. Nef declared: "The total wars of our time have been the result of a series of intellectual mistakes. . . ."

If the formative power in the media are the media themselves, that raises a host of large matters that can only be mentioned here, although they deserve volumes. Namely, that technological media are staples or natural resources, exactly as are coal and cotton and oil. Anybody will concede that a society whose economy is dependent upon one or two major staples like cotton, or grain, or lumber, or fish, or cattle is going to have some obvious social patterns of organization as a result. Stress on a few major staples creates extreme instability in the economy but great endurance in the population. The pathos and humor of the American South are embedded in such an economy of limited staples. For a society configured by reliance on a few commodities accepts them as a social bond quite as much as the metropolis does the press. Cotton and oil, like radio and tv, become "fixed charges" on the entire psychic life of the community. And this pervasive fact creates the unique cultural flavor of any society. It pays through the nose and all its other senses for each staple that shapes its life.

That our human senses, of which all media are extensions, are also fixed charges on our personal energies, and that they also configure the awareness and experience of each one of us, may be perceived in another connection mentioned by the psychologist C. G. Jung:

> Every Roman was surrounded by slaves. The slave and his psychology flooded ancient Italy, and every Roman became inwardly, and of course unwittingly, a slave. Because living constantly in the atmosphere of slaves, he became infected through the unconscious with their psychology. No one can shield himself from such an influence (*Contributions to Analytical Psychology,* London, 1928).

NORTHROP FRYE

1912-

Northrop Frye, like Marshall McLuhan, is one of the few Canadian men of letters to make and deserve an international reputation.

Born in 1912 in Sherbrooke, Quebec, Frye was educated in Moncton, New Brunswick, and at Victoria College and Emmanuel College, University of Toronto. He was ordained a minister of the United Church in 1936. After completing his post-graduate work at Oxford and the University of Toronto, he became a member of the English Department at Victoria, where he was associated with Dr. Pelham Edgar and the poet, E. J. Pratt.

In the late thirties and early forties he contributed articles on Canadian literature to *The Canadian Forum,* which he later edited. From 1950 to 1960 he wrote the poetry reviews to the *University of Toronto Quarterly's* annual survey, "Letters in Canada."

Frye's international reputation as scholar and critic began with the appearance of *Fearful Symmetry: a Study of William Blake,* published by the University of Princeton Press in 1947. The writing of this book involved Frye in a thorough re-examination of the function of symbol, myth, and ritual in imaginative literature, and prepared the way for Frye's second seminal critical work, *Anatomy of Criticism* (1957). This book showed him as a brilliant analyst of forms, genres, and motives, whose romantic ideas are poured into a thoroughly classical mold.

Frye's critical essays have often appeared in the *University of Toronto Quarterly* and various American scholarly journals. Many of these as well as the lectures and addresses he has given at American universities have been reprinted in a number of significant volumes. Among them are: *Culture and the National Will* (1957); *By Liberal Things* (1960); *Fables of Identity, The Well-tempered Critic, The Educated Imagination,* and *T. S. Eliot,* a short critical study in the Writers and Critics series (four volumes published in 1963); and two books which appeared in 1965, *The Return of Eden* (five essays on Milton), and *A Natural Perspective* (a study of Shakespeare's romantic comedies). Frye turned his attention again to Canadian literature in the characteristically brilliant "Conclusion" to the monumental *Literary History of Canada* edited by Carl F. Klinck in 1965. His essays on Canadian literature were collected in 1971 under the title of *The Bush Garden: Essays on the Canadian Imagination.*

ORDINARY SPEECH, VERSE, AND PROSE

It is a well known principle of thought that the most elementary problems are the hardest, not only to solve, but even to see. The other day an inspector of elementary schools said to me: "In grade four nearly all the children are enthusiastic about poetry: in the adult world hardly anyone bothers to read it. What happens?" This question struck me as a perversion of nature: everybody knows that literary critics are supposed to ask searching questions of educators, not the other way round. The conviction that I ought to be asking the question, however, clearly would not supply me with an answer. There are any number of automatic or cliché answers, ranging from "Schoolteachers kill the child's interest in poetry by analyzing it" to "Modern poetry is out of touch with modern life"; but such pseudo-statements, however consoling, get us nowhere.

While I do not have an answer, I can at least see the place at which the answer must start. Here again an educational problem is bound up with a critical one. Very early in our education we are made familiar with the distinction between verse and prose. The conviction gradually forces itself on us that when we mean what we say we write prose, and that verse is an ingenious but fundamentally perverse way of distorting ordinary prose statements. The conviction does not come to us from school so much as from the general pressure of our social environment. Embedded in it is the purely critical assumption that prose is the language of ordinary speech. This is an assumption of very long standing: one of the most reliable jokes in literature concerns the delight of M. Jourdain, in Molière's *Le Bourgeois Gentilhomme*, at discovering that he had been speaking prose all his life. But M. Jourdain had not been speaking prose all his life, and prose is not the language of ordinary speech. In the history of literature we notice that developed techniques of verse normally precede, sometimes by centuries, developed techniques of prose. How could this happen if prose were really the language of ordinary speech?

The language of ordinary speech is called prose only because it is not distinguished from prose. Actual prose is the expression or imitation of directed thinking or controlled description in words, and its unit is the sentence. It does not follow that all prose is descriptive or thoughtful, much less logical, but only that prose imitates, in its rhythm and structure, the verbal expression of a conscious and rational mind. Prose, therefore, is not ordinary speech, but ordinary speech on its best behavior, in its Sunday clothes, aware of an audience and with its relation to that audience prepared beforehand. It is the habitual language only of fully articulate people who have mastered its difficult idiom. And even they will avoid stilted speech, or "talking like a book," as we say, and when they do, their speech rhythm shows the influence of something that is not prose.

If we listen to children talking, we do not hear prose: we hear a heavily accented speech rhythm with a great deal of chanting in it, or whining, depending on the mood of the child. If we are lost in a strange town and ask someone for directions, we do not get prose: we get pure Gertrude Stein, a speech rhythm that is prolix and repetitive, and in which the verbal unit is no more a prose sentence than it is a villanelle. The teenager issuing mating calls over a telephone is not speaking prose, although the speech rhythm he uses is as formalized as prayer, which it somewhat resembles. The lady screaming amiabilities at a crowded cocktail party is not allowed to speak prose, for her hearers are not listening for sentences, but for a single rise and fall of the voice. The other day a student came to consult me about a failure in English, and what he said, as I recorded immediately after he left, was this:

Y'know, I couldn' figure what happened, cause, jeez, well, I figured, y'know, I had that stuff cold—I mean, like I say, I'd gone over the stuff an' I figured I knew it, and—well, jeez, I do' know.

I submit that this is not prose, and I suspect he had failed because he had not understood the difficulties of translating his speech into prose. He was, of course, "taking" English. But English was not taking him: fifteen years of schooling had failed to make any impression on his speech habits. He represents an educational problem, but not one that school or university can directly solve, because the only effective improvement would be through social snobbery. If, as at least formerly in England, habits of speech were built into the social structure: if it were taken for granted that the lower classes spoke one way and the middle classes another, middle-class speech would certainly conform to a middle-class pattern from infancy onwards. But Bernard Shaw's *Pygmalion* could hardly be written in North America, for the social facts it deals with are very different here.

Ordinary speech is concerned mainly with putting into words what is loosely called the stream of consciousness: the daydreaming, remembering, worrying, associating, brooding and mooning that continually flows through the mind and which, with Walter Mitty, we often speak of as thought. Thus ordinary speech is concerned mainly with self-expression. Whether from immaturity, pre-occupation, or the absence of a hearer, it is imperfectly aware of an audience. Full awareness of an audience makes speech rhetorical, and rhetoric means a conventionalized rhythm. The irregular rhythm of ordinary speech may be conventionalized in two ways. One way is to impose a pattern of recurrence on it; the other is to impose the logical and semantic pattern of the sentence. We have verse when the arrangement of words is dominated by recurrent rhythm and sound, prose when it is dominated by the syntactical relation of subject and predicate. Of the two, verse is much the simpler and more primitive type, which accounts for its being historically earlier than prose.

One can see in ordinary speech, however, a unit of rhythm peculiar to it, a short phrase that contains the central word or idea aimed at, but is largely innocent of syntax. It is much more repetitive than prose, as it is in the process of working out an idea, and the repetitions are largely rhythmical fillers, like the nonsense words of popular poetry, which derive from them. In pursuit of its main theme it follows the paths of private association, which gives it a somewhat meandering course. Because of the prominence of private association in it, I shall call the rhythm of ordinary speech the associative rhythm.

Traditionally, the associative rhythm has been used in tragedy to represent insanity, as in some speeches in *King Lear*, and in comedy to represent the speech of the uneducated or the mentally confused. Mrs. Quickly and Juliet's nurse are Shakespearean examples. But it is only within the last century or so, with the rise of mimetic fiction, that literature has made any systematic effort to explore the rhythms of ordinary or of inner speech. Such effort practically begins, for English literature, with the entry of Alfred Jingle into the *Pickwick Papers* and his account of the stage coach and the low archway:

> Terrible place—dangerous work—other day—five children— mother—tall lady, eating sandwiches—forgot the arch—crash— knock—children look around—mother's head off—sandwich in her hand—no mouth to put it in—head of a family off— shocking, shocking!

Jingle begins the series of associative speakers that includes the Bloom and Molly Bloom of Joyce's *Ulysses*. Wyndham Lewis, in *Time and Western Man*, has noted the connection between Jingle and Bloom, although the inferences he draws from the connection are pseudo-critical. Bloom's interior monologue falls into a series of asyntactic phrases, like Jingle's speech, except that the rhythm is a little slower and stodgier, as befits the speaker's physical type:

> Confession. Everyone wants to. Then I will tell you all. Penance. Punish me, please. Great weapon in their hands. More than doctor or solicitor. Woman dying to. And I schschsch-schschsch. And did you chachachachacha? And why did you? Look down at her ring to find an excuse. Whispering gallery walls have ears. Husband learns to his surprise. God's little joke. Then out she comes. Repentance skin deep. Lovely shame. Pray at an altar. Hail Mary and Holy Mary.

Here, however, a further distinction arises. When an author represents a character as speaking or thinking in this way, the author is aware of his audience even if his character is not; consequently he will impose on the speech of that character a third type of conventionalization. Jingle and Bloom are literary comic humors, not people drawn from life, and their monologues are more regularized in rhythm than those of any people resembling them in life would be.

There are, then, three primary rhythms of verbal expression. First, there is the rhythm of prose, of which the unit is the sentence. Second, there is an associative rhythm, found in ordinary speech and in various places in literature, in which the unit is a short phrase of irregular length and primitive syntax. Third, there is the rhythm of a regularly repeated pattern of accent or meter, often accompanied by other recurring features, like rhyme or alliteration. This regularly recurring type of rhythm is what I mean by verse. "Poetry," however indispensable a word in literary criticism, can hardly be used in the technical sense of a verbal structure possessing a regular, recurrent, and in general predictable rhythm. All verse is "poetry" as that word is generally used, except when "poetry" implies a value-judgement. It does not follow that all poetry is verse. Any jingle or doggerel that approximately scans is verse in my sense, however unpoetic: no free verse, such as Whitman's, is verse in my sense, however important as poetry.

All three rhythms are involved in all writing, but one is normally the dominating or organizing rhythm.

I I

Ideally, our literary education should begin, not with prose, but with such things as "this little pig went to market"—with verse rhythm reinforced by physical assault. The infant who gets bounced on somebody's knee to the rhythm of "Ride a cock horse" does not need a footnote telling him that Banbury Cross is twenty miles northeast of Oxford. He does not need the information that "cross" and "horse" make (at least in the pronunciation he is mostly likely to hear) not a rhyme but an assonance. He does not need the value-judgement that the repetition of "horse" in the first two lines indicates a rather thick ear on the part of the composer. All he needs is to get bounced. If he is, he is beginning to develop a response to poetry in the place where it ought to start. For verse is closely related to dance and song; it is also closely related to the child's own speech, which is full of chanting and singing, as well as of primitive verse forms like the war-cry and the taunt-song. At school the study of verse is supplemented by the study of prose, and a good prose style in both speech and writing is supposed to be aimed at. But poetry, the main body of which is verse, is always the central powerhouse of a literary education. It contributes, first, the sense of rhythmical energy, the surge and thunder of epic and the sinewy and springing dialogue of Shakespearean drama. It contributes too, as the obverse of this, the sense of leisure, of expert timing of the swing and fall of cadences. Then there is the sense of wit and heightened intelligence, resulting from seeing disciplined words marching along in metrical patterns and in their inevitably right order. And there is the sense of concreteness that we can get only from the poet's use of metaphor and of visualized imagery. Literary education of this kind, its rhythm and leisure slowly soaking into the body and its wit and concreteness into the mind, can do something to develop a speaking and writing prose style that comes out of the depths of personality and is a genuine expression of it.

As education proceeds, the student finds himself surrounded with what purports to be prose, and naturally gives this rhythm more of his attention. Prose becomes the language of information, and it becomes increasingly also the language of information about poetry, which now tends to recede as a direct experience of words. As a result of colliding with *The Lady of the Lake* in grade nine, I shall associate Scott with unmetrical footnotes all my life:

> *The stag at eve had drunk his fill*
> *Where danced the moon on Monan's, one, rill:*
> *And deep his midnight lair has made*
> *In lone Glenartney's, two, hazel shade.*

I am not disapproving the practice of writing footnotes to the proper names in verse, that being one of the ways by which I make my own living. What I regret is the growth of a tendency to find the footnote easier to read, and which in universities takes the form of dealing with a course in literature by reading books about poetry and skipping the quotations. The process, however, is by no means merely one of transferring literary experience from poetry to prose. What more frequently happens is that, faced with the enormous mass of verbiage on all sides, and having to come to terms with the constant sense of panic that this inspires, the student is taught, or develops by himself, a technique of reading everything quickly and off the top of his head. He no longer responds to the rhythm of the sentence, or to any rhythm at all, but reads with a mechanical express-train efficiency, dealing only with what that kind of effi-

ciency can handle—the main ideas, the gist of the argument, the
general point of view, and the like. This means that the process of
reading is, like the rhythms of undeveloped speech, becoming purely
associative. It is appropriate for a committee's report, or similar
expendable document, where there is one essential sentence on page
forty-two and the reader wants only to get some notion of its context; but it is inadequate for prose, and impossible for poetry.

Meanwhile, in all the attention put on techniques of teaching
students to read, ordinary speech is largely left to original sin. A
standard grammatical form of English prose is taught at school,
and the student learns to read it after a fashion, but it does not
follow that he learns to speak it habitually. Learning to speak on
this continent is often associated with "cultivating an accent," and
it is generally agreed that anyone who does that is a sissy, a snob,
a square, or whatever other abusive term is in vogue at the moment.
I am not myself speaking of accent, or of the actual production of
the sounds of speech, which is a social convention only. I am
speaking of the kind of oral verbal framework that one must develop
if one is to convey ideas or communicate any sense of personality.
Prose is founded on the sentence, and the sentence is, at least in
form, logical, communicable and periodic: it is difficult to use unless
one has something to say and means what one says. We notice that
associative speakers have a great aversion to the definiteness and
full close of the sentence: if they produce a sentence by accident,
they will add unnecessary words to the end of an apology for having
uttered it, like.

On my desk is the report of a conference transmitted by that
sobering register of the spoken word, the tape recorder. The question at issue is the teaching of American literature in foreign countries: *Huckleberry Finn* has been suggested, and the speaker is, I
think, warning us that it contains the word "ain't":

> Now, I'm rather more inclined to stick my neck out on things
> of this sort, therefore, I'm sticking my neck farther than a lot
> of people here would, in saying that I would also not see any
> objection to including such a supposedly sub-standard term as
> ain't in the sense of am not, is not, are not at a relatively early
> level of work for teaching English, but in this case with a
> specific indication that this is an extremely frequent form
> which the learner is very likely to hear in any part of the

English speaking world but that he had better be careful about using it himself unless he has more of a feel for the situations in which it is permissible and those in which it "ain't."

This kind of style, once one gets more of a feel for it, is easy to recognize as the quiz programme or buzz session style. Its unit is not the sentence, but the number of words that it is possible to emit before someone else breaks in. A discussion based on such a speech rhythm cannot achieve conversation, but only distributed monologue.

The schools, of course, will be of little help if they have been corrupted by project methods and other anti-verbal perversities. If a standard language is taught in school without conviction, it is unlikely to make much positive impression on the language spoken during recess. I say positive impression, because there does seem to be a negative one. Much of the colloquial language spoken in our society is a curious mixture of associative monologue and childhood resentments. I often revert to a little scene that made a considerable impression on me once: in a grocery store, where the clerk was showing me two things much alike, he remarked: "It doesn't make any difference," then looked me full in the face and instantly corrected himself to: "It don't make no difference." This second form was an improvement on the first, having a higher degree of what literary critics call texture. It meant (a) it doesn't make any difference (b) you look to me like a schoolteacher, and nobody's going to catch me talking like one of them. If he said: "It don't make no difference," it was not because he did not know the accepted form, but because he did know it. His speech was not ungrammatical; it was anti-grammatical. Whatever unconscious resentment may be involved in such rhetoric is not directed against a higher social class: it is directed against eggheads or longhairs or however the people are described who take their education seriously. The language taught at school is taught only there, which is why it is associated with teachers and schoolrooms. It would never have occurred to the student whose ragged speech I have quoted to be anything but clean and well dressed. But no major business is engaged in selling speech, and the example of good speakers is not reinforced by advertising, with its judicious mixture of flattery and threats.

The standard English of schoolrooms is prose, and being prose it can be analyzed grammatically, hence the body of grammatical "rules" which so many students associate with correct English. When anyone starts reflecting, as I am doing, on ordinary habits of speech, it is usually assumed that it is the correctness of one's grammar that is being impugned. But while standard speech is grammatical, it would be silly to judge it solely by its conformity to some alleged grammatical model. For one thing, the strain of constructing prose sentences is clearly marked even in the speech of the most articulate people. That is to say, the point I want to make is, all of us use, sort of, filler phrases to conceal our nervousness, or something, in working out our, you know, sentence structure. Standard English cannot be learned without the study of formal grammar. The little learning of linguistics which prompted some "educators" a few years ago to try to get rid of grammar proved to be a very dangerous thing indeed. Further, those who know language know its logical distinctions and subtle nuances, and have a duty to insist on their usefulness. The notion that the teacher of language has nothing to do but follow "usage" is one of the more miserable forms of academic self-deprecation. But still grammar is the servant and not the master of language, and speech, like handwriting, has to be allowed to find its own rhythm and character.

The hazy general notion that illiteracy is the technical inability to read and write, and that an education which teaches everybody to read and write has overcome illiteracy, is clearly nonsense. One may fully agree with everything that has been said about the futility of teaching dead languages at school. Except for some aspects of scholarly research, dead languages have no place in education. But this does not commit us to making the simple-minded and ill-considered identification of dead languages with the Classical languages. A dead language is a language that one learns to read but never thinks of as spoken. What shows that it is dead is the third factor, the writing of the language. The professor of Latin does not think of Latin as a dead language except when he is marking students' proses. Similarly, a student who has learned to read English prose, and continues to speak only associative jargon, will, when he tries to write English, find himself struggling with a language much more effectively dead than Julius Caesar. Good writing must be based on good speech; it will never come alive if it is based on reading alone.

Many people are puzzled by the fact that only the most disciplined writers are simple writers. Undeveloped writing is not simple, even in the sense of reproducing the associative speech patterns that I have quoted earlier. Writing that did that would achieve, if not simplicity, at least a kind of startling nakedness. Such writing is to be found in examination papers, of the sort that exclude their authors from a university education. Here is an example at random, from a student who was asked to compare Chaucer's Chanticleer with one of the characters in the General Prologue:

> The discription of the cock is like that of the Prioress, for we are told lots about her appearance, just as of the cock. The discription is general, typical of a Prioress, just as the discription is typical of a cock. We are told that she also could sing good, just as the cock. We know she was beautiful and care much about her manners. This is funny, for a prioress should not be concerned with such, but should pay more attention to her religion. It is funny. The discription of the cock being beautiful is also funny, especially the part about his nails compaired to a lilly. He is interested in love, having seven hens, and so is the Prioress . . .

Everybody engaged in teaching has marked bushels of such offerings: my only purpose in quoting it is to call attention to the murmuring, repetitive, asyntactic phrasing of the rhythm of association. But associative speakers are largely unaware of their own speech habits, and unless they are as naive as this student, they do not use them as a basis for writing. Now if we write in a way that we never speak, the first thing that disappears is the rhythm. It is hardly possible to give any spring or bounce to words unless they come out of our own bodies and are, like dancing or singing, an expression of physical as well as mental energy. The second thing that disappears is the color. It is hardly possible to use vivid language unless one is seeing the imagery for oneself: even abstract words, if they are genuinely possessed by the person using them, will still retain something of the concrete metaphor that they originally had. The third thing that disappears is the sense of personality, which only a basis in personal speech can ever supply. These are all, we have said, the results of a literary education centered in poetry. It is natural that associative speakers, for whom even English prose is a dead language, should regard English poetry with the baffled stare of a stranger accosted by a lunatic. I suspect that much of the difficulty complained of in contemporary poetry is really due to its use of simple and concrete language.

I feel, therefore, that there is a close connection among three aspects of language in our society. First is the associative squirrel-chatter that one hears on streets, and even in college halls, jerking along apologetically or defiantly in a series of unshaped phrases, using slang or vogue words for emphasis and punctuation. Second is the poetic illiteracy which regards anything in verse as a verbal puzzle, not even a puzzle to be worked out, but a disdainful and inscrutable puzzle without an answer. Third is the dead, senseless, sentenceless, written pseudo-prose that surrounds us like a boa constrictor, which is said to cover its victims with slime before strangling them. This last, under the names of jargon, gobbledygook, and the like, has often enough been recognized as a disease of contemporary language and ridiculed or deplored as such.

Two features of pseudo-prose seem to me of particular importance. One is that colorless and rhythmless writing is designed to obliterate the sense of personality: we write this way when we want to speak with some kind of impersonal or anonymous voice. It is not a healthy tendency, for, as Kierkegaard reminds us, the impersonal (in this context) is essentially demoralizing. The other is its underlying assumption that the idea is substantial and that the words which express the idea are incidental. This is a fallacy developed from the habit of associative reading. The words used are the form of which the ideas are the content, and until the words have been found, the idea does not fully exist. It seems to me that the fallacy of the substantial idea has a great deal to do with the bewildering woolliness of so much discursive writing today where (as in literary criticism, philosophy and much of the social sciences) the essential conceptions are verbal rather than mathematical, as mathematical language is doubtless used more accurately.

Elsewhere on my desk, which is a very untidy one, I find the following:

> In matters of curriculum, textbooks, or methods of study, variety is the spice of education and decentralization can be even more readily provided than under the small unit system because the resultant stability of teaching personnel means that the central authorities no longer have to keep so tight a grip upon a shifting texture of educational personnel.

The clanging repetition of "personnel" and the huddle of mixed metaphors at the end indicate that the author is writing in his sleep, and there is the usual absence of rhythm and color. But here we notice something else: the cliché or ready-made phrase ("variety is the spice of education") is beginning to make itself felt as a unit of thought and expression. A student of mine recently found herself at a conference of people who write (and talk) like this, and came back muttering a sentence that had, understandably, got stuck in her mind: "Jobwise, are we structured for this activation?" What is striking about this sentence is that it consists entirely of ready-made vogue or jargon words. The cliché is no longer an occasional resource: it has taken over as the only form of expression, and consequently as the only form of thought. A century ago Flaubert explored, with horrified fascination, the cultural life of Bouvard and Pécuchet, whose intellects moved entirely within the orbit of what he drew up as a supplement to his research, the Dictionary of Accepted Ideas. But Bouvard and Pécuchet were still a long way from the verbal automatism, a language based on the conditioned reflex, that we have reached with this sentence. The similar jargon used in Marxist countries looks more philosophical at first glance, but it comes from the same part of the nervous system.

GEORGE WOODCOCK

1912-

George Woodcock, the best if not the only example in Canada of an all-round man of letters, is the author of more than a score of books on a wide variety of subjects and of many sorts — biography; criticism, social, political, and literary; travel; poetry; and radio drama, including the libretto of a Centennial opera. Among the most important of these are biographical studies of William Godwin, Aphra Behn, and Oscar Wilde in the late forties and early fifties, followed by studies of the "anarchist prince," Peter Kropotkin and of the French social theorist Proudhon, and more recently of the modern English writers George Orwell, Aldous Huxley, and Herbert Read. His study of George Orwell, entitled *The Crystal Spirit* (1966), won a Governor General's Award; his most recent critical study, *Herbert Read, The Stream and the Source,* was published in 1972. The travel books include accounts of his journeys in western Canada, Mexico, Peru, India, and the Far East. His most significant work in the field of social criticism and historical studies is perhaps *Anarchism: A History of Libertarian Ideas and Movements* (1962), while a more popular work is *Civil Disobedience,* a series of seven radio talks delivered over the CBC. For the student of Canadian history and literature his *Canada and the Canadians* (1970) and a collection of his essays drawn mainly from *Canadian Literature,* the quarterly he founded in 1959 and has edited since then, entitled *Odysseus Ever Returning* (1970), are indispensable. The latter volume contains the best short essays yet written on the novelists Morley Callaghan and Hugh MacLennan and the poet Irving Layton. A newer collection of essays, *The Rejection of Politics*, was published in 1972.

George Woodcock was born in Winnipeg and spent his early life in England, receiving a grammar school education there. During the thirties he was associated with the left wing poetry movement and the early struggle against Fascism in Spain, Italy, and Germany. He contributed verse to magazines edited by Julian Symons and Geoffrey Grigson and edited his own poetry magazine *Now*. He published three small collections of verse in the early forties and his *Selected Poems* more recently in Canada. He returned to Canada in 1949 and, after teaching for a short time at the University of Washington, he joined the staff of the University of British Columbia, devoting himself after 1963 solely to writing and to the editing of *Canadian Literature*.

The essay that follows was originally published as the Introduction to *A Choice of Critics* (1966). It was reprinted in the slightly amended form used here, in *Odysseus Ever Returning*, where it had the title "Views of Canadian Criticism: 2/ in 1966."

ON CANADIAN CRITICISM

Canadian criticism tends to take as its most characteristic form the thinly masked dialogue — the critic debating, as it were, with the author, and gently drawing the reader into the discussion by the atmosphere of intimacy which he creates. All this, of course, partakes very strongly of the "personal fallacy" and the "intentional heresy" and all the other errors which, according to the recently dominant schools of criticism, particularly in the United States, arise when we allow anything beyond the finished work of literature to enter our critical vision. But Canadian criticism has arisen outside the general North American neo-critical pattern; when I search for purely analytical or purely aesthetic Canadian critics, I find it impossible to offer a single name of any significance. The great names of New Criticism may be rather distantly respected, but it is one sign of cultural independence that our writers have taken from them only as much as fits their peculiar requirements, which have been dictated far more than literary purists care to admit by historical circumstances.

What A. J. M. Smith has to say in his essay, "Eclectic Detachment" is particularly meaningful in this context:

> The function of personality in the poet is to create a thing, a
> *persona*, a poem; and in Canada the problem of the critic, if
> not of the poet, has been to relate this thing to its place and to
> its time. For the scholar, watching the critic as the critic
> watches the poet, the Canadian literary scene offers an almost
> classic instance of an easily isolable phenomenon: the quick
> and almost forced development of a compact and self-contained
> literary tradition — arising from the practice of the poets —
> and of an orthodoxy (rather rapidly changing) — arising from
> the sensibility of readers and the cogitations of critics.

In this brief paragraph Smith is in fact making two statements which reflect essential features of the situation that every Canadian critic has to face. First there is the necessity by which he feels him-self bound to relate works of literature to place and time — in other words to consider them geographically as well as historically. More immediate in the line of reflection I am now pursuing is Smith's observation of "the quick and almost forced development of a compact and self-contained literary tradition."

The emergence of the Canadian literary tradition, and the nature of what has emerged, relate closely to the quality of intimacy I have noted in much Canadian criticism. This intimacy has often been regarded as evidence of the provincial incestuousness of the Cana-dian literary world, in which most writers of any significance are personally acquainted with a very large proportion of their literary colleagues. The distances that divide literary centres — Montreal, Toronto, Vancouver — are undoubtedly great. But Canadian writers tend to be travellers; I find that even if I sit for a whole year in the western isolation of Vancouver, by the end of it I will have accu-mulated a considerable number of meetings with visiting poets, novelists and critics, not to speak of the acquaintances established and nurtured through correspondence. At the same time, a small, close, literary world need not necessarily be narrow or sterile, pro-vided it is always enlarging and varying itself by recruitment from outside; the London of Shakespeare, Dryden and Johnson, the Paris of *la belle époque*, developed networks of literary acquaintance just as intimate as those of Canada in the 1960's, without in any way detracting from the achievements of individual writers or diminish-ing the rigours of critical judgment.

That a "compact and self-contained literary tradition" has emerged in Canada during the past generation there is no doubt; one can admit it without necessarily giving comfort to nationalist politicians or to the wavers of maple-leaf flags. Canadian writers of course belong in one way to the broad general tradition of writing in English, and this they recognize by feeling unfulfilled if they have not published their works in the metropolitan centres of London and New York, and have thus failed to enter into full and equal competition with their British and American peers.

At the same time, in a geographical and to a great degree in a cultural sense Canadian writers are American writers, since they share certain influences common to intellectuals in the whole sub-continent. But this does not mean that, as Mordecai Richler and a few other Americanophiles have argued, Canadian writing is merely an extension of the tradition that has grown up in the United States, in much the same way as, in the mid-nineteenth century, it was merely a colonial offshoot of the British tradition. Even in the United States, historical and geographical circumstances help to differentiate writers and their work, so that a Negro bred in Harlem is unlikely to write like a white man bred in Georgia, and a San Franciscan of Italian descent is unlikely to write like either; these differences of tradition exist in addition to the personal qualities that distinguish every original writer from all his colleagues and competitors.

In Canada, the factors that differentiate intellectual life from that in the rest of North America are even greater than those distinguishing one American region from another. The fact that we all live in the supermarket, hire-purchase, high-living-standard environment that extends from El Paso north to Yellowknife, that we are subjected to the same kind of pressures from mass media and mass advertising as our neighbours south of the forty-ninth parallel, that Canada is even an economic and military satellite of the United States, does not mean that we think or react individually or even communally like Americans. Our political life, for example, is quite different from that of the United States; our world view is that of citizens of a precariously independent middle power rather than that of participants in a new crypto-imperialism; and we see ourselves more ironically than Americans do, and more humbly and tentatively, awed by our spaces, our unpeopled distances, the unrealized and unnerving potentialities of our land. We have, by luck rather than deliberation, evaded the temptations of Messianism.

Culturally, and in literary terms especially, these differentiating factors are compounded by the existence of influences we do not share with our fellow North Americans. A third of us do not even speak English, and look to Paris as our literary metropolis; and the presence of Quebec affects the outlook of even the most remote of our communities, uniting Canadians through the very problem that most divides them. The link with Britain remains strong, and it is only within the last decade that our younger poets and prose-writers have tended to turn towards the United States rather than towards London for examples and for the theoretical justifications of them. This has happened largely because British writing in recent years has been singularly dull and conservative; it will be interesting to see the reaction in Canada if a movement as vigorous as that of the

Thirties emerges in England during the next decade.

Finally, one cannot evade the fact that Canada is still a country of immigration in a way the United States has long ceased to be; a very high proportion of its population still consists of people born and educated abroad. While before 1945 immigrants tended to be predominantly farmers and industrial workers, since that time they have included many professional men and intellectuals. Patrick Anderson, arriving during the 1930's, was the precursor of a long succession of British and continental writers — Malcolm Lowry, Brian Moore and Kildare Dobbs prominent among them — who have contributed greatly to the development of Canadian writing over the past twenty years, both by their own writings and by the influence they have wielded as editors, publishers and critics. To an extent the British migration has been balanced by the migration to Canadian universities of American writer-scholars, some of whom have stayed to add their contribution to Canadian writing and particularly to criticism, so that Warren Tallman's American voice has counterpointed the English voices of such critics as Paul West. There is no doubt that the immigrant writers have not only brought the stimulus of new viewpoints, but have also helped to introduce more rigorous and objective critical attitudes, so that the "double standard" by which a book tended at one time to be immoderately praised (or sometimes damned) because of its Canadian origin is now, except in the columns of provincial newspapers, a thing of the past. But only of the recent past.

This brings us to the standing of criticism in Canada today. In the later Fifties a change took place in the structure of the Canadian literary world. There was a knitting together of the various disparate influences, so that though in some ways Canadian literature retained and still retains a provincial relationship to the literatures of both Britain and the United States, its core of individuality was strengthened, and it emerged as a clearly defined regional tradition. I use the word *regional* quite deliberately for two reasons. Firstly because it emphasizes that Canadian writers still belong within the greater tradition of Anglo-Saxon literature and have to establish a place there as individuals; and secondly because *national* is a political term and, though a literature may share the geographical terrain of a nation and even to an extent its historical past, the link is not a necessary one: there are multi-lingual nations like India that have several literatures, and Canada itself has two. The distinction is necessary if only to emphasize that, when we talk of a Canadian literature, our purpose is not one of chauvinism, of contribution to the national glory, but merely of critical and scholarly definition. Because of complex and not always easily detected circumstances, a certain region produces its own type of literature, as a certain climate produces its own flora; that is all.

One of the signs of the change in the character of writing in Canada during the Fifties was the double process of sophistication and differentiation that took place. It had been possible to see even the late poems of Pratt and the early poems of Birney in the context of a pioneer tradition, in which experience is recorded and glorified in robust speech, in which geography dominates and the demands of the land are still important. Other writers of the time, like Hugh MacLennan, worked under the spell of a history specifically Canadian. Only a few Canadian writers who had deliberately cultivated international affiliations, like Morley Callaghan and A. J. M. Smith, seemed at this time able to overcome the limiting factors of the environment. The new generation of the Forties and more particularly of the Fifties — represented by writers as varied as Northrop Frye and the later Birney, Margaret Avison and Douglas Le Pan, Irving Layton and James Reaney — carried out an astonishing liberation of both techniques and content from this recent past. The intellectual content of poetry and prose became more important and more complex, the actual craft of writing received far closer and more deliberate attention than ever before, and as each writer departed on his own experimental course — schools forming and breaking up into militant individualities — the pattern of Canadian literature underwent a rapid and progressive variegation.

Such phases of maturing, when attention swings to language and form and intellectual complexity, occur in the developments of all literatures, and they are times when writers talk more than they did in the past about writing — their own and other men's — and when criticism becomes not merely an outside commentary on writing but also an interior dialogue carried on by poets and novelists whose interest spreads out beyond their own work to the contemplation of the literary setting to which it belongs. The critical essays of poets like James Reaney and Louis Dudek, A. J. M. Smith and Miriam Waddington, are admirable examples of such dialogue. The critic no longer stands detached in the same way as the professional book columnist or the scholarly historian of literature; he takes his place as a creator, and we have the extraordinary phenomenon of a Northrop Frye not merely building elaborate and fascinating structures of literary theory which are in themselves works of creative imagination, but also providing a seminal impulse that helps a whole group of poets to find their individual paths of creation. The world of writing is, in fact, a unity in which criticism, understood in its broadest and deepest aspects, has a necessary place once a literature has passed beyond its most elementary stages. Nothing seems to me more pernicious than the neo-romantic doctrine — itself, of course, a perverted critical dogma — which seeks to isolate certain literary forms and set them apart from and above the rest under the title of "creative writing," as if other categories, such as history and biography and criticism, were not also in their own ways creative. The attempt to divide poetry or fiction hierarchically from the rest of literature is as devitalizing and as futile as the aesthetic attempt to divide literature from life, and so it would have been understood by the great poets and novelists who have also practiced the craft of criticism, from Dryden and Coleridge down to Eliot and James and Orwell. A good critical essay is as much a work of literary art as a good story or a good poem; the only difference lies in the criteria by which each literary category is to be judged.

The critic as artist — Wilde's phrase is still the best — belongs in Canada to the past half-generation. A glance at any critical anthology that spans a long period of Canadian literary history — like A. J. M. Smith's two collections, *Masks of Poetry* and *Masks of Fiction* — shows that what passed for criticism in the early days of writing in Canada tended to be disguised history or biography or merely rhetorical appreciation, with almost no attempt at imaginative analysis. During the Thirties and the early Forties, the period of militancy, when poets like Smith and Scott, and later Anderson and Sutherland, Dudek and Souster, were conducting their rebellions against colonial traditions in Canadian poetry, criticism took on a new form, that of the manifesto, with its tone of defiant apology; it was a matter of stating positions rather than contemplating and analysing actual works of literature.

Probably the two most important developments in the breakthrough towards a new and more analytical form of criticism were Northrop Frye's annual commentaries on Canadian poetry which began in 1952 in the Letters in Canada supplement to the *University*

RAMSAY COOK

1931-

Ramsay Cook was born in Saskatchewan and educated at the universities of Manitoba, Queen's, and Toronto, and is at present professor of history and social science at York University. He was editor of the *Canadian Historical Review* from 1963 to 1968 and is the author of a number of important books on Canadian history and current politics. Among these are *The Politics of John W. Dafoe and the Free Press* (1963), *Canada: A Modern Study* (1964), *Canada and the French Canadian Question* (1966), and most recently the book from which the chapter below has been selected, the perhaps ironically titled *The Maple Leaf Forever* (1971). This chapter is included here for its perceptive analysis of some of the Canadian historians whose writings appear in this section, to which it serves as an illuminating summary and conclusion.

LA SURVIVANCE ENGLISH-CANADIAN STYLE

"Nationalist historiography desires not only to describe a people's life but to help form it and make its history appear as the fulfillment of a supposed national destiny."

Hans Kohn, *American Nationalism*

There is a widespread assumption that while French Canadians have used history as a weapon in the endless struggle for survival, English Canadians, including their historians, have looked upon their past with a supreme detachment and objectivity. The primary implication of this assumption is that while French-Canadian history is little more than high-level propaganda, English-Canadian history is an unbiassed record of the developing Canadian reality. The unstated major premise of this view is that while Canadian nationalism is a valid and enlightened expression of the human spirit, French-Canadian nationalism is narrow and parochial. One of the reasons for this view of the difference between French- and English-Canadian history is that French Canadians have, in fact, placed their 'national' historians on a pedestal, while English Canadians have never had a 'national' historian. This, then, has led to a view which may be summed up in the words of Professor C. B. Macpherson:

> For the French Canadian historians, history is an instrument in the service of the survival of the French Canadian community and culture. It is deliberately a moralizing history, drawing from the proud record of French Canada lessons of strength in adversity and of the supreme importance of treasuring the traditional French Canadian values.
>
> English Canadian historians, more pragmatic and unattached to a philosophy, have not been in a position to see themselves as guardians of a culture. For them history has

rather been a way of discovering the interplay of forces that have made the political institutions and the whole life of Canada what they are now. They do not write in the imperative mood.

To some extent, it must be admitted, Professor Macpherson modifies this stark comparison when he concludes the paragraph with this remark: 'But since they differ in their assessment of the formative forces and do not conceal their high or low opinions of motives and policies they are in effect generally arguing a case for one line of national development rather than another. And in doing so they contribute, in their various perspectives, to the development of the Canadian national consciousness.' This last distinction is an important one—indeed, so important as to destroy much of the basis of the original contrast between French- and English-Canadian historical writing. It is quite true that there are deep differences of interpretation among English-speaking historians. But the difference, basically, is about the means of survival, not about the ultimate value of survival itself. In short, English-Canadian historians have also made history the foundation-stone of survival.

English Canada has not had a Garneau, a Groulx, or even a Brunet; it has not had a single nationalist doctrine. Nevertheless, English-Canadian historians, in a manner similar to French-Canadian historians, have used the concept of survival as a primary criterion of historical judgment. No contemporary English-Canadian professional historian has been as explicit as Henri D'Arles, who wrote, 'History is the conscience of a nation. It is from our history that we ought to draw the means of resistance to the forces that threaten our dissolution as a race.' Yet is that remark really very different from the following sentence taken from the preface to A. R. M. Lower's well-known study *Colony to Nation?*

The author hopes that a careful reading of his pages will help Canadians to some of that self-knowledge so necessary if they are to take their rightful place in the world, and still more, if they are to be a happy people at peace with themselves. If he has not succeeded in this task, then someone else must take it up, for it is imperative. It may be performed by the statesman, by the novelist or the poet, or it may be performed by the historian. Certainly on no one is the duty of revealing to the people reasons for the faith that is in them more directly laid than on the historian, for by its history a people lives. This book is an attempt to discharge that duty.

Professor Lower's denial of the existence of a Canadian 'nation' in no way weakens his own nationalism. Indeed, it rather underlines the point since his history is a contribution to the building of that nation. 'Writing Canadian history,' he says, 'is an act of faith, the substance of things hoped for.'

Lower is very clear in the statement of his faith. Others have been much less so. But an examination of recent Canadian historical writing will reveal the extent to which other English-Canadian histrrians have been guided at least implicitly by a nationalist faith similar to Lower's. There are several other possible approaches to the work of English-Canadian historians. Some of these have been very fruitful. But for the most part analyses in the past have stressed the differences that have separated English-Canadian historians. While these differences are important, that approach disguises the unifying, dominating, and even stultifying preoccupation of the writers examined. That unifying element has been the doctrine of survival. Perhaps the differences among English-Canadian historians have been overemphasized because of their common commitment to the nationalist criterion of survival. This has meant that the conflict has been a battle of patriots, each brandishing his particular recipe for national greatness. And as every student knows, there is no war more bitter than a civil war, a war between patriots, even if the battle is restricted to a battle of the books. Therefore, an analysis of the preoccupations of English-Canadian historians should begin with an examination of the fundamental presuppositions that guide the writers.

The necessary starting-point for any clear understanding of the outlook of contemporary English-Canadian historians is Harold Adams Innis. Innis's most important work was in the field of economic history. His later work in the nebulous field of communications may some day be judged his greatest achievement, but for historians of Canada his early studies, especially *The Fur Trade in Canada* and *The Cod Fisheries*, will always remain the most prominent monuments in the Innis revolution.

That revolution had two aspects. In the first place, when Innis began his career as a teacher, researcher, and writer of Canadian history, very little work of significance had been done in the field of economic history. Therefore, quite apart from the interpretation that he gave to Canadian history, Innis would have made an enormous contribution to Canadian studies by his massive accounts of the staple trades and transportation alone. But Innis did something more important than merely filling gaps—large as they were—in our knowledge of Canadian history. At this point the second aspect of the Innis revolution must be sketched in.

Not only was most Canadian history, before Innis, political and constitutional; it was also, especially in the 1920s and 1930s, based on two quite generally accepted assumptions. The first assumption was that the chief theme in Canada's development was the winning of autonomy from Britain. The second assumption was that Canada was basically part of a common North American community divided by political boundaries but united by geography, economics, and even world interests. Both of these ideas, if they have any single source, were derived from the writings of that nineteenth-century English liberals-in-exile, Goldwin Smith. The best statement of Smith's continentalism—a faith that made him a proponent of union of Canada and the United States—is found in his gloomy *Canada and the Canadian Question*, published in 1891. Innis's studies of Canadian economic growth led him to challenge Smith's thesis head-on. In the first place Innis insisted that, whatever political history might show about relations with Britain, economic history displayed the interdependence of the Canadian and European economies. Canada's very existence had depended not on separation from Britain, but on a close relationship with her. Secondly, he argued that, from the time of New France, Canada was a geographic and economic unit. He saw, what now seems so obvious, that the geographic lines of the country were as much east-west as they were north-south. He concluded that the country's primary axis, the axis upon which successive economic developments from the fur trade to the Canadian Pacific Railway had been based, was the extension of the St. Lawrence system.

In Innis's view, then, Canada was not an artificial entity established by historical accident. It was a geographically and economically natural community. The Innis philosophy, expressed in its boldest fashion in the concluding chapter of *The Fur Trade in Canada*, is summed up in these famous sentences:

Canada emerged as a political entity with boundaries largely determined by the fur trade. These boundaries included a vast north temperate land area extending from the Atlantic to the Pacific and dominated by the Canadian shield. *The present Dominion emerged not in spite of geography but because of it.* The significance of the fur trade consisted in its determination of the geographic framework. Later economic developments in Canada were profoundly influenced by this background.

The importance of the Innis revolution is obvious. It gave the Canadian nation a geographic and economic foundation that it had previously been thought to lack. There can be no doubt that its author and those who accepted this new view were fully aware of its nationalist implications. Innis himself was a Canadian nationalist but he was also a tough individualist. His interpretation of Canada's 'Europeanness' ran radically counter to the more popular 'North American' views that held sway in those years when Mackenzie King was slaying imperial paper tigers. What Innis was telling his countrymen, as they withdrew into a North American shell confident that the only challenge to their survival as a nation came from Europe, was that the country's fundamental strength lay in its European roots. Moreover, he implied, their history showed that the true threat to their survival had always come as much or more from within North America—from the United States, that is—than from Europe. This latter strain, the anti-American strain, became increasingly persistent in Innis's later writing. In the years after the Second World War, when it became painfully obvious that the power of Europe, especially of Britain, had declined, Canadian intellectuals became profoundly concerned about the threat of the United States. Innis shared these fears. Indeed, his understanding of Canadian history forewarned him of the danger. Not long before his death he warned that 'The pride taken in improving our status in the British Commonwealth of Nations has made it difficult for us to realize that our status on the North American continent is on the verge of disappearing. Continentalism assisted in the achievement of autonomy and has consequently become more dangerous. We can only survive by taking persistent action at strategic points against American imperialism in all its attractive guises.' While

Innis was never narrowly Canadian in his outlook or approach—in his later studies in communications he was probably more wide-ranging than any other scholar in the country—there is no need to labour the point that his interpretation was profoundly nationalist in its implications.

All the other major English-Canadian historians may be measured by their attitude to the central Innis thesis. Closest to Innis in age, though not in ideas, is A. R. M. Lower. Like Innis, indeed, in collaboration with Innis, Lower began his study of Canadian history by turning his attention to economic questions. In this field he produced several important studies, notably *The North American Assault on the Canadian Forest*. But he was soon drawn from economic to political history, from narrow monographic studies to broad general themes. Unlike Innis, Lower is eclectic in his ideas, epigrammatic in his writing, and, most important, 'North American' in his approach. While the growth of Canadian nationalism is Professor Lower's overriding concern, two sub-themes run through his exposition. The one, exemplified in the title of his provocative general history, *Colony to Nation*, is the old story of developing dominion status. Like many men of his generation, Lower was convinced that Canada should acquire full national autonomy. He participated in the steps leading to that goal and he proudly celebrated the triumph of Canadian autonomy in his historical writing. The winning of full national status became one aspect of the story of Canadian survival.

One of the reasons for Lower's strong insistence on the need for full national autonomy was his belief that the imperial relationship represented a fundamental barrier between English and French Canadians. That barrier could only be removed if all Canadians, French and English, gave their first loyalty to Canada. For Lower, then, there was an obstacle to Canadian national development that was greater even than Britain. That was the 'colonial mentality' of English Canadians. If only English Canadians could become as 'North American' in their outlook as French Canadians, a large step towards a true Canadianism would be taken.

This concern with the ideas of French and English Canada suggests the second main theme in Lower's concept of Canadian history and Canadian nationality: the 'two ways of life.' With more perception than any other English-Canadian historian, Lower depicted the two Canadian peoples attempting to develop a common life. He believed that the difference had its origins in religion, since English Canadians were committed to social values based on Calvinist doctrines, while French Canadians viewed life from a Roman Catholic perspective. Lower's analysis owed a good deal to R. H. Tawney's brilliant study of religion and the rise of capitalism, which Lower saw worked out in both its Protestant and Catholic phases in Canada. Lower realized that added to this gulf between the value systems of the two communities was the scar of the Conquest, which he described as 'a type of slavery' for French Canadians. From these conditions every other difference between French and English Canadians followed logically. For Lower the only way that this division could be erased, the only conceivable synthesis that could replace the 'primary antithesis,' was a 'common Canadianism.' And what would be the basis of this new nationality? In a lyrical passage at the close of *Colony to Nation* Lower offers his formula for Canadianism in terms that are interesting both as an example of late-flowering romantic liberal nationalism, and for their explicit rejection of Innis's geographic determinism. The passage deserves full quotation:

Canada with its division of races presents no common denominator in those profundities which normally unite, in race, language, religion, history and culture. If a common focus is to be found, it must come out of the common homeland itself. If the Canadian people are to find their soul, they must seek for it not in the English language, or the French, but in the little ports of the Atlantic provinces, in the flaming autumn maples of the St. Lawrence Valley, in the portages and lakes of the Canadian Shield, in the sunsets and relentless cold of the prairies, in the foothill, mountain and sea of the west and in the unconquerable vastness of the north. From the land, Canada, must come the soul of Canada. That it may be so is not so fanciful as one might think. When in 1763 the experiment was begun in the northern wilderness no one foresaw the strong state that was to be. Canada has been built in defiance of geography. Its two coasts were bridged by a transcontinental railway almost in defiance of common sense. Canadian statesmen reconciled the irreconcilable when in the 1840s they joined dependence to independence. They accomplished one of the greatest acts of state-building in history when in 1867 they brought together scattered provinces and two peoples into one country. Though extremists would more than once have wrecked it, the structure built has never failed in time of crisis to rally to it the support of moderate men from both races. It has stood through the storms of two world wars. In every generation Canadians have had to rework the miracle of their political existence. Canada has been created because there has existed within the hearts of its people a determination to build for themselves an enduring home. Canada is a supreme act of faith.

For Lower, then, the struggle for survival had to be fought on two fronts. First there was the thrilling story of the development of a nation from a mere colony. Then there was the ever-repeating story of cultural accommodation between French- and English-speaking Canadians. Should that latter struggle ever fail, the country's survival would be threatened as seriously as it would if faced by an external enemy. No English-Canadian historian has been as explicitly nationalist as Lower, and none so willing to admit openly that historical writing must play a leading part in the development of the Canadian national consciousness. In this sense Lower is more similar to the French-Canadian 'national' historians than any other English Canadian. It is perhaps for this very reason that Lower has come closer than any other English-Canadian historian to a full, sympathetic understanding of the French-Canadian outlook.

F. H. Underhill, like Lower, was a contemporary of Harold Innis. All three served in the First World War and it is perhaps not without significance and interest that while Innis served in the Canadian Expeditionary Force as an infantryman, both Lower and Underhill served in the British forces as officers. Underhill, like Lower but unlike Innis, developed an attitude of intense suspicion toward British power. In Underhill's case it is a little difficult to distinguish between the scholar and the polemicist. In both capacities, however, he was fulfilling a third role which, for him, is even more important: that of the teacher. If it can be said that Lower is the English-Canadian Garneau, Underhill is perhaps the English-Canadian Brunet. Both express themselves best in the public speech or lecture, both are iconoclasts, both use history as an armoury of weapons to be used against their complacent compatriots. Both, finally, have seemed to act according to Underhill's dictum that 'Just as war is too important to be left to generals, politics is too vital a matter to be left to politicians.'

Two things, above all others, have interested Underhill: political ideas and political parties. These have been his pre-occupations both as an historian and as a commentator on, and participant in, contemporary events. His own politics have always, at least until recently, been radical: he was one of the founders of the League for Social Reconstruction and of the Co-operative Commonwealth Federation in the 1930s. With these political interests it is not surprising that Underhill the historian turned his attention to such subjects as radical opinion in Upper Canada in the nineteenth century and more particularly to the career of the highly intellectual but politically inept Edward Blake. These interests were accompanied by a constant concern about the nature of political parties and political leadership in Canada. Almost always his sympathies have been with the dissenters and third parties: the Clear Grits, Edward Blake, Goldwin Smith, J. W. Dafoe, the c.c.f., Henri Bourassa, and above all, J. S. Woodsworth, the first leader of the c.c.f. It is true that he has finally become a grudging admirer of two of Canada's most successful politicians, Sir Wilfrid Laurier and W. L. M. King, but these are views tempered by the realization that neither can ever achieve power again.

Like Lower, Underhill was a staunch supporter of the drive for Canadian autonomy within the British Commonwealth. This, in his view, was an affirmation of Canada's true 'North Americanism.' Yet he seemed to yearn for something more exciting than the slow march from fisheries treaty to fisheries treaty that marked the growth of Canadian self-government. Reviewing Lower's Colony to Nation in 1947, Underhill wrote:

Some critics would say that Professor Lower is too prone to emphasize the self-centred attitude of British imperialism and the essential colonialism of Canadians throughout. But it is useful for us to be repeatedly reminded of the invigorating effects which independence has had upon our American neighbours, of the vitality which they have enjoyed from fully accepting their North American destiny. While we would not have survived as a separate individual Canadian people through the nineteenth century without the protection of the British connection, at the same time we have paid a heavy price for that protection in the slowness with which our national spirit grew and in the weakness of that national spirit today.

That revolution which had given the United States its national foundation had also given it a radical tradition that was, in Underhill's view, lacking in Canada. In 1946 he stated that

> For this weakness of the left in Canada the ultimate explanation would seem to be that we never had an eighteenth century of our own. The intellectual life of our politics has not been periodically revived by fresh drafts from the invigorating fountain of the Eighteenth Century Enlightenment . . . All effective liberal and radical democratic movements in the nineteenth century have had their roots in this fertile eighteenth century soil. But our ancestors made the great refusal in the eighteenth century. In Canada we have no Revolutionary tradition . . .

Underhill, like so many other English-Canadian nationalists in the 1930s and later, believed that the British connection was the factor which stifled Canadian initiative and creativity. So, despite the fact that he helped found a party whose philosophy owed more to British than to American influences, Underhill emphasized the 'North Americanness' of the Canadian experience and urged his fellow countrymen to accept closer relations with the United States. He described the Clear Grits as a typical example of a North American frontier protest movement, and the more closely he examined Canadian political parties the more convinced he became that they were more similar to American parties than to their British counterparts. Gradually he concluded that the ultimate secret of Mackenzie King's political success was his recognition of Canada's 'North Americanness,' as exemplified in King's attitude both to the British connection and to the nature of political parties. This meant that Canada should draw as far away as possible from European, especially British, influences and also that Canadian politics should be guided by American rules. In 1950, after W. L. M. King's death Underhill wrote:

Mr. King's leadership in domestic affairs was based upon two fundamentals ... One was that Canada cannot be governed without the consent and cooperation of the French Canadians; and the other was that in a loosely knit continental community like ours, with all its diverse interest groups, a political party that aspires to the responsibility of government must not be a class party, but must be a loosely knit representative collection of voters from all groups, such as the Liberal party has generally been under himself and Laurier. In other words, the federalism which is the essence of both North American countries must be reflected in their political parties.

As is befitting an admirer of Goldwin Smith, Underhill has constantly insisted on the essential unity of purpose of Canadians and American. While he was fully aware that the changed balance of power in the post-war world has placed Canada in a precarious position in her relations with the United States, he refused to indulge in the criticisms of the United States that many of his contemporaries were making. In reply to those who insisted on the close connection between Canada and Europe, Underhill claimed that the relations between the United States and Europe have really been much closer, and, more important, that the U.S.-Europe relationship has been one of equals, while the Canada-Europe relationship has been more 'colonial.' 'One of these days,' he wrote in 1959, 'we Canadians are going to wake up and discover with a shock that the Americans have for a long time been closer to Europe than we have been. This will leave our conservative social philosophers in an embarrassing state of cultural nudity.' Those who, like Professor W. L. Morton of Winnipeg, tried to depict Canadian society as qualitatively different from the United States received no support from Underhill. Reviewing Professor Morton's *Canadian Identity*, Underhill wrote:

In fact this little volume is Tract for the Times No. 1. Professor Morton is casting himself in the role of a Canadian Newman. Just as Newman in Oxford in the 1840s confronting with horror the monster of Liberalism, set himself with his companions in the Oxford Movement to save his society from the modernism of the nineteenth century, so Morton in Winnipeg is launching a Manitoba Movement to save his society from the Americanism (i.e. modernism) of the twentieth century.

Where does this put Underhill in the pattern of *la survivance?* It is perhaps more difficult to categorize him than some of the other English-Canadian historians, not least of all because in his writing there is no very clear line dividing the historian from the preacher or moralist. In the last analysis, however, he is a nineteenth-century liberal, unrevised and unrepented. The essence of his views, as they are found in his three recent books *The British Commonwealth* (1957), *In Search of Canadian Liberalism* (Toronto 1960), and *The Image of Confederation* (1964), is the story of Canada's emergence from colony to nation in terms that have more in common with Lower than with Innis. Underhill's contribution as an historian has been his emphasis on ideas; but his preoccupation has been with nationalist ideas, whether in the 'Canada First' movement or in the Progressive Party's 'New National Policy.' Despite his appeal at the close of *The Image of Confederation* for a broad, outward-looking attitude on the part of all Canadians, the predominant undertone of the book, occasionally muted but always present, is a nagging concern about *la survivance,* English-Canadian style.

No one better exemplifies the profound opposition to the Lower-Underhill 'school' of liberal nationalist historians than D. G. Creighton. Donald Creighton is at once the chief disciple of Harold Innis and English Canada's finest historian. No other practitioner of the historian's craft in Canada, past or present, can match the list of Creighton's work: *The Commercial Empire of the St. Lawrence* (1937), *British North America at Confederation* (1939), *The Dominion of the North* (1944), *John A. Macdonald* (1953 and 1955), *The Road to Confederation* (1964), and *Canada's First Century* (1970). The careful research and penetrating insight of each of these works is matched by a flowing prose and sense of the dramatic that makes Creighton's history unique.

If Innis was the first to present a documented study of the Laurentian thesis, Creighton first made it intelligible. In *The Commercial Empire of the St. Lawrence* he set out and extended the Innis thesis in majestic terms. In the preface to the second edition of the work Creighton remarked that 'the idea of the St. Lawrence as the inspiration and basis of a trans-continental, east-west system, both commercial and political in character, is still central to my interpretation of Canadian history.' The thesis had three essential ingredients: first, the east-west trading system founded on the St. Lawrence; second, the inevitable conflict between the system and its competitors to the south—a competition which was not politically or nationally determined, but rather which was built into the geography and economics of the continent; third, the connection between the 'empire' of the St. Lawrence and Europe—first France, and later Britain. It was upon the success of this system that the survival of Canada, whether French or British, depended. In *Dominion of the North* Creighton summed up the origins:

> Talon began it. No doubt he had gone out to Canada with his head full of neat, orderly Colbertian assumptions about the future of New France.... And yet, almost from the beginning, something began to happen to him.... He had suddenly become conscious of the river and of the enormous continent into which it led. He had yielded to that instinct for grandeur, that vertigo of ambition, that was part of the enchantment of the St. Lawrence.

The heroes of all Professor Creighton's books are the men who recognized the potential of the St. Lawrence: the Talons, the Montreal merchants, Sir John A. Macdonald, and the builders of the Canadian Pacific Railway. The villains are those who stood in the way of the fulfilment of the Laurentian dream: the Roman Catholic Church, the French-Canadian habitant and his liberal bourgeoisie leaders, the Americans, and the short-sighted Liberal critics of the c.p.r.

In his great biography of Macdonald, Creighton humanized the impersonal, economic determinism of the Laurentian thesis. Macdonald became a modern, successful Talon who built the state and formulated the policies—policies which were a modern version of Talon's 'mercantilism'—that were designed to stimulate the growth of 'a new nationality' on the basis of that economic empire, stretching from Atlantic to Pacific. In his more recent study, *The Road to Confederation,* Creighton passed over this familiar ground again, this time treating the Confederation movement almost biographically, in the same literary fashion that proved so successful in the Macdonald biography.

In his restoration of Macdonald, Creighton was also, openly, fighting to revise the standards of Canadian historical interpretation. Too long, he believed, Canadian historical writing had been dominated by the 'liberal nationalist' writers. 'The chief characteristic of nationalist history,' he wrote in 1948, 'amounting almost to an obsession, is with the twin achievements of Responsible Government and Dominion Status.... The achievement and maintenance of Canadian separateness on the American continent have either been neglected, or have been represented, in the main, as an easy and perfunctory business, in sharp contrast with the unending and acrimonious conflict by which autonomy within the British Empire has been achieved.' Past of Macdonald's greatness, in Creighton's eyes, was that he had recognized very clearly that the winning of freedom from Great Britain was far less important, or at least far less difficult, than maintaining Canadian independence in North America. 'Of the two imperialisms, American and British, the former was by far the more dangerous.' Indeed, one of the main features of the heroic political struggle that led to Confederation was the explicit will of British North America to survive the threat of a hostile United States. 'The desire to unite grew out of the will to survive,' Creighton says; 'survival was threatened by the marked hostility of the Americans; and dislike and distrust of the United States became a potent force in the growth of the new British American nationalism.'

The greatest sin of the 'liberal nationalist' school was that its members had forgotten or ignored the American danger and had taught Canadians to believe that Britain was the real, even the only, enemy. This view falsified Canada's past, for the country had not developed, in any marked degree, through conflict with Britain but rather with the aid of Britain. Without British capital and military strength, British North America would never have survived the southward pull of the American Republic. Unlike the United States, Canada had never cut the silken bonds that united her to Europe and it was Harold Innis who had shown this fact most effectively. Through Innis's work, Creighton maintained, 'Canadian scholars had made a rediscovery of Europe, and in the process had gone a long way towards discovering Canada itself.'

In Creighton's view, moreover, the 'liberal nationalist' in their emphasis on Canada's 'North Americanness' had not merely falsified history; they had taught lessons that left Canadian independence more vulnerable to American corrosion than ever before:

> In Europe NATO is a collective defence enterprise but in North America it is a two-power organization in which Canada can accept only the assistance and the direction of the United States. In the north, Americans build and man our radar installations; and in the east, in Newfoundland and Labrador, they hold and occupy military bases. The foreigner sits firmly astride the eastern approaches to our country; and the base, a primitive form of military imperialism, grimly questions Canada's claim to control her own destiny.

Thus Creighton's indictment of the 'liberal-nationalist' historians was not that they had used history to teach nationalist lessons, but rather that their interpretation of Canadian history had taught the wrong lessons. Neither side questioned the contention that *la survivance* was the main theme of Canadian history. The only, but bitterly disputed, question was about the identity of the enemy.

Canada's First Century rings all the changes on the survival theme, and draws a foreboding conclusion. This tension-filled book is an extended account of the rise and decline of Creighton's Canada. The triumph of 'continentalism', engineered by Mackenzie King's Liberals, and of provincial autonomy, led by the province of Quebec, has produced near collapse. In Creighton's judgment, the basic shape of Canada was defined in Macdonald's 'national' policies: a centralized federalism, a severely limited bilingualism, and an east-west economy defended by the tariff. Creighton's conclusion describes the destruction of these principles:

> The long association of Canadians with the government and people of the United States, their dependence upon American capital, their reliance upon American initiative and technology, their gradual acceptance of American standards and values, had given the Republic a large equity in the Canadian nation and a potent influence upon the Canadian national character. Continentalism had divorced Canadians from their history, crippled their creative capacity, and left them without the power to fashion a future for themselves. Even the will to

defend their independence and protect their national identity
had been weakened: they seemed scarcely to be aware of the
danger in which they stood. The problem of a separate Quebec
had come to obsess and monopolize the minds of both English
and French Canadians. It had distracted them from other
and more vital tasks. It blinded them to the peril that threatened their existence as a separate nation in North America.

There is much sadness in the sight of a great historian fallen to
such depths of despair. Yet does he himself not recognize that the
lines have been drawn too darkly? Has not the despair a purpose:
to warn and reawaken the Canadian people to their true destiny?
The lessons of survival in the past bear a moral for the present and
the future.

Professor Creighton's main ally in the reinterpretation of
Canadian history has been W. L. Morton. But if Morton has made
his peace with the Laurentian approach, it is only after a long,
agonizing search. No English-Canadian historian has been so explicit in his attempt to formulate a 'philosophy' of Canadian history
as Morton, and at every stage along the road to his present stopping
place the postulates of his nationalist outlook have been clearly expressed. For this reason his work is perhaps the most interesting
example of the theme of *la survivance* in English-Canadian historical writing.

Twenty-five years ago Morton made his first excursion into the
field of interpretation with a provocative essay entitled 'Clio in
Canada: The Interpretation of Canadian History,' in which he
vigorously criticized the Innis-Creighton-Laurentian school. His
chief criticism is extremely interesting, for it reveals Morton's view
of the function of history. It was not the accuracy or the inaccuracy
of the thesis that he questioned but rather its implications for Canadian nationalism. Its leading implication, in Morton's judgment,
was that it justified an imperialism, based in Montreal and Toronto,
which held the rest of Canada in a colonial position. In essence, his
protest was that of the westerner against eastern domination. 'For
Confederation,' he wrote, 'was brought about to increase the wealth
of central Canada and until that original purpose is altered and the
concentration of wealth and population by national policy ceases,
Confederation must remain an instrument of injustice.' The country's survival was dependent upon a recognition of legitimate

regional differences, and a successful Confederation could never be the instrument of central Canadian imperialism. He even went so far as to suggest a 'three nations' thesis which suggested that Canada could best be understood in terms of sharp regional, even national, differences between French Canada, Ontario, and the West. The only successful public philosophy for Canada, then, was an Actonian one that would allow for diversity within a single community.

It was the western 'nationalist' thesis that dominated Professor Morton's first three major historical works. In his *Progressive Party in Canada* he sympathetically, though not uncritically, explored the rise and fall of the farmers' protest movements of the 1920s. While he recognized the shortcomings of the movement, he nevertheless accepted the justice of the 'basic thesis' of the Progressive revolt that 'in a federal union of free citizens and equal communities, there must be such equality of economic opportunity and equality of political status as human ingenuity may contrive and goodwill advance.' It was in the colonial subordination of the West that Professor Morton discovered the explanation of the bias of prairie politics.

In 1956 he published an excellent analysis of the first important attempt by westerners to assert their section's equality with the older parts of Canada. In his introduction to the *Red River Journal of Alexander Begg* he analysed the tragic events of the Rebellion of 1869-70. Then, the following year, he published his best work— *Manitoba: A History*. His western consciousness shone through the pages of this superb volume as he wove together the social, cultural, political, and economic pattern of his native province. But he recognized that the 'imperialism' of the East was gradually triumphing as Manitoba became increasingly Ontarian in outlook. Nevertheless, a deep-rooted heritage remained as a microcosm of Canada's variety. 'Manitobans are made,' he concluded, 'as Canadians have been made of those who by endurance in loyalty to older values than prosperity have learned to wrest a living from the prairie's brief summer and the harsh rocks and wild waters of the north.'

In these lines there was a hint of a new mood that was shaping Morton's outlook. It was a mood characterized by two new interests: first, an interest in conservative political philosophy and politics; and secondly, a concern about the history, and survival, of the country as a whole. Morton's new conservatism was characteristic of both the West in particular and the country in general as

Canada moved from the long years of the Liberal ascendancy into the days of the first, heady intoxication with Diefenbaker Conservatism. There was, as yet, no forewarning of the inevitable hangover.

The application of this philosophic conservatism can be seen in each of Morton's works beginning with *The Guardian Identity*. Here his former emphasis on the pluralism of Canadian society was in large measure replaced by a view that insisted on the unity of Canadian history, a unity that implied a pan-Canadian nationalism. In opposition to Lower's dualism, Morton now declared that 'By Canadian history also is to be understood not one French and one British, but the entire history of all Canada. There are not two histories, but one history, as there are not two Canadas, or any greater number, but only one. Nor are there two ways of life, but one common response to land and history expressed in many strong variants of the one, it is true, but still one central substance.'

Coupled with the insistence upon the unity of the Canadian experience came a new preoccupation with those characteristics that distinguish Canada from the United States. The distinction, in essence, was that the United States was a society born of revolution, while Canada was a society that had evolved slowly according to prescriptive rather than natural rights and had retained the values of the past. The Burkean tones predominated in the sentences, 'Not life, liberty and happiness, but peace, order and good government are what the national government of Canada guarantees. Under these it is assumed life, liberty and happiness may be achieved, but each according to his taste. For a society of allegiance admits of a diversity the society of compact does not, and one of the blessings of the Canadian way of life is that there is no Canadian way of life, much less two, but a unity under the crown admitting a thousand diversities.'

Here, in this new formulation, the old and the new Morton, so to speak, are joined together. But there remains an unanswered question of the compatibility of Acton and Burke. On the one hand, the denial of a 'Canadian way of life' harks back to the earlier rejection of the nationalist-state (i.e., a state committed to a monolithic Canadianism). On the other hand, there is a new insistence on the unity of Canadian history, a unity based on acceptance of the Laurentian thesis that was earlier rejected and to which has been added the 'monarchical principle.' These new ingredients in the

Mortonian prescription raise the question of whether the author has not given with one hand what he takes back with the other. Or, to put the same point in another way: is not this society of 'allegiance' really a society in which monarchy is merely another name for British-Canadian nationalism?

These two ideas—the non-nationalist state and the monarchical principle—dominate Morton's most extended treatment of Canadian history in a volume characteristically entitled *The Kingdom of Canada* (1963). And again in this volume it is notable that the early, gentlemanly western protest against the domination of the east is replaced by a full acceptance of the Innis thesis. Replying to Underhill's criticism of his new position, Morton wrote, 'It seems to me that if Professor Underhill had studied Marion Newbigin and Harold Innis with the same devotion that he has Goldwin Smith, he would know that Smith has been answered in his own terms. Canada is "naturally" and to a decisive degree, a geographic, economic and political entity.' And Morton then proceeded to state in the most straight-forward terms the theme that had been the constant refrain of English-Canadian historical writing: 'Despite this tremendous competition [from the United States] Canada has survived and by surviving deserves to survive.'

For Morton, Canada is not the North American nation of the 'liberal nationalists' vision. Rather, it is what he calls 'Canadian-American': a society with European roots and attachments growing in North American soil. Naturally, then, the politician who best exemplifies the 'liberal nationalist' North Americanism, W. L. M. King, becomes the object of the harshest criticism of Morton and those who think like him—whereas Macdonald represents the epitome of Canadian statesmanship.

Since Confederation is the chief political expression of pan-Canadian nationalism, it is not surprising that Morton's latest book is an examination of the critical years between 1857 and 1873. He offers his view of the nature of Confederation in the concluding sentence of the volume, in which he sums up the years ending with the entry of Prince Edward Island and British Columbia into the union. 'The moral purpose of Confederation,' he writes, 'the union of the provinces in a partnership of English and French, was at last embodied in a territory reaching from sea to sea.' Here again a new note has been allowed to creep into Morton's philosophy of Canadianism, and it is perhaps a disquieting one. The political and constitutional machinery established in 1867 by a group of capable and supremely practical politicians has, in Morton's analysis, acquired a 'moral purpose.' That 'moral purpose' is surely yet another way of expressing the concept of *la survivance*; it explicitly transforms a pragmatic arrangement into an ideological principle. And that principle, described by Morton as 'the conservative principle,' is that 'the central government was supreme and as such the guarantor of the welfare of the whole country. . . .' The principle further postulates that 'two cultural communities we have and shall maintain, but we are one political community and shall remain so.' And what is the justification, the necessity which compels Canadians to accept a union sanctified by morality? The answer, by this time, will come as no surprise: '. . . the simple truth is that neither of us, English or French, can reasonably hope to exist apart as distinct communities in the North America of the twentieth century. Either we remain united and exist as English and French Canadians, or we separate and become Americanized and American.' The now familiar leitmotiv of English-Canadian historical writing has once again become dominant.

Thus, while the theme of survival in English-Canadian history has several variations, it is none the less nearly as all-pervading as it is in French-Canadian history. Its variants include the struggle for survival against the pressure of the United States, the struggle of a colony to achieve nationhood, and, finally, the struggle to maintain Canadian unity. Each one of these themes is legitimate, just as French-Canadian historians have a legitimate duty to describe *la survivance*. That is to say, the historian has not invented the theme; it does have a basis in reality. But the question which arises is obvious: how can the historian prevent his work from being transformed from an accurate description of reality into a weapon in the struggle for survival? English-Canadian historians have often accused their French-Canadian fellow historians of misusing history for nationalist purposes. French-Canadians might make the same criticism of their English-language colleagues. Only Michel Brunet has noted this tendency, but consistency makes it difficult for him to criticize those who follow principles similar to his own.

Yet the weaknesses and dangers of the nationalist approach to history are obvious. As Creighton and others have been quick to point out, the 'liberal nationalists,' in their obsession with the struggle for dominion status, distorted the true nature of the triangular relationship that has characterized Canada's contact with the outside world. But have not the new or 'conservative nationalists,' in their obsession with the threat of the United States, also been prone to read present concerns into past realities? Finally, has not the often repeated emphasis on 'national unity' been a reflection as much of the historian's present wish as of his perception of the past? (It is worth noting in passing that English-speaking nationalist historians and French-speaking nationalist historians are agreed on at least one thing: the virtue of 'national unity' or *union nationale.*' The terms, however, refer to radically different objectives.) In short, the nationalist historian is always in danger of committing the sin of making present objectives the standard by which he judges past actions.

The overriding concern with survival, with nationalism, has placed several other limitations on English-Canadian historical writing. The most obvious is that it has led to an over-emphasis on constitutional and political history. While some work has been done in the economical field, especially by Innis and his disciples, much of our economic history remains untouched. The excellent work that has been done in 'entrepreneurial history' in the United States, work that has enormously deepened our understanding of modern industrial society, has been practically ignored in Canada. Social history, apart from Lower's *Canadians in the Making*, is hardly even begun. One of the reasons for this gap is that in a country as large and varied as Canada social history must, at least at first, be 'local' history. But 'local' history seems so inferior to national 'history' that nationally conscious historians avoid it, turning instead to look again at the War of 1812 or the signing of the Halibut Fisheries Treaty. One last example, though there are others, is that the concentration on nationalism, which is largely a middle-class phenomenon, has meant that lower-class history and even the history of trade unions have received very little attention.

Having made these criticisms, certain extenuating circumstances must now be admitted. Historians are, after all, human. Their preoccupations are those of their fellow citizens. Because Canada is a small, fragile country, historians have quite naturally been concerned about its survival. But one wonders if that very concern has not contributed to the country's difficulties. If English-Canadian historians harness history to the cause of Canadian nationalism, why should not French-Canadian historians do the same? Without raising the question of the validity of nationalist values, it is necessary to raise the question of the validity of nationalism—Canadian, English-Canadian, French-Canadian, or New Canadian—as a criterion of historical judgment.

In the twentieth century our faith in reason has been badly shaken by Freud, Jung, and Marx, to say nothing of two ferocious world wars. With this dethronement of reason, historians have lost much of their nineteenth-century predecessors' faith in the possibility of scientific history. A strong subjective element must now be admitted in all historical judgment. But too often this admission has allowed historians to reject all hope of achieving objectivity and to make history the servant of some ideology. For obvious reasons, history provides the very substance out of which nationalist ideology is constructed. In their obsession with various brands of *la survivance*, both French- and English-speaking historians have often come dangerously close to making history the servant of whatever brand of nationalism—liberal, conservative, clerical, or anti-clerical—is currently popular.

The concerns of the present can never be entirely excluded from the historian's mind. Yet it is fundamental to his creed that he understand that his first duty is to assess the past in its own terms and that to be constantly combing the past to discover lessons for the present is the very antithesis of the historian's *métier*. 'Whatever concessions the historian is prepared to make to the doctrine of relativism,' Professor C. Vann Woodward has written, 'he must retain a fundamentally unshakable conviction that the past is real —however hard it may be to define its nature and write an unbiassed record of it. Fully conceding those difficulties, the historian must never concede that the past is alterable to conform with present convenience, with the party line, with mass prejudice, or with the ambitions of powerful popular leaders.' I would simply add nationalism—which is not necessarily the same as 'mass prejudice.'

FREDERICK PHILIP GROVE

1871-1948

Born in Russia of wealthy and cultivated Swedish parents,. Frederick Philip Grove spent his early life in extensive travel in Europe, Siberia, Africa, and Australasia. His earliest education was by tutors in Berlin, where he was under the care of his mother. After her death in 1887 he studied archaeology at the University of Paris and in Rome, before embarking on his foreign travels. In 1892 he found himself in Toronto, when he learned that his father had died bankrupt in Sweden. For the next twenty years he worked as a harvest laborer in Kentucky during the summer and wrote during the winter, producing several novels, for which he could find no publisher. In 1912 he became a rural school teacher in Manitoba. After the publication of two books of nature essays, descriptive of rural life in Manitoba, *Over Prairie Trails* (1922) and *The Turn of the Year* (1923), he was able to attract publishers for the series of novels he had written and continued to write. Among these were *Settlers of the Marsh* (1925), *Our Daily Bread* (1928), *The Yoke of Life* (1930), and *Fruits of the Earth* (1933). These are naturalistic studies of the hard struggle between elemental man and the obdurate earth, belonging to the school of Thomas Hardy, Knut Hamsun, and, in some particulars, of D. H. Lawrence. These are powerful novels that did much to open up the harsher aspects of Western Canadian life to the novel-reading public and to free the Canadian writer from the restrictions of provincial morality. Later works by Grove are *The Master of the Mill* (1944), a study of the changes undergone by the owners and workers in a family industry from pioneer days to the present machine age, and *Consider her Ways,* an allegorical narrative of the communal life of the ant. *It Needs to be Said* (1929) contains a number of pertinent essays and addresses on cultural and literary subjects.

Except for the two volumes of prairie essays, a few short stories, and isolated episodes such as "I Come in Contact with Humanity Again," Grove's style is naive and clumsy in the extreme; while his thinking, though honest and intense, lacks the distinction of a great novelist. Nevertheless, he has been highly honored in his adopted country. In 1934 he was awarded the Lorne Pierce Medal for Literature by the Royal Society of Canada and was elected a member of the Society in 1941. In 1946 he was given the Governor General's Medal for *In Search of Myself.*

An interesting recent biographical study by D. O. Spettigue, *F. P. Grove* (1968), questions the authenticity of many of the "facts" of Grove's life, as presented above and as documented in his autobiographical works, *A Search for America* (1927), from which comes the vivid character sketch reprinted here, and *In Search of Myself,* an account of his hard struggle to make his way as a novelist and a defence of his realism.

I COME INTO CONTACT WITH HUMANITY AGAIN

The valley of the river widened out; the islands which divided it were larger now; sometimes one of the two arms was closed by a weir, the other, by a lock.

I was more and more getting used to going hungry. Sometimes I felt a weird intoxication with hunger; at other times my mind seemed to see things with extraordinary clearness and logic.

One day, about noon, I came to a place where a large island, in outline like a pear, densely wooded, was connected at its upper end by a narrow strip of sandbank with the shore along which I travelled.

An impulse of exploration made me cross over the island. Below the sandbank which I followed there was a dead arm of the river. No doubt the sandbank was flooded after heavy rains, and the water in this dead arm was swept out. But the river was low at the time, and with the big trees—sycamores mostly—overhanging the stagnant water in the autumn sun, there was something infinitely quiet, soothing, sadly reminiscent about the place. I felt a desire to linger. The island proved a veritable trap for driftwood which I had to climb over in order to penetrate into the sanctuary of its recesses.

Suddenly I heard a noise, the cracking of a dry limb, or the snapping of a dead sapling. I stopped and listened. Not a breath seemed to stir. It was a perfect day for the season—clear, cool, crisp, yet gratefully warm. I felt as if I were confronted with a great, decisive leave-taking. Soon, soon I had to go back to the world of man. I wanted to drink to the dregs the last cup of freedom vouchsafed.

The noise was repeated; and when I carefully scanned the trees, I became aware of a man who was gathering wood, breaking dry limbs and picking up drift. I did not care to be interfered with in my present mood; so I started on a silent, infinitely cautious retreat.

I returned to the northern river-bank and continued my way downstream. By the time I reached the lower end of the island it was late in the afternoon; and I was watching the way the current on the far side broke into an eddy where it touched the stagnant water of the dead arm when a strange sight caught my eye.

From under the overhanging trees of the island a boat detached itself. It was loaded with brushwood. The sticks had been laid crosswise over the boat—making a load twelve to sixteen feet wide; they were piled across its whole length, to a height of three feet or more above the gunnel. The load was so heavy that, where the gunnel of the boat ran lowest, in the centre, there was not more than one or two inches of freeboard above the water, the ends of the lower sticks on both sides dipping into it. On top of this load stood, gingerly poised in mid-air, a tall, gaunt man who held a long, straight pole with a boathook fastened to its end. With this pole which he moved slowly and carefully—balancing the while—he guided the craft. It looked as if he were performing a feat on the tight-rope. Fascinated, I watched.

He pushed out into the dead arm of the river, guiding his boat by the lightest and deftest touches of the pole on limbs and trunks of trees. I marvelled at this exhibition of skill and strength required for handling the enormously long pole without disturbing the equilibrium of the overloaded boat.

All went well till he reached the end of the island. But there he miscalculated a motion. The sticks of wood, where they reached out on the far side, just dipped into the furious current that shot out from beyond the point of the island; the next second his craft gave a lurch, settled down, was caught in the eddy. In order to recover his balance, the man made a step to the side; the whole load tilted over, and with a curious, grotesque twist of his body, he slipped down into the water which splashed up high. It looked so funny that I burst out laughing.

But my laugh changed into a gasp: the man had gone down like a stone. Then his head bobbed up again—he was in the quiet water of the dead arm; his boat had gone off, careering, with the current. When he appeared at the surface, I saw that he was fighting wildly. He went down again, a burst of bubbles showed the exact spot where he was: he could not swim!

The weird feature of this life-and-death struggle was the absolute silence in which it proceeded. There had been no shout, no sound beyond that of the splashing water.

Now I am—or was—by nature nearly amphibious, swimming and diving being my favourite pastimes. So, the moment I realized his danger, I dropped what I was carrying, stripped off my coat, and plunged in.

When I got him, he seemed to have given up; but as soon as I jerked him to the surface, he started to fight, grabbing wildly, impeding my arms. I shouted at him, but he did not cease. So I whirled him around, getting one hand under his chin and forcing his head back; and simultaneously I lifted the other hand and brought it down, edgewise, on the root of his nose. He hung limp for a minute, long enough for me to reach shallow water. I hauled him ashore. He sat up, in a dazed, half-unconscious way. I left him.

This was an adventure for me, and I was pleasurably excited. I did not mean to leave my work half done. I ran downstream, caught up with the boat which had capsized, swam out, found its rope, took it ashore, and tied it.

Then I returned to the man. He got to his feet and shook himself in a strange way, just as a dog would shake himself after a wetting, or a horse when you pull his harness off after a hard day's work. I had never seen a man shake the water out of his artificial pelt in just that way. It had something contagious; I found myself rehearsing the thing in anticipatory impulses; I came near trying to imitate him.

There were other queer things about him. His hair was long, like that of a woman, grey; it was braided into a stout, long braid which was twice laid around his head, like a turban. His face, as I see it very clearly in my memory, closely resembled the face of Mark Twain in Carroll Beckwith's portrait, only that mustache and eyes and shaggy brows were grey, and there was absolutely no expression in his features. He was fully as tall as I was—and I am over six feet.

Again and again he shook himself, but when he stood still, there was something of the stiff and silent dignity of the turkey-buzzard about him. His expressionless face had an albino-like look.

You would expect a man to say a word or so when you have just saved his life—"Much obliged, old chap"—or, "Thanks for going to all the trouble"—but this man didn't. He merely looked me over and allowed his dead eagle-eye to rest for a moment on my things, the kettle, the tin cans, my bundle, all of which I had been carrying slung to a stick which rested on my shoulder.

His glance made me look down at myself. His eye had been halting for the fraction of a second on my knees. They were shaking violently. I became aware that I was sick with hunger and weak with fatigue from my exertion. Also, of course, I was wet through; and the evening was turning chilly.

The man walked off, up the bank, stepping with a strange leg-action and an uncanny, nearly supernatural dignity. Never a word he said. I looked after him, dumbfounded. But neither did I say a word.

Then, just as he was about to disappear in the willowbrush of the upper bank, he looked back for a moment before he went. There was no expression in his vacant, bold eye even then. I could take that look or leave it, just as I pleased. I might interpret it as a look of fear or as a summons.

I chose to take it for a summons. I quickly picked up the shoulder-stick with my things attached, threw my coat over its ends and followed him.

There was a wide band of shore-brush; through it led a narrow path which I followed in the wake of the man. The brush changed in character: from the willows of the bank to the thickets of the hillside—honey-locust predominating.

At last, half way up the hill, we came to a shoulder in the rising ground which was cleared. The path now led through a tiny corn-patch to a hut beyond. I could look out here to right and left, for the corn had been cut and shocked. There was no other human habita-tion within miles on either side. The sun was touching the horizon exactly in the river-gap.

We entered the house. It was built of lumber, unpainted, with that silky-grey appearance which testified to the weather and the rains of many years. A large slab of stone served for a doorstep.

The arrangement of the room into which we came was as follows. The wall opposite the entrance held a small window, one and a half feet square. To the right there was a fireplace, built of the rough stones of the hillside embedded in mortar. Beyond it, a homemade door of thin boards led into an adjoining room. Along the wall to the left stood a homemade table; for a seat, in front of it, an up-ended box. In the corner, behind the door through which we entered, a rough bed was strewn on the floor: straw, covered with a rag-blanket: at its foot two or three more blankets lay in a crumpled pile. At a glance you knew it for a bachelor's establishment.

My host crouched down, squatting stiffly on his heels and built a pyre of woodsticks in the grateless fireplace. Then he stood again, whittled a small piece of soft, white wood into a fan-shaped flower-head of shavings, disappeared through the door into the adjoining room, and reappeared in a minute or so with his stick ablaze. He applied it to the wood in the fireplace; the flame licked upward.

He took his smock off and hung it on a nail. His shoes and coarse cotton socks he removed, too, and laid them on the floor, close to the fireplace, along the wall. He did not pay the slightest attention to me. He moved about in a sober, grave way, slow and deliberate, with no unnecessary flourishes or bendings.

Thus he squatted down again, in front of the fire, but this time with his back to it, warming himself. His shirt began to steam over his shoulders; then he turned and sat a while longer. At last he got up and went out.

I began to feel "creepy."

But, while he was outside, I stripped my wet clothes off and slipped into my raincoat which was dry. I looked out of the window. The tiny yard of this hermitage contained a well and a large pile of just such wood as the man had lost. It was closed on the far side by a low building which seemed to serve for a pig-pen; I saw the man throwing feed into its rail-enclosure and heard the grunting of swine.

The man returned into the house and room before I had had time to pick up my wet clothes. He bent down and carefully hung them on nails in the fireplace wall. That was the first indication of the fact that he was aware of my presence.

Next he busied himself at the table, pushing things about and re-arranging them. He reached up somewhere into the now dark corner over the bed and brought down a mug, knife, and fork. It seemed so much like a conjurer's trick that I nearly jumped. But when I looked closely, I saw that a box was nailed to the wall there, serving for a cupboard. Then he took a tin kettle from the table, shook it—I heard the swish of water—took it to the window, peered into it, and, finding the contents satisfactory, placed it on top of the blazing wood in the fireplace, pressing it down to keep it from tilting.

Then he went out again.

I felt strange. Had I saved a lunatic from drowning? His actions were sane enough. As for his head-gear, that hair when unrolled must have reached down to his knees! It looked as if he took care of it; but that might be because it was wet. There was a reddish glint in his eye which was not really grey but whitish. It reminded me somehow, when at rest, of the eye of white rabbits; when it moved, of that of an eagle; it was so imperious.

When he came in again, this time, he dropped something large and light which rustled in the adjoining room and kicked the door open. He carried a sooty lantern and an empty box. The lantern he suspended from a hook in the ceiling; the box he dropped close to the door. Then he pulled the table out from the wall, put his box on one side of it, pushed the other with his foot to the opposite side, and lifted the tin kettle, which was spouting steam, with the help of a stick passed through its handle. At last he sat down on his box.

Again he looked at me with a brief glance: take it or leave it; again I took it and sat down. He poured some of the contents of the little kettle into a mug and pushed it as well as a pan of unraised corn-bread and a tin of molasses across the table to my place. The beverage was tea, bitter with many stewings. He started to eat; and I, too, ate a little, very carefully, for I was no longer used to such sumptuous fare, and more from courtesy than from appetite, though I was hungry.

I concluded that the man was deaf and dumb.

When he had satisfied his hunger with great bites of corn-bread soaked in molasses—he had a splendid set of teeth—he got up; and, passing into the darkness of the adjoining room, gathered what he had dropped there before. It proved to be an armful of straw, good, clean oat-straw too.

This he threw into the corner opposite his own bed, spreading it out with a kick or so of his foot. On it he dropped one of the blankets which he picked up from the crumpled heap on his own side; and he stood and looked thoughtfully at me.

Suddenly he reached up and took the lantern from its hook. When he entered the adjoining room, leaving the door open, I saw for the first time that from its ceiling there were hanging down great bunches of half-dried and entirely wilted "hands" of tobacco. So I was in the tobacco-belt! It also proved to be tobacco that he went after; for when he came back, he held a large "braid" of it in his hand; from which, after disposing of the lantern, he cut a generous chew.

Again we sat for a while in utter silence. I had found some cigarette paper in a pocket of my raincoat, had rubbed some of his "long-green" into granules and was smoking. I pondered a problem. I wished to speak, to say something. But, after having been silent so long, it seemed inconsiderate to start speaking now; there was something indelicate about words; I gave it up.

His large, heavy hands were resting on his knees; his shoulders were bent forward; he was staring into the fire which he fed from time to time. Suddenly I became aware that he was going to sleep. His eyelids fell; he began to nod; his head shot forward; and he pulled himself back, aroused.

As I got up, a sudden temptation was too strong for me.

"Suppose I'll turn in," I said.

I repented at once, the color mantled my face; but not a flicker in his features betrayed that he had heard.

Yet, seeing my motion, he, too, got up, slowly, stiffly, reached for the lantern, and waited for my next move. When he saw that I turned to the litter of straw, he gave the lantern an expert jerk which extinguished its flame. Thus he deposited it on the floor and rolled in. There was enough light from the fire for me to lie down by.

You can imagine that I lay awake a long while. The mere fact that I was under a roof was exciting. Here I lay in the same room with this man of sixty or more who looked like an oak-tree, lived like a hermit, and was either a lunatic or a deaf-and-dumb cripple. Even now he was weirdly silent. He lay like a log, without stirring. I had expected to hear him snoring; I did not even hear him breathe. Instead I heard mice and rats go through a veritable carnival of running and jumping, capering and dancing. At first I had pulled the patch-blanket merely over my knees; but it turned pretty cold; and when I did get drowsy, I forgot all squeamishness and rolled up.

I awoke with a start, becoming conscious of the fact that somebody was moving about in the room.

The man had relighted the fire and was leaving through the door when I opened my eyes. I jumped up and felt my clothes which I found dry. While dressing, I looked around and wondered no longer that I had been cold overnight. There were large cracks in the single boarding of the walls; lack of fresh air was no vice of this habitation. The wood used in building was sycamore lumber; it warps and twists when exposed to the weather.

The man gave no sign of recognition when he entered. He had two eggs in one hand, which he put on the table. In the other he held the little kettle, apparently freshly filled, for it dripped with water; it he placed on the fire.

He went out again, and this time I noticed a peculiarity of his footfall. I found that, whenever he put his foot down, his heel touched the floor first; and, after lifting it again, he brought his whole sole down with a thump, walking in a knock-kneed way; he was a high-stepper.

After breakfast he seemed in doubt what to do. He moved aimlessly about. At last he went to the front door, opened it as if to go out, hesitated for a second, and waited for something to be said or done.

I was going to hang on to him. He was not going to get off as lightly as all that! I had saved him from drowning, he was going to keep me for a day or two!

So I made as if to follow him; and he held the door till I took hold of it.

In the open, a subtle change in the landscape struck me very forcibly. There had been hoarfrost on the ground before; but today the crust of the ground itself was frozen. In the corn-patch the stalks and weeds north and west of the shocks were still furred with white. The leaves of the honey-locust and the great sycamores in the distant river valley were tinged with yellow. Overnight the season had changed from late fall to early winter. The next storm would bring snow!

My host wended his way down to the river and, beyond the willows, along the pebbly shelf of the beach.

We went down to his boat. He first pulled it up quite a piece on the sandy shore. It was a strong, heavy boat. Then, with a powerful heave, he turned it on its keel. He, I say; for though I made a pretence at helping him, I was so weakened by my late mode of life that my efforts, had they been needed, would not have counted for much. Then he launched the boat back into the water, took the rope in, and laid it down in the bow. For a moment he stood helpless, looking around. Apparently he was baffled because the pole was lost, which he had not realized so far. He went up to the edge of the beach, where the ribbon of the high-water drift was deposited, and selected a pole there. When he came back, he climbed into the boat.

Again, as at the door, he hesitated awkwardly. I climbed in after him; and at once he began poling upstream.

When we came to the quiet water in the dead arm, he landed; but since he did not fasten the boat beyond running it onto the sand, I did not follow him. He disappeared into the willow-brush; and after a short interval he returned, carrying another long pole and a tin dipper. He tilted the boat, climbed in and bailed the water out.

Then we went for a load of wood. He piled it just as high as the day before, possibly feeling safe in my presence; but he pushed across the dead arm before we reached the point of the island. This dead arm was strangely deep.

I stayed all day, and the next day, too. We kept at work; he carried the wood up with the help of a rope, slinging it on his back in huge bundles.

The third morning, while we had our breakfast, I thought I saw a change, an ever so slight change in his manner. I cannot define it in detail. One trifle lingers in my memory.

When I had helped myself to molasses, he took the tin and, before helping himself, he looked into it, hesitating.

Maybe he considered that by two days and three nights of hospitality he had paid for the slight service I had been able to do him. It is true, I helped him with his work; but when a person can do a piece of work by himself, he cannot afford to hire help at the expense of a diminishing supply of molasses in the tin. I agreed with this unspoken argument and made up my mind to leave.

When, after breakfast, he went to feed his pig, I rolled my bundle and tied my things to the stick.

He returned after a while but did not pay any attention to my preparations beyond a casual glance at the bundle on the floor. I sat for a while longer. Apparently he was getting ready to bring in another boat-load of firewood against the winter. At last he opened the door and stepped out, holding it for a moment, as was his custom, till I made a move. I picked the shoulder-stick up and followed. And down we wended our way to the river.

I felt soft in my heart. We had not made friends, but I had enjoyed his quiet, matter-of-fact hospitality. I should have liked to shake hands, to say a word of thanks to this man with the braided hair whose life I had saved.

When we reached the boat, we stood for a moment, awkwardly, he holding the pole in one hand, the rope of his craft in the other, and looking out to the water, as if waiting. I did not know what to do; with a shrug of my shoulders I turned.

Then I stopped and said, "I suppose it's about time for me to be moving."

And something startling happened. The man spoke. He spoke

with an effort, twisting his whole body in the act, the words sounding like those of an overgrown boy when he is changing his voice,
hoarse, unexpectedly loud and husky. It looked and sounded as if
he were heaving the words up from, let me say, his abdomen and
ejecting them forcibly.

What he said, was, "I reckon."

Then he climbed into his boat and pushed off without as much as
once looking back.

That was my first encounter with a human being in more than
three months.

It affected me profoundly, probably because it came at a critical
moment. As for the peculiarities of this representative of the genus
homo, I did not feel called upon to judge him. I did no longer
forget that possibly my own mentality would seem abnormal to
most people with whom I might come into contact. Certain conceptions which were dimly forming in my mental recesses made me
question the value of much that was highly prized by other men. I
had found, for instance, that talking largely keeps you from thinking. Without reading as yet, certain passages in the story of Jesus
had taken on a profound and new significance for me. A deep-
rooted suspicion of all that is called learning, progress, culture pervaded all my thinking. I was no longer so sure of my superiority
over those who had not received my "education." I had come to
regard education as pretty much the opposite of what, in a sane
world, it should be. It seemed to me to be a process of filling old
wine into new skins. I began to suspect that there might be more
wisdom in this "hermit's" mode of life than in that of the most refined and cultured scholar. Yes, I sometimes doubted whether he
might not have deeper, truer thoughts than anyone I had ever met
before. Certain sayings of Christ's—in the sermon of the Mount,
during the last supper—sayings which in the common interpretation
were just words without meaning—gradually grew upon me. More
and more my thoughts began to circle around Jesus.

But I had gone out on a search when I started these tramps; I
began to see that the search had been beside the point. So long as
my search remained geographical, it must of necessity be a failure;
at the same time this geographical search, though it might not
bring me nearer to the thing sought for, was slowly fitting me to
undertake the real search. Also, it taught me toleration.

Still, the give-and-take of the world was not to be forgotten. I should have to give as well as to take. These three days at the hermit's house were earned. What I had done for him was in my own estimation worth what he had done for me—though, what I had done for him seemed trifling indeed because it had been so easy for me. But I came to the conclusion that in the long run only one kind of work would do for me—and that was precisely work which did come easy: work which I should choose as play, as a pastime if I were not driven to it by necessity. If I could have earned a permanent living by pulling out of the river a dozen drowning people a day, I should have been glad to go to work right then. Unfortunately people were not reckless enough to risk their lives in order to provide a living for somebody else. So I could not rely on finding off-handedly what I was looking for.

MORLEY CALLAGHAN

1903-

For more than forty years Morley Callaghan has devoted himself to the writing of novels and short stories with a single-ness of purpose and an artistic integrity rare in modern letters. Born in Toronto, he was educated at St. Michael's College of the University of Toronto, from which he was graduated in 1925. He then worked briefly as a reporter on the *Toronto Daily Star*, where he became friendly with Ernest Hemingway, who was with the paper at that time. Soon after, Callaghan's first short stories began appearing in the Paris *avant-garde* magazines *transition* and *This Quarter*. In 1928 he was admitted to the bar on completing his studies at Osgoode Hall. He did not practise, however, and on the publication of his first novel, *Strange Fugitive*, in the same year, he determined to devote himself to writing. After eight months in Paris (1929), where he renewed his acquaintanceship with Hemingway and met other writers such as Scott Fitzgerald, Gertrude Stein, and James Joyce, he returned to Toronto, where he has lived ever since, supporting himself by his pen and by free-lancing as a reviewer and commentator for the CBC. In 1970 his career was crowned by the award of both the Molson and the Bank of Montreal prizes given annually to a distinguished Canadian.

Callaghan has won equal distinction for his short stories and for his novels. The best of his stories have appeared in three volumes, *A Native Argosy* (1929), *Now that April's Here* (1936), and a retrospective survey called *Morley Callaghan's*

Stories (1959). These tell, in a deceptively simple style, of some seemingly ordinary moment of crisis or tragedy in the lives, usually, of working-class people in a city like Toronto or the neighboring rural communities. If there is an affinity, it is with such a sober realist as Sherwood Anderson rather than with the more flashy Hemingway. The American critic Edmund Wilson, one of Callaghan's staunchest admirers, has compared his stories to the tales of Turgenev.

Of the novels the best and most characteristic are *Such is My Beloved* (1934), *They Shall Inherit the Earth* (1935), *More Joy in Heaven* (1937), and, after a long period of lying fallow, the works of what the critic Robert Weaver described as "the postwar explosion of his talents," *The Loved and the Lost* (1951), *The Many Coloured Coat* (1960), and *A Passion in Rome* (1961)—the only novel in which Callaghan has deserted the local scene. In 1963 he published *That Summer in Paris*, a rather simple and curiously parochial account of his experiences as a young man among the expatriate writers and artists on the Left Bank.

Of Callaghan's best work in fiction, whether short or long, it can be said that it gives a dignity to the commonplace and expresses a realistic philosophy that is not incompatible with an almost classic spirit of pity and irony.

ANCIENT LINEAGE

The young man from the Historical Club with a green magazine
under his arm got off the train at Clintonville. It was getting dark
but the station lights were not lit. He hurried along the platform
and jumped down on the sloping cinder path to the sidewalk.

Trees were on the lawns alongside the walk, branches drooping
low, leaves scraping occasionally against the young man's straw hat.
He saw a cluster of lights, bluish-white in the dusk across a river,
many lights for a small town. He crossed the lift-lock bridge and
turned on to the main street. A hotel was at the corner.

At the desk a bald-headed man in a blue shirt, the sleeves rolled
up, looked critically at the young man while he registered. "All
right, Mr. Flaherty," he said, inspecting the signature carefully.

"Do you know many people around here?" Mr. Flaherty asked.

"Just about everybody."

"The Rowers?"

"The old lady?"

"Yeah, an old lady."

"Sure, Mrs. Anna Rower. Around the corner to the left, then
turn to the right on the first street, the house opposite the Presbyterian church on the hill."

"An old family," suggested the young man.

"An old-timer all right." The hotel man made it clear by a twitching of his lips that he was a part of the new town, canal, water
power, and factories.

Mr. Flaherty sauntered out and turned to the left. It was dark
and the street had the silence of small towns in the evening. Turning a corner he heard girls giggling in a doorway. He looked at the
church on the hill, the steeple dark against the sky. He had forgotten whether the man had said beside the church or across the
road, but could not make up his mind to ask the fellow who was

watering the wide church lawn. No lights in the shuttered windows of the rough-cast house beside the church. He came down the hill and had to yell three times at the man because the water swished strongly against the grass.

"All right, thanks. Right across the road," Mr. Flaherty repeated.

Tall trees screened the square brick house. Looking along the hall to a lighted room, Mr. Flaherty saw an old lady standing at a sideboard. "She's in all right," he thought, rapping on the screen door. A large woman of about forty, dressed in blue skirt and blue waist, came down the stairs. She did not open the screen door.

"Could I speak to Mrs. Anna Rower?"

"I'm Miss Hilda Rower."

"I'm from the University Historical Club."

"What did you want to see Mother for?"

Mr. Flaherty did not like talking through the screen door. "I wanted to talk to her," he said firmly.

"Well, maybe you'd better come in."

He stood in the hall while the large woman lit the gas in the front room. The gas flared up, popped, showing fat hips and heavy lines on her face. Mr. Flaherty, disappointed, watched her swaying down the hall to get her mother. He carefully inspected the front room, the framed photographs of dead Conservative politicians, the group of military men hanging over the old-fashioned piano, the faded greenish wallpaper and the settee in the corner.

An old woman with a knot of white hair and good eyes came into the room, walking erectly. "This is the young man who wanted to see you, Mother," Miss Hilda Rower said. They all sat down. Mr. Flaherty explained he wanted to get some information concerning the Rower genealogical tree for the next meeting of his society. The Rowers, he knew, were a pioneer family in the district, and descended from William the Conqueror, he had heard.

The old lady laughed thinly, swaying from side to side. "It's true enough, but I don't know who told you. My father was Daniel Rower, who came to Ontario from Cornwall in 1830."

Miss Hilda Rower interrupted. "Wait, Mother, you may not want to tell about it." Brusque and businesslike, she turned to the young man. "You want to see the family tree, I suppose."

"Oh, yes."

"My father was a military settler here," the old lady said.

"I don't know but what we might be able to give you some notes," Miss Hilda spoke generously.

"Thanks awfully, if you will."

"Of course you're prepared to pay something if you're going to print it," she added, smugly adjusting her big body in the chair.

Mr. Flaherty got red in the face; of course he understood, but to tell the truth he had merely wanted to chat with Mrs. Rower. Now he knew definitely he did not like the heavy nose and unsentimental assertiveness of the lower lip of this big woman with the wide shoulders. He couldn't stop looking at her thick ankles. Rocking back and forth in the chair she was primly conscious of lineal superiority; a proud unmarried woman, surely she could handle a young man, half-closing her eyes, a young man from the University indeed. "I don't want to talk to her about the University," he thought.

Old Mrs. Rower went into the next room and returned with a framed genealogical tree of the house of Rower. She handed it graciously to Mr. Flaherty, who read, "The descent of the family of Rower, from William the Conqueror, from Malcolm 1st, and from the Capets, Kings of France." It bore the *imprimatur* of the College of Arms, 1838.

"It's wonderful to think you have this," Mr. Flaherty said, smiling at Miss Hilda, who watched him suspiciously.

"A brother of mine had it all looked up," old Mrs. Rower said.

"You don't want to write about that," Miss Hilda said, crossing her ankles. The ankles looked much thicker crossed. "You just want to have a talk with Mother."

"That's it," Mr. Flaherty smiled agreeably.

"We may write it up ourselves some day." Her heavy chin dipped down and rose again.

"Sure, why not?"

"But there's no harm in you talking to Mother if you want to, I guess."

"You could write a good story about that tree," Mr. Flaherty said, feeling his way.

"We may do it some day but it'll take time," she smiled complacently at her mother, who mildly agreed.

Mr. Flaherty talked pleasantly to this woman, who was so determined he would not learn anything about the family tree without paying for it. He tried talking about the city, then tactfully asked old Mrs. Rower what she remembered of the Clintonville of seventy years ago. The old lady talked willingly, excited a little. She went into the next room to get a book of clippings. "My father, Captain Rower, got a grant of land from the Crown and cleared it," she said, talking over her shoulder. "A little way up the Trent River. Clintonville was a small military settlement then . . ."

"Oh, Mother, he doesn't want to know all about that," Miss Hilda said impatiently.

"It's very interesting indeed."

The old woman said nervously, "My dear, what difference does it make? You wrote it all up for the evening at the church."

"So I did too," she hesitated, thinking the young man ought to see how well it was written. "I have an extra copy." She looked at him thoughtfully. He smiled. She got up and went upstairs.

The young man talked very rapidly to the old lady and took many notes.

Miss Rower returned. "Would you like to see it?" She handed Mr. Flaherty a small gray booklet. Looking quickly through it, he saw it contained valuable information about the district.

"The writing is simply splendid. You must have done a lot of work on it."

"I worked hard on it," she said, pleased and more willing to talk.

"Is this an extra copy?"

"Yes, it's an extra copy."

"I suppose I might keep it," he said diffidently.

She looked at him steadily. "Well . . . I'll have to charge you twenty-five cents."

"Sure, sure, of course, that's fine." He blushed.

"Just what it costs to get them out," the old lady explained apologetically.

"Can you change a dollar?" He fumbled in his pocket, pulling the dollar out slowly.

They could not change it but Miss Rower would be pleased to go down to the corner grocery store. Mr. Flaherty protested. No trouble, he would go. She insisted on asking the next-door neighbour to change it. She went across the room, the dollar in hand.

Mr. Flaherty chatted with the nice old lady and carefully examined the family tree, and wrote quickly in a small book till the screen door banged, the curtains parted, and Miss Hilda Rower came into the room. He wanted to smirk, watching her walking heavily, so conscious of her ancient lineage, a virginal mincing sway to her large hips, seventy-five cents' change held loosely in drooping fingers.

"Thank you," he said, pocketing the change, pretending his work was over. Sitting back in the chair he praised the way Miss Rower had written the history of the neighbourhood, and suggested she might write a splendid story of the family tree, if she had the material, of course.

"I've got the material, all right," she said, trying to get comfortable again. How would Mr. Flaherty arrange it and where should she try to sell it? The old lady was dozing in the rocking-chair. Miss Rower began to talk rather nervously about her material. She talked of the last title in the family and the Sir Richard who had been at the court of Queen Elizabeth.

Mr. Flaherty chimed in gaily, "I suppose you know the O'Flahertys were kings in Ireland, eh?"

She said vaguely, "I daresay, I daresay," conscious only of an interruption to the flow of her thoughts. She went on talking with hurried eagerness, all the fine talk about her ancestors bringing her peculiar satisfaction. A soft light came into her eyes and her lips were moist.

Mr. Flaherty started to rub his cheek, and looked at her big legs, and felt restive, and then embarrassed, watching her closely, her firm lower lip hanging loosely. She was talking slowly, lazily, relaxing in her chair, a warm fluid oozing through her veins, exhausting but satisfying her.

He was uncomfortable. She was liking it too much. He did not know what to do. There was something immodest about it. She was close to forty, her big body relaxed in the chair. He looked at his watch and suggested he would be going. She stretched her legs graciously, pouting, inviting him to stay a while longer, but he was standing up, tucking his magazine under his arm. The old lady was still dozing. "I'm so comfortable," Miss Rower said, "I hate to move."

The mother woke up and shook hands with Mr. Flaherty. Miss Rower got up to say good-bye charmingly.

Half-way down the path Mr. Flaherty turned. She was standing in the doorway, partly shadowed by the tall trees, bright moonlight filtering through the leaves touching soft lines on her face and dark hair.

He went down the hill to the hotel unconsciously walking with a careless easy stride, wondering at the change that had come over the heavy, strong woman. He thought of taking a walk along the river in the moonlight, the river on which old Captain Rower had drilled troops on the ice in the winter of 1837 to fight the rebels. Then he thought of having a western sandwich in the café across the road from the hotel. That big woman in her own way had been hot stuff.

In the hotel he asked to be called early so he could get the first train to the city. For a long time he lay awake in the fresh, cool bed, the figure of the woman, whose ancient lineage had taken the place of a lover in her life, drifting into his thoughts and becoming important while he watched on the wall the pale moonlight that had softened the lines of her face, and wondered if it was still shining on her bed, and on her throat, and on her contented, lazily relaxed body.

A PREDICAMENT

Father Francis, the youngest priest at the cathedral, was hearing confessions on a Saturday afternoon. He stepped out of the confessional to stretch his legs a moment and walked up the left aisle toward the flickering red light of the Precious Blood, mystical in the twilight of the cathedral. Father Francis walked back to the confessional, because too many women were waiting on the penitent bench. There were not so many men.

Sitting again in the confessional, he said a short prayer to the Virgin Mary to get in the mood for hearing confessions. He wiped his lips with his handkerchief, cleared his throat, and pushed back the panel, inclining his ear to hear a woman's confession. The panel slid back with a sharp grating noise. Father Francis whispered his ritual prayer and made the sign of the cross. The woman hadn't been to confession for three months and had missed mass twice for no good reason. He questioned her determinedly, indignant with this woman who had missed mass twice for no good reason. In a steady whisper he told her the story of an old woman who had crawled on the ice to get to mass. The woman hesitated, then told about missing her morning prayers. . . . "Yes, my child yes, my child . . ." "And about certain thoughts . . ." "Now, about these thoughts; let's look at it in this way . . ." He gave the woman absolution and told her to say the beads once for her penance.

Closing the panel on the women's side, he sat quietly for a moment in the darkness of the confessional. He was a young priest, very interested in confessions.

Father Francis turned to the other side of the confessional, pushing back the panel to hear some man's confession. Resting his chin on his hand after making the sign of the cross, he did not bother trying to discern the outline of the head and shoulders of the man kneeling in the corner.

The man said in a husky voice: "I wanna get off at the corner of King and Yonge Street."

Father Francis sat up straight, peering through the wire work. The man's head was moving. He could see his nose and his eyes. His heart began to beat unevenly. He sat back quietly.

"Cancha hear me, wasamatter, I wanna get off at King and Yonge," the man said insistently, pushing his nose through the wire work.

On the man's breath there was a strong smell of whiskey. Father Francis nervously slid the panel back into position. As the panel slid into place he knew it sounded like the closing of doors on a bus. There he was hearing confessions, and a drunken man on the other side of the panel thought him a conductor on a bus. He would go into the vestry and tell Father Marlow.

Father Francis stepped out of the confessional to look around the cathedral. Men and women in the pews and on the penitents' benches wondered why he had come out of the confessional twice in the last few minutes when so many were waiting. Father Francis wasn't feeling well, that was the trouble. Walking up the aisle, he rubbed his smooth cheek with his hand, thinking hard. If he had the man thrown out he might be a tough customer and there would be a disturbance. There would be a disturbance in the cathedral. Such a disturbance would be sure to get in the papers. Everything got in the papers. There was no use telling it to anybody. Walking erectly he went back to the confessional. Father Francis was sweating.

Rubbing his shoulder-blades uneasily against the back of the confessional, he decided to hear a woman's confession. It was evading the issue—it was a compromise, but it didn't matter; he was going to hear a woman's confession first.

The woman, encouraged by many questions from Father Francis, made an extraordinarily good confession, though sometimes he did not seem to be listening very attentively. He thought he could hear the man moving. The man was drunk—drunkenness, the over-indulgence of an appetite, the drunken state. Scholastic psychology. Cardinal Mercier's book on psychology had got him through the exam at the seminary.

"When you feel you're going to tell a lie, say a short prayer to Mary the mother of God," he said to the woman.

"Yes, father."

"Some lies are more serious than others."

"Yes, father."

"But they are lies just the same."

"I tell mostly white lies," she said.

"They are lies, lies, lies, just the same. They may not endanger your soul, but they lead to something worse. Do you see?"

"Yes, father."

"Will you promise to say a little prayer every time?"

Father Francis could not concentrate on what the woman was saying. But he wanted her to stay there for a long time. She was company. He would try and concentrate on her. He could not forget the drunken man for more than a few moments.

The woman finished her confession. Father Francis, breathing heavily, gave her absolution. Slowly he pushed back the panel—a street-car, a conductor swinging back the doors on a street-car. He turned deliberately to the other side of the confessional, but hesitated, eager to turn and hear another confession. It was no use—it couldn't go on in that way. Closing his eyes he said three "Our

Fathers" and three "Hail, Marys," and felt much better. He was calm and the man might have gone.

He tried to push back the panel so it would not make much noise, but moving slowly, it grated loudly. He could see the man's head bobbing up, watching the panel sliding back.

"Yes, my son," Father Francis said deliberately.

"I got to get off at King and Yonge," the man said stubbornly.

"You better go, you've got no business here."

"Say, there, did you hear me say King and Yonge?"

The man was getting ugly. The whiskey smelt bad in the confessional. Father Francis drew back quickly and half closed the panel. That same grating noise. It put an idea into his head. He said impatiently: "Step lively there; this is King and Yonge. Do you want to go past your stop?"

"All right, brother," the man said slowly, getting up clumsily.

"Move along now," Father Francis said authoritatively.

"I'm movin'; don't get so huffy," the man said, swinging aside the curtains of the confessional, stepping out to the aisle.

Father Francis leaned back in the confessional and nervously gripped the leather seat. He began to feel very happy. There were no thoughts at all in his head. Suddenly he got up and stepped out to the aisle. He stood watching a man going down the aisle swaying almost imperceptibly. The men and women in the pews watched Father Francis curiously, wondering if he was really unwell because he had come out of the confessional three times in a half-hour. Again he went into the confessional.

At first Father Francis was happy hearing the confessions, but he became restive. He should have used shrewd judgment. With that drunken man he had gone too far, forgotten himself in the confessional. He had descended to artifice in the confessional to save himself from embarrassment.

At the supper-table he did not talk much to the other priests. He had a feeling he would not sleep well that night. He would lie awake trying to straighten everything out. The thing would first have to be settled in his own conscience. Then perhaps he would tell the bishop.

A whisper had gone the rounds that Greenwich Village was washed up: Paris was the new frontier. In the early twenties living had been inexpensive, and if you wanted to be a publisher and have a little magazine the printing costs were cheap. Above all, Paris was the good address. It was the one grand display window for international talent, and if you were at all interested in the way the intellectual cloth of the time was being cut you had to be there, even if you couldn't do more than press your nose against the window.

Looking back on it, what American writer of the twenties or thirties, or the fifties, from Gertrude Stein to Faulkner to Henry Miller or Tennessee Williams didn't feel compelled to drop into the great style center to look around. It is not quite the same today. New York has challenged the Paris influence, and Rome has come into the picture and so has London. But some of the magic still remains in the word from Paris. If you want to know what it was like in the late twenties you only have to recall what has gone on in the forties and fifties. How these French writers get blown up so the international public is persuaded to listen and believe something new is being said is probably a carefully guarded French national trade secret. Through the late forties and fifties; now is the time for the writer to be engaged with society; then later; now is the time for disengagement. And Existentialism! Today in the North American universities thousands of students are worrying and wondering if there is anything new in Existentialism, or perhaps deciding that they too ought to look at the world with Sartre's "disgust and anguish."

The word from Paris. It's not the voice of the turtle today but it was in the twenties. It offered the climate, the ambience, the importance of the recognition of the new for the artist. In those days a writer coming to Paris could believe he would find contemporaries and it didn't seem to matter to him that the French themselves paid no attention to him. In no time you learned that the oddly parochial French took it for granted you were absorbed in their culture. If

not, what were you doing there in their style center? Stealing a
style or two? Why not? It was the international custom. The
burglars of French literature and painting.

We are born, we live a while, and we die, and along the way the
artist keeps looking at the appearance of things, call it concrete
reality, the stuff of experience, or simply "what is out there." Now
I think that for intellectuals, writers and artists, the Paris of those
days had become like a giant crystal; like a crystal with many
facets, and the French had a genius for turning and ever turning
the crystal so the light would fall on a new facet, and then from
the cafés would come the announcement, "This is the way it is
being looked at now." Naturally the writer or painter in far-off
cities is charmed and interested. And yet, when you think about it,
the question arises, "Were any of those French writers of the time,
aside from the intellectual gowns they were wearing, as good as the
strangers in town?" Cocteau, Breton, Aragon and Co.? In a sense
they were in the millinery business. And the great Gide? He was
a moralist, he sounded the moral tone, or rather the tone of no
morality at all beyond the aesthetic approach to life. His great
strength was in his stylish comment on life, not in the creation of
it. But Joyce and Hemingway, the foreigners, were to have a world
influence. And just as in the nineteenth century the world capital
for the novelist turns out to have been Moscow, well, where was it
in twenty-nine?

The capital did seem to be in Paris, sitting at the café with the
young businessman. The marks of the quick and wonderful French
intelligence seemed to be all around one in this city with its open
beauty, its elegance, and that splendid indifference of the French
citizen at the next table to your private life. And above all, in every
corner of this lovely Babylonian capital was stuck the national
symbol, the shrewd-eyed watchful madame at the cash register. I
could see her there in black near the café door, reminding me of the
eternal verities.

By ten in the evening the whole corner would take on the fullness
of its own life with the terraces crowded and the well-known
drunken poets or painters, celebrated for their stupor rather than
their art, wandering across the road from café to café, making the
taxis dodge them. A tourist bus would pass, the tourists gawking,
and Flossie Martin, the ex-Follies girl, plump, but still golden-haired
and pink-and-white complexioned, who refused to go home to the

States, would stand up and yell out an obscenity at the staring tourists in their bus. Or a visiting movie star, like Adolph Menjou, would be sitting at the Coupole with his new wife. While people lined up and moved slowly by his table where he sat, incredibly impassive, we, watching him from across the road, would snicker patronizingly. In the neighborhood was an American Jewish writer named Ludwig Lewisohn, who had written a successful book *Upstream* and had gone on to do novels. He looked like an important elderly professor. His friends, so I heard, had persuaded him to "show himself to the people," so now he would come slowly along the street. The others? Hundreds of others! Lawrence Vail, so blond and so sunburned; Kay Boyle, Michael Arlen, then rich and famous, having written *The Green Hat*, would be there with his beautiful wife, the Grecian countess. I liked Arlen. A shrewd, cynical, dapper dark man, he knew exactly what he was doing. For him, D. H. Lawrence was the only writer in the world and not to be compared with other writers. "The man is willing to live in a mud hut so he can write," he would say. Disdainful of this opinion, I argued with him. "You need a haircut," he said, looking at me quizzically. "You'd better get it cut or you'll think it's a halo."

We got used to the night street cries, too. Cheerful little old women, selling newspapers, would cry out, *"Ami du Peuple."* A male newspaper vendor hurrying by would be muttering in a deep hoarse voice, *"Intransigeant, Paris Soir, Paris Soir."* Another vendor in a high falsetto voice, *"Chocolat, fruits glacés, cacahouettes, messieurs, dames."* Walking home at two in the morning we would pass that crowded little dance hall, The Jockey, with the jazz blowing from the open door. One night three little girls came skipping out, giggling and pushing each other. They were trying to sing the American popular song, "Constantinople." On the street, just ahead of us, they would shout out, "Constantinople" and as the song required, try to spell out—"c-o-n-s-t-" and get no further. Shoving each other, they screamed with laughter.

On the way home we might pass Ford Madox Ford, the plump and portly president of a whole group of writers, who would be taking the night air all by himself, his hands linked behind his back. Old Ford, as Hemingway called him. Why did I always feel a little ashamed of my lack of sympathy for him; the friend of Henry James, the collaborator of Joseph Conrad? I had called him "Ford of many models." I hadn't felt drawn to him that time I had met him in New York; maybe it was his portly and heavy-mustached aloofness, his whispering voice. Yet I knew no man loved good contemporary writings more than he did. And one night at a dinner I heard him make a remark I have never forgotten: "No writer can go on living in a vacuum." It took me some years to discover how true this was; not just of writers, but of all men who would stay alone in their hearts. There must be someone somewhere you count on for approval, someone whose praise would be dear to you. When finally there is no one you might as well hand in your ticket. . . .

The May weather was so fine I didn't want to stay in the apartment in the afternoons and work. Bit by bit, looking at paintings had become part of our daily fare. Everybody in Paris seemed to paint, and in store windows in strange little streets you would see reproductions of Matisse, Derain, Rouault, Chirico, Modegliani, Picasso, Utrillo, and in the Quarter the surrealists Picabia and Miro were famous names. At that time there was still a common language of painting: the language hadn't got broken up. The painters hadn't quite entered their tower of Babel.

Some writers like to sit for long hours at their desks. Not me. At that time the *New Yorker* had written asking if I had any stories. I began to work on some. And I was also working on the novel that was to be called *It's Never Over*. But the Paris streets were my workshop. While loafing along the streets ideas for the stories would grow in my head. Little street scenes would seem to distract me, would indeed get my full attention: the intent expression on the faces of men hurrying to the street urinals; workingmen quarreling under the eyes of a gendarme, each seeking the triumph of provoking the other to strike the first blow and get arrested. Or some little street whore would make me wonder, "Why are so many of these girls of the same short solid build as the whores Lautrec loved to paint?" A writer is always working. I can remember watching the ease and style with which Lacoste and Cochet handled Big Bill Tilden in the Davis Cup tennis matches and telling myself it had something to do with style in writing. When I got back to the apartment I would sit by the window overlooking the prison wall and write rapidly, most of the work having been done in my head before I came home. Often it rained. It was the time for reading. Very late at night was also a good time. From the window I could watch the bicycle patrol, the three tough French cops no one wanted to tangle with, come peddling slowly down the street.

Even when reading a writer is busily at work watching how an effect is achieved on the page. But whether I was reading D. H. Lawrence or Tolstoi or Virginia Woolf I would notice that when I hit certain scenes I would be so carried away I would cease to be aware of style or method. What then made good writing good? That was always the question. Freshness? Verbal felicity? No, there always seemed to be some other quality. There had been at the time a quarrel about the methods of Arnold Bennett and Virginia Woolf; Bennett's or Zola's camera eye and Virginia Woolf's interior flow of impressions. But it seemed to me, reading so late at night in my room overlooking the prison wall, that there could be no quarrel at all. The temperament, the character, the very identity of the writer was in his kind of eye. Virginia Woolf had a sensibility so fragile it must have been always close to the breaking point; she couldn't have written any other way. And Lawrence? Again the writer's own character gave his work its identity. He must have been an Anglo-Saxon puritan with an inborn uneasiness about female flesh; he must have hated this uneasiness, and hungered for the expression of ecstasy; therefore the natural poetry of sex. But then I would wonder why Lady Chatterley's correct copulations didn't move me as much as one surrender by Anna Karenina, or one of poor Emma Bovary's fugitive rolls in the hay.

At the cafés, of course, one could always get an argument on these questions. But I knew what I was seeking in my Paris street walks, and in the typing hours—with Loretto waiting to retype a chapter. It was this: strip the language, and make the style, the method, all the psychological ramifications, the ambience of the relationships, all the one thing, so the reader couldn't make separations. Cézanne's apples. The appleness of apples. Yet just apples.

Wandering around Paris I would find myself thinking of the way Matisse looked at the world around him and find myself growing enchanted. A pumpkin, a fence, a girl, a pineapple on a tablecloth—the thing seen freshly in a pattern that was a gay celebration of things as they were. Why couldn't all people have the eyes and the heart that would give them this happy acceptance of reality? The word made flesh. The terrible vanity of the artist who wanted the word without the flesh. I can see now that I was busily rejecting even then that arrogance of the spirit, that fantasy running through modern letters and thought that man was alien in this universe. From Pascal to Henry Miller they are the children of St. Paul.

HUGH MacLENNAN

1907-

Hugh MacLennan, widely recognized at home and abroad, along with Morley Callaghan, as one of Canada's leading novelists, was born in Glace Bay, Cape Breton Island, and educated in Classics at Dalhousie University. He was a Rhodes Scholar and entered Oriel College, Oxford, in 1929; he was graduated B.A. and M.A. He continued his studies at Princeton University obtaining his Ph.D. in 1935. He has taught Latin and history at Lower Canada College in Montreal and, since 1951, has been a member of the English Department at McGill University. He was awarded the Lorne Pierce Medal for literature by the Royal Society of Canada in 1952 and the following year was elected to the Society.

MacLennan is a prolific writer, the author of six novels, three books of essays, and a travel book, *Seven Rivers of Canada* (1961), in which the geographical and historical background becomes as important as the contemporary foreground. Clearly and vividly written as they are, the volumes of essays, *Cross-Country* (1949), *Thirty and Three* (1954) and *Scotchman's Return* (1960) must give place to the novels, upon which, however, they provide a useful commentary. Of the novels, the most ambitious and the most successful are *Barometer Rising* (1941), an exploration of the problem of Canadian identity, set in Nova Scotia at the time of the first world war, *Two Solitudes* (1945), a dramatic presentation of the tensions between English and French in Quebec, and *The*

Watch that Ends the Night (1959), a rich and complex study of psychological and spiritual struggle, from which the fine narrative included here is taken. This novella-like passage ranks with the brilliant description of the Halifax explosion of 1917 in *Barometer Rising* as the high-water mark of MacLennan's achievement as a writer of pure narrative. Although all the novels are in a sense "problem novels" it is for their dramatic working out of plot and situation quite as much as for the handling of ideas that they are to be praised. Two novels of MacLennan's middle period remain to be named: *The Precipice* (1948), a tale in which the quiet virtues of a small town in Canada are seen as superior to the frenzied life and distorted values of an American city; and *Each Man's Son* (1951), a psychological study of the conflict between reason and violence in love set in a Cape Breton mining town.

MacLennan's most recent novel, *The Return of the Sphinx* (1967), takes up the theme of *Barometer Rising* and examines the later developments of the French-English confrontation in Canada. This is worked out through the conflict between an Ottawa-Liberal father and a Montreal-Separatist son.

I know that part of New Brunswick now. I have driven through it and flown over it and looking down from the aircraft I have seen those steely rivers winding through the somber green of the spruce and the outcroppings of rock and sometimes on a fine day, looking down from 14,000 feet in the TCA aircraft, I have seen a sort of shimmering in the green mat of the land and recognized it as sunshine reflected upward through the trees from the water of thin swamps. I also know those little fishing ports and lumber towns along the Gulf shore and in my mind I can smell them. Such ripe combination of smells they give out; balsam, lobster pots, drying fish, oakum, new lumber, bilge and the stench of fish-offal on beaches under umbrellas of screaming gulls. But inland, even four miles inland in that country, there is no sense of ocean at all, but only of this primeval forest of spruce with the tangle of deadfalls and the sound-absorbing carpet of spruce needles that have accumulated over the centuries. The rivers run through it teeming with trout and salmon, and moose, bear, deer and all the northern animals large and small are at home in the tangle of trees. So are blackflies and mosquitoes in the spring, and in winter so is the snow. In winter this whole land is like Siberia.

The camp where Jerome lived as a child was an old one; for all I know, men worked there a century and a half ago when the Royal Navy harvested this forest for masts. He grew up in a works-barracks where his mother was the cook and almost the only woman; *almost* the only woman because, so Jerome said, it is impossible for a body of men to be located anywhere without at least a few women finding them. The camp lay on the left bank of one of the larger rivers and was bordered by a branch of quieter water flowing down through the woods from the north. Around a barn-shaped cookhouse in the centre of a chip-covered clearing were the log bunkhouses of the lumberjacks, a stable for horses and an unpainted shack housing a stationary engine which drove the power saws. There were corduroy roads leading off in various directions into the woods, some of them for miles, but all of them ended in forest. Between the camp and the river estuary there was no road at all in those days, though I believe there is one now. In winter the men went down on the ice and in summer in boats and canoes, and when Jerome was a boy the first motorboat appeared on the river.

Those days are gone in Canada. Now the lumbermen eat fresh meat and fare reasonably well, and in some camps they tell me they sleep between sheets. But in those days it was pork and beans, scouse and salted horse, and lime juice against the scurvy, it was boils and the savagery of melancholy temper which comes when men live and eat like that. The workmen wore red and black mackinaws and caps, broad leather belts and oiled leather top boots with metal hooks for the laces, and Jerome told me that some of them could be utterly silent for days and would never talk unless there was drink in them. Then they talked violently and fought. Rum got into the camp smuggled up the river, and raw alcohol and essence of lemon, and when the liquor came the fights broke out.

"Those fights were a substitute for sex," Jerome said. "That greedy look of a crowd of sex-hungry men watching a fight. It's in us, George, it's in us. Once I saw a man flogged. He was seized up just like the fleet sailors used to be, and the man who did the flogging was a white-haired man who'd been a bosun's mate in the Royal Navy. Why the man was flogged I never knew, but he was, and the men were for it. I heard him scream. Yes, that was in this country. Not now but then. I saw it and I heard it, George."

There was no school in the camp, no store or church or any other boys for Jerome to play with, and when he was a child he thought this was how it was for all children, for he knew nothing different. Yet in a way he was privileged, not only because he was the only boy but because his mother was the principal woman.

He lived with her in the kitchen attached to the eating barn, the bedroom they shared being a narrow room back of the kitchen, and not even the foreman could enter their quarters without his mother's permission. She was absolute ruler of the kitchen, and more than once she drove men out of it by throwing boiling water at them or threatening them with a carving knife. At meals the men lined up outside in the main cookhouse with tin plates in their hands and Jerome, helping his mother inside, would watch her ladling out the food from the big pot and dispensing it to each man as he held his plate through the hole in the wall between the kitchen and the eating barn itself. It was in this posture that he best remembered her:

a short, square, powerful woman with moist beefy arms and a bead
of sweat around the line of her yellow hair. Behind her in the kitch-
en was the big, wood-burning stove, the sink with the pump that
drew water from the river, and the walls of the kitchen were yellow
pine stained with dark knots and festooned with black pots and
pans.

"That's what I meant by saying I don't know who I am," said
Jerome. "I don't know anything about my mother at all. Where did
she come from? I don't know. Was she local? Somehow I don't
think so. A Balt? A Norwegian or a Swede? Somehow I think she
was a Balt though I don't know. Who was my father? He'd disappeared long before I could remember anything about him. I don't
suppose he was ever married to my mother, but he may have been."

It haunted Jerome that he did not know her surname. The men
called her "Anna" or "Mrs. Anna" and he remembered her presence
in certain smells like porridge and salt codfish and the strong yellow
kitchen soap they called Surprise Soap in the Maritime Provinces.
She had a wide, straight mouth with thin lips, and as his own lips
were rather full, and his stiff hair was dark brown while his mother's
had been yellow, he had conjured up a picture of his unknown
begetter as a swarthy man, Portuguese in his swarthiness, surly,
haughty and sly, and probably quick with a knife. But this was
pure fantasy, for nobody ever told him what his father was like and
his mother never mentioned his name.

Some of the men in the camp Jerome remembered very well, better
even than he remembered his mother. There was an old sailor, proud
of being an Englishman, who used to tell him stories of Africa and
India and China and who tried to make him promise that when he
grew up he would take to the sea. Another man he particularly
liked was a gigantic French-Canadian with a freckled face, a red
complexion and the hairiest arms he had ever seen on anyone.

"He spoke French most of the time, but with his looks he must
have been descended from one of the Highland soldiers who settled
in Quebec after Wolfe. He was the strongest man in the camp and
he was a seasonal worker, for he had a wife and children on a farm
somewhere in Quebec. He loved children, and I was the only kid
in the place and he used to look after me. On nights when the
accordion man played in the cookhouse I used to sit on his knee."

This red-headed giant was also a master craftsman. He built tiny
ship models inside bottles, and it was he who built Jerome's first

canoe. It must have been one of the strangest canoes ever made, for it was boy-size, its strakes of varnished birch bark, its frame of thin pine, and there were air cans under the thwarts to keep it afloat if it capsized. When the river was open, Jerome used to paddle in the branch and go considerable distances into the forest, but he was never allowed to take the canoe into the main stream that poured down in front of the camp, for the current was so strong he could never have paddled back against it.

"My mother," he said to Catherine once, "I still dream about her sometimes and usually it's a nightmare. Whoever she was, she must have had character, for she was the queen of that camp and make no mistake about it. She had power over those men, and the power went far past her control of their food. It came out of something inside of her that used to frighten me. Did she love me? I'm sure she thought she did. She was as possessive as a female bear with a cub, and I never had to worry about being molested by the men with her there. With her there I didn't even know there are men who molested little boys. She'd have taken the carving knife to any man who so much as looked at me sideways. She hated men as a group and she despised them, too. 'They're no good,' she used to say I don't know how many times. 'All they want is one thing. That and drink is all they want. And they're all the same.' "

Catherine told me years later that Jerome's abnormal fear of displeasing a woman came from his mother.

Cyclically, this man-hating female required a man, and when she wanted one she took him. There would be weeks when she cooked for them and hardly noticed them, or bothered to answer them when they spoke, and then Jerome would see a certain look on her face and await the night with dread.

"The nights she had a man in were bad nights for me. I was always afraid. I'd be asleep—I used to sleep in the same bed with her—and I'd wake up with her carrying me out of the bedroom in her arms. She used to put me down on a palliasse she kept beside the stove in the kitchen and she left me there under a blanket with the dog. Sometimes when it was over and the man went away she'd take me back to bed with her, and when that happened I'd lie awake all night. But generally she left me till morning under the blanket with the dog.

"Was she a whore? I mean, did she take money for it? Somehow I don't think she did, though she may have. Maybe I just don't want to think she did. I don't know. I can't really remember what she was like. But I'll never forget the nights when she had a man in. I think I remember every one of them in my last year in the camp."

He would lie on the palliasse listening to the lift of the lock of the kitchen door, he would hear the muttered announcement of some man that he was there. Sometimes the man's boots would creak on the boards and sometimes his thumbs would snap at his leather belt and sometimes he'd give a throaty little laugh and sometimes he'd stand in the dark like a moose in the woods. In the deep of winter when moonlight reflected from the snow brightened the kitchen, Jerome would recognize the man as he stood among the shadows cast by the table and chairs and the pots and pans hanging on the wall. After the bedroom door closed, Jerome would lie tense on the palliasse with the dog nuzzling at him, watching the thin slip of light that struck out from under the bedroom door, waiting for the sounds.

"Oh God," he said, "men are such slaves to themselves! None of them, not one of them, wanted my mother for herself any more than she wanted any of them for themselves. And all of them were better than her. Oh yes they were, because I remember some things well. They wanted a woman—yes. But more than the sex they wanted sympathy and some woman to talk to. If she'd ever given them any of that, most of them would have taken it instead of the sex if there was any choice. I used to hear some of them talking about their mothers to her. Trying to talk about them, that is, for she'd never let them do it for long. I used to hear some of them trying to tell her about their wives and children. And I remember her saying—mean and sharp—'What do I care if you love your wife or not? What's it to me?'

"All she wanted from any of them was the sex, and by God she could be noisy about that. I'd lie there listening and driving my fingernails into my palms hoping to God the man she had that night would be able to satisfy her. Not many did, and she was cruel to them afterwards. I used to hear her sneering and mocking them. Usually she never talked unless she had to. But if she had a man, and he didn't give her what she wanted, then she talked and I knew what her face would look like. I used to see some of those men creeping out like whipped dogs and I used to hate her for what she did to them. There was only one man that last winter who satisfied her, and he was a mean-looking, wiry little foreigner who could hardly speak a word of English. No, she didn't like him, and in the daytime she never even looked at him, but he used to come in pretty often. Then without warning he went down the river and never came back."

It was Jerome's last year in the camp, the year he was a husky boy of ten with the strength and robustness of a boy of thirteen, that he remembered best. What happened before that last year he could hardly remember at all, but the last year was vivid.

"There was a man that winter," he said, "that used to frighten me the way a snake frightens me now. There was nothing snakelike about his appearance, but there was a look in his eye, the way he had of looking at everybody. He never talked at all, and when he drank he drank sullenly. We all called him the Engineer because he was in charge of the stationary engine and he was the only man in the camp who could keep the motorboat in repair. He was dark and lean and he had this queer, drawn look in his face, and he used to carry a spanner wherever he went as though it proved he wasn't an ordinary lumberjack like the rest of them. He carried it in a loop attached to his pants and he even wore it to meals. Maybe he even slept with it.

"One March morning, about three weeks after the little foreigner went down the river, the Engineer said something to me while I was watching him work on the engine. I used to be fascinated by the engine and I would have watched more if I hadn't been afraid of him. I knew all about the work the men did. I used to go out on the sleighs with them and come back on top of the cut logs. It was easy for me with most of the men. But this was the first time the Engineer had ever spoken to me. All he said was, 'I want to eat pancakes tonight. Tell your old lady I want to eat pancakes and syrup.'

"So I went back into the kitchen and told her the Engineer wanted to eat pancakes and syrup, and when she made them I knew I'd soon be seeing him in the kitchen."

But "soon" turned out to be quite a long time, for the Engineer stayed solitary all through the long spring breakup and through all of April into early May. In those days the cutting season ran from late September till April, and before the river opened the logs were piled on the banks. When the ice went out they floated the logs down in two big drives, the long, timber logs going first and the short pit-props following. As soon as the logs were in the river, most of the men left camp and went back to their farms for the spring

322 THE TWENTIETH CENTURY

work. Now only a handful of men remained, the permanent maintenance crew and the men who went down the river after the drives
to float off the logs which had stuck on the banks or piled up on
some of the little islands on the way to the sea. One of the men who
remained was the Engineer, for there was still a large pile of logs
to be cut into lengths for pit-props.

It began peacefully, Jerome's last night in the camp. It was one
of those magic Canadian spring evenings that seem like a miracle
when they arrive, one of those times in early May when a tide of
southern air pours up from the United States and seems tropical over
the half-frozen earth and around the sticky, unopened buds of the
trees. All day long the forest had been hot. The few men remaining
worked in a holiday mood stripped to the waist in spite of the blackflies and by evening some of their bodies looked like broiled lobsters
wealed all over by flybites. Some of them went swimming in the
water of the branch, water as cold as melted snow, and one of them
took a cramp and had to be hauled out on a rope. Supper time came
and there were pancakes and syrup to follow the pork and beans.
After the men had eaten, in the long spring evening just six weeks
from the June solstice, they sat about in the clearing and watched the
sun roll down out of sight into the forest. The accordion man took
his place on the cookhouse steps and played song after song, some
of the men sang, and the others lounged about, fly-bitten, hot and
tired, their backs propped against stumps on the forest fringe while
they listened and drowsed and drank. There was liquor that night,
but in the magic of the evening, the purest kind of evening we ever
have in this northern country, the men sipped at their liquor without swilling it and nobody got drunk. Jerome's mother came out in
her apron and leaned in the doorway of the cookhouse listening to
the singing, finally it fell dark and one by one the tired men got up
and drifted off to the bunkhouse to sleep. When Jerome went to bed
it was much later than his usual hour and the camp was so still the
only sounds were the ringing of frogs and the slow sigh of the
river in flood.

He guessed it was an hour before midnight when he woke in his
mother's arms, his hands about her neck and his chest against her
warm, heavy breasts. His face was still hot from the sun and his
ears were swollen and hot from the blackfly bites and he woke so
slowly it was only when the spaniel nuzzled and licked his face that
he opened his eyes. He saw moonlight pouring into the kitchen in

three separate shafts through the three high windows that faced the moon, and between those shafts of light he saw the Engineer standing still. The bedroom door opened, his mother stood there, and he heard her say, 'What are you waiting for?' Then the man followed her in and the door closed.

This time the encounter was different. The Engineer he had feared so much began talking in a low, earnest stream of conversation, talking about himself and how lonely he was and how wretched was his life, and how different everything would be if she would go away with him. Jerome could only partly hear his words, and hardly any of them could he remember, but he knew that of all the lonely men in the camp this was the loneliest of all, and he yearned for some gentleness to come into his mother's voice in place of the withholding silence or the sneer he was afraid would come if the Engineer continued to talk like this. He wanted the Engineer to break through his mother's refusal to some kindness inside, to some safe kindness inside.

After a while the Engineer stopped talking and the usual noises began. They ceased almost at once and Jerome heard his mother's voice flare in a jeer of unspeakable contempt.

"So that's the best you can do! A kid could of done better!"

He heard the man groan and cry something out, and then he heard his mother mock and scorn him, and Jerome remembered thinking: Don't let her treat you like that, Engineer! Please, please, please do something to make her stop treating you like that!

The Engineer did. Suddenly his voice changed as the woman drove back his longing for tenderness into the pride and hatred Jerome had feared in him all winter. The man began to curse the woman in a stream of obscenity using every word Jerome had ever heard the men apply to the women they called whores. There was a short struggle, the pant of his mother's breath, then a loud smack as she hit him across the face and Jerome thought: Please, please don't let her do that again!

What happened next was as sudden as a bottle exploding. Jerome and the dog sprang up together at the scream of enraged fear that came from his mother. Something bumped and fell in the bedroom, there was a heave of bodies, then the crack—crack—crack of hard fists driven expertly home. This was followed by a yelp from the man, a gasp of pain, then a crunching shock more terrible than a fist blow. Then silence.

This silence, as abrupt and profound as the end of the world, was soon filled with a multitude of sweet noises. Mating frogs were singing high and happy in the night, so loud and high that the whole kitchen was filled with their joy. Then came another sound, the sobbing breath of a frightened man in agony.

Jerome put his hand on the knob of the bedroom door and pulled it open. He saw the Engineer bent double clutching his groin and he knew where his mother had hit him that last time. Beyond the Engineer's hunched body he saw his mother's legs and thighs naked in the moonlight, but the hunched man was between the boy and her face.

It was the dog who betrayed Jerome's presence. Whining into the room, the spaniel rubbed against the man's legs and made him turn. The Engineer gasped, his face came around distorted with his sick pain and was horrible with the knowledge of what he himself had just done. But he saw Jerome and recognized him, and the moment he saw him he plunged. The boy dodged back and the Engineer stumbled and hit the floor with a crash, his spanner rattling away from his right hand. Jerome saw that his pants were down about his lower legs and that it was these which had tripped him. On the floor the Engineer looked up, his mouth shut, his violence as silent as that of a fish in the sea. Jerome turned to run, escaped from the room, reached the kitchen door, felt the dog against his legs and had the presence of mind to push him back before he himself went out. He closed the door behind him and with his nightshirt fluttering and his feet bare he ran across the moonlit, chip-strewn clearing into the darkness of the forest. When he was in the trees the undergrowth began cutting his bare feet, he stopped, turned and lay flat.

Nothing moved in the clearing. The long cookhouse with the two metal pipes that served as chimneys stood silent, its sloping roof whitened by the moon, its walls dark, its windows glittering like gun metal. He heard the sigh and gurgle of the river as it poured among the tree trunks along the flooded banks, but there was no sound of men and no light in any of the bunkhouses. He could not see the bunkhouse which was still occupied, but if there had been lights in it he would have seen their glimmer through the trees.

With the instinct of an animal Jerome got up and changed his position, slinking through the shadows among the stumps at the edge of the forest-fringe to a place he knew about thirty feet away. He found it, a depression in the ground about ten feet from the edge of the moonlight, and lay down and scooped pine needles over himself to conceal the whiteness of his shirt and skin. Lying flat with his chin in his hands and his elbows in the needles, he stared at the kitchen door and listened to the pounding of his heart.

The Engineer was only ten feet away when Jerome first saw him. He was skirting the forest-fringe with the spanner in his hand, staring into the darkness of the trees and stopping to take quick looks behind him. He wore no cap, his mackinaw shirt was open and in the moonlight Jerome saw the splash of dark hair rising out of his shirt to his throat. The man stopped directly in front of him and Jerome kept his head down, pressing his face into the needles, the needles itching in his hair. Once he lifted his eyes and saw the man's feet and noticed they were small feet even in those high leather boots. There was a crunch of bracken as the man entered the woods, one of his boots came down within a yard of Jerome's head, but the engineer was staring into the total darkness of the forest and did not look down at his feet. In the cool air of the night Jerome could hear the man pant and thought he could feel the heat of his body. The boots turned and went back out of the forest into the clearing and as they crunched farther away Jerome looked up and saw the man's shoulders go around the corner of the cookhouse and down the path to the bunkhouses.

"I knew for certain that he was after me. He was putting himself between me and the men asleep in the bunkhouse. He knew I couldn't get around through the woods without making a noise. He knew the path was the only way I could hope to go."

Jerome wondered if he ought to call out, but he knew how hard the men slept and he knew who would be the first to hear him. In any case he was too frightened to call. Except for that single jeering laugh of his mother and the man's single outburst of obscenity, what had been done that night had been done with the silence of animals killing each other in the dark.

Jerome lay still until he began to shiver and when the shivering came it was so violent it seemed to shake the ground. It was like being tied up in the cords of his own muscles shaking the earth so that everyone living on it must know where to find him.

Getting to his feet, he beat the pine needles off his nightshirt and scraped some more of them out of his hair. Others chafed the tender skin between his thighs, but these he disregarded as he stepped slowly out of the forest into the moonlight. He stopped, waiting for the man to appear and give chase, but the only sound he heard was the pounding of his own heart and the only man he saw was the man in the moon. He believed there was a man in the moon who saw everything and didn't care, who sat up there seeing and not caring and laughing to himself, and he thought he was laughing now. With his nightshirt fluttering, the boy ran across the clearing, opened the kitchen door and went in. This time he forgot about the dog, who jumped outside and ran away before Jerome could close the door.

Inside the bedroom the blind was drawn and the darkness was total. Jerome found the match box, lit the lamp and turned to look. His mother's body lay like a sack under the blankets because the engineer had covered her and pulled the blind before going out. Jerome lifted the blanket, put his hands to her face, and felt the fingers of his right hand sink into a warm stickiness. He jerked them back as though he had put them into fire and stood frozen.

"The bad wound was on the left side of her head and her left eye was bruised by his fist. Her mouth was open and her clear eye was open and angry. She looked far angrier than frightened. My mother died in a rage."

Her body was not yet cold, but it had lost some of its warmth and the blood barely oozed now that the heart had ceased to pump it. Blood was dark and wet all over the pillow and wetly thick in her hair; her breasts were like chalk-white balloons when he tried to shift her body. It was only then that he knew absolutely that she was dead. He cried out to her, he beat her naked breasts with his palms to wake her and all the time he did this he understood she was dead. Knowing she was dead he called to her to come alive again and take care of him, yet all this while he was glad the Engineer had not been like the other men whom she had humiliated.

Then he froze once more, for a step creaked outside. He blew out the lamp and turned to run into the darkness of the cookhouse where there were tables to hide under, but he was too late. The kitchen door creaked open and he crawled under the bed and crouched there against the wall with the sag of the spring just over his head.

The man entered and when Jerome heard him sniff, he knew he was smelling the snuffed wick of the lamp. When the man lit a match it was like an explosion of sound and light simultaneously, but the man did not carry the match to the lamp. Jerome saw his boots standing by the bed as the light slowly died. Then darkness again.

Then the Engineer let out a slow, choking sob and went away. Jerome heard his feet go away noisily, heard him bump into a chair in the kitchen, open the door and leave.

He crouched, shivering with cold and fright, and he might have stayed there for hours if the dog had not returned to the room. The dog came under the bed whining and nuzzling, and Jerome felt his long, wet tongue licking his feet. The feeling of the dog's tongue horrified him and he rolled over and pushed the animal away, pressing his hands against its muzzle. The beast whined appreciatively and Jerome's hair bristled when he knew the dog was licking his mother's blood off his fingers. He hit the dog and heard him whine. He hit him as hard as he could on the muzzle and the dog let out a yelp and left him alone. Then Jerome came out from under the bed and stood up.

Years afterwards he told Catherine that this was the first of many occasions when a sudden, clear-headed coolness came to him after moments of paralyzing terror. He was only ten years old, but he knew exactly what had happened and what else would happen if his mother's murderer caught him. He knew the murderer had left the bedroom because he was in terror of what he had done there, but he also knew he would be on the watch outside. The Engineer would almost certainly be watching by the kitchen door, for that was the natural way for Jerome to get out and it would also be the shortest route to the bunkhouse where the rest of the men were sleeping.

Jerome had to escape from the horror of that room where his mother lay dead. He took his clothes from the hooks where they hung: his shirt, stockings, pants, sweater and cap, and the heelless larrigans of cowhide he wore all year round. He took them out to the kitchen and dressed beside the stove which still was warm, with the dog nuzzling and whining, and he had to push the dog away several times as he pulled on his stockings. After he was dressed he washed the remaining blood from his hands under the pump and dried them on a roller towel. Very clear in the head now, he opened the big ice chest where the food was and took out the first thing he found. It was a garland of blood sausage much too clumsy and big to carry, so he cut it into lengths and stuffed a length of sausage into each of the side pockets of his pants. He left the kitchen and entered the long eating barn where the benches and trestle tables were, heading for the door at the far end, a door rarely used, and when he reached it he found it unbarred. He guessed that the Engineer had used this door when he had first gone into the clearing to search for him.

"It must have been the dog that saved me that first time. When I ran out into the clearing, the dog must have gone into the eating barn and when the Engineer heard him moving there, he must have mistaken him for me. That was the mistake that gave me time to hide."

The dog was with Jerome now and this time Jerome made no error; he caught him by the long hairs at the back of his neck, held him while he stepped out, then pushed him inside and closed the door on him.

From this corner of the cookhouse the distance to the edge of the forest was no more than twenty yards and nobody was in sight as Jerome ran across it and disappeared into the trees. He worked his way silently through trees and deadfalls until a quick coolness touched his cheeks and he knew he was near the water on the edge of the northwest branch where his canoe was beached. In flood time the branch invaded the forest a distance of thirty yards or so, and now it was pouring through the trunks of the trees, gurgling and sighing as it strained through the scrub and deadfalls, and Jerome saw quick flashes of light as the moon struck here and there against the living water.

He worked his way along, his oiled larrigans keeping the moisture off his soles, but once his foot sank into a hole and the icy wetness poured in through the laceholes and his foot felt cold and soon went numb. After a few minutes he reached the place where the canoes and rowboats were beached, his own little canoe among them. The camp motorboat was moored to a jetty about a hundred yards downstream in the main river, but the canoes and rowboats were moored where the current was weak, and now he saw their snouts projecting out of the blackness of the woods into the moonlight. He stepped out, looked up to see the sky a wide open dome with a moon in the middle of it and a vast circle of light shining around it.

"I knew I was going to make it. Every time afterwards when I was older, every time when I've been in danger and everything seemed hopeless, some moment like this always came. Suddenly I'd hear myself saying, 'You're going to make it. You're going to make it after all.'"

The short birchbark canoe with the air cans under the thwarts was easy to lift, he turned it over and ran it out into the water. He found his own paddle made to fit his height, and with a single movement he pushed the canoe off and swung himself over into the stern seat, then crept forward and settled down just about midships, got the paddle working and guided the canoe past a tree trunk and clear of some fallen branches. The movement of the current kept pressing him inshore, but he paddled hard on the left into a back-wash that took the canoe gently out, he changed sides and gave two hard thrusts on the right, and then the canoe floated silently out into the great wash of moonlight where the branch widened into the main course of the river. The current of the branch carried him far out from the shore and when he felt himself making leeway he knew he was in the central stream at last. He gave two more thrusts and pointed the bow downstream, and at once he began to move fast on a river wide, firm, silver and alive bearing him down past the silent camp, utterly alone for the first time in his life, bearing him down under that wide open sky through the forest to the open sea which he knew was at its end.

SINCLAIR ROSS

1908-

Sinclair Ross was born on a homestead near Prince Albert, Saskatchewan, and spent his boyhood on a farm in the West. For most of his life he has worked in a bank, in Winnipeg and in Montreal. During the war he served overseas with the Canadian Ordnance Corps.

He first gained recognition in the forties with a number of realistic short stories of western farm life that appeared mainly in the *Queen's Quarterly*. These are now available in *The Lamp at Noon and Other Stories*, which was added to the New Canadian Library in 1968. Ross is the author of three novels, the now classic *As for Me and My House* (1941), *The Well* (1958), and *Whir of Gold* (1970). His themes in the short stories as well as the novels are most often the psycho‐logical effect of the restrictive life in small puritanical com‐munities on the western prairies. The most recent novel is a study of loneliness and frustration in which a boy from the Prairies and a girl from the Maritimes come together for a little while in Montreal but fail to resolve the emptiness of their lives. The simplicity and directness of structure and style give the book much of its distinction. The skill with which Ross combines realism with an almost unbearable suspense is well illustrated in the story reprinted below.

THE PAINTED DOOR

Straight across the hills it was five miles from John's farm to his father's. But in winter, with the roads impassable, a team had to make a wide detour and skirt the hills, so that from five the distance was more than trebled to seventeen.

"I think I'll walk," John said at breakfast to his wife. "The drifts in the hills wouldn't hold a horse, but they'll carry me all right. If I leave early I can spend a few hours helping him with his chores, and still be back by suppertime."

She went to the window, and thawing a clear place in the frost with her breath, stood looking across the snowswept farmyard to the huddle of stables and sheds. "There was a double wheel around the moon last night," she countered presently. "You said yourself we could expect a storm. It isn't right to leave me here alone. Surely I'm as important as your father."

He glanced up uneasily, then drinking off his coffee tried to re-assure her. "But there's nothing to be afraid of—even supposing it does start to storm. You won't need to go near the stable. Every-thing's fed and watered now to last till night. I'll be back at the latest by seven or eight."

She went on blowing against the frosted pane, carefully elongating the clear place until it was oval-shaped and symmetrical. He watched her a moment or two longer, then more insistently repeated, "I say you won't need to go near the stable. Everything's fed and watered, and I'll see that there's plenty of wood in. That will be all right, won't it?"

"Yes—of course—I heard you—" It was a curiously cold voice now, as if the words were chilled by their contact with the frosted pane. "Plenty to eat—plenty of wood to keep me warm—what more could a woman ask for?"

"But he's an old man—living there all alone. What is it, Ann? You're not like yourself this morning."

She shook her head without turning. "Pay no attention to me. Seven years a farmer's wife—it's time I was used to staying alone."

Slowly the clear place on the glass enlarged: oval, then round, then oval again. The sun was risen above the frost mists now, so keen and hard a glitter on the snow that instead of warmth its rays seemed shedding cold. One of the two-year-old colts that had cantered away when John turned the horses out for water stood covered with rime at the stable door again, head down and body hunched, each breath a little plume of steam against the frosty air. She shivered, but did not turn. In the clear, bitter light the long white miles of prairie landscape seemed a region alien to life. Even the distant farmsteads she could see served only to intensify a sense of isolation. Scattered across the face of so vast and bleak a wilderness it was difficult to conceive them as a testimony of human hardihood and endurance. Rather they seemed futile, lost, to cower before the implacability of snow-swept earth and clear pale sun-chilled sky.

And when at last she turned from the window there was a brooding stillness in her face as if she recognized this mastery of snow and cold. It troubled John. "If you're really afraid," he yielded, "I won't go today. Lately it's been so cold, that's all. I just wanted to make sure he's all right in case we do have a storm."

"I know—I'm not really afraid." She was putting in a fire now, and he could no longer see her face. "Pay no attention. It's ten miles there and back, so you'd better get started."

"You ought to know by now I wouldn't stay away," he tried to brighten her. "No matter how it stormed. Before we were married— remember? Twice a week I never missed and we had some bad blizzards that winter too."

He was a slow, unambitious man, content with his farm and cattle, naïvely proud of Ann. He had been bewildered by it once, her caring for a dull-witted fellow like him; then assured at last of her affection he had relaxed against it gratefully, unsuspecting it might ever be less constant than his own. Even now, listening to the restless brooding in her voice, he felt only a quick, unformulated kind of pride that after seven years his absence for a day should still concern her. While she, his trust and earnestness controlling her again :

"I know. It's just that sometimes when you're away I get lonely—— There's a long cold tramp in front of you. You'll let me fix a scarf around your face."

He nodded. "And on my way I'll drop in at Steven's place. Maybe he'll come over tonight for a game of cards. You haven't seen anybody but me for the last two weeks."

She glanced up sharply, then busied herself clearing the table. "It will mean another two miles if you do. You're going to be cold and tired enough as it is. When you're gone I think I'll paint the kitchen woodwork. White this time—you remember we got the paint last fall. It's going to make the room a lot lighter. I'll be too busy to find the day long."

"I will though," he insisted, "and if a storm gets up you'll feel safer, knowing that he's coming. That's what you need, maybe— someone to talk to besides me."

She stood at the stove motionless a moment, then turned to him uneasily. "Will you shave then, John—now—before you go?"

He glanced at her questioningly, and avoiding his eyes she tried to explain, "I mean—he may be here before you're back—and you won't have a chance then."

"But it's only Steven—we're not going anywhere."

"He'll be shaved, though—that's what I mean—and I'd like you too to spend a little time on yourself."

He stood up, stroking the heavy stubble on his chin. "Maybe I should—only it softens up the skin too much. Especially when I've got to face the wind."

She nodded and began to help him dress, bringing heavy socks and a big woollen sweater from the bedroom, wrapping a scarf around his face and forehead. "I'll tell Steven to come early," he said, as he went out. "In time for supper. Likely there'll be chores for me to do, so if I'm not back by six don't wait."

From the bedroom window she watched him nearly a mile along the road. The fire had gone down when at last she turned away, and already through the house there was an encroaching chill. A blaze sprang up again when the draughts were opened, but as she went on clearing the table her movements were furtive and constrained. It was the silence weighing upon her—the frozen silence of the bitter fields and sun-chilled sky—lurking outside as if alive, relentlessly in wait, mile-deep between her now and John. She listened to it, suddenly tense, motionless. The fire crackled and the clock ticked. Always it was there. "I'm a fool," she whispered, rattling the dishes in defiance, going back to the stove to put in another fire. "Warm and safe —I'm a fool. It's a good chance when he's away to paint. The day will go quickly. I won't have time to brood."

Since November now the paint had been waiting warmer weather. The frost in the walls on a day like this would crack and peel it as it dried, but she needed something to keep her hands occupied, something to stave off the gathering cold and loneliness. "First of all," she said aloud, opening the paint and mixing it with a little turpentine, "I must get the house warmer. Fill up the stove and open the oven door so that all the heat comes out. Wad something along the window sills to keep out the draughts. Then I'll feel brighter. It's the cold that depresses."

She moved briskly, performing each little task with careful and exaggerated absorption, binding her thoughts to it, making it a screen between herself and the surrounding snow and silence. But when the stove was filled and the windows sealed it was more difficult again. Above the quiet, steady swishing of her brush against the bedroom door the clock began to tick. Suddenly her movements became precise, deliberate, her posture self-conscious, as if someone had entered the room and were watching her. It was the silence again, aggressive, hovering. The fire spit and crackled at it. Still it was there. "I'm a fool," she repeated. "All farmers' wives have to stay alone. I mustn't give in this way. I mustn't brood. A few hours now and they'll be here."

The sound of her voice reassured her. She went on: "I'll get them a good supper—and for coffee after cards bake some of the little cakes with raisins that he likes. . . . Just three of us, so I'll watch, and let John play. It's better with four, but at least we can talk. That's all I need—someone to talk to. John never talks. He's stronger—doesn't need to. But he likes Steven—no matter what the neighbours say. Maybe he'll have him come again, and some other young people too. It's what we need, both of us, to help keep young ourselves. . . . And then before we know it we'll be into March. It's cold still in March sometimes, but you never mind the same. At least you're beginning to think about spring."

She began to think about it now. Thoughts that outstripped her words, that left her alone again with herself and the ever-lurking silence. Eager and hopeful first, then clenched, rebellious, lonely. Windows open, sun and thawing earth again, the urge of growing, living things. Then the days that began in the morning at half-past four and lasted till ten at night; the meals at which John gulped his food and scarcely spoke a word; the brute-tired stupid eyes he turned on her if ever she mentioned town or visiting.

For spring was drudgery again. John never hired a man to help him. He wanted a mortgage-free farm; then a new house and pretty clothes for her. Sometimes, because with the best of crops it was going to take so long to pay off anyway, she wondered whether they mightn't better let the mortgage wait a little. Before they were worn out, before their best years were gone. It was something of life she wanted, not just a house and furniture; something of John, not pretty clothes when she would be too old to wear them. But John of course couldn't understand. To him it seemed only right that she should have the clothes—only right that he, fit for nothing else, should slave away fifteen hours a day to give them to her. There was in his devotion a baffling, insurmountable humility that made him feel the need of sacrifice. And when his muscles ached, when his feet dragged stolidly with weariness, then it seemed that in some measure at least he was making amends for his big hulking body and simple mind. Year after year their lives went on in the same little groove. He drove his horses in the field; she milked the cows and hoed potatoes. By dint of his drudgery he saved a few months' wages, added a few dollars more each fall to his payments on the mortgage; but the only real difference that it all made was to deprive her of his companionship, to make him a little duller, older, uglier than he might otherwise have been. He never saw their lives objectively. To him it was not what he actually accomplished by means of the sacrifice that mattered, but the sacrifice itself, the gesture—something done for her sake.

And she, understanding, kept her silence. In such a gesture, however futile, there was a graciousness not to be shattered lightly. "John," she would begin sometimes, "you're doing too much. Get a man to help you—just for a month—" but smiling down at her he would answer simply, "I don't mind. Look at the hands on me. They're made for work." While in his voice there would be a stalwart ring to tell her that by her thoughtfulness she had made him only the more resolved to serve her, to prove his devotion and fidelity.

They were useless, such thoughts. She knew. It was his very devotion that made them useless, that forbade her to rebel. Yet over and over, sometimes hunched still before their bleakness, sometimes her brush making swift sharp strokes to pace the chafe and rancour that they brought, she persisted in them.

This now, the winter, was their slack season. She could sleep sometimes till eight, and John till seven. They could linger over their meals a little, read, play cards, go visiting the neighbours. It was the time to relax, to indulge and enjoy themselves; but instead, fretful

and impatient, they kept on waiting for the spring. They were compelled now, not by labour, but by the spirit of labour. A spirit that
pervaded their lives and brought with idleness a sense of guilt.
Sometimes they did sleep late, sometimes they did play cards, but
always uneasily, always reproached by the thought of more important things that might be done. When John got up at five to attend
to the fire he wanted to stay up and go out to the stable. When he
sat down to a meal he hurried his food and pushed his chair away
again, from habit, from sheer work-instinct, even though it was only
to put more wood in the stove, or go down cellar to cut up beets and
turnips for the cows.

   And anyway, sometimes she asked herself, why sit trying to talk
with a man who never talked? Why talk when there was nothing
to talk about but crops and cattle, the weather and the neighbours?
The neighbours, too—why go visiting them when still it was the
same—crops and cattle, the weather and the other neighbours? Why
go to the dances in the schoolhouse to sit among the older women,
one of them now, married seven years, or to waltz with the work-
bent, tired old farmers to a squeaky fiddle tune? Once she had danced
with Steven six or seven times in the evening, and they had talked
about it for as many months. It was easier to stay at home. John never
danced or enjoyed himself. He was always uncomfortable in his good
suit and shoes. He didn't like shaving in the cold weather oftener
than once or twice a week. It was easier to stay at home, to stand at
the window staring out across the bitter fields, to count the days and
look forward to another spring.

   But now, alone with herself in the winter silence, she saw the
spring for what it really was. This spring—next spring—all the
springs and summers still to come. While they grew old, while their
bodies warped, while their minds kept shrivelling dry and empty like
their lives. "I mustn't," she said aloud again. "I married him—and
he's a good man. I mustn't keep on this way. It will be noon before
long, and then time to think about supper—— Maybe he'll come
early—and as soon as John is finished at the stable we can all play
cards."

   It was getting cold again, and she left her painting to put in
more wood. But this time the warmth spread slowly. She pushed a
mat up to the outside door, and went back to the window to pat
down the woollen shirt that was wadded along the sill. Then she
paced a few times round the room, then poked the fire and rattled

the stove lids, then paced again. The fire crackled, the clock ticked. The silence now seemed more intense than ever, seemed to have reached a pitch where it faintly moaned. She began to pace on tiptoe, listening, her shoulders drawn together, not realizing for a while that it was the wind she heard, thin-strained and whimpering through the eaves.

Then she wheeled to the window, and with quick short breaths thawed the frost to see again. The glitter was gone. Across the drifts sped swift and snakelike little tongues of snow. She could not follow them, where they sprang from, or where they disappeared. It was as if all across the yard the snow were shivering awake—roused by the warnings of the wind to hold itself in readiness for the impending storm. The sky had become a sombre, whitish grey. It, too, as if in readiness, had shifted and lay close to earth. Before her as she watched a mane of powdery snow reared up breast-high against the darker background of the stable, tossed for a moment angrily, and then subsided again as if whipped down to obedience and restraint. But another followed, more reckless and impatient than the first. Another reeled and dashed itself against the window where she watched. Then ominously for a while there were only the angry little snakes of snow. The wind rose, creaking the troughs that were wired beneath the eaves. In the distance, sky and prairie now were merged into one another linelessly. All round her it was gathering; already in its press and whimpering there strummed a boding of eventual fury. Again she saw a mane of snow spring up, so dense and high this time that all the sheds and stables were obscured. Then others followed, whirling fiercely out of hand; and, when at last they cleared, the stables seemed in dimmer outline than before. It was the snow beginning, long lancet shafts of it, straight from the north, borne almost level by the straining wind. "He'll be there soon," she whispered, "and coming home it will be in his back. He'll leave again right away. He saw the double wheel—he knows the kind of storm there'll be."

She went back to her painting. For a while it was easier, all her thoughts half-anxious ones of John in the blizzard, struggling his way across the hills; but petulantly again she soon began, "I knew we were going to have a storm—I told him so—but it doesn't matter what I say. Big stubborn fool—he goes his own way anyway. It doesn't matter what becomes of me. In a storm like this he'll never get home. He won't even try. And while he sits keeping his father company I can look after his stable for him, go ploughing through snowdrifts up to my knees—nearly frozen——"

Not that she meant or believed her words. It was just an effort to convince herself that she did have a grievance, to justify her rebellious thoughts, to prove John responsible for her unhappiness. She was young still, eager for excitement and distractions; and John's steadfastness rebuked her vanity, made her complaints seem weak and trivial. She went on, fretfully, "If he'd listen to me sometimes and not be so stubborn we wouldn't still be living in a house like this. Seven years in two rooms—seven years and never a new stick of furniture. . . . There—as if another coat of paint could make it different anyway."

She cleaned her brush, filled up the stove again, and went back to the window. There was a void white moment that she thought must be frost formed on the window pane; then, like a fitful shadow through the whirling snow, she recognized the stable roof. It was incredible. The sudden, maniac raging of the storm struck from her face all its pettishness. Her eyes glazed with fear a little; her lips blanched. "If he starts for home now," she whispered silently—— "But he won't—he knows I'm safe—he knows Steven's coming. Across the hills he would never dare."

She turned to the stove, holding out her hands to the warmth. Around her now there seemed a constant sway and tremor, as if the air were vibrating with the shudderings of the walls. She stood quite still, listening. Sometimes the wind struck with sharp, savage blows. Sometimes it bore down in a sustained, minute-long blast, silent with effort and intensity; then with a foiled shriek of threat wheeled away to gather and assault again. Always the eave-troughs creaked and sawed. She stared towards the window again, then detecting the morbid trend of her thoughts, prepared fresh coffee and forced herself to drink a few mouthfuls. "He would never dare," she whispered again. "He wouldn't leave the old man anyway in such a storm. Safe in here—there's nothing for me to keep worrying about. It's after one already. I'll do my baking now, and then it will be time to get supper ready for Steven."

Soon, however, she began to doubt whether Steven would come. In such a storm even a mile was enough to make a man hesitate. Especially Steven, who was hardly the one to face a blizzard for the sake of someone else's chores. He had a stable of his own to look after anyway. It would be only natural for him to think that when the storm blew up John had turned again for home. Another man would have—would have put his wife first.

But she felt little dread or uneasiness at the prospect of spending the night alone. It was the first time she had been left like this on her own resources, and her reaction, now that she could face and appraise her situation calmly, was gradually to feel it a kind of adventure and responsibility. It stimulated her. Before nightfall she must go to the stable and feed everything. Wrap up in some of John's clothes—take a ball of string in her hand, one end tied to the door, so that no matter how blinding the storm she could at least find her way back to the house. She had heard of people having to do that. It appealed to her now because suddenly it made life dramatic. She had not felt the storm yet, only watched it for a minute through the window.

It took nearly an hour to find enough string, to choose the right socks and sweaters. Long before it was time to start she tried on John's clothes, changing and rechanging, striding around the room to make sure there would be play enough for pitching hay and struggling over snowdrifts; then she took them off again, and for a while busied herself baking the little cakes with raisins that he liked.

Night came early. Just for a moment on the doorstep she shrank back, uncertain. The slow dimming of the light clutched her with an illogical sense of abandonment. It was like the covert withdrawal of an ally, leaving the alien miles unleashed and unrestrained. Watching the hurricane of writhing snow rage past the little house she forced herself, "They'll never stand the night unless I get them fed. It's nearly dark already, and I've work to last an hour."

Timidly, unwinding a little of the string, she crept out from the shelter of the doorway. A gust of wind spun her forward a few yards, then plunged her headlong against a drift that in the dense white whirl lay invisible across her path. For nearly a minute she huddled still, breathless and dazed. The snow was in her mouth and nostrils, inside her scarf and up her sleeves. As she tried to straighten a smothering scud flung itself against her face, cutting off her breath a second time. The wind struck from all sides, blustering and furious. It was as if the storm had discovered her, as if all its forces were concentrated upon her extinction. Seized with panic suddenly she threshed out a moment with her arms, then stumbled back and sprawled her length across the drift.

But this time she regained her feet quickly, roused by the whip and batter of the storm to retaliative anger. For a moment her impulse was to face the wind and strike back blow for blow; then, as suddenly as it had come, her frantic strength gave way to limpness and exhaustion. Suddenly, a comprehension so clear and terrifying that it struck all thoughts of the stable from her mind, she realized in such a storm her puniness. And the realization gave her new strength, stilled this time to a desperate persistence. Just for a moment the wind held her, numb and swaying in its vise; then slowly, buckled far forward, she groped her way again towards the house.

Inside, leaning against the door, she stood tense and still a while. It was almost dark now. The top of the stove glowed a deep, dull red. Heedless of the storm, self-absorbed and self-satisfied, the clock ticked on like a glib little idiot. "He shouldn't have gone," she whispered silently. "He saw the double wheel—he knew. He shouldn't have left me here alone."

For so fierce now, so insane and dominant did the blizzard seem, that she could not credit the safety of the house. The warmth and lull around her was not real yet, not to be relied upon. She was still at the mercy of the storm. Only her body pressing hard like this against the door was staving it off. She didn't dare move. She didn't dare ease the ache and strain. "He shouldn't have gone," she repeated, thinking of the stable again, reproached by her helplessness. "They'll freeze in their stalls—and I can't reach them. He'll say it's all my fault. He won't believe I tried."

Then Steven came. Quickly, startled to quietness and control, she let him in and lit the lamp. He stared at her a moment, then flinging off his cap crossed to where she stood by the table and seized her arms. "You're so white—what's wrong? Look at me——" It was like him in such little situations to be masterful. "You should have known better—for a while I thought I wasn't going to make it here myself——"

"I was afraid you wouldn't come—John left early, and there was the stable——"

But the storm had unnerved her, and suddenly at the assurance of his touch and voice the fear that had been gripping her gave way to an hysteria of relief. Scarcely aware of herself she seized his arm and sobbed against it. He remained still a moment unyielding, then slipped his other arm around her shoulder. It was comforting and she relaxed against it, hushed by a sudden sense of lull and safety. Her shoulders trembled with the easing of the strain, then fell limp and still. "You're shivering,"—he drew her gently towards the stove. "It's all right—nothing to be afraid of, I'm going to see to the stable."

It was a quiet, sympathetic voice, yet with an undertone of insolence, a kind of mockery even, that made her draw away quickly and busy herself putting in a fire. With his lips drawn in a little smile he watched her till she looked at him again. The smile too was insolent, but at the same time companionable; Steven's smile, and therefore difficult to reprove. It lit up his lean, still-boyish face with a peculiar kind of arrogance: features and smile that were different from John's, from other men's—wilful and derisive, yet naïvely so— as if it were less the difference itself he was conscious of, than the long-accustomed privilege that thereby fell his due. He was erect, tall, square-shouldered. His hair was dark and trim, his lips curved soft and full. While John, she made the comparison swiftly, was thickset, heavy-jowled, and stooped. He always stood before her helpless, a kind of humility and wonderment in his attitude. And Steven now smiled on her appraisingly with the worldly-wise assurance of one for whom a woman holds neither mystery nor illusion.

"It was good of you to come, Steven," she responded, the words running into a sudden, empty laugh. "Such a storm to face—I suppose I should feel flattered."

For his presumption, his misunderstanding of what had been only momentary weakness, instead of angering quickened her, roused from latency and long disuse all the instincts and resources of her femininity. She felt eager, challenged. Something was at hand that hitherto had always eluded her, even in the early days with John, something vital, beckoning, meaningful. She didn't understand, but she knew. The texture of the moment was satisfyingly dreamlike: an incredibility perceived as such, yet acquiesced in. She was John's wife—she knew—but also she knew that Steven standing here was different from John. There was no thought or motive, no understanding of herself as the knowledge persisted. Wary and poised round a sudden little core of blind excitement she evaded him, "But it's nearly dark—hadn't you better hurry if you're going to do the chores? Don't trouble—I can get them off myself——"

An hour later when he returned from the stable she was in another dress, hair rearranged, a little flush of colour in her face. Pouring warm water for him from the kettle into the basin she said evenly, "By the time you're washed supper will be ready. John said we weren't to wait for him."

He looked at her a moment, "You don't mean you're expecting John tonight? The way it's blowing——"

"Of course." As she spoke she could feel the colour deepening in her face. "We're going to play cards. He was the one that suggested it."

He went on washing, and then as they took their places at the table, resumed, "So John's coming. When are you expecting him?"

"He said it might be seven o'clock—or a little later." Conversation with Steven at other times had always been brisk and natural, but now all at once she found it strained. "He may have work to do for his father. That's what he said when he left. Why do you ask, Steven?"

"I was just wondering—it's a rough night."

"You don't know John. It would take more than a storm to stop him."

She glanced up again and he was smiling at her. The same insolence, the same little twist of mockery and appraisal. It made her flinch, and ask herself why she was pretending to expect John—why there should be this instinct of defence to force her. This time, instead of poise and excitement, it brought a reminder that she had changed her dress and rearranged her hair. It crushed in a sudden silence, through which she heard the whistling wind again, and the creaking saw of the eaves. Neither spoke now. There was something strange, almost frightening, about this Steven and his quiet, unrelenting smile; but strangest of all was the familiarity: the Steven she had never seen or encountered, and yet had always known, always expected, always waited for. It was less Steven himself that she felt than his inevitability. Just as she had felt the snow, the silence and the storm. She kept her eyes lowered, on the window past his shoulder, on the stove, but his smile now seemed to exist apart from him, to merge and hover with the silence. She clinked a cup—listened to the whistle of the storm—always it was there. He began to speak, but her mind missed the meaning of his words. Swiftly she was making comparisons again; his face so different to John's, so handsome and young and clean-shaven. Swiftly, helplessly, feeling the imperceptible and relentless ascendency that thereby he was gaining over her, sensing sudden menace in this new, more vital life, even as she felt drawn towards it.

The lamp between them flickered as an onslaught of the storm sent shudderings through the room. She rose to build up the fire again and he followed her. For a long time they stood close to the stove, their arms almost touching. Once as the blizzard creaked the house she spun around sharply, fancying it was John at the door; but quietly he intercepted her. "Not tonight—you might as well make up your mind to it. Across the hills in a storm like this—it would be suicide to try."

Her lips trembled suddenly in an effort to answer, to parry the certainty in his voice, then set thin and bloodless. She was afraid now. Afraid of his face so different from John's—of his smile, of her own helplessness to rebuke it. Afraid of the storm, isolating her here alone with him. They tried to play cards, but she kept starting up at every creak and shiver of the walls. "It's too rough a night," he repeated. "Even for John. Just relax a few minutes—stop worrying and pay a little attention to me."

But in his tone there was a contradiction to his words. For it implied that she was not worrying—that her only concern was lest it really might be John at the door.

And the implication persisted. He filled up the stove for her, shuffled the cards—won—shuffled—still it was there. She tried to respond to his conversation, to think of the game, but helplessly into her cards instead she began to ask, Was he right? Was that why he smiled? Why he seemed to wait, expectant and assured?

The clock ticked, the fire crackled. Always it was there. Furtively for a moment she watched him as he deliberated over his hand. John, even in the days before they were married, had never looked like that. Only this morning she had asked him to shave. Because Steven was coming—because she had been afraid to see them side by side—because deep within herself she had known even then. The same knowledge, furtive and forbidden, that was flaunted now in Steven's smile. "You look cold," he said at last, dropping his cards and rising from the table. "We're not playing, anyway. Come over to the stove for a few minutes and get warm."

"But first I think we'll hang blankets over the door. When there's a blizzard like this we always do." It seemed that in sane, commonplace activity there might be release, a moment or two in which to recover herself. "John has nails to put them on. They keep out a little of the draught."

He stood on a chair for her, and hung the blankets that she carried from the bedroom. Then for a moment they stood silent, watching the blankets sway and tremble before the blade of wind that spurted around the jamb. "I forgot," she said at last, "that I painted the bedroom door. At the top there, see—I've smeared the blankets."

He glanced at her curiously, and went back to the stove. She followed him, trying to imagine the hills in such a storm, wondering whether John would come. "A man couldn't live in it," suddenly he answered her thoughts, lowering the oven door and drawing up their chairs one on each side of it. "He knows you're safe. It isn't likely that he'd leave his father, anyway."

"The wind will be in his back," she persisted. "The winter before we were married—all the blizzards that we had that year—and he never missed——"

"Blizzards like this one? Up in the hills he wouldn't be able to keep his direction for a hundred yards. Listen to it a minute and ask yourself."

His voice seemed softer, kindlier now. She met his smile a moment, its assured little twist of appraisal, then for a long time sat silent, tense, careful again to avoid his eyes.

Everything now seemed to depend on this. It was the same as a few hours ago when she braced the door against the storm. He was watching her, smiling. She dared not move, unclench her hands, or raise her eyes. The flames crackled, the clock ticked. The storm wrenched the walls as if to make them buckle in. So rigid and desperate were all her muscles set, withstanding, that the room around her seemed to swim and reel. So rigid and strained that for relief at last, despite herself, she raised her head and met his eyes again.

Intending that it should be for only an instant, just to breathe again, to ease the tension that had grown unbearable—but in his smile now, instead of the insolent appraisal that she feared, there seemed a kind of warmth and sympathy. An understanding that quickened and encouraged her—that made her wonder why but a moment ago she had been afraid. It was as if the storm had lulled, as if she had suddenly found calm and shelter.

Or perhaps, the thought seized her, perhaps instead of his smile it was she who had changed. She who, in the long, wind-creaked silence, had emerged from the increment of codes and loyalties to her real, unfettered self. She who now felt his air of appraisal as nothing more than an understanding of the unfulfilled woman that until this

moment had lain within her brooding and unadmitted, reproved
out of consciousness by the insistence of an outgrown, routine
fidelity.

For there had always been Steven. She understood now. Seven
years—almost as long as John—ever since the night they first danced
together.

The lamp was burning dry, and through the dimming light,
isolated in the fastness of silence and storm, they watched each other.
Her face was white and struggling still. His was handsome, clean-
shaven, young. Her eyes were fanatic, believing desperately, fixed
upon him as if to exclude all else, as if to find justification. His were
cool, bland, drooped a little with expectancy. The light kept dimming, gathering the shadows round them, hushed, conspiratorial. He
was smiling still. Her hands again were clenched up white and hard.

"But he always came," she persisted. "The wildest, coldest nights
—even such a night as this. There was never a storm——"

"Never a storm like this one." There was a quietness in his smile
now, a kind of simplicity almost, as if to reassure her. "You were out
in it yourself for a few minutes. He'd have it for five miles, across
the hills—— I'd think twice myself, on such a night before risking
even one."

Long after he was asleep she lay listening to the storm. As a check
on the draught up the chimney they had left one of the stove lids
partly off, and through the open bedroom door she could see the
flickerings of flame and shadow on the kitchen wall. They leaped and
sank fantastically. The longer she watched the more alive they seemed
to be. There was one great shadow that struggled towards her threat-
eningly, massive and black and engulfing all the room. Again and
again it advanced, about to spring, but each time a little whip of light
subdued it to its place among the others on the wall. Yet though it
never reached her still she cowered, feeling that gathered there was
all the frozen wilderness, its heart of terror and invincibility.

Then she dozed a while, and the shadow was John. Interminably
he advanced. The whips of light still flickered and coiled, but now
suddenly they were the swift little snakes that this afternoon she had
watched twist and shiver across the snow. And they too were advancing. They writhed and vanished and came again. She lay still,
paralysed. He was over her now, so close that she could have touched

him. Already it seemed that a deadly tightening hand was on her throat. She tried to scream but her lips were locked. Steven beside her slept on heedlessly.

Until suddenly as she lay staring up at him a gleam of light revealed his face. And in it was not a trace of threat or anger—only calm, and stonelike hopelessness.

That was like John. He began to withdraw, and frantically she tried to call him back. "It isn't true—not really true—listen, John——" but the words clung frozen to her lips. Already there was only the shriek of wind again, the sawing eaves, the leap and twist of shadow on the wall.

She sat up, startled now and awake. And so real had he seemed there, standing close to her, so vivid the sudden age and sorrow in his face, that at first she could not make herself understand she had been only dreaming. Against the conviction of his presence in the room it was necessary to insist over and over that he must still be with his father on the other side of the hills. Watching the shadows she had fallen asleep. It was only her mind, her imagination, distorted to a nightmare by the illogical and unadmitted dread of his return. But he wouldn't come. Steven was right. In such a storm he would never try. They were safe, alone. No one would ever know. It was only fear, morbid and irrational; only the sense of guilt that even her new-found and challenged womanhood could not entirely quell.

She knew now. She had not let herself understand or acknowledge it as guilt before, but gradually through the wind-torn silence of the night his face compelled her. The face that had watched her from the darkness with its stonelike sorrow—the face that was really John— John more than his features of mere flesh and bone could ever be.

She wept silently. The fitful gleam of light began to sink. On the ceiling and wall at last there was only a faint dull flickering glow. The little house shuddered and quailed, and a chill crept in again. Without wakening Steven she slipped out to build up the fire. It was burned to a few spent embers now, and the wood she put on seemed a long time catching light. The wind swirled through the blankets they had hung around the door, and then, hollow and moaning, roared up the chimney again, as if against its will drawn back to serve still longer with the onrush of the storm.

For a long time she crouched over the stove, listening. Earlier in the evening, with the lamp lit and the fire crackling, the house had

seemed a stand against the wilderness, a refuge of feeble walls wherein persisted the elements of human meaning and survival. Now, in
the cold, creaking darkness, it was strangely extinct, looted by the
storm and abandoned again. She lifted the stove lid and fanned the
embers till at last a swift little tongue of flame began to lick around
the wood. Then she replaced the lid, extended her hands, and as if
frozen in that attitude stood waiting.

It was not long now. After a few minutes she closed the draughts,
and as the flames whirled back upon each other, beating against the
top of the stove and sending out flickers of light again, a warmth
surged up to relax her stiffened limbs. But shivering and numb it had
been easier. The bodily well-being that the warmth induced gave
play again to an ever more insistent mental suffering. She remembered the shadow that was John. She saw him bent towards her, then
retreating, his features pale and overcast with unaccusing grief.
She re-lived their seven years together and, in retrospect, found them
to be years of worth and dignity. Until crushed by it all at last,
seized by a sudden need to suffer and atone, she crossed to where
the draught was bitter, and for a long time stood unflinching on the
icy floor.

The storm was close here. Even through the blankets she could
feel a sift of snow against her face. The eaves sawed, the walls
creaked, and the wind was like a wolf in howling flight.

And yet, suddenly she asked herself, hadn't there been other storms,
other blizzards? And through the worst of them hadn't he always
reached her?

Clutched by the thought she stood rooted a minute. It was hard
now to understand how she could have so deceived herself—how a
moment of passion could have quieted within her not only conscience, but reason and discretion too. John always came. There could
never be a storm to stop him. He was strong, inured to the cold. He
had crossed the hills since his boyhood, knew every creek-bed and
gully. It was madness to go on like this—to wait. While there was
still time she must waken Steven, and hurry him away.

But in the bedroom again, standing at Steven's side, she hesitated.
In his detachment from it all, in his quiet, even breathing, there was
such sanity, such realism. For him nothing had happened; nothing
would. If she wakened him he would only laugh and tell her to listen
to the storm. Already it was long past midnight; either John had
lost his way or not set out at all. And she knew that in his devotion

there was nothing foolhardy. He would never risk a storm beyond his endurance, never permit himself a sacrifice likely to endanger her lot or future. They were both safe. No one would ever know. She must control herself—be sane like Steven.

For comfort she let her hand rest on Steven's shoulder. It would be easier were he awake now, with her, sharing her guilt; but gradually as she watched his handsome face in the glimmering light she came to understand that for him no guilt existed. Just as there had been no passion, no conflict. Nothing but the sane appraisal of their situation, nothing but the expectant little smile, and the arrogance of features that were different from John's. She winced deeply, remembering how she had fixed her eyes on those features, how she had tried to believe that so handsome and young, so different from John's, they must in themselves be her justification.

In the flickering light they were still young, still handsome. No longer her justification—she knew now—John was the man—but wistfully still, wondering sharply at their power and tyranny, she touched them a moment with her fingertips again.

She could not blame him. There had been no passion, no guilt; therefore there could be no responsibility. Looking down at him as he slept, half-smiling still, his lips relaxed in the conscienceless complacency of his achievement, she understood that thus he was revealed in his entirety—all there ever was or ever could be. John was the man. With him lay all the future. For tonight, slowly and contritely through the day and years to come, she would try to make amends.

Then she stole back to the kitchen, and without thought, impelled by overwhelming need again, returned to the door where the draught was bitter still. Gradually towards morning the storm began to spend itself. Its terror blast became a feeble, worn-out moan. The leap of light and shadow sank, and a chill crept in again. Always the eaves creaked, tortured with wordless prophecy. Heedless of it all the clock ticked on in idiot content.

They found him the next day, less than a mile from home. Drifting with the storm he had run against his own pasture fence and overcome had frozen there, erect still, both hands clasping fast the wire.

"He was south of here," they said wonderingly when she told them how he had come across the hills. "Straight south—you'd wonder how he could have missed the buildings. It was the wind last night, coming every way at once. He shouldn't have tried. There was a double wheel around the moon."

She looked past them a moment, then as if to herself said simply, "If you knew him, though—John would try."

It was later, when they had left her a while to be alone with him, that she knelt and touched his hand. Her eyes dimmed, it was still such a strong and patient hand; then, transfixed, they suddenly grew wide and clear. On the palm, white even against its frozen whiteness, was a little smear of paint.

HUGH GARNER

1913-

Born in Yorkshire, England, Hugh Garner was brought to
Toronto at the age of six. During the Depression he worked
at various jobs, and in 1937 fought in Spain as a gunner in the
International Brigade. He had already published his first short
stories in *The Canadian Forum,* but on the outbreak of World
War II after a short period in the army he enlisted in the R.C.N.
and served at sea from 1940 to 1945. From this experience came
his first novel, *Storm Below* (1949), a realistic account of life
on a corvette during four days of submarine attack on an
Atlantic convoy. Garner's life as a working man in the industrial quarters of Toronto gave him material for a series of
sensitive and sympathetic novels and short stories dealing for
the most part with the lives of the poor in a Canadian city.
Among these are *Cabbagetown* (1950), *Waste no Tears,* published under the name of "Jarvis Warwick" (1950), *Present
Reckoning* (1951), *The Yellow Sweater and Other Stories*
(1952), *The Silence on the Shore* (1962), and *Men and Women*
(1966). A selection entitled *Hugh Garner's Best Stories* won
the Governor General's Award in 1963. Garner's most recent
novels, *The Sin Sniper* and *A Nice Place to Visit,* both published in 1970, are realistic and sometimes bitter studies of life
in urban Ontario. The latter deals with the experiences of a
middle-aged journalist investigating the case of an eighteen
year old youth imprisoned, perhaps in error, for the murder of
a pregnant girl. *Violation of the Virgins* (1971), his latest
collection of short stories has consolidated his position as one
of Canada's finest writers in this field.

After they had eaten, Big Tom pushed the cracked and dirty supper things to the back of the table and took the baby from its high chair carefully, so as not to spill the flotsam of bread crumbs and boiled potatoes from the chair to the floor.

He undressed the youngster, talking to it in the old dialect, trying to awaken its interest. All evening it had been listless and fretful by turns, but now it seemed to be soothed by the story of Po-chee-ah, and the Lynx, although it was too young to understand him as his voice slid awkwardly through the ageless folk-tale of his people.

For long minutes after the baby was asleep he talked on, letting the victorious words fill the small cabin so that they shut out the sounds of the Northern Ontario night: the buzz of mosquitoes, the far-off bark of a dog, the noise of the cars and transport trucks passing on the gravelled road.

The melodious hum of his voice was like a strong soporific, lulling him with the return of half-forgotten memories, strengthening him with the knowledge that once his people had been strong and brave, men with a nation of their own, encompassing a million miles of teeming forest, lake and tamarack swamp.

When he halted his monologue to place the baby in the big brass bed in the corner the sudden silence was loud in his ears, and he cringed a bit as the present suddenly caught up with the past.

He covered the baby with a corner of the church-donated patch-work quilt, and lit the kerosene lamp that stood on the mirrorless dressing table beside the stove. Taking a broom from a corner he swept the mealtime debris across the doorsill.

This done, he stood and watched the headlights of the cars run along the trees bordering the road, like a small boy's stick along a picket fence. From the direction of the trailer camp a hundred yards away came the sound of a car engine being gunned, and the halting note-tumbles of a clarinet from a tourist's radio. The soft summer smell of spruce needles and wood smoke blended with the evening dampness of the earth, and felt good in his nostrils, so that he filled his worn lungs until he began to cough. He spat the resinous phlegm into the weed-filled yard.

It had been this summer smell, and the feeling of freedom it gave, which had brought him back to the woods after three years in the mines during the war. But only part of him had come back, for the mining towns and the big money had done more than etch his lungs with silica: they had also brought him pain and distrust, and a wife who had learned to live in gaudy imitation of the boom-town life.

When his coughing attack subsided he peered along the path, hoping to catch a glimpse of his wife Mary returning from her work at the trailer camp. He was becoming worried about the baby, and her presence, while it might not make the baby well, would mean that there was someone else to share his fears. He could see nothing but the still blackness of the trees, their shadows interwoven in a sombre pattern across the mottled ground.

He re-entered the cabin and began washing the dishes, stopping once or twice to cover the moving form of the sleeping baby. He wondered if he could have transmitted his own wasting sickness to the lungs of his son. He stood for long minutes at the side of the bed, staring, trying to diagnose the child's restlessness into something other than what he feared.

His wife came in and placed some things on the table. He picked up a can of pork-and-beans, she had bought and weighed it in the palm of his hand. "The baby seems pretty sick," he said.

She crossed the room, and looked at the sleeping child. "I guess it's his teeth."

He placed the pork-and-beans on the table again and walked over to his chair beside the empty stove. As he sat down he noticed for the first time that his wife was beginning to show her pregnancy. Her squat form had sunk lower, and almost filled the shapeless dress she wore. Her brown ankles were puffed above the broken-down heels of the dirty silver dancing pumps she was wearing.

"Is the trailer camp full?" he asked.

"Nearly. Two more Americans came about half an hour ago."

"Was Billy Woodhen around?"

"I didn't see him, only Elsie," she answered. "A woman promised me a dress tomorrow if I scrub out her trailer."

"Yeh." He saw the happiness rise over her like a colour as she mentioned this. She was much younger than he was—twenty-two years against his thirty-nine—and her dark face had a fullness that is common to many Indian women. She was no longer pretty, and as he watched her he thought that wherever they went the squalor of their existence seemed to follow them.

"It's a silk dress," Mary said, as though the repeated mention of it brought it nearer.

"A silk dress is no damn good around here. You should get some overalls," he said, angered by her lack of shame in accepting the cast-off garments of the trailer women.

She seemed not to notice his anger. "It'll do for the dances next winter."

"A lot of dancing you'll do," he said pointing to her swollen body. "You'd better learn to stay around here and take care of the kid."

She busied herself over the stove, lighting it with newspapers and kindling. "I'm going to have some fun. You should have married a grandmother."

He filled the kettle with water from an open pail near the door. The baby began to cough, and the mother turned it on its side in the bed. "As soon as I draw my money from Cooper I'm going to get him some cough syrup from the store," she said.

"It won't do any good. We should take him to the doctor in town tomorrow."

"I can't. I've got to stay here and work."

He knew the folly of trying to reason with her. She had her heart set on earning the silk dress the woman had promised.

After they had drunk their tea he blew out the light, and they took off some of their clothes and climbed over the baby into the bed. Long after his wife had fallen asleep he lay in the darkness listening to a ground moth beating its futile wings against the glass of the window.

They were awakened in the morning by the twittering of a small colony of tree sparrows who were feasting on the kitchen sweepings of the night before. Mary got up and went outside, returning a few minutes later carrying a handful of birch and poplar stovewood.

He waited until the beans were in the pan before rising and pulling on his pants. He stood in the doorway scratching his head and absorbing the sunlight through his bare feet upon the step.

The baby awoke while they were eating their breakfast.

"He don't look good," Big Tom said as he dipped some brown

sauce from his plate with a hunk of bread.

"He'll be all right later," his wife insisted. She poured some crusted tinned milk from a tin into a cup and mixed it with water from the kettle.

Big Tom splashed his hands and face with cold water, and dried himself on a soiled shirt that lay over the back of a chair. "When you going to the camp, this morning?"

"This afternoon," Mary answered.

"I'll be back by then."

He took up a small pile of woven baskets from a corner and hung the handles over his arm. From the warming shelf of the stove he pulled a bedraggled band of cloth, into which a large goose feather had been sewn. Carrying this in his hand he went outside and strode down the path toward the highway.

He ignored the chattering sauciness of a squirrel that hurtled up the green ladder of a tree beside him. Above the small noises of the woods could be heard the roar of a transport truck braking its way down the hill from the burnt-out sapling covered ridge to the north. The truck passed him as he reached the road, and he waved a desultory greeting to the driver, who answered with a short blare of the horn.

Placing the baskets in a pile on the shoulder of the road he adjusted the corduroy band on his head so that the feather stuck up at the rear. He knew that by so doing he became a part of the local colour, "a real Indian with a feather'n everything," and also that he sold more baskets while wearing it. In the time he had been living along the highway he had learned to give them what they expected.

The trailer residents were not yet awake, so he sat down on the wooden walk leading to the shower room, his baskets resting on the ground in a half circle behind him.

After a few minutes a small boy descended from the door of a trailer and stood staring at him. Then he leaned back inside the doorway and pointed in Big Tom's direction. In a moment a man's hand parted the heavy curtains on the window and a bed-mussed unshaven face stared out. The small boy climbed back inside.

A little later two women approached on the duckboard walk, one attired in a pair of buttock-pinching brown slacks, and the other wearing a blue chenille dressing gown. They circled him warily and entered the shower room. From inside came the buzz of whispered conversation and the louder noises of running water.

During the rest of the morning several people approached and stared at Big Tom and the baskets. He sold two small ones to an elderly woman. She seemed surprised when she asked him what tribe he belonged to, and instead of answering in a monosyllable he said, "I belong to the Algonquins, Ma'am." He also got rid of one of his big forty-five cent baskets to the mother of the small boy who had been the first one up earlier in the day.

A man took a series of photographs of him with an expensive-looking camera, pacing off the distance and being very careful in setting his lens openings and shutter speeds.

"I wish he'd look into the camera," the man said loudly to a couple standing nearby, as if he were talking about an animal in a cage.

"You can't get any good picshus around here. Harold tried to get one of the five Dionney kids, but they wouldn't let him. The way they keep them quints hid you'd think they was made of china or somep'n," a woman standing by said.

She glanced at her companion for confirmation.

"They want you to *buy* their picshus," the man said. "We was disappointed in 'em. They used to look cute before, when they was small, but now they're just five plain-looking kids."

"Yeah. My Gawd, you'd never believe how homely they got, would you, Harold? An' everything's pure robbery in Callander. You know, Old Man Dionney's minting money up there. Runs his own soovenir stand."

"That's durin' the day, when he's got time," her husband said.

The man with the camera, and the woman, laughed.

After lunch Big Tom watched Cooper prepare for his trip to North Bay. "Is there anybody going fishing, Mr. Cooper?" he asked.

The man took the radiator cap off the old truck he was inspecting, and peered inside.

"Mr. Cooper!"

"Hey?" Cooper turned and looked at the Indian standing behind him, hands in pockets, his manner shy and deferential. He showed a vague irritation as though he sensed the overtone of servility in the Indian's attitude.

"Anybody going fishing?" Big Tom asked again.

"Seems to me Mr. Staynor said he'd like to go," Cooper answered.

His voice was kind, with the amused kindness of man talking to a child.

The big Indian remained standing where he was, saying nothing. His old second-hand army trousers drooped around his lean loins, and his plaid shirt was open at the throat, showing a grey high-water mark of dirt where his face washing began and ended.

"What's the matter?" Cooper asked. "You seem pretty anxious to go today."

"My kid's sick. I want to make enough to take him to the doctor."

Cooper walked around the truck and opened one of the doors, rattling the handle in his hand as if it were stuck. "You should stay home with it. Make it some pine-sap syrup. No need to worry, it's as healthy as a bear cub."

Mrs. Cooper came out of the house and eased her bulk into the truck cab. "Where's Mary?" she asked.

"Up at the shack," answered Big Tom.

"Tell her to scrub the washrooms before she does anything else. Mrs. Anderson, in that trailer over there, wants her to do her floors." She pointed across the lot to a large blue and white trailer parked behind a Buick.

"I'll tell her," he answered.

The Coopers drove between the whitewashed stones marking the entrance to the camp, and swung up the highway, leaving behind them a small cloud of dust from the pulverized gravel of the road.

Big Tom fetched Mary and the baby from the shack. He gave his wife Mrs. Cooper's instructions, and she transferred the baby from her arms to his. The child was feverish, its breath noisy and fast.

"Keep him warm," she said. "He's been worse since we got up. I think he's got a touch of the 'flu."

Big Tom placed his hand inside the old blanket and felt the baby's cheek. It was dry and burning to his palm. He adjusted the baby's small weight in his arm and walked across the camp and down the narrow path to the shore of the lake where the boats were moored.

A man sitting in the sternsheets of a new-painted skiff looked up and smiled at his approach. "You coming out with me, Tom?" he asked.

The Indian nodded.

"Are you bringing the papoose along?"

Big Tom winced at the word "papoose", but he answered, "He won't bother us. The wife is working this afternoon."

"O.K. I thought maybe we'd go over to the other side of the lake today and try to get some of them big fellows at the creek mouth. Like to try?"

"Sure," the Indian answered, placing the baby along the wide seat in the stern, and unshipping the oars.

He rowed silently for the best part of an hour, the sun beating through his shirt causing the sweat to trickle coldly down his back. At times his efforts at the oars caused a constriction in his chest, and he coughed and spat into the water.

When they reached the mouth of the creek across the lake, he let the oars drag and leaned over to look at the baby. It was sleeping restlessly, its lips slightly blue and its breath laboured and harsh. Mr. Staynor was busy with his lines and tackle in the bow of the boat.

Tom picked the child up and felt its little body for sweat.

The baby's skin was bone dry. He picked up the bailing can from the boat bottom and dipped it over the side. With the tips of his fingers he brushed some of the cold water across the baby's forehead. The child woke up, looked at the strange surroundings, and smiled up at him. He gave it a drink of water from the can. Feeling reassured now he placed the baby on the seat and went forward to help the man with his gear.

Mr. Staynor fished for a half hour or so, catching some small fish and a large black bass, which writhed in the bottom of the boat. Big Tom watched its gills gasping its death throes, and noted the similarity between the struggles of the fish and those of the baby lying on the seat in the blanket.

He became frightened again after a time, and he turned to the man in the bow and said, "We'll have to go pretty soon. I'm afraid my kid's pretty sick."

"Eh! We've hardly started," the man answered. "Don't worry, there's not much wrong with the papoose."

Big Tom lifted the child from the seat and cradled it in his arms. He opened the blanket, and shading the baby's face, allowed the warm sun to shine on its chest. He thought, if I could only get him to sweat; everything would be all right then.

He waited again as long as he dared, noting the blueness creeping over the baby's lips, before he placed the child again on the seat and addressed the man in the bow. "I'm going back now. You'd better pull in your line."

The man turned and felt his way along the boat. He stood over the Indian and parted the folds of the blanket, looking at the baby. "My God, he is sick, Tom! You'd better get him to a doctor right away!" He stepped across the writhing fish to the bow and began pulling in the line. Then he busied himself with his tackle, stealing glances now and again at the Indian and the baby.

Big Tom turned the boat around, and with long straight pulls on the oars headed back across the lake. The man took the child in his arms and blew cooling drafts of air against its fevered face.

As soon as they reached the jetty below the tourist camp, Tom tied the boat's painter to a stump and took the child from the other man's arms.

Mr. Staynor handed him the fee for a full afternoon's work. "I'm sorry the youngster is sick, Tom," he said. "Don't play around. Get him up to the doctor in town right away. We'll try her again tomorrow afternoon."

Big Tom thanked him. Then, carrying the baby and unmindful of the grasping hands of the undergrowth, he climbed the path through the trees. On reaching the parked cars and trailers he headed in the direction of the large blue and white one where his wife would be working.

When he knocked, the door opened and a woman said, "Yes?" He recognized her as the one who had been standing nearby in the morning while his picture was being taken.

"Is my wife here?" he asked.

"Your wife; Oh, I know now who you mean. No, she's gone. She went down the road in a car a few minutes ago."

The camp was almost empty, most of the tourists having gone to the small bathing beach farther down the lake. A car full of bathers was pulling away to go down to the beach. Big Tom hurried over and held up his hand until it stopped. "Could you drive me to the doctor in town?" he asked. "My baby seems pretty sick."

There was a turning of heads within the car. A woman in the back seat began talking about the weather. The driver said, "I'll see what I can do, Chief, after I take the girls to the beach."

Big Tom sat down at the side of the driveway to wait. After a precious half hour had gone by and they did not return, he got to his feet and started up the highway in the direction of town.

His long legs pounded on the loose gravel of the road, his anger and terror giving strength to his stride. He noticed that the passengers in the few cars he met were pointing at him and laughing, and suddenly he realized that he was still wearing the feather in the band around his head. He reached up, pulled it off, and threw it in the ditch.

When a car or truck came up from behind him he would step off the road and raise his hand to beg a ride. After several passed without pausing he stopped this useless time-wasting gesture and strode ahead, impervious to the noise of their horns as they approached him.

Now and again he placed his hand on the baby's face as he plodded along, reassuring himself that it was still alive. It had been hours since it had cried or shown any other signs of consciousness.

Once, he stepped off the road at a small bridge over a stream, and making a crude cup with his hands, tried to get the baby to drink. He succeeded only in making it cough, harshly, so that its tiny face became livid with its efforts to breathe.

It was impossible that the baby should die. Babies did not die like this, in their father's arms, on a highway that ran fifteen miles north through a small town, where there was a doctor and all the life-saving devices to prevent their deaths.

The sun fell low behind the trees and the swarms of black flies and mosquitoes began their nightly forage. He waved his hand above the fevered face of the baby, keeping them off, while at the same time trying to waft a little air into the child's tortured lungs.

But suddenly, with feelings as black as hell itself, he knew that the baby was dying. He had seen too much of it not to know now, that the child was in an advanced stage of pneumonia. He stumbled along as fast as he could, his eyes devouring the darkening face of his son, while the hot tears ran from the corners of his eyes.

With nightfall he knew that it was too late. He looked up at the sky where the first stars were being drawn in silver on a burnished copper plate, and he cursed them, and cursed what made them possible.

To the north-west the clouds were piling up in preparation for a summer storm. Reluctantly he turned and headed back down the road in the direction he had come.

It was almost midnight before he felt his way along the path through the trees to his shack. It was hard to see anything in the teeming rain, and he let the water run from his shoulders in an unheeded stream, soaking the sodden bundle he still carried in his arms.

When he reached the shanty he opened the door and fell inside. He placed the body of his son on the bed in the corner. Then, groping around the newspaper-lined walls, he found some matches in a pocket of his mackinaw and lit the lamp. With a glance around the room he knew that his wife had not yet returned, so he placed the lamp on the table under the window and headed out again into the rain.

At the trailer camp he sat down on the rail fence near the entrance to wait. Some lights shone from the small windows of the trailers and from Cooper's house across the road. The illuminated sign said: COOPER'S TRAILER CAMP — Hot And Cold Running Water, Rest Rooms. FISHING AND BOATING — INDIAN GUIDES.

One by one, as he waited, the lights went out, until only the sign lit up a small area at the gate. He saw the car's headlights first, about a hundred yards down the road. When it pulled to a stop he heard some giggling, and Mary and another Indian girl, Elsie Woodhen, staggered out into the rain.

A man's voice shouted through the door, "See you again, sweetheart. Don't forget next Saturday night." The voice belonged to one of the French-Canadians who worked at a creosote camp across the lake.

Another male voice shouted, "Wahoo!"

The girls clung to each other, laughing drunkenly, as the car pulled away.

They were not aware of Big Tom's approach until he grasped his wife by the hair and pulled her backwards to the ground. Elsie Woodhen screamed, and ran away in the direction of the Cooper house. Big Tom bent down as if he was going to strike at Mary's face with his fist. Then he changed his mind and let her go.

She stared into his eyes and saw what was there. Crawling to her feet and sobbing hysterically she left one of her silver shoes in the mud and limped along towards the shack.

Big Tom followed behind, all the anguish and frustration drained from him, so that there was nothing left to carry him into another day. Heedless now of the coughing that tore his chest apart, he pushed along in the rain, hurrying to join his wife in the vigil over their dead.

HUGH HOOD

1928-

Hugh Hood was born and grew up in Toronto. He attended
the University of Toronto and received a Ph.D. in literature
in 1955. He taught for a number of years in Connecticut and
since 1961 has been a member of the English Department at
the University of Montreal.

He is best known for his short stories contributed to *Esquire*,
The Tamarack Review and other periodicals. One of them,
"Flying a Red Kite" was filmed by the National Film Board
and has been shown on television by the cbc. He has published
several collections of his stories and sketches, among them
Flying a Red Kite (1962), *White Figure, White Ground* (a
novel published in 1964), and *Around the Mountain: Scenes
from Montreal Life* (1967). *The Camera always Lies,* a psychological study of a film star, was also published in 1967. It
was followed by *A Game of Touch* (1970).

THE END OF IT

*In their eyes I have seen
the pin men of madness in marathon trim
race round the track of the stadium pupil.*
P. K. Page

"Sixty seconds," said a voice in the dark.

"Landy ran the first quarter in a minute flat, he set a killing pace and held it. I never thought he'd hold it."

The four men sat silently in the projection room and watched the film of the famous race, "the mile of the century." They heard the crowd noises on the sound track and began to pulse with them, but the film never showed the crowd, it followed the runners as they circled the track. The rhythm of the crowd noises grew steadily more insistent.

"There's Rich Ferguson in third place. He ran his best mile ever and finished third in 4:01 and change. Watch now, here comes Bannister."

The runners seemed to be racing around the edge of the screen, leaving the centre blank. You followed the runners intensely and were aware of the great blank space, the stadium infield, at some inferior level of consciousness.

"You haven't cut once," said Sanderson, "you've simply kept them in focus, and panned all the way round." He grew excited: "Watch now, this is the great part!" Bannister picked up a cue from his coach at the end of the third quarter and lengthened his stride.

"I wanted to zoom in on Landy but we couldn't. A news photographer caught him when he wobbled. Here it comes, there, there, see that? He had a bad heel that he didn't tell anyone about." They all saw him wobble, lose his rhythm momentarily and pick it up as Bannister went by. Perfectly involuntarily the four men began to pound on the arms of their seats and chant in the runner's rhythm "GO, GO, GO, GO, GO, GO, GO, GO," and the sound in the small projection room bounced from the walls and rebounded into their chant, reinforcing it, "GO, GO, GO, GO, GO, GO, GO, GO," it was bedlam as Bannister broke the tape and the film ended, the lights came on,

they saw where they were, they glanced at each other with embarrassment and amusement. They had been naïve; they had let what they
did for a living move them.

"That's exactly what happened on the day of the race," said
Sanderson, "I was sitting in a beer parlour with a crowd of total
strangers, we were glued to the set, and the moment Bannister
pulled out to pass everybody in the room picked up his rhythm. By
God, you talk about ritual art, it *was* ritual, I've never seen anything
like that in my life." He was shaking with pleasure and excitement.
"And it happens every time, that's the important thing." He turned
to the CBC man from whom they had borrowed the film. "How did
you get that, Wilfrid, that's an important piece of film? You could
win prizes with it."

"We did win prizes with it, we got an award for photo-journalism
that same year. It's a very nice sequence, isn't it?"

"Nice? It's a classic," said Sanderson. He turned to the others.
"See what I told you? It runs four minutes and it's a single sequence.
He doesn't cut or dissolve at any point, and look what he gets!"

"It was pure accident," said the CBC man, Wilfrid Wallace, who
felt terribly pleased to hear Sanderson saying these things, the Dean
of the Film Board, the best man on documentary since Grierson and
Flaherty. Of course, he told himself in qualification, these guys are
all either Socialists or nuts. I don't know why but they have this
large bleeding sense of the heart of the folk. Comes of shooting all
those close-ups of gnarled faces. But he listened carefully to what
Sanderson was saying and felt flattered.

"We'll have him run it again," said Philip Sanderson to his
editor and cutter, "and I want you to watch and see how the effect
builds, it has a starting point, you become aware of the crowd at
the same moment every time. I've got a stop-watch here and I'm
going to clock it. I think it comes towards the end of the second
quarter. Just at that instant the audience gets in there with the runners, that's the first important movement. Then for about a minute
we can't keep our eyes off Landy, but we sense that Bannister is
there. We don't pay any attention at all to Ferguson because we
know he isn't a threat, he's straining and straining. Even at this
distance we can see him strain to stay in the running. But Bannister
is hanging off there in third place full of power." He broke off,
struck with another train of thought.

"You see what it is? The motion casts the film *for* you. It writes your script and makes Landy the villain, and he was a nice fellow, I'm told, and it makes Bannister the hero and for all I know he's just a decent British doctor, which is what he is. But the motion gives you a script and a cast and an action. Oh, I'm going to do something about this film; it can't be allowed to moulder away in a library."

"It had to be a single sequence because we broke the other camera," said Wallace, laughing.

"Is that what happened, truly?"

"You know how these athletic meets are, they have officials milling around all over, more officials than runners. And one of these guys— I never knew his name, but he had a badge of some kind—got his foot caught in our cable just as the race started and disconnected Camera Two. Then while he was apologizing, he and the cameraman knocked the damned thing over. I swear to God that's what happened, so I couldn't use it at all. I'd had a shooting schedule, just a little bit of a thing on the back of an envelope, and my zoom lens was on Two. It shouldn't have been. It should have been on One, but I just didn't know how to shoot a footrace."

Sanderson smote his brow. "And you got this great thing by accident? If you'd had the other camera working, you'd have messed it up zooming in and out. Oh, Wilfrid, Wilfrid, you lucky bloody bastard!"

"That's life for you. I had to shoot it on One. There was nothing else to do."

"You see," Sanderson said with real bitterness and without humour, "he gets by accident what I've racked my brain for twenty years to figure out."

"It's a remarkable piece of work," said his cutter obsequiously, "it's purely cinematic."

Sanderson stared at him coldly, "Kitcheff," he said, "I know that you are fresh from the University Film Society and I can make certain allowances, but would you really mind not using phrases like 'purely cinematic,' I mean really?"

Kitcheff was wounded and showed it; that was one thing about Sanderson, he didn't mind your letting him see what you felt. "How else would you say it?" demanded Kitcheff rebelliously.

"Say it some way that means something. Who knows what 'cinematic' is? Nobody knows. You don't have to talk like that."

"All I mean is what you said yourself," said Kitcheff, "it's the art form of timed movement in space, and it dictates the shape of the given piece of work."

"This is a sterile discussion," said the editor, sanctimoniously.

Sanderson reversed his field, rounding on the editor and defending Kitcheff. "We've got to try to say these things some way, otherwise how will we know what we're doing?"

"Leave it to the critics," said the editor, who hoped one day to be a producer himself in a secure situation where he wouldn't have to listen to Sanderson who, genius though he might be, was feckless, undependable in argument, apt to change his mind at any point, and full of crazy ideas.

"Timed movement in space," he was saying just now, weighing it, "it's a nice phrase, Kitcheff boy, but I don't know what it means."

"Don't you tell him, Kitcheff," said the editor hastily, "don't try to tell him or we'll be here all afternoon. Are we going to run it again?"

"We are," said Sanderson, taking up his lecture where he'd dropped it, "and I want you to notice precisely when we feel like pounding the arms of the chairs, and when we actually begin to do it."

"I can tell you that," said Wilfrid Wallace, "it's just where——"

"Shut up for God's sake," said Sanderson, "I want them to find out for themselves. This proves an important point and it's going to make *A Walk Home from School* great documentary, something we've never done before. Purely cinematic, huh!" He walked back to the booth and told the projectionist to run the film again. As the lights dimmed he drew a stop-watch from his pocket and concentrated on the screen with enormous intensity. Kitcheff and the editor, Vasko, glared at him with mutinous envy. He had really extraordinary powers of concentration and could remember every detail of every shot, cut, sequence, angle, from every one of the thousands of movies he'd seen and made. It caused them trouble all the time.

"They used that in *Une Fille pour L'Eté*," he would say, and then they had to spend hours figuring another way to do it. In the dark they heard him fiddling with the stop-watch, clucking and mumbling to himself.

"It's the empty space they're running around," they heard him say, "that's what gives you the effect, you want to get in there beside the runners." Nobody answered him.

"Of course I'm not a psychologist," he said to nobody in particular, "a psychologist would likely tell you differently." And then they all began to beat on the arms of their seats again and only Kitcheff wondered if this was because Sanderson was willing them to do it, and the race was over, the tape breasted, Bannister home and cooled out, lights on. Vasko and Kitcheff smiled happily at Sanderson, and he pumped Wilfrid Wallace's hand with the disinterested pleasure he always took in really good work, his own or another's.

"I'm so glad you could get down to talk to us," he said, "I had the hell of a job worming the piece out of the CBC Library, and the boys had to see it. They're giving me a very bad time just now." He stared expressionlessly at Vasko and Kitcheff, making them fidget. He wasn't vindictive but he would say anything, absolutely anything, with terrifying candour, and they never knew what to expect. "Can you have dinner with Margery and me?" He was leaving them out of the invitation quite openly, but he had meals with them all the time, meals which they never remembered eating, though the food stains were on their clothes and they didn't feel hungry. They had been arguing over *A Walk Home from School* for three weeks now, and their office was full of coffee containers that nobody would admit ordering.

"I'm catching the five o'clock out of the Windsor Station," said Wallace, "I've got to do a football game tomorrow."

"What can you do with a football game?" said Sanderson interestedly.

"Not a hell of a lot. CBS pretty well established the conventions ten years ago."

"I'd like to do one," said Sanderson, "or fool around with the tape."

The others guffawed. "The audience would love it," said Wallace, "but they wouldn't know the score."

Vasko and Kitcheff were hilarious and Sanderson looked innocent. "I have no idea what you mean," he said and then he laughed and put his arm around Wallace's shoulder, walking him out of the projection room and making pleasant chat.

"Do you mean Margery Endicott?" said Wallace as they went out. "I'm in love with Margery Endicott, always have been, always will be. She played Juliet at Hart House my first year in college. I guess she was in fourth year then, but she really looked fourteen, only Juliet I've ever seen who looked fourteen, *ka-bong, ka-bong.*"

Vasko and Kitcheff sat looking at each other as their chief left the room. "She's thirty-four now," they heard him say, "and it's no secret, she tells everybody. You never saw such a thirty-four year old in your life. Did you know we were married for a while?" His voice passed out of hearing.

"He *is* crazy," said Vasko, "it can't be done, nobody will watch it. It's a waste of the taxpayer's money."

Kitcheff chuckled around his pipe-stem; he was an insecure young man who doubted that he could carry off a pipe *and* tweeds, so he settled for the pipe without the tweeds and even at that was afraid. "Who gives a shit about the taxpayers?" he said.

"I know, it's just an expression. But I tell you, Ted, if he shoots a film that runs to one fifteen-minute sequence—and I don't care about the angles, anybody can figure out impossible angles—for one thing we'll be out of a job, figuratively speaking, I mean, if you don't mean to cut and edit the film, where does that leave us?"

"The Film Board never fires anybody," said Kitcheff equably.

"Oh, I'm not worried about my job. They aren't all like him, thank God, none of the other producers think that way."

"None of them are as good."

"Oh, he's good all right, up to a certain point, I'll grant you that, but lately, I don't know, lately I've been wondering about him, some people are great artists and some are just plain crazy, and it's hard to tell the difference. Maybe he's a fraud."

"That has nothing to do with you—you just follow instructions, you're not a policy-maker. And as for me, I'm just a little guy fresh from the University Film Society. We don't have to worry, we aren't responsible, and anyway the world won't stop revolving just because one fifteen-minute documentary is a flop. What difference does it make?"

Vasko was looking around for his topcoat, not paying much attention. "Maybe it's a question of artistic principle."

Kitcheff said, "That's Film Society talk. Sanderson would vomit if he heard you say that."

"He can have principles, why can't we?"

"We can't afford them. Wait till you're a producer, then you can have all the principles you want."

"Yeah, I guess you're right. Let's go over to The Seven Steps and check the talent." They left the projection room, feeling glad that they didn't have to go back upstairs, they were through for the day.

"How did Sanderson ever get into Margery Endicott? He's twice her age," said Vasko.

"Genius, Vasko boy, pure genius."

"Huh!" said Vasko.

As he waited for the operator to locate Miss Endicott, through a bewildering tintamarre of crossed wires, clicks, half-heard confused voices, Sanderson let his thoughts run peaceably along without conscious control, letting his ear, a hot sore ear pressed against a sweaty receiver, direct his associations. His life with Margery had been fed through a switchboard with a clumsy operator making a bad connection every time they tried to reach each other. It was an idea for a poem, the poet is trying to reach somebody, probably a girl, but he keeps getting "one moment, please," and at length hangs up. He hadn't written a poem for fifteen years, preferring the visual medium; but you couldn't put that idea on film. It wasn't "purely cinematic," there was nothing to it visually.

How do you express the imperfect tense on film?

I used to try and reach her. We used to go around together. We were going to the movies quite a lot in those days. The imperfect, despite its name, is the tense for the good old days back there. It's a flashback, a montage, a long close-up, and a slow dissolve.

I'm being frivolous, he thought, and anyway that's another man's idea, not mine, but you could figure out the appropriate film technique for every tense, not excluding the *plus-que-parfait* and the *conditionnel antérieure*. The French, he thought, who worries about such notions but the French?

Movies have no tense, he decided, movies are all in the present just as you see them, even flashback gives us a present past. That's my problem, he realized all at once, that's my disease. I'm trying to seize the whole present, but literature keeps sneaking in and giving me history. I don't want history, and I don't want to think about Margery ten years ago.

Then the operator found her and she came on the line sounding irritated as all hell. "What are you trying to do to me, Phil? I've got work to do, I'm a busy girl and I'm menstruating like mad."

She doesn't waste any time, he thought. "Take a two-twenty-two," he said and she laughed. Their medicine cabinet had been full of vials of two-twenty-twos, his and hers. "I just want to check about dinner, same time, same place?"

"Oh, sure, sure, *poulet rôti, farci, garni,* this is 'Festival,' you know, and it's all balled-up. I don't know why I do these things, except by now they know how to shoot me."

"I'm the only one who knows how to shoot you," he said, "because I've got first-hand experience of your best angles." The operator click-click-clicked the line.

She chuckled. "I'm not that angular."

"Margery, are you feeling all right? You're not working too hard? You look so thin."

"You should see me in the flesh," she said, and added sententiously, "the camera adds ten pounds."

"Chez Stien, Mackay Street, quarter to eight."

"I've got to run, lover, they're calling me. I'll see you then." Click-click-click the switchboard in the middle, he thought, it's a good idea for a poem but you can't get it on film, they tried it in *Sorry, Wrong Number* and it stank. He came out of the phone booth, looked at his watch and decided to go home and put on a necktie, formal wear, a necktie, and nipping out to the sidewalk he stole a cab from under an administrator's nose.

In his apartment he was God Almighty, Montreal apartments for the upper-income brackets are all like that, always on the side of the mountain with a view of the river. His was way way up almost at the Lookout and all the kingdoms of the earth were spread at his feet. I've never offered them to anybody, he thought, they don't belong to me. What am I doing wrong with *A Walk Home from School?* Is it built on a fundamentally wrong premise? He began to meditate seriously on his current assignment; he had nearly three hours to kill and Margery was notorious for her tardiness, always had been, always would be. I'll have two drinks in the bar and then she'll come, and I'll be two drinks ahead all night, another bad connection.

Now the first angle will determine the whole film, just like Wilfrid's footrace, the lucky bastard, the man came along and buggered up his shooting schedule by accident. I can't have somebody come in and smash my lens when I'm not expecting it. How the hell do you get that gratuitous quality? When they made *The Lady in the Lake* they made a big stink about the camera as the eyes of the hero, and some schnook kept punching the camera. They got it all wrong. If I'm going to try something the same in *A Walk Home from School* I'd better figure out what went wrong with that movie. Where can I get a print? Making a mental note to research *The Lady in the Lake*, he went on to his own problems.

Vision is binocular. Maybe I should use two cameras and super-impose the results, would that do it? No. That just gives me a cheap 3-D process effect. I wish I were a psychologist, that's what I need to be at this point. How do we see? What makes the whole field of vision cohere and mean something, alive space? The trouble is I don't know. I don't even know if I can find out. Let me think, let's try to pin the thing down. I remember twenty years ago Grierson used to say that film was the supreme medium for rendering reality because it imitated consciousness so perfectly. Was that a tautology?

Grierson. A cantankerous man, hard to deal with, opinionated, gifted, but I'm better than he was; he was too literal-minded. You can't get life itself by copying it; you have to arrange it.

Consciousness is a single sequence, why can't Kitcheff and Vasko understand that? There's no technique to consciousness, we make our arrangements because of who we are; it's a seventy-year sequence, and yet they claim a fifteen-minute sequence will drive people out of the theatre. I've wanted to do this film all my life, and it's going to be my walk home from school, we'll shoot it in Toronto and we'll end up at 27 Cornish Road.

A softball slamming into a left-handed shortstop's glove for the last out, the game is over, and we see the empty field with the players in the middle distance walking slowly away in all directions. We see a forgotten bat lying in the dust beside home plate, we get the sense of emptiness and then we pan around and dolly towards the steps, we climb the steps——

——how am I going to get that last out, the ball coming into the glove? It was the only decent play I ever made in high-school, I was too young for the guys in my grade, and too small, and they didn't like me because I was too goddam smart. I couldn't help that, but I'm going to get that sense of desertion into the opening frames——

——a left-handed shortstop, wouldn't you know——

——we'll shoot it from below and get the sense of reaching up for the ball, if we could get the pitcher first, then the batter swinging, the flight of the ball, then the catch, no hand, no arm, just the dark mass of the big glove in the bottom picture, then the ball, then the merge with the ball, then where do we go?

I'm not certain how to get that shot, and in any case why am I trying to recreate my own recollections? The camera is for actuality, but perhaps I can get the actuality of the recollections, to hell with theory, I'm not Dr. Kracauer. I wonder if this idea is built on a false premise? I've been drifting around it for years, and if I don't try it now, I might lose it and it's the best script I ever had. I'll just go to the location and shoot it, coming along Farnham Avenue, the trees, I used to bend my head back and look up into the trees and through the trees at the sky, that would be in May and I could see the clouds parading through the dark green, and behind them the blue, dark green on white on blue, heraldic, and all moving as I moved with my head back, except the background of blue, it never moved, it was the field of reference.

The sky is the condition of movement; that's where the light comes from, white through blue.

And on past the stuccoed apartment houses to Yonge Street, to the left past the Packard showroom, now it's a Volkswagen showroom. I wonder if I ought to ask them to put some Packards in the window? Where could we find Packards as of this date? We'd better stick to Volkswagens but in that case I falsify my recollection, and then the Dodge dealership, Mills and Hadwin, across the street. I never walked along the east side, I stayed on the west, past the Esso station, the two candy stores, the Rosehill Barber Shop, God, it's all there in my head, I can see it as if I were there.

Am I by any chance making this picture out of pure regressiveness? I might be. Is that bad?

Maybe all movies are made that way. Grierson used to say "never let your memory get into the picture, stick to actualities, otherwise you've got both feet in literature" and how he hated literature. It was the Scotch in him, or that puritanical reformer's streak, he was an original-sin man if ever there was one. I'm not an original-sin man, I'm an Eden man, we never really left home. *A Walk Home from School.*

When we get to the corner of St. Clair and Yonge, we'll have a big brilliant ball, we'll peek inside the bank and wonder what they do in there, we'll look behind the stagings where they're putting a new Vitrolite storefront on The Osgoode Grill, we'll stand on the corner waiting for the light to change watching the maze of streetcars. There are no streetcars on Yonge anymore but they still run along St. Clair. We'll look up the street to see what's playing at the Kent and the Hollywood, then we cross, east then north, I always walked on the north side of St. Clair, and in a minute we're out of the shopping district past Loblaws and halfway home.

In the distance we see the red dome of Our Lady of Perpetual

Help away down the street across the St. Clair bridge. Now here's where the motion has to write the script for us. Kitcheff was quite right, we can't tell the audience in so many words that it's the church of our mother of perpetual help. Is there any way to communicate the feeling visually? In any case I never walked that far, unless I was going to see Philly Daniels, I turned away before I got that far, what I'm heading for now is the bridge, ah, divine bridge, this is where we open out the picture, we come to the bridge and we show them the length and span of it, the few afternoon cars wheeling idly across, we get that sense of open space and sunny air and distance. Then.

We don't cross the bridge. We climb over the rail at the near end as the ground slopes away down underneath the ravine, and we give them the luxuriance of the ravine, foliage, the brook at the bottom, the sound of streetcars rumbling overhead, mud on my shoes, stepping stones in the brook, a boy's whole world, we pan up the bridge-supports, massive concrete grey inhuman ghostly, then we follow the brook north by winding paths through shady groves and we climb back up to Heath Street on the other side.

I want that sunny space and air and then the dark ravine, the foliage, the brook, and to hell with psychoanalysis, I just want it for the picture. I hope. We have a little coda as we climb out of the ravine, walk up Heath Street past kids on their bikes, turn onto Cornish Road, we'll shoot the house, the veranda, the screen door, and that'll be the end of it. I wonder who lives there now, and whether they'll let me inside, or even onto the veranda. It's supper time when we get home. Supper time!

He looked at his watch, seven-ten, my God, where did it go? Time for Margery and dinner. As he rose and went into the bathroom to wash his face and hands and straighten his tie, he thought suddenly, *maybe I can't get it, maybe I'll never get it, maybe John was right and nobody can get it.* I can't put streetcars on a street where they've torn up the tracks. I can't put vanished Packards into Volkswagen showrooms.

He began to whistle softly, a thing he always did when badly worried; then he left the bathroom, put on his jacket, checked to be sure that he had some money, and went to keep his date.

She was not there, naturally, but she had phoned to say that she would be delayed. That they didn't give him the message when he first appeared in the foyer puzzled and at last faintly annoyed him.

He had to poke around into all the little rooms, nooks, niches, in which the famous old house abounded, a tiny place, a hole in the wall on Mackay Street and the *fons et origo* of the higher cuisine of Montreal; there were diners who held that Cafe Martin surpassed the little place in the excellence of its wine list, and particularly in the virtuoso treatment of veal. Anyone could make a great dish of beefsteak, but the test of cookery was the cook's approach to the problem of veal.

Sanderson thought Cafe Martin overrated, the magnificence of its *sommelier*, the glow of its chandeliers, its Aubusson, false reinforcements for a middling-to-good table. He wasn't a gourmet, thinking the pastime trivial and even pagan, but he was by trade a *metteur-en-scène* and a shrewd critic of other peoples' decors. He had always preferred Chez Stien for its sly and understated humility, its air of astonishment at its own perfection, its continual ability to surprise its clientele. Since the Film Board had moved to Montreal, Sanderson had become a devotee of the little place. He had always come here, of course, from his first callow times in Montreal when he was young and hopeful, fresh out of college, and afterwards when he'd settled into film production and begun to make a great name, and later still when he was married to Margery and his pictures were winning at Cannes and Venice, and these days, with his marriage six or seven years behind him and his work growing progressively more sure and obscure. Why didn't they simply hand him his messages as he came in, instead of requiring him to pursue his quest through all the purlieus of the labyrinthine old house? He put his head into the owner's rooms, walked past the kitchens, idled in the foyer, and finally demanded of the *maître d'hôtel* whether anything had been heard from Margery.

"A message from Miss Endicott for Mister Sanderson?" he asked diffidently. He wasn't a name dropper, least of all of his own name.

"I will see, sir," said the grand personage, courteously enough. His names was Gilles. He had been here for years and certainly must know Sanderson by sight if not by name; but he gave no sign, perhaps pursuing a policy of the house and tactfully ignoring the celebrity of the celebrities who came here. It was a place where you could be inconspicuous, if that's what you wanted. In a moment he came back with a slip of paper in his hand.

"Yes, sir," he said, handing it to Sanderson, "this came an hour ago."

Sanderson examined the note; she would come at eight-fifteen.

"Will you keep my table free, please? For two, Mr. Sanderson, and we'll go in about eight-thirty."

Gilles scanned his reservations anxiously. "That will be arranged, Mr. Sanderson. We are rather busy tonight, as you see, but there will be a table."

Sanderson gave him money; he was awkward at such things, having an oppressive sense of the other man as a fellow human being, not caring to treat him as anything less than free. But Gilles put the bill away with a fine ease, turning from him to greet a Toronto writer and his wife who came in on the crest of an expense-account weekend. Some magazine will pay for that, thought Sanderson critically as he eyed the writer, whom he knew slightly and didn't like, as the couple were bowed to a table. My table, he guessed, and they'd damned well better be finished by eight-thirty. He wandered off disconsolately to the downstairs bar to kill forty-five minutes.

He wasn't a heavy drinker, but he liked to drink and decided that there would be time for two slow-to-slowish nibbles before she came. He ordered his first and stationed himself in a corner on an uncomfortable stool. When his drink came he drank half of it on the instant, a Manhattan because he loved cherries, surprising himself with his unaccustomed haste. He let the second half stand for a moment.

She'll have some joke to make about that, he thought, she'll say "you're way ahead of me" or "I'll have to catch up" or something like that. It was not drink that had led to their divorce but work, an innocent enough pastime, they had supposed, although nowadays one was beginning to see in the papers and magazines pieces about "workoholics" who did with their jobs what others accomplish through drugs or drink. He was no workoholic and neither was she, though they had traded accusations to that effect before the term had been invented. He could hear her now.

"I'm so damned tired, Phil, I just can't respond," and he would stand there, desiring her and knowing that he mightn't in charity insist on his rights. When she got fine-drawn like that from overwork she was so fatally provocative, at least to him. Some like them plump, but he had adored her fragile shoulderblades, the huge eyes in the perfect cheekbones, that Picasso line to her jaw. And her other parts were so sweetly harmonious. Her buttocks, he remembered with his dazzling visual imagination, had been those of a child, no bigger than the outspread palm of his hand, and though she was mainly a composition in angles, in that place she was wonderfully curved in a curve without grossness.

"Damn you," she used to say towards the end of it, "you love only my composition, you're always photographing me with your eyes. It's just that you work too hard and I'm not an abstraction."

"If you lose any more weight you will be," he said. "Who works too hard? Who is it that's too tired all the time?" She began to weep quietly.

"We're both too nervous; other men don't make me feel like this, but I love you, Phil, believe me, I love you."

"And I love you," he had murmured sadly, "but perhaps you're right. I don't mean to drive you to exhaustion."

She sat up angrily on their bed. "Do you want to be rid of me?"

"I only want what's right for both of us."

"No, you just want to love everybody by way of the movies. I warn you, Phil, you can't do it. One real woman is better than a strip of celluloid, even if it plays every house in the world, and what you want, you can't get on film. Don't be a power-lover, darling, you're not Nehru."

He laid his cheek against her buttocks and held it there. Whose skin was feverish, his or hers? You could not put this on film; there were lots of things that wouldn't go. He closed his eyes for a second, then opened them and swallowed the other half of his drink, signalling for the second as he swallowed.

He had timed her perfectly, so well that he remembered her in-clinations—they might almost have been his own, they were at least mysteriously inside him, dictating the shape and tone of his conduct towards her. As he finished the second glass, he probed the crystal cup to the bottom with his toothpick, pricking and fixing the cherry and finally swallowing it with pleasure, and after that he rose, paid the bar check and went upstairs to find her standing at the door, her coat melting mysteriously from her shoulders—she never took things off, they simply melted invisibly away, and one didn't notice the attendants who cared for them.

"Yes," she said, "well, I said I'd be late."

"It's worth the wait. I'm very glad to see you. I've been wanting to talk to you. I think—— no, let's go in." They were ushered to their table and Sanderson was relieved to note that the Toronto writer was still sitting on the other side of the room. At least they were not following that crabbed act. After some low comedy in French they succeeded in making their wishes known and first drinks, and then a series of dishes, began to arrive in a broadening and deepening flow. There were side-tables everywhere, and four attendants, and in an instant, plainly, the chef would epiphanize from the kitchen. They had identified Margery which was odd because she appeared very rarely on the French network.

"What is all this?" he said crossly.

"I did a commercial for Comet Cleanser and Huguette Lamarche dubbed the voice, they've been using it for years on CBFT."

He had internationally fifty times his wife's—he checked himself because she was no longer his wife—fifty times Margery Endicott's reputation. He had been coming here for twenty years and they had not caught his name. In the Montreal Film Festival last summer his *Sonata da Chiesa* had been ecstatically received, and even lauded.

Who gives a damn about it, who cares? But it was a part of his gripe, he was aware, the want of overt recognition. He couldn't have been an actor, and wouldn't if he could. She was laughing at him.

"What's the matter, Phil, do you want my autograph? Don't be afraid to speak up."

He had to laugh with her. "The CBC has a 'no star-system' policy. You'd better be careful with your autographs."

"They've changed all that since they've been losing everybody to the States. I've got a billing clause now, and if they don't meet it, I don't do the show. People seem to want to see Margery Endicott."

"It's unfair," he said, knowing that he sounded like a small boy; she had always been able to force him into this corner.

"Oh, stop horsing around, you know you don't care."

He was glad to see that she was eating, and sorry to see how thin and overtired she seemed, and of course she was seeing him after some lapse of time, and would be thinking about his looks.

"I haven't gained an ounce," he said.

"No, I've shrunk." She put her hand across the table, palm upwards, and he took it gently and pressed it. "Dear Phil," she smiled with her lovely kindness, "my good man."

He was gruff. "I'm in a mess as you'd expect."

"Socialism, or theory of film?"

"I haven't been a Socialist since before we were married, I've dropped all that stuff, ideology is no good for me."

"Would you mind very much not using words like 'ideology'?"

He remembered young Kitcheff and blushed. "I'm just an old comedian," he said, kidding himself, "just an old clown who's been around and who knows all the tricks, just faking my way through."

"And I'm a clean young girl from Swift Current in a starched gingham check."

"Once you were," he said seriously.

"Yes, I was. God, that was awful." Then they both had another drink. "What's the matter?"

"You act," he said, "and you're a good actress, for what it's worth, and when you're older you'll be better because you're going to hang on to your looks, the bones are there. . . ."

"Never mind about my bones."

"——they're what you live on. Listen, what I want to know is, can you tell how you're getting better. I watch your shows, and I see you do things you wouldn't have dreamed of trying when we were married, and yet, you don't really *think* about it at all, do you?"

"No. My head is for hats to go into. I can't think at all."

"But you get better. How do you do it?"

"Practice. It was always there, now I know how to use it." She was suddenly grave. "I started to know after we broke up."

"Yes, I suppose so."

"We love each other, we're a mutual admiration society. You know, my dear, I see your things, I've never missed one, and you are so good. *You are getting so good.*" Her eyes were wet.

"Don't do that, Margery," he said.

"You fool," she said, "you're a great man." That hurt him very much. "You're a great man and I'm a cute girl on a regional television network."

Of course he was not a great man and would never be a great man.

"What it is," he said, "is that I can't do it, I don't believe. I can't get it. I cannot get what I want."

"Why you've been getting it right along. I wish you'd use me."

"Can't use actors in documentary."

"Actors are people."

"You can only use them when they aren't looking, in documentaries about actors."

"So make a picture about my *métier*! Show me rinsing out a sweaty bra and pants in the ladies' room at the studio, all my hard life and times. Artists have lives."

"I'm sick of making paradoxes about art and life. It all falls into place." And he quoted:

> . . . that which suits a part infects the whole,
> And now is almost grown the habit of my soul.

"What is it, Phil, what's wrong?"

"I'm fifty," he said soberly, "and I've been on the wrong track.

What I've wanted to do can't be done on film."

She was resisting the understandable temptation to say "I told you so." Instead she said, "Let's get married again," and it was the nicest gift anybody had ever offered him; but life is not composed of gifts, though it is itself gratuitous, and though it hurt him to smile he did so, saying, "I really do love you, you know, and I wouldn't put you through that again for the world." They both knew that there was nothing to it and taking their time over a bottle of wine they smiled at each other and in the end decided to catch the late showing of *L'Année Dernière à Marienbad* at the Elysée.

"Resnais is very good," said Sanderson magisterially.

"Not as good as you are."

"It's true."

They found the film pellucid, crystalline, because they knew how it had been put together, and on what good grounds.

In the middle of the following afternoon, having risen very late, having gotten to bed very very late indeed, Sanderson came slinking into the Film Board building like a cat who has breakfasted on gold-fish. He was determined to avoid Kitcheff and Vasko if at all possible, he didn't want to face their cross-questionings today, and he had arranged another showing of "the mile of the century" without telling them.

He glanced into the coffee shop to see if they were there, but they weren't, not they, and they certainly wouldn't be in the office, so he figured he was home free and he went directly to the projection room where the projectionist was waiting for him, glancing at his watch. Sanderson was not normally a hard man to deal with but today he harassed the poor technician continually. He made him show fifty feet, stop, run it again, another fifty feet, stop, re-wind, run it again, stop there please, until the poor man was ready to tell him to go to hell. He had never seen Sanderson act like that.

"All right," said Sanderson after some time, with an odd air of triumph, "now I want to see the end of it, the last minute, keep running it over and over, please." He trotted back and forth between the seats and the booth like a distracted man. "Just show me the end of it, that's all I want to see."

The projectionist felt an obscure fright, but as he began to run the footage he saw Sanderson settle into a seat and begin to smoke idly, alone in the dark.

This time he didn't cheer aloud, feeling no sense of community; it had been better in the beer parlour, when he'd seen it first. But he sat on, ostensibly quietly, nursing his cigarette, and in his head, in sympathy with the soundtrack, in sympathy with the pulse in his temple, his disembodied interior voice was screaming: "GO, GO, GO, GO, GO, GO, GO, GO." It would go on screaming until the race was over.

3. Character and Comedy

ETHEL WILSON
1890-

Born in South Africa, Ethel Wilson was brought to Canada at the age of eight to live with relatives in Vancouver. After an English schooling she became a teacher in Vancouver until her marriage in 1920 to a prominent physician. She did not begin writing until fairly late in life, her first published story being a contribution to *The New Statesman and Nation* in 1937. Since that time she has written many stories, sketches, and novellas, and several novels, among them *Hetty Dorval* (1947), *The Innocent Traveller* (1949), *The Equations of Love* (1952), consisting of two novelettes, "Tuesday and Wednesday" and "Lilly's Story," *Swamp Angel* (1954), and *Love and Salt Water* (1956). *Mrs. Golightly and Other Stories,* a retrospective collection, was published in 1961.

Ethel Wilson possesses a sharp but innocent eye for character and background, an urbane wit, and a sense of irony that have placed her among the most civilized of Canadian writers of fiction. Her distinction of mind and clarity of style give her peculiarly feminine studies of the human comedy a cogency they share with the English novels of Elizabeth Bowen and Muriel Spark.

In two revealing essays, "A Cat among the Falcons" and "The Bridge or the Stokehold," published in 1959 and 1960 in *Canadian Literature,* Mrs. Wilson has discussed the principles of her art with engaging informality.

THE INNUMERABLE LAUGHTER

"What a lovely morning! Oh look, there's a bird!" said Aunt Topaz as she hastened down the steps from the verandah of the small summer cabin which her nephews had caused to be built upon the high rocky shores of Benbow Island. "And the sea, oh look!" she said to no one in particular, for there was no one there. " 'The many-twinkling smile of ocean!' 'The innumerable laughter of the sea!' Just like the Greeks I do declare! I wouldn't be at all surprised! Who would think that this is the Pacific Ocean! Much the same rocky—— What is that? Voices? Voices? Who *can* it be?" and she quickened her steps towards the rock which overlooked the lonely bay.

Aunt Topaz, hurrying forwards, reached the rock and looked down. "Well!" she said.

On the smooth expanse of the little bay below her floated two small yachts, and in the bay, swimming about with lusty and happy shouts, were several young men with nothing on.

"Well I never!" exclaimed Aunt Topaz, bending down so as to see better. "Nothing on! Very pleasant I'm sure! Oh can that be Mr. Morland? Good-morning, Mr. Morland, good-morning! And *can* that be that nice young man in the Bank? I do believe it is!" said Aunty, delighted to recognize two young men of her acquaintance so far from home, even though they had nothing on.

At the sight of Aunty who smiled and called and waved the handkerchief which she had rummaged from the front of her blouse, Mr. Morland and the nice young man in the Bank uttered warning cries. All the swimmers immediately turned face downwards and swam about, vainly trying to escape from the orbit of Aunty's vision. Aunty now saw nothing but posteriors swimming vainly away.

"Oh," said Aunty, vexed, "if only they'd turn right side up, I'd be able to see if it really *is* Mr. Morland! I must tell Rachel!"

Aunt Topaz, who was a great imparter of news, turned and went back at top speed to the cottage, where she saw her niece Rachel standing in the doorway.

"Rachel, Rachel, what *do* you suppose," she cried, "there are nine young men swimming about the bay with nothing on, and I *do* believe that one is Andrew's friend Mr. Morland, and I *do* believe that one of them is that nice young man in the Bank! If they would only turn right side up I might be able to see! I called and called, but they did not reply!"

"What does it matter if it *is* Mr. Morland?" said Rachel wrathfully. "A great pity if young men can't have a bit of a swim without people staring at them. I sometimes think, Anty, that you have no modesty."

"*Me!* No modesty!" exclaimed Aunty with indignation. "Well really! Here I am clothed from head to foot, and they haven't got a stitch on! Who's immodest, I'd like to know! Oh Annie, so *there* you are! What do you think, there are nine——"

Just as the Grandmother appeared at the door, Yow, the domineering Chinese cook, came round the corner with a large breakfast tray.

"I puttem breakfast verandah. Plenty sun," he announced, without asking them whether they wanted to have breakfast on the verandah or not.

"Ah, bacon, bacon! How nice!" said Aunty. "Delicious! Annie, did you know that there are nine young men—— Oh dear me, there's a serpent!"

"Why, there's a snake!" said Rachel, looking over the verandah railing at a snake which lay curled on the warm grass.

"A serpent?" said the Grandmother in surprise.

The garter snake slid, coiled, stopped. It slid, coiled, stopped and slid shining away through the grasses.

"Well!" said the ladies, who had seldom seen snakes before except in a zoo.

"Can it be poisonous?" asked Rachel.

"Is it venomous, do you think?" asked the Grandmother. They all left their bacon and peered over the verandah railing after the vanished snake.

"Mr. Oxted says that snakes in this part of the world are never poisonous," said Aunt Topaz. "Mr. Oxted has lived in British Columbia for years and years and years. Mr. Oxted says that Mrs. Oxted——"

"*Anty*," said Rachel in extreme exasperation, "if I hear you mention Mr. Oxted once more—— if I hear you quote Mr. Oxted once more—— I've heard nothing but Mr. Oxted ever since we started coming up here, for two whole months. You'd think that no one but Mr. Oxted had ever gone camping before!"

"Mr. Oxted is a very nice man and a very *fine* man," said Aunt Topaz. And then she proceeded to give a good example of the way she could shift an argument to suit herself. Since no one could prove whether the snake was poisonous except by being bitten by it, and being sent down as a corpse to Vancouver, Aunty adroitly shifted her stand.

"His wife is a very handsome woman, and she sings in St. Andrew's choir. A fine contralto. Some people say that St. Andrew's choir is the best choir in Vancouver."

This was not kind of Aunty. Rachel had been for five years a faithful choir member and a leading soprano in Wesley Church. But Aunty achieved her end, which was to irritate Rachel just a little. Rachel had rebuked her in the matter of the young men, and Aunty was still mildly annoyed. She succeeded in irritating Rachel.

"How can you say such a thing!" cried Rachel. "Everyone who is anyone and knows anything about music knows quite well that Wesley Church choir is the leading choir in Vancouver, and if St. Andrew's——"

The Grandmother held up her hand. "Let us have no rivalry," she said gently. "Although we do not belong to the Presbyterian Church, there is no doubt but that, in their own way, the Presbyterians praise God with equal——"

"Oh do look at Yow!" exclaimed Aunt Topaz.

Yow stood nonchalantly in the doorway. He looked at the ladies with his peculiar facial cynicism. This was not difficult, as his right eyelid drooped by nature with a sinister effect, and gave to his face a cynical and even diabolical appearance without any effort on Yow's part. Between his fingers he held the tail of a snake. The snake, hanging head downwards, looked uncomfortable, and squirmed in an angular and unnatural manner, quite unlike its usual fluid performance.

"I catchem snake. I puttem stew," said Yow, looking with indifference upon the breakfast party. Cries arose, but Yow did not stay to listen. He departed, taking the snake with him.

"I do believe he will!" they breathed one to another.

It was the habit in this family of three ladies that even the slightest move on anyone's part should be prefaced by a brief and candid explanation. If Rachel should at any time arise, and go out of the room without some such announcement as "I am going to get my sewing cotton," the Grandmother and Aunt Topaz would say mutually in amazement,

"Where *can* Rachel have gone?" as if she might have gone to China or to Peru or to bed.

Aunt Topaz therefore did not surprise anyone when she said, "I have a call," and got up and walked in her hasty pounding fashion in the direction of the rear of the cottage.

She returned by way of the lean-to kitchen where Yow was making loud noises in the dishpan.

"Yow," said Aunt Topaz, "you wouldn't *really* put that serpent into the stew, would you?"

"Sure," said Yow rudely, and went into the house.

As Aunty returned dismayed to the verandah, Rachel arose and said, "I am going to get some more hot water." She then repaired to the lean-to kitchen. Yow looked at her malevolently.

"Yow," said Rachel, using her mixture of pidgin-English, which she admired but could not achieve, and the King's own English, "I absolutely forbiddem you puttem snake in stew. If you puttem snake in stew, I shall tell Mr. Andrew when he comes next Saturday. If you puttem snake in stew, Mr. Andrew will be extremely angry."

"I no care," said Yow, and went on being noisy.

When Rachel got back to the breakfast table, the Grandmother stood up in all her small dignity and said, "I am going to speak to Yow about that serpent," and sailed like a little black schooner into the house.

"Yow," she said, lifting her limpid brown gaze to the Chinaman, "*please* don't put that little serpent into the stew! I shall not relish my stew at all if you do. Please, Yow!"

Yow looked upon his darling. "I no puttem snake stew, Missy Hasting," he said. "You no likee, I no puttem. I makem little fun. I foolem. They heap clazy. They no savvy nothing. I no puttem stew."

"Oh I do thank you, Yow," said the Grandmother gratefully. She returned, saying to her sister and daughter, "Yow declares that he does not intend to put the serpent into the stew. He says——" but her sister and her daughter did not hear her.

"I have every intention of doing so!" declared Aunt Topaz. "Mr. Oxted says that Mrs. Oxted says that she finds it most beneficial. She says that he says I mean he says that she says——"

"Oh, for goodness *sake*, Anty!" said Rachel.

"What can this be?" asked the Grandmother, diverted from the serpent.

"I am going to sleep on this verandah tonight," said Aunt Topaz. "It will be most delightful. Mrs. Oxted sleeps on their summer cottage verandah all summer. She sleeps like a top. I shall sleep like a top too. I shall sleep on this little couch. It will be quite comfortable and it will be very invigorating."

"Yes, and you will be going around with one of your sniffly colds for the rest of the summer. *I* know," said Rachel, "and breakfasts in bed and the wash full of those pocket-handkerchiefs of yours."

"Now, love," said the Grandmother mildly, "let Aunty do what she likes. Let her try it for one night. I'm sure if I were young I should enjoy it."

"Young!" said Rachel, and she looked at the shining spacious sea, and the sky, and at the fringe of the dark bright forest. *If I had been here when I was young. If I had come here before I was an elderly woman looking after two older women, and my brother, and my sister's child—— all this beauty. If I had married Tom Shaw, or Mr. Calverley when he asked me, I might have been a married woman and important like my sisters-in-law—— but I could never have married Tom Shaw or anyone else. Only this life that I lead is tolerable to me. I could not endure to be other than I am. Oh, what a beautiful beautiful morning!*"

There was within Rachel a virgin well into which beauty silently seeped. She could receive the beauty of the morning without speaking. She did not have to transmute this beauty into conversation. So, now, she did not need to say to her mother "Look, the smooth bark of the arbutus tree is like copper in the sunshine, isn't it? See how the draped branches of the cedars wave seriously! Listen to 'the innumerable laughter of the sea'!" But she turned to her mother, content, and then cried in her anxious way, "Mother, what *are* you doing! Come Anty, let us move Mother's chair out of the sun!"

When the evening came, Aunty's plans for the night caused so much confusion that no one could sit upon the verandah couch without being asked, several times, to get up. Even the mild Grandmother felt that the experiment demanded too much fuss.

"I shall take my walking-stick," declared Aunty, pounding in and out with her busy tread.

"Whatever for?" asked Rachel.

"Well, I might want to walk down the steps in the night. And I shall take my umbrella and my parasol that belonged to Elijah's wife."

"Both of them, love?" asked the Grandmother.

"Yes, both of them. In Case. Because it might rain in on me, or in the morning the sun might prevent my sleeping. And, you see, I shall take a glass of milk."

"That will attract slugs," said Rachel.

The slugs of Benbow Island are large and gross. They appear to be inert, but are really very mobile; they cover long distances at night and may be found in the morning glued to the edges of containers of food. They are very intelligent, although they do not look it.

"Slugs! Oh. Then I shall take some biscuits and a little bit of chocolate instead," Aunty announced.

Rachel did not say "That will attract mice," although she felt that it should be said.

"I shall take my quilt and Grandfather's shawl," continued Aunty, plumping up her pillow. "And I shall take a hat."

"A hat! Whatever for?" enquired Rachel.

"Because I should like to have my hat with me. In Case. I might wish to sit up during the night, and then it would be nice to have my hat on," said Aunt Topaz.

"Anything else?" asked Rachel.

Night drew on, and the coal oil lamp was lighted. Yow, the protector, had gone to bed in his outside room. Night finally declared itself, dark and moonless. The lamp shone reflected in the jet-black windows. This was the time when the three women felt within themselves a turning towards sleep. The Grandmother was settled by Rachel; Rachel settled herself, and Aunt Topaz at last closed the door on the warm small room, instinct with habitation, and went out into the uncharted dark. She was excited.

After some stumbling, and some rearrangement on the floor of her equipment, she turned back her neatly made bed, got in, and pulled the bedclothes up to her chin. She looked up into the dark. "This is most delightful," she announced to herself.

She lay for some time looking into the darkness which did not become less opaque. Objects did not emerge from this darkness. Sometimes she turned and regarded a patch of starred sky which the slope of the verandah roof disclosed. All was very still, except for the small continuous sound of ocean upon the rocks. There had been a wind earlier in the day. The wind had died, but a slight wash of the salt sea remained, and with the wash against the shore only a small continuing sound, which grew more faint. The usual commotion and breeze caused by Aunt Topaz in the business of living had ceased abruptly with getting into bed and pulling up the bedclothes. She would have liked to cough, for something to do, but the austere solitude of the night forbade her. Her own stillness and the dark cosmic and planetary silence outside the cabin really disturbed and deprived Aunty a good deal, but she determined to enjoy herself.

"This is indeed *most* delightful," she thought again, but she was restive, feeling a need of someone to express herself to. There was no one. Even the young men in the bay had long since sailed away. She lay awake. She was not afraid, but, with her genius for communication, she felt deeply the need of a listener, to whom she, Aunty, could explain how delightful everything all was. This became more needful as she continued to lie awake. But there were no human ears at hand to oblige her; so she conversed with herself, within, or fell silent, pinioned in the bedclothes.

There are on Benbow Island many deer of small and medium size. These beautiful bucks and does—with their elegant heads, their poetic and nonsensical eyes, their delicate feet and their fine russet or beige rumps—together with their pretty dappled children inhabit the forest where they stray safely, because there are no predatory beasts indigenous to Benbow Island. The only predatory beast is man, occasional man, and the deer are reasonably safe from man except for a few months in the year. Knowing and suspecting man, the deer stray in the forest in the day-time, but when night comes they emerge from the woods, and enjoy cropping tender shoots in the grass that often surrounds the small houses where men seem to keep themselves at night; and, if possible, the deer enter men's enclosed vegetable gardens and eat up their green peas, and sometimes get shot out of season for doing this.

Around Aunt Topaz's nephews' cottage, which was in solitude, there were no green peas, but there was some good lush grass. The deer knew this, and because they were as conversant with the dark as with the day, they came out by night one by one, to the number of three or four, and cropped this good grass undisturbed, but Aunt Topaz did not know this. She soon heard an alien sound.

For there were now, near her, sounds as of small careful footsteps, a little movement, a little rustling. Aunty raised herself cautiously on her elbow and peered. She could see nothing, nothing. These small sounds came from in front of the cottage, and from either end of the verandah. They were closing in. Crop, crop, crop. Rustle, chump, and a nipping of grasses. "Dear me," thought Aunty, "it sounds like a very little cow! But there are no cows. Or a sheep! Certainly it sounds like a grass-eating animal. Could it be a deer? Or an elk? Or a moose? Or *could* it be a bison? Is it dangerous if surprised? However, since it seems to be a vegetarian it is unlikely to attack me." She began nevertheless to feel nervous. The sounds ceased. They began again. Aunty strained her eyes this way and that into the unrevealing night.

In the woods, so near the cottage, owls began to cry. Hoo-oo-oo, came the sweet quavering cry. Hoo-oo-oo, came the answer ort of the forest. "Owls," thought Aunt Topaz, "I do believe! I hope indeed that they will not think of pecking out my eyes!—— And if owls, then mice, and what else—rats, perhaps, and weasels. This is, when all is said and done, a very wild country, and only newly inhabited. Truly the New World. Oh there's the owl again!" She began to wish that she had never met Mr. Oxted, and as the unexplained unexplainable rustlings continued near the verandah, she wanted to gather up her bedclothes and go in from the unknown and elemental to the comfortable familiarity of the cabin. She was wide awake, and her usually impercipient senses were alert. But she was too proud to get up and go inside.

A great shooting star tore red across the patch of silent sky and went out. Aunty felt elated, and then subdued. "And to think that Rachel is sleeping, and Annie too!" she reflected, bitterly.

"If I thought about Father, perhaps I could go to sleep," she decided, and reverted easily to her life's habit of youngest daughter. She saw at once his noble bearded head. "What a fine beard! You never see a beard like that now. How queer those nine young men would have looked today swimming about with beards on! Very odd. Very much in the way. There must be some reason for it, I suppose." She now indulged her favorite habit of enumeration. "Let me see, beards, beginning with Father. And then Uncle Montague. And Uncle Edward. And Sam Rathbone—all long and well-combed except Uncle Edward's, a very unpleasant beard. And *not* Matthew Arnold—side-whiskers when we knew him, very peculiar. And all my brothers, little pointed ones—the decline of the beard, I suppose. Mrs. Porter's husband hadn't got a beard, but then he was a very unprincipled man. And, oh, William Sandbach—the most *beautiful* beard!" She tried to evoke tenderness at the thought of Mr. Sandbach and his beard, his benign, deceiving, heartless, hypocritical beard. But no, her love for him was long dead. She who had wept so much could not now evoke even a spurious sigh. "How could he have made me so unhappy?" she asked herself with surprise. A dreadful cry grated and rent the night. Aunt Topaz stiffened and her eyes started. She did not know that a blue heron was protesting as it awoke, and was now beating its great wings slowly against the adjacent air. She had never heard of a blue heron. The harsh and frightful cry was repeated near at hand. "That is not human!" thought Aunty trembling, and, of course, it was not. What Aunty meant was that it was hellish, which it was. All her bearded company had flitted, like the lot of silly shadows that they were. They had never been. The only reality was the dark and preposterous night. "If I turn over," thought Aunt Topaz unhappily, seeking refuge in a phrase, "I shall sleep like a top."

The owls had ceased their whistling, the deer had moved slowly on, and with the passing of time even the slight sound of the sea against the rocks was stilled. Aunt Topaz turned over, and it was when she began to pull the flannelette sheet about her ears that she heard the voice.

A voice? Voices? Sweet, high, clear, and very faint. A dropping cadence of semitones. A foreign tongue? A sound never heard before, followed by a light sigh, a groan. Aunty listened with her whole being. Again the sweet descending unmeaning cry, followed by a sigh, a groan. It came from the shore. No, it came from the ravine. No, it was nearer than that. It was farther away. In the dark was no proportion, no guide. Whence did it come? From the ravine? Again! Is it a voice, is it a cry, or is it music. Is it a flute? Yes, it is a flute. "Oh, My God!" thought Aunty, and cowered in the dark, remembering.

(*Yes, said Mrs. Porter when she had finished reading to her young pupils sitting safely about her beside the fire, now, girls, you under-*

stand where the word Panic comes from. The Greeks, you see, believed that whoever should hear the fluting of the pagan god Pan was in danger of a revelation which would turn him mad, and whoever should see Pan—who was not even a human type of god, if I may say so, but resembled also a goat—might die from the experience. How much more fortunate are we than the Greeks—we who have the benefits of the Christian religion, that we do not suffer from these and other unsatisfactory superstitions!

But, Mrs. Porter, asked Eliza Pinder and Topaz Edgeworth, both speaking together, and only half convinced, wasn't there really a god Pan in those days? The Greeks were quite sure of it!

No, certainly not, replied Mrs. Porter turning her fine eyes upon them, except——well——it may be possible——that before they had the benefit of the Christian religion, when their world of rocks and trees was so new——and in its natural state——who can say ——no, we cannot say——why, even Homer——Benbow Island is as new as Greece ever was, and newer, newer, much newer.) Again the descending notes of the flute, and a groan, dropping into the night.

Inside the white satin body of Topaz—satin-white until the day of her death—there opened a dark unknown flower of fear. Slowly it opened, and through the orifice of this flower fear poured into the darkness. Her whole body dissolved listening into fear which flowed into the terrible enclosing night. She, all alone, became only a frightened part of the listening elements.

The high sweet sound continued again into a groan. She could not tell whether the fluting came now at regular intervals. It came. It came. It was light but clear, and stronger than the silence into which it fell. "Oh God Our Help. Oh God Our Help," said a residuum of Topaz blindly. She could not remember anything more to say. But the sweet sound came again, undefeated and unperturbed by the Holy Name. *Then I must go or I am lost, this is Panic, I have heard it, now, at any moment, I shall see him close in the darkness, I shall feel his breath!* And she sprang up, not knowing what she did, and seized soft quilt and Grandfather's shawl, and stumbling, trailing, upsetting, she found the door. She wrenched the door open and rushed in. She shut the door and locked it. How dark was the room.

"What on earth *are* you doing?" said Rachel crossly from the bedroom.

Topaz stood against the wall, breathing heavily, her quilt fallen about her. Directly she stood within this frail unlit shelter of walls, doors, windows, and humanity, even before she heard the comfortable crossness of Rachel's voice, Pan, so very near at hand, became impotent and withdrew into his own place. Her living family and all her bearded memories rushed about her in confusion.

Rachel lit a candle and, blinking from sleep, saw Topaz standing there, white and staring. "Were you frightened, Anty? What frightened you?" she asked curiously.

"I have a cold, I think," said Topaz, chattering. "I think I have a chill." She labored across the floor and cast herself upon her naked and deserted bed. She pulled the quilt over her.

Rachel got up and stood with the candle in her hand. "Would you like a bit of a rub?" she asked.

"Yes," said Topaz, with her eyes closed, and still shivering, "I would like a bit of a rub." She longed to feel the hard comfort of Rachel's capable hand upon her.

"What is it, love?" murmured the Grandmother, stirring distantly in sleep.

"Nothing, Mother, turn over, turn over."

Rachel bent over and rubbed and rubbed. She wondered amazedly "She isn't talking! She isn't saying a word! Why is she so quiet?" Her knowing capable hands swept up and down the flaccid white back and shoulders of her lively, voluble, silent aunt. Aunt Topaz felt their solace, mournfully.

"There then," said Rachel, and stood up. She looked down on Topaz who still lay without speaking. "She looks as though she were suffering," she thought.

"Anty," Rachel said at last, "why did you lock the door?"

But Topaz did not answer.

The wind having so long dropped, the ocean became at last still, and there was no movement at all in the waters of the bay. Long before dawn broke and there came the sounds of birds and of day, the faint regular musical rub of the boom log against the little wharf, wood against wood, wood against wood with the slow sway of the water, ceased its clear petulant cry, its chime, its rhythmical sighing.

THOMAS RADDALL

1903-

Thomas Head Raddall came to Nova Scotia from Kent at the age of ten and was educated at the Halifax Academy. When his father died in 1918, he left school and became a wireless operator with the Canadian merchant marine both on board ship and at various coast-guard stations on the eastern seaboard. From 1922 to 1938 he was employed in the office of a Nova Scotia paper mill. On the publication of a number of his short stories in *Blackwood's Magazine* and in various Canadian and American periodicals, he retired in order to devote himself entirely to writing. His first of several collections of short stories, *The Pied Piper of Dipper Creek* (1939), was published with a eulogistic introduction by John Buchan, who recognized in Raddall a spirited writer of historical tales who combined romance and realism with something of the same verve as he himself had done. Other collections of stories, first published in such magazines as *Maclean's*, the *Saturday Evening Post*, and *Colliers*, are *Tambour and Other Stories* (1945), *The Wedding Gift and Other Stories* (1947), and *A Muster of Arms and Other Stories* (1954). *At the Tides Turn,* a selection of Raddall's best tales was added to the New Canadian Library in 1959, with an introduction by Allen Bevan.

Even more interesting to the student of Nova Scotian history than the short stories is the series of well-researched and vividly written romances, which includes *His Majesty's Yankees* (1942), based in part on historian J. B. Brebner's *The Neutral*

Yankees of Nova Scotia and on the diaries of Simeon Perkins; *Roger Sudden* (1944), a tale of the Seven Years' War and the seige of Louisbourg; *Pride's Fancy* (1946), a romance of privateers in the West Indies; and *The Governor's Lady* (1960), the story of an aristocratic Loyalist family in the days of the American War of Independence.

Novels of contemporary life include *The Nymph and the Lamp* (1950), a book based on Raddall's experiences as a wireless operator at Cape Sable and, along with *His Majesty's Yankees*, perhaps Raddall's finest achievement; *Tidefall* (1953); and *Wings of the Night* (1956). Raddall is also the author of a brilliantly written history of Nova Scotia's capital, *Halifax: Warden of the North* (1948, revised and enlarged 1965).

Raddall is a popular and immensely successful commercial writer, but he has achieved his success without compromising the rigorous standards of good writing and artistic faithfulness. The story printed here is a somewhat rare example of the critical and ironic spirit taking over from the romantic and is actually a fictionalized exposure of one of the great impostors of all time, George Stanfield Belaney (1888-1938), better known as "Grey Owl" (Wa-sha-quon-asin). Belaney, though born in Hastings, England, posed as an Indian, became a trapper and guide, lived among the Ojibwa Indians, married and was left by an Indian woman, served in the first world war, returned to Canada with an English wife, deserted her and lived with an Ojibwa woman, became a ranger and an authority on conservation, and a popular writer of nature books dealing with the Indian and the wild animal life of the north and west. He was a nature writer of considerable ability. (For an appreciation of his work see Carl F. Klinck, *et al.*, *Literary History of Canada*, pp. 376-378.) Two interesting biographies of Belaney are H. Cory, *Grey Owl and the Beaver* (1935) and Lovat Dickson, *Half-breed: the Story of Grey Owl* (1939).

BALD EAGLE

I have seen the ghost of Selby Higgins. I am quite sure, because it wore the shape of his totem and hovered high in the blue over the little cluster of Micmac hovels at Eel River, where he made his first astounding metamorphosis. It is a lovely place. The Eel River writhes down to the Fundy tide through a deep rift in the wooded ridge we call South Mountain, and from the red dust of the mountain road you look down upon grey shingled roofs of the Indian village half hidden in trees beside the stream.

Downstream, where the small rushing river pours itself over the half-tide flats, a pair of ospreys hover and flash, white under parts gleaming as they fish in the shallows, and the lone bald eagle waits to pounce and rob them as they bring the catch towards their untidy stick nest in a dead tree above the settlement. That is the bald eagle's habit, of course. He eats offal, too, when he can find it.

Sage American writers have pointed out these weaknesses in their national bird and suggested the turkey for better choice, a bird of unblemished character, nationally venerated, the foremost feature of Thanksgiving Day. I fancy the early Americans were carried away by the noble appearance, for the bald eagle is not really bald, and his white head and neck and tail, his dark brown, almost black body, his capable claws, his strong beak and fierce uncompromising eye all make a very fine picture.

Undoubtedly that picture carried Selby Higgins away in his choice of a totem. But in no other way did Selby imitate the feathered bandit of Eel River. Selby never stole a thing in his life, and if he practised to deceive it was a charming deception, a rather magnificent deception, and the public had good value for its money.

He was eighteen when he first came to Canada, a tall, thin youngster with eager dark eyes, a high nose and a cockney accent that rang in the ear like a peal of Bow bells. He wore shoddy tweeds, badly wrinkled, and carried a battered old portmanteau. He had twenty-five shillings in his pocket. He was an orphan, brought up by a maternal aunt and educated in the London County Council schools.

From the age of ten his chosen reading had been the literature of the penny shockers, tales of the Wild West for choice; and one evening in 1906 he had found himself in Steinway Hall, sitting rapt, while a handsome red Indian woman recited poems that breathed the air of the Canadian woods.

Her white name was Pauline Johnson, but she had another and better, a Mohawk name, long and sonorous and beautiful—Tekahionwake—and she wore fringed garments of deerskin and a necklace of bear claws, with a little cluster of eagle feathers drooping from a shining mass of dark hair. The recital was under distinguished patronage, but Pauline Johnson needed none as far as the boy in the back row was concerned.

He came away from the hall filled with visions of a savage and delightful life in the woods beyond the sea, and three years later the aunt—in desperation I suppose—purchased a steerage passage to Halifax and let him go.

Upon arrival in Nova Scotia he did not come down the gangway clutching a shotgun to fend off the savages, as the proverbial English greenhorn is supposed to do; but he confessed long afterwards that he fully expected to see the Northwest Mounted Police, horses and all, drawn up on the wharf, and was disappointed to find the capital of Nova Scotia in 1909 a small, dusty, rather shabby version of London, with noisy one-story trams careering up and down the hilly streets, and bobbies wearing what he termed "American" uniforms.

He told the immigration people he was going to "hunt and trap" —preferably with an Indian partner. Nowadays that would cause a raising of official eyebrows, but immigration in 1909 was a simple affair. They looked at his vaccination certificate and directed him to the Green Market, where he would find the only Indians they knew.

In those remote days Halifax had no public market of echoing brick and glass. Country folk drove their wagons into the business district of a Saturday morning and displayed their wares along the sidewalk outside the post office. There, amongst carrots and cabbages and fresh string beans, Selby Higgins found a group of stolid brown people selling baskets and little birchbark canoes, and toy bows and arrows and souvenirs of that sort. They were dressed like anybody else in the Green Market. One or two of the older men wore their hair in a pair of small pigtails.

Selby stared at them for a long time. His heart sank. These? The tramp over hot sidewalks from the old Deepwater Terminal had made his feet ache. The portmanteau dragged his left hand. A throng of vegetable-shopping housewives jostled him unmercifully. The sidewalk was narrow and the country people and their wares occupied most of it. A stream of Saturday morning traffic, horse and foot, poured up from the Dartmouth ferry past the corner. Another stream surged along Hollis Street. Business men fought their way in and out of the post office through a scrum of hucksters and baskets. The air was full of the price of vegetables and eggs and the clamor of live chickens, ducks and geese. The fun and flavor went out of the Green Market during the first German war, when the city erected a market building under the shoulder of Citadel Hill and compelled the truck farmers to display their goods inside.

Selby fixed his dark eye on one of the older Indians, one of the pigtailed men. He wondered how to begin. The penny literature had insisted on a sonorous "How!" with a schoolboy gesture of the right arm. That seemed absurd in this miniature Covent Garden.

Selby was no fool. He knew this was not the Wild West. But he had only twenty-five shillings and the railway fare to the West was something fabulous in dollars. Somewhere outside this dusty, thirsty city lay a green forest, with wild animals to be had for the hunting. Everyone on the boat had assured him of that, and the immigration officials confirmed it. It was their indifference that astonished him. They had said there was no money in trapping these days, young fella, and he'd better hunt about the city for a job. In these glum Micmacs of the market place Selby Higgins saw his sole hope of the dream life.

He bought a toy canoe for a start. The Indian examined his shilling with care, bit it, stowed it away in a trouser pocket, and stared once more over the passing heads at the soldier on the South Africa monument. Selby was discouraged. But after the noon gun of the Citadel sounded its thunderclap over the roofs there was a lull, the throng of shoppers melted into the higher streets, the hucksters drifted behind the post office where their wagons were parked wheel to wheel, and pulled out sandwiches and bottles of cold tea. There Selby found his Micmac and a fat old squaw eating corned beef and bread in the shade of the building. They had forgotten him but he waved the toy as a talisman and squatted beside them with his back to the wall.

The talk was slow and devious. They saw that he was poor like themselves, though he showed them a handful of silver to prove his independence. They offered him bread and meat, which he ate. At the afternoon's end he crossed the harbor on the Dartmouth ferry and vanished into the woods with them.

They had a shack beside one of the lakes behind Dartmouth town, with two or three other families of their people in similar dwellings, and lived in a state of comfortable uncleanliness, making baskets of maple splints and souvenirs of birchbark and beads and dyed porcupine quills for the Halifax market. They caught trout in the lake and earned a dollar or two when city men wanted guides for fishing or hunting. They set snares for rabbits and traps for wildcats and bears, on which the county paid a bounty. The women did a lot of begging at Dartmouth's back doors.

It was not the life Selby wanted but it gave him a taste of the woods and showed him the path to better things. That path was the highway which ran by the Shubenacadie valley to the other side of the province. The Micmacs, a people with great taste for wandering, do not care for reservations like their brethren to the west. Here and there are considerable communities but for the most part they live in small groups on the edge of country towns, and there is a perpetual visiting back and forth—to the despair of the Department of Indian Affairs, which likes to keep track of its wards.

Often you will see a man and woman trudging the highroad burdened with baskets for sale in the next town. And at county exhibitions and affairs of that sort there is sure to be a family, sprung from nowhere, squatting in a bark wigwam somewhere on the grounds, making and selling baskets and the rest, and wearing a quaint dress modeled from Western moving pictures, with bonnets of tall feathers such as no Micmac ever wore except in heraldry.

From the movies, too, they have evolved a "war dance" with much shuffling and weird cries. They are not to be blamed. White folk expect it and the Indian gives it to them—and passes the hat.

In these theatricals Selby Higgins joined with gusto. He was naturally dark, with prominent cheekbones and coarse black hair. A few months of wandering amongst his chosen people gave his sallow cheeks a convincing swarthiness. He passed readily for a Micmac at the fairs. Amongst themselves they spoke their ancient tongue and he picked it up quickly, and from the older ones a good deal of Indian legend, which afterward he made famous. And he changed his English, substituting the grunting intonation of the Micmacs for his old cockney twang. All this with much pains.

He learned to trap mink and otter and the forbidden beaver, and how to spear salmon under a sawmill dam at night when the fish wardens were asleep, and he shot moose and caribou in and out of season in the blithe Indian fashion. Caribou were then dwindling to the vanishing point in Nova Scotia. Selby Higgins always claimed, with magnificent remorse, to be the man who killed the last caribou in the province. Perhaps it was true—caribou were last seen on the mainland in 1912, although they hung on in Cape Breton island a few more years—but true or not it was one of the distinctions which in later years made Selby Higgins what he was.

He loved this gipsy life, the picking up and going wherever he took the notion, his scant possessions slung to his back in a corded gunny sack, the winding road that played hide-and-seek with the endless coast, the nights in friendly barns or over a smolder of twigs in the edge of the woods.

Country folk never grudged food or lodging to a wanderer; but he relied chiefly on the little Indian villages, often no more than a trio of ramshackle huts beside a stream, with a white settlement in the offing. It was possible in most parts to plan the journey in stages from one settlement to another, sleeping in an old blanket by the stove like any other guest of the blood. He stayed a day or a month as he chose, and made himself useful in the way of firewood, and joined them in their hunting and fishing, and made axe handles, canoe paddles, lobster traps and other popular products of the peculiar Micmac crooked-knife.

He was a supersalesman of these things. There was none of the usual gentle rap on the door, the staring off into space, the murmured "Baskit, leddy?" Selby gave a postman's knock, looked the householder engagingly in the eye and told the virtues of his wares in a voice whose possibilities he was beginning to realize, a deep and melodious voice as different from the husky Micmac treble as a bass viol from a half-hearted flute.

He was tall and young, he was lean as a lance, with dark flashing eyes, and thick black hair hung straight to his shoulders under a wide-brimmed black felt hat. He wore moccasins always, and corduroy trousers and a red flannel shirt. Townsmen said of his departing back, "Looks superior to the others. Must be a pure blood. A chief, who knows, if he had his rights?" Women wondered if he could sing, and bought baskets they did not want and paddles their husbands would never use, and paid outrageous prices without a haggle.

Not once in those days did Selby Higgins say he was an Indian. People looked at him and his wares and jumped to the obvious conclusion. One might almost say the deception was thrust upon him, but there is no denying he played up to it and revelled in it.

The ease with which he had slipped into an Indian skin in the course of two or three years delighted him. As he told me long afterward, white people are easily deceived anyhow. The truth is that they know nothing of Indians. After three centuries of white contact the Micmac remains as aloof and mysterious as ever. He slips along the busy street, as quiet, as anonymous as a shadow, and then he is swallowed up in the woodland that touches the skirt of every Nova Scotia town.

You might live within a mile of his hovel for a year without suspecting his existence, if it were not for the occasional soft knock on the door and the reedy voice intoning "Baskit? Axe hundle?"—or in the berry season, "Br'arb'ry? Ras'b'ry? Blueb'ry?"

Selby never fooled an Indian for a minute, though some considered him a half-breed. But he fooled white people without effort, because they wanted to be fooled, because in his person he dramatized for them the Indian of the storybooks.

For five years he roamed the province. The aunt in England never heard from him and gave him up for dead. In a sense he was. But Selby the Englishman returned to life for a time. In the summer of 1914 the first German war sent its echoes across the Atlantic. He was at Eel River then, a transient guest of the Indians. He walked down to the town and enlisted in the Canadian army under his own name.

Of his war service nobody knows much. Selby preferred to cloak it in the mystery that was part of him. When he became famous the public invented legends which he did not trouble to deny; there were tales of sparkling valor, of wounded officers—preferably colonels—rescued under fire, of singlehanded captures of machine-gun nests. It was devoutly believed that he had been the crack sniper of the Canadian Corps, with an incredible number of notches cut in the stock of a special Ross .303.

All that is definite is that he went overseas with the first Canadian contingent in 1914 and returned unwounded in 1919. That a private of infantry could have survived four years of the Western Front without a scratch is doubtful, though not impossible. The inference is that he spent much of the time somewhere else. As for the sniper legend, Selby Higgins was a fair shot, no more; no better or worse than half a million others who passed through the ranks of the Canadian Corps.

Probably he saw service in the trenches, but his lungs were shaky even then. I know he was ill for a time, and I suspect that he spent a large part of those four years in one of the Canadian reserve camps —in England, the land of his birth. In after years he attributed his cough to "a touch of gas on active service," with a little smile of apology for mentioning his sacrifice for king and country, and female interviewers always devoted a lyric paragraph to the incident. But it was tuberculosis, the curse of Micmac hospitality, acquired in stuffy winter hovels from Cape Sable to Cape North in those years before the war.

It would be interesting to know all he did in England during that time. He made no attempt to hunt up his aunt. It was his fancy to call himself an Indian when talking to English people, and he regaled them with tales of the woods and streams, and the Micmac legends with which his mind was stored; and it must have been then that he conceived the postwar career which made him a figure in the world. Those people hung on his every word, fascinated with his keen dark face and the brown tragic eyes, bemused by the slow rich voice.

He had a gift for words. He improved it with much reading of poetry. When he returned to Canada in 1919, a slim dark man in faded khaki and polished ammunition boots, he could recite Shakespeare, Keats, Browning, and Wordsworth by the hour. And so the great idea which began as a humble seedling in Steinway Hall in 1906 now burst into flower at last.

He went about it quietly, with imagination and enormous patience. His discharge gratuity bought a plot of timberland on the high flank of the South Mountain above Eel River, and there he built a cabin of peeled pine logs overlooking the stream and the Indian huts like specks beside it. You could see it from the motor road on the other side, a small yellow cube against the green woods, the color changing slowly to grey with the weathering of the logs.

It was a perfect setting for him, withdrawn like himself but at the same time visible, a challenge to human curiosity. The time came when a curious world literally beat a path to that far high door. He trapped and tamed a bear cub, a porcupine that would come at his whistle and nibble slices of apple from his hand, a skunk—skillfully disarmed—which never failed to send lady visitors into nervous ecstasies. He made for himself a shirt of buckskin and close-fitting trousers of the same, with dangling points of leather along the seams

from ankle to thigh and from shoulder to wrist. He made neat moccasins of moose hide and decorated them tastefully with colored
beads. He made a leather bag to sling on his back, ornamented with
a bright design in dyed porcupine quills. He let his hair grow long
once more, parted it carefully in the middle and gathered it into two
braids, tied with narrow red ribbon. Finally he shot a bald eagle and
stuck one of the stiff white tail feathers at the back of his head.

To the close-cropped, store clothed Micmacs of Eel River he was
an utter stranger. He had been a passing guest in 1914, part of the
eternal procession of Indian tramps, and five long years had gone by.
Those who remembered him at all remembered him vaguely. They
gave him a queer name—Esaak—which means literally The Half
Man. Perhaps they meant half-breed, perhaps half-wit, although they
have a different word for that.

They became used to the sight of Esaak walking past their shacks
to the town in this eye-filling costume. Visitors stared. But he looked
so tall and stern, and carried himself with such dignity, that nobody
dared to laugh. He spoke very little to his Micmac brethren, and
then always in their own tongue, looking down upon them kindly
but mysteriously like an incarnation of Gluskap, the whimsical god
of the olden time.

To white folk he talked even less, but let it be known that his
name was Bald Eagle. This was just as strange as his costume, for the
Micmacs dropped such fancy names generations ago. But Bald Eagle
thrived on astonishment.

In summer he left his cabin and small menagerie in the care of an
Indian boy and travelled the highways, timing his arrival in every
town with the skill of a born stage manager—always in the late afternoon of a fine day, when the day's work neared its end and the
townsfolk began to think of tea and evening and the things of the
spirit. At first they thought he was advertising something, but his
lofty silence chilled the thought of anything so crass. Who was he?
"Bald Eagle," he said, and passed on.

It was not long before he began to appear in the country newspapers, and then in the country-correspondent columns of the Halifax dailies.

"Bald Eagle, the colorful Micmac Indian, passed through town
today."

"Bald Eagle, the Micmac chief, was an overnight guest of the Rev.
Harry Corum at the parsonage."

"The Thursday evening meeting of the Young People's Society was addressed on 'The Tragedy of the Beaver' by Bald Eagle, the well-known Indian philosopher, who is a guest of Mr. and Mrs. Fairchild."

So it went. Bald Eagle was accepted at his face value, which was considerable. Nobody asked why he did not call himself Joe Something-or-other like the rest of the Micmacs. And nobody questioned the "chief"—for Micmac "chiefs" are as common in the Maritime Provinces as colonels in Kentucky. By 1925, when he was thirty-four, Bald Eagle had become an accepted fact in a hundred white communities. And he was an honored guest wherever he went. No more the barns and the roadside clearings, never again the borrowed blanket on the shanty floor!

For hospitality he gave entertainment of the finest sort. Visitors flocked to that fortunate home which Bald Eagle honored with his presence. In the evening in the crowded parlor, where his lean dark face and figure held all eyes and his picturesque garments filled the air with a scent of strange leather, he held forth on the life of the forest, the old entrancing myths, the mournful saga of the red man's decline and fall. For variation he recited poetry in his wonderful voice—Keats, Shakespeare, and the rest—and then, always under pressure and with a grave modesty, "a little bit of my own rhyming."

On this careful foundation his fame spread like the shade of a maple in the easy open of a hillside pasture. The legends began to grow about him—the legends which he always dismissed with a shrug and a solemn smile.

In 1926 Kirby Eddy made that superb photograph of him, head and shoulders, the face all strong lights and shadows, the tip of the eagle feather catching the light, which won the Grand Prize at Montreal's Exhibition of Art Photography. The newspapers made prints of it, and in October of that year a Toronto paper published beside it the first of his poems. It was the haunting *Lament for Summer*, which begins:

On Blomidon behold the hunter's moon!
This night is pricked with frost, and crisp the leaf
Dies underfoot, and Kwemoo the mad loon
Disturbs the shadowed water with his grief
At summer's passing.

It was followed soon after by his *Hymn to the Sun of God,* and then *By the Waters of Pescawa.* Then a mentor appeared. As Pauline Johnson had her Watts-Dunton, so Bald Eagle received public homage from Eustace Parminter, and with it the homage of *littérateurs* over the English-speaking world.

Periodicals began to clamor for his verse, newspapers sent special reporters. The world began to climb the path from Eel River to his lonely cabin, armed with autograph album and camera. His log shack, his strange pets and not least himself, were made familiar to readers from Sheerness to Shanghai.

In the spring of 1927 appeared the first collection of his verse, *Autumn Leaves in Acadie,* followed six months later by *Footprints On the Trail,* which contained amongst many good things the tender *Gluskap's Farewell,* the *Ode to the Southwest Wind,* and the stirring *Warpath Song* which Siegfrid Tansley set to music and which was broadcast on the radio, and made into records, and finally ousted Mandalay from the programs of concert baritones.

Agents in London and New York attended to the business side of all this. From a hundred sources money trickled to form a fat stream pouring into his account. He cared nothing for it. With him the role was everything, the money less than the dust. He lived simply, as always. The simple life came naturally to him now, for he had ceased to be a white man in Indian dress; he *was* an Indian, he was Bald Eagle! But because his shack was now a shrine for literary tourists, the very simplicity of his life had a theatrical touch about it. In a box in the cabin he kept small sheets of birchbark on which, for favored visitors, he scribbled a line or two of his verse. This bark autography was characteristic. All he said and wrote and did had the sure touch of the supreme actor he was.

In 1928 he began the famous tours, using airplanes whenever possible, all over the continent. Reporters were quick to link his name with his chosen mode of travel. He covered Canada and the United States with speed and éclat.

He was a sensation even in California, where nothing under the eternal sun is strange. He recited in halls, in theaters, in great out-door stadiums with sound equipment blaring through the crowd. He intoned over the American broadcasting chains, with queer tinkling music and the beating of tom-toms for a background. He caused a traffic jam on Broadway merely by walking a hundred yards.

Wherever he found an Indian reservation he visited in state, with a scampering platoon of press photographers and newsreel men, and bestowed largess on his less fortunate brothers with a generosity that was real if rather public. But once, in the Oklahoma oilfields, he found Indians richer than himself and left in disgust.

Everywhere he wore the moccasins, the buckskins, the single dramatic feather, and carried his modest baggage on his back in the decorated knapsack. But he stayed at the best hotels—not for luxury as such but because he loved to stride soft-footed through those cathedral-like foyers and feel the stares of the world's elite. That was the eternal cockney in his soul, which he never quite suppressed.

And a spark of the lusty cockney humor glowed within him to the last. In October 1928, when he was at the height of his meteoric career, appeared the long narrative poem *The Legend of Kedooske*. The praise of the critics rose about it like a chorus of cicadas on a Canadian summer morning. One diligent soul discovered a lake of the name, hidden in the woods of Western Nova Scotia, and devout pilgrims visited the spot for years.

Nobody troubled to ask an Indian what it meant—and if they had he would have told them something quick and imaginative, for the Micmac is nothing if not a gentleman. When lady visitors went into raptures over *Kedooske*, behind Bald Eagle's impassive mask I fancied the cockney chuckle of Selby Higgins.

By this time he was signing himself *Wo-bu-lot-pa-jit*—"Big White Headed Hawk" which is the Micmac picture word for his totem, and his books were appearing in red-leather editions with the design of the Bald Eagle stamped in gold. By this time, too, some enthusiasts were calling him "the greatest Indian since Hiawatha," a phrase that originated with Eustace Parminter, who honestly believed it.

His London agent implored him to tour the British Isles. "I realize," he wrote, "that an ocean journey will seem distasteful to you who have lived always so close to the earth; but then you came over here for the war, and first-class passage on the *Mauretania* (say) is not to be compared with a slow convoy passage in a crowded troopship. You must come. People here will flock to hear you."

His English publishers added their entreaties. It must have amused their client. Nothing was more fixed in Selby's mind than the intention to re-visit the land of his birth—in his chosen time. That haunting memory of Pauline Johnson in Steinway Hall was as fresh as ever. He saw himself on the stage of the Albert Hall—so very much

bigger and better than the Steinway—holding a London audience
spellbound as that strange and beautiful Mohawk half-blood had
held them more than twenty years before. He saw it as the climax
of his career, the satisfying of a lifelong desire. All that followed
would be tasteless. So he put off the fulfillment as long as possible.
In this he was abetted by the New York agent, who frankly considered the British trip a waste of time and money.

"You want to keep me in American circulation like a silver dollar," said Bald Eagle scornfully.

The agent squirmed a little. He had come from his lair in New
York, had even climbed this uncomfortable hill in the rain, to persuade the poet into a winter tour of the Southern States. He was a
hard-boiled man with a vast experience of public entertainers. He
had handled Indians before—after all, the stunt was as old as America—and he remembered them mostly as brown humbugs with a
vast greed for cash, which they spent on whisky and blond young
women. Bald Eagle's indifference to all these things puzzled him. It
was an admirable pose, of course, but it could be carried too far. It
made Bald Eagle extraordinarily difficult to handle.

"Look here," urged the man from New York. "The U.S. has
never been so prosperous. Some say it's permanent but that's bunk!
It's a boom, and now's the time to cash in, if you've got something
the public wants. Of course, I know you don't like to talk about
money."

"I have more money now than I can possibly use," returned the
deep calm voice. "And I must have a certain amount of leisure and
solitude for writing. On tour I am yours, I do what you say. Here"—
he swept his long brown hand to include the interior of moss-chinked
logs, the simple pine bookcase and table, the unpainted birch chairs,
the fireplace deep in ashes, the bare plank floor, the bearskins on the
wall, the bed of brushwood carelessly heaped in a corner with a pair
of Hudson's Bay blankets—"here I am me, Bald Eagle!" He
thumped himself on the chest for emphasis. The gesture made him
cough.

The agent regarded him curiously. "That's a nasty hack you've
got, Bald Eagle."

Of sheer habit the gentle, beautiful smile spread over the aquiline
face, the tragic glow appeared in the dark eyes. "A little touch of
gas," Bald Eagle said, "that I got in the last war."

"Spending your winters in this shack don't do it any good,"

warned the agent bluntly. He knew a lunger when he saw one. All his Indians had been lungers except the one who died of delirium tremens in Wichita.

"Nevertheless, here I spend this winter, my friend. In the spring— in the spring I shall go to London. It is time I went to London."

And in the spring he went to London. It was the spring of 1929, a momentous year in many ways, although Bald Eagle did not live to see its sequel, the great crash and the incidental ruin of the New York bank that held his fortune.

He had written very little in that lonely winter at Eel River. He must have been ill for weeks on end, lying on the brushwood in the corner like a sick animal, resigned and patient, a little curious, perhaps, about the outcome.

When he boarded the *Mauretania* in his famous fringed buckskins, the object of all eyes, Bald Eagle was erect as ever, with the same lithe spring in his step; but his face had shrunk against the high cheekbones and the dark eyes glistened deep in their sockets. His long lips clung like wet paper to the handsome false teeth, the two-hundred-dollar teeth acquired in San Francisco on his first tour. The gaunt ascetic look was no longer a pose. The mask had set. He was thirty-eight and looked a haggard fifty.

He traveled first class and held himself aloof. Fellow passengers often noticed him at the rail, staring forward, his hawk face outthrust as if to urge the great ship on. He was asked to take part in the usual ship concert, and refused, without giving any reason, although he gave a hundred dollars to the Seamen's Orphans' Fund.

At the dock he was met by the London agent and a covey of reporters and photographers, the beginning of a build-up for the London appearance, conducted with great skill. He called at the gate of Buckingham Palace, with photographers busy in the offing, and delivered a pair of beaded moccasins for the King and a volume of his poems for the Queen. He was photographed at the Horse Guards; in the Tower; feeding the Canadian bears at the Zoo; laying a wreath of maple leaves on the tomb of Pocahontas.

It irked him that his agent could not secure the Albert Hall. He went into a fit of un-Indian petulance which surprised that worthy man. But he got the Queen's Hall, off Regent Street, which as the agent pointed out was not to be despised, and secured patronage distinguished enough to satisfy his wildest dreams.

On the great night every seat was taken, with a mass of starched shirts and glittering evening dress in front where the subdued light fell. The body of the hall was almost in darkness, with a warm amber glow upon the stage where Bald Eagle stood tall and splendid in his deerskins.

The program included a dozen of Bald Eagle's poems, separated by some Indian transpositions by Lieurance, played by the most brilliant young pianist in London, with an interval for the singing of the *Warpath Song* by four handsome young men in white ties and tails. It was all a tremendous success, and when the four young men reached the swinging blood-tingling chorus of the *Warpath Song* the whole assembly joined in—a marked surprise to Bald Eagle, who had expected stiffness in a London audience.

Then, as the song ended and the hush fell, a voice cried from the middle of the hall. "That's 'im! That's my 'usband, Selby 'Iggins! I'd know 'im in a million!" It was a woman's voice and shrill, but no one could see until the lights came on suddenly and revealed her, a stout red-faced person standing in the aisle, a female of the costermonger species, the kind you see spangled with mother-of-pearl buttons on London holidays and entitled *A Pearly Queen* in the *Daily Mirror*.

She was flanked by a tall pimply youth with water-plastered black hair, and a plump girl who looked, in a fresher way, exactly like herself. Together they made a small phalanx in the aisle, facing the stage. Ushers bore down upon them from all sides amid a babel of well-bred astonishment. On the stage the male quartet, half way to their seats, turned and stared. The brilliant pianist goggled over his impeccable Bond Street shoulder. Only the distinguished patronage retained its self-command—consulting the program with an air of bright interest that was flawless.

There was a slight scuffle in the aisle and the voices of ushers were heard, low and urgent, and the woman insisting, "Married me durin' the war, 'e did, and went orf and left me with two children on me 'ands, and not so much as a soldier's farewell! And 'ere 'e is, makin' pots o' money, and me still scrubbin' me fingers to the bone! Callin' 'imself an Injian!"

It was seen that she flourished a scrap of newsprint, one of the numerous informal photographs taken of Bald Eagle's progress about London. It was one of those pictures which through some accident of light, of pose, of expression, cast a man back ten or twenty years.

As if drawn by a cord, all the heads now turned to the stage, where Bald Eagle was slowly rising from his chair. A lesser actor would have ignored her, or demanded that the ushers put her out. Bald Eagle strode to the front of the stage. Dignity clothed him like an armor. He was calm. He was superb. The rustle of his garments sent a little gust of aromatic leather to the people in the front seats. He flung up a fringed buckskin arm, and there was a great silence.

"Let the woman come," he said in his deep voice. "Let her speak to me."

The ushers stood back, and she came down the aisle tossing her head defiantly, but for all that frightened a little by her own boldness. She had the air of a woman who has started something and regrets it but is resolved to see the thing through. She kept muttering, "Got me pride, I 'ave," as she came. She smelled of beer.

At the front in the full light she halted, staring up at him, twitching the news picture in her fingers. Her clothes were not so much shabby as ill-chosen, and stuck rather than hung over a body that bulged in all the wrong places. She wore a rather good hat but you could see how common she was. She stood there, flustered but determined, and at a tremendous disadvantage from a theatrical point of view. With the height of the stage added to his own lean length Bald Eagle stood over her like a colossus.

"You want something?" he said.

She hesitated, and waved the fragment of paper uncertainly. "This 'ere—this is my 'usband, Selby 'Iggins. It says 'ere—" She saw his hand uplifted in that imperative gesture for silence.

"I am *Wo-bu-lot-pa-jit*, Bald Eagle"—in a serene voice that carried to the farthest seats. Then, kindly, "Look at me, madam. A man is more important than a photograph. You see me clearly now that you have come up here. Do you say I am anyone but Bald Eagle of the *Meeg-a-mahg* people?"

She stared for a long half minute, stared at the haggard brown face, the lined cheeks and brow, the strong sunwrinkles at the eye corners, the lips that clung as if by suction against the teeth, and the eyes, sunken but splendid, that stared back at her unwinking.

"I—I dunno," she faltered. "You don't look the same, some'ow. Summink about you frightens me, some'ow." She fluttered the paper again. "This 'ere—that's my 'usband, Selby 'Iggins. But you—you ain't 'im. Not you. You're a bloody Injian all right. I never saw you before. Don't understand it. I don't." She turned her face away from the glittering eyes, partly because it hurt her neck to look up so, and said to the people in the nearby seats, "There's summink bloody queer about all this," and began to cry. Those who looked up the aisle perceived that the son and daughter had fled. The ushers bore down once more.

"Gently, gently," Bald Eagle said. "This woman has a sorrow of some kind. There has been an unhappy mistake, I think."

She was led, weeping noisily, to the main exit. The front seats, with an audible crumple of shirt fronts, turned to watch her go.

In a moment Bald Eagle was filling the hall with his passionate *Prayer To The Great White Father*, and the incident was forgotten. It was not mentioned in the next day's papers. There were columns of praise for the Indian poet and his works.

It was never understood why Bald Eagle broke off so suddenly what was obviously destined to be a triumphal tour. The fact is that he spent nearly the whole night walking, bareheaded and alone, on Hampstead Heath, and the results were fatal. There was a period of silence and then it was announced abruptly that the great Red Indian poet was ill and returning to his native Canada. That was true, but not even the concerned London agent guessed how ill he was.

Bald Eagle boarded the steamer at Liverpool on his own moccasined feet, erect and with the famous knapsack slung on his back. He went at once to his cabin and there, with the cliffs of Holyhead sliding past the porthole, he collapsed. A steward found him lying on the floor. Thirty-six hours later Bald Eagle opened his eyes in the ship's hospital. In the old soldier slang he asked, "It's all up with me?"

" 'Fraid so," the ship's doctor said.

A silence. Then, "Bury me at sea."

"What about your relatives?"

"None."

"I must notify your friends."

"None."

It staggered the doctor. But it was the truth. Whom could Bald Eagle truly call "friend"? The agents, aware that a comfortable source of income had gone dry for ever? The public? People make pilgrimages to the tomb of poets, they do not weep at their funerals. The Micmacs? They had known him for a charlatan from the first. Fortunately they did not write to newspapers. No, better at sea, a decent exit from the world, with the big ship stopped for a time, the ship's company ranked at attention in the disciplined British way, and the captain reading the burial service. It would make good reading in the newspapers. He smiled at that, and he was smiling when he died.

It is given to few men to play on the world's stage with lines they write themselves, and these surely look upon the lines as their ultimate monument. Yet to Selby Higgins his poetry was no more than the eagle feather or the romantic cabin on the hillside or his decontaminated skunk.

Looking back, this is the most amazing thing about him—that man could be so blind. For *The Warpath Song, The Lament for Summer, By the Waters of Pescawa*—yes, even *The Legend of Kedooske* with its securely hidden ribaldry will live when Selby Higgins and his great deception have been forgotten or decently obscured by the passage of time.

There was a curious omen in the fate of his home at Eel River. At the news of his death his pets were turned loose into the forest. The door of his shack had only a simple wooden latch and was left to swing in the wind. The windows were shattered by mischievous boys from the settlement. Rain and snow came in. The inevitable rot began and flourished. Nothing was taken. The Indians held the place haunted.

When Jim Shaw, the farmer who is Indian agent at Eel River, walked up there out of curiosity a year or two ago the path had vanished, the clearing grown up in a thicket of scrub maple. The shack was a sagging ruin, the rotten floor covered with dead leaves and a litter of porcupine dung. In a corner he found a stained sheet of paper with a few scribbled lines, flung aside when the owner left for England—the last thing Bald Eagle wrote this side the Happy Hunting Grounds.

The words were phonetics of the Micmac tongue, inscribed to *Ap-che-nem-ka-wa—Death Everlasting*. So far as I know it was the only attempt Bald Eagle ever made at verse in the Indian speech. Translated, the fragment ran:

Gently bear my light bark, Mighty One,
Swiftest of rivers, Thou!
The night is cold. . . .

JOHN GLASSCO

1909-

John Glassco was born in Montreal, and at the age of eighteen, while still an undergraduate at McGill, he abandoned his courses and shipped on a freighter to Europe. After paying a visit of homage to George Moore in London, he joined the group of American literary exiles in Paris. He soon became a member of the group that included the novelists Robert McAlmon and Kay Boyle, the poet Robert Desnos, and the painter Hilaire Hiler. More than thirty-five years later his reminiscences of the twenties scene in Paris were completed from contemporary notes and published as *Memoirs of Montparnasse* (1970). Vividly written and very amusing sketches of literary and Bohemian figures including Gertrude Stein, James Joyce, and Glassco's fellow Canadian Morley Callaghan as well as many colorful hangers-on make the book what the American critic Malcolm Cowley has called the sharpest and most authentic picture of an international literary epoch.

It was not until middle age that John Glassco became known as a distinguished poet and man of letters in Canada. He has published three volumes of verse *The Deficit Made Flesh* (1958), *A Point of Sky* (1964), and *Selected Poems* (1971). He has also edited *The Poetry of French Canada in Translation* (1970). He has translated the *Journals* of Saint Denys Garneau and is at present working on a translation of Garneau's complete poems.

"A Season in Limbo" originally appeared in the *Tamarack Review* (1962) under the anagrammatic pseudonym of Silas N. Gooch.

A SEASON IN LIMBO

DIAMOND JUBILEE HOSPITAL, MONTREAL
March 15
Everybody is really very kind. But cases like mine—with no dramatic accompaniment of haemorrhage, extreme emaciation, tantrums, hysteria, or drug addiction—are so common here they aren't even interesting. This disaster is a novelty to no-one but myself.

How long am I in for? They're supposed to tell me in a day or so. That probably means in a week. Anyway, all the sentences here are indeterminate. The doctors differ, they can't say, they don't know: we must wait and see.

The other patients talk listlessly of their own cases in terms of years—as if 1955 were last month. I'm not going to listen to them. This is only my third day in this place which still seems like a kind of lazaretto.

"Don't do that, Mr Gooch! Don't cough in kleenex, please. It's too absorbent. Use the proper wipes provided by the hospital and put them *at once* into the paper bag by your bed. Remember, your sputum is highly infectious. You wouldn't want one of the nurses or orderlies or ward-maids to catch t.b., would you? Do try and bear this in mind." A flinty smile. "Think of *us*."

Canny Miss McClang. She is in charge of the whole floor, does the paper-work, keeps track of the drugs, harries the help, nags the nurses, sees that the meals are kept hot, the toilets kept clean, the linen changed, the new patients quickly reduced to impotence and desperation. She has the eye of a hawk, the energy of a machine, the aplomb of a professional golfer. Long ago she grasped the grand principle of hospital administration: see that the patient gives as little trouble as possible. For instance, she knows there is no real danger from my coughing in kleenex, and that everyone here does it all day long; but she is making her pounce while I am still groggy and biddable. She is a busy woman, saving herself time and effort in the foreseeable future.

And she's right: it's the only way to run a public hospital. And how easy when the patient is being treated free! He hasn't a leg to stand on. Not only is he at the psychological disadvantage of getting something for nothing, but there's nowhere else for him to go. It's as a punishment. All the same, I had a bit of luck: the orderly absolutely free treatment in a state hospital, I'm discovering the real aspect of socialized medicine from the patient's point of view: he's a charge, not a customer.

Disturbing too to have your clothes taken away and hidden in some unknown region five floors down. In pyjamas and dressing-gown you feel defenceless, infantile, forlorn, especially in the middle of the day: probably a childhood reminiscence of being sent to bed as a punishment. All the same, I had a bit of luck: the orderly somehow overlooked my trousers, which are now locked away safely in my bedside cupboard, instantly available.

And so this evening things are not so bad, the world is not absolutely shut out, a quiet flight is still possible. The fire-escape is only a few yards away. I could slip out and run through the streets of Montreal without being stopped by a policeman. . . .

But of course I am still technically at liberty. I can demand my clothes and walk out of here any time. In Ontario, I would be picked up by the police and put back here under guard or taken to jail. Good old Quebec, still on the honour system! The knowledge that you are at least *physically free* does wonders for the morale at a time like this, in this atmosphere which breeds a strange mood of terror and infantile protest. So far, I think it has saved me from going mad.

But now I'm beginning to think I'll go mad if I have to stay here for more than a month. Everything here smells of death, boredom, despair. . . .

April 1
Well, now I know. I'll be in this place—or this kind of place—for at least a year.

Since Dr Czablonski, the house-doctor, told me this last week, I've kept no record of any kind. . . .

To note: that there are at least four stages in the process of accepting any sudden disaster. The first, the shock, is hardly describable, it's even difficult to recall: you remember almost nothing but a few unimportant features of the actual scene when the blow fell—

a face, a sound, a voice, the light, the look of a landscape or a room—
and of them you only understand, at that moment, that they are
now fixed forever as mnemonics, and if they should ever be repro-
duced they will in turn recall the disaster itself. This is probably
why absolute monarchs were given to immediately executing the
bearers of bad tidings and destroying all vestiges of the scene: *this
must not happen again*. My own scene is made up of Dr Czablonski's
bush of grey hair, his mid-European accent, his curious air of triumph, and the froglike spread of his mouth emitting, "For you a
year, at least a year!"—and dusk in St Origène Street five storeys
down, the mountain seen from the ward window and the lights
just coming out on the electric cross on top of it. That was the
moment when I, as an absolute monarch, would have had Dr
Czablonski's head cut off and the cross torn down.

The next stage is attempted disbelief: "This cannot be." You have
only to close your eyes, clench your teeth, tighten the muscles of
scalp and ears once or twice, and wake up. It's a great temptation,
but as an indulgence should be strictly limited, for the return to
reality is so much the worse by so far as you have refused, though
only for a few seconds, to accept it. This game of refusal to believe
is, however, I believe, almost necessary in certain circumstances; and
I understand now how indispensable it is to people who are, say,
blinded or judicially sentenced to death, in other words how it helps
them retain their sanity during the "difficult period" (as hospital
and prison chaplains call it) before they can accept the sad fact
that they are not going to see any more or are going to be legally
murdered on a certain date. Dickens has some fine pages on this
alternation of disbelief and realization, this desperate fluttering between dream and fact, in his description of the last days of Fagin
in Newgate, and, though with a slight falling off in power, of those
of the hangman Dennis in *Barnaby Rudge*: it seems to have been
a favourite subject of his.

This phase then tends to merge and *diffuse* into what might be
called that of comparison or collation (really only a variant of disbelief), which consists in *comparing* the disastrous present with the
happy past, that is, before the blow had fallen. *Nessun maggior
dolore*, etc. It's best to go easy on this too.

These three stages, though brief enough, are highly unpleasant,
and you can wander back and forth through them for three or four
hours at a time. *The important thing is to keep moving from one*

to another. My own other palliatives were simple, but, like most extemporized things fairly effective: at the beginning, I found tears gave some relief, and also walking slowly up and down; a deep sigh also helped, and, when all these failed, the occasional reiteration under my breath of the common word for the human faeces. But everyone will find his own method, and I have noticed a reserved, silent, elderly man, who was admitted a few days before me, using nothing but the classic "Swann gesture"—taking off his spectacles, breathing on them deeply, then wiping them and replacing them on his nose. In his case it would seem that the "business" of the spectacles is merely a kind of cover-activity for the deep breath or sigh, as it may have been for Swann also. A few of the other patients are also still in one or other of these three preliminary stages: some of them groan deeply or even howl into their pillows from time to time; the Chinaman in the bed beside me grinds his teeth all night long, with a sound like a kitchen match being struck on sandpaper; many sleep all day; and there are a few who simply lie in bed with a happy smile and a glassy stare. (Can these be the lunatics who are sent here as part of the liaison between the Diamond Jubilee and the Vimy Ridge Insane Asylum? I don't like to ask.)

I am now entering on a fourth stage, that of irrational anger. A great improvement on the other three, and one I seem to share with many of the hardier patients. With them, sudden unpredictable storms of anger are directed against a variety of objects: the heating system, the internes (brisk, efficient, brutal young men), the alleged bluntness of the hypodermic needles, the food, Mrs Puncheon the night nurse. No-one seems to have it in for Dr Czablonski, so I have him all to myself. I indulge in fantasies of boxing his ears, smashing his glasses, kicking him. "Take that, you grinning hyena! And that, you piddling pill-pusher! And that, you two-bit sadist!" He picks himself up and comes at me, his fists doubled. I floor him with a hook to the mid-section. He's down, he's out! "Anger," as Achilles said, "is sweet as honey," and in cases of personal disaster is superior to day-dreaming, self-pity, or regret.

Today my anger has dwindled into simple irritation and a kind of fatuous disgust.

I can get used to sleeping in the same room with three other men, to queueing up for a toilet every morning, to facing a meal of boloney, noodles, and tinned peaches at five o'clock, even to being called "a good boy" by a student nurse for eating some of it, but not to the smell of this place, that peculiar hospital smell so indistinguishable from the greasy, sweetish smell of ear-wax. It's everywhere, lying on the air like a coating of oil on water: everywhere, that is, except in the bathroom where the smell of man is supreme, heated and intensified by the steam from the showers, almost cloacal in its power to evoke the human, all-too-human—the smell of the locker-room and barracks, that stupefying blend of cheap soap, cigarette-butts, toothpaste, chewing-gum, and dried sweat.

—God, how did I get into this kind of place?

Listen: this means you haven't yet accepted the fact you really have this disease. Think of your cavity, the size of a small egg. Think of that. Remember what Dr Y— said, in his best death-bedside voice, "You're a far advanced case, Mr Gooch. . . ."

And how did it start? Working too hard, not eating or sleeping enough, getting a little run-down, then having someone with the active germ sneeze or cough nearby. It's quite simple. There's no punishment, no nemesis involved. You've done nothing wrong, nothing to "pay for." It's not like gonorrhoea at all. There's no excuse for it, no rhyme or reason. As Camus would say, it's absurd. As for the unknown party I got it from, I don't want to see a law passed that will put him in a place like this by force: I still remember my own first night here! Anyway, that kind of thing simply ends by putting all kinds of sick people behind bars. Contagious diseases, like ideas and universal brotherhood and Shelley's kind of love, are even signs of the essential solidarity of mankind. You can't fence yourself off from the bugs of your fellow-man. Nothing human is alien to us, worse luck.

I'll soon be out of here, anyway. I'm to serve my year in the Jubilee Sanatorium at Ste-Misère-du-Lac.

I don't know whether I've really faced this yet.

In the meantime I'm in search of solitude, or at least quiet. But the Chinaman beside me is wedded to his radio, and the two other men talk bubblingly and interminably in Yiddish. There is a small sitting-room near the nurses' desk, but alas, it has a television set. This leaves the toilet, the telephone-room and the corridor itself, but with the first two in constant use, I'm simply reduced to walking up and down or standing around until Miss McClang calls our cheerily, "Come now, Mr G., mustn't tire yourself out that way!" Back to

Mr Miller and Mr Nudleman and Mr Wang, with their human and
mechanical noises.

Notes on Noise in Music and Life. I always thought noise in
music was all right. I used to like Ives, Antheil, Cage, Boulez,
musique concrète. But I could never, until now, agree with Russolo's
Manifesto, that "today Noise is triumphant, and reigns supreme
over the senses of man." He was right. Music must combine and
give continuity to these sounds, liberate them. The task is of course
endless.

For this constant row is almost too much. In fact, I don't see how
music can take it all into account. For instance, the endless grinding
away of the human voice. How is it that this, simply as one of life's
most persistent, monotonous, and nerve-racking noises, whether produced naturally or mechanically, as *the sound of words* altogether
divorced from what they mean, has been so neglected among the
transposed horrors in modern music? Something will have to be
done, I see.

By now I know by heart every program over the worst radio
station in Montreal from seven in the morning till ten at night: the
music either sentimental or hillbilly, the sung or spoken commer-
cials, the endless repetition of firm-names, products, street-addresses,
telephone numbers, and the jackpot affairs where they telephone a
housewife and ask her a question. I've learned to screen out the
actual meaning of the words, but that's not enough. For the worst
feature of all this mechanical noise is its fearful sameness: each set
of sounds is standardized. Every announcer has the same light tenor,
the same mouthing delivery, the same deceptive air of having
finished just as he's drawing breath to start in again. Even the
housewife who answers the telephone has the same flat, reedy
miaoul, the same giggle; she might be the same woman.

One of the private rooms reserved for serious or post-operative
cases has just been vacated. I ask Miss McClang if I can have it.
"Oh no. I'd like to, but Mr Legendre is coming back tomorrow."

"A serious case, I suppose?"

"No, but all transferees from Bordeaux Jail must be isolated. That
is one of the rules."

"Miss McClang, surely crime is not as contagious as all that."

"You don't understand. Mr Legendre must be *watched*, that is
the law. He is serving a two-year term for selling narcotics, and last

year the poor man developed t.b. in prison. He came here for minor surgery, and was sent back to Bordeaux a few months ago, with a tube to drain his pleura. Recently, however, he appears to have pushed the tube back into the cavity, and peritonitis may have set in."

"Poor fellow. But why should he push the tube back?"

She gives me one of her rare twinkles. "Mr Legendre prefers the Jubilee to the jail, Mr Gooch."

"Oh, I see. But who watches him here?"

"That is done by the police, of course."

I feel rather put out. This dope-peddler, this jailbird, is going to get that nice single room!

Terrible depression today. A reversion to my first week's feelings. I see you can go through all that again and again. Only this time claustrophobia has been added, and a growing feeling of personal uncleanness. Also moments of fear: am I going to spend the rest of my life in places like this? A few friends have telephoned, but I won't speak to them. Some visitors too, J— and S—, A—, E—, but I'm not at home. I would be ashamed to be seen in a place like this. . . .

Three old men have arrived, tubercular recidivists, perpetual returnees of the past twenty years. All of them grey, shaking, tight-lipped. They all wear thick, tubular, ankle-length woollen bathrobes, heavy grey socks, carpet slippers. They are very quiet and walk without lifting their feet, sliding their slippers along the waxed linoleum like little boats. Their daylong occupation is fixed by the demands of their kidneys. To and fro they go, to the toilet and back, their eyes fixed on the ground, carrying their urinals. There is something ominous about these elderly Danaids.

They have their own special smell, too—a mixture of unaired beds and rotted leather, and another ingredient I can't place: the smell of dried sour milk, the insides of old hats?

They all cough patiently, horribly.

Coughs. There are four kinds here: the hard, dry, metallic cough, more a bark; the interminable, gasping, wheezing cough, like a broken bellows; the deep powerful mucous cough which ends with the phlegm being hurled into the mouth to be spat, generally with a report like the stroke of an outboard motor, into one of the little waxed cardboard boxes supplied for the purpose; and finally the soft, loose, furry cough which is not really a cough at all but only a kind of cautious agitation of air in the bronchus, not designed to bring the mucus up but just to shift its position, turn it over, blow it around a bit: this is the way the three old men of the urinals cough, the old professionals.

Some of the patients don't cough at all. They are the ones with the smile and the glassy stare. I know about them now; they are the goofball artists, up on their little pink clouds.

Mr Legendre arrived today with his suite of a sheriff and two husky plainclothesmen. Quite young, black-haired, plump, eyelashes like a deer. He greets all the nurses by name. They all smile and twitter: he's a great favourite. Dr Czablonski, grinning his frog-smile, goes into his room with him. The two policemen get chairs, sit down outside the door, and light up cigars. A nice quiet assignment.

The patients discuss Mr Legendre.

"Falls on his feet, Gerry does."

"Christ, he was here only three months ago."

"His time must be pretty near up by now."

"No, for Christ's sake, he's got six months to serve yet."

"He'll serve it here some way. If he has to lose three lobes doing it."

You begin to realize what a hell Bordeaux jail must be, compared to this place. Everyone feels comforted, almost content.

Legendre is the life of the floor. Wearing a white foulard and a sky-blue satin dressing-gown appliquéd with dragons, he does the rounds of the wards every day in a wheel-chair, pushed by one of his guards. He has the gift of pleasing. He speaks to his guard in French, to Mr Miller and Mr Nudleman in Yiddish, to Mr Wang in Chinese, to me in English. He remembers everyone's personal affairs, like a politician in the country. "How is your little boy, Mr Huntziger? Good, Good.—And your wife's rheumatism, that is better, eh, Mr Pestalozzi? That's fine.—What happened to old Mr Thibaut? Dead, you say? Well, that is indeed too bad. Mr Papastratos, your cough seems much better, my friend. You say you're here for surgery? Good! That will cure you in permanence. Like it did me. Ha! ha!—Mr Gooch, you are going to Ste-Misère, I hear. A beautiful place, you will be in the heart of nature there,

sir.—Ah, my dear Mr Overmire (this is one of the old men of the
urinals), do I see you again? You are looking a little pale, but that
will soon pass; we will build you up again." And so on, with a
pause to listen gravely, attentively, to everyone. You see all the new
information being filed away in his head, the heavy-lidded eyes miss
nothing. He seems to have a passion for detail. You can't help liking
him, even with those big shifty eyes of his, that unmistakable air of
the underworld. He is, you feel, on the job—some job or other—all
the time.

Otherwise everything is dull. I'm only waiting till there is a free
bed for me at Ste-Misère. . . .

Waiting, always waiting. Everyone here is waiting. I already see
that this is the life of the tubercular—waiting for something or
other, the results of something, of a test, a culture, an x-ray, the
closing of a cavity, the disappearance of a shadow, for weeks and
months and years. Time has ceased to exist for these listless, mild,
slippered, slow-moving dwellers in limbo of whom I am now one.
I have a year of waiting ahead of me. And then—No, I won't think
past that.

"Mr Gooch, I think I'll be able to let you have that single room in
a day or two. While you're waiting to go to the San. Isn't that nice?"

"That is indeed good news, Miss McClang. But what about Mr
Legendre?"

She shakes her head sadly. "Mr Legendre has nothing wrong with
him at all. Dr Kinch extracted the tube, and there's no infection.
Of course we will take X-rays and tests as a matter of routine. But
I'm afraid Mr Legendre will have to go back to jail."

Poor fellow.

He catches me in the toilet, takes my arm. "In here," he says, and
leads me into the shower stall and pulls the curtain.

"Mr Gooch, today you have the opportunity of doing your
fellow-man a great service. I can see you are a man of refinement,
you have a good heart, yes, you are a real gentleman or I would not
ask this little favour."

It's a touch, I think. "Well—"

"No, not money, my dear sir! Merely a kindness, something that
will cost you nothing. I have heard your sputum is highly positive

—lousy with germs. Pardon me, but is that correct? Ah, then all I desire is your co-operation in the little matter of my sputum-test which they will take tomorrow. I, alas, am negative! You understand? Yes, it is such a small service, and it will save me from that goddam jail. . . ."

He already has the little glass specimen-bottle out and uncapped. He holds it out with a frank, winning gesture.

Well, why not? I take a deep breath, cough heartily, and deposit my little offering.

He grips my hand, pockets his bottle and slips out.

I've been trying to salve my conscience for this unsocial, almost immoral action.

And after all, who will be the worse for what I did? The doctors? One case more or less doesn't matter to them in the slightest. The community? But Mr Legendre is still in durance. The government, the taxpayer? I have seen statistics showing it costs more to keep a man in jail than in a hospital. No, as far as I can see, almost everyone stands to gain: Legendre, his guards, the patients, the Provincial treasury, even the nurses and Miss McClang who like having him around. Everyone in fact except myself, who won't be getting the private room. That is, if the scheme really works.

It worked. I fancy most of Legendre's schemes work. I heard him yelling in his room this morning as Miss Brébeuf gave him his first shot of streptomycin. He hates the needle, poor fellow. Or perhaps this is only another act.

He has given me a little present. Five goofballs. "To show my *ap*-preciation, sir. These are the real stuff, the real McCoy, as we say. When you are feeling sad, Mr Gooch, you have only to take one of these," he holds it up like a salesman on a television program, "and your troubles will melt away for three hours. You will have some very fine mental experiences, believe me, my friend. And these are guaranteed. No hangover or nothing. No diarrhoea. No 'abit of formation. With my compliments."

Already the bread I cast upon the waters is beginning to come back.

I'm going to Ste-Misère tomorrow, and I have a private room there. A lunatic has just been moved out of one and sent back to the Vimy Ridge, making room for me.

STE-MISÈRE-DU-LAC

April 15

"But just wait till you see the place in summer! Once all the snow's gone, it's simply beautiful! All that out there is lawn, beautiful green grass, and the hillside is all lovely maples. Over there is the clock golf. . . ."

Miss Duckless is the official greeter. Her voice has a synthetic softness and reverberance, an elocutionary, almost inspirational drawl, recalling both the political meeting and the kindergarten. We go along a bright corridor to the elevator.

"But I understand I won't be allowed off the fourth floor for three months."

"Exactly! You'll be able to look out at everything. Your room has a beautiful view of the Nurses' Residence too. Where *I* live. . . ."

She insists on carrying my bag. I notice she has the familiar lopsided build of all the receptionists, clerks, technicians, and even half the doctors in the Jubilee—one shoulder carried higher than the other, the wry, permanent shrug left by thoracoplasty; they're all former t.b. surgical cases. This disease seems to have a fascination for people who have had it, as if they wanted to hang around it for the rest of their lives.

We get off at the fourth floor and I meet Miss McTavish, the head floor-nurse. She seems just right—sharp, nasal, Nova Scotian, a figure like a ramrod, white hair coiled on her crown, the eyes and beak of an eagle.

Miss Duckless, still discoursing sweetness and light, takes me along another corridor past rows of closed doors; everything is wonderfully quiet. Right at the end she opens a heavy door, and I see my home: a bright square cell with a bed, a table, two chairs. And there is the famous view of the hillside and the Nurses' Residence—my own view for god knows how long.

"Isn't it beautiful! Just wait till everything is green, you'll love it. And in the fall the whole hillside is a glory, simply a riot of colour!"

In the fall. Hmmm-mm.

That first effect of hush and quiet was deceptive. It was merely the afternoon cure-period. At half-past three the whole place comes to life with shouts and laughter. In the four-bed room opposite mine there is a man who can imitate a barking dog, another who can play the mouth-organ.

I haven't yet sorted out the lunatics from the others. It's not too easy. Most of the patients are new citizens—Greek, Italian, Hungarian—with all that happy European faculty for noise, music, and sustained argument. The lunatics are native produce. I'm lucky in having one of them in the single room next to mine.

My neighbour, Mr Brown, is a model patient; he speaks to no-one, never smiles, sleeps twenty hours a day. His appearance, of course, is rather against him: his head is enormous, he has no shoulders, a Neanderthal jaw, and only one eye. He is from the Ridge, which sends him up here whenever his chronic t.b. becomes infectious. He's rather a favourite with Miss McTavish, who has been seeing him here, off and on, for the last twenty years. "Mr Brown," she tells me, "is not really insane. He is merely mentally disturbed. He has no family, and not a friend in the world. But he is really a good man, except when he drinks."

"Drinks? I thought all liquor was forbidden here."

She looks down her handsome Nova Scotian nose. "Yes, but there are some men who bring the stuff in, and who *use* it, Mr Gooch. And sometimes they give it to Mr Brown. He then becomes very excited, and he sings and shouts, and is sick all next day. I call them men, though they are not worthy of the name. But then a man who uses liquor is little better than a beast."

I think of the bottle of gin cached under my shirts. I have the momentary illusion that she knows it is there, and is warning me not to give any to Mr Brown. . . .

Good God, this has to last a year.

Anyway, there can't be too much wrong with me at the moment. I've been here for three days and I haven't even seen Dr Teach yet.

Dr Teach. A name, as they say, to conjure with. He is the Grand Old Man of Tuberculosis, the man who built this place almost single-handed, the apostle and father of bed-rest. You think of him in the clichés and cadences of a nineteenth-century newspaper editorial: Now well over seventy and of independent means, he continues to guide the destinies of the Sanatorium because he has long since lost interest in anything but the sick. He has never touched liquor or tobacco, and is childless; his whole life has centred around the idea of keeping people in bed, for years if necessary, and while disposed to admit the efficacy of drugs, and even to countenance surgery, he retains his original faith in the inexorable passage of

Time as the great healer. He has been on the point of retiring for the last fifteen years, but has not been able to make up his mind. "How can I rest," he asks, "when so many others should be doing so?" Such is the man who rules the Jubilee of Ste-Misère. He paid a visit to my cell yesterday afternoon, flanked by Miss McTavish, a staff-doctor, and two gazelle-like student nurses.

He is certainly every inch the grand old man: portly, grey at the temples, brown-cheeked with twinkling blue eyes; dressed from head to foot in spotless white, he has the air of deep seriousness and omniscience of a doctor in the movies; his voice is deep and measured.

He looks at me lying in bed for at least half a minute.

"I hear you write poetry," he says at last, making his lips twitch as if there were something irresistibly funny in the idea. One of the student nurses lets out a giggle.

I incline my head solemnly.

"Modern stuff, I suppose. Without the rhymes or punctuation marks, hey?"

I incline my head again. Easy does it.

He chuckles. "Well, you'll have a long way to go before you can beat Robert Service. Look, why don't you fellows write poetry like that any more? Can't do it, I suppose?"

"I'm afraid not."

He draws a deep breath and clears his throat. For a moment I have the feeling he is going to recite; the moment passes, and I'm so relieved to see him suddenly and unpredictably nod, wheel, and depart that I don't say another word.

Well, I suppose there was really nothing for him to say. . . .

But for the first time in my life I have grasped the conception of The Doctor of Molière, Le Sage, Goldoni, opéra bouffe: *il Dottore*, with his fleam and syringe, an absurd but sinister figure.

I wish I were out of here. . . .

Come now, remember what Dr Y— said in Montreal. "Your cure is absolutely a matter of routine. T.b. is a simple disease, the treatment calls for no special care, it's a matter of drugs and rest. You'll have the drugs at Ste-Misère, and the rest (ha! ha!) is up to yourself."

Sunday. This is hangover day. When last night's drinkers at the village hotel lie abed and groan and the bathroom reeks of vomit.

It seems that alcohol, especially beer, doesn't sit well with the drugs for t.b. A recent arrival across the way is puzzled.

"Jeez, what the hell's gone wrong? Two bottles of beer last night and I'm puking like a sailor. Look, before I come up here I could—"

"It's the bloody pills, man. Don't take any for two days ahead and you'll be all right."

"No kidding!"

"Sure, right down the f—ing toilet with them. That's the way. Only don't let them catch you, or they'll throw you out."

Alcohol also has a special effect on Mr Brown. I listened to him roaring like a wild animal last night. After a while a crash. Nurses scurrying up and down. "Mr Brown has fallen out of bed!"

It seems difficult to put him back in. The night nurse is frail and elderly, the student nurse is terrified: Good Heavens, Mr Brown has nothing on! "Get the night orderly!"

This takes time, of course. In the meantime Mr Brown keeps on roaring. Now that his door is open I can hear what he is saying.

"Jesus Christ! Jesus Christ! Christ, Christ, Jesus Christ!" Not an appeal or a protest or an invocation, simply a persistent mindless rhythmic chant, like the fans at a football game.

The orderly comes and puts him back in bed; metal bars are attached to the sides of his bed, the orderly goes away cursing. Mr Brown keeps calling for Christ. I go out and look into his room. Still naked, he is squatting in his newly constructed crib, his hands gripping and shaking the bars. His face is nothing but a hook nose, a jaw with no teeth, a mop of hair; his one good eye is staring at me like the face of a wrist-watch.

"Jesus Christ, Jesus Christ. . . ."

Mr Paquette, the dog-imitator, appears beside me in flowered pyjamas, grinning. He shakes his fist at Mr Brown; *"Ta gueule, toai!"* Then, as a clincher, he lowers his head and gives a few deep growls.

Mr Brown falls silent, peers at us, and lies down.

Three weeks here already. What tedium. Meals, bed, meals, bed. Loads and loads of warm, tasteless food. Drugs and more drugs. I am getting twenty para-aminosalicylic acid tablets a day, which give me diarrhoea, two shots of streptomycin a week, which bring on a blinding headache, three kinds of vitamin pills, which give me heartburn, and I'm even told there's something in the soup to inhibit sexual desire. One hears of new drugs constantly being developed to subdue this sturdy, unkillable t.b. germ, but the fact is the researchers are on the wrong tack. What is really needed is a pill to abolish consciousness altogether for say six months at a time, put the brain into a kind of deep freeze, seal off the senses from the noise and the smell and the food and the intolerable succession of the days, something to turn the patient into a zombie, an all-day sleeper—like Mr Brown.

May 30th

Good news. My sputum has turned negative. I have a double feeling of accomplishment, for it took me two weeks' persistent asking to get this information. I thought it was bad news they were keeping from me; now I see it was good. Or perhaps it is just any news at all. I'll never understand the system on which this place is run.

Now that I'm negative I'm allowed to go down to the first floor where the Library and canteen are. The library is an enormous, marvellous collection of Edwardian, Georgian, and modern rubbish, made up of the kind of books people give away or leave behind in hotels and trains. Philip Gibbs, Gertrude Atherton, A. J. Cronin, Frances Keyes, T. B. Costain, Nevil Shute. Mazo de la Roche takes up more space than anyone else: eight feet of her books, all battered, rubbed, and worn by hundreds of loving hands. Plenty of in-betweeners too, the deadbeats like Galsworthy, Walpole, Charles Morgan, Joyce Cary. This is where all the dull books of England end up, their own private limbo. In a few years the shelves will be filled with Graham Greene, Iris Murdoch, William Sansom, Anthony Powell, C. P. Snow. This is the literary potter's field, the tomb of passable trash. As Garneau said of the tombs on Côte des Neiges, *d'autres prendront la place des morts et les mêmes caveaux les abriteront.* Among them a few well-worn Canadian books: Ralph Connor, L. M. Montgomery, Thomas Raddall, Pierre Berton; they blend in nicely. There are also a lot of nineteenth-century French novels: Halevy, Jules Claretie, Octave Feuillet, Cherbuliez; there were dwarfs, too, in those days. With all this, a number of oddities: *The English Governess,* a work of domestic flagellation; Strindberg's *The Inferno; Memoirs of a Dope Fiend* by Aleister Crowley; *Nadja* by André Breton, with the original illustrations. How on earth did these fantastic, vicious creatures ever get up here, cheek by jowl with our Hugh MacLennan, F. P. Grove, Ethel Wilson, and Morley Callaghan, the purest of the pure?

But most of the time I gorge on detective stories. The hard-boiled, fast-moving kind, featuring some lean, symbolic, trench-coated indestructible,

> *The universal private "I"*
> *Whose foot and .45 conjoin*
> *To pulverize the hoods and sluts;*
> *Who kicks the killer in the groin*
> *And drills the lovely in the guts.*

They suit my mood.

A general clearance of the drunks this morning. Miss Duckless is the hatchet woman.

"Mr Pinsonneault, Mr Twite, Mr Paquette, Mr Dudley (the pill-destroyer), Mr Mellors (who couldn't keep his beer down), you're all to pack up now and go. To the Beth Israel in Ste-Apathie. You were warned by Dr Teach, you know, that this is not a hotel or a base for drinking. The bus is leaving in ten minutes."

A chorus of schoolboy groans.

"Ten minutes, gentlemen."

It takes longer than that, of course. But at last they all file out with bundles, suitcases, paper shopping-bags. I go out to the sun-porch and watch them pile into the bus. Mr Twite is playing his mouth-organ defiantly. Mr Paquette gives a few barks, but his heart isn't in it. As they go off, Mr Dudley shouts, "Teach, Teach, the son of a beech!" The others, laughing, take up the words like a college cheer as the bus grinds through the gates.

Miss McTavish is already superintending the sweepers with buckets of lysol, the orderlies are stripping the beds. She comes out and smiles.

"Children, Mr Gooch, children."

"But what about the Jewish hospital? Is there room for them there?"

"Oh yes, the Beth is sending us a busload of similar cases in return. They're on their way now."

"The same kind?"

"We maintain a close liaison with the Beth Israel."

As I go in, one of the orderlies grins at me. "Those bastards going to be sorry. No nice pork chops there. No butter at dinner. See how they like that for a while."

The lot from the Beth Israel are not too bad. Almost all of them have been here before in the last five years. *Qu.*: Doesn't anybody ever leave this place for good?

They seem rather subdued. Probably the experience of being thrown out has a sobering effect to begin with, though they know they'll always be taken in somewhere.

Note. T.b. patients, like lunatics, aren't covered by the Hospital Insurance Act, their sanatoria and asylums are subsidized by the Public Charities Fund on a per-patient-day basis, so each of these men is worth about six dollars a day to any recognized institution; so that ten patients a year, more or less, could affect the break-even point in a hospital's operations, because their actual keep can't come to more than fifty cents a day. Every empty bed represents a loss. When the patients get out of hand they just shift them about in busloads, the way the Soviets do with refractory peasants. . . .

My God, I suddenly realize I'm in the same boat. I, Silas N. Gooch, 38, minor poet, single, unemployed, am worth over $2,000 a year to the Diamond Jubilee. And I don't make a noise, walk in my sleep, wet the bed, quarrel, complain, criticize. A model patient. What chance have I got of ever getting out?

I'm certainly into something. . . .

Come now, use your head. And where is your trust in human nature, in medical ethics, in common humanity? Wake up, man, you're just having an Orwell nightmare. You have to trust somebody in this world.

Still, $2,000 a year. . . .

I am growing softer, I am adjusting, accepting, and it frightens me. At this rate I will soon be like everyone else here, shuffling around in the gloom of indifference, letting the days go by, growing more and more like the old crocks who have been here so long they don't want to leave.

To reawaken my feelings of rebellion, reactivate my hatred of this place, simply in order to keep alive. And this is getting harder every day. There is the same soft layer of fat around my feelings as on my body.

I think back to the early stages of this horrible adventure. A little of that anguish or anger is what is needed now. I'm being stifled, slowly and painlessly, in this cotton-wool of restraint and routine, among these listless, slippered shades of men, these bland, uncommunicative doctors, these cheerful little ward-maids, in all this hideous disregard of the passage or value of time, this whole way of life summed up in the unfailing solicitude of the older nurses, these withered virgins with hearts of gold, these dedicated old pill-bearers on squeaky rubber feet.

"None of this medical business bothers me," says old Mr Thackeray who arrived last week. "I'm a high-grade moron."

He's not joking, he really is one.

"Sure I can read, but the words don't mean a thing! I can pick up a newspaper and read it right through without taking in a word! And tell me anything *deep*, it just goes in one ear and out the other. No, what I miss here is occupation, there's nothing to do. Nothing to do here, that's the trouble."

Still, he does what he can. He delivers the newspapers every morning, helps with the meal-trays, fills the sugar-casters, sweeps the floors, swabs out the toilets, runs up and down the corridors all day long looking for odd jobs, until Miss MacTavish tells him to stop, he's here to rest. But he can't rest; he secretly collects everyone's shoes and polishes them, beautifully; he repairs the window-blinds; he sews on buttons.

But what he really likes to do is talk. Unfortunately his conversation has neither sense nor continuity, it's simply an articulated stream of consciousness that begins by being fascinating and ends by leaving you dizzy. It's like Leopold Bloom, without Joyce.

"Nothing to do here, that's the trouble. I've been a busy man all my life. I specialize in construction work, engineering, gardening, horses, jackhammers, driving, I can drive anything on wheels, I used to be a motorman with the old Montreal Street Railway Company, Car 83, the downtown loop. Those were the days!" He works imaginary levers, stamps on the floor. "Full speed ahead, give her the old bell, ne parlez pas au garde-moteur! Going up Beaver Hall Hill was the only tough spot—that was before they graded it back in 1931, back in the days before they pulled down the Angelican church at the corner of Belmont where the Bell Telephone building is now, and do you know, sir, the site of that building has something wrong with it to this day, they're always having trouble, I know they are, I've spoken to the workmen myself. Quicksands, seepage, *weakness*," he leans forward and drops his voice, "in the basement. You know why? Consecrated ground!" And so on.

July 10

Three months now.

Tonight I feel as if I were right back where I started on St Origène Street in Montreal, looking out of the fifth-floor window at the electric cross on the mountain. The same sense of horror and unreality. What am I doing here? What has become of my real life?

After another week's frantic asking, I've found out I have made no progress at all in the last two months. My cavity is apparently not closing.

Miss McTavish has gone on her holidays. Miss Labrosse has taken over. A new broom. Always dropping in for a chat.

"You seem blue, Mr Gooch. Have you had bad news?"

"Well, they say my last x-ray shows no improvement at all."

"Ah, that often happens. You must be patient. Above all, you mustn't get gloomy, that's bad. They will take another x-ray in another two months, and perhaps that will be better! Come now, a little smile. Two months, what is that? Why, there are patients who've been here for two years, and they're not downhearted." She leans forward, her voice becomes deep and resonant. "Just tell yourself you aren't giving up hope, just tell yourself," she clashes her false teeth and smites her fist in her palm, "you are not going to lay down under this thing, no, you are going to *beat* this bug!"

"Yes, yes."

"Would you like to try some o.t.?"

"?"

"Miss Withering in the shop will show you how to do leatherwork, or you can make some ornaments in brass leaf. Wouldn't you like to make a pair of cosy slippers for someone? Miss Withering will be delighted to show you how."

Miss Madrigal, the incredibly beautiful student nurse, comes in breathlessly: "Mr Gooch, you're to go down to see Dr Teach right away!"

I slip on my dressing-gown and slippers and pad down after her to the main corridor, where she tells me to sit on a bench. Dr Teach's latest secretary, another lopsided woman, peers out and whispers, "The Doctor will see you in five minutes."

After half an hour on the bench I am quite calm, my knees have stopped shaking. Through the door I can hear Teach's deep, measured voice and his deep, measured chuckle. There is no other voice audible. At last the door opens and Mr Brown is ushered out. What relief! Apparently we're all just being taken in order.

Dr Teach, in his snow-white sanitary suit, stares at me from behind his desk, then makes his eyes twinkle, his mouth twitch: the old routine. "Well, how do you find you're getting along? Writing a lot of modern poetry, hey?"

"Not a great deal, doctor. I'm a little worried about my progress. I'd like to know—"

"Not writing. A caged bird, hey? Well, that happens, that happens." He sinks back in his chair, picks up what must be my dossier and studies it intently for a full minute. At last he shakes his head, sighs deeply, looks up. A terrible silence.

"Let me ask you a question, Mr Gooch."

"Yes . . ."

"Are you a fisherman?"

"No."

But Dr Teach is. He is, it appears, an ardent, an inexorable fisherman. For five minutes he tells me of his prowess in the lakes and streams. The deep, measured voice rolls on, with the occasional matching chuckle, as he recalls how he out-witted some particular fish. But the little blue eyes fix me intently for a second or two every now and then. Is this some kind of psychology? No, he's just a thundering old bore. During a pause I try to break up the flow of his bragging and reminiscence.

"I understand my cavity is not closing, Dr Teach. Does this mean that surgery is the answer? And if so, how long will it be before you know?"

Dr Teach looks up sharply, then lets his hands fall heavily on his desk. When he speaks, his voice is rasping and as if barely under control.

" 'How long.' You ask me, 'How long'! Don't you understand by now, Mr Gooch, that this is one question we simply cannot answer, that cannot be answered?"

"Why not?"

His face gets a little pinker. He makes a gesture expressive of the utter impossibility of explaining such a question to a layman. Then, however, the fine old smile is brought out again as he gets up.

"You must be patient, Mr Gooch. Let me see," he consults my dossier, "you have been here four months now, haven't you? Well, now, I think we can allow you a little liberty. I will tell Miss McTavish to give you a pass to go out on the grounds for two hours on Sunday. How will that be?"

Every Sunday now I wander around the grounds. I see more and more of the old regulars, the patients who have nothing wrong with them and refuse to leave, unable to face the world outside; they are given light jobs looking after the grounds. There are lots of flowers here, mainly petunias, all disposed with the grim regularity of the floral arrangements at country railway-stations. Some of the younger patients are playing clock golf.

I sneaked off to the village the other day. It's forbidden, but why not?

Notes on Ste-Misère. A hotel, four stores, a bank, three garages, a movie-house, and a church bigger than all of them put together. Prevalence of the genuine French-Canadian types: the thin, straight-haired, shrill-voiced little girls with narrow mouths and hard ratlike eyes: these girls will be good at arithmetic, sewing, and catechism; the swarthy, wide-hipped youths, good-humoured, furtive, caught between the attraction of the American movies and fear of the priest: they will make good breeders; the priest himself, with his cummerbund, black varnished straw hat, cigar, and one of the biggest crucifixes I have ever seen on anyone (of black wood inlaid with brass, it could actually accommodate a small monkey); the old men, small, brown, bandy-legged, wrinkled like prunes, a pipe stuck in the lipless mouth like a catheter in a wound, eyes that miss nothing.

This is back country. In the optometrist's window is a special vision-chart for illiterates. Instead of the E and F, the P and D, there are pictures of a horse and a pig, a wagon-wheel and a clock-face, a church and a house, a table-knife and an oar.

August

Once again this feeling of utter misery, of abandonment, of lost-ness. It is midsummer now, and spring has at last come to Ste-Misère. In the woods below me, opposite my cage, the thrushes are singing. What did they come all the way up here for? Already, at home, they will have raised their first brood and gone off to the deep woods to sing by themselves. And at night, now, there are whip-poor-wills, my unfavourite bird. All evening long I hear that monotonous *pirri-pip, pirri-pip, pirri-pip*. A dreary note.

Now the old crocks, the drunks, the addicts have ceased to touch me with pity or sadness. After five months I have developed an immunity to whatever is pitiable or exasperating in them, like this hardy tuberculosis bacillus of mine which seems to be adjusting to all kinds of attack. To hell with them, let them die, and the sooner the better: let them fall downstairs, roar like bull-calves, cough their rotten lungs out—that's their business and it may be all they're good for. They will leave a gap in the television audience, that's all. It's all the same to me.

This must be the process of adjustment. . . .

You adjust, yes: that is, you harden, dry up, withdraw, become indifferent to mankind, pump all your vitality and interest back into yourself, simply in order not to wither away or go mad. Prolonged, stupid, unsensational suffering like this is the proper school for selfishness, I guess. . . .

I broke off here last week in an absolute of dejection and despair. I could have lain down on my bed and howled, beat my fists on my pillow like a child. But I did something much more sensible. I got out Legendre's goofballs and swallowed one of them with a good long swig of water.

"When you are feeling sad, Mr Gooch. . . ."

An enormous, an unqualified success! Good God, no wonder the prisoners in a jail will do anything for one of these things. Every afternoon for the last five days I have had a succession of the most extraordinary experiences of well-being in my whole life. Alcohol simply cannot touch it.

First you feel nothing at all, except that things seem to become oddly *quieter*; then there is a faint, delicious tickling in the skin of the feet, hands, and shoulder-blades, which doesn't increase or fade during the whole experience. Only gradually do you become conscious of how simply and supremely *happy* you are. All worry, concern, feelings of duty or obligation have disappeared; the process is slow, orderly, everything is temperate. You feel well-disposed to everyone, you think of your friends with boundless affection, of your enemies with forgiveness and a sense of having misunderstood them entirely. Then comes the feeling of confidence, of perfect, equable self-satisfaction in everything you have ever done in your whole life. The future is abolished, you luxuriate in an immediate sense of achievement. You are a success! At this point the ideas come thronging, all in perfect order. You survey your thought-processes with a fatuous delight. You have never been so brilliant.

Yesterday, lying in bed, I even took a few notes on the spot, since it was my last goofball. Here they are, just as I jotted them down in my own homemade shorthand:

—There's Dr Teach on the steps of the Nurses' Residence. All in white, his hands behind his back, overlooking the hospital buildings and grounds with a broad brown smile on his brown old face. He is perfectly happy. He looks on his work and sees it is good. His dreams have all come true! No brains, charm or push, but he has succeeded. Rich, happy, respected. And he owes it all, all to tuberculosis! He has a vested interest in this disease, you might say. What a wonderful thought this is. . . .

A vested interest in disease. Vested interests and the professions.

> *Medicine: in disease*
> *Armed Forces: in war*
> *Law: in crime, injustice*
> *The Church: in fear, awe, suffering.*

Eliminate the latter, you eliminate the former. This is *irrefutable*. No doctors, soldiers, lawyers, judges, priests; no nurses or policemen.
—All right: what about my own profession?
Literature's vested interest: in what?
(Pause)
Problem: The elimination of what condition, misfortune, evil, appetite or disposition would make serious literature unnecessary? I.e., why does a man read? (Self-improvers excluded.) Better, why doesn't he simply *not* read?
A. Because man must do something.
Q. What, for instance?
A. Either work all the time (E. P. Taylor, the corner grocer, the Pope); play all the time (children, Duke of Windsor, etc.); drink all the time (skid-row types); love all the time (Julie de l'Espinasse, newlyweds); sleep all the time (Mr Brown). But anyone can read.
Q. Yes, but why must he do something?
A. To escape from thinking.
Q. What's wrong with thinking?
A. Thoughts.

Q. What kind of thoughts?

A. Gloomy thoughts. Worries, fears, forebodings, feelings of discontent, ambition, undeserved neglect, guilt, envy, inferiority, failure, horror of death: in a word, Unhappiness.

∴ Reading is a simple, cheap but intelligent way of escaping from unhappiness.

∴ Literature has a vested interest in unhappiness. *Quod erat explicandum.*

(Rider: A happy people has no literature. ∴ Canadians are a happy people, or were until recently.)

—That is five minutes of a goofball reverie. At the time you think how marvellously, how exquisitely lucid. . . .

The rains have come. This makes life a little better. I begin to notice things again.

The curious and infinite variety of nurses' caps. Some like sauce-boats, some like water-lilies, some combining features of the funnel and the dunce's cap, some like a boy's Eton collar turned backward and put on upside down, some bordered with black like old-fashioned mourning notepaper, some that recall the classic milk-maid's coif, others the bonnet on the woman in the Old Dutch Cleanser advertisements. Mrs Thwaites, the Superintendent, has something really exotic. She is a graduate of King Lud's Hospital in London, and her cap is shaped like an inverted bird's nest with a square of hemmed linen hanging down at the back and covering her nape like the sunstroke-protector on the képi of a Foreign Legionnaire. Seen striding along the corridor with her mediaeval jaw out-thrust and this vestigial monastic veil flying behind, she is really impressive. Miss Terrier, the Head Nurse, on the other hand, wears a very mean-looking cap: it is only half starched and looks home-made, especially the way the folds are drawn together at the back like the opening of a skin purse or a centenarian's mouth; but to make up for this, she wears a mysterious gold medal on her right breast.

Many changes now. Old patients go and the new ones come. Some are shifted down to the Third Floor. I am now the second-oldest inhabitant of the Fourth, outranked only by Mr Brown.

Mr Thackeray has been put in a room by himself, and is almost crazed with loneliness. It seems he was talking too much. All day long he runs around trying to buttonhole people to talk to, but they break away, walk away, fade away.

"It's just like they say, Mr Gooch, 'I'll take the high road and you'll take the low road,' only now it happens to be me that's on the low road, there I'm going along, *phut-phut-phut*, down and down and down and the guys on the high road they don't see you any more, to hell with you Thackeray, they're thinking, sure I know what they're thinking, it's only Bill Thackeray he's lost his marbles anyway, now what a way is that for the world to act to a man like me who's always paid his taxes and done his civic duty, by God Mr Gooch I once found a stray dog run over on the highway and took it twenty miles in my own car to the nearest vet and now there's not a guy in this whole place who'll listen to a word I say, to hell with you, that's what they're thinking, to hell with you Thackeray, go roll your hoop you old bastard you're just a stationary engineer, yes that's their attitude and by God it's getting me down."

Things are getting me down too. I can't get any information out of anyone. I might be getting better, getting worse, getting nowhere, I might be cured or be going to die: how do I know? I can't even get near Dr Teach. Ever since that talk I had with him he has been blind and deaf. Every time I see him in the corridor he turns and walks away. Am I incurable? Or is it just that $2,000 a year?

I've just seen their financial statement here. Almost a quarter of the government grant goes to paying the interest on the bank loans they negotiate every year to cover the deficit. The setup is crazy. . . .

At night, now, I nourish terrible fancies. The fits of claustrophobia are getting worse, they leave me dizzy, almost physically sick. What with that, the smells in the toilets and the corridor and the revolting food, I've almost stopped eating. I suppose that can't go on indefinitely or I will have a relapse of some kind. Or is the place really as bad as I imagine it? Am I really going mad? Am I talking like Mr Thackeray, am I looking like Mr Brown? I begin to fancy Miss McTavish is regarding me oddly. I have nightmares of dying in this place, of being sent to the Vimy Ridge. . . .

It's a far cry from my original dislike and distrust of Teach. The shameful truth is, he terrifies me now.

"Now then," says Dr Teach from behind his desk, "just what is it you want to know?"

"I want to know when I can get out of this place."

"Hmmm. How long have you been here?"

"Five months."

He takes a deep breath, pretends to explode. "Five months! What do you expect to happen in five months? Do you know, sir, there are patients who have been here, who still are here, after five *years?*"

"That's just it."

His jaw comes out. We face each other grimly. He glares for a few seconds, then controls himself and goes into the lip-twitching routine. He puts his elbows on the desk, clasps his hands.

"There's no use your getting impatient, Mr Gooch. In fact I'm surprised to find this attitude in someone like yourself. You must realize you are being kept here for your own good."

"Dr Teach, there is nothing I am doing here that I can't do better in my own home."

He grins, shakes his head silently.

"I suggest I go home, continue taking the drugs and following the same régime I have been following for the past five months, and check in here or at the hospital in Montreal whenever necessary."

He keeps shaking his head. "No, no, we don't do things that way here. That's all too complicated and irregular. And I know all about patients who go home. They all come back here in a month or two, in worse condition than they left."

"In that case they must skip the drugs or the cure-periods or go on a bat or something."

"Very likely. That is only human nature, Mr Gooch."

"Then I'm being kept here because I can't be trusted to behave rationally anywhere else?"

Dr Teach makes no reply; he simply gives me the steady twinkle. He has all the statistics.

I suddenly see it's hopeless. I see why I'm being kept here: to cover Teach in case I have a relapse, and to save everyone in the Jubilee a lot of extra trouble when it's time for the regular x-rays and tests.There's also that little matter of the provincial grant. It all makes sense. No, I'm in the machine now, in the hopper, along with Thackeray and Brown and Paquette, Twite and Dudley. There's no way out. I'm a patient of the state, a public charge, which means I've simply got caught up in something on which a lot of people's jobs depend.

Dr Teach is giving me the deep, measured chuckle. He's back in the saddle now. "Just let me tell you, sir, that we in this hospital know what is best for you. Make no mistake about that. It's the opinion of medical men all over the world that the best place for a t.b. patient is in a sanatorium. Of course, you're at perfect liberty to leave here at any time." A twitch of the lips. "And start in all over again somewhere else."

What I'm doing still frightens me at times. But I know it's the right thing. Another six months here and I would go literally mad. And Teach isn't the kind of man you tell that to: not with any safety. Any more than you could tell him about the noise and the smell and the food here, the claustrophobia and creeping mental paralysis induced by this self-contained antiseptic slum. It just wouldn't make sense to him. This place is his baby, his pride and joy.

No, I've got to get out. No matter what it means. I'll take private treatment somewhere, if I have to go in hock for it for the rest of my life.

I'm all packed, the train leaves tomorrow morning. I've drawn up and signed a paper releasing the Jubilee from all responsibility. . . . I'm leaving quietly, secretly: no arguments, discussions, protests, pleas, words, words, words. . . .

Already I have the peculiar feeling one always has just before leaving any place one has lived in for a long time, the feeling as if one had just arrived and was seeing it with the same eyes one saw it with the first time. A few minutes ago I put my waste-basket out in the hall as per regulations; I looked up and down this hushed, darkened corridor for the last time, with the gloomy little night-light above the nurses' desk at the far end and the red light above the fire-escape stairs almost over my head, and the impression came over me once again of having just arrived and still asking myself, "What am I doing here?" It's neither unpleasant nor pleasant, simply *strange*.

For now that I'm going, I find I've no hard feelings towards anyone or anything. It's not a bad hospital, all it needs is a new set of patients. And this free state-medicine is really a wonderful thing. It's the essence of fairness, it insists on everyone being treated the same. It presumes that all men are equal—that is, equally imbecile and irresponsible. Mr Brown has established the norm. And rightly so: how else could he qualify? He at least has nothing to complain of. And if I were in his mental condition I would have nothing to

440   THE TWENTIETH CENTURY

complain of either. I'd be staying right here. Right here until I died. . . .

All that was yesterday. It's ancient history now, part of a long night's nightmare.

Dr Teach with his full entourage has just left my cell. "Your last x-ray shows enormous improvement, Mr Gooch. I think we'll be able to let you out soon. Say in three months. You can wait that long, hey?"

I can hardly speak. "Of course, of course . . . ."

Everybody is smiling. Even Miss McTavish's wintry Nova Scotian lips are curved upward. Miss Madrigal, wearing a Botticelli simper, looks more beautiful than ever.

Good God, they are actually glad I am getting better! How I've misjudged them. Especially old Teach. What a fine old fellow he is after all!

Three months more. Only 90 days. Less time than I've already been here. I can be out of here before Christmas. It's nothing, simply nothing. I can do it on my head.

Oh how good everybody is, how kind!

ROBERTSON DAVIES

1913-

Robertson Davies was born in Thamesville, Ontario, and educated at Upper Canada College, Queen's University, and Bal-
liol College, Oxford. He has had a varied and brilliant career
as actor, stage manager, and director with the Old Vic Reper-
tory Company in England and as a journalist, publicist, and
educator after returning to Canada in 1940. He was for a time
literary editor of *Saturday Night*, Toronto, and in 1942 became
editor of the *Peterborough Examiner*. A knowledgeable and
urbane lecturer on literature and the theatre, Davies taught
English at Trinity and University College, Toronto, and in
1962 was appointed Master of Massey College.

Davies' first books grew out of his experience in the theatre
in England. They are *Shakespeare's Boy Actors* (London,
1939) and *Shakespeare for Young Players* (Toronto, 1942),
and they were followed by a number of plays, the earliest of
which have been collected in *Eros at Breakfast and other Plays*
(1949). These were followed by *Fortune my Foe* (1949), *At
My Heart's Core* (1950), a historical play dramatizing the
plight of Susanna Moodie and her sister Mrs. Traill in the
cultural wilderness of Peterborough in pioneer days, and *A
Jig for the Gypsy* (1954), a political play set in England in the
1880's. Davies has also written two masques for youthful actors
and, in collaboration with Tyrone Guthrie and the artist Grant
Macdonald, three books about the Stratford festival.

As editor of the *Peterborough Examiner*, Davies contributed a series of whimsical essays, which were subsequently published as *The Diary of Samuel Marchbanks* (1947) and *The Table Talk of Samuel Marchbanks* (1949). These led to Davies' later discursive and humorous novels, *Tempest-Tost* (1951), *Leaven of Malice* (1954), and *A Mixture of Frailties* (1958), which satirized provincialism and pretentiousness in various aspects of artistic, theatrical, and academic life in the Dominion. His most recent novel, *Fifth Business* (1970), is an attempt to explore imaginative reality and to reveal an inner and secret identity by means of comedy, melodrama, and metaphysical speculation in the form of a memoir, the *apologia pro vita sua*, of a retired schoolmaster. A book of literary essays, *A Voice from the Attic* (1960), was well received in England and the United States.

The quality of Davies' contribution to Canadian literature may be summed up in a sentence or two quoted from the present editor's note in *Masks of Fiction* (1961): "Mr. Davies brings the virtues of urbanity, sophistication, good humor, and a certain consciousness of superiority to bear on books, food, wine, and social behavior." He is "an old-fashioned novelist who is more advanced than many new-fashioned novelists."

In the episode from *A Mixture of Frailties* that follows, a naive and rather vulgar young Canadian singing student from a small town in Ontario on a scholarship in London has an embarrassing but instructive interview with a sophisticated and somewhat contemptuous British musical figure who agrees to accept her as a pupil.

Thirty-two Tite Street was a gloomy house across the road from a large Infirmary, from whose windows came an unceasing sound which Monica at first thought was the weeping of baby chicks, but which she later learned was the crying of infants in the nurseries. A rack of cards in the hall told her that Giles Revelstoke was on the top floor, and she was about to press the bell beneath his name when she heard someone coming down the stairs very rapidly and noisily, shouting "Sorree, sorree" in a loud voice. It was a very tall young man with tousled hair, who arrived beside her as her finger was poised to push.

"You want Giles?" said the young man. "Don't ring; don't dream of ringing; you'll cut him to the heart if you ring. Go right up, and right in without knocking, and if you don't see him about give a cooee. Most informal fellow in the world. Hurry up, old girl; up you go."

Monica had dressed herself elegantly for this first meeting with her new teacher, and had worked up a sense of the dignity of the occasion. She did not want to burst upon him without all the proper formalities. But the tall young man was not to be gainsaid, so she went up two flights of long dark stairs, and found a door at the top which opened into what was plainly a studio, an extremely crowded and untidy room furnished with a large work table and an upright piano, and beyond that nothing recognizable as furniture, but with heaps of books, papers, and music piled on the floor and all the other flat surfaces. The only pleasing thing about the room, apart from a large black cat asleep on the piano top, was a dormer window set in the sloping roof which gave a view, through chimneypots, toward the Thames.

Should she sit down? But where? She stood for a few minutes, then picked her way through the debris on the floor to the window and looked out of it for a while. But she was disturbed by the sense that she was in somebody else's room. She must not make free. But where was Mr. Revelstoke? Had he forgotten that she was to come at four? The tousled young man had said that he was at home. This was quite unlike a visit to Molloy, who was as punctual as the clock, or to Sir Benedict, whose valet was always at hand to take her at once to the great man. What had Molloy called Revelstoke? "Quite the little genius." This looked like a genius's room. But how to inform the genius of her presence?

She coughed. Nothing happened. She coughed again, and walked about heavily, making a noise with her feet and feeling a fool. Should she go downstairs again, and ring the bell?

No; she would play the piano. She seated herself and played what came first into her head, which was her one-time favorite, *Danse Macabre*. The cat roused itself, yawned at her, and slept again.

She had played for perhaps three minutes, when a voice said very loudly behind her, "Stop that bloody row!" She turned, and standing in the doorway was a man. He was utterly naked.

Nothing in Monica's previous experience had prepared her for such a spectacle, and it was the most shocking sight, within the bounds of nature, that could have confronted her. The Thirteeners, and everybody else with whom she had ever been intimately acquainted, thought very poorly of nakedness. Courtships, even when carried to lengths which resulted in hasty and muted weddings, were always conducted fully dressed. The intimacies of married life were negotiated in the dark, under blankets. Shame about nakedness was immensely valued, as a guarantee of high character. It is true that, when in Paris, Monica had been taken to the Louvre several times by Amy Neilson, and she had learned to look at naked statuary— even the Hermaphrodite—without betraying the discomfort she felt in the presence of those stony, bare monsters; but that was art and idealized form—no preparation for what she now saw—a naked man, not especially graced with beauty, coloured in shades which ranged between pink and whitey-drab, patchily hairy, and obviously very much alive.

He was smiling, which made it all worse. He seemed quite at his ease; it was she—she who was in the right, she the clothed, she the outraged one, who was overset. Monica had never fainted in her life, but she felt a lightness in her head now, an inability to get her breath, which might well rob her of consciousness.

"You're the Canadian Nightingale, I suppose," said he. "I forgot you were coming. Hold on a jiffy, while I get some clothes. But don't play that trash any more."

And a jiffy it was, for he was back again almost at once, wearing flannel trousers, and with his bare feet thrust into worn slippers, buttoning his shirt; he went behind the piano, picked up a bundle of woman's garments and threw them through the door into the next room, shouting, "Come on, Persis, you lazy cow, get up and make us some tea." The reply, which came through the door in a rich and well-bred contralto, was brief, and couched in words which Monica had never heard spoken in a woman's voice before. "Shut up," replied Revelstoke, "can't you behave yourself when we have company —a distinguished guest from the Premier Dominion, our mighty ally in peace and war? Be a good girl and get some tea, and we shall have music to restore our souls."

He took the cat in his arms and stroked it, as he turned again to Monica. "You mustn't mind a degree of informality here which you haven't met in the elegant environs of Sir Benedict Domdaniel. Brummagem Benny, as we sometimes call him in the musical world —without a hint of malice, mind you—likes to do himself very well. And properly so. He must keep up a position commensurate with his great and well-deserved reputation. But I, you see, am a very different sort of creature. You are now in the editorial offices of *Lantern*, undoubtedly the most advanced and unpopular critical journal being published in English today. The significance of the name will not escape you. *Lantern*—it is the lantern of Diogenes, searching for the honest, the true and the good, and it is similarly the lantern, or lamppost, referred to in the good old Revolutionary cry "A la lanterne!" —because from this *Lantern* we suspend the hacked corpses of those whom we are compelled to judge harshly; you will not miss, either, the allusion to that Lantern Land which Master Francis Rabelais describes in his *Pantagruel* (with which I presume that you are amply acquainted) and which was the habitation of pedants and cheats in all branches of the arts; we allude to it slyly in our title by a species of gnomic homophony which will at once be apparent to you. This is a workroom, and workrooms are apt to be untidy. This will soon be your workroom, too, if we get on as well as I hope we shall. You had better meet my friend, Pyewacket, a delightful but musically uncritical cat."

He was interrupted by the entry, from the bedroom, of a tall girl of twenty-three or four, wearing a not very fresh slip and nothing else; her long dark hair was hanging down her back and she had the tumbled look of one who has risen from bed.

"Match," said she to Revelstoke. He found one on the table and gave it to her.

"Allow me to introduce Miss Persis Kinwellmarshe, daughter of Admiral Sir Percy Kinwellmarshe, retired, now of Tunbridge

Wells. Miss Kinwellmarshe is one of my principal editorial assist-
ants. We have been engaged in a type of editorial conference known
as scrouperizing. You do know Rabelais? No? Pity!"

Monica disliked Miss Kinwellmarshe on sight. She had Bad Girl
written all over her, and in addition she was extremely handsome,
with a finely formed nose, through the crimson-shadowed nostrils of
which she now seemed to be looking at Monica.

"It's a pleasure to meet any acquaintance of Mr. Revelstoke's,"
said she.

Monica knew when she was being mocked, but Amy's prime in-
junction—"You can never go wrong by being simple, dear"—came
to her rescue. So she bowed her head slightly toward Miss Kinwellmarshe, and said "How do you do?"

Miss Kinwellmarshe, taking the match, turned and went to the
kitchen. *She's got a butt-end on her like a bumble-bee*, said the voice
of Ma Gall, very clearly, inside Monica's head—so clearly that
Monica started.

"Now, let's do some work," said Revelstoke, who appeared to
have enjoyed this encounter. "You've been with the ineffable Molloy
for a while, Sir Benny tells me. An admirable coach, with a splendid,
policeman-like attitude toward the art of song. Sing me a few of the
things he's taught you."

Unlike Molloy, he made no move to accompany her, so Monica
sat at the piano and sang half-a-dozen English folksongs. She could
not have explained why it was so, but the knowledge that Miss Kinwellmarshe was within earshot had a tonic effect on her, and she sang
them well.

"The accompaniments are charming, aren't they?" said Revelstoke. "Cecil Sharp had a delightful small talent for such work. But
of course folksongs are not meant to be accompanied. Just sing me
Searching for Lambs without all that agreeable atmospheric deedle-
deedle."

So Monica sang the song again. If he thinks I've never sung this
without accompaniment he certainly doesn't know Murtagh Molloy,
she thought.

"Not bad. You have a true ear, and a nice sense of rhythm.—Ah,
here is dear Miss Kinwellmarshe with the tea. I won't ask you to
take a cup, Miss—I forget for the moment—yes, of course, Miss Gall,
but you shall have one when you've finished singing. Now, Brum
Benny tells me you have a special line in Victorian drawing-room
ballads—such a novelty, and so original of you to have worked it up

in a time when that kind of music is so undeservedly neglected. I understand that Tosti's *Good-Bye!* is one of your specialties. I can hardly wait. Will you sing it now, please. You won't mind if we have tea as you do so? The perfect accompaniment for the song, don't you think?"

Miss Kinwellmarshe had laid herself out voluptuously on the work table, pillowing her head on a pile of manuscript and permitting her long and beautifully wavy hair to hang over the edge; the splendour of her figure in this position was somewhat marred by the dirtiness of the soles of her feet, but it was clear that she aimed at large effects, and scorned trifles.

"I haven't sung that song for several months," said Monica. Indeed, she had learned to be thoroughly ashamed of Tosti under the rough but kindly guidance of Molloy. How could Sir Benedict have mentioned it! These English! Sly, sneaky, mocking! You never knew when you had them.

"But after we have put a favorite work aside for a time, we often find that we have unconsciously arrived at a new understanding of it," said Revelstoke, and he was smiling like a demon.

"I'd really rather not," said Monica.

"But I wish it. And I dislike having to remind you that if I am to teach you anything, you must do as I wish." His smile was now from the teeth only.

He just wants to roast me in front of that grubby bitch, thought Monica. I'll walk out. I'll tell Sir Benedict I won't bear it. I'll go home.

But she met Revelstoke's eyes, and she sang. She was angrier than she had ever been in her life. She hated this man who dared to show himself naked, and whose talk was one smooth, sneering incivility after another; she hated that nearly naked tart lolling on the table. She hated Sir Benedict, who had been making fun of her behind her back. She was so full of passionate hatred that her head seemed ready to burst. But she had not spent six months with Murtagh Molloy for nothing. She took possession of herself, she breathed the muhd, and she sang.

She finished, and the seven bars of *diminuendo* regret on the piano were completed. There was silence. The first to break it was Miss Kinwellmarshe, and her comment was a derisive, dismissive, derogatory monosyllable.

"Not at all," said Revelstoke; "and let me remind you, Persis, that I am the critic here, and any comment will come from me, not you.

Take yourself off, you saucy puss, and do some typing, or wash up, or something." Rising, he hauled Miss Kinwellmarshe off the table and pushed her toward the kitchen, giving her a resounding slap on her splendid buttocks. She repeated her previous comment with hauteur, but she went.

"Now," said he, "let's get down to business. What's that song all about?"

Monica had occasionally been questioned in this way by Molloy, and she always hated it. A song was a song, and it was about what it said; it was almost bad luck to probe it and pull it to pieces, for it might never regain its shape. But Revelstoke had made her sing against her will, and she knew that he could make her speak. Might as well give in at once and get it over.

"It's about people saying good-bye."

"People?"

"Lovers, I suppose."

"Why are they saying good-bye?"

"I don't know; the song doesn't say."

"Doesn't it? Who wrote it?"

"Tosti."

"The music, yes. When did he live?"

"Oh, quite recently; Mr. Molloy once saw him."

"Who wrote the words?"

"I—I don't know."

"Oh, then I assume that you consider the words of small importance in comparison with the music. Do you think it is good music?"

"No, not really."

"How would you describe it?"

"A sort of drawing-room piece, I suppose."

"Yes, yes; but technically?"

"A ballad?"

"No, not a ballad. It is hardly a tune at all—certainly not a hummable sort of tune like a ballad. It's what's called an *aria parlante.* Know what that means?"

"A sort of speaking song?"

"A declamatory song. So there must be something to declaim. The words were written by a Scottish Victorian novelist and poet called George John Whyte-Melville. I see that your copy of the song gives his initials as 'G.T.' and robs him of his hyphen; just shows what the firm of Ricordi thought about him. Ever heard of him?"

"Never."

"An interesting man. Quite successful, but always underestimated his own work and was apt to run himself down, in a gentlemanly sort of way. Wrote a lot about fox-hunting, but there is always a melancholy strain in his work which conflicts oddly with the subjects. His biographer thought it was because his married life was most unhappy. Does that seem to you to throw any light on that song?"

"It's very unhappy. You mean that perhaps it wasn't lovers, but himself and his wife he was writing about?"

"I am charmed by your implied opinion of the married state. Married people are sometimes lovers, and lovers are not always happy. Why are they unhappy, do you suppose?"

"Well, usually because they can't get married. Or because one of them may be married already."

"There can be other reasons. Read me the first verse."

In a constricted tone, and without expression, Monica read:

> Falling leaf, and fading tree,
> Lines of white in a sullen sea,
> Shadows rising on you and me;
> The swallows are making them ready to fly
> Wheeling out on a windy sky—
> Good-bye, Summer,
> Good-bye!

"You see? A succession of pictures—the fall of the leaf, the birds going south, a rising storm, and darkness falling. And it all adds up to—what?"

This is worse than Eng. Lit. at school, thought Monica. But she answered, "Autumn, I suppose."

"Autumn, you suppose. Now let me read you the second verse, with a little more understanding than you choose to give to your own reading—

> Hush, a voice from the far away!
> 'Listen and learn', it seems to say,
> 'All the tomorrows shall be as today.
> The cord is frayed, the cruse is dry
> The link must break and the lamp must die.
> Good-bye to Hope,
> Good-bye.'

What do you make of that?"

"Still Autumn?"

"An Autumn that continues forever? Examine the symbols—lamp gone out, chain broken, jug empty, cord ready to break, and all the tomorrows being like today—what's that suggest? What is the warning voice? Think!"

Monica thought. "Death, perhaps?"

"Quite correct. Death—perhaps: but not quite Death as it is ordinarily conceived. The answer is in the last verse—

> *What are we waiting for?*
> *Oh, my heart!*
> *Kiss me straight on the brows!*
> *And part—again—my heart!*
> *What are we waiting for, you and I?*
> *A pleading look, a stifled cry—*
> *Good-bye forever,*
> *Good-bye!*

There it is! Plain as the nose on your face! What is it all about? What are they saying Good-bye to? Come on! Think!"

His repeated insistence that she think made Monica confused and mulish. She sat and stared at him for perhaps two minutes, and then he spoke.

"It is Death, right enough, but not the Death of the body; it is the Death of Love. Listen to the passion in the last verse—passion which Tosti has quite effectively partnered in the music. Haste—the sense of constraint around the heart—the pleading for a climax and the disappointment of that climax—What is it? In human experience, what is it?"

Monica had no idea what it was.

"Well, Miss Lumpish Innocence, it is the Autumn of love; it is the failure of physical love; it is impotence. It is a physical inadequacy which brings in its train a terrible and crushing sense of spiritual inadequacy. It is the sadness of increasing age. It is the price which life exacts for maturity. It is the foreknowledge of Death itself. It is the inspiration of some of the world's great art, and it is also at the root of an enormous amount of bad theatre, and Hollywood movies, and the boo-hoo-hoo of popular music. It is one of the principal springs of that delicious and somewhat bogus emotion—Renunciation. And Whyte-Melville and old Tosti have crammed it into

twenty lines of verse and a hundred or so bars of music, and while
the result may not be great, by God it's true and real, and that is why
that song still has a kick like a mule, for all its old-fashionedness.
Follow me?"

Monica sat for a time, pondering. What Revelstoke had said struck
forcibly on her mind, and she felt that it would have opened new
doors to her if she had fully understood it. And she wanted to understand. So, after a pause, she looked him in the eye.

"What's impotence?"

Revelstoke looked at her fixedly. Ribald comment rose at once to
his tongue, but Monica's seriousness asked for something better
than that. He answered her seriously.

"It is when you want to perform the act of love, and can't," he
said. "The difficulty is peculiar to men in that particular form, but
it is equally distressing to both partners. The symbolism of the poem
is very well chosen."

There was silence for perhaps three minutes, while Monica pondered. "I don't see the good of it," she said at last. "You take an old
song that hundreds of people must have sung and you drag it down
so it just means a nasty trouble that men get. Is that supposed to
make it easier for me to sing it? Or are you making fun of me?"

"I am not making fun of you, and I have not done what you said.
I have related quite a good poem to a desperate human experience
which, in my opinion, is the source from which it springs. If you
think of a poem as a pretty trifle that silly men make up while
smelling flowers, my interpretation is no good to you. But if you
think of a poem as a flash of insight, a fragment of truth, a break in
the cloud of human nonsense and pretence, my interpretation is
valid. When you sing, you call from the depth of your own experience to the depth of experience in your hearer. And depth of
experience has its physical counterpart, believe me; we aren't disembodied spirits, you know, nor are we beautiful, clear souls
cumbered with ugly indecent bodies. This song isn't about 'a nasty
trouble that men get'—to use your own depressingly middle-class
words; it is about the death of love, and the foreknowledge of death;
it is an intimation of mortality. As you say, hundreds of people have
sung it without necessarily looking very deeply into it, and thousands
of listeners have been moved without knowing why. Poetry and
music can speak directly to depths of experience in us which we
possess without being conscious of them, in language which we

452   THE TWENTIETH CENTURY

understand only imperfectly. But there must be some of us who understand better than others, and who give the best of ourselves to that understanding. If you are to be one of them, you must be ready to make a painful exploration of yourself. When I came in here just now, you were playing a rather silly piece in a very silly way. You sang your folksongs like a cheap Marie Antoinette pretending to be a shepherdess. Domdaniel wants you to be better than that, and so he has sent you to me."

"Do you think Sir Benedict thinks about songs and poetry the way you do?"

"Sir Benedict dearly loves to play the role of the exquisitely dressed, debonair, frivolous man of the world. But he's no fool. And he thinks you are no fool, too. He told me so. Here's your cup of tea that I promised you."

It was very nasty tea. Monica drank it reflectively. After a time, during which Revelstoke had stared intently at her, he said—

"What are you thinking about?"

"I was thinking that you're not really *simpatico*."

"I've no time for charm. Many people think me extremely unpleasant, and I cultivate that, because it keeps fools at a distance."

"Mr. Molloy says you're quite the genius."

"Mr. Molloy, in his limited way, is quite right—Well, are you coming to me for lessons?"

"Yes."

"All right. Give me thirty shillings now, for your subscription to *Lantern*. Here's a copy of the latest number. And next time you come here, have the politeness to ring the bell. It'll spare your blushes."

W. O. MITCHELL

1914-

W. O. Mitchell was born in Weyburn, Saskatchewan, and for many years has lived at High River, Alberta. He was educated at the Universities of Manitoba and Alberta, and gratefully acknowledges the assistance of "a stringent English Professor," F. M. Salter of Alberta, in becoming a successful writer. He has contributed short stories of prairie life to *The Atlantic Monthly*, *Maclean's*, *The Ladies Home Journal*, *Liberty*, and *The Canadian Forum*, and was for a time fiction editor of *Maclean's*. He is now writer in residence at University of Calgary.

Mitchell's first novel, *Who has Seen the Wind*, appeared in 1947 and was immediately recognized as a minor classic of western local color. The passage from it included here was originally a prize-winning short story in *The Atlantic Monthly*. Mitchell was the author of a popular radio series "Jake and the Kid," set in the imaginary town of Crocus, Saskatchewan. In 1961 it was published as an episodic novel and won the Leacock medal for humor in 1962. A third novel, *The Kite*, was published in 1962. In spite of a somewhat conventional plot, the book is remarkable for the vivid characterization of old Daddy Sherry, an incorrigible centenarian of Selby, Alberta.

FROM *Who Has Seen the Wind*, 1947

SAINT SAMMY

Saint Sammy, Jehovah's Hired Man, lifted the sacking from the front of his piano box and looked out over the prairie sweeping to the horizon's bare finality.

Today was the fifth day.

The first day after Bent Candy's visit had not been the day; the Lord had been busy; for one thing he had been lightening and darkening His earth by slipping the melting edges of slow clouds over the prairie.

The second day after Mr. Candy's visit had not been the day. Saint Sammy had known that as he walked to the corner of the poplar pole corral, one shoulder high, walking as though he had a spring under one heel. Far to the West, he decided, the Lord was occupied with a honing wind and a black dust-storm that needed His attention.

The third day after Bent Candy's visit had not been the day. That day there had been no frightened feeling in the pit of Sammy's stomach. So the third day had not been the day.

Nor was the fourth day. That day had been the Lord's hail day. He had been mixing up a batch of hail. Hail to the Lord that was mixing hail! Hail to the bunging brown grasshopper that leaped! Hail to his bulging shanks! Hail to Saint Sammy too!

Today, the fifth day, was the day. As he watched Habbakuk and Haggar cropping the grass by the empty wagon box and the others, Hannah, Naomi, Ruth, Hosea, Joel, Malachi, and the two colts, Corinthians One and Two, in the far corner of the pasture, Saint Sammy knew that today was the Lord's day to punish Bent Candy. The Lord wasn't letting him get any Clydes!

Bent Candy, the caterpillar man, had added another five sections to his holdings that year; he had put all his land into flax, and with his usual luck had managed to have a moderate amount of rain fall on his crops. Some of it was burned, but most of it would still return him enough to show a profit, small though it was. He was called the Flax King now.

As Sammy walked over the prairie toward the Lord's corner of the pasture he was aware of a rising wind in the grasses; the stitching ring of crickets was in his ears like the pulsing of his own blood. He heard a meadow lark sing. A gopher squeaked.

Whatever the Lord did to Bent Candy, it would serve him right; he ought to have known better than to fool around with the Lord and Saint Sammy. Going to church and passing the collection plate were not going to help him now; it hadn't helped the Pharisees. After the Lord had smited him for coveting the Clydes, Bent Candy wouldn't be called the Flax King any longer.

Time and again since Candy had first made an offer for the horses Sammy had been visited by the voice of the Lord, reminding him always of the day ten years ago. That had been the bad hail year, when Sammy had stood on the edge of his ruined crop, looking at the countless broken wheat heads lying down their stalks.

As he had stared, the wind turning upon itself had built up a black body from the top soil, had come whirling toward him in a smoking funnel that snatched up tumble-weeds, lifting them and rolling them over in its heart. The voice of the Lord had spoken to him.

"Sammy, Sammy, ontuh your fifty-bushel crop have I sent hail stones the size a baseballs. The year before did I send the cutworm which creepeth an' before that the rust which rusteth an' the saw-fly which saweth.

"Be you not downcast, fer I have prepared a place fer you. Take with you Miriam an' Immaculate Holstein an' also them Clydes. Go you to Magnus Petersen, who is even now pumping full his stock trought. He will give ontuh you his south eighty fer pasture, an' there will you live to the end of your days when I shall take you up in the twinkling of an eye.

"But I say ontuh you, Sammy, I say this—don't ever sell them Clydes, fer without them ye shall not enter. I will take them up with you when I shall fill the air with Cherubim an' Serubim from here to the correction line.

"Even as I did ontuh Elijah an' Elisha an' John, will I speak ontuh you just like now. So git, Sammy—git to Magnus Petersen before he's finished of pumping full that stock trought an' shall commence to stook the oats which I have made ready for him.

"There will you find the box off of Miss Henchbaw's pianah,

which Magnus will give ontuh you together with his stone boat fer hawlin' it.

"Hail, Saint Sammy!" the Lord had said. "Hail, Jehovah's Hired Man!

"Mr. Candy must not get the Clydes!"

And today was the Lord's smiting day, decided Sammy as he walked over the prairie to the Lord's corner. It was a perfect smiting day.

Ahead of Saint Sammy the sun had haloed the soft heads of fox-tails bending in the rising wind; it glistened from the amber wings of a red-bodied dragon-fly hovering; it gleamed from the shrunken surface of the slough. High in the sky a goshawk hung, over the prairie flat as the palm of a suppliant hand, inscrutable and unsmiling, patched dark with summer fallow, strung long with the black crosses of telephone poles marching to the prairie's rim.

The vengeance of the Lord upon Bent Candy would be awful. Mr. Candy would wish he'd never tried to get Saint Sammy's horses; he'd wish he had never ordered them off the Petersen pasture. The vengeance of the Lord would be enough to give a badger the heart-burn.

Saint Sammy thought of the day that Bent Candy had called on him.

He had climbed under the barbed wire and had said, "I come to see was you gonna sell them there Clydes."

"Over the breadth a the earth there ain't no horses like mine!" Saint Sammy cried, "an' the voice a the Lord come ontuh me sayin', 'Sammy, Sammy, don't you sell them there Clydes.' An' moreover I say ontuh you, I ain't!"

"Like I thought. Figgered to give you one more chance. You ain't takin' it. Got a week to git off of here."

Saint Sammy's mouth made a little round hole in his grey beard, and as he looked into Bent Candy's expressionless red face under white hair, the wildness of panic came to his eyes. "All a this here land was give ontuh me an' the Herb thereoff fer me an' my critters! Magnus Petersen he——"

"Sold her."

"But—the Lord, He wouldn't——"

"No blaspheemy. Sell er git off. My land now. Them horses ain't no good to anybody—way they are. You ain't broke 'em. You don't work 'em. Sell er git off!"

"But—Magnus—he wouldn't——"

"He did."

"From here to the ridge there ain't no pasture fer—the Lord hath mighty lightnin', Bent Candy."

"Mebbe He has."

"An' He moves in——"

"Sell er git off!"

"The Lord hit a man I knew an' it come to pass between the well an' the back stoop an' the Lord's lightnin' burnt every stitch of clothin' from off of him an' left him standin' bare-naked with a bucket of water in each hand—once."

"I got no time to listen——"

"An' his wife she arose an' she went fer tuh emp'y the slop pail an' she was sore afraid when she saw him there an' she yelled an' he come to with a great start an' spilt the water from them red-hot buckets over him an' got scalded nigh ontuh death."

"You got a week."

"The Lord will——"

"Sell er git off!"

After Mr. Candy had gone, Saint Sammy had been afraid. He had gone into his piano box and lain there. He plunged his hand deep into the raw sheep's wool and binder twine bits to bring out the tin box with its broken glass and pebbles and twigs and empty match boxes and labels. He had counted them as he always counted when troubled. Count your labels, count them one by one.

It did not help. He put the red and blue underwear labels back, and for a long time he watched the wedge face of a field mouse sitting just outside the piano box opening.

When the fence post shadows lay long over the prairie and the whole pasture was transfigured with the dying light of day, he went out to milk Miriam and turn the calf loose on Immaculate. Then he started across the prairie to Bent Candy's. He found him in the act of rolling gasoline barrels off his truck, that stood by the barn. It was a new barn, hip-roofed and painted red, a thing of beauty and of pride. One looked at the flawless, red siding and felt as a child must feel in gazing upon a new, red wagon. The metal runner and pulleys on the broad door were hardly rusted yet, since Candy had built the barn only that spring. It was the barn that was to become the home of Saint Sammy's Clydes, a barn built by a man who did his farming by tractor, and who, although he had no use for horses, had been obsessed for years by a desire to possess Sammy's.

He turned upon Saint Sammy. "Whatta you want?"

"I come to see would you—ain't there any way me an' my critters could dwell on——"

"Jist sell me them ten head a horses—stay as long as you please."

"But—the Lord He won't take me up in the twink——"

"You got a week."

"The Lord might knock yer flax flatter'n a platter a——"

"You heard me."

Saint Sammy's long arm came slowly up, and the finger pointing at Bent Candy trembled. "The glory of the Lord come out a the East an' His voice was the wind a-comin' over the prairie's far rim!"

On Mr. Candy's red face there was a look of discomfort; in the district, he enjoyed the reputation of a religious man; he was serving his fifteenth year as Baptist deacon. "Now—don't you go startin' none a that——"

"An' the voice a the Lord come ontuh me, sayin', 'I kin do the drouthin' out an' the hailin' out an' the hopperin' out an' the blowin' out till Bent Candy gits good an' tired out! She shall come to pass——' "

Mr. Candy reached behind himself and knocked with his knuckles against the manure fork handle leaning against his new barn. He *was* a religious man, and years of prairie farming had deepened in him faith in a fate as effective as that of Greek drama. There had been a mental struggle through the years since he had first seen and wanted the Clydes. Before he could go to Magnus Petersen and secretly buy the land, it had been necessary for him to want the horses badly.

" '—sorra an' sighin' shall come to Bent Candy, for he hath played the sinner in the sight a the Lord, an' it shall come tuh pass the horned owl mourneth an' the kiyoot howleth!' " Saint Sammy's arm had come down.

For a long time after Sammy had left, Bent Candy stood by his shining barn. Then as he walked back to his house he looked up to the evening sky where high clouds still caught the lingering light of day and held it unexpected there. His Baptist conscience told him that the Clydes were horses after all. A killdeer sadly called. The church, thought Bent Candy, could use new pews.

Coin clear, the sun had sunk to leave an orange stain behind on clouds above the prairie's western line.

And now, thought Saint Sammy, waiting in the Lord's corner of the pasture, the fifth day was the day. He said it aloud to the weasel a short distance away with his slant head bolt upright in Presbyterian propriety, his toy ears round.

The rising wind tossed the prairie grasses now, stirring Saint Sammy's long and tangled beard, lifting the grey hair that hung to his shoulders. A butterfly came pelting by to pause on one of the dusty leaves laddering up a goldenrod's stem, its wings, closed up like hands held palms together; it untouched itself to go winking and blinking, now here, now there, echoing itself over the empty, wind-stirred prairie.

And off toward the town a small boy's figure could be seen, leaning into the strengthening wind, as it walked toward Saint Sammy's. Brian wished that he had not decided to call on Sammy; he would have turned back now in the face of the threatening windstorm, but he was closer to the Petersen pasture than he was to the town. So, while Saint Sammy waited for the Lord to button up the top button of His work smock, give a hitch to His Boss of the Road pants, and call for a whirlwind, Brian walked on, the grasses all around him, tossing like demented souls, their sibilance lost in the voice of the strengthening wind.

Brian reached the Lord's corner of the pasture just as Sammy shaded his eyes with his hand and looked out over the prairie.

"An' the Heavens will be opened up!" Saint Sammy cried, "just south a the correction line! Sorrah an' sighin' shall come to Bent Candy today!"

"It's going to storm, Sammy!" shouted Brian.

Sammy plucked the yellow head from a flower at his feet, crushed it, and stared down at the threads of gum stringing from the ball of his thumb. "The vengeance of the Lord shall be tenfold on Bent Candy—an' it shall be somethin' fearful!"

Calm and peace were in Sammy now; the terror had left him as he watched the far cloud hung low on the horizon, perceptibly spreading its darkness up the sky. "The Lord is on His way! He shall smite Bent hip an' thigh an' shin, an' there shall be none to comfort him!"

A tumble-weed went bounding past the boy and the old man, caught itself against the strands of the fence, then, released, went rolling on its way. An unnatural dusk that had grown over the whole prairie made Brian strain his eyes to see through the spread

darkness of dust licked up by the wind in its course across the land.
His ears were filled with the sound of the wind, singing fierce and
lost and lonely, rising and rising again, shearing high and higher
still, singing vibrance in a void, forever and forever wild.

As far as the two could see, the grasses lay flat to the prairie earth,
like ears laid along a jack rabbit's back. They could feel the wind
solid against their chests, solid as the push of a hand. It had plastered
Sammy's beard around his cheek. Brian felt it sting his face with
dust and snatch at his very breath. He was filled again with that
ringing awareness of himself that he had experienced so often before.

He looked at Saint Sammy and saw that the old man had his head
cocked on one side in a listening attitude. From the darkness all
around, scarcely distinguishable from the throating wind, the voice
of the Lord came to Saint Sammy :

"Sammy, Sammy, this is her, and I say ontuh you she is a dandy!
Moreover I have tried her out! I have blew over Tourigny's hen-
house; I have uprooted Dan Tate's windbreak, tooken the back door
off of the schoolhouse, turned over the girls' toilet, three racks, six
grain wagons; I have blew down the power line in four places; I
have wrecked the sails on Magnus Petersen's windmill!

"In two hours did I cook her up; in two hours will I cook her
down! An' when she hath died down, go you ontuh Bent Candy's
where he languishes an' you shall hear the gnashing of teeth which
are Bent Candy's an' he shall be confounded! Thus seth the Lord
God of Hosts, enter intuh thy pianah box an' hide fer the fear a the
Lord! Take the Kid with you!

"Count yer labels, Sammy, count them one by one!"

"C'mon!" cried Sammy to Brian, and as the boy stared questioningly up to him, "He's invited you in! C'mon!" He took Brian by
the shoulder and led him toward the piano box.

In the dark depths of Sammy's house, they crouched, and Sammy
did the Lord's bidding, going over his collected underwear labels by
the light of the flickering lantern.

In town, a bounding garbage can flung by the wind, clanged
against the bars of the town hall basement window plastered with
papers and tumble-weed. For the first time in his jail term the Ben
was still, standing in the centre of his cell, his wild eyes up to the
swirling darkness outside.

By her open window on the second floor of the O'Connal house,
Brian's grandmother sat quite still in her rocker, her hands black

with blown dust driven into the room between frantic curtains. Maggie O'Connal entered, struggled with the window, then turned anxiously to her mother.

Mrs. Abercrombie and Mr. Powelly, their planning of the Auxiliary garden party interrupted, stared at each other from uncomfortable throne chairs; they felt the large frame house around them shake like a spaniel after a swim. Over the sound of the wind came a rending crash; the house jumped.

"Let us pray!"

"What!"

"Let us pray!" Mr. Powelly called again.

"Oh."

The two got down on their knees with elbows on the rich velvet of Renaissance chairs.

The light of Sammy's lantern had become weak, and outside, the light of day had become strong again. Saint Sammy lifted the sacking.

The wind was discreet in the grass; Brian saw that just the loose blow dirt piled slightly higher, sharply rippled as the sand of a creek bed engraved by the water's current, showed that the Lord's wind had passed. Silence lay over everything, Brian and Sammy stood just outside the piano box. A gopher squeaked hesitantly. A suave-winged hawk slipped his shadow over the prairie's face, and a jack rabbit, startled, ears erect, went off past the fence in an exuberant bounce.

With his right shoulder high and his walk punctuated as though he had a spring under one heel, his arm swinging wide, Saint Sammy started off over the pasture. Brian, drawn, followed. The prairie grass clung at their pant legs; looping grasshoppers sprang sailing ahead of them and disappeared to lift again in brief, arcing flight. Here and there the yellow petals of black-eyed susans hung about their chocolate domes.

They crossed the road before Bent Candy's farm.

Mr. Candy stood where his new, red barn had been.

Sammy and Brian halted; they stared at the utter, kindling ruin of what had once been a barn. No stick stood. In the strewn wreckage not even the foundation outline was discernible. The result was what might have been expected if the barn had been put through a threshing machine and exhaled through the blower. Certainly the Lord's vengeance had been enough to give a gopher the heartburn.

There was awe in the old and quavering voice of Saint Sammy as it lifted in the hush of Bent Candy's farmyard.

"The Lord hath blew! He hath blew down the new an' shinin' barn of the fundamental Baptist that hath sinned in His sight! Like He said, 'Sorra an' sighin' hath cometh to Bent Candy!'"

Candy turned to Saint Sammy; he looked into the old man's eyes, water-blue, mildly wild with a fey look which said that he was either childlike, senile, or gently insane. He looked at the squeezed intensity of Sammy's face, and he thought of the spreading fields of flax he had planted, even now thirsting for moisture; he thought of the years of drouth and rust and hail and the many wheat plagues which had touched him only lightly. He said:

"You kin stay."

Brian watched Saint Sammy lift his arms wide.

"I looked an' I beheld! The Heavens was opened up, an' there was a whirlwind a-comin' outa the East, liftin' like a trumpet a-spinnin' on her end, an' there was fire inside a her, an' light like a sunset was all around about her! Plumb outa the midst a her come the voice a the Lord, sayin' 'Sammy, Sammy, git up from offa thy knees fer I am gonna speak ontuh you! The prairie shall be glad, an' she shall blossom like the rose! Yay, she shall blossom abundantly! The eyes a the blind shall see, an' the ears a the deaf shall hear! The lame is gonna leap like the jack rabbit, an' the water shall spout ontuh the prairie, an' the sloughs shall be full—plumb full!'"

Saint Sammy's arms came down.

"Amen," said Mr. Candy.

JACK LUDWIG

1922-

Born in Winnipeg and educated at the Universities of Manitoba and California (Los Angeles), Jack Ludwig has lectured
at several colleges in the United States and is a member of the
English Department at the State College of New York at
Stony Brook, Long Island. During 1967-1968 he was Writer
in Residence at the University of Toronto.

He is chiefly noted for his short stories of urban Jewish life
and has had award winning stories in the *Atlantic Monthly*,
Martha Foley's *Best American Short Stories* (1961), and *The
O. Henry Prize Stories* (1961). He has contributed stories to
Tamarack Review and various Canadian anthologies. He was
a co-founder and editor of the American avant-garde periodical, *The Noble Savage,* and is the author of a small book *On
Recent American Novelists* (1962). His most ambitious work
is his comic picaresque novel *Confusions* (1963) in which
West-Coast American academic life is satirized from the point
of view of a young Jewish instructor from Harvard. *Above
Ground*, his most recent novel was published in 1968. Ludwig
in his rough humor and satirical wit has something in common with two other Canadian-born Jewish novelists, Saul
Bellow and Mordecai Richler.

REQUIEM FOR BIBUL

Once upon a time—if we counted time not by calendars but by assimilated history and scientific change I'd be tempted to say four or five thousand years ago: before total war and all-out war, before death camps, Nagasaki, before fusion and fission, jets, moon shots, aeronauts, Luniks in orbit, before antibiotics, polio vaccine, open-heart surgery, before T.V., carburetors, and other wonders of auto-mation, before dead-faced hoods on motor-cycles, dead-faced beat-niks on maldecycles—once upon *that* kind of time lived a boy and his horse.

The year was 1939. This is no pastoral tale. The boy and the horse are both dead.

Twenty years late, counting time by the calendar, I write you of this boy Bibul and his horse Malkeh, of Bibul's ambition and his sad sad end. In time-sorrowed perspective I record for you the im-print Bibul left on my mind and feeling—his tic-like blink, his coal-black hair in bangs over his forehead, his emerycloth shaver's shadow, his ink-stained mouth, his immutable clothes that wouldn't conform to style or the seasons: always black denim Relief-style pants whitened by wear and washing, always a brown pebbled car-digan coiled at the wrists and elbows with unravelled wool, always a leather cap with bent visor, split seams, matching the color and texture of Bibul's hair. An old ruined Malkeh, scorned before lamented, making her daily round under Bibul's urging, dragging his creak of a fruit-peddler's wagon through Winnipeg's "island" slum north of the Canadian Pacific Railway Yards.

Bibul peddled while my time burned: in 1939 all of us high-school boys owlish with sixteen- and seventeen-year-old speculation, almost missed seeing this Bibul foxy with world-weary finagling. We were out to save the world, Bibul a buck. Hip-deep in reality, trying to beat tricky suppliers, weasely competitors, haggling cus-tomers, Bibul couldn't believe in us vaguesters. Peddling had forced him to see, hear, and judge everything. By his practical measure we were simply unreal. We'd speculate: Bibul would respond with *yeh-yeh*—the Yiddish double affirmative that makes a negative. He didn't have to say a word, or raise a sceptical eyebrow, or even frown with that tic. His smell alone argued a reality out of reach of our politely neutral Lux, Lifebuoy, Vitalis middle-class sweetness: "effluvium Bibul" we called that mixture of squashed berries, bad turnips, dank pineapple crates, straw, chickens, sad old horsey Malkeh. Bibul had a grand gesture to sweep away our irrelevance, a sudden movement of the hand like a farmwife's throwing feed to chickens, his nose sniffing disgust, his sour mouth giving out a squelching sound, "aaaa." Sometimes he sounded like a goat, other times a baby lamb—just "aaaa," but enough to murder our pushy pretentions.

We were a roomful of competitive sharks—math sharks, physics sharks, English, Latin, history sharks, secretly, often openly, sure we surpassed our teachers in brain and know-how. Joyfully arrogant we shook off the restricting label of high-school student, considering ourselves pros—mathematicians, scientists, writers, artists. In our own minds we had already graduated from the University, had passed through Toronto or Oxford, were entangled in public controversies with the great names in our respective fields, ending right but humble, modestly triumphant. But where was Bibul in this league? As loud as we pros hollered Bibul heard nothing. He only yawned, slouched, even snoozed, gave out with that killing yeh-yeh, poked his greyish nose into his peddler's notebook red with reality's ooze of tomato.

"Bibul," we'd say in the break between classes, "do semantics mean nothing to your knucklehead? An intellectual revolution's coming. You've got to stand up and be counted. What'll it be? Are you for Count Korzybski or against him?"

"Aaaa," aaed Bibul, and his chicken-feeding motion sent us back to ivory towers.

"You' nuddin' bud gids," he'd say haughtily whenever we disturbed his audit of fruit-and-vegetable reality, "a 'ell of a lod you guys know aboud live."

Though we jeered and mocked, treated him like a clown, he was one of us, so how could we disown him? Kings of St. John's High, lording it from our third-floor eminence over the giants and dwarfs living the underground life in the school's basement a-screech with whirling lathes and milling machines, or those second-floor, salt-of-the-earth commercial students dedicated to bookkeeping, typing, the sensible life, we of course wanted to pass our nobility on to Bibul. We ran the yearbook and could have established him there—

466 THE TWENTIETH CENTURY

but on the "island" English ran a poor second to Ukrainian, Polish, German, or in his case, Hebrew. We could have made him captain of the debating team, but peddling wrecked that: wrought up he stammered, angry he slobbered, no way to win arguments. Being a businessman, like his breed he had no time for politics; being tone-deaf he was a flop at glee-club try-outs. At sports he was dreadful. He couldn't swim a stroke, or skate, was flubbyknuckled at baseball, slashing pigeon-toed at soccer, truly kamikaze going over a hurdle. And women? He had no time for them in his practical life: his old mare Malkeh and the ladies who haggled with him were the only females Bibul knew.

In recognition of his memo-book involvement we made Bibul our room treasurer.

After classes we theoreticians sprawled on the school green and took pleasure from long-limbed, heavy-thighed, large-breasted girls thwarting an educator's pious wish that the serge tunic neutralize the female form. Bibul was never with us. At the closing bell he'd run off to his horse and wagon, set to run the gauntlet of his customers (*shnorrers*, pigs he called them); and early on a morning, when we theoreticians-turned-lover, weary after a long night of girl-gaming, sat in Street Railways waiting houses knocking ourselves out over noisy reading of Panurge's adventure with the Lady of Paris, Bibul, up and dressed since 4:00 a.m., struggled at the Fruit Row for bruised fruit and battered vegetables in competition with wizened peddlers and their muscular sons. At nine, bleary-eyed all, theoretician and practical man rose to greet the morn with a mournful *O Canada*.

Lost in abstraction, and me, I thought little of Bibul in those days. He was a clown. A mark. A butt. The peddling was part of the sad desperate struggle for money every family in the depression knew. Bibul was the eldest of four children, his widowed ma supporting them on what she could make out of a tiny grocery store, doing the best she could, the dear lady, known throughout the "island" as "The Golden Thumb" and the "Adder," the latter reference ambiguous, meaning either snakes or computation, Bibul's ma being famous for a mathematical theorem that said $5 + 6 = 12$ or 13, whichever was higher.

Not till the year of our graduation did I discover why Bibul peddled with such dedication, why he rode out like a teen-age Don Quixote to do battle with those abusive, haggling, thieving *shnorrers*.

And what a riding-out that was! His paintless wagon listed like a sinking ship, sounded like resinless fiddles in the hands of apes, each wheel a circle successfully squared. Bibul sat on a tatter of leatherette bulging at the ends like a horsehair creampuff; over his wilted greens and culled fruit Bibul's faultless-in-his-favor scales made judgment, this battered tin scoop more dented than a tin B-B target. And what was more fitting than a nag like Malkeh to drag that crumbling wagon on its progress?

As grim as Don Quixote's Rosinante would look next to elegant Pegasus, that's how Malkeh would have looked next to Rosinante: she was U-shaped in side view, as if permanently crippled by the world's fattest knight lugging the world's heaviest armor. She sagged like a collapsed sofa with stuffing hanging low. She was bare as buffed mohair, her shoulders tanned from the rub of reins, her color an unbelievable combination of rust, maroon, purple, bronze, found elsewhere only in ancient sun-drenched velvets. Her tail was a Gibson Girl's worn discarded feather boa, its fly-discouraging movements ritualistic, perfunctory, more to let flies know that Malkeh wasn't dead than that she was alive. Her legs, like a badly carpentered table, were of assorted lengths, which made Malkeh move by shuffling off like a pair of aged soft-shoe dancers in final farewell. Her hooves were fringed with fuzzy hairs like a frayed fiddle-bow abandoned to rain and sun, her horseshoes dime-thin, rusty as the metal hinges on her wagon's tail-gate. To encourage Malkeh to see Bibul covered her almost-blind eyes with a pair of snappy black racing-horse blinkers trimmed with shiny silver rivets, a touch to her décor like a monocle in the eye of a Bowery bum.

Out of compassion, out of loyalty to this wreck of a horse, Bibul let his wagon go to ruin: wood could be camouflaged with paint or varnish but where was covering to hide or revive sad old mortal Malkeh?

One day I came to school early, and saw her.

She was the horse version of "The Dying Gaul." On Bibul's "island" Malkeh suffered no invidious comparisons, but on a main thoroughfare like St. John's High's Salter Street Malkeh was exposed to the cruelty of horse hierarchy, and her submarginal subproletariat hide was bared. High-stepping, glossy-flanked, curried and combed T. Eaton Company horses, middle-class cousins of aristocratic thoroughbreds seen only on race tracks, veered their rumps sharply as they passed, hooves steelringing, traces white as snow. Their tails were prinked out with red ribbon, their wagons chariots spar-

468 THE TWENTIETH CENTURY

kling in red, white, gold against blue-blackness that could mean only good taste. These bourgeois horses had the true bourgeois comforts —warm blankets, stables with hay wall-to-wall, feedbags that offered privacy and nourishment. Their drivers looked like sea-captains, neat contrast to a slop like Bibul. And their commercial feed was gastronomical compared with the bad lettuce, wilted carrot tops, shrivelled beets Bibul shoved at Malkeh in a ripped old postman's pouch.

Malkeh took their snubs without flinching. It was part of the class struggle. What hurt was the heavy powerful working-class Percherons and their stinking garbage scows, when *they* avoided kinship with Malkeh, acting like a guest at a high-toned party ignoring a waiter who's a close relative.

Pity old Malkeh's vengeful heart: the only pleasure she got from her enforced station on Salter Street came from knowing flies used her as an aerodrome from which to launch vicious attacks on the elegant department-store horses passing.

I saw her. The Principal too saw her, slouched with resignation, a "Don't" in an SPCA exhibit, her right foreleg flatteringly fettered by a cracked curling stone to give Malkeh the impression she had the vim and youth to turn runaway horse. Malkeh died a long time ago, but years before she did the Principal had her one visit gnomically memorialized and graven in metal: early next morning, where Malkeh had stood, this marker went up: "No Parking At Any Time."

Bibul never again brought her to school.

Which is not to say that life on the "island" was without its grim side: what accounted for an almost-blind horse wearing blinkers? *Shnorrers!* Those women with bare feet stuck hurriedly into their husbands' outsize felt slippers, their hair uncombed, faces unmade, women in nightgowns at four on a sunshiny afternoon, hands clenching pennies and silver Bibul had to charm away from them with hard-sell and soft-soap. Singly they waited, in concert plotted, en masse moved in on him. Their purpose was simple—*get much, pay little*. To the victor went Bibul's spoiled spoils.

"Giddy ahb, Malgeh," Bibul would holler from his high seat on the wagon, and his cry sounded to a *shnorrer's* ears like a warring clarion.

Into the lists Malkeh dragged the keening wagon, onto the "island" in ruins like a medieval town (Canadian history is short but our buildings add spice by getting older faster). Foundationless hovels kids might have built out of assorted-sized decks of cards sagged, leaned at crazy-house angles to astound Pisa. Gates tipsy as Malkeh's wagon swung on one hinge from a last lost post; dry, cracking wood fences leaned in surrender towards the ground, begging like old men in sight of a grave to be allowed to fall the rest of the way; windows were tarpaper-patched, like pirate's eyes, ominous as the blackness left in the streets by uninsured fires.

Behind every window or screen opaque with dust, behind every door splintered from kids' kicking waited the *shnorrers*, trying to make Bibul anxious, make him sweat a little, a cinch for persistent hagglers.

"Ebbles, ebbles, den boundz f'a quadder," Bibul shouted.

Crafty with stealth the *shnorrers* didn't bite.

Unflustered, unfooled, Bibul took advantage of the phony war, biting off the only three unspotted cherries in his entire stock while Malkeh dragged the exposed tin rims of the wagonwheels into the frost heaves and back-lane crevices. That cramped stinking back lane was mutually agreeable as a Compleat Battlefield—for Bibul because the solid pall of chicken droppings and horse dung was fine camouflage for the imperfections Time and Decay wrought his produce, for the *shnorrers* because the narrow quarters made tampering with the scale easier, detection harder, filching a hot possibility.

"Whoa beg, whoa der Malgeh," Bibul ordered, oblivious of the spying women.

There, among rusted bedsprings hung up like huge harps, torn mattresses resembling giant wads of steel wool, in a boneyard of Model T's, Malkeh and the wagon rested. Dogs scooted in darts of nervous yapping, cats hissed down from rust-streaked corrugated rooftops, pigeons wheeled high above Bibul's untroubled head, returning to perch on overhanging eaves like fans anxious to get close to a scene of scuffle.

The *shnorrers* tried to read Bibul's face: the text was that Sphinx-like tic of a blink. Stalling he made entries into that memo-book, peeled an orange, scratched himself with casual but maddening thoroughness.

The *shnorrers'* united front crumbled. A foot slipped out from behind a door. Then a head.

"Wha' you gonna cheat me on t'day, Bibul?" rasped out of an impatient throat.

The war was on! Horseflies, the depression having made pickings so sparse they dropped their high standards and declared Malkeh a host, left the depressing fare of uncovered garbage cans (each lid long ago commandeered to be target in the minor-league jousts of the *shnorrers'* unknightly kids), and, hiding behind the *shnorrers* sneaking up to do Bibul battle, launched assault on old Malkeh's flat weak flanks.

The siege began, swiftly, deftly: a red-haired old woman flipped two-cent oranges into the one-cent bins, her other hand pointed up at the sky to make Bibul raise his eyes and predict weather.

Her accomplice brought Bibul back to reality, picking the bargains up before they'd even stopped rolling.

"Boyaboy Bibul, you god good tings in y' usually stinkin' stock, look here, Mrs. Gilfix, at such oranges."

Bibul's tic-like blink snapped like a camera shutter on their mischief.

"Give over here dem oniges," he reproved them, "*yoisher*, show a liddle resdraind," and the sad old innocents watched the two-cent numbers fall back into the two-cent bins.

On the other side of the wagon a pair of raspberry hands crushed away at lettuce greens.

"How much off f' damaged goods" the criminal hollered, wiping lettuce juice off on her gaping nightgown.

But the red-haired old woman hadn't given up on oranges.

"Black head means black heart, robber," she cried out. "Perls d'fruit man who has a white head and eight kids and supports two unmarried sisters in Russia, from *him* I get fresher cheaper by two coppers—ha come, ha? Ha come?"

"My oniges are Sundgizd, Blue Gooze," Bibul, a sucker for brand names, came back huffily. "Berls' oniges grow on ebble drees."

One man's quarrel is another woman's smoke screen. The *shnorrers* moved in, squeezing the fruit, poking, tapping, complaining with shrieks and curses that sent the pigeon-hearted pigeons high off their perches. Like a bucket brigade the ladies passed fruit up and down the length of the wagon, each nose an inspector, those with teeth taking their duties more seriously, tasters whose opinions Bibul could live without.

"*Shnorrers* dad youz are," he hollered, holding up a nipped apple, a chewed-up orange, "you god no gare vor my brovides?"

"Low how he's independent," mocked the red-haired one, lunging fruitless after a fistful of cherries, "look how he holds hisself big! His fadder's a doctor, maybe? Or the mayor?"

Bibul was a lone guard defending his fortress from desperate pillagers; ubiquitous as Churchill, many-handed as Shiva, he had to be compassionate as Schweitzer. Though *I* didn't know what Bibul's dedication to peddling was all about, the *shnorrers* did: Bibul was saving up to become a Rabbi. Bibul immersed himself in the practical, pedestrian, material life because of a Great Cause—the Yeshiva in New York, eventual immersion in a spiritual life dedicated to comfort suffering mankind.

How the *shnorrers* used that Great Cause in their war with Bibul! It was all double: in sincerity they poured out their hearts to him— an educated boy, soon to be a Rabbi, maybe he'd understand *their* side—the husband who had taken off and never come back, the bad-hearted rich relatives, the ungrateful kids, the treacherous friends, root, trunk, branch of a Jewish Seven Deadly Sins. They dizzied him with complicated stories, unsettled his strong stomach with demonstrations of human frailty—missing teeth, crossed eyes, wens, tumors, needed operations.

As a bonus to sincerity they hoped the tales would divert Bibul long enough for their aprons to fill with filched fruit.

Crying real tears Bibul would free an apricot from a fist already stained with cherry.

"A religious you call yourself?" the caught thief howled. "God should strike me dead if I stole ever in my life one thing!"

Glancing up at the sky she moved closer to the other ladies: who knew what kind of pull with God a boy-studying-to-be-a-Rabbi had?

"Bibul, sveethard," cooed one Mrs. Itzcher, blemished but bleached, "give off ten cents a dozen by oranges and Tillie'll show plenty appreciation."

Bibul used his chickenfeed gesture to ward off temptation.

The *shnorrers* prayed God to give Bibul good enough ears to hear their laments but to compensate with a little dimming of the eyes so he wouldn't catch them stealing. When they lost they cursed in tones loud enough to be heard above the world's fishwifery in action.

No wonder Bibul considered us sharks irrelevant. After those *shnorrers* poured it on what was left to be said?

"My brudder's second wibe's kid wid da hump in back, Rabbi Bibul, has already her third miscarriage."

In the midst of haggle they rained down proofs of suffering and absurdity—banged heads, cut knees, singed eyelashes, hands caught in wringers, slippery floors, broken steps, toppling ladders. The compensation they asked was meagre. Pity, a buy on a busted watermelon.

When we sharks, hot for culture, cool for Schoenberg, long on judgments, short on facts, turned our abstract expressions Bibul's way how else could he respond but with that "aaaa"? What did our books and ideas have to compete with a *shnorrer*'s lament? Now when I think of that "aaaa" I translate it "When I was a child I spake as a child——" (may Bibul forgive me for quoting Saint Paul); "aaaa" said "vanity of vanities; all is vanity"; in explanation of the term for Mammon so that the rest would be with Abraham, Isaac, and Jacob; "aaaa" said "To everything there is a season, and a time to every purpose under the heaven."

On St. John's High School's Graduation Day Bibul was already at least half a Rabbi. The cardigan was gone, so too the denims and the black leather cap. He wore a fancy blue serge suit so new it still smelled of smoke. His sideburns were growing religiously into side curls, his emerycloth shadow was now a beardlike reality. But it was Bibul's eyes I remember, excited, gay, snapping under that tic. He looked incredibly happy.

"Bibul," I said seriously, "you look beautiful in that suit!"

"Damorra, Joe," he said low and secretive, "damorra I go d'Noo Yorick an' d'Yeshiva."

I talked to him without clowning. He told me what he wanted, explained the peddling.

"Bibul," I said seriously, as we were walking out to our waiting parents, "doesn't the idea of a city the size of New York scare you? You'll be strange. Winnipeg's a village——"

"Wadz t'be asgared?" Bibul said with that wave of his hand. "Beoble iz beoble. I zeen all ginds already."

He told me he'd sold Malkeh to Perls the peddler. His mother walked proudly towards Bibul as we reached the street.

"Bibul," I shouted as parents came between us, "you'll be a terrific Rabbi! Good luck!"

He gave that chickenfeed flourish, but with new style, and with modesty.

"Aaaa," I heard above the shouting congratulations of parents, the last time I heard or saw Bibul.

That fall we sharks entered the University, and Canada the war. Winnipeg was transformed, full of aircrew trainees from places I knew about before only through postage stamps, men with yellow

skins, red, brown, black, Maori tribesmen from New Zealand, bush-
men from Australia, strange-sounding South Africans, carved-faced
Indians thronging the streets and beer parlors. But far off in New
York, Bibul, who had known war with the *shnorrers*, paid little
attention to this latest struggle. He studied Torah and Talmud. He
made his spending money selling fruit to Lower East Side *shnorrers*
at the Essex Street Market.

Bibul's old Winnipeg customers haggled half-heartedly with old
man Perls and old horse Malkeh, the one mercifully deaf, the other
nearly blind. The depression seemed over: money came easier.

Once in a long while I checked in at Bibul's mother's store and,
gleaning news of Bibul, let her weigh me up a light pound of corned
beef. She wore her hair Buster Brown, carried a huge buxom body
on little feet in grey-white tennis shoes.

She shoved a letter at me.

"Look how a educated boy writes?" she said, pugnaciously proud.
"Who but a Rabbi could understand such words?"

She pulled it back before I could answer.

"See him only, just look," she pushed a picture at my eyes.

Bibul huddled against a bare Williamsburg wall grinning the
same grin as the three other Bibuls in the picture, all of them bearded
and wild as Russians, in black beaver hats bought with money they
had earned tutoring the Americanized grandchildren of rich
Chassidim.

"Some boy, my Bibul," his mother called to me as I was leaving.

Winter passed and the war grew grimmer. Spring was beautiful,
the war more dreadful. Summer was hot, particularly in New York
where Bibul divided his time between the Yeshiva and Essex Street's
shnorrers. For days the temperature was in the high nineties. Bibul
had never known such heat. He couldn't study, sleep, sell. In desperation he took himself one evening to the "Y," forgetting in the
heat that he'd never learned to swim.

An attendant, going off duty, warned Bibul away, told him not
to enter the pool. Who can be blind to Bibul's response?

"Aaaa," and that gesture.

He drowned.

His *shnorrers* on the "island," being told, wept and lamented.
We sharks, even in the midst of war's casualties, were moved and
stricken. Bibul was the first of us to die.

I cannot find Bibul's like in Winnipeg today.

Somebody waved a T-square wand over the old "island," bringing it the ninety-degree angle unknown in Bibul's far-off day. Progress pretends Bibul's "island" never really existed: the lanes are paved, the rot-wood of wall and fence has been sloshed over with paint. A few sneaky signs of the old world are around: a clothes-line pole, exhausted from long years of soggy fleece-lined underwear to support, seems ready to give up the ghost; an outside staircase, impermanent as a hangman's scaffold, mocks the fire commission that asked for greater safety and got greater danger.

Malkeh is dead. The wagon is all bits and crumble.

Motorized peddlers in trucks like Brink's Cars zoom through the reformed "island" late at night with the remnants of produce picked over by ringed and braceleted hands on the day route—River Heights, Silver Heights, Garden City, places of Togetherness, Betterness, Spotlessness, the polite answers Comfort has given to the sad old questions of Civilization.

"Apples, apples, two pounds for a quarter," the peddlers call, but not too loudly, and the women once poor enough to be *shnorrers* (few are still alive), the women who have replaced the departed *shnorrers* in remodelled rebuilt houses, look over the fruit and vegetables (ironically like Bibul's old rejects and reduced-to-clears because of prior though elegant pawing), buy a little, haggle not at all, or withdraw with a snub at peddling, a bow in favor of the superior refrigeration of supermarkets.

Through the streets old Malkeh drew that creaking wagon urged on by leather-capped Bibul, chrome-trimmed cars speed in unending gaggle, their sport-capped, stylishly-hatted drivers in control of power the equivalent of four hundred un-Malkeh horses. The Mayor tells Winnipeggers to "Think Big," bid for the Pan-American Games, hang out more flags and buntings. Slums like Bibul's "island" and the City Hall are fortunately doomed: Winnipeg is obviously a better place to live in.

Who doesn't welcome prosperity?

But the fact remains: I cannot find Bibul's like in Winnipeg today.

And that is why here and now, in this, his and my city, I write you this requiem for Bibul, for his face, for his Great Cause, his tic, his wave, his "aaaa." In love and the joy of remembering I sing you this Bibul and all that's past and passing but not to come.

When the City Hall is torn down they will build Winnipeg a new one; but where, O where shall we find more Bibuls?

MORDECAI RICHLER

1931-

With the publication of *The Apprenticeship of Duddy Kravitz*, his fourth novel, in 1959, Mordecai Richler found a theme that was both close to his own experience and extremely significant—the rise of a "smaller hero" from poverty and subjection to wealth, independence, and a kind of glory—through smartness, ruthlessness, obstinacy, self-esteem, and luck. The apotheosis of the heel is not a new or unusual story in American letters, but the colorful local background and the wealth of Jewish characterization make the novel a very special and convincing study. St. Urbain Street and its pulsating life are seen with a detachment that is never cold or superficial, and the book falls into place with the poetry of Klein and Layton and the fiction of Adele Wiseman and Jack Ludwig as part of the rich literary interpretation of the Hebraic culture of the modern Canadian city. Richler brings to it a hard-boiled sardonic humor, which can be seen at its most concentrated in the short story included here. This theme is developed with even greater power in Richler's latest and most ambitious novel *St. Urbain's Horsemen,* which won the Governor-General's Award for 1971.

Richler's earlier novels were *The Acrobats* (1954), *Son of a Smaller Hero* (1955), and *A Choice of Enemies* (1957). These deal with left-wing Canadian expatriates in London and Europe, whose sexual, Jewish, and political aspirations and frustrations are sometimes movingly but often somewhat superficially related. The Canada that most of his exiles reject is a small and narrow segment—even of his city and his province.

Much of Richler's recent work has been in the field of satire. *The Incomparable Atuk* (1963) and *Cocksure* (1968) are comic extravaganza which excoriate the arty Bohemian set that exploits Canadianism in literature and commercialized art. The savage intensity of the author's contempt makes these novels valuable contributions to Canadian self-awareness. Other recent books by Richler are his collection of journalistic essays *Tigers Under Glass* (1969) and his autobiographical sketches of St. Urbain Street published as *The Street* (1969).

Mordecai Richler was born in Montreal in 1931 of Jewish parents who had come to Canada from Russia and Poland. He was educated at Baron Byng High School and Sir George Williams University. He has lived in London and Montreal, where he has worked as a script writer for the BBC and the CBC. In 1958 he lived in the south of France, where with the aid of a Canada Council grant he wrote *Duddy Kravitz*. An engaging account of his literary career can be found in *Canadian Literature* 41, under the title "The Uncertain World."

MORTIMER GRIFFIN, SHALINSKY, AND HOW
THEY SETTLED THE JEWISH QUESTION

I was, at the time, beginning my first scholastic year as a lecturer in English literature at Wellington College in Montreal. You've probably never heard of Wellington. It's a modest institution with a small student body. There's the Day College, comprised, for the most part, of students who couldn't get into McGill, and the Evening College, made up of adults, most of them working at full-time jobs and trying to get a college education after hours. I was responsible for two Evening College courses, English 112 (Shakespeare) and English 129 (The Modern Novel). Shalinsky registered for both of them.

Until my fourth lecture I was only aware of Shalinsky as a ponderous presence in the third row. My fourth lecture dealt with Franz Kafka and naturally I made several allusions to the distinctively Jewish roots of his work. Afterwards, as I was gathering my notes together, Shalinsky approached me for the first time.

"I want to tell you, Professor Griffin, how much intellectual nourishment I got out of your lecture tonight."

"I'm glad you enjoyed it."

I'm afraid I was in a hurry to get away that night. I was going to pick up Joyce at the Rosens'. But Shalinsky still stood before my desk.

His wisps of grey curly hair uncut and uncombed, Shalinsky was a small, round-shouldered man with horn-rimmed spectacles, baleful black eyes, and a hanging lower lip. His shiny, pin-striped grey suit was salted with dandruff round the shoulders. A hand-rolled cigarette drooped from his mouth, his eyes half-shut against the smoke and the ashes spilling unregarded to his vest.

"Why did you change your name?" he asked.

"I beg your pardon. Did you ask me why I changed my name?"

Shalinsky nodded.

"But I haven't. My name is Griffin. It always has been."

"You're a Jew."

"You're mistaken."

Shalinsky smiled faintly.

"Really," I began, "what made you think—"

"All right. I'm mistaken. I made a mistake. No harm done."

"Look here, if I were a Jew I wouldn't try to conceal it for a moment."

Still smiling, blinking his eyes, Shalinsky said: "There's no need to lose your temper, Professor *Griffin*. I made a mistake, that's all. If that's the way you want it."

"And I'm not a professor, either. *Mr.* Griffin will do."

"A man of your talents will be famous one day. Like—like I. M. Sinclair. A scholar renowned wherever the intelligentsia meet. Thanks once more for tonight's intellectual feast. Good night, Mr. Griffin."

In retrospect, on the bus ride out to Hy and Eva Rosen's house, I found the incident so outlandishly amusing that I laughed aloud twice.

Joyce had eaten with the Rosens, and Eva, remembering how much I liked chopped liver, had saved me an enormous helping. I told them about Shalinsky, concluding with, ". . . and where he ever got the idea that I was Jewish I'll never know." I had anticipated plenty of laughter. A witty remark from Hy, perhaps. Instead, there was silence. Nervously, I added: "Look, I don't mean that I'd be ashamed—or that I was insulted that someone would think I was—Christ, you know what I mean, Hy."

"Yes," Hy said sharply. "Of course."

We left for home earlier than usual.

"Boy," Joyce said, "you certainly have a gift. I mean once you *have* put your foot in it you certainly know how to make matters worse."

"I thought they'd laugh. God, I've known Hy for years. He's one of my best friends. He—"

"*Was*," Joyce said.

"Look here," I said, "you don't seriously think that Hy thinks I'm an anti-semite?"

Joyce raised one eyebrow slightly—an annoying, college-girl habit that has lingered.

"Don't be ridiculous," I said. "Tomorrow, the day after, the whole thing will be forgotten, or Hy will make a joke of it."

"*They* have an excellent sense of humour," Joyce said, "haven't they? There's Jack Benny and Phil Silvers and—"

"Oh, for Christ's sake!"

Two days later a copy of the magazine called *Jewish Thought* came
in the mail. Attached was a printed note, WITH THE COMPLIMENTS OF
THE EDITOR, and underneath, penned with a lavish hand, *Respectfully, J. Shalinsky*. It took me a moment or two to connect Shalinsky, the editor, with Shalinsky, my student. I began to flip through
the pages of the little magazine.

The editorial, by J. Shalinsky, dealt at length with the dilemma
of Jewish artists in a philistine community. The lead article, by
Lionel Gould, B.Comm. (McGill), was titled "On Being a Jew in
Montreal West." Another article, by I. M. Sinclair, M.D., was titled
"The Anti-Semite as an Intellectual: A Study of the Novels of
Graham Greene." There were numerous book reviews, two senti-
mental poems translated from the Yiddish, a rather maudlin Israeli
short story, and, surprisingly, "Stepan Zweig and J. Shalinsky: A
Previously Unpublished Correspondence."

That night, as soon as my Eng. 112 lecture was finished, Shalinsky
loomed smiling over my desk. "You got the magazine?" he asked.

"I haven't had time to read it yet."

"If you don't like it, all you have to do is tell me why. No eva-
sions, please. Don't beat around the bush." Shalinsky broke off and
smiled. "I have something for you," he said.

I watched while he unwrapped a large, awkward parcel. The
string he rolled into a ball and dropped into his pocket. The brown
wrapping paper, already worn and wrinkled, he folded into eight
and put into another pocket. Revealed was an extremely expensive
edition of color plates by Marc Chagall.

"It occurred to me," he said, "that a man so interested in Kafka
might also find beauty in the art of Marc Chagall."

"I don't understand."

"Would you be willing," Shalinsky said, "to write me a review,
a little appreciation, of this book for the next issue of *Jewish
Thought*?"

I hesitated.

"We pay our contributors, of course. Not much, but—"

"That's not the point."

"And the book, it goes without saying, would be yours."

"All right, Mr. Shalinsky. I'll do it."

"There's something else. You have no lectures next Wednesday
night. You are free, so to speak. Am I right?"

"Yes, but—"

"Next Wednesday night, Mr. Griffin, the Jewish Thought Literary Society will be meeting at my house. It is a custom, at these meetings, that we are addressed by a distinguished guest. I was hoping—"

"What would you like me to talk about?" I asked wearily.

"Kafka," he said. "Kafka and Cabbalism. Refreshments will be served."

The address Shalinsky had given me was on St. Urbain Street. His house smelled of home-baked bread and spices. The living-room, almost a hall once the double doors had been opened, was filled with folding chairs, all of them vindictively directed at the speaker's table. The walls were laden with enormous photographs of literary giants protected by glass and encased in varnished wooden frames. Tolstoi, a bearded scarecrow on horseback, glared at the refreshments table. Dostoyevsky and Turgenev, their quarrels forgotten, stood side by side. Opposite, Marcel Proust smiled enigmatically.

At dinner I was introduced to Shalinsky's wife and daughter. Mrs. Shalinsky was a round rosy-cheeked figure with a double chin. The daughter—plump, plum-cheeked Gitel Shalinsky—wore a peasant blouse laced tightly over a tray of milky bosom, and a billowy green skirt. Her thick black hair she wore in an upsweep; glittering glass ear-rings dripped from her cup-shaped ears. A wooden clasp, GRETA, rode one breast, and a rose the other. Throughout dinner Gitel never said a word.

I handed Shalinsky my twelve-hundred-word article on Chagall, titled—rather brightly, I thought—*The Myopic Mystic*. My editor pondered the piece in silence, waving his hand impatiently whenever his wife interrupted him, a frequent occurrence, with remarks like, "Chew your meat, Jake," and, in an aside to me, "If I gave him absorbent cotton to eat, you think he'd know the difference?" and again, baring her teeth in a parody of mastication, "Chew, Jake. *Digest*."

Shalinsky read my article unsmilingly and folded it neatly in four.

"Is there anything the matter?" I asked.

"As an intellectual exercise your article is A-1, but—"

"You don't have to print it if you don't want to."

"Did I say I wouldn't print it? No. But, if you'll let me finish, I had hoped it would be a little more from the soul. Take the title, for instance. *The Myopic Mystic*," he said with distaste. "Clever. Clever, Mr. Griffin. But no heart. Still, this is a fine article. I wouldn't change a word. Not for the world."

The first of Shalinsky's guests arrived and he went into the living-room with him. Mrs. Shalinsky excused herself, too, and so I was left alone with Gitel. "Your father," I said, "is quite an extraordinary man. I mean at his age to take university courses and edit a magazine—"

"*The Ladies' Home Journal*," Gitel said. "*There's* a magazine for you. But *Jewish Thought*. An eight-hundred-and-forty-two circulation, counting give-aways—that's no magazine."

"Your father tells me he's printed work by S. M. Geiger. He's a very promising poet, I think."

"Some poet. He comes up to here by me. Alan Ladd—there's another twerp. How long are you going to speak tonight?"

"I'm not sure."

"Make it short, Morty. The blabbers never get invited back."

Three-quarters of an hour after my lecture was supposed to have started, only twelve people, all middle-aged men, had turned up, though many more had been prepared for. "It's the rain," Shalinsky said. A half-hour later six more people had drifted into the living-room: eight, if you counted the woman with the baby in her arms. Her name was Mrs. Korber. She lived upstairs and, in passing, I overheard her say to Mrs. Shalinsky, "Tell Mr. Shalinsky it's no trouble. Harry and the boy will be here the minute *Dragnet* is finished."

At that moment my jacket was given a fierce tug from behind. Whirling around, I was confronted by a small, wizened man with rimless glasses. "I am I. M. Sinclair," he said.

Retreating, I said: "You are a doctor, I believe."

"Like Chekhov."

"Oh. Oh, I see."

"I'm the only poet in Canada. Go ahead, laugh." Then, as though he were composing on the spot, I. M. Sinclair said: "I am an old man —an old man in a dry mouth—waiting for rain."

"You ought to write that down," I said.

"I have turned better lines. We have a lot to talk about, Griffin. The moment in the draughty synagogue at smokefall. . . ."

I broke away just in time to see Harry and the boy arrive. Shalinsky quickly called the meeting to order. There were three of us at the speaker's table—Shalinsky, myself, and a thin man with a fat ledger open before him. Shalinsky gave me a fulsome introduction, and Harry's boy—a fourteen-year-old with a running nose—poked two grimy fingers into his mouth and whistled. The others applauded politely. Then, as Mrs. Korber fed her baby with a bottle, I began.

"Louder," barked a voice from the back row.

So I spoke louder, elaborating on Kafka's difficulties with his father.

"What does he say?" somebody shouted. I waited while the man next to him translated what I had said into Yiddish. "Nonsense," his neighbour said. "A Jewish education never harmed anybody."

I rushed through the rest of my lecture, omitting half of it. A short question period was to follow. A Mr. Gordon was first.

"Mr. Griffin, my son is studying at McGill and he wishes to become a professor too. Now my question is as follows. How much can my Lionel expect to earn after five years?"

I had barely answered Mr. Gordon's question when a man in the back row began to wave his arm frantically.

"Yes," Shalinsky said. "What is it, Kaplan?"

Kaplan shot up from his seat. "I move a vote of thanks to Mr. Griffin for his excellent speech. I also move no more questions. It's nearly a quarter to eleven."

"Second both motions," cried a little man with thick glasses. "Segal. s, e,—no i—g, a, l. Get that in the minutes, Daniels."

A moment later Shalinsky and I were abandoned on one side of the room. Everyone else crowded round the refreshments table. I asked for my coat. At the door, Shalinsky thanked me profusely for coming.

"It's you I ought to thank," I said. "I enjoyed myself immensely."

"You see," Shalinsky said, "it's good to be with your own sometimes."

"Just what do you mean by that?"

Shalinsky smiled faintly.

"Look, will you please get it through your head that I'm not Jewish."

"All right, all right. I'm mistaken."

"Good night," I said, banging the door after me.

Joyce was waiting up for me in bed. "Well," she asked, "how did it go?"

"Skip it."

"What's wrong?"

"I don't want to talk about it, that's all."

"I don't see why you can't tell me about it."

I didn't answer.

"I mean you don't have to bite my head off just because I'm curious."

"There's nothing to tell."

"You've left a cigarette burning on the bureau."

"Oh, for Christ's sake. It would be so nice not to have all my filthy little habits pointed out to me for once. I know there's a cigarette burning on the bureau."

Retreating into the bathroom, I slammed the door after me. But even a bath failed to soothe my nerves. I lit a cigarette and lingered in the tub.

"What on earth are you doing in there?" Joyce shouted.

"Writing a book."

"Isn't he witty?"

"And next time you use my razor on your blessed armpits, kiddo, I'll thank you to wash it and replace the blade."

"Now who's pointing out whose filthy habits?"

I don't like mirrors. I make a point of never sitting opposite one in a restaurant. But tonight I had a special interest in studying my face.

"Mortimer!"

Mortimer, of course, could be a Jewish name.

"What are you doing in there?"

I'm a tall man with a long horse-face. But my nose is certainly not prominent. Turning, I considered my face in profile. When I finally came out of the bathroom I asked Joyce: "Would you say I had a Jewish face?"

She laughed.

"I'm serious, Joyce."

"As far as I'm concerned," she said, "there's no such thing as a Jewish face."

I told her about the lecture.

"If you want my opinion," she said, "you wouldn't mind Shalinsky's notion in the least if you weren't a sublimated anti-semite."

"Thank you," I said, switching off the light.

An hour later, sensing that I was still awake, Joyce turned to me in bed.

"I've been thinking, darling. Look, if—now please don't get angry. But *if* you were Jewish—"

"*What?*"

"I mean, if you have got Jewish blood I'd love you just as—"

"Of all the stupid nonsense. What do you mean, *if* I'm Jewish? You've met my parents, haven't you?"

"All I'm saying is that if—"

"All right. I confess. My father's real name is Granofsky. He's a goddam defrocked rabbi or something. Not only that, you know, but my mother's a coon. She—"

"Don't you dare use that word."

"Look, for the tenth time, if I had Jewish blood I would not try to conceal it. What ever made you think——?"

"Well," she said. "You know."

"Goddam it. I told you long ago that was done for hygienic reasons. My mother insisted on it. Since I was only about two weeks old at the time, I wasn't consulted."

"O.K.," she said. "O.K. I just wanted you to know where I would stand if—"

"Look, let's go to sleep. I've had enough for one day. Tomorrow first thing I'm going to settle this matter once and for all."

"What are you going to do?"

"I'm going to start a pogrom."

"Some of your jokes," Joyce said, "are in the worst possible taste."

"Yes. I know. I happen to be cursed with what Hy calls a Goyishe sense of humour."

The next morning I phoned Shalinsky.

"*Jewish Thought* here. Mr. Shalinsky is in Toronto. I'll have him get in touch with your office the minute he returns."

"Shalinsky, it's *you*."

"Ah, it's you, Griffin. I'm sorry. I thought it was Levitt the printer. He usually phones at this hour on Thursday mornings."

"Look, Shalinsky, I'd like you to come over here at three this afternoon."

"Good."

Taken aback, I said: "What do you mean, *good*?"

"I was hoping you'd want to talk. Speaking frankly, I didn't expect it to happen so soon."

"Just be here at three," I said. "O.K.?" And I hung up.

By the time Shalinsky arrived I had amassed all manner of personal documents—my army discharge papers, passport, driving license, McGill graduation certificate, marriage license, a Rotary Club public speaking award, my unemployment insurance card, vaccination certificate, Bo-lo Champion (Jr. Division) Award of Merit, three library cards, a parking ticket, and my bank book. On all these documents was the name Mortimer Lucas Griffin. Seething with suppressed anger, I watched as Shalinsky fingered each document pensively. He looked up at last, pinching his lower lip between thumb and index finger. "Facts," he said. "Documents. So what?"

"So what? Are you serious? All this goes to prove that I was born a white Protestant male named Mortimer Lucas Griffin."

"To think that you would go to so much trouble."

"Are you mad, Shalinsky?"

"I'm not mad." Shalinsky smiled, blinking his eyes against the smoke of his cigarette. "Neither do I want to make problems for you."

"What do I have to do to prove to you that I'm not Jewish?"

Shalinsky sifted through the papers again. "And what about your father?" he asked. "Couldn't he have changed his name without you knowing it? I mean, this is within the realm of possibilities, is it not?"

"Or my grandfather, eh? Or my great-grandfather?"

"You're so excited."

"I'd take you to see my parents, but they're both dead."

"I'm sorry to hear that. Please accept my condolences."

"They died years ago," I said. "A car accident."

"Is that so?"

"I suppose you think I'm lying?"

"Mr. Griffin, please."

"You're ruining my life, Shalinsky."

"I hardly know you."

"Do me a favour, Shalinsky. Cut my courses. I'll be grateful to you for the rest of my life."

"But your lectures are marvellous, Mr. Griffin. A delight."

"Some delight."

"Why, some of your epigrams I have marked down in my notebook to cherish. To memorize, Mr. Griffin."

"I've got news for you, buster. They're not mine. I stole them from my professor at Cambridge."

"So what? Didn't Shakespeare, may he rest in peace, steal from Thomas Kyd? The oral tradition, Mr. Griffin, is—"

"Shalinsky, I beg of you. If you won't quit my courses, then at least don't come to classes. If you'll do that for me I promise to pass you first in the class."

"Absolutely no."

Emptied, undone, I collapsed on the sofa.

"You don't feel so hot?" Shalinsky asked.

"I feel terrible. Now will you please go."

Shalinsky rose from his chair with dignity. "One thing," he said. "Among all those papers, no birth certificate. Why, I ask myself."

"Will you please get the hell out of here, Shalinsky!"

My parents were very much alive. But I hadn't lied to Shalinsky because I was afraid. There were my mother's feelings to be considered, that's all. You see, I was born an indecent seven months after my parents' marriage. They never told me this themselves. They always pre-dated the ceremony by a year, but once I accidentally came across their marriage license and discovered their deception. Not a very scandalous one, when you consider that they've been happily married for thirty-two years now. But the secret of my early birth belonged to my parents and, to their mind, had been carefully kept. There was something else. My father, a high-school teacher all these years, had been a poet of some promise as a young man, and I believe that he had been saving his money to go to Europe as soon as he graduated from McGill. He met my mother in his senior year, alas. I was conceived—suspiciously close to the Annual Arts Ball, I put it—and they were married. (A shock to their friends for, at the time, my mother was seeing an awful lot of Louis Cohen, a famous judge today.) Next year, instead of Europe, my father enrolled for a teacher's course. I have always been tormented by the idea that I may have ruined their lives. So I was certainly not going to open a belated inquiry into the matter for Shalinsky's sake. Let him think I was Jewish and that I was afraid to show him my birth certificate. I knew the truth, anyway.

But as far as Shalinsky was concerned, so did he.

Beginning with my next lecture, he contrived to make life a misery for me.

"It seems to be your contention—correct me if I'm wrong—that Kafka's strict Jewish upbringing had a crippling effect on the man. Would you say, then, that this was also true of Hemingway, who had a strict Catholic upbringing?"

Another day.

"I may have misinterpreted you, of course, but it seems to me that you place Céline among the great writers of today. Do you think it possible, Mr. Griffin, that anti-semitism goes hand in hand with literary greatness? Answer me that."

Shalinsky filled all my dreams. He attacked me in alleys, he pursued me through mazes and, in a recurring nightmare he dragged me screaming into the synagogue to be punished for nameless iniquities. Many an afternoon I passed brooding about him. I saw myself being led up the thirteen steps to the hangman's noose, the despised strangler of Shalinsky, with—because of my ambiguous state—neither minister nor rabbi to comfort me. Because I was sleeping so badly, I began to lose weight, dark circles swelled under my eyes, and I was almost always in an unspeakable temper.

Fearful of Shalinsky, I cut *The Merchant of Venice* from Eng. 112.

"Ah, Mr. Griffin, a question please."

"Yes, Shalinsky."

"It seems to me that in our study of Shakespeare, may he rest in peace, we have so far failed to discuss one of the Bard's major plays, *The Merchant of Venice*. I wonder if you could tell me why."

"Look here, Shalinsky, I do not intend to put up with your insolence for another minute. There are other problems besides the Jewish problem. This is not the Jewish Thought Literary Society, but my class in English 112. I'll run it however I choose, and damn your perverse Jewish soul."

With that, and the sharper exchanges that were to come, my reputation as an anti-semite spread. Soon I found myself being openly slighted by other lecturers at Wellington. Several students asked to be released from my classes. It was rumoured that a petition demanding my expulsion was being circulated among the students with, I must say, huge success. Eventually, Joyce found out about it.

"Mortimer, this can't be true. I mean you didn't call Shalinsky a meddling Jew in class last week. . . ?"

"Yes, I did."

"Is it also true, then, that you've stopped taking our newspapers from Mr. Goldberg because . . . you want to transfer our business to a Gentile store?"

"Absolutely."

"Mortimer, I think you ought to see an analyst."

"I'm crazy, eh?"

"No. But you've been overworking. I don't know what's come over you."

"Is this Hy's idea?"

She looked startled.

"Come off it. I know you've been seeing Hy and Eva secretly."

"Mortimer, how could you have written that article on Chagall for *Jewish Thought*?"

"What's wrong with it?"

"Did you have to call it 'A Jewish Answer to Picasso'? Hy's furious. He thinks that was so cheap of you. He—"

"I'll kill that Shalinsky. I'll murder him."

Joyce, holding her hands to her face, ran into the bedroom. Three days later, when I sat down to the tiresome job of correcting the Eng. 129 mid-term essays, I was still in a rage with Shalinsky. But I swear that's not why I failed him. His essay on Kafka was ponderous, windy, and pretentious, and deserved no better than it got: F-minus. Unfortunately for me, Dean McNoughton didn't agree.

"Not only do I consider this failure unwarranted, Griffin, but frankly I'm shocked at your behaviour. For the past two weeks charges of the most alarming nature have been flooding my office. I've been in touch with your wife who tells me you've been overworking, and so I prefer not to discuss these charges for the present. However, I think you'd best take the second term off and rest. Hodges will take your courses. But before you go, I want you to mark this paper B-plus. I think Shalinsky's essay is worth at least that."

"I'm afraid that's impossible, sir."

Dean McNoughton leaned back in his chair and considered his pipe pensively.

"Tell me," he said at last, "is it true you offered to mark Shalinsky first in your class if he only stopped attending your lectures?"

"Yes, sir."

"I'm afraid I have no choice but to mark this paper B-plus myself."

"In that case I must ask you to accept my resignation."

"Go home, man. Rest up. Think things over calmly. If after three weeks you still want to resign——"

I started impatiently for the door.

"I don't understand you, Griffin. We're not prejudiced here. If you're Jewish, why didn't you say so at first?"

Pushing Dean McNoughton aside roughly, I fled the office.

Joyce wasn't home when I got there. All her things were gone, too. But she had left me a note, the darling. It said, in effect, that she could no longer put up with me. Perhaps we had never been right for each other. Not that she wished me ill, etc. etc. But all her instincts rebelled against sharing her bed with a fascist—worse, a Jewish fascist.

I don't know how Shalinsky got into the house. I must have left the door open. But there he stood above me, smiling faintly, a hand-rolled cigarette in his mouth.

"My wife's left me," I said.

Shalinsky sat down, sighing.

"Joyce has left me. Do you understand what that means to me?"

Shalinsky nodded his head with ineffable sadness. "Mixed marriages," he said, "never work."

All this happened two years ago, and I have married again since then. I don't earn nearly as much money in my new job, and at times it's difficult to live with my father-in-law, but next spring, God willing, we hope to rent an apartment of our own (not that I don't appreciate all he's done for us).

I don't see any of my old friends any more, but my new life offers plenty of rewards. I. M. Sinclair, for instance, composed a special poem for our wedding and read it after the rabbi's speech.

> Lay your sleeping head, my love,
> human on my faithless arm. . . .

When the last issue of *Jewish Thought* appeared, imagine my delight when I read on the title page: EDITED BY J. SHALINSKY AND M. GRIFFIN. Our circulation, I'm pleased to say, is rising steadily. Next year we hope to sell 1,500 copies of each issue. Meanwhile it's a struggle for Gitel and me. For me especially, as I am not yet completely adjusted to my new life. There are nights when I wake at three a.m. yearning for a plate of bacon and eggs. I miss Christmas. My father won't have anything to do with me. He thinks I'm crazy. Hy's another matter. He's phoned a couple of times, but I no longer have much use for him. He's an assimilationist. Last week my application for a teaching job with Western High School was turned down flatly—in spite of my excellent qualifications.

It's hard to be a Jew, you see.

ALICE MUNRO

1931-

Born in a small town in Ontario, Alice Munro now lives in Victoria, British Columbia. For more than a decade she has been attracting the attention of connoisseurs for the excellence of her sharply observed and sympathetic short stories in such journals as *Tamarack Review* and the *Canadian Forum* and in various anthologies. These were collected in *Dance of the Happy Shades*, which won the Governor-General's Award in 1968. In a short but appreciative Foreword, the novelist Hugh Garner spoke of the artistry with which Mrs. Munro depicted the lives of ordinary people. "You'll find at least one member of your family in these stories," he wrote, "probably the one you have most despised all along. He or she will be married to the one who jilted you or didn't even notice you in your new dress at the high school dance. You'll notice that your mother was once a girl, and that your father once had a girl friend. But most of all you'll notice some of the profound though probably unpalatable truths about yourself." The promise (though it was actually much more than that) shown in the book of short stories was amply fulfilled in the full length novel *Lives of Girls and Women* that followed in 1971. This book is worthy to rank among the greatest triumphs of sensitive and subtle realism in modern fiction, British or American as well as Canadian.

THE DANCE OF THE HAPPY SHADES

Miss Marsalles is having another party. (Out of musical integrity, or her heart's bold yearning for festivity, she never calls it a recital.) My mother is not an inventive or convincing liar, and the excuses which occur to her are obviously second-rate. The painters are coming. Friends from Ottawa. Poor Carrie is having her tonsils out. In the end all she can say is: 'Oh, but won't all that be too much trouble, now?' *Now* being weighted with several troublesome meanings; you may take your choice. Now that Miss Marsalles has moved from the brick and frame bungalow on Bank Street, where the last three parties have been rather squashed, to an even smaller place — if she has described it correctly — on Bala Street (Bala Street, where is that?). Or: now that Miss Marsalles's older sister is in bed, following a stroke; now that Miss Marsalles herself — as my mother says, we must face these things — is simply getting *too old*.

'*Now?*' asks Miss Marsalles, stung, pretending mystification, or perhaps for that matter really feeling it. And she asks how her June party could ever be too much trouble, at any time, in any place? It is the only entertainment she ever gives any more (so far as my mother knows it is the only entertainment she has ever given, but Miss Marsalles's light old voice, undismayed, indefatigably social, supplies the ghosts of tea-parties, private dances, At Homes, mammoth family dinners). She would suffer, she says, as much disappointment as the children, if she were to give it up. Considerably more, says my mother to herself, but of course she cannot say it aloud; she turns her face from the telephone with that look of irritation — as if she had seen something messy which she was unable to clean up — which is her private expression of pity. And she promises to come: weak schemes for getting out of it will occur to her during the next two weeks, but she knows she will be there.

She phones up Marg French who like herself is an old pupil of Miss Marsalles and who has been having lessons for her twins, and they commiserate for a while and promise to go together and buck each other up. They remember the year before last when it rained and the little hall was full of raincoats piled on top of each other because there was no place to hang them up, and the umbrellas dripped puddles on the dark floor. The little girls' dresses were crushed because of the way they all had to squeeze together, and the living-room windows would not open. Last year a child had a nose-bleed.

'Of course that was not Miss Marsalles's fault.'

They giggle despairingly, 'No. But things like that did not use to happen.'

And that is true; that is the whole thing. There is a feeling that can hardly be put into words about Miss Marsalles's parties: things are getting out of hand, anything may happen. There is even a moment, driving in to such a party, when the question occurs: will anybody else be there? For one of the most disconcerting things about the last two or three parties has been the widening gap in the ranks of the regulars, the old pupils whose children seem to be the only new pupils Miss Marsalles ever has. Every June reveals some new and surely significant dropping-out. Mary Lambert's girl no longer takes; neither does Joan Crimble's. What does this mean? think my mother and Marg French, women who have moved to the suburbs and are plagued sometimes by a feeling that they have fallen behind, that their instincts for doing the right thing have become confused. Piano lessons are not so important now as they once were; everybody knows that. Dancing is believed to be more favourable to the development of the whole child — and the children, at least the girls, don't seem to mind it as much. But how are you to explain that to Miss Marsalles, who says, 'All children need music. All children love music in their hearts.' It is one of Miss Marsalles's indestructible beliefs that she can see into children's hearts, and she finds there a treasury of good intentions and a natural love of all good things. The deceits which her spinster's sentimentality has practised on her original good judgement are legendary and colossal; she has this way of speaking of children's hearts as if they were something holy; it is hard for a parent to know what to say.

In the old days, when my sister Winifred took lessons, the address was in Rosedale; that was where it had always been. A narrow house, built of soot-and-raspberry-coloured brick, grim little ornamental balconies curving out from the second-floor windows, no towers anywhere but somehow a turreted effect; dark, pretentious, poetically ugly — the family home. And in Rosedale the annual party did not go off too badly. There was always an awkward little space before the sandwiches, because the woman they had in the kitchen was not used to parties and rather slow, but the sandwiches when they did appear were always very good: chicken, asparagus rolls, wholesome, familiar things — dressed-up nursery food. The performances on the piano were as usual, nervous and choppy or sullen and spiritless, with the occasional surprise and interest of a lively disaster. It will be understood that Miss Marsalles's idealistic view of children, her tender-or simple-mindedness in that regard, made her almost useless as a teacher; she was unable to criticize except in the most delicate and apologetic way and her praises were unforgivably dishonest; it took an unusually conscientious pupil to come through with anything like a creditable performance.

But on the whole the affair in those days had solidity, it had tradition, in its own serenely out-of-date way it had style. Everything was always as expected; Miss Marsalles herself, waiting in the entrance-hall with the tiled floor and the dark, church-vestry smell, wearing rouge, an antique hair-do adopted only on this occasion, and a floor-length dress of plum and pinkish splotches that might have been made out of old upholstery material, startled no one but the youngest children. Even the shadow behind her of another Miss Marsalles, slightly older, larger, grimmer, whose existence was always forgotten from one June to the next, was not discomfiting — though it was surely an arresting fact that there should not be one but two faces like that in the world, both long, gravel-coloured, kindly, and grotesque, with enormous noses and tiny, red, sweet-tempered and short-sighted eyes. It must finally have come to seem like a piece of luck to them to be so ugly, a protection against life to be marked, in so many ways, *impossible,* for they were gay as invulnerable and childish people are; they appeared sexless, wild, and gentle creatures, bizarre yet domestic, living in their house in Rosedale outside the complications of time.

In the room where the mothers sat, some on hard sofas, some on folding chairs, to hear the children play 'The Gypsy Song,' 'The Harmonious Blacksmith,' and the 'Turkish March,' there was a picture of Mary, Queen of Scots, in velvet, with a silk veil, in front of Holyrood Castle. There were brown misty pictures of historical battles, also the Harvard Classics, iron fire-dogs, and a bronze Pegasus. None of the mothers smoked, nor were ashtrays provided. It was the same room, exactly the same room, in which they had performed themselves: a room whose dim impersonal style (the flossy bunch of peonies and spiraea dropping petals on the piano was Miss Marsalles's own touch and not entirely happy) was at the same time uncomfortable and reassuring. Here they found themselves year after year — a group of busy, youngish women who had eased their cars impatiently through the archaic streets of Rosedale, who had complained for a week previously about the time lost, the fuss over the children's dresses, and above all, the boredom, but who were drawn together by a rather implausible allegiance — not so much to Miss Marsalles as to the ceremonies of their childhood, to a more exacting pattern of life which had been breaking apart even then but which survived, and unaccountably still survived, in Miss Marsalles's living-room. The little girls in dresses with skirts as stiff as bells moved with a natural awareness of ceremony against the dark walls of books, and their mothers' faces wore the dull, not unpleasant look of acquiescence, the touch of absurd and slightly artificial nostalgia which would carry them through any lengthy family ritual. They exchanged smiles which showed no lack of good manners, and yet expressed a familiar, humorous amazement at the sameness of things, even the selections played on the piano and the fillings of the sandwiches; thus they acknowledged the incredible, the wholly unrealistic persistence of Miss Marsalles and her sister and their life.

After the piano-playing came a little ceremony which always caused some embarrassment. Before the children were allowed to escape to the garden — very narrow, a town garden, but still a garden, with hedges, shade, a border of yellow lilies — where a long table was covered with crepe paper in infant's colours of pink and blue, and the woman from the kitchen set out plates of sandwiches, ice-cream, prettily tinted and tasteless sherbet, they were compelled to accept, one by one, a year's-end gift, all wrapped and tied with ribbon, from Miss Marsalles. Except among the most naïve new pupils this gift caused no excitement of anticipation. It was apt to be a book, and the question was, where did she find such books? They were of the vintage found in old Sunday-school libraries, in attics, and the basements of second-hand stores, but they were all stiff-backed, unread, brand new. *Northern Lakes and Rivers, Knowing the Birds, More Tales by Grey-Owl, Little Mission Friends.* She also gave pictures: 'Cupid Awake' and 'Cupid Asleep,' 'After the Bath,' 'The Little Vigilantes'; most of these seemed to feature that tender childish nudity which our sophisticated prudery found most ridiculous and disgusting. Even the boxed games she gave us proved to be insipid and unplayable — full of complicated rules which allowed everybody to win.

The embarrassment the mothers felt at this time was due not so much to the presents themselves as to a strong doubt whether Miss Marsalles could afford them; it did not help to remember that her fees had gone up only once in ten years (and even when that happened, two or three mothers had quit). They always ended up by saying that she must have other resources. It was obvious — otherwise she would not be living in this house. And then her sister taught — or did not teach any more, she was retired, but she gave private lessons, it was believed, in French and German. They must have enough, between them. If you are a Miss Marsalles your wants are simple and it does not cost a great deal to live.

But after the house in Rosedale was gone, after it had given way to the bungalow on Bank Street, these conversations about Miss Marsalles's means did not take place; this aspect of Miss Marsalles's life had passed into that region of painful subjects which it is crude and unmannerly to discuss.

'I will die if it rains,' my mother says. 'I will die of depression at this affair if it rains.' But the day of the party it does not rain and in fact the weather is very hot. It is a hot gritty summer day as we drive down into the city and get lost, looking for Bala Street.

When we find it, it gives the impression of being better than we expected, but that is mostly because it has a row of trees, and the other streets we have been driving through, along the railway embankment, have been unshaded and slatternly. The houses here are of the sort that are divided in half, with a sloping wooden partition in the middle of the front porch; they have two wooden steps and a dirt yard. Apparently it is in one of these half-houses that Miss Marsalles lives. They are red brick, with the front door and the window trim and the porches painted cream, grey, oily-green, and yellow. They are neat, kept-up. The front part of the house next to the one where Miss Marsalles lives has been turned into a little store; it has a sign that says GROCERIES AND CONFECTIONERY.

The door is standing open. Miss Marsalles is wedged between the door, the coatrack, and the stairs; there is barely room to get past her into the living-room, and it would be impossible, the way things are now, for anyone to get from the living-room upstairs. Miss Marsalles is wearing her rouge, her hair-do, and her brocaded dress, which it is difficult not to tramp on. In this full light she looks like a character in a masquerade, like the feverish, fancied-up courtesan of an unpleasant Puritan imagination. But the fever is only her rouge; her eyes, when we get close enough to see them, are the same as ever, red-rimmed and merry and without apprehension.

My mother and I are kissed — I am greeted, as always, as if I were around five years old — and we get past. It seemed to me that Miss Marsalles was looking beyond us as she kissed us; she was looking up the street for someone who had not yet arrived.

The house has a living-room and a dining-room, with the oak doors pushed back between them. They are small rooms. Mary Queen of Scots hangs tremendous on the wall. There is no fireplace so the iron fire-dogs are not there, but the piano is, and even a bouquet of peonies and spiraea from goodness knows what garden. Since it is so small the living-room looks crowded, but there are not a dozen people in it, including children. My mother speaks to people and smiles and sits down. She says to me Marg French is not here yet, could she have lost too?

The woman sitting beside us is not familiar. She is middle-aged and wears a dress of shot taffeta with rhinestone clips; it smells of the cleaner's. She introduces herself as Mrs Clegg, Miss Marsalles's neighbour in the other half of the house. Miss Marsalles has asked her if she would like to hear the children play, and she thought it would be a treat; she is fond of music in any form.

My mother, very pleasant but looking a little uncomfortable, asks about Miss Marsalles's sister; is she upstairs?

'Oh, yes, she's upstairs. She's not herself though, poor thing.'

That is too bad, my mother says.

'Yes it's a shame. I give her something to put her to sleep for the afternoon. She lost her powers of speech, you know. Her powers of control generally, she lost.' My mother is warned by a certain luxurious lowering of the voice that more lengthy and intimate details may follow and she says quickly again that it is too bad.

'I come in and look after her when the other one goes out on her lessons.'

'That's very kind of you. I'm sure she appreciates it.'

'Oh well I feel kind of sorry for a couple of old ladies like them.

They're a couple of babies, the pair.'

My mother murmurs something in reply but she is not looking at Mrs Clegg, at her brick-red healthy face or the — to me — amazing gaps in her teeth. She is staring past her into the dining-room with fairly well-controlled dismay.

What she sees there is the table spread, all ready for the party feast: nothing is lacking. The plates of sandwiches are set out, as they must have been for several hours now; you can see how the ones on top are beginning to curl very slightly at the edges. Flies buzz over the table, settle on the sandwiches and crawl comfortably across the plates of little iced cakes brought from the bakery. The cut-glass bowl, sitting as usual in the centre of the table, is full of purple punch, without ice apparently and going flat.

'I tried to tell her not to put it all out ahead of time,' Mrs Clegg whispers, smiling delightedly, as if she were talking about the whims and errors of some headstrong child. 'You know she was up at five o'clock this morning making sandwiches. I don't know what things are going to taste like. Afraid she wouldn't be ready I guess. Afraid she'd forget something. They hate to forget.'

'Food shouldn't be left out in the hot weather,' my mother says.

'Oh, well I guess it won't poison us for once. I was only thinking what a shame to have the sandwiches dry up. And when she put the ginger-ale in the punch at noon I had to laugh. But what a waste.'

My mother shifts and rearranges her voile skirt, as if she has suddenly become aware of the impropriety, the hideousness even, of discussing a hostess's arrangements in this way in her own living-room. 'Marg French isn't here,' she says to me in a hardening voice. 'She did say she was coming.'

'I am the oldest girl here,' I say with disgust.

'Shh. That means you can play last. Well. It won't be a very long program this year, will it?'

Mrs Clegg leans across us, letting loose a cloud of warm unfresh odour from between her breasts. I'm going to see if she's got the fridge turned up high enough for the ice-cream. She'd feel awful if it was all to melt.'

My mother goes across the room and speaks to a woman she knows, and I can tell that she is saying Marg French *said* she was *coming*. The women's faces in the room, made up some time before, have begun to show the effects of heat and a fairly general uneasiness. They ask each other when it will begin. Surely very soon now; nobody has arrived for at least a quarter of an hour. How mean of people not to come, they say. Yet in this heat, and the heat is particularly dreadful down here, it must be the worst place in the city — well you can almost see their point. I look around and calculate that there is no one in the room within a year of my age.

The little children begin to play. Miss Marsalles and Mrs Clegg applaud with enthusiasm; the mothers clap two or three times each, with relief. My mother seems unable, although she makes a great effort, to take her eyes off the dining-room table and the complacent journeys of the marauding flies. Finally she achieves a dreamy, distant look, with her eyes focused somewhere above the punch-bowl, which makes it possible for her to keep her head turned in that direction and yet does not in any positive sense give her away. Miss Marsalles as well has trouble keeping her eyes on the performers; she keeps looking towards the door. Does she expect that even now some of the unexplained absentees may turn up? There are far more than half a dozen presents in the inevitable box beside the piano, wrapped in white paper and tied with silver ribbon — not real ribbon, but the cheap kind that splits and shreds.

It is while I am at the piano, playing the minuet from *Berenice*, that the final arrival, unlooked-for by anybody but Miss Marsalles, takes place. It must seem at first that there has been some mistake. Out of the corner of my eye I see a whole procession of children, eight or ten in all, with a red-haired woman in something like a uniform, mounting the front step. They look like a group of children from a private school on an excursion of some kind (there is that drabness and sameness about their clothes) but their progress is too scrambling and disorderly for that. Or this is the impression I have; I cannot really look. Is it the wrong house, are they really on their way to the doctor for shots, or to Vacation Bible Classes? No, Miss Marsalles has got up, with a happy whisper of apology; she has gone to meet them. Behind my back there is a sound of people squeezing together, of folding chairs being opened; there is an inappropriate, curiously unplaceable giggle.

And above or behind all this cautious flurry of arrival there is a peculiarly concentrated silence. Something has happened, something unforeseen, perhaps something disastrous; you can feel such things behind your back. I go on playing. I fill the first harsh silence with my own particularly dogged and lumpy interpretation of Handel.

When I get up off the piano bench I almost fall over some of the new children who are sitting on the floor.

One of them, a boy of nine or ten years old, is going to follow me. Miss Marsalles takes his hand and smiles at him and there is no twitch of his hand, no embarrassed movement of her head to disown this smile. How peculiar; and a boy, too. He turns his head towards her as he sits down; she speaks to him encouragingly. But my attention has been caught by his profile as he looked up at her — the heavy unfinished features, the abnormally small and slanting eyes. I look at the children seated on the floor and I see the same profile repeated two or three times; I see another boy with a very large head and fair shaved hair, fine as a baby's; there are other children whose features are regular and unexceptional, marked only by an infantile openness and calm. The boys are dressed in white shirts and short grey pants and the girls wear dresses of grey-green cotton with red buttons and sashes.

'Sometimes that kind is quite musical,' says Mrs Clegg.

'Who are they?' my mother whispers, surely not aware of how upset she sounds.

'They're from that class she has out at the Greenhill School. They're nice little things and some of them quite musical but of course they're not all there.'

My mother nods distractedly; she looks around the room and meets the trapped, alerted eyes of the other women, but no decision is reached. There is nothing to be done. These children are going to play. Their playing is no worse — not much worse — than ours, but they seem to go slowly, and then there is nowhere to look. For it is a matter of politeness surely not to look closely at such children, and yet where else can you look, during a piano performance, but at the performer? There is an atmosphere in the room of some freakish inescapable dream. My mother and the others are almost audibly saying to themselves: No, I know it is not right to be repelled by such children and I am not repelled, but nobody told me I was going to come here to listen to a procession of little — little idiots for that's what they *are — what kind of a party is this?* Their applause however has increased, becoming brisk, let-us-at-least-get-this-over-with. But the program shows no signs of being over.

Miss Marsalles says each child's name as if it were a cause for celebration. Now she says, 'Dolores Boyle!' A girl as big as I am, a long-legged, rather thin and plaintive-looking girl with blond, almost white hair, uncoils herself and gets up off the floor. She sits down on the bench and after shifting around a bit and pushing her long hair behind her ears she begins to play.

We are accustomed to notice performances at Miss Marsalles's parties, but it cannot be said that anyone has ever expected music. Yet this time the music establishes itself so effortlessly, with so little demand for attention, that we are hardly even surprised. What she plays is not familiar. It is something fragile, courtly, and gay, that carries with it the freedom of a great unemotional happiness. And all that this girl does — but this is something you would not think could ever be done — is to play it so that this can be felt, all this can be felt, even in Miss Marsalles's living-room on Bala Street on a preposterous afternoon. The children are all quiet, the ones from Greenhill School and the rest. The mothers sit caught with a look of protest on their faces, a more profound anxiety than before, as if reminded of something that they had forgotten; the white-haired girl sits ungracefully at the piano with her head hanging down, and the music is carried through the open door and the windows to the cindery summer street.

Miss Marsalles sits beside the piano and smiles at everybody in her usual way. Her smile is not triumphant, nor modest. She does not look like a magician who is watching people's faces to see the effect of a rather original revelation; nothing like that. You would think, now that at the very end of her life she has found someone whom she can teach — whom she must teach — to play the piano, she would light up with the importance of this discovery. But it seems that the girl's playing like this is something she always expected, and she finds it natural and satisfying; people who believe in miracles do not make much fuss when they actually encounter one. Nor does it seem that she regards this girl with any more wonder than the other children from Greenhill School, who love her, or the rest of us, who do not. To her no gift is unexpected, no celebration will come as a surprise.

The girl is finished. The music is in the room and then it is gone and naturally enough no one knows what to say. For the moment she is finished it is plain that she is just the same as before, a girl from Greenhill School. Yet the music was not imaginary. The facts are not to be reconciled. And so after a few minutes the performance begins to seem, in spite of its innocence, like a trick — a very successful and diverting one, of course, but perhaps — how can it be said? — perhaps not altogether *in good taste*. For the girl's ability, which is undeniable, but after all useless, out-of-place, is not really something that anybody wants to talk about. To Miss Marsalles such a thing is acceptable, but to other people, people who live in the world, it is not. Never mind, they must say something, and so they speak gratefully of the music itself, saying how lovely, what a beautiful piece, what is it called?

'The Dance of the Happy Shades,' says Miss Marsalles. *'Danse des Ombres Heureuses,'* she says, which leaves nobody any the wiser.

But then driving home, driving out of the hot red-brick streets and out of the city and leaving Miss Marsalles and her no longer possible parties behind, quite certainly forever, why is it that we are unable to say — as we must have expected to say — *Poor Miss Marsalles?* It is 'The Dance of the Happy Shades' that prevents us; it is that one definite glimpse of the other country where she lives.

HOWARD O'HAGAN

1902-

Howard O'Hagan was born in Lethbridge, Alberta, and educated at McGill University, graduating in law in 1925. He has
worked as a journalist and publicist in Montreal, Edmonton,
and Sydney, Australia. In the early thirties he spent three years
in Buenos Aires as chief of publicity for the Central Argentine
Railway. He has spent summers as a Rocky Mountain guide
at Jasper and now lives on Vancouver Island.

O'Hagan's remarkable western novel *Tay John* was published by a small London firm on the eve of the outbreak of
war in 1939 and has received little of the attention it deserves,
though it was republished in America in 1960 with an introduction by Harvey Fergusson who calls the book "one of the
most distinctive novels I have ever read, a novel to delight
those who can appreciate a fresh vision of life."

O'Hagan's short stories and sketches of the Rocky Mountain
country have appeared in *The Tamarack Review*, *Prairie
Schooner*, *New Mexico* quarterly, *Maclean's*, *Story*, and
Esquire, and have been collected in two volumes, *Wilderness
Men* (1958) and *The Woman Who Got On at Jasper Station*
(1963).

Although one of his stories in *The Tamarack Review* was
awarded the President's Medal at the University of Western
Ontario, Howard O'Hagan is perhaps the least-known Canadian writer of superior excellence. The episode from *Tay John*
included here is an unforgettable masterpiece.

FROM *Tay John*, 1939

THE FIGHT WITH THE BEAR

In the year 1904, and in the years that followed, a new name blew
up against the mountains, and an idea stirred like a wind through
the valleys.

The name was the name of the new railway, the Grand Trunk
Pacific, and the idea was that of a new route to the Pacific—a northern route, bringing the eastern cities, where money bred, closer to
the Orient than they had ever been. The smell of Asia was in the
air, and men thirsted still for the salt water beyond the mountains.

It would be an imperial route, and in time of war Britain could
rush troops across Canada well back from the American border. "It
will show these damned Yankees," a Member of Parliament shouted
in Ottawa, "that what independence we have we mean to keep."

Out on the prairies the white man's breath had blasted the Indian
and the buffalo from the grasslands, now his plough turned the
grass under. In small towns, set in half-circles of worship round
railway stations, under a sun that laboured across the sky all day, and
set at the day's end, great and red and bloated, as though slowly
consumed by the fire of its own creating—farmers and settlers and
ranchers met. "The Grand Trunk Pacific," they said, "will break
the monopoly of the Canadian Pacific. It will bring our freight-rates
down. It will give our country back to those who are its rightful
owners."

The snow-topped mountains, seen from the plains like the tents of
giants pitched to contend man's westward way, would be pierced
again. Man would find a pass, lay his rails, and send his trains roaring down to meet the tides. There was Pine Pass, and there was the
pass at the head of the Wapiti—but these were far north, close to
the tight white line of the Arctic.

Yet if a man looked west from Edmonton, where the forest of the
foothill steps upon the plain, to Prince George beyond the first range
of the mountains, and beyond that again to the Pacific shore, Yellowhead Pass was in the path of his vision. It was a low pass. Its

contours were gentle. It was a gateway opening to the west.

Still, in those days, no man knew. Surveys were sent out to find the way, to besiege the fortress of the mountains, to follow rivers and to pause by lakes set like moats below rocky walls. Men saw themselves cast in strange shapes by their shadows flung upon untutored ground. They felt the hot breath on their shoulders of those who would come after, with steel rails for the valleys, bridges for the rivers, and ploughs for the fields, and houses for the new clearings in the forest. They shouted words back and went on.

They went on till the hills and peaks closed after them, and behind they saw only what waited ahead. They went on so far into troubled and unearthly land that they wondered, some of those who were young, that their shadows still were with them. They were men carried on the wind of an idea. They found themselves blown up a canyon where man had never been and words never lived before. Nameless river water tugged their saddle stirrups. In the winter silence was about them on the snow like a name each had heard whispered in his mother's womb.

One man who had been out to the country of Yellowhead Pass came back to Edmonton in the days when the railway had been pushed well into the mountains, with a tale. He was a lanky man in his forties, who seemed older. He kept his brown beard tightly clipped. Pouches hung heavily beneath his eyes so that the red of his lower eyelids showed, and someone said of him once, seeing him in his old tweed suit, that he resembled a somewhat thoughtful Saint Bernard dog. He walked along the wooden sidewalks, taller than average, a slouch hat over his eyes, moving at leisure through the world with a long careful stride, appearing to take a step just once in a while.

His name was Jack Denham, but he was known generally as Jackie—a man whose pride was in his past, of which he seldom spoke, but over which loomed the shadow of a great white house in the north of Ireland, in the county of Tyrone. From the past, and because of it, he received four times a year a remittance. Then, in funds, he put up at the Selkirk—Edmonton's first hotel—lived and dined in the style of which the town was capable. His remittance gone, he would be no more seen for a time. He would return to cheap lodgings across the Saskatchewan River, where he cooked his own meals in an unplastered room. He often hired out with outfits going west to the mountains, or north to the Peace. He was a good man with horses and on the river, and once had made a long trip alone by canoe along the north fork of the Peace to its source up against the Arctic Circle. He said he knew the valleys of the mountains and the way the rivers ran better than he knew the lines on the wide, calloused palm of his hand.

He owed money no longer than it took him to make it on the trail. He accepted no drink at the bar unless he could return it. He treated others with no more respect than he regarded as due to himself in turn. Coming back from his journeys to the foothills and the mountains, from that country where words were too often outdistanced by the actions which gave them rise, he was heard with tolerance and interest—one who had held his own in the places he spoke of, whose speech and life were close to events.

All his years in the west, Jack Denham had lived in the midst of events. Yet they had somehow passed him by. He had not given them their shape, and they left him apparently only the man he had always been. He had gone into the Yellowhead country with a survey party scouting a route for the new railway, to swing an axe or handle the rod before the transit of the engineer. To the mountains he had returned to see the rails put down. Up there, he said, at one time only the width of a mountain stream kept him from the adventure of his life.

He would talk about it anywhere—in a pause during dinner at the hotel. He would allude to it suddenly at the bar among strangers over the second glass of whisky. Two tall pale glasses of whisky were his limit. One drink of whisky was good for you, two were too many, three were not enough. "I always take too many," he explained with a laugh and a wide gesture.

He might meet a friend at the street corner and follow him to his destination, talking, stretching his story the length of Edmonton. It became known as "Jackie's Tale." It was a faith—a gospel to be spread, that tale, and he was its only apostle. Men winked over it, smiled at it, yet listened to its measured voice, attentions caught, imaginations cradled in a web of words.

"I almost had an adventure there," Jack Denham would burst forth, referring to the mountain stream, drawing his chin down against his shoulder, jutting out his lower lip and running his fingers over his soft, fur-like beard.

Do you see what I mean? (The tale continued.) An adventure. A real one. Blood in it. It was a close call. I would have been in on it too, but there was the creek in the way—and a man besides.

It would have taken courage to cross that creek. I don't think it was possible to cross. I don't know now. Hard to tell. At the time, anyway, it was impossible. It wasn't wide. Twice as wide as a man, standing, might jump perhaps, but deep and swift. Boiling. There were rapids. That creek—it was white. It was jagged. It had teeth in it. I felt it would have cut me in two. I would have hesitated even with a horse—and I was afoot.

And what I saw was worth more than what I would have done. What would I have done had I been on the other side of the creek? That's what I don't know. That's what no man would know, unless he knew what he had always done and could see himself as clearly as I saw that other man across the water from me. But he knew. At least he had no doubts—this other man. No doubts about himself. And there was no doubt about what he saw before him, or, for that matter, about that river at his back. He could no more have forded the river than I, and he had no time. It was a matter of moments, I tell you; split seconds. It was the stuff of a nightmare come alive in broad daylight and throwing its shadow on the ground before you.

Do you see? No matter—for him, for this other man I mean, it must have seemed like a nightmare. Yet I doubt if he, a man of his type, would ever have had a nightmare in his life. No, his sleep would be sleep—just sleep—like a deep shadow between each of his days. Nothing more than that. No place of visions. No birth of creatures to stay with him when he woke and stand between him and the sun. With me it was different. I was an onlooker. I saw what he didn't see. I saw him, for instance. Yet he was aware, it appears to me now, long before I, that something waited for him, although his back was towards it.

You see, I had gone up that valley alone, on foot. It was Sunday, and I left the three of them in camp: Burstall, the boss; Hank, the horse wrangler—we had twelve head of horses with us—and Sam, the cook. We were well up into the mountains, and were on one of the rivers, the Snake Indian. It flows into the Athabaska. There were any number of passes there, and any number of unnamed streams. It is a good game country, too, and on the alplands I could see caribou and flocks of mountain sheep. I had my glasses with me, so that I could have a good look at the high country, also a revolver —only a twenty-two—on the chance of knocking over a few grouse. It was a busman's holiday for me, a walk. It was nothing unusual for us to walk twenty miles in a working day—but here was this valley, with no name, a clear flow of water, clear and cold as spring water, coming from it through a lane of spruce-trees by our camp, and I wanted to see where it led to. A new mountain valley leads a man on like that—like a woman he has never touched.

His experience tells him it will be much like others he knows—a canyon to go through, a meadowland or two, some forest, and its head up against a mountain wall or trickling from a grimy glacier. Yet still he goes up it hoping vaguely for some revelation, something he has never seen or felt before, and he rounds a point or pushes his head over a pass, feeling that a second before, that had he come a second earlier, he would have surprised a creator at his work —for a country where no man has stepped before is new in the real sense of the word, as though it had just been made, and when you turn your back upon it you feel that it may drop back again into the dusk that gave it being. It is only your vision that holds it in the known and created world. It is physically exhausting to look on un-named country. A name is the magic to keep it within the horizons. Put a name to it, put it on a map, and you've got it. The unnamed —it is the darkness unveiled. Up in those high places you even think you can *hear* the world being made. Anyway you can hear the silence, which is the sound of the earth's turning.

At any rate I had gone up this river, or creek, or whatever you want to call it, and its valley had surprised me. It was tight and narrow all the way. A canyon at first where I had some pretty rock climbing to do. After that a long belt of forest. Near the end of this forest belt I found a dead tree that spanned the stream and crossed to the other side where the going appeared better. There was no sign of man up there at all—no old stumps, no blazes—nothing. Beside the caribou and sheep far above the timber I saw not a living thing— not a squirrel, nor a mouse, nor a humming fly. I came almost to the headwaters where a great green glacier moved down, when I turned around to reach camp before dark. It got on my nerves a bit, I guess, that river, being penned up with it all day long and having its roar in my head. It filled my head, my thoughts. It was enough to make me stagger. I crossed the river again on the dead tree, and about two miles below that tree and about the same dis-tance above the canyon through which the river broke out into the main valley where we had our camp, I stopped to have a smoke and to look up a side valley coming down from the north. A stream came in from the north across from me and spread in shallows over a gravel flat. Tall green grass grew there on a sort of island, and behind was the forest leading up a narrow valley between two towering mountains. Somewhere up there I remember was a waterfall. I could see it, but though it was quite close, a long white line against the rock, the sound of its fall was drowned by the river before me. As I say, it wasn't wide, that river I was following. Twice as wide as a man might jump, perhaps, but it was swift, and I could hear the boulders rolling in the surge of its waters.

Then across from me, as though he had grown there while my eyes blinked, I saw a man. He was stripped to the waist, wearing only moccasins and a pair of moose-hide leggings. Behind him some little distance I saw his rifle stacked against a tree and beside it his pack with a shirt of caribou hide, the hair still upon it, tossed upon the ground. He had come down the creek opposite me. What he was doing there when I saw him, standing out on that flat among the grasses, I don't know. About to make his camp for the night perhaps.

Anyway, he saw me. He doubtless saw me before I saw him. He would have, that sort of fellow. He looked at me, yet gave no sign of recognition. He was tall, dark of skin as an Indian, yet his hair was full and thick and yellow, and fell low to his shoulders. His eyes were black, and I was so close to him that I could see their whites, and his nostrils flex ever so slightly and his white teeth showed when he breathed. From behind me the shadows of the trees were reaching across the water, but he stood full in the sun. His brown skin glowed, and his muscles were a pattern of shadows across his chest and belly. He had a build, that fellow. Still, there was something, it is hard to say, something of the abstract about him—as though he were a symbol of some sort or other. He seemed to stand for something. He stood there with his feet planted apart upon the ground, as though he owned it, as though he grasped it with them. When he moved I would not have been surprised to have seen clumps of earth adhere to the soles of his moccasins and the long shadows of his muscles across his body—they weren't strength in the usual sense of being able to lift weights and that kind of thing. They represented strength in the abstract. Endurance, solitude—qualities that all men search for. It was in his face, too, long and keen as though shaped by the wind, and beardless as a boy's—those fellows ('*buch*' they are called)—seldom if ever have a beard. I felt I was an intruder, and could I have spoken to him I believe I would have tried to excuse my presence there, along the lonely river.

But I couldn't speak to him. There was too much noise with that confounded water. I shouted. "Hallo!" I shouted; "Hallo!" I waved my arms and shouted again. It seemed absurd. I was so close to him that he should have been able to hear a whisper. He stood there across from me, too, with his head tilted a bit as though he were listening. Yet even then it seemed he wasn't listening to me at all, but to something else I couldn't hear. Had he been able to hear me, for all I knew then, he wouldn't have understood what I said. But, still, he wasn't all Indian. There was that yellow hair. It was long and heavy. A girl would have been proud of it, and he had it held with some sort of a band around his forehead. A black band, like a strip of hide cut from some small fur-bearing animal. A piece of marten, say.

Yes, his hair shone. It seemed to shed a light about him. Then he looked directly at me. I was still gesturing, throwing my arms about, trying to draw attention to myself. In short, making a very vulgar display. He looked as though he thought so, anyway. My arms dropped to my side. I tell you, I was ashamed. I have no doubt he would have spoken to me had we met in the usual way. But here was this rushing torrent between us. We couldn't cross it. Our voices couldn't be heard above it. He accepted that for the impossibility it was, while I was making frantic efforts at evasion. When he looked at me I could see the reflected light of the sun burning deep down in his dark eyes. Then he turned slowly, as if in disgust at what he saw, and took a step back towards his rifle.

And in that moment, while his foot was lifted for his second step, and his back towards me, it happened. Suddenly it seemed to me like a play being put on for my benefit, with the forest and mountains for backcloth, the gravel bar where this Yellowhead was for stage, and the deep river with its unceasing crescendo for the orchestra pit.

A bear was there above him, between him and his rifle. It may have been there for some time. Anyway it was there now, no question about it. A grizzly bear at that, a silver tip, with a great roll of muscle over its shoulders and the hair slowly rising in fear along the length of its backbone. For the bear was frightened, make no mistake about that. Later when it stood up I saw it was a she-bear. She probably had a cub cached somewhere close by. As a rule, of course, a bear won't attack a man—but this was a she-grizzly, and she was trapped. There was the pack behind her, you see, with its human smell. There was the man before her. Her cub was somewhere near by. If she hadn't been frightened or angered—and the cause and often the result of the one is much the same as the other —she would have turned around and left a situation she was unprepared to meet. But, no, she stood her ground.

And my Yellowhead across from me stood his. He slowly, ever so slowly, put his foot back upon the ground and waited. He stood, a bronze and golden statue planted among the grasses that rose up to his knees. This was the sort of thing I had sometimes dreamed of —of meeting a bear one day close up, hand to hand so to speak, and doing it in. An epic battle: man against the wilderness. And now I saw the battle taking form, but another man was in my place and with the river between us I could give no help. None at all. My revolver? I might have hit the man, but against the bear it was worth no more than shooting peas. I waited.

Something was going to happen. The grizzly opened her mouth. I saw her sharp white teeth. She flicked the grass with her long-nailed fore-paw. That paw seemed suddenly to sprout out from her body, then to be drawn back. She advanced a step. I saw the right hand of this Yellowhead fellow move gently to his waist and come out with the handle of a gleaming knife in his fist. The muscles along his shoulders rippled. His rifle was beyond his reach, past the bear. He glanced not once at the river nor at me behind him. His eyes I knew were on the bear. She swung her head low, from side to side, as though she cautioned him to be careful. Her mouth opened and she roared. I could hear that across the river. It came to me faintly, like a cough.

Then Yellowhead moved quickly. His left hand swiped the band off his head and threw it towards the grizzly, not directly at her, but just above her head. She reared up, and then I saw the hang of her laden teats. She stood so that she towered above Yellowhead. That's what I called him now. I found myself saying "Yellowhead," "Yellowhead." I had to give him a name so that I could help him— morally, you know. I had to align him with the human race. Without a name no man is an individual, no individual a man.

There she was above him, immense and unassailable as a mountain side. She clawed the air after this black thing that flew towards her. And when she swung he sprang beneath her arm. I saw his left hand grab the long fur around her neck, and I saw his right swing twice with the long-bladed knife, and the knife stayed there the second time, a flash of light embedded in her side, searching for the great, slow beat of her heart. It was a matter of moments. Then they were on the ground rolling over and over. I caught glimpses now and then of that yellow mass of hair, like a bundle the she-grizzly held with affection to her breast. It was his only chance. If he had stepped back from her those claws would have ripped his belly open, torn his head from off his shoulders. He did the one thing, the only thing he could have done, and did it well.

They rolled to the very edge of the stream on whose other bank I stood. They were quiet there. Yellowhead was beneath. "If he's not dead," I said, "he's drowned." The great mass of fur was quiescent before me, and from its side a stream of dark blood flowed into the hungry river.

Then the mass quivered. It heaved. A man's head appeared beside it, bloody, muddied, as though he were just being born, as though he were climbing out of the ground. Certainly Man had been created anew before my eyes. Like birth itself it was a struggle against the powers of darkness, and Man had won. Like birth, too, it was a cry and a protest—his lips parted as though a cry, unheard by me, came from them. Death, now that is silence—an acceptance—but across this creek from me was life again. Man had won against the wilderness, the unknown, the strength that is not so much beyond our strength as it is capable of a fury and single passion beyond our understanding. He had won. *We* had won. That was how I felt. I shouted. I did a dance. Then I calmed down. I wanted more than anything I knew to go across and touch this man, this Yellowhead, to tell him, "Well done!" But I couldn't cross that river. I might have gone back to the foot log, but that would have taken more than an hour, and it would seem that I was leaving him in his moment of victory—when no man wishes to be alone. A victory is no victory until it has been shared. Defeat? Well, that is another matter.

But Yellowhead was damaged. Somehow the grizzly had clawed his face. One side of it streamed blood. It looked raw like meat. For a time he sat there on the ground, among the grasses, and the blood ran off his shoulder, down his arm, down between his very fingers. He didn't look at me. Seemed to have forgotten all about me. He stared with wonder, I think, at the body of the bear lying half in the river. He spat some of her fur out, caught between his teeth. Then he washed his face, found the band for his hair and bound it back. After that he took his knife, still caught between the she-grizzly's ribs, cut her head off, neatly severing the vertebrae at its base, climbed with it up a tree and left it there, caught in a crotch so that it gazed upon the scene of its dismay.

He came down to the side of the river, bathed his face again. It still bled. I shouted, but he didn't hear me, or didn't care to. He disdained me, that fellow, absolutely.

It was growing dusk now. He went back to the edge of the forest where his pack and rifle rested. He staggered once and leaned against a tree. Then he pulled on his caribou-hide shirt, hoisted his pack and shouldered it. He picked up his rifle and stepped, without one backward glance, behind the trees. He vanished, as though he were leaving one form of existence for another. For a moment or two I saw his yellow head, a gleam of light being carried away through the timber. He had come down from the high country to do his job, and having done it, left. Entering the forest his pack brushed against a branch of spruce. The branch moved there before my eyes, swayed gently, touched by an invisible hand after he had gone. It moved. The river flowed. The headless trunk of the she-grizzly swung out a bit from the bank, rolled over in the force of the current, as if in her deep sleep she dreamed. Night's shadow was on the valley. Trees creaked in a new wind blowing. An owl hooted somewhere close to me.

It was late when I got back to camp. It was dark, black as the inside of a bear. Night was about me like a covering from which I tried to escape. My hands wandered far from me feeling my way. My fingers touched branches, the harsh bark of trees. I pulled them back to me, held them against my sides. They were some company for me in the darkness.

Days passed before I told them in the camp of what I had seen on the banks of the river that streamed clear and fresh and nameless before our tents. It took me a time to find the words.

If there had been a glass of whisky—Whisky. Another victory of man against the powers of darkness, whatever they may be.

A. M. KLEIN

1909-1972

Abraham Moses Klein was born in Montreal and educated at McGill University and the University of Montreal. He became interested in Talmudic studies and was active in the Zionist movements. He was called to the bar in 1933 and at one time sought to enter politics as a CCF candidate for parliament. From 1930 to 1933 he edited the *Canadian Zionist*, and in the forties and fifties he made several visits to Israel.

Klein's early poems were published in the late twenties in *The Canadian Forum* and *The Menorah Journal*, and he was associated with the group of Montreal poets who produced *Preview* and *Northern Review* in the thirties and forties. He was one of the six poets included in the group anthology *New Provinces* (1936). His first book of poems *Hath not a Jew . . .* was published in New York in 1940. It was followed by a savage satirical poem *The Hitleriad* (1944) and *Poems* (1944). His last book of poems, *The Rocking Chair*, in which Jewish themes are replaced by analogous ones drawn from Quebec culture, appeared in 1948. For three years in the forties he was a lecturer in poetry at McGill.

Klein began an exhaustive chapter by chapter analysis of Joyce's *Ulysses*, three parts of which appeared in American literary journals. These studies turned his attention to the structure of fiction and bore fruit in his own novel, *The Second Scroll*, which was published in 1951. Here a richly symbolist prose has been used to develop the theme of the Jews' search for a Messiah who might lead them to rise

Phoenix-like from the Nazi pyres and reassume the promised ancestral home in Palestine.

Klein was awarded the Lorne Pierce Medal of the Royal Society of Canada in 1957. During his last years he lived in retirement in Montreal and did not publish, though the reputation of his poetry and of *The Second Scroll* has grown steadily in popular as well as critical favor. He died in Montreal after a long illness in 1972.

FROM *The Second Scroll*, 1951

"ON FIRST SEEING THE CEILING OF THE SISTINE CHAPEL"

ET LEVAVI OCULOS MEOS : ET VIDI ET
ECCE VIR, ET IN MANUS EJUS FUNI-
CULUS MENSORUM.

. . . to the Sistine Chapel; and so to me the long passage through the marble corridors leading to the beatific door was no more than a flotation upon a channel of foam, a transit between walls of wind forgotten as soon as blown. The white statuary of that ghostly gauntlet I recall as but a series of pale shadows, a spectral escort. I do not even remember my walking; like something dreamed in a dream of walking on water, such and such feebly the recollection of that calm wan floor. The ceiling—was there really a ceiling above these interminable candid galleries?—the ceiling even then was less than a thought, a mere scalp's awareness: and all, ceiling, floor, and walls, all vanished for me as I reached the threshold of that door and, the long umbilical cord of corridors behind me, pressed forward with infant eagerness to enter this new world, truer than sculpture, not tunnelled, but global-ceilinged.

I entered, and I lifted my eyes to the cosmic vault, and scanned its expanse, panelled, pullulant, populate. Head flung back—this heaven breaks even the necks of the proud—I paced up and down the alexandrine floor, circling the chapel, casting my gaze from miracle to miracle, pursuing the arrowheads of the spandrels to each pointed particular wonder. At first saw only geometry: triangle consorting with square, circle rolling in rectangle, the caress parabolic, the osculations of symmetry: as if out of old time Euclid were come to repeat his theorems now entirely in terms of anatomy. Theorems they are, but theorems made flesh; for at last it is not the whirlwind of forms but the tornado of torsos that abashes the little homunculus below, puny before the myriad bodies instant, ambulant, volant, who in their various attitudes and postures are turned and contorted to make of the ceiling the weighted animate corpus of humanity.

High and central in the chapel's empyrean the throned twenty bear down with an almost palpable imminence. Young men, handsome and marvellously sinewed, wonderful in their proportions, they are the prototypes of the human kind; and whether face-to-face conversant or januarial back-to-back, or in their serpentinings musclerippled, there is upon them everywhere the glory of God's accolade. Brooding nudities, they are themselves like gods. Long-limbed, Atlas-shouldered, lyre-chested, each body is a song echoing the Creator's voice. *Fiat!* The dew of paradise is still upon them, they are ichor-fresh, ambrosia-scented; their gaze is Eden-rapt, all are adonic, almost adonaic! It is also to be seen that they know themselves earthlings, earthlings involved in concatenations far from celestial: group after group of them is perceived tangled in the circuit of those murderous medallions rolling before their feet, from which they recoil back horror-struck. Circle-racked! Caught in these wheels the color of dried blood, it is clear that they have an awareness of the ambiguity of their plight: their pristine unmarred felicity ever in peril of cicatrice and brand-mark. That peril, however, is below them, below their knees, and even there dark and obscured; about their countenances another aura reigns, the memory of the fingertouch, of God's lifegiving fingertouch, which through each pulsating vein and every quickened limb proclaims divine origins and makes of this adamic-seraphic ceiling a pantheon of gods.

This—these men writ big—this is the flesh majuscule: there are also the charming minor ones, the lesser clan springing from the heels of the giants—a stance of caryatids, a conjugation of cherubim. But the idiom of the twins and doubles—affectionate damonandpythias, most loving davidandjonathan—though not of a lordly utterance, still speaks its tribute to the divine quickness of the mortal flesh. Belly to belly, to buttock buttock, hand by thigh, and on nipples palm, it is in gross comic terms, almost in terms of parody that the mischievous pairs advert to the condition of their immortality—an itch, not an afflatus. It is out of this itch, the rub and yearning of their essence, that they fashion, like coupled philosophers, the dialogue of being. Out of upholding heaven, which is their proper duty, they make a game, these gemini in a zodiac of delight, and their tête-à-têtes are sibilant of the secrets of the universe they brace. They embrace, ambivalent *bambini*, and their contacts and touchings are copy, an ingratiating and pathetic imitation, of that first famous fingertouch. The ceiling sounds with their diphthongs.

518 THE TWENTIETH CENTURY

The whole ceiling is indeed in all its parts and divisions, its bur-
dens and canticles, but a tremendous pæan to the human form
divine, a great psalter psalmodizing the beauty and vigor and worth
of the races of mankind. It is the parable of the species that is pend-
ent over me, and nowhere can I scan that ceiling but I must encounter my semblable and like. For four long years suffering the
ordeal of the scaffold Michael Angelo—say rather the Archangel
Michael—inscribed this testament, his pinion for a brush; and one
sole word it was that stood him for lexicon; one word from the
changes and declensions of which he phrased the Law and the
Prophets: *The Flesh*. (Twelve score and eight the limbs, parts, and
members of the body, and eighteen score and five its organs and
sinews—the sum all-embracing of commands and forbiddings, the
six hundred and thirteen, *curriculum taryag*!) In that altitude one
temperature prevails—the temperature of the human body. One
color dominates this ceiling—the color of living skin; and behind
the coagulation of the paint flows the one universal stream of everybody's blood.

It well may be that Michelangelo had other paradigms in mind:
there is much talk of *zimzum* and retractations; but such is the
nature of art that though the artist entertain fixedly but one intention and one meaning, that creation once accomplished beneath his
hand, now no longer merely his own attribute, but Inspiration's very
substance and entity, proliferates with significances by him not conceived nor imagined. Such art is eternal and to every generation
speaks with fresh coeval timeliness. In vain did Buonarotti seek to
confine himself to the hermeneutics of his age; the Spirit intruded
and lo! on that ceiling appeared the narrative of things to come
which came indeed, and behold above me the parable of my days.

ET EUM, QUI AB AQUILONE EST,
PROCUL FACIAM A VOBIS, ET
EXPELIAM EUM IN TERRAM
INVIAM ET DESERTAM; FACIEM
EJUS CONTRA MARE ORIENTALE.
ET ASCENDET FETOR EJUS, ET
ASCENDET PUTREDO EJUS, QUIA
SUPERBE EGIT.   *Joel*

ET FILIOS JUDA ET FILIOS
JERUSALEM VENDIDISTIS FILIIS
GRAECORUM.   *Delphica*

Certainly I could not look upon
those limbs, well fleshed and of
the color of health, each in its
proper socket, each as of yore ordained, without recalling to mind
another scattering of limbs, other
conglomerations of bodies the dis-
jected members of which I had
but recently beheld. For as I regarded the flights of athletes above
me the tint subcutaneous of well-
being faded, the flesh dwindled,

the bones showed, and I saw again the *relictae* of the camps, entire cairns of cadavers, heaped and golgotha'd: a leg growing from its owner's neck, an arm extended from another's shoulder, wrist by jawbone, ear on ankle: the human form divine crippled, jack-knifed, trussed, corded: reduced and broken down to its named bones, femur and tibia and clavicle and ulna and thorax and pelvis and cranium: the bundled ossuaries: all in their several social heap-ings heaped to be taken up by the mastodon bulldozer and scaven-gered into its sistine limepit.

And so that I might understand the meaning of this wreckage, the poet set between his unmaimed heroes his painted homilies of sin and crime. It may have been wine that brought old Noah to shame and uncovering; a headier liquid, as red as wine and more potent, intoxicated my generation's men of blood. This is the great drunkenness that whirls in the wheels of the medallions, of treachery smiting under the fifth rib, of bodies cast upon a plot of ground to be trodden underfoot, of carcasses diminished to skull, and feet, and the palms of the hands, of murder, murder, murder that cutteth off all life. For even as wine lifts man up a little higher than his stature, so too was the shedding of life for the sons of Belial vanity's tempta-tion. They would be like gods; but since the godlike touch of crea-tion was not theirs, like gods they would be in destructions. To kill wantonly, arrogantly to determine that another's term is fulfilled— with impunity to do these things and be deemed therefore gods— such were their vain imaginings, the bouquet and flavor of their drink. It was the sin against our incarnate universality. Comes then Michelangelo to teach us that he who spills but a drop of the ocean of our consanguinity exsanguinates himself and stands before heaven by that much blanched, a leper; that such beginnings have terrible ends: it is the first murder that is difficult: and that the single gout released sets cataracts of carnage on to flood.

Such were the imaginations of the thoughts of the hearts of men who denied the godliness of all flesh but their own. A survivor of the Ark, I fled the deluge of the uncontained blood; the scenes and flights that Michelangelo forecast onto this ceiling, I beheld them, I was part of them. Well has the prophet done to depict the victims in their nudity; always it was, always it is in nakedness that one meets one's fate. That fate in its hundred engulfing forms I saw; I saw the husband in flight from the mounting flood carrying his wife on his shoulders, she looking in terror back; and saw both turned to salt and chemicals. Witness was I to the father bearing his dead son to the mother that bore him, and they enduring but long enough to wish their death. Women I saw convert blessing to curse, seeking to live in their blood; they, too, perished. I was privy to the many devices of escape; the most were futile. The victims themselves I saw fighting one another, struggling in blood, for that additional hour of survival. And of all I heard their weeping, which was drowned.

ET TIMEBUNT ET CONFUNDENTUR AB AETHIOPIA SPE SUA. *Erithraea*

QUO MIHI MULTITUDINEM VICTIMARUM VESTRORUM, DICIT DOMINUS. . . . PLENUS SUM: HOLOCAUSTA. . . . NOLUI, INCENSUM ABOMINATIO EST MIHI.   *Esaias*

With what sibylline intuition did the poet look forward into the dark future, there to discern the burning rituals that filled our sky with smoke! He has not been able to bring himself to paint them in their barbaric literalness; through the medallion shadowing the babes of Moloch sent into the fire and through that adumbrating the innocent man made sacrifice and put in the forefront of battle, he has hinted, he has pointed at his as yet unconflagrated meaning. Explicitness would have shrivelled his palette; wherefore it is the creature animal, brute and beast, that we are offered for a burnt offering upon Noah's altar, and see Noah himself raising his index finger—the finger now blaspheming life! —to adduce the scenes before. They are all of a piece; only now it is not blood that is the tale, but the white leukemia of ash. How could this scene—this cattle issued from what cattle-cars, these sheep to slaughter led, these goats, these azazels—speak otherwise to me than of recent furnaces and holocausts? Only before those latter fires it was the human form that lay prostrate and bound, bleating; while the cornute heads readied the blade and the faggot. The horror of his own prophecy abashed him, this scene the angel would not limn; there rises, therefore, before the nostrils of Noah the incense of the fat of fed beasts. But the odor is the odor of the fume of humanity.

From flood and fire those who could flee fled. It is a flight into a limbo of neither life nor death, an expulsion from the earth no-whitherwards. This, too, out of his secular presentiments Michelangelo imaged upon the ceiling. It is not a paradise from which he shows expulsion: no flowers spring from the earth, no lush vegetation, no crystal streams; it is a landscape infertile of barren soil and unyielding rock where no thing grows save the malefic tree on which hermaphrodite evil sits and loves itself. It is the landscape of our life on earth; no Eden, but the little to which we cling. Yet even from this little my generation was cut off.

By an angel? Not angel is he wielding the expelling sword: see! from the rib of the Serpent, like Eve from Adam's rib, he rises. They are one person. But the apple? There is no apple. In that entire frame there is no apple. There are gestures as of rondures grasped, reached, held; but there is no apple in that scene. There is only the subtil illusion of apples.

In the writ whence Michelangelo drew his moral there surely was that fruit. By what intervention, then, did it come to pass that the apple was lost from that tree, from those hands, from this the world's first parable? Design was it or forgetfulness? It was the spirit of prophecy. It was the spirit of prophecy that veiled the painter's memory and took hold of his brush and changed a chapter of genesis into the vision apocalyptic: mankind from mankind wresting the habitation of earth, by guile and by violence, and my kinsmen set forward in flight, their backs forever shuddered with pursuit. Oh, bitter homelessness that owns not even its isle of banishment!

TU AUTEM, FILI HOMINIS, VATICINARE ADVERSUM GOG, ET DICES: HAEC DICIT DOMINUS DEUS: ECCE, EGO SUPER TE, GOG. *Ezechiel* IBI IDUMAEA ET REGES EJUS, ET OMNES DUCES EJUS . . . QUI DESCENDUNT IN LACUM. *Cumæa*

We approach now a fuller explication—an unfolding—of the ugly heinousness of killing. Like a plant growing against a wall Adam lies croziered and convolute, and from his body, at the behest of God, Eve blossoms forth. The chain of generation is thus figured; we know now, seeing Adam, seeing Eve, that man is not born for a day, but for all time; that under the guise of fecundation, immortality is symboled; and that man, being also a seed, may between his thighs compass eternity. It is murder of the codes to snap the thread of a man's life. Such homicide the sons of Belial committed in thousands of thousands, a thousand thousand for each day of the six days of creation. Alas, alas for their victims, and alas for them, that their crime did not end with this slaughter but is forever repeated and multiplied: as the constellations move in their courses and the years and decades pass and the generations that should have been born are not born, the hand that slew is seen again to be slaying, and again, and again;

frustrate generation after frustrate generation, to all time, eternal murder, murder immortal! Peruse the circles circling the tableau of the risen Eve—you would not say that so idyllic a conjuration—man as one with his helpmate—should be rounded on the one hand by the house of Abner brought to naught and on the other by the prophet exclaiming: *Thou Art the Man!* Yet so it is; the deed is named: the hand of the Lord is lifted, beckoning levitation, and what horror shall be affixed to the hand that slaps His down?

Lies on the ground the body of Adam anticipative. It has its due limbs, its due members, its quantum of blood in the veins. It resembles a man. Its length is extended and curved, its arm is fixed outright, its hand hippocratic in hue hangs limp. Awaits its completion, languid, a hemisphere; awaits; and encircled by spheres and cycles of potency, robed in the draped whirlwind, the future under His cloak and all possibles in His ambience trembling, with flight of power and might of majesty, with beauty, with splendor. He brings to the earthen mold recumbent His finger's imminence— oh, benedictive touch!—life, and the glory of His countenance! And in his eyes is imaged God. . . . He dared not transliterate it, Michelangelo, he dared not point the burden of his charge. But I read it plain and spell it out—summation and grand indictment— the unspeakable nefas—deicide.

EGO OSTENDAM TIBI, QUAE FUTURA SUNT IN NOVISSIMO MALEDICTIONIS, QUONIAM HABET TEMPUS FINEM SUUM . . . ARIES . . . REX MEDORUM EST ATQUE PERSARUM. *Persicha*

But deicide—its syllables contradict each other—this is the evil possible only in its attempt, not in its perpetration. A covenant stands between man and his destruction, the covenant of sea and sky: the bow in the cloud. Not

ECCE, EGO VIDI QUATUOR VIVOS SOLUTOS ET AMBULANTES IN MEDIO IGNIS, ET NIHIL CORRUPTIONIS IN EIS EST, ET SPECIES QUARTI SIMILIS FILIO DEI. *Daniel*

otherwise than by this, God's seal, were the people spared. Though bloody coursed the red and orange fevered bright, though the pus yellow yeasted, the gangrene green and the smitings waxed

bruise-blue contused to indigo and the virulent violet, violet waned, the indigo fled, the veins throbbed azure, and green was the world once more and golden, high sanguinary, and the body ruddy with health. The remnant would be whole again. And that this would come and in this wise come Michelangelo signified it, writing on a

ceiling his seven-sealed token ADAM PALSYN ZAHAV YEREQ KOHL
ISOTHYS ADAM—SAPIRI, signified it and between God's palms stablish-
ing sea and sky preserved it. All colors melled to hope; the spectrum
fused to white.

The people endured; floated out the flood, defied the furnace.
With their foretold salvation fulfilled, there revived also into existence and shone bright the worlds and planets which without man
their beholder are as if they were not. The clouds vanished, and the
sky was starred again; the clouds vanished, and the sun shone. Upon
the breath of little children is the whole globe poised, say the Tal-
mudists; and say: every human soul is weighted against worlds
three hundred and ten. Oh, the proliferation in the heavens as the
dry bones stirred! Oh, the enkindled suns the moons gilded the
splendiferous satellites and the aureoled glories that sprang forth
luminous, scintillant, extant! as a swooned generation opened its
eyes once more to see . . . to see the Author of their Days, not in
the image of man made—with
what triumphant orthodoxy does
Michelangelo at last in peroration
doff his metaphor to breathe upon
the ceiling the true concept—the
form of formlessness, unphrasable,
infinite, world-quickening anima,
the shaped wind!—not in any
manner image, not body, nor the
similitude of body, but pure pervasive Spirit intelligential, the One

ET REDUCAM ISRAEL AD
HABITACULUM SUUM ET
PASCITUR CARMELUM ET BASAN,
ET IN MONTE EPHRAIM ET
GALAAD SATURABITUR ANIMA
EJUS.   *Iheremias*
ASCENDITE EQUOS ET EXULTATE
IN CURRIBUS ET PROCEDANT
FORTES ÆTHIOPIA, ET LIBYES
TENENTES SCUTUM.   *Lybica*

(oh, musculature of flame!) the First, the Last (oh, uncontainable
fire unconsumed!) Cloud numinous with Creation, Omnipotent,
yes, and All-Compassionate, who in the heavens resides and in the
heart's small chambers (beating little heart of Isaac on the fag-
gots . . .) magnanimous with Law, and who even to the latest of
generations fulfils His prophets' prophecies, rebuking, rewarding,
hastening for them who wait him who tarries, merciful-munificent
with ascensions, aliyoth, resurrections, authorizing Days. . . .

Hence the illumination of the four corners squared and rounded.
From east, from west, from north and south, the quadruplicate
communiqué of heaven, the prophecy in four salvation scenes made
clear, made eternal: not ever shall He utterly forsake! It is a
covenant.

It is a covenant, here of the fourfold type, confirmed through the
grace even of the young stripling who slang his one smooth stone,
the shepherd's mite, to lay low and dented the six cubits and a span
of Gath's Gogmagog, gigantical Goliath. Thus in the hour of challenge is Israel saved.

Or even through a female. Judith, the maid of Bethulia, who in
the valley of Esdraelon rendered acephalous the headstrong Holo-
fernes, the arrogance of Persia that henceforth at the shoulders
ceased. Thus in the hour of threatening is Israel spared.

Through a dream, the dream that remembered Mordecai who did
remember Esther who brought to remembrance the Lord's pact,
whereby the man Haman was destroyed, his design confounded.
Thus in the hour of peril does Israel triumph.

And even through a fiery serpent, when that it is looked upon,
and named by name. Thus in the hour of brass, thus in the round of
serpents, by God's grace, Israel lives.

The sigils, talismans, and magic circles of Michelangelo to this
purpose did I read; and when at last I stood beneath the sign of the
gourd and whale's head, the prayer of Jonah in the fish's belly spoke
for me:

> The waters compassed me about, even to the soul: the depth
> closed me round about, the weeds were wrapped about my
> head. I went down to the bottoms of the mountains; the earth
> with her bars was about me for ever: yet hast thou brought up
> my life from corruption, O Lord my God. . . . I will sacrifice
> unto thee with the voice of thanksgiving, I will pay that that
> I have vowed.

Thus did I leave the chapel, noting for the last time the series of
rams' skulls of which the poet had made a device to signify, some
say, descent to mortality. But to me, through the long marble corridors hurrying back, they were rams' horns, sounding liberation.

MALCOLM LOWRY
1909-1957

Malcolm Lowry was born in England, but became a Canadian citizen and lived in Canada for the most creative years of his life. He made the Pacific Coast near Vancouver the setting of some of the most powerful of his stories and novellas as he made Mexico the setting of one of the great modern novels, *Under the Volcano*, written for the most part at Lowry's squatter's cabin at Dollarton on the North Arm.

At seventeen Malcolm Lowry went to sea as a deck-hand on a freighter and sailed to the Far East. He returned in 1929 and graduated from Cambridge University with honors in English and classics in 1932. His first novel *Ultramarine*, based on his experiences at sea, was published in 1933. Meanwhile Lowry travelled in Spain, the United States, and Mexico, where in Cuernavaca he began the writing of *Under the Volcano*. In 1939 he came to British Columbia, where he settled down with his second wife, Margerie Bonner, at Dollarton. Here he worked and reworked *Under the Volcano*, which was finished in 1947 and published in 1949. Lowry remained in Canada until 1954, when he was evicted from his cabin at Dollarton. He went to Sicily and later to England, where he died accidentally in 1957.

After his death his papers and unrevised tales and novels were published by his widow. These included the novellas published in *Hear Us O Lord from Heaven Thy Dwelling Place* (1961); *Lunar Caustic*, a novel set in the psychiatric ward of Bellevue Hospital, New York, (1968); and *October Ferry to Gabriola* (1970). A small collection of *Selected Poems* was edited by Earle Birney in 1962, and *Selected Letters,* edited by Mrs. Lowry and Harvey Breit, appeared in 1965.

In the *novella* "Through the Panama," the last part of which appears below, Lowry gives us through the experiences of a fictional protagonist an account of an actual voyage he made with his wife in a French freighter from Vancouver through the Panama Canal to Rotterdam. The hurricane-like storm they encountered has been rendered with a vivid intensity not excelled by Conrad. Some of the reflections on modern novelists and the art of writing are of great interest to a student of Lowry's philosophy of art.

FROM *Hear us O Lord from Heaven*
Thy Dwelling Place, 1961

THROUGH THE PANAMA

... We make the Anegada Passage and are in the Atlantic.

Seaweed like gold tinsel, says Primrose. Sargasso Sea directly north. *Isle of Lost Ships,* featuring Stuart Rome, Moreton Cinema, Cheshire, England, Matinee at 3 p.m. My brother and I missed 26 years ago. Now we enter the Western Ocean and the 4,000 miles before we sight land at Bishop's Point, at Land's End. But to what end?

The Atlantic Highlands—long deep swell. Atlanterhavet.

Montserrat not far away to starboard where I altered geography books by climbing Chance's Mountain in 1929, in company with two Roman Catholics: Lindsey, a Negro, and Gomez, a Portuguese.

One albatross.

Six bottles of beer on top of mountain.

Primrose says, I'm afraid of this boat, thrown together in wartime by makers of washing machines—— But for myself, I like her, though she rolls worse than the ship Conrad loaded with one third of the weight "above the beams" in Amsterdam. It is wrong to suppose the poor old Liberty ship hasn't got a soul by this time, just because she was thrown together in forty-eight hours by washing machine makers. What about me?—thrown together by a cotton broker in less than 5 minutes. 5 seconds perhaps?

Another ship to starboard: *Flying Enterprise.* Pretty name.

Dec. 3. Great storm to leeward near sunset, sweeping diagonally past.

Commandant, meaning well, hunts out old American magazines for me. Old *Harper's.* Terrifying ancient brilliant and even profound article by De Voto on later work of Mark Twain. (Mem: Discuss this a little: problem of the double, the triple, the quadruple "I".) Almost pathological (I feel) cruelty to Thomas Wolfe. Would De Voto like to know what I think of him, in his Easy Chair, lambasting a great soul—and why? because he is a man—who, as N. might say, cannot answer? Mem: quote Satan in *The Mysterious Stranger*. And then on top of this obsession with Wolfe's weaknesses to come across a statement like: "I am (I hope) a good Joycean." Why? To keep in with whom? Coming from De Voto it's almost enough to make you hate Joyce. And indeed I do sometimes hate Joyce.

—Reason for Thomas Wolfe's lapses, De Voto himself probably analyzed perfectly elsewhere, about someone else he didn't hate, like De Voto: reason was Thomas Wolfe was in a hurry, knew he was going to die, like N., in same sort of hurry. And what about what is disciplined about him, his marvelous portraits, his humor, savagery, sense of *life*. There is far more sense of life actually felt in Wolfe than in all Joyce for that matter. I myself consider it unjust too to criticize Wolfe for seeming to have nothing fundamentally to say (as they say). He had not time to get a real view of life. A giant in body, he might not have really matured till he was sixty. That he had not time was, for literature, a tragedy: and I myself feel that one should be grateful for what he has given us. Much to be learned in De Voto's articles however; agonizing about Mark Twain. Possibly De Voto had troubles of his own though, in that uneasy chair. Enough to give one delirium Clemens.

The sea is worse than before to me, its expanse, rough, gray blue or rainy, and without seabirds, says nothing to me at the moment: though well do I understand now Joyce's fear of the sea: (who knows what lives in it? Don't want to think about this—frightening thought occurred to me last night, when Primrose says I woke her up saying: "Would they put Mother back in the sea?" What awful thing did I mean? Belief in mermaids?). It seemed to Martin he had offended some of the good Frenchmen too—both the second engineer and the third mate stern to him, curiously more formal: La Mer Morte, a sea that comes following a day of high wind when the wind has dropped, leaving behind the great dead swell of the day before: hangover within and without.

Position Report
S.S. *Diderot*
Date: 5 Dec. 1947
Latitude: 27° 24′ N.
Longitude: 54° 90′ W.
Course: Rv. 45
Distance: 230 m.

To go: 2,553 m.
Length of Day: 23H. 40M.
Average Speed: 9nds 7
Wind: N. 6
Sea: Houleuse, du vent
Signed: CH. GACHET 1st Lieut.

Two squalls: cobalt thunderstorms. Wind catches spray and blows it across the sea like rain, a tiny squall of rain.

Martin was gloomy and savage, lying all day in his bunk predicting death and disaster.

During these last days, since going through the Anegada Passage, have been through some important spiritual passage too—what does it mean?

Afternoon squall hit suddenly with a million hammers. The ship shakes, shudders. The sea is white, sparkling, sequined—it is over in a flash.

Terrific squall toward sunset. Thunder. Cobalt lightnings reveal a sizzling sea——*vision of creation.*

For some reason this made Martin happy. He rose from his bunk and went down to dinner in a jovial mood. He even played games afterwards with the Mais, Andrich and Gabriel.

—am glad to be welcomed by skipper again—really believe I have now got through some spiritual ordeal——though a little hard to see what.

Dec. 6. My mother's birthday. In getting out of bed this morning I seemed to be edging out of the table after dinner.

—utter forgetfulness whether one had gone to lavatory or not.

—finally one doesn't bother; for five whole days—result: a pain in back: no wonder: forgetfulness of teeth, hatred of teeth, continually muttering little phrases like—I wonder——couldn't have been as if——

—Tragedy of someone who got out of England to put a few thousand miles of ocean between himself and the non-creative bully-boys and homosapient schoolmasters of English literature only to find them so firmly entrenched in even greater power within America by the time he arrived (Martin thinks), and responsible for exactly the same dictatorship of opinion, an opinion that is not based on shared personal or felt experience or identity with a given writer, or love of literature, or even any intrinsic knowledge of *writing*, and is not even formed independently, but is entirely a matter of cliques who have the auxiliary object of nipping in the bud any competitive flowering of contemporary and original genius, which however they wouldn't recognize if they saw it. What! A person like myself—Martin went on to write—who discovered Kafka for himself nearly 20 years ago, and Melville 25 years ago, when about 15, and went to sea at 17, becomes disgusted in a way not easy to explain. Kafka meant something spiritually to me then: no longer. Melville like-wise: I find it almost impossible to share what they meant to me with these people. They have ruined these writers for me. In fact I have to forget that there is such a thing as so-called "modern literature" and the "new criticism" in order to get any of my old feeling and passion back. How can I help remembering that no fewer than seventeen years ago it was I myself who had to *point out* to one of the editors of the *Nouvelle Revue Française* that they actually *had* published Kafka's *The Trial.* On reading it—for no, of course he hadn't read it—the fellow said to me: "Did you write that book?" "What? Didn't you like it?" "Not much—the bar part was quite funny—but I got the feeling I was reading about *you.*" (His boss made a play out of it fifteen years later.) Then again, fifteen years ago, I couldn't find a single book of Kierkegaard's in the New York Public Library save *The Diary of a Seducer.* (Some years later we found this book in the market in Matamoros, Guerrero, Mexico). Now he is all the rage and there is probably even a waiting list in the best-sellers department for *Fear and Trembling.* And yet what right have these English junior housemasters of American literature to Kafka and Melville? Have they been to sea? Have they starved? Nonsense. They probably haven't ever even been drunk, or had an honest hangover. Nor did they even discover Kafka and Melville themselves——etc. etc.

A brilliant piece of scorn, thought Martin (who suffered slightly from paranoia), regarding what he had written, and with his mouth almost watering. Then he added:

Now you see how easy it is to be carried away by an impulse of hatred! There is some truth in what I say (that is, it is certainly true that I hate these people) but what of this whole thing, read aright? What testimony to my inadequacy, my selfishness, my complete confusion indeed! Worse than that. Suppose we take it to pieces, starting at the end, and see what our persistent objective self makes of such a thing. First it seems apparent that the writer feels that literature exists for his personal benefit, and that the object of life is to get drunk, to go to sea, and to starve. (As well it may be?)

Moreover we feel sure that the writer wants us to know he has *had* many hangovers, *been* drunk very often, and *has* starved. (Though this last is doubtful because it is immediately qualified by the word Nonsense.) Certainly we must feel, if we read him aright, that he is a most unusually dog-in-the-manger sort of fellow, because for some undisclosed reason, among other things, he wishes to prevent the "English junior housemasters of American literature" from reading Kafka and Melville. Perhaps the writer wanted to be just such a curious junior housemaster himself, and failed (either in England, or in America, or even in both)? Mystery. Mystery too clothes the mention of *Fear and Trembling* and the *Diary of a Seducer*, though that the author evidently feels himself to be singularly misused (to the extent that it even causes him to have some sort of mystical experience in the New York Public Library), at the same time feels himself to be some sort of unrecognized pioneer, who maybe even lives himself in a state of Fear and Trembling, perhaps even is undergoing some sort of Trial at the moment, seems manifest here too. And how proud he is of being mistaken in his youth for the author of *The Trial*, though this little story looks like a lie. (Or does it? The little story in question is not a lie, Martin knows, the trouble is that he has told so many lies now he has become incapable of making the truth not look like a lie.)

—Alas, before we can arrive at any real view of the undoubted truth that seems shadowily contained in some of these damaging phrases, certain syntactical deficiencies in this first paragraph oblige us to question the writer's own "love of literature" (it looks as though it isn't very wide—perhaps he has only read the three books he mentions, though we may doubt even that)—we may wonder why, if he despises these schoolmasters so much he bothers himself about their "power," wonder too if he has not even secretly thought of himself as being "a non-creative bully-boy and homosapient schoolmaster," at which rate we may feel that it is no wonder if he has failed to put a thousand miles of ocean between himself and himself (however schizophrenic) and come down finally to what seems to be the one undoubted unequivocal brute fact in the whole thing, which is that it looks indeed as though some sort of tragedy were involved.

What? Neurosis, of one kind and another, is stamped on almost every word he writes, both neurosis and a kind of fierce health. Perhaps his tragedy is that he is the one normal writer left on earth and it is this that adds to his isolation and so to his sense of guilt. (But without Primrose he wouldn't be a writer of any kind, or normal either.)

Just the same it is necessary for people to stand in judgment every now and then, and not allow themselves to be crippled by such smashing self-criticism as the above, or all talent—though we note with a smile he called it genius—would be "nipped in the bud" and the world get nowhere. And this brought Martin to the business, the question rather, of equilibrium.

No one likes it (indeed it seems so intangible how can you discuss it?) and the people who recommend it, if one can so phrase it, are nearly always bastards who have never known what was more than enough anyway—(there Martin went again). And yet there has never been a time in history when there was a greater necessity for the preservation of that seemingly most cold-blooded of all states, equilibrium, a greater necessity indeed for sobriety (how I hate it!). Equilibrium, sobriety, moderation, wisdom: these unpopular and unpleasant virtues, without which meditation and even goodness are impossible, must somehow, because they are so unpleasant, be recommended as states of being to be embraced with a kind of passion, as indeed passions themselves, as the longing for goodness itself is a passion, and thus invested somehow with all the attractions and attributes of qualities rare and savage (though you personally can be as drunk as a cock on blackberry brandy for all I care, albeit your chances of equilibrium, unless you are a veritable Paracelsus, become increasingly fewer in that state). Without such equilibrium, be it then only mental, Martin thought, all reactions, public and personal, will tend to react too far. Whereas before we had sadism in literature, for instance, now an equal kindness, a distaste for cruelty in any shape or form will be evinced: but we shall not believe it presages a universal change in man, because this apparent kindness will be allied with other qualities in themselves dull or wicked—albeit so far as cruelty is concerned this is one point upon which man should allow the pendulum to swing to its furthest reach of compassion for all God's creatures, human and animal, and there remain.

And yet one should be able passionately to impugn the wanton slaughter of wild creatures as something essentially cowardly, unworthy, contemptible and even suicidal without at the same time feeling bound in the same breath to attack your Hemingway; one should realize that your Hemingway has a right to shoot wild creatures and while he is engaged in that dubiously masculine occupation he is not, at least for the moment, shooting anyone else.

Bully-boys and schoolmasters now go to church, instead of Communist meetings, and obediently popular opinion follows, prayer book in hand. Into the church of myth go the other bloody lot—Oh shut up.

But the people really responsible for the spread of interest in Kierkegaard, stemming out of the interest in Kafka, for which they are equally to be thanked, Edwin and Willa Muir, the brilliant translators of Kafka, responsible by virtue of the preface to *The Castle*, have never received the credit. Since but for that preface Kierkegaard would no doubt have remained in oblivion, and the bully-boys and —Oh shut up. Shut up. Shut up.

When Martin starts to study French, after a difficult period of abstinence, but still with a hangover, he is confronted, to say the least, in his French grammar, with the following phrases:

Traduisez en français:

1. The man was not dead but his wife told him that he had died two days ago.

2. She dressed herself as the Goddess of Death.

3. She opened the door and offered to the drunkard a dinner that was not very appetizing—(all this stemming from a lecture on the page headed *L'Ivrogne Incorrigible*——and beginning, Un homme revenait tous les soirs à la maison dans un état d'ivresse complet— below this was a photo of La Bourse, Paris, taken circa 1900).

4. You must suffer for your vice, said she. I shall come each day to bring you the same meal.

5. The meal does not matter, but I am suffering from thirst, you must come every hour to bring me 3 glasses of wine.—On the back of this rusty-colored book an embossed cock (perhaps the one I mentioned earlier as being drunk on blackberry brandy) greeting the dawn, beneath it the words: *Je t'adore, ô soleil*, in gilt letters—— *What does this portend?*

Kindly remark of Lorca's: I'd like to pour a river of blood on her head.

Dec. 9. Bloody weather! Slow, dark daylight. The salle-à-manger is depressing, porthole covers down and electric lights going at noon, and noisy, with sea thundering tons of water across foredeck.

The poor little Mais, who've huddled, arms entwined, on deck, chattering like little gibbons, are now sad and sick; they could not eat lunch and finally all lay down on bench behind table.

Only Gabriel is still gay: "I have been eating 5, 6, and 8 because I am always hungry when the sea is bad."

Crash! Coffee, milk, etc. falls into Primrose's lap and on floor. I fear she will be scalded (she was too) but she is wailing because her pretty new red corduroy slacks are stained.

Godawful storm is on the wing (a good line) unless I have been a seaman for nothing. As a matter of fact I was a seaman for almost nothing, as wages go these days.

King Storm whose sheen is Fearful.

Huge seas, snow-capped mountains, but a south wind en arrière so that the sea is following us; the *Diderot* riding it wonderfully (but rolling so everything in cabin is banging about) like a Nathaniel Hawthorne blowing along in the wind to see the devil in manuscript, or windjammer running before the wind: passed another Liberty ship, going in the opposite direction, pitching way up in the skies, could not be making more than 20 miles per day.

Our rescue ship—coming to meet us.

The crew, in oilskins and sou'westers, battling the driving rain and wind, stretch lifelines on the afterdeck, terrific seas beyond and astern. Beyond and astern of time.

At sunset, tremendous sight of sprays and seas breaking over ship, black smoke pouring out of galley chimney straight to bâbord shows, however, that wind has gone to west——

Dec. 10. Gale increasing. And in fact what we seem in for is one of those good old Conradian Southwesterlies, dreaded by sailors, first read about at school by torchlight, where the moon, sun, and stars disappear for seven days, and oneself finally beneath the blankets.

Primrose says: well, this is the Atlantic, the Western Ocean as I always imagined it.

Low, wild sky with now and then a muted sun; gray, gray sea with a huge roll (grosse houle), but confused and breaking in every direction, some waves breaking like combers *He heareth sounds* on a beach with a crash, with curving snowy *and seeth strange* crests from which the wind lifts the spray like *sights and* a fountain. Some waves collide, rising to *commotions in the* jagged peaks high above the ship, where the *sky and the* top breaks, and even spouts. Most weirdly *element.* beautiful of all, once in a long time a light comes through the top: beneath the spray appears a pale luminous brilliant green like phosphorescence, as though the wave were lighted from within by a green flame.

Standing on the passerelle, Charles tells us the wind was Force 8 at 1 a.m. but has now dropped a little. There is a bad storm ahead all right but travelling faster than we are. We are making 11 knots.

Later, near sunset, the wind has risen, is still rising, and radio reports it is shifting to a southwesterly quarter. The radio operator and the third engineer, on passerelle with us, obviously don't like it and mutter together, predicting a dirty night.

They have posted an extra lookout on the bridge.

Gabriel points to the # 3 hatch just below, over which waves are constantly breaking (they are almost breaking over the bridge) and says: "Flour! But ze cover eez waterproof." "Why?" says Primrose. "What does he mean?"

The Commandant scampers up and looks around: "She isn't rolling—not too much. A good ship, eh?" Good, fine, we say, and he is pleased.

Le vent chant dans le cordage.

Later. The wind is now Force 9 and still rising, also has shifted, and is abeam. Wind flickering the spray like smoke along the face of the water. We are making 9 knots.

Rilke comes to Martin's aid, via *The Kenyon Review*: "The experience with Rodin has made me very timid toward all changing, all diminishing, all failure—for those unapparent fatalities, once one has recognized them, can be endured only so long as one is capable of expressing them with the same force with which God allows them. I am not very far off work, perhaps, but Heaven forbid that I should be called upon (right away at least) for insight into anything more painful than I was charged with in Malte Laurids. Then it will just be a howl among howls and not worth the effort. . . ."

But Martin has not, as a matter of fact, read a line of Rilke, and the whole thing, on his part, is simply an illusion of grandeur.

And, "Things must become different with us, from the ground up, from the ground up, otherwise all the miracles in the world will be in vain. For here I see once more how much is lavished on me and just plain lost. The Blessed Angela had a similar experience—'quand tous les sages du monde,' she says, 'et tous les saints du paradis m'accablereraient de leurs consolations et de leurs promesses, et Dieu lui-même de ses dons, s'il ne me changeait pas moi-même, s'il ne commençait au fond de moi une nouvelle operation, au lieu de me faire du bien, les sages, les saints et Dieu exaspéraient au delà de toute expression mon désespoir, ma fureur, ma tristesse, ma douleur et mon aveuglement!' This (says Rilke) I marked a year ago in the book, for I understand it with all my heart and I cannot help it, it has since become only the more valid. . . ."

Frère JACQUES—Frère JACQUES—
Sonnez les MATINES! Sonnez les MATINES!

Dec. 11. Gale still worse. Poor Salvadoreans and Dutchmen stuck in their cabins on after deck: seas breaking right over: they can't get to salle-à-manger. Try to help but turns out couldn't matter less, they are all seasick and it's impossible to eat anyhow with dishes jumping off table onto floor—nearly impossible to drink too, should one want to: have to brace back against wall, clutch bottle in one hand and glass in other and pour teaspoonful at a time, for Primrose too. Have to write standing up too.

STORM OVER ATLANTIS. Martin had a dream of seeing mad pictures of Bosch, in Rotterdam. Probably I have seen them somewhere, or reproductions of them, particularly the dreadful St. Christopher. Real dream was preceded by a vision of a gigantic cinema, also apparently in Rotterdam, otherwise catastrophic ruin, a great queer slim tower, at the top of which church bells were ringing ceaselessly.

Then barrel organs as big as shops, and cranked with the kind of energy one associates with a coal trimmer, i.e., myself, winding up ashes from the stokehold on a winch—— I once knew a man, who in thus dumping the ashes overboard, went overboard himself with the ashcan. That chap not unlike me either.

Then the St. Christopher, carrying Christ on his back, and a fish in his right hand, a dog barking on the opposite bank, old women, cocks, and a sort of gnome house up a tree where the gnome has hung up washing in near background, someone enthusiastically hanging a bear, on the other side of another kind of river, with a background of castles, old Rotterdam, etc. (will we make it?), but rather modern; some sort of naked fiend apparently dancing by his clothes, preparing to bathe from the river bank—the general effect one of the inerrable horror, and Satanic humor. But why should Martin be dreaming about it? perhaps clairvoyant—

THE BEAST.—The abomination of desolation, standing in the holy place.

But the Bosch picture of most importance to *La Mordida* I might describe as follows: in the foreground there is the same detailed figure, to whom I will return, in the background is a house, with some rafters missing from the roof, panes missing in the windows, etc., but giving a sense of even greater inerrable evil and horror and at the same time poverty and utter debauchery: in the doorway a man and a woman are discussing some matter that one knows is gruesome and terrible, without being able to say quite why: on the right of this house, which also on examination shows some signs of having been recently partially burned, an old man is peeing lustily; to return to the figure in the foreground: he has the air of a pilgrim, his goods slung over his shoulder, cadaverous he is likewise, and one leg is bandaged (like Death in my other dream); up a rather nice-looking tree between him and the man peeing are various objects that turn out upon close inspection to be demons of one sort and another, the most remarkable being an extremely wide, cat-like of visage, yet seemingly bodiless creature a bit like the Cheshire Cat in the illustrations to Lewis Carroll. This should occur in *La Mordida* in Trumbaugh's dream: for the meaning of this horror—a horror this time almost without humor unless it is the pissing man—is indeed that of the Pilgrim—even Bunyan's if you like, though the imagery is far more deeply religious, the man in the foreground in fact is the Protagonist, turning his face from damnation, as he thinks, and limping off into the unknown, and leaving his poor house, though he is making a great mistake as it happens, for his poor house was his salvation—like an image of his niche in the next world he was presented with in advance—and his business was to purify it and rebuild it, before setting forth—— To hell with this—— I think the trouble with Martin is that Hieronymus Bosch is literally the only painter he can appreciate at all, and at that not much, because he seems vaguely to recognize—well, whatever it is he does recognize, poor devil. Or was it because he was a pre-Adamite?

—What I'm really getting at with Martin, is to try and plot his position of isolation, not merely in society, but from all other artists of his generation. Though an Englishman perhaps, in reality he belongs to an older tradition of writers, not English at all, but American, the tradition of Jamesian integrity and chivalry, of which Faulkner and Aiken, say—though both Southerners, which raises other questions—are about the last living exponents, albeit their subject matter might sometimes have scared their elders. However,

Martin is quite incapable of their kind of chivalry and tolerance toward writers of that same generation, of whose souls the cover on
Esquire might be considered the outward semblances, and who tend
to divide mankind into two categories: (a) those who are regular,
(b) the sons of bitches, the bloody bully-boys, who——

Bah, but what I mean is something like this. I am capable of con-
ceiving of a writer today, even intrinsically a first-rate writer, who
simply cannot understand, and never has been able to understand,
what his fellow writers are driving at, and have been driving at, and
who has always been too shy to ask. This writer feels this deficiency
in himself to the point of anguish. Essentially a humble fellow, he
has tried his hardest all his life to understand (though maybe still
not hard enough) so that his room is full of *Partisan Reviews, Kenyon Reviews, Minotaurs, Poetry* mags, *Horizons,* even old *Dials,* of
whose contents he is able to make out precisely nothing, save where
an occasional contribution of his own, years and years ago, rings a
faint bell in his mind, a bell that is growing ever fainter, because to
tell the truth he can no longer understand his own early work either.
Yet he still tries, for the hundredth thousandth time, to grasp *The
Love Song of Alfred Prufrock,* for the nine millionth time to grapple
with *The Waste Land,* of which the first line—though he knows it
by heart of course!—is still as obscure to him as ever, and in which
he has never been able to understand why Christ should have been
compared to a tiger, though this has caused him to read William
Blake (he had really been drawn to William Blake in childhood
because he'd read in his father's London *Times* that Blake was
cuckoo) whose poem about the little lamb is perhaps the only thing
in all literature that he has thoroughly grasped, and even in that
case maybe he's fooling himself. I am partly joking, for in fact my
writer has a thorough grounding in Shakespeare. H'm. Anyhow,
when he really faces up to matters, he finds his taste has been formed
not necessarily by things that he has liked, but by things that he has
understood, or rather these are so pitifully few that he has come to
identify the two. Is this a fantastic portrait? Because it isn't that this
man is not creative, it is because he *is* so creative that he can't understand anything; for example, he has never been able to follow the
plot of even the simplest movie because he is so susceptible to the
faintest stimulus of that kind that ten other movies are going on in
his head while he is watching it. And it is the same way with music,
painting, etc. At the age of thirty-seven, having acquired a spurious

fame for various pieces that, as I say, he has long ceased to understand himself, he wakes up to the fact that he has really only enjoyed with aesthetic detachment four things in his life. A poem by Conrad Aiken, a performance of *Richard II* when he was ten years old at the Birkenhead Hippodrome, a gramophone record of Frankie Trumbauer's with Eddie Lang, Venuti and Beiderbecke, and a French film directed by Zilke (rhymes with Rilke?) called *The Tragedy of a Duck*. Despite this, he still heroically reads a few pages of William Empson's *Seven Types of Ambiguity* each night before going to sleep, just to keep his hand in, as it were, and to keep up with the times——

There is a truth contained in this portrait, for this man, while a genuine artist—in fact he probably thinks of nothing but art—is yet, unlike most artists, a true human being. For alas this is the way the majority of human beings see other human beings, as shadows, themselves the only reality. It is true these shadows are often menacing, or they are angelic, love may move them, but they are essentially shadows, or forces, and the novelist's touch is missing in their human perception. Nothing indeed can be more unlike the actual experience of life than the average novelist's realistic portrait of a character. Nonetheless Martin's blindness, isolation, anguish, is all for a reason. I can see that on that road to Damascus, when the scales drop from his eyes, he will be given the grace to understand the heroic strivings of other artists too. Meantime he must slug it out, as they say, in darkness, that being his penance.

(Note: it must be said somewhere that Martin had been on this planet for so long that he had almost tricked himself into believing he was a human being. But this he felt with his deeper self not to be so, or only partly so. He could not find his vision of the world in any books. He had never succeeded in discovering more than a superficial aspect of his sufferings or his aspirations. And though he had got into the habit of pretending that he thought like other people, this was not the case. It is thought that we made a great advance when we discovered that the world was round and not flat. But to Martin it was flat all right, but only a little bit of it, the arena of his own sufferings, would appear at a time. Nor could he visualize the thing going round, moving from west to east. He would view the great dipper as one might view an illuminated advertisement, as something fixed, although with childish wonder, and with thoughts in mind of his mother's diamonds. But he could not make anything move. The world would not be wheeling, nor the stars in their courses. Or when the sun came up over the hill in the morning, that was precisely what it did. He was non-human, subservient to different laws, even if upon the surface he was at best a good-looking normal young man with rather formal manners. How else explain the continual painful conflict that went on between him and reality, even him and his clothes. "There is a continuous cold war between me and my clothes." Like a man who has been brought up by apes, or among cannibals, he had acquired certain of their habits; he looked like a man, but there the resemblance ended. And if he shared some of their passions, he shared these equally with the animals. Describe The Getting Up of Martin Trumbaugh, in the complications, futility, complications with clothes, reality, etc. And yet, also, in his deepest self, he possessed aspirations that were neither animal, nor, alas, any too commonly human. He wished to be physically strong, not in order to defeat people, but in order to be more practically compassionate. Compassion he valued above all things even though he saw the weakness in that desire. In fact anybody who said anything like this would immediately seem to be condemned for some sort of hypocrisy in his eyes just as he felt himself condemned at that moment. That weakness of self-pity he wished to correct too. He valued courtesy, tact, humor. But he wanted to find out how these could be put into practice in an uncorrupted form. But above all he valued loyalty—or something like loyalty, though in an extreme form—loyalty to oneself, loyalty to those one loved. Above all things perhaps he wanted to be loyal to Primrose in life. But he wanted to be loyal to her beyond life, and in whatever life there might be beyond. He wanted to be loyal to her beyond death. In short, at the bottom of his chaos of a nature, he worshipped the virtues that the world seems long since to have dismissed as dull or simply good business or as not pertaining to reality at all. So that, as in his lower, so in his higher nature too, he felt himself to be non-human. And he was in general so tripped up by the complexities of his own nature that too often he exhibited no virtues whatsoever, and all the vices, once glaring but now obscure; sins, that for all her victory, Protestantism is responsible for rendering less deadly than they in fact are. And he had good cause——)

Another dream of a huge desolate cathedral, yet involved marvelously with life, pissoirs underneath it, shops living within its very architecture, the great unseen triptychs of Rubens in the gloom, and

the gigantic tinkling of a huge bell——the peace, and the distant
bowed priests in white, carrying ingots.

The wireless operator praying lonely in the church: and I too,
am he.

—Delirium of sea under moon—

Dec. 11. Night

Al stereless within a boot am I
Amid the sea, betwexen windes two
That in contrarie standen evermo

Chaucer's comment is to be taken seriously: something has gone
west in our steering gear. That is what I think at least, though I can
gain no information and to my humiliation I have no knowledge of
the hydraulic contraption we're dependent on. But the ship did not
answer her helm from the upper bridge earlier, and there is something evilly wrong. Nearly all hands seem working down below,
and I suspect the second mate of having gone down the propeller
shaft, which is a bad sign—— Al stereless within a stormboot are
we.

—Tonight, in a full gale, off the Azores, our cabin—the Chief
Gunner's—being on the lee side and the wind from the south-west,
with tremendous seas, but being driven down wind, it was possible
to leave our porthole wide open, through which one could see, as
the ship lurched down to leeward, great doc-
tor of divinity's gowns of seas furling to leeward, the foam like lamb's wool: the wind
rose to a pitch of wailing in the cordage so
extreme that it sounded almost false, like
movie wind about a haunted house: and indeed the whole ship sounded like an immense
exaggeration of the same thing: clankings of
chains, unearthly chimes, inexplicable tinker-
ings clinkings and chatterings and sudden
horrid whistlings: from down below in the

*The Mariner
hath been cast
into a trance;
for the angelic
power causeth
the vessel to
drive northward
faster than
human life
could endure.*

engines, there issued an unimaginable noise of battering, whistling
and thumping, accompanied too, for whatever reason, and at regular
intervals, and as if were concealed down there some of mystic Ahab's
secret harpooners engaged in forging their weapons, a tremendous

sound of hammering that always ceased after a while, and doubtless was concerned some way with the propeller but so fearsome that I could explain it to Primrose only by saying that indeed it was the custom during gales for the chief engineer to keep his intransigent greasers employed in chipping rust (she didn't believe me but nodded gravely), that they might not become discouraged or bored and lose their nerve: on top of this, and also at regular intervals, there was the noise that seemed to come out of the wall between myself and the wireless operator's cabin, as of a jack being cranked up, which Sacheverell Sitwell has taught us to associate with the signing off or evening greeting of a poltergeist. Beneath one, lying in the bunk, when this was possible, the ship squirmed and twisted, at moments of crisis, like a woman in an agony of pleasure, and looking out at the storm, and observing the gigantic seas, rising all above us as if we were in a volcano, it seemed impossible the ship could survive the punishment she was receiving; horrible detractable noises too

The supernatural motion is retarded; the Mariner awakes, and his penance begins anew.

came from the closed galley two decks below where that day the cook had been badly burned: and yet the sea never visited us through the porthole, we were safe in the midst of chaos, the wind rose to a howl of wolves as we plunged on, leaving me not merely a feeling that it was impossible to be experiencing this but, at every moment, the feeling that one had not experienced it at all.

We have had to change our course, the skipper says, and are going by dead reckoning.

—Mad game of chess with skipper in his cabin: tables and chairs are mostly anchored to deck (nearly said floor), other chairs etc. and so on are lashed, so the cabin resembles escapologist's "rumpus" room—how I hate that phrase!—everything goes over from time to time anyhow: giacomo piano opening: chessmen peg into board like cribbage board—bottle of whisky in skipper's furred sea-boot beside table, because sea-boot won't fall over, is for me, he scarcely touches it; this chess is his idea of an hour's relaxation instead of sleep—he has summoned me to play in the middle of the night as if I were a medieval courtier subject to the King's wishes: dash to the chartroom something like one of those dashes, when scrum half on opponent's twenty-five, over the try-line—opposing xv in this case being not human beings but objects, fortunately static: wireless operator hasn't turned in for three days, looks half dead, poor fellow, keeps fighting uphill into skipper's cabin every now and then with idiotic reports of fine weather and light winds in the Baltic, meantime the scene outside, when I can see it, is like a descent into the maelstrom. Other, more serious radio reports, to the skipper's sardonic amusement, are always accompanied by some such remark as "These reports have nothing to do with navigation." We are evidently in a bad way though skipper has no intention of telling me what is wrong, or at least not yet; anyhow we can't hear ourselves speak. Skipper looks damned grave, however; despite which, after a long game, he beats me very decisively. Grisette, the little cat, is delighted with all these escapologist's arrangements, "for her benefit." I was so concentrated on the game that I forgot to look on the bridge, which seemed unnaturally dark, to see if there was a man at the wheel. However I tell Primrose that there was. But so help me God, I don't think there was.

—Game of chess now seems to me utterly unreal and something like that eerie wonderful absurd scene in the French movie by Epstein of *The Fall of the House of Usher* in which Roderick Usher and the old doctor are reading by the fire, the house has already caught fire, not only that but cracks are opening in the walls and the house is in fact coming to pieces all around them, while flames creep toward them along the carpet, and insane electric storm moreover is discharging its lightnings outside in the swamp, through which Mrs. Usher, née Ligeia, having just risen from the grave, is making her way back to the house with some difficulty; nonetheless, absorbed in the story, Usher and the good doctor go on reading: the unspeakably happy ending of that film, by the way, Martin thought, under the stars, with Orion suddenly turned into the cross, and Usher reconciled with his wife in this life yet on another plane, was a stroke of genius perhaps beyond Poe himself, and now it occurs to me that something like that should be the ending of the novel.——

Roderick Usher rose at six
And found his house in a hell of a fix.
He made the coffee and locked the door,
And then said, what have I done that for?
But had poured himself a hell of a snort
Before he could make any kind of retort,
And poured himself a jigger of rum
Before he heard the familiar hum

Of his matutinal delirium
Whose voices, imperious as a rule,
Were sharper today, as if at school :
Today, young Usher, you're going to vote.
Said Roderick, that's a hell of a note.
So he packed his bag full of vintage rare,
His house fell down but he didn't care,
And took the 9:30 to Baltimore
And was murdered, promptly, at half past four.

—Three flying Dutchmen.

Later. In vain attempt to get some information I am informed by the fourth mate—the sort of information I might have given myself in a similar situation—that all hands are engaged in putting a ceinture around the ship to prevent its falling apart. (Indeed this is not so funny as it sounded—get from newspaper cuttings Pat Terry's story of the ship that used chains in this regard : also it is an electric welded ship; danger of breaking in two or cracking hull very real.) Charles says, smiling, "These Liberty ships, you know, Sigbjørn, they all fell in two in the Atlantic, in the war." Then, seeing Primrose's face, he added, "Do not worry, Madame, we have put a ceinture around its middle."

Later.—My sailor's instincts tell me, all of a sudden—and it is amazing with what suddenness such a crisis is upon one—that it will actually be an unusual bloody miracle if we pull through. The worst is being able to do nothing. Worse still, can't tell what they're doing, or if they think they are doing anything, what they imagine it can be. Despite the fourth mate's joke, there is an actual sound as of the ship breaking up. On an old type of ship such as I knew, if the steering gear went, there was still an old-fashioned windjammer wheel on the poop that could go into direct action. On top of that—believe it or not—even as late as 1927, we carried sails on board : and the lamptrimmer, one of the petty officers, and a rating they seem to have no longer, corresponded to the old sailmaker. Here there is no windjammerlike wheel, and as certainly there are no sails. But there are two wheels, one above the other, on the upper and lower bridge, and so far as I can gather, both of these are out of commission. Yet we still have steerage way, of a kind, and are not hove to. The thing to be thankful for is that we haven't lost our propeller. Yet.

—Martin took his ignorance of the nature of the crisis to heart, telling himself that it was because these Liberty ships were not like the old ships where you could see what was going on, that there was an almost Kafka-like occlusion, everything closed, ghastly, so that in the Chief Gunner's cabin, while it connected with the bridge, you might as well have been hidden away on the upper deck of one of the Fall River Line paddlesteamers for all that you were in contact; but no matter what he told himself, it seemed all part and parcel of his wider isolation, and in fact like the ultimate ordeal of——

Primrose is assured, whenever she washes up against anyone, that everything is all right and there's nothing to worry about. She can't possibly be fooled but pretends she is. She's a good sailor, spends her time eating sandwiches, for there's been no hot food for two days, and watching the storm from the lower bridge. What else to do? Can't get into bunk or you're thrown out. The poor Salvadoreans, the Hungarian sportsman, and the Mynheer Peeperhorns are all half dead of seasickness and there is nothing anyone can do to help them. Our store of liquor, however, takes on a dimension of social utility for once. Second mate reports all lifeboats to starboard smashed. You'd think one would notice this, but somehow one didn't. One lifeboat to port is still possible—Côté à l'Abri du vent——etc. While wheel is functioning again on the lower bridge.

Later. The wind is now 100 miles an hour. Seems unbelievable but I've forgotten whether this is Force 10 or 12. Wireless weather report: overcast sky, some rain.

Dec. 12. Position Report. S.S. Diderot. There is no position report. (As Stephen Leacock would say.)

Dec. 13. 3 a.m. Wind is now Force 10-11. On lower bridge with Primrose and Commandant, who says to Primrose, laughing:

"Well, there is now nothing I can do. But if you like, Madame, you can pray."

—The storm, paralyzing scene from bridge, of the ship in anguish shipping sea after sea of white drifting fire, after each smash the spume smoking mast high above the foremasthead light.

Later. We have now had no sleep for two nights—I think it has been two nights—impossible to lie down, or even sit down. We stand, bracing ourselves and holding on. This desk thank God is strongly anchored, so I hang on with one hand to desk, write with other. Hope I can read this scrawl later. Primrose spends most of her time on lower bridge. I know she is frightened but she won't say so. She comes staggering in every so often to reassure me, or give latest report. Primrose——

She tells me: Everyone is on duty except first mate, who is asleep! Skipper sends man to wake him. Impossible. Finally skipper himself stamps down in a rage. They shout and shake him but, says André, "He was like a dead corpse."

Absolute blackness and wild water all around. Our rudder trouble has started all over again. Uncanny scene of completely useless wheel in bridgehouse spinning round, with the ship going like a bat out of hell. Or did I dream it?

Ship seems to jump out of water, shudder from end to end.

Sonnez les matines!

Sonnez les matines!

Back in Chief Gunner's cabin I remember Gerald once saying, "when in doubt make a memorandum." So I do—— Death compared to a rejected manuscript. Am my grandfather's son, who went down with ship—do I have to do that? Ship not mine anyhow—— Seems unnecessary. Would be downright awkward, in fact. Embarrassment of skipper. A short story: "The Last Apéritif."

Martin reflected that these kind of idiotic thoughts were simply a mechanism in forced inaction to short-circuit anxiety about Primrose. This anxiety, when one gives way a bit, seems less anxiety than an inoculation against intolerable and appalling grief, a grief indeed that seems exactly like this sea——

Primrose, laughing, manages to shout to me: "Do you know, I just had the most idiotic thought, if we have to take to the lifeboat I mustn't wear my beautiful fur coat—I don't want to ruin it!"

But, as a matter of fact, there are now no lifeboats.

No use trying to get into bunk—we are pitched out on the floor.

Another way of confronting death is to conceive of it as a Mexican immigration inspector: "Hullo. What's the matter with you, you look as though you'd swallowed Pat Murphy's goat and the horns were sticking out of your arse."

(That is what the Manx fisherman admirably observed to the skipper of the liner, who not only nearly ran his boat down, but started yelling at him apoplectically for not keeping out of his way. So I tell Primrose this story which diverts her a lot. In fact, it is enough to make God laugh, that story, I always think. Possibly something like this anecdote—which I had from a Manx fisherman—is the origin of someone's threat—Bildad's?—in *Moby Dick*: "I'll swallow a live goat, hair and horns and all.")

Our house. Incredible jewel-like days in December sometimes.

Such radiance for December. Celestial views. Then a bell ringing in the midst. Would like someone to have it, live in it, without fear of eviction.

—Thou god of this great vast, rebuke these surges
Which wash both Heaven and Hell: the seaman's whistle
Is as a whisper in the ears of death,
Unheard.

But one should be grateful that there are not *six short* whispers followed by one *long* whisper.

In fact, as I surmise, many lives have been saved by the weather's being too bad to abandon ship.

Sonnez les matines!

Sonnez les matines!

Three S.O.S going at once. Radio next door crackling like small storm within a storm inside. Operator tells me—how many hours ago?—Costa Rican tanker has been sinking for three days. A Greek and a Finn also in distress. And now a Panamanian. Greek ship is called ΑΡΙΣΤΟΤΕΛΗΣ just to give us our unities presumably, since Aristotle's personal destiny is not much help. (Note: Aristotle drowned himself.) We are all too far away from one another, all too far down the drain ourselves, to do any good. Still, it is a comfort to each other to know we are not alone. This is apparently one of the worst storms in living history in the Atlantic. Though messages still come through, "having nothing to do with navigation."

Ventilators singing in wild organ harmony: Hear us, O Lord, from heaven thy dwelling place!

—No ship would stand many more seas like that—in old type of steamer half crew would be cut off in the fo'c'sle. Now it is the poor passengers, the Salvadoreans, etc., who are cut off.

Popular illusions to spike about French, officers and crew of this ship anyhow (message in a bottle):

That they are predominantly homosexual. (There are seemingly none aboard this ship. Though a Frenchman is capable of living a balanced and even chivalrous life with a female giraffe, without inflicting it on you.)

That they are predominantly unfaithful to their wives. (There is one longing in common among all the married men, officers and sailors to whom I have spoken, to be home with their wives for Christmas. Though this may be a virtue peculiar to married sailors.)

That they are mean. (Your concièrge may be so. Madame P.P. is so.)

No matter what yoke they were reeling under, no matter how starved, I believe you would never see in France, or among Frenchmen, the appalling sights of despair and degradation to be met with daily in the streets of Vancouver, Canada, where man, having turned his back on nature, and having no heritage of beauty else, and no faith in a civilization where God has become an American washing machine, or a car he refuses even to drive properly—and not possessing the American élan which arises from a faith in the very act of taming nature herself, because America having run out of a supply of nature to tame is turning on Canada, so that Canada feels herself at bay, while a Canadian might be described as a conversationist divided against himself—falls to pieces before your eyes. Report has nothing to do with navigation. Instead of ill this very extremity in Canada probably presages an important new birth of wisdom in that country, for which America herself will be grateful.

That they are not good sailors. (Even Conrad, in his most whiskery mood admitted in *The Rover* that they were among the best.)

That they have no, or a prissy, or a precise or merely urbane sense of humor. (Rabelais' "roaring arm chair" has never been vacated.)

Prosper Mérimée writing on the Scots. And on the Americans placed at different tables on the Riviera (during the American Civil War) "to prevent them eating each other." Similar illusions should be spiked re Americans, English, Jews, Mexicans, Negroes, etc., etc. An example of humor to be appreciated in any language: Grisette is now in heat.

Greatest fault of the French is that they do not listen to what each other say. No wonder their governments fall—or rather they are talking so much all at once they can't even hear them fall, perhaps.

Prayer to the Virgin for those who have nobody them with.

For she is the Virgin for those who have nobody them with.

And for mariners on the sea.

And to the Saint of Desperate and Dangerous Causes.

For the three El Salvadoreans. For the one Hungarian sportsman. And for the three Mynheer von Peeperhorns.

Plight of an Englishman who is a Scotchman who is Norwegian who is a Canadian who is a Negro at heart from Dahomey who is

married to an American who is on a French ship in distress which
has been built by Americans and who finds at last that he is a Mexican dreaming of the White Cliffs of Dover.

Mystical objection to changing one's religion. But let the whole
world make a fresh start. A universal amnesty (extending even to
the bullies, the Mexican immigration inspectors, the schoolmasters,
and finally myself, who have never lifted a finger to speak against
the death in life all about me till this moment). Society is too guilty
in the eyes of God to hold any man permanently to account in a
larger sense for a crime against it, no matter how wicked: collec-
tively, who have always—these donkey, these man—done something
worse.

The day in Bowen Island we found the bronze bells and saw the
harlequin ducks.

Prayer for Einar Neilson, who saw us off, singing "Shenandoah."

"And from the whole earth, as it spins through space, comes a
sound of singing." (C.A.)

Sonnez les matines!

Sonnez les matines!

¿ Le gusta esta jardin? ¿ Que es suyo?

Vanity of human beings is terrific, stronger than fear, worse than
that story in Schopenhauer.

S.O.S going on next door. Battement de tambours!

God save the Fisher King.

Can't tell what's happening on deck at all. And there is absolutely nothing, for the moment, that can be done, which is never
how you visualize it. Nevertheless, Martin reflected, this is a position
all novelists find themselves in eventually. Put on your life jacket,
your arms through the shoulder straps. Damned if I will. Couldn't
if I tried. Have always had trouble with things like that. Put life
jacket on Primrose, Martin thought. But Primrose, eating a sandwich, has already decided she wants to return to the bridge. So meanwhile we manage a drink. It is a rather good, strange drink.

à ce signal:

—Go to your cabin.

—Cover yourself warmly.

—Put on your gill-netting of sauvetage, and letting yourself be
guided by the personnel render yourself at the Bridge of Embarca-
tions, on the side secluded from the wind——

The signal of abandon—— Couldn't hear it given in this noise.

Chief Gunner's cabin.

Martin swore that if he survived he would never willingly do another injurious action, or a generous one for an ulterior motive, unless that were an unselfish one. But the thing to do was *not to forget this*, like the character in William March's story, if you ever got out of the jam. God give me, he asks, a chance to be truly charitable. Let me know what it is You want me to do——

—Wish old Charon was here——

The whole is an assembly of apparently incongruous parts, slipping past one another—

Something like our steering gear in fact.

—law of series.

Sonnez les matines!

Sonnez les matines!

Miraculous such nights as these——etc.

Great God—we seem to be steering again.

And the ancient Mariner beholdeth his native country.

The second mate says to Primrose, laughing, "All night we have been saving your life, Madame."

Dawn, and an albatross, bird of heaven, gliding astern.

And to teach by his own example, love and reverence to all things that God made and loveth.

A 9nds. arrivée Bishop Light, Angleterre, le 17 Dec. vers 11 H.

—S.S. *Diderot*, left Vancouver November 7 —left Los Angeles November 15—for Rotterdam.

Frère Jacques
Frère Jacques
Dormez-vous?
Dormez-vous?
Sonnez les matines!
Sonnez les matines!
Ding dang dong!
Ding dang dong!

GEORGE WHALLEY

1915-

George Whalley is a scholar, literary critic, and poet and is at
present a member of the English Department at Queen's University. Born in Kingston, Ontario, he was educated at Bishop's
University, Lennoxville, Quebec, and at Oriel College, Oxford,
where he was a Rhodes Scholar. After the war, during which
he served as a Commander in the Royal Canadian Navy, he
took his Ph.D. at King's College, London.

On returning to Canada he taught for three years at Bishop's
University before going to Queen's. He published two volumes
of verse, *Poems* 1939-1944 (1946) and *No Man Is an Island*
(1948), and in 1953 a work of theoretical criticism, *The Poetic
Process*, upon which his international reputation mainly rests.
Associated with Kathleen Coburn in her studies of Coleridge,
he has published *Coleridge and Sara Hutchinson and the Asra
Poems* (1955) and is one of the editors of a forthcoming complete edition of Coleridge's works. In 1955 he edited *Writing
in Canada*, a compilation of the papers and discussions given
at the Canadian Writers' Conference held at Queen's University, and in 1964 *A Place of Liberty: Essays on the Government
of Canadian Universities*. The spirited narrative included here,
printed in *The Cornhill* and, in this slightly revised form, in
The Tamarack Review (1957), is a short version of *The Legend
of John Hornby*, published in 1962.

THE LEGEND OF JOHN HORNBY

Perhaps that vivid photograph of John Hornby was taken in the summer of 1918 at Fort Norman, near the entrance to Great Bear Lake. Whoever took it—it may have been Guy Blanchet—caught precisely the physical image of the man in a rare instant of repose, shock-headed, bearded, hawk-nosed, moccasined, the strong lean hands holding an illustrated catalogue. He is reading with almost insolently withdrawn concentration. What the picture does not show is that John Hornby is a short wiry man, little more than five feet tall; that his eyes are intensely blue, memorable, and disconcerting because vague and always (it seems) looking at something a long way away. It was ten years since he had first come into the North. Within the next five years he was to become a legend in his own lifetime.

In the first quarter of this century there were plenty of colourful characters in the Northwest Territories: old Klondikers, beach-combers, remittance-men, frantic solitary men who got bushed and stayed behind, men of good family with a past and men of good family with no future, and men of no family with neither past nor future; braggarts, ruffians, visionaries, unscrupulous men. These provided a variegated contrast to the respectable and hard-working people who were simply and quietly committed, through choice or birth, to living in an inhospitable country: grave, self-reliant Scots and Orcadians who served the interests of the great trading companies, and sometimes their own; and morose businesslike trappers—often of Scandinavian or German stock—who wrung a living from the country dangerously, relying on skill, experience, and their dogs. Restlessness, endurance, energy, cunning are the hallmarks of the best of them. Against such a background the small lithe Chaplinesque figure—pathetic and endearing, with the laconic smile and piercing blue eyes—would seem slender material for the making of a legend.

But John Hornby eluded all the categories. He had no commercial or scientific ambitions, no will-o'-the-wisp dream of gold or fur. His past was not notably disreputable. He was said to be wealthy—and that, at times, was about half-true. He was well educated, a Harrovian, spoke in a soft scholarly voice, was not given to profane language, and was even suspected of being a learned man because he knew a few words of French, German, and Italian. Professionally he was not an explorer, a trapper, a prospector; he was something of all these, but a caricature of them all. By instinct and habit he was most like a trapper, and could have been a good trapper but for his love of animals and his hatred of steel traps. He never killed except for food and even in that matter was notoriously improvident. He was not a particularly good shot with a rifle, yet managed to keep himself alive. And his name persists on the maps. The bay where he first wintered on Great Bear Lake; the elegant canoe passage he discovered through the confusing islands and peninsulas at the eastern end of Great Slave Lake; the double turn in the Thelon River where he built a cabin and died—all these still bear his name. And although his name is now overshadowed by the manner of his death, he lives still in the long Northern memory.

The legend is mostly to do with Hornby's feats of strength and endurance, and with behaviour which, even in the Northwest Territories, was regarded as eccentric. Stories were told of him as a young man working with the railway gangs around the Yellowhead Pass, how he would go hatless in winter, and barefoot if need arose; and how, when he was at Onoway, he would frequently run the forty-odd miles to or from Edmonton, had once trotted fifty miles beside a horse, and on another occasion ran a hundred miles from Edmonton to Athabaska Landing in under twenty-four hours for a wager of a bottle of whisky (although he was not a drinking man). It was said that he could outrun an Indian, and pack more than his own weight at a portage; and his untiring crooked jog-trot was the despair of anybody who had the misfortune to travel with him. When the Hudson's Bay Company was celebrating its 250th anniversary, an impromptu football match was mounted at Fort Smith—with other delights—to celebrate the occasion; and Hornby had injured his leg in the game but set off on the 300-mile canoe trip to Reliance alone, with his leg in splints. He had the reputation of fearing no man, of being crazily quixotic; and this was illustrated by the story of his kidnapping a woman from a brutal and dangerous common-law husband, and hiding her and her two children in a furniture warehouse in Edmonton, and setting them safely on their way to England.

On the whole he preferred the company of Indians to white men,

and liked to travel light. His standard outfit even for a journey of
indefinite duration—he was inclined to boast—was a rifle, a fishnet,
and a bag of flour. Because he despised "white man's grub," other
men were suspicious of travelling with him; yet it was said that he
had several times kept indigent Indians alive by starving himself.
Altogether his reputation for starving and for being impervious to
hunger and hardships was impressive. He had even wintered once
in a wolf-den south of Chipewyan when the freeze-up caught him
on the way to Slave Lake. And stories more genial and fanciful were
also told: how he refused to travel with any brown-eyed man; how
he had once turned up at Resolution with a group of Indians to
collect Treaty Money, and would have got away with it but for his
eyes; how he knew of fabulous deposits of gold and silver but refused to form a company for fear of spoiling the country; and how
he had been the first man to bring samples of pitchblende out of
Bear Lake.

Many of these legendary stories about Hornby had some root in
fact; but they suffered accretion and transmutation in passing from
one story-teller to another; for heroic elaboration of the truth is one
of the chief forms of emotional release in the North, and a good
story travels quickly. The story of the pitchblende, for example, has
no reliable basis; the myth-making faculty, here as elsewhere, had
fused some genuine piece of Hornby lore with detail from other
men's stories. Hornby did not deliberately manufacture or distort
his own legend; but he was too human to destroy it, and intelligent
enough to understand the rhetorical force of deftly managed silences.
He delighted in providing his few friends with a fund of outrageous
stories about himself. To gain his effect, elaboration was seldom
necessary.

Consider the Arden story, for example. Not many weeks before
the Fort Norman photograph was taken, Hornby had been "rescued" by a young Englishman named D'Arcy Arden. Arden lives
in Yellowknife now and tells the story himself. "That was in the
winter of 1917–18. It was at Dease Bay and Jack had come through
from Norman and went straight on to his old house on Hornby
Bay. I visited him early in the winter and found him half-starving.
There were moose almost within rifle-shot of his cabin; but he insisted that winter on doing all his hunting with a small-bore pistol.
He said he was all right and there were Indians there, so I went back
to Dease Bay. Later in the winter an Indian named Bay-u-Na

brought back a dog I had given Hornby. It was a very fine dog and I told him not to give him to the Indians; now the dog was almost starved to death. So Pat Klinkenberg and I took a dog-team with food to Hornby Bay. We saw plenty of caribou on the way; but Jack had no food except some old fish-bait. He had lost most of his stove-pipe through a fish-hole in the ice earlier in the season. His cabin stove therefore was propped up several feet off the floor so that what was left of the stovepipe would go through the roof. We had a lot of trouble persuading him to come back with us: he said he was all right and didn't need company. But he came in the end."

There were other reasons why Hornby did not want to go back with Arden, even if it did mean a warm house and plentiful food. For Dease Bay was the headquarters of his own modest empire, his natural home, and Arden the usurping monarch. Hornby's own account of that winter is less assuming than Arden's. The Indians with him had starved, and he fed them staples until there were none left. He crippled his leg with an axe and for some time "could only crawl about my business." The Indians left him and no doubt he would have died if Arden had not intervened. We have Arden's story of the pistol and the stovepipe. It is some measure of Hornby's reticence and bitterness that Arden did not know the rest of the story. For Hornby had been away from Bear Lake for three years serving in the Army in France, had been decorated, then severely wounded. Somehow he got back to Canada and, neglecting to report for duty, withdrew from the Army in a way which the military authorities regarded as unorthodox but venial. For he was discharged in December 1916 "on account of ill-health caused by wounds," with the honorary rank of Second Lieutenant—a courtesy not reserved for deserters. Like a wounded animal finding a quiet place to die, he had turned towards Great Bear Lake, setting off with practically no outfit, "a desperate man running away from civilization, looking like death, making the tremendous trip in a little boat no better than a broken-down packing-case." Alone and ill he managed the journey of more than 1,100 miles, escaped drowning more than once, and arrived at Dease Bay "with a much depleted outfit" to find many changes. It was no home-coming. He felt deep affection for the Sastudene Indians that, years before, he had brought from Norman back to their ancestral caribou-grounds; these gentle, guileless, still unspoiled people matched his own temperament. Now D'Arcy Arden held among them the position Hornby had held before. The gear Hornby had left in his cabin was destroyed or stolen; the cabin near the Dismal Lakes had been looted and burned since the two Oblate Fathers Rouvière and Leroux had been murdered by the Eskimo; trappers had overrun the country and were working the whole area down the Coppermine to the Gulf and along the Arctic coast. His land was violated; he could no longer live there. He made his way with a few Indians, temporarily loyal, to his old base on Hornby Bay, on the edge of the Barren Ground where he had first wintered with Cosmo Melvill in 1908. Even after the Arden rescue, he spent one more desolate winter there, and nearly died of it; then left Great Bear Lake never to return.

By 1923 the legend had reached Edmonton. Whenever he came "outside" he could usually be seen in the King Edward Hotel, his weather-beaten clean-shaven face and almost conventional dress an intriguing contrast to the lurid stories that were told about him. From Bear Lake he had turned to the east end of Great Slave Lake, and twice had nearly died of starvation there. He never learned to swim: yet he had nearly drowned himself in trying to explore the torrential Taltson River with an equally inexpert canoeist. Because the Barren Ground—the open shelterless tundra—is the most savage part of the North, Hornby's name became linked with the Barrens, although he had seen little of that country. One photograph shows him in winter wearing an old jacket with tattered sleeves, the trouser-knees monstrously baggy from crouching on his heels like an Eskimo at a fish-hole, his headgear a bizarre affair with strings and ear-flaps, the fruit of a succession of inspired improvisations to meet the whim or need of the moment. Another photograph shows him sitting on a large rock blissfully cracking caribou bones with an axe to get the marrow from them. Edmonton journalists—their romanticism fired by hearsay and the mute evidences supplied by the machine that never lies—described this second picture as "John Hornby, the Hermit of the Barrens, examining scientific specimens." Because he was reticent and enigmatic—and not least reticent when most voluble—he was called a hermit and a mystic. Because he refused to plan, and did whatever he did with bland self-confidence, he was said to be a man of diabolical skill and daredevil courage, a man capable of surmounting any difficulty by deft improvisation. The fact that he survived year after year did nothing to undermine the legend.

But all this, like the Arden episode, had its darker side. In the

Bear Lake years before the war—the six years with Melvill and the Douglas party and the Oblate Fathers—Hornby had been content (at least until Leroux brought malice and intrigue to Dease Bay); he had suffered no acute hardships, had never starved, had found satisfaction in activities which, if they lacked distinguishable rational basis, were at least appropriate to the country and its people. But it was distaste for "civilization" that had brought him to Canada at twenty-three and then taken him into the North four years later. Growing up in his Nantwich home was, he said, intolerable: all the talk was of cricket, and horses, and hunting—if this was civilization he could not regard it very seriously. The war had sharpened and deepened all his suspicions. He had had to use his hunter's skill to murder men. The world had run wild; civilization was in a suicidal state of decay, and all its ways were unclean. And even when he had placed the length of the Mackenzie River and the breadth of Bear Lake between himself and civilization, he had found fresh bitterness, a shattering desolation. He had been amiable, gregarious, amenable before; suddenly he becomes solitary, resentful, inscrutable. Casual observers sometimes thought him mad; perhaps he was from time to time. In the winter of 1920–1 (first starving winter near the ruins of Back's old Fort Reliance) he had written in his diary:

> At times this life appears strange. I never see anyone, no longer have anything to read, and my pencil is too small to let me do much writing. It is not surprising that men go mad. I have long been *mentis non compos*. . . . Unquestionably my mind has become somewhat vacant, for there is nothing to sharpen the intellect. . . . It is very easy to lie down and give up, but an entirely different matter to bestir oneself and move about.

After the war his travels had become more and more arduous: not that he went to more inaccessible places, but that he took no pains to avoid discomfort and disaster. Hardships and starvation seemed to take on a positive value, as though they were the only substantial values left for him, as though an ascetic or masochistic spirit were driving him to some impossible consummation with the country he loved. He courted death because he did not fear death. He went into the North alone and with little provision, because he loved the unfenced land to the point of obsession and felt that any other approach defied the integrity of the land. If he was deliberately seeking death he had many opportunities to gratify such a wish. But his supreme self-confidence allowed him to do impossible things as a child would do them—without bravado, absent-mindedly, without delight in skill. His exploits were feats of endurance, miracles of survival. Yet he was no daredevil: his mind did not deal in calculated risks. You either got through or you didn't. If you ignored pain and hunger and exhaustion, the issues were horribly simple: as long as you weren't dead you were alive, and some last tendril of the will-to-live could cling to the most improbable surfaces. What some men will suffer to make a living or a fortune or a reputation, or to extend the limits of knowledge or to alleviate the human condition, Hornby endured continuously, alone, without encouragement, for no reason that anybody could see. He got into predicaments that nobody else would have courted; but he survived them as nobody could have been expected to survive.

As long as he travelled alone—which he almost invariably did from choice—his eccentricities were harmless enough. Oldtimers and trappers who knew and liked him never mistook him for a Super-man of the North. Anybody who did was in danger. Bullock's ad-venture with Hornby in 1924-5 is particularly interesting: Bullock was the only man who ever acted on the assumption that the Hornby legend was true and survived.

Malcolm Waldron in his book called *Snow Man* gives a touching account of the first meeting between Hornby and Bullock: he had the story from Bullock. Like most of Hornby's memorable meetings, this took place in an Edmonton hotel. James Charles Critchell-Bullock, at twenty-five, had just retired from the Indian Army after five years' service and somehow or other had wound up, with the remnant of an inherited annuity, in Edmonton in search of some new way of life. Amazed at the small commanding figure that Hornby cut, and by the precision and softness of his voice, Bullock advanced without introduction to congratulate the little stranger upon his uncorrupted English accent. Hornby, eighteen years older than Bullock, was not embarrassed by this affront. "Harrow," he murmured. "Sherborne," said Bullock in reply. And that was the beginning of a lifelong friendship—or almost.

Bullock quickly found out who Hornby was; almost anybody in the lobby could tell him some part of the legend. As their acquaint-ance grew, he disclosed his state of mind to the famous man. He was weary of the ways of the world and wanted to do something bold and clean—anything, no matter how dangerous, so that it took him into the Far North. Hornby listened quizzically and patiently, and replied ambiguously. Did Bullock realize how hard life was in the North? Bullock, six foot two and proud of his physique, replied that he reckoned he could stand any hardships. So they made a short, inconclusive, and unnecessarily strenuous trial run into the Mount Coleman country. Hornby talked a good deal on that trip and gave Bullock the impression that he would like him to be his biographer. Thereafter Bullock collected a quantity of information about Hornby, some of it unique but much of it unverified and inaccurate. Bullock wrote elatedly to his brother: "Hornby is a wonder man—can go off into the blue goodness knows where with half a dog, a couple of fish, and only the clothes he stands up in." A trip into the North with Jack Hornby was "on"; and Bullock started to prepare himself for it by eating raw fish and going bare-headed in cold weather. He also began, with his own money, to make elaborate preparations under the fantastic belief that what Hornby called a "trip" was what Bullock would call an "expedition."

The diverting preliminaries to the Hornby-Bullock expedition are too intricate to be rehearsed here. Temperamentally two men could not have been worse assorted. Bullock's idea was that he would be the first man to winter on the Barrens and to take meteorological observations there; he would also be the first man to take motion pictures of the rare and almost extinct musk-oxen in their natural habitat. In Hornby's absence he laid in equipment consonant with such ambitions, had a little instruction in meteorology and geology, and wrote some preposterous letters to the Northwest Territories and Yukon Branch in Ottawa seeking support and encouragement. Hornby withdrew to England, cancelled the expedition by cable, then returned, looked up Bullock almost (it seems) by accident, shouted with laughter when he saw all the gear Bullock had collected, and agreed with puckish ambiguity to go with him to the east of Slave Lake—not that he approved of the scheme but because he could not bear to think of a greenhorn "messing about in my country." He promised to meet Bullock at Smith on an agreed date and turned up at Resolution six weeks late; by then Bullock was having trouble with his hired hand and wondering whether they would get to their destination before the freeze-up. When Hornby arrived, Bullock got his first severe shock. Hornby had brought four trapper friends with him and gaily introduced them. They were all coming. Wouldn't that be fun, he said. Bullock fumed and sulked;

but Hornby showed him then and later, obliquely but without qualification, that Hornby not Bullock was in charge of the party.

The legend, on very slender evidence, had linked Hornby's name
with the Barrens. It was the thought of wintering on the Barrens, and
of gaining some notoriety thereby, that had seized upon Bullock's
imagination. The half-million square miles of Canadian tundra
were a no-man's-land that called out—like other desolate places—
for a small devoted *élite*; among these Bullock longed to be numbered. The Athabaskans call that country *De-chin-u-way*: no trees.
Samuel Hearne had given it the haunting name of The Barren
Ground, a name still preferred by purists to the more colloquial
term "Barrens." The northernmost limit of trees—the Timber Line
—almost reaches the Arctic coast 150 miles east of the Mackenzie
Delta. From there it runs southeasterly to the northern tip of Great
Bear Lake and crosses the Arctic Circle about a hundred miles to
the eastward. Tongues of small timber run northerly down the river
valleys—the Coppermine particularly; but the line trends steadily
southeast in a slight curve, crossing Artillery Lake east of Great
Slave, and meeting Hudson Bay at Churchill. Beyond the Timber
Line is the Barren Ground: open rolling plains eroded by wind and
frost, broken by soft ridges, ground down by the ice-cap into slashes
of lake and muskeg, scoured out in long striations; for the few weeks
of summer, a blaze of flowers and brilliant lichens, and the haunt
of drab butterflies and—the worst enemy—blackflies and mosquitoes;
and a terrible desolation in winter when there is no shelter anywhere from the winds. In the stillness the temperature may drop
to 60 degrees below zero. And the sky is a vast commanding presence
there as it is at sea. The only features are the eskers, the long
gravel ridges—sometimes looking like railway embankments—
dropped by the receding ice-cap. The lifeblood of that country is the
caribou migrations. Back and forth from the timber to the Barren
Ground the caribou range in an unpredictable rhythmic life-flow:
splay-footed, deer-legged, antlered creatures, wonderful swimmers.
They are food and clothing. "They are like ghosts," runs an Indian
saying; "they come from nowhere, fill up all the land, then disappear." A season when "the caribou did not come" is a black
season; much misery, many deaths.

The party of eight made a quick passage of Slave Lake. There
were more shocks for Bullock here too. First Hornby insisted that
Bullock leave his hired man and wife behind in one of his old

cabins, then he made a caché of all Bullock's cherished gear, allowing him to keep only a couple of cameras and a typewriter. It was,
he pointed out, rather a lot of gear to take over a 25-mile portage;
and when Bullock protested about the waste of such expensive equipment, Hornby asked whether money was really of any ultimate importance. Bullock sulked all the way over Pike's Portage. But the
winter caught them when they had scarcely entered Artillery Lake
and Bullock could no longer indulge the luxury of wounded feelings.
Two of the trappers built a cabin just inside the timber; the other
two built a stone dugout nearer the head of the lake, later replacing
it with a cabin a little to the southward. Hornby and Bullock went
on into the Barrens, some six miles north of the head of the lake,
and dug a cave in the top of an esker. The dwelling, when finished,
was seven by ten feet, with nominal headroom of six feet. The whole
cave had to be revetted inside with spruce-brush and ground-willow,
and caulked with moss to keep the sand out. The roof was supported
by thirty green poles no bigger than an inch and a half in diameter,
and the whole loaded with a heavy layer of sand. "It is comfortable,"
Bullock wrote at first, "except for there being sand in everything."
But the roof creaked dangerously and Hornby brought more wood
from the south—the first instalment of a network of small crooked
poles that grew in the pure fantasy of improvisation, never quite
keeping the sand at bay, and in the end making movement in the
cave almost impossible. A detail that Hornby had probably not
overlooked was that he stood five foot two and was nimble on his
feet. Bullock stood six feet two and though proud of his physique
lived up to his name very well.

   If one supposed that wintering in the Barren Ground in the grand
manner was their objective, one would have expected them to settle
down to a winter of stoical endurance, the trappers acting as a support party in case of need. Bullock hoped that that would be the
case; but Hornby had no such intention. Indeed the winter was devoted to trapping—the only occasion when Hornby is known to
have trapped seriously—probably because fur was the only way of
offsetting Bullock's large and ill-considered outlay. After only five
days in the cave, Bullock wrote: "Our discomforts are certainly
appalling, almost squalid. Poor Hornby is becoming daily more untidy. His only care is in setting traps, cutting up meat, and chasing
and talking about caribou." A few days later he found Hornby "too
communistic—this rich and poor stuff gets me." When he tried to

argue Hornby into good conservative sense, Hornby would open a book and start reading.

Bullock had hoped for something more romantic; but their longest continuous period in the cave was a month—and even then there were interruptions, usually at five-day intervals, when Hornby through restlessness or in self-defence would withdraw to the trappers' place for a couple of days. Bullock was too inexperienced to travel far alone in winter, and at first kept to the cave as headquarters; but both spent a good deal of time with the trappers. In the cave everything offended Bullock's fastidious nature like a cold blast on a raw nerve. They argued about the Battle of the Somme, about religion, about money, about table manners, about books, about how to write diaries. Hornby's pocketknife exasperated Bullock. Bullock remonstrated; for a day or two they were "not particularly communicative;" but Hornby went on using his knife exactly as before. "I loathe skinning foxes on my bed," Bullock wrote again. "Blood everywhere—sand everywhere—" and as an inevitable if banal echo of Blasco Ibanez—"Blood and Sand." But there was nowhere else. And when Hornby would vanish for a day or two, Bullock would heave a sigh of relief, tidy up the cave, get out his typewriter, and write long self-communing letters that he never posted but once tried to publish. For a time he busied himself with trapping and hunting—and they were never short of food—but the hallucinatory solitude bothered him. One day he contemplated suicide because he could find no shadow on the snow. His humiliation was complete. From January onwards, whenever he was alone in the cave, his apathy increased, his attention relaxed, he slept for dangerously long periods.

Once in the middle of December Hornby collapsed outside the cave, either from poisoning or from a heart attack. Bullock stumbled over him in the dark, dragged him into a cave, and nursed him for two days and nights expecting him to die. Then Hornby sat up and demanded food and never referred to the incident again. Twice Hornby went out to Reliance for stores and ostentatiously neglected to bring back the meteorological instruments Bullock wanted. At Christmas, Hornby left Bullock alone in the cave. Wood ran out; Bullock wrote some long heroic passages in his diary and finally, when he found his beard freezing to his sleeping-bag, set off for the nearest trappers' shack, in a blizzard, led by a dog with a frost-bitten and gangrenous paw. He suffered the crowning insult to his eloquence by surviving the journey. But the dangers were real enough.

The most notorious incident was the arrival of a Mounted Police patrol on All Fool's Day 1925. On the second trip to Reliance Hornby was asked by Bullock's hired man whether it was true, as Indian rumour had it, that Bullock was insane. Hornby loved a mystery and had plenty of reason to feel concern for Bullock's deterioration; he replied impatiently that "The police had better come and see for themselves." By the time the patrol arrived from Resolution, the days were lengthening out again, the trappers were counting their skins and thinking of pulling out, and Bullock was delightedly busying himself with his cameras. The police were greatly impressed with the squalor of the cave, but after sizing up Bullock and hearing Hornby's story decided that, although Bullock didn't seem a very suitable person for Northern travel, he was not dangerously insane.

The police left and the trappers set off for Resolution, and Bullock made a journey alone with dogs—as he had longed to do all winter—to Reliance to settle with his man and say goodbye to his expensive gear now to be abandoned; and injured his back on the return journey travelling through a wet spring blizzard. When he reached the cave the spring thaw was well advanced and the squalor of the cave indescribable. Hornby was burning old clothes for lack of fuel. So they demolished the rickety structure, dumped all the loathsome garbage of the winter into the pit and set it afire. The winter was over, with no solid accomplishment, no genuine heroism. But they had taken 353 white foxes, the skins worth at least $10,000. And they had got through the winter without killing each other.

The journey out was another marvel—of confused purpose and futile hardship. If they were to take the Thelon route to the east—as Hornby was determined despite the contrary advice of the police—they could only do it safely by travelling light. If they wanted to be sure of the furs, a 600-mile journey through poorly mapped country was whimsical security. But Hornby had not yet made the observations he had promised to make for the Government, and Bullock had not yet filmed the musk-oxen—his last shred of self-respect: and these jobs could only be performed on the Thelon. So they settled for the Thelon. Through the early days of May they eyed the fickle weather, trying to keep their smouldering tempers under control, while they sorted and weeded out their accumulation of gear and skins and threw away whatever they could—including much food—and still could not get their load much below a ton. At two-thirty on the morning of May the 12th they finally set off with all this, and two canoes, precariously mounted on one toboggan, four dogs and two men hauling; and pulled their hearts out, packing and double-packing and manhauling, to shift it all two miles in that first day.

The Hanbury River—the northern branch of the Thelon—starts as an imperceptible current running northerly through a vertiginous confusion of lakes and standing water east of Artillery Lake. Hornby knew that once they were into the Hanbury they would have a straight run—except for portages—into the Thelon. Instead of taking the classic northerly route into the Hanbury, he decided to travel due east until he struck Campbell Lake (which is actually much farther to the south) and pick up the Hanbury from there. He had no accurate map. One of Hornby's most endearing qualities—and his most dangerous—was his bland disregard for brute fact. His favourite reply to an insuperable difficulty was "What does it matter?" Now that the thaw had started, and the ice was not out of the lakes, he would travel by sled at night when the ground and snow would be frozen. He reckoned that they could make 200 miles in five days. There were obstacles to this spirited plan: their prodigious load, Bullock's injured back, the lack of night-frost, then a very heavy fall of wet snow. Their progress was pitifully slow. And when they struck what they thought was Campbell Lake, having travelled fifteen miles in twelve days, they were completely lost for a fortnight; and in any case the condition of the lake and the land prevented travel of any sort. Hornby, reconnoitring far to the North, eventually found the Hanbury by the simple expedient of dropping bannock crumbs in the water. Once into the Hanbury they made a better time. But when, at one o'clock on the morning of July the 23rd, they ran out of the Hanbury into the Thelon, they had travelled 150 miles in seventy-two days; and even this speed had been achieved by taking unnecessary risks in running rapids single-handed in laden canoes. They still had 400 miles to go.

At the junction of the Hanbury and Thelon they stopped for a few days to photograph musk-oxen and ran through a large caribou migration. Refreshed and well-fed, they made forty miles the first day under way. Then Bullock nearly amputated several toes with an axe. For a day he kept going, then collapsed. Hornby, who had borne the burden of most of the portaging, was in nearly as bad condition as Bullock. In the summer heat their stock of meat suddenly went bad. Two of their dogs had run away; one had had to be shot; now they shot the last one. Somehow they rallied and went on, sometimes living off trout and "poor" caribou, and most of the time feeble and half-starved. Two or three times they narrowly escaped drowning in the rapids. But towards the end of the journey they travelled 260 miles in twenty-six days on thirteen of which bad weather prevented them from moving.

On the afternoon of August the 27th they pulled out of the Thelon into Baker Lake and sighted the cluster of buildings to the north-east—the Révillon Frères post. According to Northern custom, they tidied themselves as best they could, and paddled across to the post. Somebody at the landing stage, startled by the bewhiskered filth of the two men in the canoes, asked where the hell they had come from. "Edmonton," said Hornby.

From their winter-quarters to Baker Lake they had travelled 535 miles in 107 days: a feat of endurance perhaps, an act of folly certainly, but not a notable journey by any rudimentary standard of judgment or skill. The only remarkable thing about it is that they survived. As a final merry quip of fortune, they found that all the furs, imperfectly cleaned in the dark cave and in the rapid thaw, had spoiled on the journey and were worthless. With remarkable pre-science Bullock had written his epitaph on this journey after only a few days in the cave on the Barrens: "With Hornby one travels by hook or crook. The greatest distance with the minimum of comfort, a maximum of energy expended with often least accomplished."

Hornby's parting shot—an aside written in his characteristic elliptical style in his report on the caribou written in Ottawa in November 1925—is much more light-hearted: "The day of hardships and exploration in the Arctic regions is now a thing of the past. One can realize what difficulties and hardships were to be met with (in earlier days). Now the routes are mapped, transportation is easy and instead of months it is only a question of days (to get anywhere). Previously it was the explorer (who travelled this country), now it will be the American tourist." "I intend," he said, "to retire from active life and become only an armchair critic"; and because his father was mortally ill he returned to England at the turn of the year.

Hornby still had hankerings for "one more trip." He had discussed this with Bullock; but by the time they had extricated themselves from Hudson Bay, made Newfoundland in a little trading vessel, and parted in Ottawa, Bullock had had enough. Apart from anything else, Bullock had lost all his money and Hornby had scarcely reached England when the first of a series of cables from Bullock arrived demanding funds. Some authorities have said that if it had not been for these cables, Hornby would never have gone into the North again; that he went back to "settle" with Bullock. But even when he went back to Canada he made no attempt to find Bullock (who was then in New York in straitened circumstances). All the evidence shows that he could never have come to rest in Nantwich—or indeed anywhere else in "civilization."

Perhaps, after so many solitary privations, he was now looking for a travelling companion; and in his young cousin Edgar Christian, a boy of sixteen who had just finished school and was thinking of going to South Africa, he found an eager and devoted hero-worshipper. But in fact it was Edgar's father, Colonel Christian, who urged Hornby to take Edgar on a Northern journey; it would be a priceless opportunity for the boy before coming to grips with the troubled world of the middle twenties. In the winter of 1926 Hornby's reminiscent talk—one imagines—flowed compellingly. He would sit forward, at once alert and indolent, gazing into the fire; and you would swear he was sitting by a campfire on one of the eastern islands of Great Slave Lake. He talked perhaps about the spell of the Barren Ground and of the Upper Thelon; of how few men had really penetrated beyond the timber, and how—though he had seen only threads of the country—he knew it perhaps better than any man. He talked about the fur-animals, and the lakes and rivers teeming with great salmon; and how the caribou at migration moved in solid bands of thousands—millions perhaps—their eyes glazed, their hooves grinding the ice to fine powder, the air shaking with their bemused grunting, crowding each other to death in the rapids and at shallow river-crossings. Some day he would write a book about the country and his travels and all he had learned: it was to be called *In the Land of Feast or Famine*. He had made several starts at it and now had much of the material collected. More interesting things kept interrupting this intention; but this winter on the Thelon he was going to take things easy, and writing his book would give him something to do in the dark hours.

What Colonel Christian could not know—and there was probably nobody in England who could have told him—was that Hornby, for all his fabulous experience and rhapsodic talk, was an extremely dangerous man to travel with. He refused to plan; he had never shown any organizing ability or forethought; the trip with Bullock shows that his humour could run to grim, even cynical, extremes; his judgment, focused continually upon the present, was seriously distorted because he rejected—as manifestations of the "civilization" he loathed—everything that thought, analysis, skill, and purpose could add to the purely animal business of Northern living. He had never yet had any clear purpose to give shape or direction to his activities. And although this may in some way be admirable as an absent-minded return to primordial existence, it was a precarious enough thread to hang anybody else's life on. His earliest travels are the putterings of a man in love with the country; after the war an element of melodrama enters; the Bullock episode was macabre comedy. Everything shows that Hornby was a gentle-hearted man who shrank from the suffering of animals and would not willingly have harmed anybody he loved or respected. Yet he was intensely self-preoccupied, isolated in a world which was nobody else's world. And the next and final episode was tragedy—a tragedy of which Hornby was the instrument but in which Edgar Christian was the protagonist.

In April 1926 Hornby landed in Montreal with Edgar Christian. Both were in holiday mood and Edgar wrote home to say that in Montreal they had met a man who told him he was "with one of Canada's best and anybody who is with J. Hornby can never go wrong." What Edgar did not understand, because his admiration would not let him see it, was that Hornby's friends were appalled at the prospect of Hornby taking the boy into the North. It was one thing for Hornby to survive incredible privations alone: the addition of one ineffective hunter to the party could destroy the infinitesimal margin that Hornby always operated on. In Ottawa, in Toronto, in Winnipeg, in Edmonton, wherever they stopped on their trip westward, different people tried to dissuade Hornby and warn Christian. But neither would listen. The record of one of these warnings is preserved. "In the spring of 1926 Hornby cabled me in Ottawa that he was on his way and presently arrived with Edgar Christian. He was full of plans to winter far out on the Barrens where no trapper had been before and trap white foxes. I tried to persuade him that this was a *summer* breeding ground but not a winter range, that there would be no fish in the Thelon and that the

caribou pass through in the autumn and late spring only. He did not
argue but put on his puckish grin: he knew better. Christian
resented any question of Jack's knowledge and ability. Again in
Edmonton we talked about it, then I left for the North. I was at
Fort Chipewyan when Hornby and the two boys arrived by canoe.
I tried to persuade him to join me with Christian on my exploration
of the Upper Dubawnt, but Hornby was determined to make a final
journey down the Thelon and then give up northern travel."

In Edmonton Hornby had run into Harold Adlard, a retired
English Air Force man of twenty-six whom Hornby had declined
to take on the Bullock trip. Adlard had never been farther north
than Onoway. But now Hornby said he would redeem his promise
and take him into the North. Edgar was perhaps jealous at first but
also a little cheered that there should be another greenhorn in the
party besides himself. From Fort Smith he wrote home final words
of encouragement. "Don't get worried about me because I am as safe
as a house with Jack. . . . I have seen lots of trappers who have been
on the trail with Jack and many won't go again because he is too
tough, although they like [him] more than any man. I shall be with
someone whose name runs through Canada with highest praise
which makes me feel absolutely satisfied about the future."

And they disappeared into country where there were not even
Indians.

One of the last men to see the party travelling eastward in their
big square-sterned canoe was an Artillery Lake trapper named Jim
Cooley. He endears himself to memory because he always travelled
into his trapping country in an impeccable suit of blue serge and a
dove-grey Stetson.

"Sure," he told an *Edmonton Journal* reporter, "I met him myself
near Reliance. It's quite true that they didn't have much grub, but
then, Jack Hornby could go farther on a diet of snow, air, and
scenery than a Lizzie can go on twenty gallons of gas. . . . While
Hornby is fond of taking chances and does many things that look
crazy to the ordinary individual, he has made trips which will be
talked about for years around northern campfires. He has reduced
the business of living off the country to a science."

Jim Cooley did not know his man well: he was merely repeating
the legend in his own vivacious style. Hornby had reduced nothing
to a science. And the story of his last journey is distressingly straight-
forward, as we have it in the grim ingenuous record written by

Edgar Christian throughout the seven and a half months it took him and his two companions to die of starvation.

For Edgar Christian the traverse of Great Slave Lake was full of wonder. At Reliance they were held up by ice, but presently made their way over Pike's Portage, into Artillery Lake, and by Hanbury's route into the Thelon. Hornby knew where he was going: he had chosen the exact spot the year before and pointed it out to Bullock. It was about 300 miles from Reliance, in one of the few sizable stands of spruce timber of the Thelon. But for no intelligible reason he travelled slowly—"from laziness" he said in one of the notes left in a cairn for the Artillery Lake trappers—reached his destination very late in the season and missed the southward migration of caribou that their lives would depend upon. They were late in getting a cabin started, and the temperature was ten below zero before they had finished it. By the end of December their position was becoming desperate: even Edgar Christian could see that.

Without dogs there was no hope of retreating westward or of advancing eastward. Hornby had starved before and was not unduly alarmed. But he was on the move all the time, remorselessly, in all weathers. For many hours at a time he would range the Barrens that lay just beyond the protecting screen of trees, or watch with binoculars from a ridge-top for a sight of caribou. He set traps for animals, and nets for birds; and even at night, in bitter temperatures, he would spend hours clearing and setting and hauling the fishnet through the ice on the river. There seemed no limit to his physical endurance, and he was incorrigibly cheerful. If sheer expenditure of effort, and dogged defiance, could have fed the party, they would have fared handsomely; but Hornby's rifle seldom killed anything. The others helped as best they could. Edgar Christian was no hunter, and once he started to starve could not endure the cold. For lack of caribou their clothing was inadequate. They saved for Christmas dinner a caribou head—a notable Northern delicacy. Thereafter they took little but a few small animals and some fish; never much, never enough to last. Adlard, greenhorn though he was, learned quickly, and soon proved himself a good shot and a tenacious hunter; but he got severely frostbitten bringing in the last caribou they shot early in February and had to keep to the cabin for almost a month; otherwise he might have saved the whole party.

They clawed their way through the first two months of the year. At the end of February Hornby realized that he must make a final effort for caribou before he was completely incapacitated; for his old wounds were now causing him intense pain. They hunted for ten days in the open and took nothing; and when they returned exhausted to the cabin they found the tracks of caribou that had passed near the house. They saw caribou only twice after that, and were too feeble by then to hunt them.

Ever since Christmas Hornby had been behaving as though he understood very clearly how serious their condition was. He had now driven himself beyond even the limits of his own endurance in his efforts to find food. But he continued to make light of the situation and in late March read to his companions part of the diary of the terrible winter of 1920–1 to show that conditions could be even worse and still not be fatal. Christian noted that now, "under similar but not severer conditions," he could appreciate the meaning of the diary, with its laconic understatements and bleak statements of shocking fact. And Christian's own diary unwittingly shows that Hornby had been consistently denying himself in order to feed the others.

Killing an occasional bird or fish, and by digging up garbage and old fish-bait thrown out in the fall, they survived March and the year was beginning to turn. But now they were confronted by a new danger. Adlard, who had all along suffered from being shut out of the deepening intimacy between Hornby and Christian, became morose, then menacing, then on the verge of mental collapse. Seventeen days passed without their taking game of any sort. By that time Hornby was dying. For nearly a week Christian and Adlard did what they could for him, which wasn't much; and Adlard was shocked back into sanity. Hornby told them what he could about how to look after themselves, and how to get out in the spring. In the morning of April the 16th he lost consciousness and died in the evening. His body, sewn in a canoe-sail, was placed outside the cabin door. For three days Adlard devoted himself to Christian's needs, but exhausted his last reserves of strength, lingered a little, and died two weeks later.

For more than a fortnight Edgar Christian recorded, day by day, the gruesome particulars of his own solitary decline, without a flicker of emotion or self-pity. Long before Adlard died Christian had faced up to his personal predicament. There was no sign of panic. If only his crazy body could assimilate the wretched garbage he grubbed up from the snow, he could hold on indefinitely. His horizon had now shrunk to an apathetic animal search for food and his resolve "to pull through and go out to let the world know of the last days of the finest man I had ever known."

The sunshine was getting warmer; he sat outside in the sun when he could, doing everything possible to regain strength. Soon the birds would be returning; he saw a raven flying north. Then cold weather came again and heavy snow; then the snow thawed. With the terrible remorselessness of a machine running down, his strength ebbed away. One day he discovered to his amazement that he was too weak to carry a rifle out of the house, and thereafter left two loaded rifles outside the door. Some days he had to den up, because of bad weather or sheer weakness; he burned floorboards and bunk poles. Then one day he tried to go out and found he could only crawl.

For the last eleven days of May the diary was silent. On June the 1st, five days before his nineteenth birthday, he entered his diary for the last time and "made preparations"—wrote a letter to his father and a note to his mother, placed carefully in the cold ashes of the stove the diary and letters and Hornby's will and some other letters and records, and left a note on top of the stove. He turned into his bunk and pulled a red Hudson's Bay blanket over his head. Almost the last words he wrote were: "Please dont Blame dear Jack."

Fourteen months after Edgar Christian died, three geologists canoeing down the Thelon noticed fresh cuttings in the wood by the riverbank. They landed and found the cabin derelict, the two bodies outside, the two loaded rifles by the door, the boy's body inside. A year later a Mounted Police patrol recovered the letters and diary from the stove, buried the three skeletons beside the cabin and set over them three crosses with initials cut in them, tidied the cabin in case somebody else should need to shelter there, and signed death certificates in quintuplicate. Only two parties are known to have passed the cabin since then.

When the story of Hornby's death was given to the world in 1929, Northern people, and particularly Hornby's friends and associates, were profoundly shocked. The publication of Edgar Christian's diary some years later received and still receives, the recognition it deserves. But about Hornby, although he is still a living legend, there has been almost a conspiracy of silence and genuine information about him is very hard to come by. One man will allow that Hornby was a lovable man of generous disposition and vivid personality; another will dismiss him as aimless, incompetent, irresponsible, a freak, a myth. Companionable as only an intensely lonely man

can be, he had many warm acquaintances, but very few intimates—
perhaps one. To his closest friends he could be as infuriating as he
was endearing.

For the rest, he was a man one met by accident; he moved like a
bird of passage, arriving without warning, leaving without apology.
With something of an animal's protective instinct, he was guilelessly
ambiguous, would announce a profusion of plans and then invent
at the last moment a quite new one. Without deliberate duplicity he
would reveal one aspect of himself to one person, to another, another;
always withdrawn, devious, unpredictable. Something vivid and
fantastic about him disarmed criticism, inspired hero-worship in
some, and in others affection; but others, on slight acquaintance,
felt only distrust and contempt. The disaster that Hornby's death
involved is a barrier almost insuperable to a sympathetic understanding. Yet the central figure in a myth or a tragedy has a stature
and power that not even accurate history can confer; and he stands
now with his back to a strong light.

When representations were made to the Committee on Historical
Documents in 1931 that some memorial should be erected on the
Thelon to commemorate John Hornby's death there, the suggestion
was rejected "inasmuch as it was the consensus of opinion that this
was not an event of sufficient national importance to receive attention in the manner suggested." Which is one way of saying, of
Hornby's life and of his death, in his own most characteristic phrase:
"What does it matter?" And what after all would one commemorate, beyond his vivid smile, his crazy generosity, his passionate sense
of the integrity of the country, his gay and birdlike inconsequence,
his childlike illogical optimism, his astonishing self-confidence,
his pitiless endurance, his tragic light-hearted courage in the face
of a disaster that he must have known his own levity and irre-
sponsibility had produced, the slow merciless killing of himself to
save two lives he knew he could not save? To say that he longed for
death and deliberately sought it is to miss the point. He once told
Denny LaNauze that he wished he had been born an Indian. And
if his philosophy could be crystallized, it would be very simple and
straightforward, rather like an Indian's—something like this:

*In civilization there is no peace. Here, in the North, in my country,
there is peace. No past, no future, no regret, no anticipation; just
doing. That is peace.*

As long as he could live by himself and to himself it was perhaps
an excellent philosophy.

SHEILA WATSON

1919-

Born in New Westminster, B.C., Sheila Watson studied at the University of British Columbia and, after her marriage to the poet Wilfred Watson, at the University of Toronto, where she worked on a biographical study of Wyndham Lewis.

She is the author of one remarkable experimental novel in the symbolist tradition, *The Double Hook* (1959), and a number of mythological-modern short stories in *Queen's Quarterly* and *The Tamarack Review*, in which the tale reprinted below appeared in 1959.

My father ruled a kingdom on the right bank of the river. He ruled it with a firm hand and a stout heart though he was often more troubled than Moses, who was simply trying to bring a stubborn and moody people under God's yoke. My father ruled men who thought they were gods or the instruments of gods or, at very least, god-afflicted and god-pursued. He ruled Atlas who held up the sky and Hermes who went on endless messages, and Helen who'd been hatched from an egg, and Pan the gardener, and Kallisto the bear, and too many others to mention by name. Yet my father had no thunderbolt, no trident, no helmet of darkness. His subjects were delivered bound into his hands. He merely watched over them as the hundred-handed ones watched over the dethroned Titans so that they wouldn't bother Hellas again.

Despite the care which my father took to maintain an atmosphere of sober commonsense in his whole establishment, there were occasional outbursts of self-indulgence which he could not control. For instance, I have seen Helen walking naked down the narrow cement path under the chestnut trees for no better reason, I suppose, than that the day was hot and the white flowers themselves lay naked and expectant in the sunlight. And I have seen Atlas forget the sky while he sat eating the dirt which held him up. These were things which I was not supposed to see.

If my father had been as sensible through and through as he was thought to be, he would have packed me off to boarding school when I was old enough to be disciplined by men. Instead he kept me at home with my two cousins who, except for the accident of birth, might as well have been my sisters. Today I imagine people concerned with our welfare would take such an environment into account. At the time I speak of most people thought us fortunate—especially the girls whose father's affairs had come to an unhappy issue. I don't like to revive old scandal and I wouldn't except to deny it; but it takes only a few impertinent newcomers in any community to force open cupboards which have been decently sealed by time.

However, my father was so busy setting his kingdom to rights that he let weeds grow up in his own garden.

As I said, if my father had had all his wits about him he would have sent me to boarding school—and Antigone and Ismene too. I might have fallen in love with the headmaster's daughter and Antigone might have learned that no human being can be right always. She might have found out besides that from the seeds of eternal justice grow madder flowers than any which Pan grew in the gardens of my father's kingdom.

Between the kingdom which my father ruled and the wilderness flows a river. It is this river which I am crossing now. Antigone is with me.

How often can we cross the same river, Antigone asks.

Her persistence annoys me. Besides, Heraklitos made nonsense of her question years ago. He saw a river too—the Inachos, the Kephissos, the Lethaios. The name doesn't matter. He said: See how quickly the water flows. However agile a man is, however nimbly he swims, or runs, or flies, the water slips away before him. See, even as he sets down his foot the water is displaced by the stream which crowds along in the shadow of its flight.

But after all, Antigone says, one must admit that it is the same kind of water. The oolichans run in it as they ran last year and the year before. The gulls cry above the same banks. Boats drift towards the Delta and circle back against the current to gather up the catch.

At any rate, I tell her, we're standing on a new bridge. We are standing so high that the smell of mud and river weeds passes under us out to the straits. The unbroken curve of the bridge protects the eye from details of river life. The bridge is foolproof as a clinic's passport to happiness.

The old bridge still spans the river, but the cat-walk with its cracks and knot-holes, with its gap between planking and hand-rail has been torn down. The centre arch still grinds open to let boats up and down the river, but a child can no longer be walked on it or swung out on it beyond the water-gauge at the very centre of the flood.

I've known men who scorned any kind of bridge, Antigone says. Men have walked into the water, she says, or, impatient, have jumped from the bridge into the river below.

But these, I say, didn't really want to cross the river. They went Persephone's way, cradled in the current's arms, down the long halls under the pink feet of the gulls, under the booms and tow-lines, under the soft bellies of the fish.

Antigone looks at me.

There's no coming back, she says, if one goes far enough.

I know she's going to speak of her own misery and I won't listen. Only a god has the right to say: Look what I suffer. Only a god should say: What more ought I to have done for you that I have not done?

Once in winter, she says, a man walked over the river.

Taking advantage of nature, I remind her, since the river had never frozen before.

Yet he escaped from the penitentiary, she says. He escaped from the guards walking round the walls or standing with their guns in the sentry-boxes at the four corners of the enclosure. He escaped.

Not without risk, I say. He had to test the strength of the ice himself. Yet safer perhaps than if he had crossed by the old bridge where he might have slipped through a knot-hole or tumbled out through the railing.

He did escape, she persists, and lived forever on the far side of the river in the Alaska tea and bulrushes. For where, she asks, can a man go farther than to the outermost edge of the world?

The habitable world, as I've said, is on the right bank of the river.

Here is the market with its market stalls—the coops of hens, the long-tongued geese, the haltered calf, the bearded goat, the shoving pigs, and the empty bodies of cows and sheep and rabbits hanging on iron hooks. My father's kingdom provides asylum in the suburbs. Near it are the convent, the churches, and the penitentiary. Above these on the hill the cemetery looks down on the people and on the river itself. It is a world spread flat, tipped up into the sky so that men and women bend forward, walking as men walk when they board a ship at high tide. This is the world I feel with my feet. It is the world I see with my eyes.

I remember standing once with Antigone and Ismene in the square just outside the gates of my father's kingdom. Here from a bust set high on a cairn the stone eyes of Simon Fraser look from his stone face over the river that he found.

It is the head that counts, Ismene said.

It's no better than an urn, Antigone said, one of the urns we see when we climb to the cemetery above.

And all I could think was that I didn't want an urn, only a flat green grave with a chain about it.

A chain won't keep out the dogs, Antigone said.

But his soul could swing on it, Ismene said, like a bird blown on a branch in the wind.

And I remember Antigone's saying: The cat drags its belly on the ground and the rat sharpens its tooth in the ivy.

I should have loved Ismene, but I didn't. It was Antigone I loved. I should have loved Ismene because, although she walked the flat world with us, she managed somehow to see it round.

The earth is an oblate spheroid, she'd say. And I knew that she saw it there before her comprehensible and whole like a tangerine spiked through and held in place while it rotated on the axis of one of Nurse's steel sock needles. The earth was a tangerine and she saw the skin peeled off and the world parcelled out into neat segments, each segment sweet and fragrant in its own skin.

It's the head that counts, she said.

In her own head she made diagrams to live by, cut and fashioned after the eternal patterns spied out by Plato as he rummaged about in the sewing basket of the gods.

I should have loved Ismene. She would live now in some pre-fabricated and perfect chrysolite by some paradigm which made love round and whole. She would simply live and leave destruction in the purgatorial ditches outside her own walled paradise.

Antigone is different. She sees the world flat as I do and feels it tip beneath her feet. She has walked in the market and seen the living animals penned and the dead hanging stiff on their hooks. Yet she defies what she sees with a defiance which is almost denial. Like Atlas she tries to keep the vaulted sky from crushing the flat earth. Like Hermes she brings a message that there is life if one can escape to it in the brush and bulrushes in some dim Hades beyond the river. It is defiance not belief and I tell her that this time we walk the bridge to a walled cave where we can deny death no longer.

Yet she asks her question still. And standing there I tell her that Heraklitos has made nonsense of her question. I should have loved Ismene for she would have taught me what Plato meant when he said in all earnest that the union of the soul with the body is in no way better than dissolution. I expect that she understood things which Antigone is too proud to see.

I turn away from her and flatten my elbows on the high wall of the bridge. I look back at my father's kingdom. I see the terraces rolling down from the red-brick buildings with their barred windows. I remember hands shaking the bars and hear fingers tearing up paper and stuffing it through the meshes. Diktynna, mother of nets and high leaping fear. O Artemis, mistress of wild beasts and wild men.

The inmates are beginning to come out on the screened verandas. They pace up and down in straight lines or stand silent like figures which appear at the same time each day ·from some depths inside a clock.

On the upper terrace Pan the gardener is shifting sprinklers with a hooked stick. His face is shadowed by the brim of his hat. He moves as economically as an animal between the beds of lobelia and geranium. It is high noon.

Antigone has cut out a piece of sod and has scooped out a grave. The body lies in a coffin in the shade of the magnolia tree. Antigone and I are standing. Ismene is sitting between two low angled branches of the monkey puzzle tree. Her lap is filled with daisies. She slits the stem of one daisy and pulls the stem of another through it. She is making a chain for her neck and a crown for her hair.

Antigone reaches for a branch of magnolia. It is almost beyond her grip. The buds flame above her. She stands on a small fire of daisies which smoulder in the roots of the grass.

I see the magnolia buds. They brood above me, whiteness feathered on whiteness. I see Antigone's face turned to the light. I hear the living birds call to the sun. I speak private poetry to myself: Between four trumpeting angels at the four corners of the earth a bride stands before the altar in a gown as white as snow.

Yet I must have been speaking aloud because Antigone challenges me: You're mistaken. It's the winds the angels hold, the four winds of the earth. After the just are taken to paradise the winds will destroy the earth. It's a funeral, she says, not a wedding.

She looks towards the building.

Someone is coming down the path from the matron's house, she says.

I notice that she has pulled one of the magnolia blossoms from the branch. I take it from her. It is streaked with brown where her hands have bruised it. The sparrow which she has decided to bury lies on its back. Its feet are clenched tight against the feathers of its breast. I put the flower in the box with it.

Someone is coming down the path. She is wearing a blue cotton dress. Her cropped head is bent. She walks slowly carrying something in a napkin.

It's Kallisto the bear, I say. Let's hurry. What will my father say if he sees us talking to one of his patients?

If we live here with him, Antigone says, what can he expect? If he spends his life trying to tame people he can't complain if you behave as if they were tame. What would your father think, she says, if he saw us digging in the Institution lawn?

Pan comes closer. I glower at him. There's no use speaking to him. He's deaf and dumb.

Listen, I say to Antigone, my father's not unreasonable. Kallisto thinks she's a bear and he thinks he's a bear tamer, that's all. As for the lawn, I say quoting my father without conviction, a man must have order among his own if he is to keep order in the state.

Kallisto has come up to us. She is smiling and laughing to herself. She gives me her bundle.

Fish, she says.

I open the napkin.

Pink fish sandwiches, I say.

For the party, she says.

But it isn't a party, Antigone says. It's a funeral.

For the funeral breakfast, I say.

Ismene is twisting two chains of daisies into a rope. Pan has • stopped pulling the sprinkler about. He is standing beside Ismene resting himself on his hooked stick. Kallisto squats down beside her. Ismene turns away, preoccupied, but she can't turn far because of Pan's legs.

Father said we never should
Play with madmen in the wood.

I look at Antigone.

It's my funeral, she says.

I go over to Ismene and gather up a handful of loose daisies from her lap. The sun reaches through the shadow of the magnolia tree.

It's my funeral, Antigone says. She moves possessively toward the body.

An ant is crawling into the bundle of sandwiches which I've put on the ground. A file of ants is marching on the sparrow's box.

I go over and drop daisies on the bird's stiff body. My voice speaks ritual words: Deliver me, O Lord, from everlasting death on this dreadful day. I tremble and am afraid.

The voice of a people comforts me. I look at Antigone. I look her in the eye.

It had better be a proper funeral then, I say.

Kallisto is crouched forward on her hands. Tears are running down her cheeks and she is licking them away with her tongue.

My voice rises again: I said in the midst of my days, I shall not see—

Antigone just stands there. She looks frightened, but her eyes defy me with their assertion.

It's my funeral, she says. It's my bird. I was the one who wanted to bury it.

She is looking for a reason. She will say something which sounds eternally right.

Things have to be buried, she says. They can't be left lying around anyhow for people to see.

Birds shouldn't die, I tell her. They have wings. Cats and rats haven't wings.

Stop crying, she says to Kallisto. It's only a bird.

It has a bride's flower in its hand, Kallisto says.

We shall rise again, I mutter, but we shall not all be changed.

Antigone does not seem to hear me.

Behold, I say in a voice she must hear, in a moment, in the twinkling of an eye, the trumpet shall sound.

Ismene turns to Kallisto and throws the daisy chain about her neck.

Shall a virgin forget her adorning or a bride the ornament of her breast?

Kallisto is lifting her arms towards the tree.

The bridegroom has come, she says, white as a fall of snow. He stands above me in a great ring of fire.

Antigone looks at me now.

Let's cover the bird up, she says. Your father will punish us all for making a disturbance.

He has on his garment, Kallisto says, and on his thigh is written King of Kings.

I look at the tree. If I could see with Kallisto's eyes I wouldn't be afraid of death, or punishment, or the penitentiary guards. I wouldn't be afraid of my father's belt or his honing strap or his bedroom slipper. I wouldn't be afraid of falling into the river through a knothole in the bridge.

But, as I look, I see the buds falling like burning lamps and I hear the sparrow twittering in its box: Woe, woe, woe, because of the three trumpets which are yet to sound.

Kallisto is on her knees. She is growling like a bear. She lumbers over to the sandwiches and mauls them with her paw.

Ismene stands alone for Pan the gardener has gone.

Antigone is fitting a turf in place above the coffin. I go over and press the edge of turf with my feet. Ismene has caught me by the hand.

Go away, Antigone says.

I see my father coming down the path. He has an attendant with him. In front of them walks Pan holding the sprinkler hook like a spear.

What are you doing here? my father asks.

Burying a bird, Antigone says.

Here? my father asks again.

Where else could I bury it? Antigone says.

My father looks at her.

This ground is public property, he says. No single person has any right to an inch of it.

I've taken six inches, Antigone says. Will you dig the bird up again?

Some of his subjects my father restrained since they were moved to throw themselves from high places or to tear one another to bits from jealousy or rage. Others who disturbed the public peace he taught to walk in the airing courts or to work in the kitchen or in the garden.

If men live at all, my father said, it is because discipline saves their life for them.

From Antigone he simply turned away.

MARGARET LAURENCE

1926-

Margaret Laurence was born in Neepawa, Manitoba, and educated at the University of Manitoba. After her marriage to an engineer she spent several years in Africa with her husband, where she found the themes for some of her novels and short stories. Among these are *This Side Jordan* (1960), set in newly-independent Ghana; *The Tomorrow-Tamer* (1963), a collection of short stories; and *The Prophet's Camel Bell* (1963), an account of her stay in Somaliland.

Her Canadian novels, *The Stone Angel* (1964) and *A Jest of God* (1966), are starkly tragic studies of the psychological havoc wrought by loneliness and isolation on the prairies. The latter enjoyed a well-deserved success as a film under the title *Rachel, Rachel*. *The Fire-Dwellers* (1969) carries on the same theme in an urban setting.

Mrs. Laurence is one of the minority of Canadian novelists who have had both critical and popular success in the United States and England as well as in Canada. She has published short stories in *Atlantic, Holiday, Saturday Evening Post, Tamarack Review, Story,* and other periodicals. *A Jest of God* was awarded the Governor-General's Medal for fiction in 1966.

A QUEEN IN THEBES

Fear of a war was not what had taken them to the cottage in the mountains. Everyone had feared war for so long that it seemed it might never happen after all. Nerves cannot be kept on edge year in and year out without a boredom taking hold of the tension, calcifying it, ultimately making the possibility of devastation seem impossible in the face of the continuing realities—the newspapers delivered each day to the door, the passing of seasons, the favourite TV serials which would, everyone somehow felt, continue in spite of the fires of hell or the Day of Judgement. No, they had simply gone to the mountains because it would be good to get the baby out of the stifling city for the summer, into the cooler air and the quiet. It was a long way for her husband to drive for the weekends, but he said he did not mind, and later in the summer he would be getting his two weeks' holiday. Her husband had built the cottage the year they were married. It was only a shack, really, and it was not close to any settlement or town. They had to bring in all their supplies, and they decided to have the tinned goods sent in all at once, by truck, enough to last the summer, so her husband would not have to bother with much shopping when he came up on the weekends. Although it was isolated, it was a place they both loved. The lake was nearby, azure, and alive with fishes, and the pine and tamarack brushed their low-sweeping boughs against the windows as the night wind stirred them. Her husband spent a day in getting enough firewood for a week, making certain everything was all right.

"You don't mind being alone here with Rex?" he said. "If anything happens, you can always walk down the hill to Benson's Garage, and phone me."

She was afraid, but she did not say so. He went back to the city then. The day after he left, the sky turned to fire, as though the sun had exploded.

The city was a long way off, down on the plains, too far for the death to reach here, but she saw it like the disintegrating sun, the light like no other light, a dark illumination and not the health which we associate with light. Then the dust cloud formed like the shape of a giant and poisonous toadstool, and she knew the thing had come which everyone had feared. She herself had feared it until it no longer seemed real, and now it had come. She did not scream or cry, after the first unbelieving cry. She hid her eyes, lest the sight damage them. She ran into the cottage and sat quite still. It grew dark, and the baby was crying. She fed him, picking him up with small stiff movements of her hands. Then she put him into his bed and he went to sleep. She did not think at all of the cloud or the light or the death, or of how it would be this moment in what had been the city. She was waiting for her husband to arrive.

In the morning, she looked out and saw the sun rising. The fire of it glowed red and quiet in the sky. For an instant she gazed at it in panic. Then she drew the curtains across the windows so the light would not infect her or the baby. Everything was all right, she calmed herself. It was only that she had never been away from people before, although she was twenty years old. Either her family or her husband had always been with her. He will soon come, she told herself. She fed the baby. Then she took out her purse mirror and combed her hair, so she would look nice when her husband arrived.

She lived this way for some days, going outside the shack only at night. Then one morning she knew the sun did not threaten her. She walked out in the daylight, although she still could not look directly at the sun. When she looked beyond the forest, in the direction of the far-off city, she remembered the death. She ran back to the shack and took the baby in her arms. She rocked him there, and for the first time she cried and could not stop. She mourned wordlessly, and when her tears were done and the violence of the pain had momentarily spent itself, she thought of herself and the baby. She set out, carrying the child, to find people.

When she reached the foot of the mountain, she found no-one at Benson's Garage. The place had been deserted. The money was gone from the till, but otherwise everything had been left as it was. The people must have felt that they were not far enough away, thinking of the dust that could enter them in the air they breathed, rotting the blood and bone. They must have fled to some more distant and uncontaminated place. She wondered dully if they had found such a place, or if they had only run into other deaths, other polluted places, other cities shattered and lying like hulked shadows on the earth. She became afraid of the air now herself, and because she felt safer on the mountain, she wanted to start back. But she thought of the telephone, and an unreasoning hope possessed her. She was certain her husband was still somewhere and that she would be granted the miracle of his voice. She lifted the receiver and dialled. There was no response. She tried again and again, but there was no sound. She replaced the phone carefully, as though it mattered. Then she took the baby and began walking up the hill.

She knew she had to find people. In the days that followed, she walked long distances through the forest, marking her way so she would not get lost. She walked down the hill on every side, through the heavy bracken and the snarled bushes, until her legs and arms were bleeding with the small incisions of thorns and branches, and her arms ached with the fatigue of carrying the child, for she would not leave him alone in the shack. But in all her treks she found no-one. At night she did not cry. She lay sleepless, her eyes open, listening to owls and wind, trying to believe what had happened.

The leaves of the poplar were turning a clear yellow, and she knew it was autumn. She looked with sudden terror at the tins of food on the shelves, and saw they were almost gone. She picked berries and cooked them on the wood stove, wondering how long they would keep. She had fished only to provide her daily needs, but now she caught as many fish as she could. She slit and cleaned them, and laid them out in the sun to dry. One afternoon she found a black bear from the forest, feeding on the outspread fish. She had no gun. At that moment she was not afraid of the animal. She could think only of the sun-dried fish, hers, the food she had caught. She seized a stick and flew at the bear. The creature, taken by surprise, looked at her with shaggy menace. Then it lumbered off into the green ferns and the underbrush.

Each evening now, when the child was asleep, she lighted one of the remaining candles for only a few minutes and looked at herself in the mirror. She saw her long brownish blond hair and her thin tanned face and eyes she hardly knew as hers. Sometimes she wondered if her husband would recognize her when he arrived. Then she would remember, and would pick up the child and hold him tightly, and speak his name.

"Rex—it's all right. We're going to be all right."

The baby, wakened by her tears, would be frightened, and then she would be sufficiently occupied in quieting him. Sometimes, after she had looked in the mirror, she would not recall what had happened. She would go to bed comforted by the thought of her husband's arrival and would sleep without dreaming of the human shadows which she had long ago heard were etched on stone, their grotesque immortality.

Only when the first snow fell did she really believe that her husband was dead. She wanted and needed to die then, too, but she could not bring herself to kill her son and she could not leave him alone, so she was condemned to life.

The winter went on and on, and she thought they would not live until spring. The snow was banked high around the shack, and in the forest the hollows were filled with white, a trap to her unsure feet. She stumbled and fell, gathering firewood, and her axe severed the leather of the old boots which had been her husband's, cutting deeply into her ankle. She bound the wound clumsily, not expecting it to heal. It did heal, but the muscle had been affected and she walked with difficulty for a long time. She and the child were always cold and usually hungry. The thought uppermost in her mind was that she had to keep the fire going. She became obsessed with the gathering of wood, and would go out and drag the spruce branches back, even when the pile of boughs outside the shack was still high.

She prayed for help to come, but none came. Gradually she stopped praying. She did not curse God, nor feel she had been deserted by Him. She simply forgot. God seemed related to what had once been and was no more. The room in her mind where the prayers had dwelt became vacant and uninhabited.

The thing she loved was the sound of the child's voice. What she missed most now was not her husband's protective presence, nor his warmth, but the sound of human voices. The child was learning to talk, and soon they would be able to speak together, as people do. This thought heartened her.

When she looked in the mirror now, she saw how bony and drawn her face had become, but the wide eyes were harder than before, and an alertness lurked in them. Her hearing was becoming keener. She could hear the deer that approached the cabin at night, and she would look out at them, but although she tried making traps, she caught only an occasional jack-rabbit. Once, seeing the deer, their bodies heavy with meat, she took the axe and went out, ready to attempt them. But they were too quick and they vanished into the night forest where she dared not follow.

The dried fish were almost gone. She lived in a semi-conscious state, drugged by exhaustion and hunger. Even her despair had lost its edge and was only a dulled apprehension of hopelessness. One day she threw the bones of a rabbit out into the snow, and for a moment sank down beside them, summoning strength to walk back into the cabin. A flock of sparrows landed on the snow beside her and began to explore the gnawed bones. She remembered dimly having once put out bread crumbs for the birds in winter. Delicately, hardly realizing she was doing it, her hands moved with a swiftness she had not known she possessed. She reached out and seized. When she drew back her hands, she had a live sparrow in each. She throttled them between thumb and forefinger, and began to tear off the feathers even before the small wings had stopped palpitating. Stolidly, feeling nothing, she cooked the birds and ate them. Then she vomited, and frightened the child with the way she cried afterwards. But the next time, when she caught birds and felt the life ebbing away between her fingers, she did not vomit or cry.

When the days began to lengthen, and spring came, she did not know whether it mattered that she and Rex were still alive. She moved only between one sunrise and the next. She could not think ahead. When the pain took possession of her heart, she still believed that she did not care whether they lived or died. Yet every day she gathered the firewood and foraged for some kind of food, and nothing was loathsome to her now, if her teeth and stomach could turn it into one more day of life.

She had kept only an approximate accounting of seasons, but one day she realized that Rex must be nearly six years old. She was much stronger than she had been—how weak and stupid she had been in the early days, after the Change—but now the boy was almost as strong as she. He was better at trapping rabbits and birds, and when he went to the lake, he never came back without fish. He would lie for hours on the shore, watching where the fish surfaced and which reedy places in the shallows were most likely to contain them. His eyes were better than hers, and his ears, and he had discovered for himself how to walk through the forest noiselessly, without allowing the ferns and bracken to snap under his feet.

At first she had tried to teach him things from that other world— how to read and how to pray. But he only laughed, and after a while she laughed, too, seeing how little use it was to them. She taught him instead what she had learned here—always to keep the fire going, always to gather wood, how to uproot dandelions and how to find the giant slugs where they concealed themselves on the underside of fallen logs. Then, gradually and imperceptibly, the boy began to teach her.

He was standing in the doorway now, and across his shoulders was a young deer with its throat slit.

"Rex—where? How?" They did not speak together tenderly and at length, as she once had imagined they would. Their days were too driven by the immediate matters of food, and in the evenings they wanted only to sleep. They spoke briefly, abruptly, exchanging only what was necessary.

The boy grinned. "I ran after it, and then I used my knife. You never tried. Why?"

"I tried," she said. She turned away. The boy was laughing softly to himself as he took the animal outside and began to skin it. She looked out the doorway at him as he squatted beside the deer, his face frowning in concentration as he tried to decide how to do something he had not done before. He took the skin off badly, and grew furious, and hacked at the slain animal with his knife. They ate meat that night, though, and that was what counted. But for the first time she felt a fear not of the many things there were to fear outside, but of something inside the dwelling, something unknown. When the boy was sleeping, she took out her mirror and looked. *I am strong,* she thought. *We can live. I have made this possible.* But her own eyes seemed unfamiliar to her, and she looked at the image in the glass as though it were separate from herself.

The years were not longer years but seasons—the season of warmth and growth, when the green forest provided deer and the lake swarmed with fish; the season of coolness and ripening, when the berries reddened on the bushes; the season of snow and penetrating chill, when the greatest fear was that the fire might die. But when, after all the seasons of care, the fire did die, it happened in spring, when the melting snow drenched into the shack one night through the weakening timbers of the roof. She had left the iron lid off the old stove so it would draw better, for the wood was not quite dry. It was her fault that the fire died, and both of them knew it. Rex was almost as tall as she was, now, and he grasped her wrist in his intensely strong hand and led her to see.

"You have killed the fire. Now what will we do? You are stupid, stupid, stupid!"

She looked at his other hand, which was clenched, and wondered if she dared draw away from his grip. Then some deep pride straightened her. She pried at the noose-like fingers which held her wrist, and she used her fingernails like talons. He let go and gazed his rage at her. Then he dropped his eyes. He was not yet full grown.

"What will we do?" he repeated.

She saw then that he was waiting for her to tell him, and she laughed—but silently, for she could not risk his hearing. She put her hands gently on his shoulders and stroked the pliant sun-browned skin until he turned to her and put his head against her in a gesture of need and surrender. Then, quickly, he jerked away and stood facing her, his eyes bold and self-contained once more.

"I have tried to strike fire from stone," she said. "We must try again."

They did try, but the sparks were too light and fleeting, and the shreds of birch bark never caught fire. They ate their meat raw that summer, and when the evenings lengthened into the cool of autumn, they shivered under the deer hides that were their blankets.

Rex became ill on meat that had spoiled. They had both been sick before, many times, but never as badly as this. He vomited until his stomach was empty, and still he could not stop retching. She gave him water and sat beside him. There was nothing else she could do. The cabin was almost a wreck now, for although they had tried to repair it, they lacked sufficient tools, and Rex was not old enough yet to invent new and untried ways of building. They hardly moved outside for many days, and in this period the shack's mustiness and disrepair came to her consciousness as never before, and she looked with fear at the feeble timbers and the buckling walls, thinking of the winter. One night, when Rex's fever was at its height, and he lay silently, contracted with pain, she tried to think back to the distant times before the Change. She had forgotten her husband. But she remembered that some words used to be spoken, something powerful when everything else had failed.

"I should—pray," she said.

He opened his eyes. "Pray?"

She felt then, in some remote and dusty room of her mind, that she had not imparted to him something which was his due. There was always too much to do. She was too tired to talk much in the evenings.

"We used to speak of God," she said. "All life comes from God. Something great and powerful, greater than we are. When many people lived, they used to say these things."

The boy looked at her vacantly, not comprehending. Later, however, he asked her again, and she attempted once more to tell him. "All life comes from God——" but she no longer understood this very well herself and could not express it.

Gradually the illness left, and Rex grew strong again. One day he came back to the shack and told her he had found a cave in the side of a cliff.

"It will be better for the winter," he said.

She knew he was right. They moved everything they had, the knives and axe, the worn utensils, the tattered blankets, the deer hides. When she left the shack she cried, and the boy looked at her in astonishment.

Late that summer there was a severe storm, and the lightning descended to earth all around them, gashes of white light streaking the sky and tearing apart the darkness. She crouched on the cave floor and hid her eyes, as she always did in the presence of a sudden violence of light. Her fear was mingled with a sorrow whose roots she could no longer clearly trace. The boy knelt beside her and put his hands on her hair, and spoke to her, not roughly but quietly. He was afraid of the lightning, too, for he had learned her fear. But he was less afraid than she. He had no memory, not even her dim and confused ones, of any other life.

When the storm was over, they saw that the lightning had set the forest ablaze, a long way off, on the crest of the hill beyond their territory. The boy went off by himself. He was away for several days and nights, but when he returned he was carrying a smouldering pine torch. Their fire came to life again, and as it flared up in the circle of stones on the floor of the dark cave, the boy made an involuntary movement, as though compelled by something beyond his own decision. He raised his hands and bowed his head. Then, as though feeling that this was not enough, he knelt on the rock of the cave floor. He looked up and saw her standing immobile beside him, and his eyes became angry. With a sharp downward motion of his hand, he signalled what she was to do.

Slowly, doubtfully, and then as she stared at him at last unresisting, she went down onto her knees beside the circle of stones that contained the living fire. Together they knelt before the god.

One day she looked at Rex and saw he was much taller than she. He killed deer now mainly with his spear, and unless it was an exceptionally dry summer when the deer moved away in search of grazing, they were always well supplied with meat. The boy's hair grew down around his shoulders, but he lopped it off with his knife when it grew too long, for it got in his way when he was hunting. The hair was growing now on his face, but he did not bother to cut this. Age had no meaning for them, but she tried to count, as they counted the dried fish and strips of dried venison for the winter. The boy would be fifteen, perhaps, or sixteen.

She told him, without knowing in advance that she was going to say it, that the time had come for them to try once more to find the people. They thought of them as *The People*, those who perhaps lived somewhere beyond the mountain. She believed in their existence, but Rex believed only occasionally.

"There are no people," he said now.

"Yes," she said. "We must try."

"Why?" he asked.

She did not reply. She could only repeat the same words, over and over. "We must try." Rex shrugged.

"You go, then."

So she went alone, walking through the forest, descending into gullies where the loose shale slid under her feet, drinking face down from mountain streams, trapping squirrel and rabbit when she could. For many days and nights she travelled, but she did not find the people. Once she came to some dwellings, a few houses with weeds grown into the doorways, but they were deserted except for the mice and rats which eyed her, unblinking, from the corners of the dusty floors. Finally she knew she could not travel far enough. She was not any longer certain, herself, that the people really existed. She turned and started back.

When she reached the mountain once more, and entered the cave, Rex looked different, or else her time away from him had enabled her to see him differently.

"You are back," he said, with neither gladness nor regret.

But that evening in front of the fire, she saw he really had changed. He knelt as before, but more hastily, more casually, as though it were not quite so important as it had been. He saw her questioning eyes.

"I was wrong," he explained.

"Wrong?" she was bewildered.

He indicated the fire. "This one is small. There is—something else."

He did not say anything more. He turned away and went to sleep.

He wakened her at dawn and told her to come outside the cave. He pointed to the sun, which was appearing now over the lake, a red globe in the pale sky of morning.

"Our fire comes from there. The voices told me when you were not here. I was alone, and I could hear them. They were waiting for you to go away. You do not hear the voices. Only I can hear them, when I am alone."

He spoke almost pityingly, and with a certainty she had not heard before. She wanted to cry out against what he said, but she did not know why, nor what she could say to him.

"Look——" he said. "You look."

He knew she could not look directly at the sun. She feared, always, that the sight would damage her. The man grinned and turned his face to the sky.

"I can look," he said. "I can look at God. The fire comes from there. He does as He wishes. If He is pleased, then all things will go well. If He is angry, then we will suffer."

He went into the cave and brought forth the liver and heart of the deer he had killed the evening before. He laid these on a raised slab of stone. He brought a pine brand and made a fire underneath the entrails. Then he knelt, not as he had inside the cave, but prostrating himself, forehead to the earth in obeisance.

"Shall I kneel?" she asked him.

"Yes," he said. "But you are not to touch this stone and this fire and this meat. That is for me to do."

She obeyed. There was nothing else she could do. When he had gone to the lake to fish, she went to the corner of the cave where the cooking pots were piled. She had dug a niche into the rock, and here her secret possession lay. She took out the bundle of dried leaves, unfolded them carefully, and held the mirror in her hands. She looked into it for a long time. It calmed her, as though it were a focus for the scattered fragments of herself. Dream and daylight hovered in uncertain balance within her, always. Only when she looked in the mirror did she momentarily know she really existed.

"What is that?" The man's voice was harsh. She glanced up and quickly tried to conceal what she held in her hands. She had never allowed him to see her looking at herself. He had never seen a mirror. He had seen his own image in the quivering lakewater, but never the sharp, painful, and yet oddly reassuring picture she had of her own cruel and gentle eyes.

"It is nothing," she told him.

He took hold of her hand and forced it open. He looked at the shining object. His face was puzzled, but only for an instant. He glanced out the cave entrance to the sky and the mid-morning sun. Then he hurled the mirror from his hand, and it shattered against the rock of the cave walls. After that, he hit her, again and again and again.

"You are unclean!" he cried.

She knew then he was afraid of her, too. They were afraid of each other.

The seasons went by, and she kept no account of time. Generally she was content. She sat crosslegged now on the wide ledge outside the cave entrance. She was scraping a deer hide with the bone blade Rex had made. He had discovered, on one of his longer trips, a place where the people used to live and where pieces of iron lay rusting, and he had brought some back and fashioned spearheads and knives and an axe. But these were kept for his use, for he needed them more in hunting than she did in scraping the hides and making them into clothes. It was slow work, this, but she did not mind. The sun of late spring warmed her, and the raw trilling of frogs from the lake made her feel glad, for this was a good time of year, with hunger gone. The fish and game were plentiful, and the roots and leaves of the dandelions were succulent and tender.

The pointed shadow of the altar stone on the rock ledge told her that he would soon be back from the forest. She must prepare food, for he would be hungry when he returned. He did not like to be kept waiting. That was as it should be. A man was hungry after hunting.

But still she sat in the sunshine, drowsing over her work. Then the insinuating voice began, humming its tune inside her, and she blinked and shook her head as though to shake the whispered song away, for when it came to her she felt threatened and unsafe and she did not want to listen. Rex said the voices came only to him. But she heard this voice occasionally, unknown to him, in the deep quietness of the morning, when the birds were suddenly still, or in the wind that brushed through the forest at night. She did not recall when the voice had begun. She did not have a name for herself, as Rex did, and although it was enough to be what she was, in some way the voice was connected with the name she had once held, the name which had been shattered somewhere, some time, like lake-water when a stone is thrown into it. She never understood what the voice was saying to her, with its jingling music, a monotonous chanting from a long way off and yet close to her as her blood. The words, familiar in form but totally unfamiliar in meaning, were like the dry and twisted shells she found on the shore of the lake, objects that had once contained live creatures, but very long ago, so that no trace of flesh remained. The voice echoed again now, hurting and frightening her.

> *Lavender's blue, dilly dilly, lavender's green,*
> *When you are king, dilly dilly, I shall be queen.*

She half shut her eyes, and listened intently, but still she could not understand and could only feel troubled by something untouchable, some mystery that remained just beyond her grasp.

Then, inside the cave, one of the children began crying, and she went to give comfort.

LEONARD COHEN

1934-

Leonard Cohen was born of a wealthy Jewish family in
Westmount and educated at McGill University. He has published five volumes of poetry, the last of which, *Selected
Poems*, 1956-1968 was awarded the Governor-General's Medal,
an honor which the poet with genuine modesty refused. He
has read his poems in night clubs and has composed words
and music which he sings to enthusiastic audiences, mainly of
young people, the best of which he has recorded on two
Columbia albums. In recent years he has spent much of his
time in the Greek islands but makes Montreal his headquarters.

Cohen's two remarkable novels, *The Favourite Game* (1963)
and *Beautiful Losers* (1966), are an even more memorable
achievement than his romantic and, as George Woodcock has
pointed out, thoroughly conservative lyric poems. The first of
these is that common *Opus* 1 of many young novelists, a
portrait of the artist as a young man, but it is very far from
being an ordinary example of the genre. Its distinction of style
and its relentless search in episode after episode for something
spiritually satisfying in sexual experience, which culminates in
the passages printed below depicting the tragically or casually
destroyed figure of the saintlike "fool of God" Martin, give
the story a power and relevance not often found in autobiogra-
phically inspired first novels. *Beautiful Losers* is a more ambitious work, more complex, more various, and more original,

but its calculated disorganization and its continuous exploitation of almost every type of sexual perversion defeats its author's intention, which is, one gathers, to explore the possibility of redemption through immersion in the destructive element of sensuous stimulation. The problem before the literary critic is this: Can one judge, on literary grounds alone, the book a success or a failure?

When would the old dialogue with Krantz resume?

The lake was beautiful in the evening. Frogs went off like coiled springs.

When would they sit beside the water like small figures in a misty scroll painting, and talk about their long exile? He wanted to tell him everything.

Krantz lectured the counsellors on Indoor Games for Rainy Days. Krantz prepared a days-off schedule. Krantz set up a new buddy system for the waterfront and drilled the counsellors for two hours. Krantz carried a clip-board and a whistle around his neck.

No crude bugle wakened them in the morning, but a recording on the PA of the first few bars of Haydn's Trumpet Concerto. Krantz's idea. On the fifth morning of the pre-camp training programme which Krantz had instituted for the counsellors, Breavman knew that this particular piece of music had been ruined for him for life.

Well, Krantz was busy. And there was this girl, Anne, who had followed him from England. Thank God she wasn't beautiful. She was a modern dancer.

After the organization was completed and the kids arrived, things would run smoothly and they would repair their old commentary on the universe.

Krantz explained the American game of baseball.

"If a guy catches a ball after it's hit, the batter's out."

"That sounds rational," said Anne, and they hugged.

He hoped the dialogue would begin soon, because there was nothing he liked about camp. Obscene. He felt it the minute he arrived. There is something obscene about a rich kids' camp. Something so obvious it disgusts. It's like an amusement park, like rows of elaborate pinball machines. He looked around at the playing fields, handball courts, bunks, boats—receptacles to hold children for a summer, relieve parents. Gangrene in the family. Living rooms back in Montreal were stinking with twisted intimacy.

He was glad that four hundred miles away Shell was waiting.

The counsellors were on the dock, lying in the sun. Breavman surveyed the flesh. Soon it would all be brown, bronze would grow around the bra straps. Now they were city-white. How the pines must despise them!

Breavman looked at a tall girl named Wanda. She was sitting at the far end of the dock, dangling her toes in the water. She had good legs and yellow hair but they didn't whip him. She wasn't quite in the great golden tradition. Wanda, you're safe from Breavman.

All the girls were very plain. And this was the joke. He knew what two months in that community would do. He'd be writing sonnets to all of them. These poems-to-be made him tired.

The Laurentian sky was jammed with stars. Breavman, who didn't know the names of constellations, judged confusion to be an aspect of their beauty.

"Counsellors' meeting," Krantz called up to the balcony.

"Let's not go, Krantz."

"Brilliant idea, except that I'm chairman."

As they walked to the Counsellors' Lounge they were joined by Ed, a first-year law student at McGill.

"First guy to make it with Wanda gets it," Ed proposed. "I mean, it's a matter of time. We're all going to make her before the summer's over, it happens every season, but this way one of us stands to collect."

Breavman hated that kind of young-buck talk. He wished he had the courage to smash his face. Maybe Krantz would do it. He was supposed to be a lover now.

"I suppose you're wondering how we can be certain when the first man claims the money." Ed, the legalist, explained the silence of the other two. Breavman searched the silence for their old unity.

"I think we can trust each other," said Krantz. "Breavman?"

Breavman called their attention to a falling star.

"A contract of cosmic significance."

They agreed that five dollars each would make the pool worthwhile.

What did you expect, Breavman, reunion on a windy hill, a knife ceremony and the exchange of blood?

The bus depot was a chaos of parents, children, fishing rods, tennis racquets, and bewildered dogs dragged to see their young masters away. Mothers who had been awaiting the great day for weeks were suddenly stricken with a certainty that their babies would starve without them. A special diet was pressed into Breavman's hand along with a five-dollar bill.

"I know you'll look after him," a woman shouted hurriedly, scanning the crowd meanwhile for someone else to bribe.

Fifteen minutes before the scheduled departure Breavman sneaked into one of the empty waiting buses. He closed his eyes and listened to the confusion beyond the window. What was he doing with these people?

"My name is Martin Stark. Capital S, small t, small a, small r, small k. No e."

Breavman wheeled around.

In the seat behind him, sitting very stiffly, was a boy of about twelve years. His eyes were incredibly white, not naturally, but as if he were straining to show as much white as possible. This gave him an expression of having just seen a catastrophe.

"Sometimes I spell it with an e and then I have to tear up the page and begin again."

He spoke in a monotone, but over-articulating each word as if it were an elocution lesson.

"My name is Breavman. Capital B, small r, small e——"

He had been warned about Martin, who was going to be one of his campers. According to Ed, Martin was half-nut, half-genius. His mother was supposed to be ashamed of him. At any rate she never came on Visiting Day. Today, Breavman learned from the boy, she had come an hour early and deposited him in the bus with the command not to stir. Thus she avoided meeting the other parents.

"I'm your counsellor this summer, Martin."

Martin registered no reaction to this information. He continued to stare beyond Breavman with a kind of vacant, unchanging terror. He had a bony face and a great Caesar nose. Because he generally clenched his teeth when he wasn't talking, the lines of his jaw were severely outlined.

"What's your favourite store?" asked Martin.

"What's yours?"

"Dionne's. What's your favourite parking lot?"

"I don't know. What's yours?"

"Dionne's Parking Lot."

The questions excited Martin because now he asked breathlessly, "How many windows are in the building Dionne's is in?"

"I don't know, Martin. How many?"

"In all the walls?"

"Of course all the walls. What good would it do to know the number of windows in only one wall or even three walls?"

Martin supplied a number triumphantly. Breavman idiotically promised himself he would check next time he was in town.

"How many cars were in the Dionne's Parking Lot last Thursday?"

"Tell me."

Fifty campers invaded the bus. There was much scrambling and bargaining for seats and Breavman's rapport with the boy was lost. Martin sat calmly through the ride, mumbling to himself. Breavman learned later that he liked to give himself four-figure numbers to multiply together.

On the way north Breavman asked him, "Do you like the countryside?"

"After I investigate it. . . ."

Martin fascinated him. He reckoned that he had misinterpreted Martin's expression. It was not vacant terror but general wonder. He was that rarest creature, a blissful madchild. The other children understood his election and treated him with a kind of bemused awe.

One afternoon they entertained themselves by encircling Martin and firing large numbers at him to multiply.

He rocked back and forth, like a man at prayer, his eyes closed. He beat his thighs with open palms as he thought, like an awkward bird trying to leave the ground, and made a buzzing sound as though his mind were machinery.

"Em-m-m-m-m-m-m-m-m-m——"

"Look at him go!"

"Em-m-m-m-m-m-m-m-m-m——"

"C'mon, Martin boy!"

"Eighty-one thousand, nine hundred and eighteen," he announced, opening his eyes. The boys cheered and hugged him.

Then he caught sight of a small pine tree. He stopped dead, stared, and walked out of the circle. Breavman followed him.

"Are you okay?"

"Oh yes. I believe I'd better count these."

Until supper he amused himself by discovering how many needles there were on an average pine tree.

Krantz was annoyed when he discovered what Breavman's afternoon activity was.

"That isn't what Mrs. Stark pays her money for."

"No?"

It was incredible that they should have put themselves into a position where one could castigate the other.

"Not to have her son used as a side-show freak."

"What does she pay her money for?"

"Come off it, Breavman. You know it wasn't healthy. She wants the kid to be like everyone else—integrated, inconspicuous. It's hard enough on her as it is."

"Okay, we'll force him into baseball."

"Infractions of the regulations will be severely disciplined Herr Breavman."

A horse-shoe of hills rose behind the bunks. On one of the hills there was an amphitheatre with wooden benches and stage. It was used for plays, singsongs, and on Sabbath as a House of Prayer.

How goodly are thy tents, O Jacob,
and thy dwelling place, O Israel . . .

They sang in Hebrew, their voices mingling with the sunlight. It was fragrant there, the pines high, blasted, and black. The camp was assembled in white clothes.

That's how we are beautiful, he thought, that's the only time—when we sing. Storm troopers, band of crusaders, gang of stinking slaves, righteous citizens—only tolerable when their voices ring in unison. Any imperfect song hints at the ideal theme.

Ed told a wonderful Sholem Aleichem story about a young boy who wanted to play the fiddle but was forbidden to by his Orthodox parents. For a minute Breavman thought he would overdo it, but no, he swayed and danced under his imaginary fiddle and everyone believed him.

The same Ed who bet with a girl's body.

Breavman sat thinking that he could never do as well, never be so calm and magical. And that's what he wanted to be: the gentle hero the folk come to love, the man who talks to animals, the Baal Shem Tov who carried children piggy-back.

He would never be able to pronounce a Jewish word with any confidence.

"Krantz," he whispered, "why weren't we allowed to cross the tracks?"

Twelve righteous faces told him to shh.

Still, and he knew it was arrogance, he often considered himself the Authentic Jew. His background had taught him the alien experience. He was grateful for that. Now he extended that experience to his own people.

What was it all about anyhow? A solitary man in a desert, begging for the inclination of a face.

Anne performed a Hasidic dance, annihilating anything womanly in her body with the crammed, ironic movements. But for a few moments they were lost in Europe, their skins untanned, waiting in narrow streets for miracles and the opportunity for revenge they would never take.

After the Sabbath services a butterfly seemed to follow him down the hill, disappearing as he left the wooded area for the hot campus. He felt the honour of it all through the day. . . .

Breavman received a letter from Mrs. Stark, Martin's mother. It wasn't customary for parents to reply to the official reports the counsellors were obliged to send.

Dear Mr. Breavman,

I'm sure my son Martin is in excellent hands.

I'm not anxious and I don't expect any further detailed communications concerning his behaviour.

Very sincerely,

R. F. Stark

"What the hell did you write her?" demanded Krantz.

"Look, Krantz, I happen to like the kid. I took a lot of trouble over the letter. I tried to show that I thought he was a very valuable human being."

"Oh, you did?"

"What was I supposed to say?"

"Nothing. As little as possible. I told you what she's like. For two months of every year she doesn't have to look at him every day and can pretend that he's a normal boy doing normal things with other normal boys at a normal camp."

"Well, he isn't. He's much more important than that."

"Very good, Breavman, very compassionate. But keep it to your-self, will you? It was Breavman you were pleasing, not the boy's mother."

They were standing on the balcony of the Administration Build-ing. Krantz was about to announce Evening Activity over the PA.

Didn't Krantz know what he knew about Martin? No, that wasn't true. He didn't know anything about the boy, but he loved him. Martin was a divine idiot. Surely the community should con-sider itself honoured to have him in their midst. He shouldn't be tolerated—the institutions should be constructed around him, the traditionally incoherent oracle.

Out in the open, tempered by the dialogue, it wouldn't sound so mad.

Krantz looked at his watch, which he wore in the inside of his wrist. As he turned to go in he caught sight of a figure lying face down in the darkness near a row of bushes at the bottom of the lawn.

"For God's sake, Breavman, that's the sort of thing I mean."

Breavman walked quickly across the lawn.

"What are you doing, Martin?"

"Twenty thousand and twenty-six."

Breavman returned to the balcony.

"He's counting grass."

Krantz shut his eyes and tapped the banister.

"What's your evening activity, Breavman?"

"Scavenger hunt."

"Well, get him over there with the rest of the group."

"He isn't interested in a scavenger hunt."

Krantz leaned forward and said with an exasperated smile, "Con-vince him. That's what you're supposed to be here for."

"What difference does it make whether he goes looking for yes-terday's newspaper or counts grass?"

Krantz leaped down the stairs, helped Martin up, and offered him a piggy-back across the field, to where Breavman's group was as-sembled. Martin climbed on gleefully and as he rode stuck his index fingers in his ears for no apparent reason, squinting as if he were expecting some drum-splitting explosion.

Every night, just before he went to sleep, it was Martin's custom to declare how much fun he had had that day. He checked it against some mysterious ideal.

"Well, Martin, how did it go today?" asked Breavman, sitting on his bed.

The mechanical voice never hesitated.

"Seventy-four per cent."

"Is that good?"

"Permissible."

He marvelled at how still he could lie.

He was stiller than the water which took the green of the mountains.

Wanda was fidgeting, pretending to write a letter in what was left of the light of the day. So her long yellow hair wasn't quite in the great tradition. Her gold-haired limbs could be worshipped individually, but they did not amalgamate into beauty. Nevertheless, how many thighs could he kiss at the same time?

If I had a really immense mouth.

The flies were very bad. They put on Six-Twelve. Wanda extended her arm to him but instead of applying the lotion himself he gave the bottle to her. His fantasy: applying the lotion with greater and greater frenzy all over her flesh.

A light rain swept across the face of the water, veiling it with a silver net. From time to time they heard the cheer of the camp, which had assembled in the mess hall for a Lassie movie.

The rain passed and the still surface recomposed itself.

"I've never really lived by a lake," said Wanda, who was given to walking barefoot.

"Now don't get into poetry, Wanda."

He absently caressed her face and hair, which was softer than he imagined.

An inner eye flying away from the boathouse like a slow high star gave him the view of a tiny plywood box in which two minuscule figures (mating insects?) made inevitable ballet movements to each other.

Wanda was trying to get her head into a position in which she could kiss his caressing fingers.

Finally he kissed her lips, mouth, stomach, all the parts.

Then something very disturbing occurred.

Her face blurred into the face of little Lisa, it was dark in the boathouse, and that face blurred into one he didn't recognize, that one dissolved into the face of Bertha, maybe it was the blonde hair. He stared hard to make the changing stop, to return to the girl beside him.

He chased the different faces with his mouth, stopping no one. Wanda mistook his exercise for passion.

They walked back up the path. The sky was mauve. A moon emerged from a gentle accumulation of clouds. The path was softened by millions of pine needles. Martin would find out how many, perhaps.

Wanda sneezed. The damp wood planks.

"It was so peaceful down there, so peaceful."

Breavman was tempted to punish her for the trite rhythm of her sentence by telling her about the pool for her body.

"Do you know what the ambition of our generation is, Wanda? We all want to be Chinese mystics living in thatched huts, but getting laid frequently."

"Can't you say anything that isn't cruel?" she squeaked as she ran from him.

He sat up all night to punish himself for hurting her. The morning birds began. In the window grew a cool grey light, the trees beyond still black. There was a light mist on the mountain but he didn't feel like following it.

A few days later he discovered that he had caught Wanda's cold. And he couldn't understand the way his campers were shoving food down their faces. They bubbled in the milk, diluting it with spit, fought over extras, sculptured out of squeezed bread.

Breavman glanced at Martin. The boy hadn't eaten anything. Krantz had warned him that he must supervise the boy's diet closely. Sometimes he went on mysterious hunger strikes, the reasons for which could never be discovered. On this occasion Breavman could have hugged him.

His head was completely stuffed. The flies were vicious. He went to bed with the campers but couldn't sleep.

He lay there thinking stupidly of Krantz and Anne, lovingly of Shell.

The horizontal position was a trap. He would learn to sleep standing up, like horses.

Poor Krantz and Anne off in the woods. How long can they lie naked before the black flies get them? His hands will have to leave her flesh and hair to scratch his own.

606 THE TWENTIETH CENTURY

"Can I come in?"

It was Wanda. Of course she could come in. He was fettered on the bed, wasn't he?

"I just want to tell you why I haven't let you see me."

She turned off the lights to give them an even chance against the flies. They mingled fingers as she talked. Just before he drew to himself and kissed her lightly, he noticed a firefly in the corner. It was flashing infrequently. Breavman was sure it was almost dead.

"Why are you kissing me?"

"I don't know. It's not what I came here for. Just the opposite."

He was taking a great interest in the firefly. It wasn't dead yet.

"Why the hell don't you know?"

She was fumbling with something under her blouse. "You've broken my bra strap."

"This is a great conversation."

"I'd better go."

"You'd better go. He'd better go. We'd better go. They'd better go."

"You can't seem to talk to anyone."

Was that supposed to make him miserable? It didn't. He had given himself to the firefly's crisis. The intervals became longer and longer between the small cold flashes. It was Tinker Bell. Everybody had to believe in magic. Nobody believed in magic. He didn't believe in magic. Magic didn't believe in magic. Please don't die.

It didn't. It flashed long after Wanda left. It flashed when Krantz came to borrow Ed's *Time* magazine. It flashed as he tried to sleep. It flashed as he scribbled his journal in the dark.

Boohoohoohoohoohoo say all the little children. . . .

He watched Martin clean his nose, his great Caesarian nose that should have sponsored historic campaigns but only counted grass and pine needles.

Every morning Martin got up half an hour early to fulfil the ritual.

Toothpicks, cotton-wool, vaseline, mirrors.

Breavman asked him why.

"I like to have a clean nose."

Martin asked Breavman to mail a letter to his brother. Mrs. Stark had given instructions that they be intercepted and destroyed. Breavman read them and they brought him closer to the boy's anguish.

Dear Bully fat Bully you dirty

I got your last thirty-four letters and saw in a second the millions of lies. I hope you starve and your boner breaks in half with lots of screams and lets the beatles out after what you told her about me. Why don't you fill your mouth with towels and razorblades. Mummy is not a stupid skull she sneaked a look in the flashlight and read the poison shit you wrote me under the blankets.

love your brother,

MARTIN STARK

... "Fifty cents for a hand on her crotch."
Krantz was joking with Breavman about selling Anne to him piece by piece. Breavman didn't like the joke but he laughed.
"An almost unused nipple for three bits?"
Oh, Krantz.
They had quarrelled over Breavman's treatment of Martin. Breavman had categorically refused to enjoin the boy to participate in group activities. He had put his job on the line.
"You know we can't start looking for replacements at this point in the season."
"In that case you'll have to let me handle him my own way."
"I'm not telling you to force him into activities, but I swear you encourage him in the other direction."
"I enjoy his madness. He enjoys his madness. He's the only free person I've ever met. Nothing that anybody else does is as important as what he does."
"You're talking a lot of nonsense, Breavman."
"Probably."
Then Breavman had decided he couldn't deliver a sermon to the camp on Saturday morning when his turn came around. He had nothing to say to anyone.
Krantz looked at him squarely.
"You made a mistake, coming up here, didn't you?"
"And you made one asking me. We both wanted to prove different things. So now you know you're your own man, Krantz."
"Yes," he said slowly. "I know."
It was a moment, this true meeting, and Breavman didn't try to stretch it into a guarantee. He had trained himself to delight in the

608 THE TWENTIETH CENTURY

fraction. "What thou lovest well remains, the rest is dross."

"Of course you know that you're identifying with Martin and are only excluding yourself when you allow him to separate himself from the group."

"Not that jargon, Krantz, please."

"I remember everything, Breavman. But I can't live in it."

"Good."

Therefore Breavman was obliged to laugh when Anne joined them and Krantz said, "Buttocks are going very cheap."

In the evening he stayed motionless on the mess hall balcony. Krantz was about to put a record on the PA.

"Hey, Anne, you want Mozart, the Forty-ninth?" he shouted. She ran towards him.

Breavman saw clover in the grass, a discovery, and mist drifting across the tops of the low mountains, like the fade in a photo. Ripples on the water moving in the same direction as the mist, from black into silver into black.

He didn't move a muscle, didn't know whether he was at peace or paralysed.

Steve, the Hungarian tractor driver, passed below the balcony, picking a white flower from a bush. They were levelling out some land for another playing field filling in a marsh.

The flute-bird had a needle in its whistle. A broken door down the hill beside the thick-bottomed pines.

> *"London Bridge is falling down*
> *falling down*
> *falling down"*

sang a file of children.

Down the pine-needled path stood Martin, motionless as Breavman, his arms stretched out in a Fascist salute, his sleeve rolled up.

He was waiting for mosquitoes to land.

Martin had a new obsession. He elected himself to be the Scourge of Mosquitoes, counting them as he killed them. There was nothing frantic about his technique. He extended his arm and invited them. When one landed, wham! up came the other hand. "I hate you," he told each one individually, and noted the statistic.

Martin saw his counsellor standing on the balcony.

"A hundred and eighty," he called up as greeting.

Mozart came loud over the PA, sewing together everything that Breavman observed. It wove, it married the two figures bending over the records, whatever the music touched, child trapped in London Bridge, mountain-top dissolving in mist, empty swing rocking like a pendulum, the row of glistening red canoes, the players clustered underneath the basket, leaping for the ball like a stroboscopic photo of a splashing drop of water—whatever it touched was frozen in an immense tapestry. He was in it, a figure by a railing.

Since his mission against the mosquitoes had begun, Martin's enjoyment percentages soared. All the days were up around 98 per cent. The other boys delighted in him and made him the ornament of the bunk, to be shown off to visitors and wondered at. Martin remained an innocent performer. He spent most afternoons down at the marsh where the tractors were preparing new fields to run on. His arm was swollen with bites. Breavman applied calamine.

On his next day off Breavman took a canoe down the lake. Red-wing blackbirds rose and plunged into the reeds. He ripped open a stalk of a waterlily. It was veined with purple foam.

The lake was glass-calm. He could make out sounds of camp from time to time, the PA announcing General Swim; recorded music filtered through the forest and crept over the water.

He went down the creek as far as he could before sandbars stopped him. The only indication of current was the leaning underwater weeds. Clams black and thickly coated with mud—an unclean food. A snap of water and the green stretched-out body of a frog zoomed under the canoe. The low sun was blinding. As he paddled back to his camp-site it turned the paddle gold.

He built a fire, spread out his sleeping bag in the moss, and prepared to watch the sky.

The sun is always part of the sky, but the moon is a splendid and remote stranger. The moon. Your eye keeps coming back to it as it would do to a beautiful woman in a restaurant. He thought about Shell. The same moment he believed he had the confidence to live alone he believed he could live with Shell.

The mist was riding slowly on the reflection of birch trees; now it was piled like a snowdrift.

Four hours later he awakened with a start and grabbed his axe.

"It's Martin Stark," said Martin.

The fire was still giving some light, but not enough. He shone his flash in the boy's face. One cheek had been badly scratched by branches but the boy grinned widely.

"What's your favourite store?"

"What are you doing out here in the middle of the night?"

"What's your favourite store?"

Breavman wrapped the sleeping bag around the boy and ruffled his hair.

"Dionne's."

"What's your favourite parking lot?"

"Dionne's Parking Lot."

When the ritual was finished Breavman packed up, lifted him into the canoe, and shoved off for camp. He didn't want to think about what would have happened if Martin hadn't been able to find him. That cheek needed iodine. And it seemed that some of the bites were infected.

It was beautiful paddling back, reeds scraping the bottom of the canoe and turning it into a big fragile drum. Martin was an Indian chief squatting beside him, bundled in the sleeping bag. The sky displayed continents of fire.

"When I'm back home," Martin said loudly, "rats eat me."

"I'm sorry, Martin."

"Hundreds and hundreds of them."

When Breavman saw the lights of the camp he had a wild urge to pass them, to keep paddling up the lake with the boy, make a site somewhere up the shore among the naked birch trees.

"Keep it down, Martin. They'll kill us if they hear us."

"That would be all right. ..."

Ed's bunk was expected to win the baseball game.

The foul-lines were marked with Israeli flags.

What right did he have to resent their using the symbol? It wasn't engraved on his shield.

A child brandished a Pepsi, cheering for his side.

Breavman passed out hot dogs. He was glad he'd learned to suspect his Gentile neighbours of uncleanliness, not to believe in flags. Now he could apply that training to his own tribe.

A home run.

Send your children to the academies in Alexandria. Don't be surprised if they come back Alexandrians.

Three cheers. Mazel tov.

Hello Canada, you big Canada, you dull, beautiful resources. Everybody is Canadian. The Jew's disguise won't work.

When it was Ed's turn to umpire, Breavman walked across the field to the marsh and watched Martin kill mosquitoes. The tractor man knew him well because he often came to see Martin fulfil his mission.

The boy had killed over six thousand mosquitoes.

"I'll kill some for you, Martin."

"That won't help my score."

"Then I'll start my own score."

"I'll beat you."

Martin's feet were wet. Some of the bites were definitely infected. He should send him back to the bunk, but he seemed to be enjoying himself so thoroughly. All his days were 99 per cent.

"I dare you to start your own score."

As they accompanied their groups back to the campus Ed said, "Not only did you lose the game, Breavman, but you owe me five dollars."

"What for?"

"Wanda. Last night."

"Oh, God, the pool. I'd forgotten."

He checked his journal and gratefully paid the money. . . .

Martin Stark was killed in the first week of August 1958. He was accidentally run over by a bulldozer which was clearing a marshy area. The driver of the bulldozer, the Hungarian named Steve, was not aware that he had hit anything except the usual clumps, roots, stones. Martin was probably hiding in the reeds the better to trap his enemy.

When he didn't show for supper Breavman thought he might be up there. He asked a junior counsellor to sit at his table. He walked leisurely to the marsh, glad for an excuse to leave the noisy mess hall.

He heard a noise from the weeds. He imagined that Martin had seen him coming and wanted to play a hiding game. He took off his shoes and waded in. He was terribly squashed, a tractor tread right across his back. He was lying face down. When Breavman turned him over his mouth was full of guts.

Breavman walked back to the mess hall and told Krantz. His face went white. They agreed that the campers must not find out and that

the body be removed secretly. Krantz went up to the marsh and returned in a few minutes.

"You stay up there until the camp's asleep. Ed will take your
bunk."

"I want to go into town with the body," Breavman said.

"We'll see."

"No, we won't see. I'm going in with Martin."

"Breavman, get the hell up there now and don't give me arguments at a time like this. What's the matter with you?"

He stood guard for a few hours. Nobody came by. The mosquitoes
were very bad. He wondered what they were doing to the body.
They'd been all over when he found it. There wasn't much of a
moon. He could hear the seniors singing at their bonfire. At about
one in the morning the police and ambulance arrived. They worked
under the headlights.

"I'm going in with him."

Krantz had just spoken to Mrs. Stark on the phone. She had been
remarkably calm. She had even mentioned that she wouldn't press
charges of criminal negligence. Krantz was very shaken.

"All right."

"And I'm not coming back."

"What do you mean you're not coming back? Don't start with me
now, Breavman."

"I'm quitting."

"Camp runs another three weeks. I don't have anybody to replace
you."

"I don't care."

Krantz grabbed his arm.

"You got a contract, Breavman."

"Screw the contract. Don't pay me."

"You phony little bastard, at a time like this—"

"And you owe me five dollars. I had Wanda first. July eleventh,
if you want to see my journal."

"For Christ's sake, Breavman, what are you talking about? What
are you talking about? Don't you see where you are? Don't you see
what is happening? A child has been killed and you're talking about
a lay—"

"A lay. That's your language. Five dollars, Krantz. Then I'm
getting out of here. This isn't where I'm supposed to be—"

It was impossible to say who threw the first punch.

DON'T SQUEEZE ANYTHING OUT OF THE BODY IT DOESN'T OWE YOU ANYTHING was the complete entry.

He banged it out on the bus to Montreal, typewriter on knees.

It was the worst stretch of the road, signs and gas stations, and the back of the driver's neck, and his damn washable plastic shirt was boiling him.

If only death could seize him, come through the scum, dignify. What was it they sang at the end of the book?

Strength! strength! let us renew ourselves!

He would never learn the names of the trees he passed, he'd never learn anything, he'd always confront a lazy mystery. He wanted to be the tall black mourner who learns everything at the hole.

"I'm sorry, Father, I don't know the Latin for butterflies, I don't know what stone the lookout is made of."

The driver was having trouble with the doors. Maybe they'd never open. How would it be to suffocate in a plastic shirt?

Dearest Shell,

It will take me a little while to tell you.

It's two in the morning. You're sleeping between the green-striped sheets we bought together and I know exactly how your body looks. You are lying on your side, knees bent like a jockey, and you've probably pushed the pillow off the bed and your hair looks like calligraphy, and one hand is cupped beside your mouth, and one arm leads over the edge like a bowsprit and your fingers are limp like things that are drifting.

It's wonderful to be able to speak to you, my darling Shell. I can be peaceful because I know what I want to say.

I'm afraid of loneliness. Just visit a mental hospital or factory, sit in a bus or cafeteria. Everywhere people are living in utter loneliness. I tremble when I think of all the single voices raised, lottery-chance hooks aimed at the sky. And their bodies are growing old, hearts beginning to leak like old accordions, trouble in the kidneys, sphincters going limp like old elastic bands. It's happening to us, to you under the green stripes. It makes me want to take your hand. And this is the miracle that all the juke-boxes are eating quarters for. That we can protest this indifferent massacre. Taking your hand is a very good protest. I wish you were beside me now.

I went to a funeral today. It was no way to bury a child. His real death contrasted violently with the hush-hush sacredness of the chapel. The beautiful words didn't belong on the rabbi's lips. I don't know if any modern man is fit to bury a person. The family's grief was real, but the air-conditioned chapel conspired against its expression. I felt lousy and choked because I had nothing to say to the corpse. When they carried away the under-sized coffin I thought the boy was cheated.

I can't claim any lesson. When you read my journal you'll see how close I am to murder. I can't even think about it or I stop moving. I mean literally. I can't move a muscle. All I know is that something prosaic, the comfortable world, has been de-stroyed irrevocably, and something important guaranteed.

A religious stink hovers above this city and we all breathe it. Work goes on at the Oratoire St. Joseph, the copper dome is raised. The Temple Emmanuel initiates a building fund. A reli-gious stink composed of musty shrine and tabernacle smells, decayed wreaths and rotting barmitzvah tables. Boredom, money, vanity, guilt, packs the pews. The candles, memorials, eternal lights shine unconvincingly, like neon signs, sincere as advertising. The holy vessels belch miasmal smoke. Good lovers turn away.

I'm not a good lover or I'd be with you now. I'd be beside you, not using this longing for a proof of feeling. That's why I'm writing you and sending you this summer's journal. I want you to know something about me. Here it is day by day. Dearest Shell, if you let me I'd always keep you four hundred miles away and write you pretty poems and letters. That's true. I'm afraid to live any place but in expectation. I'm no life-risk.

At the beginning of the summer we said: let's be surgical. I don't want to see or hear from you. I'd like to counterpoint this with tenderness but I'm not going to. I want no attachments. I want to begin again. I think I love you, but I love the idea of a clean slate more. I can say these things to you because we've come that close. The temptation of discipline makes me ruthless.

I want to end this letter now. It's the first one I didn't make a carbon of. I'm close to flying down and jumping into bed beside you. Please don't phone or write. Something wants to begin in me.

LAWRENCE

DAVE GODFREY

1938-

A native of Manitoba, Dave Godfrey attended the Universities of Toronto, Iowa, and Stanford. After leaving the university he taught in Ghana under the auspices of the Canadian University Service Overseas, from which experience came his first novel, *The New Ancestors* (1970), a major work which won the Governor-General's Award. His remarkable short stories were collected in *Death Goes Better with Coca-Cola* (1967) and *New Canadian Writing* (1968), along with stories by Clark Blaise and David Lewis Stein. Godfrey is co-author also of *Man Deserves Man: CUSO in Developing Countries* (1968) and *Gordon to Watkins to You* (1970).

'In an interview with Don Cameron in *Quire & Quill* for February 1972, Dave Godfrey speaks of the story included here. "I think 'The Hard-Headed Collector' did represent a breakthrough for me. I was reading it to my class last week — I promised them a lecture on what Canadian literature is all about, and I worked out this theory. You move from the period of heroic terror to the period of humane struggle and the period of disintegration. And as I was reading the story I realized that it was a perfect illustration of that: coming through the mountains against the wilderness, all the guys peeling off to fight their own little humane battles, and at the end it disintegrates. . . ."

Dave Godfrey is an active supporter and theoretician of the movement opposing American encroachment in the Canadian economy and in cultural fields, especially communications. Together with Robert Fulford and Abraham Rotstein he edited *Read Canadian: A Book About Canadian Books* (1972), an eloquent plea for Canadian cultural and economic independence. He wishes to state that his story appears here only out of regard for the editor and because this anthology was begun while the publisher was still Canadian owned. "All permission fees received by the author," he adds, "are being utilized in the struggle against American cultural and economic imperialism in Canada and throughout the Third World."

THE HARD-HEADED COLLECTOR

They came through the mountains themselves unscathed, although Piet Catogas nearly tumbled into the gorges beneath Yellowhead Pass when his horse skittered out from under him. The last horse. When they entered North Battleford they were all seven afoot, but they were well entertained in front of the tent of the bread baker, who kept them amused with juggling tricks and poured them many cups of hot tea in blue galvanized cups filled to the brim then with swirling milk.

The bread baker's final trick was to keep seven round oranges up in the air at once, and when the rotund man had heard enough of their clapping he gave one orange to each man. His own children clustered around and his wife walked back into the tent, so the men were careful to divide, but Pier Dela Ombre, throwing his filthy black hair out of his eyes so that the firelight could blaze back out of his pupils, asked for a second orange from Piet Catogas, the leader, and began to explain to the children why the earth did not fall into the sun. He sang to them.

Katrina, the wife of the bread maker, came out of the tent and said to her husband. "Why not offer Mr. Dela Ombre two loaves of wheat bread every morning so that he will be encouraged to stay here."

The bread maker stated the offer to Piet, but Piet refused. "We are on our way to a strange land and there is not one man that I can afford to lose. We have the return journey on our minds too."

Pier Dela Ombre's orange sun rotated around and around the orange earth held stationary by little Katrina, the bread baker's only daughter. The mother smiled.

At midnight, when all the men except Ole Siuk and Scrop Calla were seated around the fire drinking the white lightning which the Scottish whisky-maker distilled in North Battleford, Katrina came out of the tent with the bread baker.

"We will give you your own tent," she said directly to Pier Dela Ombre. "And a complete set of the *European Encyclopedia*, and after twenty years' service a golden shovel. Which will no doubt help to make you feel glorious as you clear away the blizzards from your door or clean out the many ashes from your stove. Around here we have very little anthracite."

Pier Dela Ombre smiled and said that he needed no time to consider their kindness. "We do not even know how far we now need to travel," he said to the woman, "but we must be there by May and then there is the long journey back before we can really set down to work, and for each stage I will have to learn the new strophe that the good Calla writes. In fact, if he were not out now stealing the settlement's horses, he would probably be putting one together, telling of our dangerous passage through the mountains. I cannot stay."

They both laughed at his humour of the horses and determined even more to persuade him to stay.

"Little Katrina will be disappointed you were unable to explain to her the proportions of the sun and the earth," the woman said. "At times in the summer I have heard her say that they almost seem equal. It does get very hot here in the summer, but we arrange many boat picnics on the Saskatchewan, and of course there is nothing like sawdust to keep the winter's ice safely stored."

They kept after him, gently, until the bread maker fell asleep.

Ole and Scrop came back very early in the morning, before the sun, but little Katrina had risen and was adding yeast to the sugar water for the day's baking.

"If you let him stay long enough to explain the proportions of the earth and the sun," she said to Piet, "I will not awaken my father and tell him that the man with the sunken eyes has taken possession of Elder Clough's grey horse and silver bridle. And six other poorer horses."

Piet nodded to Pier Dela Ombre. He laid the golden orange of the sun on the ashes of last night's fire and took Katrina by the hand.

"If the sun were made that small," Pier said, "let us say about a thousand to one, then the earth would still be so large that in a whole day we could not walk around its edge."

He held her hand more tightly and began walking with her away from the tent and the fire, in the gentle circle of one who is uncaringly lost.

The six men were glad to have the extra horse and the mountains behind them, with the summer not completely gone.

"He'll be in real trouble when they discover the loss," Scrop Calla said to Piet when they next stopped.

"The mother will get him out of it," Piet replied. "If the little girl

can't. God, they start them young here. I can't believe there's anywhere they start them so young. Even among the Sasarians."

Why had he decided to present the works to the United States?

*"Well, a lot of people wanted it——but I couldn't do what I did
in any other country. What I did I accomplished here in the United
States. It belongs here."*

Did he have any comment about President Johnson?

"I told him I've adopted him. I love him."

They went eastward safely for five days across the lush prairie grass
until they heard gunfire in the distance ahead and what they thought
might be a tornado, a dust storm. Coming over the rise they saw a
Nanarian Indian from one of the reserves who shouted at them as he
drove his almost collapsing wagon at a dangerous pace towards the
west. His wife and children sat on mounds of hay in the back, firing
whence they had come. The men rode on, although they knew there
was a fire ahead which would block their way.

"We can return later," Piet said, "and cross over the ashes. Or
look for the river again."

"I'm sure I can find it if you let me lead," said Torah Black.

He rode back whence they had come—the mountains were invisible—and the others followed, although Piet had said nothing.

The wagon was overturned less than a mile to the west. Besides
the wife and the four children there was a milkwhite goat among the
hay. "This will save us all," Black said and slit its throat. He held it
by the hind legs as it kicked its way to death and circumscribed a
large circle around the wagon, the men, the four children, and the
woman.

"We had better ride on," Piet said.

After a time the firing started again, and once or twice the five
men could distinguish the sound of Torah Black's shotgun. Scrop
Calla could see the gold engraving on its stock glittering in the sun.

"What does a gunsmith know about old superstitions," Piet said
as they rode back eastward over the powdery black ashes. Looky
McLaww nodded sagely.

*Mr. Hirshhorn lives with his fourth wife, Olga, in Greenwich. He
is the father of six chidren, two of them adopted, and is a grandfather several times over. He is board chairman of the Callahan
Mining Company, and the principal stockholder in Prairie Oil
Royalties, a Canadian concern.*

He has been trying to follow doctor's orders to take it easy, but finds it a trial. When he appears at Parke-Bernet, the auctioneer knows that he has to keep a sharp eye for the little man with the expressive face who signals vigorously with his program. If there is any doubt, Mr. Hirshhorn lets the auctioneer know what he is up to. He calls out his bids in a loud clear voice.

"*He's a tiger," an old, close friend said.*

Beyond the death of Torah Black they had no more difficulties until they reached Winnipeg. It was difficult to find a place that would take all of them, for the Leagues were busy, but eventually they found a large old house on the river in Ste. Vital. All of the girls spoke French so that André was kept busy as a translator; but after all, what is there to say?

"We have made it over the hard part," Piet said. "We have still eight months to go. Let us hope that the winter will be easy. Tonight you may enjoy yourselves; there is no more need of the horses in any case."

The first girl did not satisfy Looky because the pleasure of her body simply filled his head with memories of the wife he had left on Queen Charlotte Island.

"That damn Hunky won't want more than a snack," he said and walked into Ole Siuk's room and threw him out of bed. "*J'ai une qualité inestimable,*" he said to the girl and she shone with delight.

"He is afraid for his wife," Piet said to Ole Siuk. "There are many other carvers and poets on the island. She is a loving model; puts her heart into it."

"Mineur, how's about a free and equal exchange of riches," Looky later said to André. But when André tried his new girl he found her cold and exhausted. She swung a condom full of black beetles over his head and threatened him with death.

Looky took Scrop Calla's girl also, a plumper one than the first three, but when he came to Piet's room he found him gone.

The old woman, the girl provider, still lay in the bed and offered herself to Looky, but she was dark haired and hidden-eyed like Looky's wife and he could not take her.

"There's the matter of the bill," she said, "but that's not important. I have the horses. If you had slept with me those bay-tárds would have beaten you to death with horseshoes on the end of pikes and we would have put you out in the stable to freeze until spring, but as it is you will save us the cost of putting an ad in the *Free Press* for some able body to haul our ashes all winter."

"At least McLaww won't have to go about with a gold shovel in his hands," Piet Catogas said to Scrop Calla as the four men trudged on bear-paw snowshoes through the winedark snows north of Fort Frances, as the sun fell.

But, with the end of World War I, he guessed wrong on the market and found his fortune had shrunk to $4,000. Mr. Hirshhorn says he has always learned by his mistakes. At any rate, he was back on top in a few years and intuitively got out of the market with $4 million just before it broke in 1929.

When he was a child, Mr. Hirshhorn was attracted to the pictures on the Prudential Life Insurance Company's calendars.

Mr. Hirshhorn was attracted to the possibilities of Canada, bought 470 square miles of land and, by 1950 was mining uranium. His biggest coup occurred in 1952. On the advice of Franc Joubin, a geologist who had little audience elsewhere, Mr. Hirshhorn secretly put together 56,000 square miles of claims in Ontario's Algoma Basin and struck a uranium bonanza in Blind River.

When the four men were only twelve miles from Chapleau, they came across a group of Hémonites at prayers. These had built a great square wall of snowblocks out onto the lake, no more than a foot high, and at intervals, dressed in brown worsted cowls, stood women, men, and the older children, praying into the sky.

"This is a chance for Calla to use his four iamb line," said Ole Siuk, who had taken over the post of religious cynic since they had lost McLaww.

Piet could see no altar, but in the centre of the square was a tall ancient man standing above a slender circular hole cut deep into the ice down to the dark water below.

"In the summer you can see clear down thirty-two feet," the old man said.

Near him were three boys tending nine blanketed cattle. On a high easel, facing in the direction in which all prayed, was an old lithograph of an Essex County dairy farm, coated in plastic to protect it against the weather but torn in one corner so that the gold of cut hay was stuck to a piece of flapping plastic and glittered in the frosted sunlight.

"No one will do it," the old man said.

"I'm out of grass, acid, and mushrooms," said Scrop Calla, "but I know what you want and I will attempt it."

He stripped himself naked and lowered himself into the water three times so that not only his heavy beard and hair were covered with a silver of ice, but his whole body. It shone.

He held his arms outward in the direction of them all and said loudly and with no sound of rhythm: "I know, I know, I know."

Upon the horizon appeared, as though on the edge of a highly polished silver punch bowl, a simple inverted image of all: the penitents, the wall of snowblocks, the old priest, Scrop Calla, the strangers, and the forests and the snow-covered meadows behind them. With the exception that, in the inverted image, the cows were unblanketed and moved about freely: their udders thick with milk, their coats sleek as threshed grain.

"You're a genius and a half," the old priest said. "You'll have to settle here. In the summer you can see down thirty-two feet and the fishing licence's only two bucks—to natives that is."

"During the war," said Piet to Ole Siuk as they came near French River, "Calla once deserted and tried to find the enemy, but a handful of men went unknowingly after him and became so enthused with fear that they broke through the lines of the Sasarians and covered themseves with loot and glory."

At night when they stopped now, Ole Siuk read in Calla's leather-bound notebooks and occasionally was seen stamping his left foot heavily and repeatedly on the hard earth of the world.

"Poverty has a bitter taste," Mr. Hirshhorn said years later, recalling how his mother was sent to the hospital when a fire gutted their tenement on Humbolt Street, and the family was dispersed to various home in the neighborhood. "I ate garbage."

In French River the three men were fed and lodged in a building as tall as the smallest of the foothills they had long left behind them.

"Perhaps we have gone far enough," said André. "That is a building tall enough to house Egsdrull. The tools must be rusty and I long to hear the chips shatter, even a practice stroke."

All of the people there had a small exact circle of soot on each cheek, but they were kind to the voyagers, gave them fat for their stiff-thonged snowshoes, and did not laugh loudly at Ole Siuk's awkward attempts at song.

"You can see God's fish," they said at the end of the recital. "Perhaps then you will stay and teach us to sing."

Inside the tall building sat rows and rows of old men and women, all dressed in heavy blue robes, but seemingly divided into three groups.

Some had two circles of dark soot on their cheeks, so that only the blue robes distinguished them from the guide. These sat reading from a book that was passed slowly down the rows, meditating while they awaited their turn. Others had only one circle of soot, that on their right cheek, and were busy at work benches, hammering tiny marbles of gold into large, almost circular flakes. Their blue robes seemed cumbersome, and many seemed too old for such a task.

The third group had no marks on their cheeks, but on their foreheads was a slightly larger, more oval, circle of soot. These seemed to be neither reading nor hammering, but once, while the strangers were there, one of the old men among them went up to the forty-foot fish which dominated the entire building, a *mashkinoje*. Only its skeletal frame was finished; the outer covering was not yet half done. The old man laid in place on the others his own interlocking golden scale. Then fire consumed him.

"Each year," said the guide, "we get just about done before the Sasarians come raiding. We've calmed the Nanarians. One year the Sasarians will be awed by God's fish and will allow us to finish. Below God's fish, you will see the coffins of the fifty original scale craftsmen. Each holds an ivory tooth on his breast, and on the day that the Sasarians are awed, they will all arise and the teeth will complete the fish of unity."

When Piet and Ole left, André Mineur was talking in Arabic to the God's fish's tail. He was not speaking of their own voyages and their many losses.

"He's a sucker, that Mineur," said Piet Catogas to Ole Siuk as they crossed the St. Lawrence at Three Rivers. "It won't sell. I've seen men making them in Boston, twice the size, every scale machine-polished, and for half the price."

"I think you have the right reason," said Ole Siuk. "Hah, hah, hah." His teeth had all fallen out because of the bad diet they had endured during the winter and he looked very old and ugly.

"It's almost the end of April," he said.

The President added:

"Washington is a city of powerful institutions—the seat of government for the strongest government on earth, the place where democratic ideals are translated into reality. It must also be a place of beauty and learning, and museums should reflect a people whose commitment is to the best that is within them to dream. We have the elements of a great capital of beauty and learning, no less impressive than its power."

The two men avoided all contact with the Sasarians, although Piet was certain he could communicate with them if necessary, but when they arrived in Edmundston and stated that they were determined to reach the Bay of Chaleur even though only two of them remained, they ran into the united opposition of all the Town Fathers.

"The *day* of judgment is only possible as a concept because of our notions of the duration of time," the Mayor said. "In reality there is a summary court in perpetual session and we're going to beat your knackers down to your knees."

They turned upon Siuk, stripped off all his clothing, tore away his finger nails with their teeth, gnawed his fingers with the fury of famished dogs, and thrust a sword through one of his hands. They drove the two men between them in a hastily formed aisle, and beat them with clubs and thorny sticks. Then they hung them by the wrists to two of the poles that supported the Town Hall. A woman was commanded to cut off Piet's thumb, which she did; and a thumb of Siuk was also severed, a clam-shell being used as an instrument, in order to increase the pain.

In the morning the children came to castrate them, and then they were set free. Hair was pulled from their beards and their wounds were lacerated before they left.

In the night Ole Siuk wrote out a message for Piet, the leader, although he did not awaken him.

"I guess I've followed Areskoui and that crew long enough. I feel the need of those Edmundston men more than anything. My great-aunt was a nun in the Ukraine, but she was of unsound motives in her religious pursuits. When she was not made Mother Superior at a time she had appointed, she stripped herself naked during a Sunday mass and declared herself to the world as an atheist. The family has had bad luck ever since. Maybe this act of mine will atone in some way. I wouldn't visit us, however, on your way back. I'll probably be married to the woman who collects thumbs."

Piet had no-one to talk to, but he chuckled to himself as he came upon the birch bright sea.

"It's lucky old McLaww didn't make it to that part of the contest. He would have hated me for the rest of his life."

"This is a magnificent day for the nation's capital and for millions of Americans who will visit Washington in the years to come," the President said, smiling at Mr. Hirshhorn at his side.

"Throughout the world," the President said, *"Mr. Hirshhorn has sought the great art of our time—those expressions of man's will to make sense of his experience on earth, to find order and meaning in the physical world about him, to render what is familiar in a new way."*

It was late June when he arrived at the bay.

"I've come for Egsdrull," said Piet to the manager of the lumber yard. "I'm the carver from Queen Charlotte." He handed him the receipt.

"You're a *little* late," replied the manager. "And as well there's the little matter of the seven terms: shape an axe, sing its joints, engrave its shaft, bless its point, name it in ten tongues, knit soul and intent, determine where lies its enemy."

"I had men who could do all that. Ole Siuk could have shaped it out of brittle rock; Pier Dela Ombre was once with the Scalla; the best man with a graver you ever saw was Torah Black; Looky Mc-Laww would have had a libation for the blade; André Mineur knew a baker's-dozen tongues; Scrop Calla would have taught you a thing or two about serpents biting their own tails and how to hoop a barrel hoop. And I, why do you think I came all this way? Put that axe in my hands and show me the tree, show me Egsdrull, and God himself will not be able to catch the bloody chips."

"Terms is terms," the manager said. "The sea probably has fish who could do all that, but you don't see him standing there begging."

Piet could find nothing to say.

"I've got something out behind the slab pile that might do for you," the manager said. "We flooded those ten or twelve years back when we gave up hope on you."

Beyond the slab pile, where a small red fork-lift truck scurried with its swaying load of sixteen- and eighteen-foot slabs, was a scene of desolation. The creek which once had there flowed into the Bay of Chaleur was dammed. Forty feet or more on either side was flooded. All the trees that once had grown there were black stubs. Not ankle high, as a good piece of future meadowland might look waiting for the years to rot the stumps, but man high, totem high: trunks like amputated limbs.

"You're free to make something of one of those if you like," said the manager. "But I don't expect any of them is fit for a trip back to the coast. Hollow rotten."

"I did not come all that way," said Piet. He was screaming. "Lose all those men, suffer all that laceration. Father, father, I am a grown man. You promised me Egsdrull. I discovered the Pacific; I fed China for three months; I played poker with Lord Astor; I kissed the dirty Hun's lady. I courted death. You have forsworn me. Thief-man."

"Forsworn you, my ass. Terms is terms. There it is in black and white. Ninth of May or all terms void. Seven terms to be fulfilled before delivery. It's time you earned your daily bread for a change, young fellow. Don't father me. Perhaps we can fit you in on the butt-saw, if you can keep up. You're not so spry as you once were. What do you say, young fellow? Want to try Newfoundland?"

President Johnson formally accepted the Hirshhorn art collection today "on behalf of the American people" in a ceremony at noon in the Rose Garden of the White House.

Piet Catogas lasted a week at work before his death. Not on the butt-saw, which is a skilled task and requires a young and agile man, but out in the yard in the sunlight, sorting the lumber by lengths, widths, and grades.

This was a job for the young or the very old, but he found no sympathy among his comrades and was unable to speak to them of the carvings that he had made before he was half their age, back on the island.

More than one of his wounds was infected, and though he bathed in the warm sea he knew it was futile and awaited his death with great equanimity. At night he wondered if Dela Ombre would have blond sons later with Katrina or what Torah had thought about as he fired into the flame and smoke; he chuckled at the thought of Looky beaten by the horseshoes on pikes and wondered how many winters Calla would survive; he was afraid Mineur had sold out to those madmen and prayed for Ole Siuk.

In the mornings he slept later and later. He would have been fired on the morning he died if ever he had reached the yard where men sorted the sixteen-foot one-by-sixes into four grades without a passing glance at the ship which came for his body.

GENERAL REFERENCES

BIBLIOGRAPHIES

Bohne, Harold, *Canadian Books in Print, 1972* (Toronto, 1973)

Boyle, Gertrude M., *A Bibliography of Canadiana, First Supplement. Being items in the Public Library of Toronto, Canada, Relating to the Early History and Development of Canada* (Toronto, 1959)

Morse, William I., *The Canadian Collection at Harvard University* (Cambridge, Mass., 1947)

Queen's University Library, *A Catalogue of Canadian Manuscripts Collected by Lorne Pierce and Presented to Queen's University* (Toronto, 1946)

Staton, Frances M., and Tremaine, Muriel, eds., *A Bibliography of Canadiana. Being items in the Public Library of Toronto, Canada, Relating to the Early History and Development of Canada* (Toronto, 1934)

Toronto Public Library, *Landmarks of Canada: What Art Has Done for Canadian History: A Guide to the J. Ross Robertson Historical Collection*, 2 vols. (Toronto, 1917-1921)

Watters, Reginald Eyre, *A Checklist of Canadian Literature and Background Materials, 1628-1960*, 2nd ed. (Toronto, 1972)

Watters, Reginald E., and Bell, Inglis F., *On Canadian Literature, 1806-1960: A Checklist of Articles, Books, and Theses on English-Canadian Literature, Its Authors, and Language* (Toronto, 1964)

STUDIES

Atwood, Margaret, *Survival: A Thematic Guide to Canadian Literature* (Toronto: Anansi, 1972)

Baker, Ray Palmer, *A History of English-Canadian Literature to the Confederation* (Cambridge, Mass.: Harvard University Press, 1920)

Dunham, Aileen, *Political Unrest in Upper Canada, 1815-1836* with an Introduction by A. L. Burt (Carleton Library 10, Toronto, 1963)

Eggleston, W., *The Frontier and Canadian Letters* (Toronto, 1957)

Klinck, C. F. et al., *Literary History of Canada: Canadian Literature in English* (Toronto, 1965)

New, Chester, *Lord Durham's Mission to Canada,* edited and with an Introduction by H. W. McCready (Carleton Library 8, Toronto, 1963)

Pacey, D., *Creative Writing in Canada: A Short History of English-Canadian Literature,* 2nd ed. (Toronto, 1961)

Smith, A. J. M., *Masks of Fiction: Canadian Critics on Canadian Prose* (New Canadian Library 02, Toronto, 1961)

Sylvestre, G., Conron, B., and Klinck, C. F., *Canadian Writers/ Ecrivains Canadiens* (Toronto, 1964)

Waite, P. B., ed., *The Confederation Debates in the Province of Canada 1865* (Carleton Library 21, Toronto, 1965)

The Western Interior of Canada: A Record of Geographical Discovery 1612-1917, compiled and with an Introduction by John Warkentin (Carleton Library 15, Toronto, 1964)

SELECTED CRITICISM

EDWARD BLAKE

Banks, M., *Edward Blake, Irish Nationalist: A Canadian Statesman in Irish Politics, 1892-1907* (Toronto, 1957)

Bissell, C. T. (ed.), "Edward Blake" by F. H. Underhill in *Our Living Tradition* (Toronto, 1957)

Dent, J. C., *The Canadian Portrait Gallery* (Toronto, 1880)

Flenley, R. (ed.) "Edward Blake and Canadian Liberal Nationalism" by F. H. Underhill in *Essays in Canadian History* (Toronto, 1939)

Hassard, A. R., "Great Canadian Orators," *Canadian Historical Review* 1: 229

Kennedy, W. P. M., "Edward Blake," *Canadian Historical Review* 12: 455

Lemieux, Hon. R., "Edward Blake," *Canadian Historical Review* 10: 283

Longley, Hon. J. W., "Great Canadians I Have Known," *Canadian Historical Review* 2: 209

Underhill, F. H., "Edward Blake," in C. T. Bissell (ed.), *Our Living Tradition: Seven Canadians* (Toronto, 1958)

Underhill, F.H., "Edward Blake and Canadian Liberal Nationalism," in R. Flenley (ed.), *Essays in Canadian History* (Toronto, 1939)

Underhill, F. H., "Laurier and Blake 1882-1891," *Canadian Historical Review* 20: 392-408 (December 1939)

Underhill, F. H., "Laurier and Blake 1891-1892," *Canadian Historical Review* 24: 135-155 (June 1943)

E. K. BROWN

Bennet, C. L., Review of *Matthew Arnold: A Study in Conflict, Dalhousie Review* 29: 203 (July 1949)

Bennet, C. L., Review of *Rhythm in the Novel, Dalhousie Review* 31 no. 4 (Winter 1952)

Bourinot, A. S., "Selected Poems of Duncan Campbell Scott, with a Memoir by E. K. Brown," *Canadian Poetry* 14: 30-31 (Summer 1951)

Breen, M., "Man of Letters," *Saturday Night* 65: 15 (December 27, 1949)

Clarke, G. H., "Canadian Poetry," *Queen's Quarterly* 58: 455-458 (Autumn 1951)

Clarke, G. H., Review of *On Canadian Poetry, Queen's Quarterly* 50 no. 4: 435-437 (1943)

Collin, W. E., "The Stream and the Masters," *University of Toronto Quarterly* 13: 221-227 (January, 1944), 324-327 (April 1944)

Daniells, R., "Selected Poems of Duncan Campbell Scott, with a memoir by E. K. Brown," *Canadian Forum* 31: 140 (September 1951)

Duncan, C., Review of *On Canadian Poetry, Canadian Forum* 23: 237 (January 1944)

Dunn, D., Review of *Rhythm in the Novel, Culture* 12: 194-195 (juin 1951)

MacLennan, H., "Rhythm in the Novel," *University of Toronto Quarterly* 21: 88-90 (October 1951)

Martin, B., Review of *On Canadian Poetry, Dalhousie Review* 23: 478 (January 1944)

Sandwell, B. K., "The Late E. K. Brown," *Saturday Night* 66: 7 (May 8, 1951)

Sandwell, B. K., "The Poetry of the Victorians," *Saturday Night* 57: 15 (July 11, 1942)

Sandwell, B. K., "The Summing-Up," *Saturday Night* 66: 33-34 (October 1951)

Smith, A. J. M., Review of *On Canadian Poetry, Canadian Historical Review* 25: 196-197 (June 1944)

Stanley, C., "Matthew Arnold," *University of Toronto Quarterly* 19: 106-109 (October 1949)

Williams, A., Review of *On Canadian Poetry, Culture* 5: 95-96 (mars 1944)

MORLEY CALLAGHAN

Arthur, C. J., *A Comparative Study of the Short Stories of Morley Callaghan and Hugh Garner* (unpublished thesis, University of New Brunswick, 1967)

Avison, M., "Callaghan Revisited," *Canadian Forum* 39: 276-277 (March 1960)

Callaghan, M., "The Imaginative Writer," Convocation address, University of Toronto, June 3, 1966, *Tamarack Review* 41: 5-11 (Autumn 1966)

Callaghan, M., "The Plight of Canadian Fiction," *University of Toronto Quarterly* 7: 152-161 (January 1938)

Callaghan, M., "Those Summers in Toronto," *Maclean's* 76: 25-27, 37-40 (January 5, 1963)

Conron, B., *Morley Callaghan* (New York, 1966)

Conron, B., "Morley Callaghan as a Short Story Writer," *Journal of Commonwealth Literature* 3: 58-75 (July 1967)

Davis, H. J., "Morley Callaghan," *Canadian Forum* 15: 398-399 (December 1935)

Hoar, V., *Morley Callaghan* (Toronto, 1969)

McCarvell, J., *Morley Callaghan as a Short Story Writer* (unpublished thesis, Laval University, 1957)

MacGregor, R. G., *A Comparative Study of the Short Stories of Morley Callaghan and Ernest Hemingway* (unpublished thesis, University of New Brunswick, 1968)

McKellar, I. H., *The Innocents of Morley Callaghan* (unpublished thesis, Carleton University, 1968)

McPherson, H., Introduction to *More Joy in Heaven* (New Canadian Library, Toronto, 1960)

McPherson, H., "A Tale Retold," *Canadian Literature* 7: 59-61 (Winter 1961)

McPherson, H., "The Two Worlds of Morley Callaghan," *Queen's Quarterly* 64: 350-365 (Autumn 1957)

Moon, B., "The Second Coming of Morley Callaghan," *Maclean's* 73: 19, 62-64 (December 3, 1960)

Orange, J., *Morley Callaghan's Catholic Conscience* (unpublished thesis, University of Toronto, 1966)

Phelps, A. L., "Morley Callaghan," in his *Canadian Writers* (Toronto, 1951)

Ripley, J. D., *A Critical Study of Morley Callaghan* (unpublished thesis, University of New Brunswick, 1959)

Ross, M., Introduction to *Such is my Beloved* (New Canadian Library, Toronto, 1957)

Scobie, S., "Magic, not Magicians, *Beautiful Losers* and *Story of O*," *Canadian Literature* 45: 56-60 (Summer 1970)

Steinhauer, H., "Canadian Writers of To-day," *Canadian Forum* 12: 177-178 (February 1932)

Walsh, W., *A Manifold Voice* (Studies in Commonwealth Literature, London, 1970)

Watt, F. W., Introduction to *They Shall Inherit the Earth* (New Canadian Library, Toronto, 1962)

Watt, F. W., "Morley Callaghan as Thinker," *Dalhousie Review* 39: 305-313 (Autumn 1959). Also in A. J. M. Smith (ed.), *Masks of Fiction* (New Canadian Library, Toronto, 1961)

Weaver, R., "A Golden Year," *Canadian Literature* 16: 55-57 (Spring 1963)

Weaver, R., "Stories by Callaghan," *Canadian Literature* 2: 67-70 (Autumn 1959)

Weaver, R., "A Talk with Morley Callaghan," *The Tamarack Review* 7: 3-29 (Spring 1958)

Wilson, E., "Morley Callaghan of Toronto," *New Yorker* 36: 224-236 (November 26, 1960). Included in Edmund Wilson, *O Canada* (New York, 1965)

Wilson, M., "Callaghan's Caviare," *The Tamarack Review* 22: 88-92 (Winter 1963)

Woodcock, G., "The Callaghan Case," *Canadian Literature* 12: 60-64 (Spring 1962)

Woodcock, G., "Lost Eurydice," *Canadian Literature* 21: 21-35 (Summer 1964). Also in *Odysseus Ever Returning* (Toronto, 1970)

LEONARD COHEN

Anon., (portrait), *Maclean's Magazine* 81: 60 (August 1968)

Batten, J., "Leonard Cohen: the Poet as Hero," *Saturday Night* 84: 23-26 (June 1969)

Cohen, L., "Leonard Cohen: The Poet as Hero" (interview by Michael Harris), *Saturday Night* 84: 26-31 (June 1969)

Djwa, S., "Leonard Cohen: Black Romantic," *Canadian Literature* 34: 32-42 (Autumn 1967)

Duffy, D., Review of *Beautiful Losers, The Tamarack Review* 40: 75-79 (Summer 1966)

Elson, N., *Love in the Novels and Poetry of Leonard Cohen* (unpublished thesis, University of New Brunswick)

Gose, E. B., "Of Beauty and Unmeaning," *Canadian Literature* 29: 61-63 (Summer 1966)

Lyons, R., *Jewish Poets from Montreal: Concepts of History in the Poetry of A. M. Klein, Irving Layton, and Leonard Cohen* (unpublished thesis, Carleton University, 1968)

Ondaatje, M., *Leonard Cohen* (Toronto, 1970)

Owen, D., "Leonard Cohen: the Poet as Hero," *Saturday Night* 84: 31-32 (June 1969)

Pacey, D., "The Phenomenon of Leonard Cohen," *Canadian Literature* 34: 5-23 (Autumn 1967)

Purdy, A. W., "Leonard Cohen, a Personal Look," *Canadian Literature* 23: 7-16 (Winter 1965)

Robertson, G., Review of *The Favourite Game, Canadian Literature* 19: 69-70 Winter 1964)

Ruddy, J., "Is the world (or anybody) ready for Leonard Cohen?" *Maclean's Magazine* 79: 18-19, 33-34 (October 1, 1966)

Sutherland, R., "Twin Solitudes," *Canadian Literature* 31: 5-24 (Winter 1967)

Watt, F. W., "Letters in Canada, 1963," *University of Toronto Quarterly* vol. 33, no. 4, pp. 393-394 (July 1964)

Woodcock, G., "The Song of the Sirens: Notes on Leonard Cohen" in *Odysseus Ever Returning* (Toronto, 1970)

RALPH CONNOR

Beharriell, S. R., Introduction to *The Man from Glengarry* (New Canadian Library, Toronto, 1960)

Daniells, R., "Glengarry Revisited," *Canadian Literature* 31: 45-53 (Winter 1967)

McCourt, E. A., "The Sky Pilot," in *The Canadian West in Fiction* (Toronto, 1949)

Paterson, B., "Ralph Connor and his Million-Dollar Sermons," *Maclean's Magazine* 66: 26, 56-60 (November 15, 1953)

Roper, R. *et al.*, in C. F. Klinck *et al.* (eds.), *Literary History of Canada*, pp. 322-324 (Toronto, 1965)

Watt, F. W., "Western Myth—The World of Ralph Connor," *Canadian Literature* 1: 26-36 (Spring 1959)

RAMSAY COOK

Anon., Review of *Canada and the French-Canadian Question, French Canadian Nationalism: An Anthology, The Maple Leaf Forever, Canadian Dimension*, p. 51 (January, 1972)

Arès, R., "Provincial Autonomy, Minority Rights and the Compact Theory, 1867-1921. Studies of the Royal Commission on Bilingualism and Biculturalism, 4. Ramsay Cook," *Canadian Historical Review* 51: 316-318 (September 1970)

Beck, J. M., Review of *The Maple Leaf Forever: Essays on Nationalism and Politics in Canada, Dalhousie Review* 51: 288-289 (Summer 1971)

Beck, J. M., Review of *The Politics of John W. Dafoe and the Free Press, Dalhousie Review* 43: 579-581 (Winter 1963)

Bélanger, André J., Review of *French-Canadian Nationalism: An Anthology, Canadian Journal of Political Science* 3: 490 (September 1970)

Brady, A., "National and International," *University of Toronto Quarterly* 33: 454-455 (July 1964)

Fox, P., "The French-Canadian Question," *Executive* 8: 48 (October 1966)

French, G. S., Review of *Canada and the French-Canadian Question, Queen's Quarterly* 73: 445-446 (Autumn 1966)

Glazebrook, G. de T., "The Dafoe-Sifton Correspondence, 1919-1927. Edited by Ramsay Cook," *International Journal* 23: 316-317 (Spring 1968)

Graham, R., "The Dafoe-Sifton Correspondence 1919-1927. Edited by Ramsay Cook," *Canadian Historical Review* 50: 204 (June 1969)

Gwyn, J., Review of *Canada and the French-Canadian Question, Revue de l'Université d'Ottawa* 38: 175-176 (janvier-mars 1968)

Gwyn, J., Review of *The Maple Leaf Forever, Essays on Nationalism and Politics in Canada, Revue de l'Université d'Ottawa* 41: 567-568 (octobre-décembre 1971)

Hodgins, B. W., "Turning New Leaves," *Canadian Forum* 46: 182 (November 1966)

Latouche, D., "Some of the Best English Canadians are my Friends," *Canadian Dimension* p. 51 (January 1972)

McDougall, R. L., "Dualité Canadienne," *Canadian Literature* 32: 75-77 (Spring 1967)

McLeod, J. T., "Understanding Quebec," *Saturday Night* [81]: 45 (May 1966)

Morton, W. L., Review of *The Politics of John W. Dafoe and the Free Press, International Journal* 18: 381-382 (Summer 1963)

Savard, P., Review of *French Canadian Nationalism: An Anthology, Canadian Historical Review* 51: 450-451 (December 1970) [review in French]

Smiley, D., Review of *The Maple Leaf Forever: Essays on Nationalism and Politics in Canada, Canadian Historical Review* 53: 75-78 (March 1972)

Stanley, G. F. G., "Pessimistic Nationalism," *Queen's Quarterly* 77: 443-445 (Autumn 1970)

Turner, H. E., Review of *Canada and the French-Canadian Question, Commentator* 10: 29 (September 1966)

Wallot, J. P. "French-Canadian Nationalism: from Cannon Shot to Total Revolution," *Canadian Forum* 50: 22-24 (April-May 1970)

D. G. CREIGHTON

Anon., "Biographical note," *Royal Society of Canada, Transactions,* third series 45: 44 (1951)
Anon., "Nation Building 1867," *Canadian Business* 36: 22-24, 26 ff. (July 1963)
Anon., (portrait), *Saturday Night,* 70: 12 (November 26, 1955)
Anon., (portrait), *Saturday Night* 72: 41 (November 9, 1957)
Cook, R., *The Maple Leaf Forever,* pp. 153-158 (Toronto, 1971). (In the present collection.)
Crane, D., "The Man Who Revived Sir John A.," *Maclean's Magazine* 78: 2-3 (March 6, 1965)
Kent-Barber, N., La théorie du commerce principal chez M. M. Creighton et Quellet," bibliographical footnotes, *Revue d'Histoire de l'Amérique Française* 22: 401-414 (décembre 1968)
Kilbourn, W., "The Writing of Canadian History," in C. F. Klinck *et al.* (eds.), *Literary History of Canada,* pp. 496-519 (Toronto, 1965)
Marion, S., *Péchés d'omission d'un historien canadien* (Ottawa, 1966)

ROBERTSON DAVIES

Callwood, J., "The Beard," *Maclean's* 65: 16-17, 30-33 (March 15, 1952)
Dobbs, K., "Fifth Business," *The Tamarack Review* 57: 76-80 (1971)
Hall, W. F., "The Real and the Marvellous," *Canadian Literature* 49: 80-81 (Summer 1971)
Kirkwood, H., "Robertson Davies," *Canadian Forum* 30: 59-60 (June 1950)
McPherson, H., "The Mask of Satire: Character and Symbolic Pattern in Robertson Davies' Fiction," *Canadian Literature* 4: 18-30 (Spring 1960). Also in A. J. M. Smith (ed.), *Masks of Fiction* (New Canadian Library, Toronto, 1961)
Marchbanks, Samuel [Robertson Davies], "The Double Life of Robertson Davies," *Liberty* pp. 18-19, 53-58 (April 1954). Also in C. F. Klinck and R. E. Watters (eds.), *Canadian Anthology* (Toronto, 1966)
Murphy, S. M., *Self-Discovery: The Search for Values in the Work of Robertson Davies* (unpublished thesis, Carleton University, 1968)
Owen, I., "The Salterton Novels," *The Tamarack Review* 9: 56-63 (Autumn 1958)
Read, S. E., "A Call to the Clerisy," *Canadian Literature* 7: 65-68 (Winter 1961)
Roper, G., Introduction to *Marchbanks' Almanack* (New Canadian Library, Toronto, 1968)
Steinberg, M. W., "Don Quixote and the Puppets: Theme and Structure in Robertson Davies' Drama," *Canadian Literature* 7: 45-53 (Winter 1961)
Turner, J. O. F., *Robertson Davies: Critic and Author* (unpublished thesis, University of Manitoba, 1958)

SARA JEANNETTE DUNCAN

Bissell, C. T., Introduction to *The Imperialist,* (New Canadian Library, Toronto, 1961)
Burness, J. F., "Sara Jeannette Duncan—A Neglected Canadian Author," *Ontario Library Review* 45: 205-206 (August 1961)
Goodwin, R., *The Early Journalism of Sara Jeannette Duncan* (unpublished thesis, University of Toronto, 1964)

Roper, G., *et al.*, in C. F. Klinck *et al.* (eds.) *Literary History of Canada*, pp. 314-317 (Toronto, 1965)

R[oss]., M. E., "Sara Jeannette Duncan: Personal Glimpses," *Canadian Literature* 27: 15-19 (Winter 1966)

NORTHROP FRYE

Blisset, W., (review article), *University of Toronto Quarterly* 33: 401-408 (July 1964)

Dudek, L., "Northrop Frye's Untenable Position," *Delta* 22: 23-27 (October 1963

Krieger, M., (ed.), *Northrop Frye in Modern Criticism, selected papers from the English Institute* (New York, 1966)

Mandel, E. W., *Criticism: the Silent-Speaking Words*, pp. 37-46 (Toronto, 1966)

Mandel, E. W., "The Language of Humanity," *The Tamarack Review* 29: 82-89 (Autumn 1963)

Mandel, E. W., "Toward a Theory of Cultural Revolution," *Canadian Literature* 1: 58-67 (Summer 1959)

Reaney, J., "Frye's Magnet," *The Tamarack Review* 33: 72-78 (Autumn 1964)

Smith, A. J. M., "The Critic's Task, Frye's Latest Work," *Canadian Literature* 20: 6-14 (Spring 1964)

Tucker, M. C., *Toward a Theory of Shakespearean Comedy: a Study of the Contributions of Northrop Frye* (unpublished thesis, Emory University, 1963) (on microfilm)

Watt, F. W., "The Critic's Critic," *Canadian Literature* 19: 51-54 (Winter 1964)

HUGH GARNER

Anderson, A., "An Interview with Hugh Garner," *The Tamarack Review* 52: 19-34 (1969)

Arthur, C. J., *A Comparative Study of the Short Stories of Morley Callaghan and Hugh Garner* (unpublished thesis, University of New Brunswick, 1967)

Story, N., *The Oxford Companion to Canadian History and Literature* 310-311 (Oxford University Press, Toronto, London, New York, 1967)

Waddington, M., "Garner's Good Ear," *Canadian Literature* 50: 72-75 (Autumn 1971)

JOHN GLASSCO

Anon., "Unrevised and Unrepentant," *Time* (Canadian edn.) (May 4, 1970)

Cowley, M., "We Had Such Good Times," *The New Republic* (December 25, 1971)

Fethering, D., "After the Fun was Over . . .", *Saturday Night* (April 1970)

Fethering, D., "An Overqualified Poet Deserves our Notice," *Saturday Night* (April 1972)

French, W., Review of *Memoirs of Montparnasse* in Toronto *Globe and Mail Magazine* reprinted in *Book of the Month Club News* (Midsummer 1970)

Hornyansky, M., "Letters in Canada: Poetry," *University of Toronto Quarterly*, p. 335 (Summer 1972)

Kapica, J., "Memoirs of Montparnasse," *McGill Daily Supplement* (November 13, 1970)

Kattan, N., "L'aventure parisienne de John Glassco," *Le Devoir* (May 2, 1970)

Marshall, A., "Well-spent Youths," *New Statesman* (May 29, 1970)

Morgan, J.-L., "Le gentleman de Foster," *Actualité*

Richmond, J., "John Glassco — An Interview," Montreal *Star* (October 18, 1969)

Richmond, J., "Paris When It Sizzled,'" Montreal *Star* (February 21, 1970)

Showers, P., "Memoirs of Montparnasse," New York *Times Book Review* (November 29, 1970)

Thorpe, D., "Memoirs of Montparnasse," Washington, D.C., *Sunday Star* (March 8, 1970)

DAVE GODFREY

Atwood, M., *Survival, pp.* 239-241 (Toronto, 1972)

Cameron, D., "Don Cameron Interviews Dave Godfrey," *Quill & Quire* 38, 2: 3, 10-11 (February 1972)

Cameron, D., "The Three People Inside Dave Godfrey," *Saturday Night* (September 1971)

Cockburn, R., Review of *Death Goes Better With Coca-Cola, Fiddlehead* 76: 78-79 (Spring 1968)

Helwig, D., "Stories Around Death," *Queen's Quarterly* 75: 347-350 (Summer 1968)

Laurence, M., "Ancestral Voices, Prophesying . . .", *The Mysterious East* (December 1970)

Nowlan, A., Review of *Death Goes Better With Coca-Cola, Canadian Forum* 47: 282 (March 1968)

Thomas, A., "The Smell of Recognition," *Canadian Literature* 49: 78-80 (Summer 1971)

Woodcock, G., "Borderland of Truth," *Canadian Literature* 38: 91-93 (Autumn 1968)

FREDERICK PHILIP GROVE

Ayre, R., "Canadian Writers of Today—Frederick Philip Grove," *Canadian Forum* 12: 255-257 (April 1932)

Birbalsingh, F., "Grove and Existentialism," *Canadian Literature* 43: 67-76 (Winter 1970)

Clarke, G. H., "A Canadian Novelist and his Critic," *Queen's Quarterly* 53: 362-368 (August 1946)

Collin, W. E., "La tragique Ironie de Frederick Philip Grove," *Gants du Ciel* 4: 15-40 (Winter 1946)

Eaton, C. E., *The Life and Works of Frederick Philip Grove* (unpublished thesis, Acadia University, 1940)

Eggleston, W., "Frederick Philip Grove," in C. T. Bissel (ed.), *Our Living Tradition: Seven Canadians* (Toronto, 1958)

Eggleston, W., *The Frontier and Canadian Letters* (Toronto, 1957)

Ferguson, M., *A Study of the Tragic Element in The Novels of Frederick Philip Grove* (unpublished thesis, University of Manitoba, 1947)

Grant, G. M., *Frederick Philip Grove: Birth of the Canadian Novel* (unpublished thesis, Dalhousie University, 1946)

Grove, F. P., "Apologia pro Vita et Opere Sua," *Canadian Forum* 11: 420-422 (August 1931)

Grove, F. P., "In Search of Myself," *University of Toronto Quarterly* 10: 60-67 (October 1940). Also in A. J. M. Smith (ed.), *Masks of Fiction* (New Canadian Library, Toronto, 1961)

Grove, F. P., "The Plight of Canadian Fiction: A Reply," *University of Toronto Quarterly* 7: 451-467 (July 1938)

Grove, F. P., "A Postscript to *A Search for America,*" *Queen's Quarterly* 49: 197-213 (Autumn 1942)

Holliday, W. B., "Frederick Philip Grove: An Impression," *Canadian Literature* 3: 17-22 (Winter 1960)

Jackel, S., "The House on the Prairies," *Canadian Literature* 42: 46-55 (Autumn 1969)

636   THE CANADIAN CENTURY

Knister, R., "Frederick Philip Grove," *Ontario Library Review* 12: 60-62 (November 1928)
McCourt, E. A., *The Canadian West in Fiction* (Toronto, 1949)
McKenzie, R., "Life in a New Land: Notes on The Immigrant Theme in Canadian Fiction," *Canadian Literature* 7: 24-33 (Winter 1961)
McLeod, G. D., *The Primeval Element in the Prairie Novels of Frederick Philip Grove* (unpublished thesis, University of Manitoba, 1967)
McMullin, S. E., *The Promised Land Motif in the Works of Frederick Philip Grove* (unpublished thesis, Carleton University, 1968)
Nesbitt, B. H., *"The Seasons*: Grove's Unfinished Novel," *Canadian Literature* 18: 47-51 (Autumn 1963)
Pacey, D., *Frederick Philip Grove* (Toronto, 1945)
Pacey, D., *Frederick Philip Grove* (Toronto, 1970)
Pacey, D., "Frederick Philip Grove: A Group of Letters," *Canadian Literature* 11: 28-38 (Winter 1962)
Pacey, D. (ed.), *Tales from the Margin. The Selected Short Stories of Frederick Philip Grove*. Edited with Introduction and Notes. (Toronto, 1971)
Park, M. G., Introduction to *Fruits of the Earth* (New Canadian Library, Toronto, 1965)
Phelps, A. L., "Frederick Philip Grove," in his *Canadian Writers* (Toronto, 1951)
Pierce, L., "Frederick Philip Grove: 1871-1948," *Royal Society of Canada, Transactions,* third series 43: 113-119 (1948)
Ross, M., Introduction to *Over Prairie Trails* (New Canadian Library, Toronto, 1957)
Sandwell, B. K., "Frederick Philip Grove and the Culture of Canada," *Saturday Night* 61: 18 (November 24, 1945)
Sutherland, R., *Frederick Philip Grove* (Toronto, 1969)
Saunders, D. B., "The Grove Collection in the University of Manitoba: A Tentative Evaluation," *Papers of the Bibliographical Society of Canada* (Toronto, 1963)
Saunders, T., "The Grove Papers," *Queen's Quarterly* 70: 22-29 (Spring 1963)
Saunders, T., Introduction to *Settlers of the Marsh* (New Canadian Library, Toronto, 1966)
Saunders, T., "A Novelist as Poet: Frederick Philip Grove," *Dalhousie Review* 43: 235-241 (Summer 1963)
Skelton, I., "Frederick Philip Grove," *Dalhousie Review* 19: 147-163 (July 1939)
Spettigue, D. O., *Frederick Philip Grove* (Toronto, 1969)
Stanley, C. W., "Frederick Philip Grove," *Dalhousie Review* 25: 433-441 (January 1946)
Watters, R. E., Introduction to *The Master of the Mill* (New Canadian Library, Toronto, 1961)
Wilson, J. M., *A Comparative Study of the Novels of Frederick Philip Grove and Theodore Dreiser* (unpublished thesis, University of New Brunswick, 1962)

HUGH HOOD

Baldwin, R. G., Review of *White Figure, White Ground, Queen's Quarterly* 72: 204 (Spring 1965)
Dalt, G. M., Review of *Around the Mountain, The Tamarack Review* 45: 116-117 (Autumn 1967)
Dobbs, K., "Memory Transfigured," *Canadian Literature* 16: 72-73 (Spring 1963)
Erskine, J. S., Review of *Flying a Red Kite, Dalhousie Review* 43: 264-265 (Summer 1963)
Godfrey, D., "Line and Form," *The Tamarack Review* 35: 96-101 (Spring 1965)
Godfrey, D., "Turning New Leaves," *Canadian Forum* 42: 229-230 (January 1963)
Grosskurth, Ph., Review of *The Camera Always Lies, Saturday Night* 82: 55 (November 1967)

Gzowski, P., "Why Montreal is Canada's Parnassus," *Maclean's Magazine* 80: 70-71 (August 1967)
Hale, V. G., "An Interview with Hugh Hood," *World Literature Written in English* X, 1: 35-41 (April 1972)
Hornyansky, M., "Countries of the Mind II," *The Tamarack Review* 27: 80-89 (Spring 1963)
Kilgallin, T., "Hood's Montreal," *Canadian Literature* 36: 94-95 (Spring 1968)
Lane, L., Review of *Flying a Red Kite, Queen's Quarterly* 70: 451-452 (Autumn 1963)
Nowlan, A., Review of *The Camera Always Lies, Canadian Forum* 48: 46-47 (May 1968)
Pacey, D., "A First Novel," *Fiddlehead* 63: 70-71 (Winter 1965)
Percy, H. R., Review of *The Camera Always Lies, Canadian Author and Bookman* 43: 23 (Winter 1967)
Percy, H. R., Review of *Flying a Red Kite, Canadian Author and Bookman* 38: 11 (Spring 1963)
Percy, H. R., "Three Novels," *Canadian Author and Bookman* 40: 16 (Winter 1964)
Stratford, Ph., "The Artist's Life," *Saturday Night* 79: 30 (October 1964)
Warren, M., "Artist's Passion," *Canadian Literature* 25: 76-77 (Summer 1965)
Watt, F. W., Review of *Flying a Red Kite, University of Toronto Quarterly* 32: 391-394 (July 1963)
Watt, F. W., Review of *White Figure, White Ground, University of Toronto Quarterly* 34: 376-377 (July 1965)

A. M. KLEIN

Avison, M., Review of *The Rocking Chair, Canadian Forum* (November 1949)
Brown, E. K., "The Development of Poetry in Canada," *Poetry* (Chicago, April 1941)
Canadian Literature 25, "A Symposium on A. M. Klein" (Summer 1965). Includes articles by D. Livesay, T. A. Marshall, M. W. Steinberg, and M. Waddington.
Collin, W. E, "The Spirit's Palestine," *The White Savannahs* (Toronto, 1936)
Crawley, A, "Notes on A. M. Klein," *Contemporary Verse* 28: 20 (Summer 1949)
Dudek, L., "A. M. Klein," *Canadian Forum* 30: 10-12 (April 1950)
Edel, L., "Abraham M. Klein," *Canadian Forum* 12: 300-302 (May 1932)
Edel, L., "Poetry in the Jewish Tradition," *Poetry* (Chicago) 58: 51-53 (April 1941)
Fischer, G. R., "Klein's Forgotten Play," *Canadian Literature* 43: 42-53 (Winter 1970)
Gotlieb, P., "Klein's Sources," *Canadian Literature* 26: 82-84 (Autumn 1965)
Lewisohn, L., Foreword to *Hath not a Jew* ... (New York, 1940)
Marshall, T., *A. M. Klein* (Toronto, 1970)
Matthews, J., "Abraham Klein and the Problem of Synthesis," *Journal of Commonwealth Literature* 1: 149-163 (September 1965)
Smith, A. J. M., "Abraham Moses Klein," *Gants du Ciel* 11: 67-81 (printemps 1946)
Spurgeon, D. C., "Whither Green-haired Poet?" *Saturday Night* 65: 12, 46 (May 23, 1950)
Steinberg, M. W., Introduction to *The Second Scroll* (New Canadian Library, Toronto, 1961)
Steinberg, M. W., "A Twentieth Century Pentateuch," *Canadian Literature* 2: 37-46 (Autumn 1959). Also in A. J. M. Smith (ed.), *Masks of Fiction* (New Canadian Library, Toronto, 1961)
Sutherland, J., "Canadian Comment," *Northern Review* 2:30-34 (August-September, 1949)
Sutherland, J., "The Poetry of A. M. Klein," *Index* vol. i, no. 6, pp. 8-12 (August 1946)
Swados, H., Review of *The Second Scroll, The Nation* (New York, November 3, 1951)
Waddington, M., *A. M. Klein* (Toronto, 1969)
Wilson, M., "Klein's Drowned Poet," *Canadian Literature* 6: 5-17 (Autumn 1960)

MARGARET LAURENCE

Anon., "Laurence of Manitoba," *Canadian Author and Bookman* 41: 4-6 (Winter 1966)

Boyd, B., *Patterns and Parallels in the Fiction of Margaret Laurence* (unpublished thesis, Acadia University, 1968)

Callaghan, B., "The Writings of Margaret Laurence," *The Tamarack Review* 36: 45-51 (Summer 1965)

Godfrey, D., "For Bonfires/For Burning," *The Tamarack Review* 33: 92-94 (Autumn 1964)

Gotlieb, P., "On Margaret Laurence," *The Tamarack Review* 52: 76-80 (1969)

Harlow, R., "Lack of Distance," *Canadian Literature* 31: 71-74 (Winter 1967)

Jackel, S., "The House on the Prairies," *Canadian Literature* 42: 46-55 (Autumn 1969)

Kreisel, H., "The African Stories of Margaret Laurence," *Canadian Forum* 41: 8-10 (April 1961)

Kreisel, H., "A Familiar Landscape," *The Tamarack Review* 55: 91-94 (1970)

Laurence, M., "Sources," *Mosaic* 3/3: 80-84 (Spring 1970)

Laurence, M., "Ten Years' Sentences," *Canadian Literature* 41: 10-16 (Summer 1969)

New, W. H., Introduction to *The Swamp Angel* (New Canadian Library, Toronto, 1968)

Read, S. E., "Margaret Laurence, The Stone Angel," *British Columbia Library Quarterly* 28: 41-44 (July-October, 1964)

Read, S. E., "The Maze of Life: the Work of Margaret Laurence," *Canadian Literature* 27: 5-14 (Winter 1966)

Robertson, G., "An Artist's Progress," *Canadian Literature* 21: 53-55 (Summer 1964)

Sykes, P., Review of *The Fire-Dwellers, Maclean's* vol. 82, no. 6, p. 98 (June 1969)

Thomas, C., "Ascent and Agony," *Canadian Literature* 42: 91-93 (Autumn 1969)

Thomas, C., *Margaret Laurence* (Toronto, 1969)

SIR WILFRID LAURIER

Barthe, U., *Wilfrid Laurier on the Platform 1871-1890* (Quebec, 1890)

Colvin, J. A., "Sir Wilfrid Laurier and the British Preferential Tariff System," bibliographical footnotes, *Canadian Historical Association Report*, pp. 13-23 (1955)

Dafoe, J. W., *Laurier: A Study in Canadian Politics* (Carleton Library, Toronto, 1963). (Originally published 1920.)

David, L. O., *Laurier et son temps* (1905)

David, L .O., *Laurier: sa vie, ses oeuvres* (1919)

DeCelles, A. D., (ed.), *Discours de Sir Wilfrid Laurier* (3 vols., 1909-1920)

Gundy, H. P., "Sir Wilfrid Laurier and Lord Minto," bibliographical footnotes, *Canadian Historical Association Report* pp. 28-38 (1952)

La Terreur, M., "Correspondance Laurier—Mme. Joseph Lavergne, 1891-1893," bibliographical footnotes, *Canadian Historical Association Report*, pp. 37-51 (1964)

La Terreur, M., "Sir Wilfrid Laurier écrit à Emilie Lavergne," *Le Magazine Maclean* 6: 14-15, 36-39 (janvier 1966)

McArthur, P., *Sir Wilfrid Laurier* (Toronto, 1919)

Marion, S., "L'unité dite rationale du temps de Sir Wilfrid Laurier," bibliographical footnotes, *L'Action Nationale* 56: 587-602 (février 1967)

Neatby, H. B., "Laurier and Canadian Nationhood," *Canadian Forum* 37: 56-57 (June 1957)

Neatby, H. B., "Laurier and Imperialism," *Canadian Historical Association Report* pp. 24-32 (1955)

Plouffe, A. F., "Un mot sur deux lettres inédites," *Royal Society of Canada, Transactions,* third series 48 (section 1): 19-24 (1954)
Robertson, B., *Wilfrid Laurier* (Canadian Lives, Toronto, 1971)
Schull, J., *Laurier, the First Canadian* (Toronto, 1965)
Skelton, O. D., *The Day of Sir Wilfrid Laurier* (Toronto, 1916)
Skelton, O. D., *Life and Letters of Sir Wilfrid Laurier* (2 vols., Toronto, 1921; New York, 1922; reprinted Toronto, 1965)
Wade, M., "Sir Wilfrid Laurier," in C. T. Bissel (ed.), *Our Living Tradition: Seven Canadians* (Toronto, 1958)
Willison, J. S., *Sir Wilfrid Laurier* (vol. xi in the Makers of Canada series, London, 1926)
Willison, J. S., *Sir Wilfrid Laurier and the Liberal Party, a Political History* (2 vols., Toronto, 1903)

STEPHEN LEACOCK

Beharriell, S. R., Introduction to *Nonsense Novels* (New Canadian Library, Toronto, 1963)
Belanger, R., *Canadian Humorists: Leacock, Haliburton, Earle Birney, W. O. Mitchell* (unpublished thesis, Université Laval, 1968)
Cameron, D. A., "The Enchanted Houses: Leacock's Irony," *Canadian Literature* 23: 31-44 (Winter 1965)
Cameron, D. A., *Faces of Leacock: An Appreciation* (Toronto, [1967])
Cameron, D. A., Introduction to *Behind the Beyond* (New Canadian Library, Toronto, 1969)
Cameron, D. A., "Stephen Leacock: The Boy Behind The Arras," *Journal of Commonwealth Literature* 3: 3-18 (July 1967)
Cameron, D. A., "Stephen Leacock: The Novelist who Never Was," *Dalhousie Review* 46: 15-28 (Spring 1966)
Cole, D. W., Introduction to *Further Foolishness* (New Canadian Library, Toronto, 1968)
Curry, R. L., Introduction to *Arcadian Adventure with the Idle Rich* (New Canadian Library, Toronto, 1959)
Curry, R. L., *Stephen Leacock: Humorist and Humanist* (New York, 1959)
Davies, R., Introduction to *Literary Lapses* (New Canadian Library, Toronto, 1957)
Davies, R., Introduction to *Moonbeams from the Larger Lunacy* (New Canadian Library, Toronto, 1964)
Davies, R., *Stephen Leacock* (Toronto, 1970)
Davies, R., "Stephen Leacock," in C. T. Bissell (ed.), *Our Living Tradition: Seven Canadians* (Toronto, 1958). Also in A. J. M. Smith (ed.), *Masks of Fiction* (New Canadian Library, Toronto, 1961)
Dooley, D. J., Introduction to *Frenzied Fiction* (New Canadian Library, Toronto, 1969)
Dooley, D. J., Introduction to *Short Circuits* (New Canadian Library, Toronto, 1967 [?])
Edgar, P., "Stephen Leacock," *Queen's Quarterly* 53: 173-184 (Summer 1946). Also in P. Edgar's *Across My Path,* N. Frye (ed.), pp. 90-98 (Toronto, 1952)
Innis, H., "Stephen Butler Leacock (1869-1944)," *Canadian Journal of Economics* 10: 216-266 (May 1944)
Kimball, E., *The Man in the Panama Hat* (Toronto, 1970)
Leacock, S., *The Boy I Left Behind Me* (New York, 1946)
Legate, D. M., *Stephen Leacock* (Toronto, 1970)
McGill University Library School, *A Bibliography of Stephen Butler Leacock* (Montreal, 1935)

Masson, T. L., "Stephen Leacock," in *Our American Humorists*, pp. 209-229 (New York, 1931)

Nimmo, B., "Stephen Leacock: A Personal Note," Introduction to *The Boy I Left Behind Me* (London, 1947)

Pacey, D., "Leacock as a Satirist," *Queen's Quarterly* 58: 208-219 (Summer 1951)

Phelps, A., "Stephen Leacock," in his *Canadian Writers* (Toronto, 1951)

Ross, M. E., Editor's Preface to *Sunshine Sketches of a Little Town* (New Canadian Library, Toronto, 1960)

Stephen, F., *Leacock* (Jackdaw Series, Toronto, 1970)

Stevens, J., Introduction to *My Remarkable Uncle* (New Canadian Library, Toronto, 1965)

Walsh, J., *Stephen Leacock as an American Humorist* (unpublished thesis, University of Toronto, 1962)

Watt, F. W., "Critic or Entertainer: Leacock and the Growth of Materialism," *Canadian Literature* 5: 33-42 (Summer 1960)

Watters, R. E., "A Special Tang: Stephen Leacock's Canadian Humour," *Canadian Literature* 5: 21-32 (Summer 1960)

Whalley, G., Introduction to *My Discovery of England* (New Canadian Library, Toronto, 1961)

ROBINA LIZARS and KATHLEEN LIZARS

Graham, W. H., *The Tiger of Canada West* (Toronto, 1962)

Klinck, C. F., *William "Tiger" Dunlop: "Blackwoodian Backwoodsman"* (Toronto, 1958)

Story, N., *The Oxford Companion to Canadian History and Literature* (Toronto, 1967)

A. R. M. LOWER

Anon., Biographical note, *Canadian Geographical Journal* 71: iii (July 1965)

Anon., (portrait), *Maclean's Magazine* 81: 58 (January 1968)

Cook, R., *The Maple Leaf Forever*, pp. 143-149 (Toronto, 1971). (In the present collection.)

Kilbourn, W., "The Writing of Canadian History," in C. F. Klinck *et al.* (eds.), *Literary History of Canada*, pp. 496-519 (Toronto, 1965)

Underhill, F. H., "A Canadian Philosopher-Historian," *Canadian Forum* 83-84 (July 1947)

MALCOLM LOWRY

Aiken, C., *Ushant* (New York, 1952)

Anon., "The Fate of the Consul," *Times Literary Supplement*, p. 693 (October 28, 1960)

Anon., "Malcolm Lowry," *Times Literary Supplement* 3387: 57-59 (January 26, 1967)

Bates, R., "The Medium is the Message," *The Tamarack Review* 33: 79-86 (Autumn 1964)

Benham, D., "Lowry's Purgatory, Versions of *Lunar Caustic*," *Canadian Literature* 44: 28-37 (Spring 1970)

Birney, E., "First Supplement to Malcolm Lowry Bibliography," *Canadian Literature* 11: 90-95 (Winter 1962)

Birney, E., "Glimpses into the Life of Malcolm Lowry," *The Tamarack Review* 19: 35-41 (Spring 1961)

Birney, E., "Second Supplement to Malcolm Lowry Bibliography," *Canadian Literature* 19: 83-89 (Winter 1964)

Birney, E., and Lowry, Margerie, "Malcolm Lowry (1909–1957) a Bibliography," Part I,

Works by Malcolm Lowry, *Canadian Literature* 8: 81, 88 (Spring 1961); Part II, Works about Malcolm Lowry, *Canadian Literature* 9: 80-84 (Summer 1961)
Breit, H., "Malcolm Lowry," *Paris Review* 23: 84-85 (Spring 1960)
Buston, B. C., *Structural Organization in "Under the Volcano"* (unpublished thesis, University of Western Ontario, 1967)
Canadian Literature 8, "Special Malcolm Lowry Number" (Spring 1964). Includes original articles, letters, and poems by Malcolm Lowry; articles by C. Aiken, E. Birney, M.-P. Fouchet, and R. Heilman.
Chittick, V. L. O., "Ushant's Malcolm Lowry," *Queen's Quarterly* 71: 67-75 (Spring 1964)
Costa, R. H., *"Ulysses,* Lowry's *Volcano* and the Voyage Between: A Study of an Unacknowledged Literary Kinship," *University of Toronto Quarterly* 36: 335-352 (July 1967)
Doyen, V., "Elements Toward a Spatial Reading of Malcolm Lowry's *Under the Volcano,*" *English Studies* 50: 65-74 (February 1969)
Durrant, G., "Death in Life, Neo-Platonism in *Through the Panama,*" *Canadian Literature* 44: 13-27 (Spring 1970)
Edmonds, D., "The Short Fiction of Malcolm Lowry," *Tulane Studies in English* 15: 59-80 (1967)
Edmonds, D., "Under the Volcano: A Reading of the Immediate Level," *Tulane Studies in English* 16: 63-105 (1968)
Enright, D. J., "Malcolm Lowry," *New Statesman* 73: 117-118 (January 27, 1967)
Epstein, P., "Swinging the Maelstrom, Malcolm Lowry and Jazz," *Canadian Literature* 44: 57-66 (Spring 1970)
Kilgallin, A. R., "Eliot, Joyce & Lowry," *Canadian Author and Bookman* 41: 3-4, 6 (Winter 1965)
Kilgallin, A. R., "Faust and *Under the Volcano,*" *Canadian Literature* 26: 43-54 (Autumn 1965)
Lloyd, R. O., *Mexico and "Under the Volcano"* (unpublished thesis, University of Western Ontario, 1967)
Lowry, M., "Letter from Lowry," *Canadian Forum* 42: 62-63 (June 1962)
Lowry, M., "Preface to a Novel," *Canadian Literature* 9: 23-29 (Summer 1961)
McConnell, W., "Recollections of Malcolm Lowry," *Canadian Literature* 6: 24-31 (Autumn 1960). Also in A. J. M. Smith (ed.), *Masks of Fiction* (New Canadian Library, Toronto, 1961)
New, W. H., "Lowry's Reading," *Canadian Literature* 44: 5-12 (Spring 1970)
Nyland, A. C. (Sister Mary Rosalinda), *The Luminous Wheel: A Study of Malcolm Lowry* (unpublished thesis, University of Ottawa, 1967)
Prairie Schooner 37, special issue on Malcolm Lowry (Winter 1963/64). Includes articles by E. Birney, D. Day, J. M. Edelstein, J. Hirschman, C. Knickerbocker, M. Lowry, D. Markson, and G. Noxon.
Spender, S., Introduction to *Under the Volcano* (New York, 1965; Toronto, 1966)
Stern, J., "Malcolm Lowry," *Encounter* 29: 58-64 (September 1967)
Thomas, H., "Lowry's Letters," *Canadian Literature* 29: 56-58 (Summer 1966)
Tiessen, P., *"Under the Volcano": Lowry and the Cinema* (unpublished thesis, University of Alberta, 1968)
Wild, B., "Malcolm Lowry: A Study of the Sea Metaphor in *Under the Volcano,*" *University of Windsor Review* 4: 44-60 (Fall 1968)
Woodcock, G., "Four Facets of Malcolm Lowry," in *Odysseus Ever Returning* (Toronto, 1970)
Woodcock, G., "Malcolm Lowry as Novelist," *British Columbia Library Quarterly* 24: 25-32 (April 1961)

Woodcock, G., "Malcolm Lowry's *Under the Volcano*," *Modern Fiction Studies* (Purdue University) 4: 151-156 (Summer 1948)
Woodcock, G., *Malcolm Lowry, the Man and his Work* (Vancouver, 1971)
Woodcock, G., "On the Day of the Dead," *Northern Review* 6: 15-21 (December-January, 1953/54)

JACK LUDWIG

Carroll, J., "On Richler and Ludwig," *The Tamarack Review* 29: 98-102 (Autumn 1963)
Godfrey, D., "Starved in the Hour of Our Hoarding, The Conglomerate as Fiction, [a review article]," *The Tamarack Review* 48: 73-79 (1968)
James, E., "Ludwig's *Confusions*," *Canadian Literature* 40: 49-53 (Spring 1969)
Ludwig, J., "You always go home again," *Mosaic* 3/3: 107-111 (Spring 1970)
Stonehewer, L., "The Anatomy of Confusion," *Canadian Literature* 29: 34-42 (Summer 1966)

TOM MacINNES

Pacey, D., *Creative Writing in Canada* (Toronto, 1961)
Story, N., *The Oxford Companion to Canadian History and Literature* (Toronto, 1967)

HUGH MacLENNAN

Ballantyne, M. G., "Theology and the Man on the Street: A Catholic Commentary on *Cross-Country*," *Culture* 10: 392-396 (décembre 1949)
Buitenhuis, P., *Hugh MacLennan* (Toronto, 1969)
Chambers, R. D., "The Novels of Hugh MacLennan," *Journal of Canadian Studies, revue d'études canadiennes* 2: 3-11 (August 1967)
Cockburn, R. H., *The Novels of Hugh MacLennan* (Montreal, 1970)
Dalt, G. M., "Fiction Chronicle," *The Tamarack Review* 45: 114-116 (Autumn 1967)
Davies, R., "MacLennan's Rising Sun," *Saturday Night* 74: 29-31 (March 28, 1959)
Duncan, D., "My Author Husband," *Maclean's* 58: 7, 36, 38, 40 (August 15, 1945)
George, G. A., *Theme and Symbolism in the Novels of Hugh MacLennan* (unpublished thesis, Université Laval, 1966)
Gilley, R. K., *Myth and Learning in Three Novels of Hugh MacLennan* (unpublished thesis, University of British Columbia, 1967)
Goetsch, P., *Hugh MacLennan's Novels* (unpublished thesis, University of Marburg, 1960)
Goetsch, P., "Too Long to the Courtly Muses: Hugh MacLennan as a Contemporary Writer," *Canadian Literature* 10: 19-31 (Autumn 1961)
Lucas, A., *Hugh MacLennan* (Toronto, 1970)
Lucas, A., Introduction to *Each Man's Son* (New Canadian Library, Toronto, 1962)
MacLennan, H., Letter to the Editor re "A Nation's Odyssey," *Canadian Literature* 13: 86-87 (Summer 1962)
MacLennan, H., "My First Book," *Canadian Author and Bookman* 28: 3-4 (Summer 1952)
MacLennan, H., "Reflections on Two Decades," *Canadian Literature* 41: 28-39 (Summer 1969)
MacLennan, H., "The Story of a Novel," *Canadian Literature* 3: 35-39 (Winter 1960). Also in A. J. M. Smith (ed.), *Masks of Fiction* (New Canadian Library, Toronto, 1961)
McPherson, H., "Novels of Hugh MacLennan," *Queen's Quarterly* 60: 186-198 (Summer 1953)

McPherson, H., Introduction to *Barometer Rising* (New Canadian Library, Toronto, 1958)

Morley, P. A., *Puritanism in the Novels of Hugh MacLennan* (unpublished thesis, Carleton University, 1967)

New, W. H., "The Apprenticeship of Discovery," *Canadian Literature* 29: 18-33 (Summer 1966)

New, W. H., "The Storm and After; Imagery and Symbolism in Hugh MacLennan's *Barometer Rising*," *Queen's Quarterly* 74: 302-313 (Summer 1967)

New, W. H., "Winter and the Night People," *Canadian Literature* 38: 19-28 (Autumn 1968)

O'Donnell, K., "The Wanderer in *Barometer Rising*," *University of Windsor Review* 3: 12-18 (Spring 1968)

Phelps, A. L., "Hugh MacLennan," in his *Canadian Writers* (Toronto, 1951)

Spettigue, D. O., "Beauty and the Beast," *Queen's Quarterly* 74: 762-765 (Winter 1967)

Sutherland, R., "The Fourth Separatism," *Canadian Literature* 45: 7-23 (Summer 1970)

Vallerand, J., "Hugh MacLennan ou la tendresse dans la littérature canadienne," *Le Devoir* p. 11 (samedi, 28 novembre, 1959)

Watters, R. E., "Hugh MacLennan and the Canadian Character," in E. Morrison and W. Robbins (eds.), *As a Man Thinks* (Toronto, 1953)

Woodcock, G., "Hugh MacLennan," *Northern Review* 3: 2-10 (April-May, 1950)

Woodcock, G., *Hugh MacLennan* (Toronto 1970)

Woodcock, G., "A Nation's Odyssey, The Novels of Hugh MacLennan," *Canadian Literature* 10: 7-18 (Autumn 1961). Also in A. J. M. Smith (ed.), *Masks of Fiction* New Canadian Library, Toronto, 1961) G. Woodcock (ed.), *A Choice of Critics* (Toronto, 1966) and G. Woodcock, *Odysseus Ever Returning* (Toronto, 1970)

MARSHALL McLUHAN

Anon., "Operation McLuhan," *Times Literary Supplement* (September 28, 1967)

Bates, R., "The Medium is the Message," *The Tamarack Review* 33: 79-86 (Autumn 1964)

Boulding, K. E., "Medium and the Message," review article, *Canadian Journal of Economics and Political Science* 31: 269-273 (May 1965)

Compton, N., "Out of Orbit," *Canadian Literature* 47: 91-94 (Winter 1971)

Compton, N., "The Paradox of Marshall McLuhan," *New American Review* 2 (New York, 1968)

Crosby, H. H., and Bond, G. R. (compilers), *The McLuhan Explosion: A Casebook on Marshall McLuhan and "Understanding Media"* (New York, 1968)

Day, B., *The Message of Marshall McLuhan* (London, 1967)

Duffy, D., *Marshall McLuhan* (Toronto, 1969)

Emery, T., "Revolution in Communication," *Canadian Literature* 14: 65-67 (Autumn 1962)

Finkelstein, S. W., *Sense and Nonsense of McLuhan* (New York, 1968)

Hagler, R., "Out of the Tribe," bibliographical footnotes, *British Columbia Library Quarterly* 28: 12-16 (July–October, 1964)

Klousky, M., "McLuhan's Message," *New American Review* 2 (New York, 1968)

McCormack, T., "Innocent Eye on Mass Society," *Canadian Literature* 22: 55-60 (Autumn 1964)

McGeachy, J. B., "New Variety of Northern Light," *Financial Post* 59: 7 (December 4, 1965)

McLuhan, H. M., *The Interior Landscape,* (ed. by E. J. McNamara, Windsor, 1969)

Mandel, E. W., *Criticism: the Silent-Speaking Words*, pp. 34-36 (Toronto, 1966)
Maróti, L., "McLuhan's Media," *The New Hungarian Quarterly*, vol. ix, p. 29
　(Spring 1968)
Moltram, E., *et al.*, "The World of Marshall McLuhan," (a transcript of a BBC Third
　Programme, May 1966) *Journal of Canadian Studies*, vol. i, p. 21 (August 1966)
Rosenthal, R. B. (compiler), *McLuhan: Pro and Con* (New York, 1968)
Ross, A., "High Priest of Pop Culture," *Maclean's Magazine* 78: 13, 42-43 (July 3, 1965)
Sheps, G. D., "Utopianism, Alienation and Marshall McLuhan," *Canadian Dimension*
　vol. iii, p. 6 (September–October, 1966)
Smith, A. J. M., "The Taste of Space," in *Poems New and Collected* (Toronto, 1967)
Stearn, G. E. (ed.), *McLuhan: Hot & Cool:* a critical symposium (New York, 1967)
　Includes articles by A. Alvarez, J. Behar, W. Blissett, K. E. Boulding, J. Culkin, S.J.,
　D. M. Davin, B. DeMott, G. P. Elliott, A. Forge, J. Freund, H. L. Gossage,
　P. D. Hazard, D. Hymes, J. M. Johansen, F. Kermode, B. Lieberman, D. MacDonald,
　M. McLuhan, J. Miller, R. E. Morriss, W. Ong, S.J., H. Parker, C. Ricks, H. Rosenberg,
　R. Shafer, S. Sontag, G. E. Stearn, G. Steiner, D. Walker, R. Williams, and T. Wolfe.
Theall, D. F., *The Medium is the Rear View Mirror* (Montreal and London, 1971)
Wagner, G., "Misunderstanding Media: Obscurity as Authority," *The Kenyon Review*
　29: 246-255 (March 1967)
Walker, D., "McLuhan Explains the Media," *Executive* 6: 22-27 (August 1964)
Watkins, M. H., "McLuhan Is the Message," *Continuous Learning* 3: 206-209
　(September-October, 1964)

W. O. MITCHELL

Barclay, P., "Regionalism and the Writer, a Talk with W. O. Mitchell," *Canadian
　Literature* 14: 53-56 (Autumn 1962)
Belanger, R., *Canadian Humorists: Leacock, Haliburton, Earle Birney, W. O. Mitchell*
　(unpublished thesis, Université Laval, 1968)
Eggleston, W., *The Frontier and Canadian Letters* (Toronto, 1957)
Laurence, M., "Holy Terror," *Canadian Literature* 15: 76-77 (Winter 1963)
New, W. H., "A Feeling of Completion: Aspects of W. O. Mitchell," *Canadian Literature*
　17: 22-33 (Summer 1963)
Tallman, W., "Wolf in the Snow," *Canadian Literature* 5: 7-20 (Summer 1960) and
　6: 41-48 (Autumn 1960)

ALICE MUNRO

Harvor, B., "The special world of the WW's: through female reality with Alice, Jennifer,
　Edna, Nadine, Doris and all those other girls," *Saturday Night* 84: 33 (August 1969)
Helwig, D., Review of *The Dance of the Happy Shades*, *Queen's Quarterly* 77: 127-128
　(Spring 1970)
Jackson, H., Review of *Lives of girls and women*, *Canadian Forum* 51: 76-77
　(January-February 1972)
Kirkwood, H., Review of *The Dance of the Happy Shades*, *Canadian Forum* 48: 260
　(February 1969)
McAlpine, M., "An Expansive Vision, A Fulfilled Promise," *Saturday Night* 87: 36-37
　(January 1972)
Peter, J., Review of *The Dance of the Happy Shades*, *Malahat* 11 (1969)
Thomas, A., "She's only a girl, he said" *Canadian Literature* 39: 91-92 (Winter 1969)
Thompson, K., Review of *The Dance of the Happy Shades*, *Fiddlehead* 82: 71-72
　(November-December 1969)

HOWARD O'HAGAN

Anon., Review of *Tay John, Canadian Literature* 9: 65-66 (Summer 1961)
Anon., Review of *Tay John, University of Toronto Quarterly* 30: 414-415 (July 1961)
Anon., Review of *Wilderness Men, Saskatchewan History* 13: 79 (Spring 1960)
Fergusson, H., Introduction to *Tay John* (New York, 1960)

THOMAS RADDALL

Anon., Biographical note, *Canadian Library* 20: 382 (May 1964, part 2)
Anon., (portrait), *Canadian Library* 21: 72 (September 1964)
Anon., "Thomas Raddall," *Canadian Author and Bookman* 42: 17 (Spring 1967)
Bevan, A., Introduction to *At the Tide's Turn and Other Stories* (New Canadian Library, Toronto, 1959)
Bissell, C. T., "Letters in Canada, 1950," *University of Toronto Quarterly* vol. 20, no. 3, pp. 262-272 (April 1951)
Bissell, C. T., "Letters in Canada, 1956," *University of Toronto Quarterly* vol. 26, no. 3, pp. 311-318 (April 1957)
Hawkins, W. J., "Thomas H. Raddall, The Man and His Work," *Queen's Quarterly* 75: 137-146 (Spring 1968)
MacGillivray, J. R., "Letters in Canada, 1943," *University of Toronto Quarterly* vol. 13, no. 3, pp. 316-324 (April 1944)
Matthews, J., Introduction to *The Nymph and the Lamp* (New Canadian Library, Toronto, 1963)
Spicer, S. T., "Great Stories to Tell, a Profile of Thomas H. Raddall," *Atlantic Advocate* 54: 44-46 (December 1963)

MORDECAI RICHLER

Bevan, A. R., Introduction to *The Apprenticeship of Daddy Kravitz* (New Canadian Library, Toronto, 1968)
Bowering, G., "And the Sun Goes Down," *Canadian Literature* 29: 7-17 (Summer 1966)
Cameron, D., "Don Mordecai and the Hardhats," *Canadian Forum* 29-33 (March 1972)
Cameron, D., "The Professional Canadian," *Canadian Literature* 50: 103-104 (Autumn 1971)
Carroll, J., "On Richler and Ludwig," *The Tamarack Review* 29: 98-102 (Autumn 1963)
Cohen, N., "A Conversation with Mordecai Richler," *The Tamarack Review* 2: 6-23 (Winter 1957)
Kattan, N., "Mordecai Richler," *Canadian Literature* 21: 46-52 (Summer 1964)
McKenzie, R., "Life in a New Land: Notes on the Immigrant Theme in Canadian Fiction," *Canadian Literature* 7: 24-33 (Winter 1961)
New, W. H., "The Apprenticeship of Discovery," *Canadian Literature* 29: 18-33 (Summer 1966)
Richler, M., "The Apprenticeship of Mordecai Richler," *Maclean's* 74: 21, 44-48 (May 20, 1961)
Richler, M., *The Street* (Toronto, 1969)
Richler, M., "The Uncertain World," *Canadian Literature* 41: 23-27 (Summer 1969)
Scott, P. D., "A Choice of Certainties," *The Tamarack Review* 8: 73-82 (Summer 1958)
Sheps, G. D., *On Mordecai Richler* (Critical Views on Canadian Writers) (Toronto, 1970)
Tallman, W., "Beyond Camelot," *Canadian Literature* 42: 77-81 (Autumn 1969)
Tallman, W., "Richler and the Faithless City," *Canadian Literature* 3: 62-64 (Winter 1960)

Tallman, W., "Wolf in the Snow," *Canadian Literature* 5: 7-20 (Summer 1960) and 6: 41-48 (Autumn 1960)
Thomas, A., "An Off-White Horse," *Canadian Literature* 51: 83-84 (Winter 1972)
Woodcock, G., Introduction to *Son of a Smaller Hero* (New Canadian Library, Toronto, 1966)
Woodcock, G., *Mordecai Richler* (Toronto, 1970)
Woodcock, G., "The Wheel of Exile," *The Tamarack Review* 58: 65-72 (1971)

LOUIS RIEL

Anderson, F. W., "Louis Riel's Insanity Reconsidered," bibliography for *Saskatchewan History* 3: 104-110 (Autumn 1950)
Anon., "Correspondance Louis Riel—Mgr. Bourget," *Revue d'Histoire de l'Amérique Française* 15: 430-442 (décembre 1961)
Anon., "Louis Riel, Defender of the Past," *Beaver* 290: 24-29 (Spring 1960)
Bowsfield, H., *Louis Riel* (Canadian Lives, Toronto, 1970)
Coulter, J., *Riel: A Play in Two Parts* (Toronto, 1962)
Coulter, J., *The Trial of Louis Riel,* with French translations by Raynald Desmeules (Ottawa, 1968)
Dubue, J., "Correspondance . . ." *Revue d'Histoire de l'Amérique Française* 20: 430-436 (décembre 1966); 625-630 (mars 1967); 21: 112-117 (juin 1967)
Epitome of Parliamentary Documents in connection with the North-West Rebellion, 1885 (Ottawa, 1886)
Godbout, A., "Ascendance de Louis Riel d'après Tanguay," *Revue d'Histoire de l'Amérique Française* 2: 157 (janvier 1948)
Gutteridge, D., *Riel, a Poem for Voices* (Fredericton, 1968)
Mitchell, W. O., "Riddle of Louis Riel," *Maclean's Magazine* 65: 7-9, 43 (February 1); 12-13, 41-42 (February 15, 1952)
Morton, A. S., *A History of the Canadian West to 1870-1871* (Toronto, 1939)
Osler, E. B., *The Man Who Had To Hang: Louis Riel* (Toronto, 1961)
Shrive, N., *Charles Mair, Literary Nationalist* (Toronto, 1965)
Stanley, G. F. G., *The Birth of Western Canada; a History of the Riel Rebellions* (Toronto 1960)
Stanley, G. F. G., "Footnote to History: was Riel an American Citizen?" bibliographical footnotes, *Canadian Historical Review* 29: 40-43 (March 1948)
Stanley, G. F. G., *Louis Riel* (Toronto, 1963)
Stanley, G. F. G., *Louis Riel, Patriot or Rebel?* (Ottawa, Canadian Historical Association, 1954) 24 p. booklet
Wade, M., *The French Canadians, 1760-1945* (Toronto, 1955)
Wilson, A., "Riel Reconsidered," *Canadian Literature* 10: 66-69 (Autumn 1961)

SIR CHARLES G. D. ROBERTS

Anon., (portrait), *Atlantic Advocate* 54: 66 (February 1964)
Atwood, M., "Animal Victims," *Survival,* Chap. 3 (Toronto, 1972)
Burroughs, J., "Roberts' *Red Fox,*" *Outing* 48: 512a-b (July 1906)
Campbell, J. H., *The Prose of Sir Charles G. D. Roberts* (unpublished thesis, University of New Brunswick, 1963)
Cappon, J., *Charles G. D. Roberts* (Toronto, 1925)
Cappon, J., *Roberts and the Influence of his Time* (Toronto, 1905)
Edgar, P., "English-Canadian Literature," *Cambridge History of English Literature* 14 (London, 1916)

Gold, J., "Precious Speck of Life," bibliographical footnotes, *Canadian Literature* 26: 22-32 (Autumn 1965)
Keith, W. J., *Charles G. D. Roberts* (Toronto, 1970)
Lucas, A., Introduction to *The Last Barrier and Other Stories* (New Canadian Library, Toronto, 1958)
Lucas, A., "Nature Writers and the Animal Story" in Carl F. Klinck and Others, *Literary History of Canada* chapter 19: especially 383-386 (Toronto, 1965)
Marquis, T. G., "A History of English-Canadian Literature" in *Canada and Its Provinces* 12: 526-528, 557-559 (Toronto, 1913)
Pacey, D., "Sir Charles G. D. Roberts," in R. L. McDougall (ed.), *Our Living Tradition*, Fourth Series (Toronto, 1962)
Polk, J., "Lives of the Hunted," *Canadian Literature* 53: 51-59 (Summer 1972)
Pomeroy, E. M. "Canadian Author's Welcome in Italy and a Few Memories of the Poet," *Atlantic Advocate* 52: 57-59 (March 1962)
Pomeroy, E. M., *Sir Charles G. D. Roberts. A Biography* (Toronto, 1943)
Stevenson, L., *Appraisals of Canadian Literature* (Toronto, 1926)

SINCLAIR ROSS

Daniells, R., Introduction to *As for Me and My House* (New Canadian Library, Toronto, 1957)
Eggleston, W., *The Frontier and Canadian Letters* (Toronto, 1957)
Laurence, M., Introduction to *The Lamp at Noon and Other Stories* (New Canadian Library, Toronto, 1968)
McCourt, E. A., *The Canadian West in Fiction* (Toronto, 1949)
New, W. H., "Sinclair Ross's Ambivalent World," *Canadian Literature* 40: 26-32 (Spring 1969)
Ross, S., "On Looking Back," *Mosaic* 3/3: 93-94 (Spring 1970)
Stephens, D., "Fluid Time," *Canadian Literature* 48: 92-94 (Spring 1971)
Stephens, D., "Wind, Sun, and Dust," *Canadian Literature* 23: 17-24 (Winter 1965)
Tallman, W., "Wolf in the Snow," *Canadian Literature* 5: 7-20 (Summer 1960) and 6: 41-48 (Autumn 1960)

DUNCAN CAMPBELL SCOTT

Brown, E. K., *On Canadian Poetry*, pp. 108-132 (Toronto, 1943)
Brown, E. K., "Memoir," *Selected Poems of Duncan Campbell Scott* (Toronto, 1951)
Clarke, G. H., "Duncan Campbell Scott (1862-1948)", *Transactions of Royal Society of Canada*, 3rd series 39: 115-120 (1948)
Edgar, P., "Duncan Campbell Scott," *Dalhousie Review* 7: 38-46 (April 1927)
Edgar, P., "Travelling with a Poet," in *Across my Path* (ed. N. Frye) pp. 58-74 (Toronto, 1952)
Knister, R., "Duncan Campbell Scott," *Willison's Monthly* 2: 295-296 (January 1927)
Smith, A. J. M., "Duncan Campbell Scott," in McDougall, R. L. (ed.), *Our Living Tradition* (2nd and 3rd series) pp. 73-94 (Toronto, 1959)

GOLDWIN SMITH

Anon., (portrait), *Saturday Night* 72: 22-23 (July 6, 1957)
Anon., "So What Else is New," *Financial Post* 62: 6 (May 11, 1968)
Armytage, W. H. G., "Goldwin Smith: Some Unpublished Letters," bibliographical footnotes, *Queen's Quarterly* 54: 452-460 (Winter 1947-8)

Brown, R. C., "Goldwin Smith and Anti-Imperialism," bibliographical footnotes, *Canadian Historical Review* 43: 93-105 (June 1962)
Haultain, T. A., *Goldwin Smith: His Life and Opinions* (London, 1913)
McEachern, R., *Goldwin Smith* (unpublished thesis, University of Toronto, 1934)
Ross, M. E., "Goldwin Smith," in *Our Living Tradition: Seven Canadians,* C. T. Bissell (ed.), (Toronto, 1958)
Underhill, F. H., *In Search of Canadian Liberalism* (Toronto, 1960)
Wallace, E., "Goldwin Smith," *Canadian Welfare* 41: 108-112 (May-June, 1965)
Wallace, E., *Goldwin Smith: Victorian Liberal* (Toronto, 1957)
Wallace, M. E., "Goldwin Smith and Social Reform," bibliographical footnotes, *Canadian Historical Review* 29: 363-369 (December 1948)
Wallace, M. E., "Goldwin Smith: Journalist and Critic," *Canadian Forum* 35: 275 (March 1956)
Wallace, M. E., "Goldwin Smith, Liberal," bibliographical footnotes, *University of Toronto Quarterly* 23: 155-172 (January 1954)

UNDERHILL, F. H.

Careless, J. M. S., on presentation of Tyrrell medal, *Royal Society of Canada, Proceedings,* 4th series: 64-65 (1963)
Carver, H. S. M., "Premier Hepburn and the Professors," *Canadian Forum* 19: 40-41 (May 1939)
Cook, R., *The Maple Leaf Forever* pp. 149-153 (Toronto, 1971). (In the present collection.)
Kilbourn, W., "The Writing of Canadian History," in C. F. Klinck *et al.* (eds.), *Literary History of Canada,* pp. 496-519 (Toronto, 1965)
McNaught, C., "Democracy and our Universities," *Canadian Forum* 20: 333 (February 1941)

SHEILA WATSON

Child, P.,"Canadian Prose-Poem," *Dalhousie Review* 39: 233-236 (Summer 1959)
Grube, J., Introduction to *The Double Hook* (New Canadian Library, Toronto, 1966)
Jackel, S., "The House on the Prairies," *Canadian Literature* 42: 46-55 (Autumn 1969)
McPherson, H., "An Important New Voice," *The Tamarack Review* 12: 85-88 (Summer 1959)
Monkman, L., "Coyote as Trickster" in *The Double Hook, Canadian Literature* 52: 70-76 (Spring 1972)
Morriss, M., "The Elements Transcended," *Canadian Literature* 42: 56-71 (Autumn 1969)
Salter, F. M., in "A Note from the Publisher," *The Double Hook* (Toronto, 1959)
Theall, D. F., "A Canadian Novella," *Canadian Forum* 39: 78-80 (July 1959)

GEORGE WHALLEY

Blanchet, G., Review of *The Legend Of John Hornby, Beaver* 293: 58 (Spring 1963)
Bowering, G., "Hero without Motive," *Canadian Literature* 17: 72-73 (Summer 1963)
Press, J., *The Chequered Shade* 207-208, 215-216 (London, 1958)
Watson, J. L., "Business Executive and Nut," *Canadian Saturday Night* 78: 29 (May 1963)
Zaslow, M., Review of *The Legend of John Hornby, University of Toronto Quarterly* 33: 470-471 (July 1964)

ETHEL WILSON

Campbell, B., *The Fiction of Ethel Wilson: A Study in Theme and Technique* (unpublished thesis, University of Toronto, 1967)

Campbell, R. L. *Imagery and Symbolism in the Fiction of Ethel Wilson* (unpublished thesis, University of New Brunswick, 1967)

Clarke, R., *Appearance and Reality in the Fiction of Ethel Wilson* (unpublished thesis, University of British Columbia, 1964)

Kirkwood, H., "Realist with a Difference," *Saturday Night* 76: 41-42 (October 28, 1961)

Livesay, D., "Ethel Wilson: West Coast Novelist," *Saturday Night* 67: 20, 36 (July 26, 1952)

New, W. H., "The 'Genius' of Place and Time: The Fiction of Ethel Wilson," *Journal of Canadian Studies; revue d'études canadiennes* 3: 39-48 (November 1968)

New, W. H., "The Irony of Order: Ethel Wilson's *The Innocent Traveller*," *Critique* 10: 22-30 (1969)

Pacey, D., *Ethel Wilson* (Twayne world author series: Canada 33, (New York, 1968 © 1967)

Pacey, D., "Ethel Wilson's First Novel," *Canadian Literature* 29: 43-55 (Summer 1966)

Pacey, D., Introduction to *Swamp Angel* (New Canadian Library, Toronto, 1962)

Smith, M. B., "Sipped and Savoured," *Canadian Literature* 11: 67-68 (Winter 1962)

Sonthoff, H. W., "The Novels of Ethel Wilson," *Canadian Literature* 26: 33-42 (Autumn 1965)

Watters, R. E., "Ethel Wilson, The Experienced Traveller," *British Columbia Library Quarterly* 21: 21-27 (April 1958)

Wilson, E., "The Bridge or the Stokehold? Views of the Novelist's Art," *Canadian Literature* 5: 43-47 (Summer 1960)

Wilson, E., "A Cat among Falcons: Reflections on the Writer's Craft," *Canadian Literature* 2: 10-19 (Autumn, 1959). Also in A. J. M. Smith (ed.), *Masks of Fiction* (New Canadian Library, Toronto, 1961)

Wilson, E., "Reflections in a Pool," *Canadian Literature* 22: 29-33 (Autumn 1964)

GEORGE WOODCOCK

Barbour, D., Review of *Hugh MacLennan, Canadian Forum* 50: 189 (July-August 1970)

Bennet, C. L., Review of *Ravens and Prophets: An Account of Journeys in British Columbia, Alberta and Southern Alaska, Dalhousie Review* 33: ix, xi (Autumn 1953)

Bilsland, J. W., "George Woodcock, Man of Letters," *British Columbia Library Quarterly* 23: 23 (July 1959)

Brady, A., Review of *Anarchism: A History of Libertarian Ideas and Movements, University of Toronto Quarterly* 32: 448-450 (July 1963)

Cairns, J. C., Review of *Anarchism: A History of Libertarian Ideas and Movements, Canadian Historical Review* 44: 258-9 (September 1963)

Cameron, D., "Canadian Studies: A Beachhead for the Cultural Marines?" *Queen's Quarterly* 77: 282-4 (Summer 1970)

Clark, A. F. B., Review of *Ravens and Prophets: An Account of Journeys in British Columbia, Alberta and Southern Alaska, Canadian Forum* 32: 260 (February 1953)

Coldwell, J., "The Mind of the Exile," *Canadian Literature* 51: 88-90 (Winter 1972)

Daniells, R., "Microcosm of our Moving World," *Canadian Literature* 30: 63-64, 66 (Autumn 1966)

Dobbs, K., "Travellers' Masks," *Canadian Literature* 2: 85-86 (Autumn 1959)

Drury, V., Review of *Ravens and Prophets: An Account of Journeys in British Columbia, Alberta and Southern Alaska, The British Columbia Historical Quarterly* 17: 153-4 (January-April 1953)

Evans, J. A. S., "Woodcock and Cook on Canada," *Commentator* 15: 21 (April 1971)

Fowke, E., Review of *A Choice of Critics, Canadian Forum* 47: 262 (February 1968)

Fox, C. J., "Canada Portrayed," *Canadian Literature* 49: 92-94 (Summer 1971)

Harris, M., "Superthinker," *Maclean's* 80: 21 (August 1967)

Hutchison, A., Review of *Malcolm Lowry: The Man and His Work, Malahat Review* 22: 126 (April 1972)

Kattan, N., "George Orwell: une âme de cristal," *Liberté* 10: 56-58 (janvier-février 1968)

Kilgallin, T., Review of *The Crystal Spirit; A Study of George Orwell, The Canadian Author and Bookman* 43: 16 (Autumn 1967)

King, C., Review of *Canada and the Canadians, University of Toronto Quarterly* 40: 321-322 (Summer 1971)

King, C., Review of *The Crystal Spirit; A Study of George Orwell, University of Toronto Quarterly* 37: 427-429 (July 1968)

King, C., Review of *Malcolm Lowry: The Man and His Work, University of Toronto Quarterly* 41: 404-5 (Summer 1972)

King, C., Review of *Odysseus Ever Returning, University of Toronto Quarterly* 40: 322 (Summer 1971)

Lavin, J. A., "Orwell's World," *Canadian Literature* 33: 90-91 (Summer 1967)

McCormack, R., "Orwell," *The Tamarack Review* 58: 83 (1971)

Nelles, V. and Rotstein A., (eds.), *Nationalism or Anarchism? Responses to George Woodcock*, New Press (November 1972)

Nesbitt, B., Review of *Hugh MacLennan, West Coast Review* 5 no. 3 (January 1971)

Nixon, G., Review of *The Crystal Spirit; A Study of George Orwell, British Columbia Library Quarterly* 31: 37, 39-40 (July 1967)

Review of *The Paradox of Oscar Wilde, University of Toronto Quarterly* 20: 301 (April 1951)

Roht, T., "The Problems and Work of Translators," *Culture* 29: 256 (septembre 1968)

Stainsby, D., "Minority History," *Canadian Literature* 40: 78-9 (Spring 1969)

Stedmond, J., Review of *Mordecai Richler, Canadian Forum* 50: 222-3 (September 1970)

Stevens, P., "Critical Odyssey," *Canadian Literature* 47: 84-87 (Winter 1971)

Symons, J., "Man of the Thirties," *Canadian Literature* 37: 75-76 (Summer 1968)

Wainwright, A., "Art, a Critic, and a Whole Bloody Bird," *Saturday Night* 85: 33-4 (April 1970)

Watt, F. W., *Letters in Canada, University of Toronto Quarterly* 40: 320 (Summer 1971)

Weaver, R., "Remember George Orwell," *Saturday Night* 82: 33, 35 (June 1967)

Wolfe, M., Review of *Canada and the Canadians, Canadian Forum* 50: 439-440 (March 1971)

ACKNOWLEDGMENTS

E. K. BROWN "The Problem of a Canadian Literature" from *On Canadian Poetry*, The Ryerson Press, by permission of McGraw-Hill Ryerson Limited.

MORLEY CALLAGHAN "Ancient Lineage" and "Predicament" from *A Native Argosy* and and excerpt from *That Summer in Paris*, by permission of Harold Matson Co. Ltd.

LEONARD COHEN an excerpt from *The Favourite Game*. Copyright © 1963 by Leonard Cohen. Reprinted by permission of The Canadian Publishers, McClelland and Stewart Limited, Toronto, and The Viking Press, Inc.

RALPH CONNOR an excerpt from *Glengarry Schooldays,* reprinted by permission of The Canadian Publishers, McClelland and Stewart Limited, Toronto, and Fleming H. Revell Company.

RAMSAY COOK "La Survivance English-Canadian Style" from *Maple Leaf Forever*, by permission of The Macmillan Company of Canada Limited.

DONALD G. CREIGHTON "The Economy of the North" from *The Commercial Empire of the St. Lawrence, 1760-1850*, by permission of The Macmillan Company of Canada Limited.

ROBERTSON DAVIES an excerpt from *A Mixture of Frailties*, by permission of The Macmillan Company of Canada Limited and Collins-Knowlton-Wing, Inc.

NORTHROP FRYE "Ordinary Speech, Verse, and Prose" from *The Well-tempered Critic*, by permission of Indiana University Press.

HUGH GARNER "One-Two-Three Little Indians" from *The Yellow Sweater and Other Stories*, copyright by Hugh Garner, 1950, 1952 and 1972, reprinted by permission of the author.

JOHN GLASSCO "A Season in Limbo" first appeared in *The Tamarack Review* (1962) under the anagrammatic pseudonym 'Silas N. Gooch,' reprinted by permission of the author.

DAVE GODFREY "The Hard-Headed Collector," first published in *The Tamarack Review* (1966), reprinted by permission of the author.

FREDERICK PHILIP GROVE "I Come into Contact with Humanity Again" from *A Search for America*, reprinted by permission of The Canadian Publishers, McClelland and Stewart Limited, Toronto, and of A. L. Grove.

HUGH HOOD "The End of It," The Ryerson Press, by permission of McGraw-Hill Ryerson Limited.

A. M. KLEIN "On First Seeing the Ceiling of the Sistine Chapel" from *The Second Scroll*, reprinted by permission of The Canadian Publishers, McClelland and Stewart Limited, Toronto, and Random House, Inc.

MARGARET LAURENCE "A Queen in Thebes," by permission of the author and John Cushman Associates Inc.

STEPHEN LEACOCK "The Great Election in Missinaba County" and "The Candidacy of Mr. Smith" from *Sunshine Sketches of a Little Town*, "The Rival Churches of St. Asaph and St. Osoph" from *Arcadian Adventures with the Idle Rich*, reprinted by permission of The Canadian Publishers, McClelland and Stewart Limited, Toronto, Dodd, Mead and Company, and The Bodley Head.